ADVANCES IN

Experimental
Social Psychology

VOLUME 28

ADVANCES IN

Experimental
Social Psychology

EDITED BY

Mark P. Zanna
DEPARTMENT OF PSYCHOLOGY
UNIVERSITY OF WATERLOO
WATERLOO, ONTARIO, CANADA

VOLUME 28

ACADEMIC PRESS
San Diego   New York   Boston
London   Sydney   Tokyo   Toronto

Academic Press, Inc.
A Division of Harcourt Brace & Company
525 B Street, Suite 1900, San Diego, California 92101-4495

United Kingdom Edition published by
Academic Press Limited
24-28 Oval Road, London NW1 7DX

International Standard Serial Number: 0065-2601

International Standard Book Number: 0-12-015228-2

PRINTED IN THE UNITED STATES OF AMERICA
96 97 98 99 00 01 BB 9 8 7 6 5 4 3 2 1

CONTENTS

Principles of Judging Valence: What Makes Events Positive or Negative?

C. Miguel Brendl and E. Tory Higgins

Pluralistic Ignorance and the Perpetuation of Social Norms by Unwitting Actors

Deborah A. Prentice and Dale T. Miller

People as Flexible Interpreters: Evidence and Issues from Spontaneous Trait Inference

James S. Uleman, Leonard S. Newman, and Gordon B. Moskowitz

Social Perception, Social Stereotypes, and Teacher Expectations: Accuracy and the Quest for the Powerful Self-Fulfilling Prophecy

Lee Jussim, Jacquelynne Eccles, and Stephanie Madon

Nonverbal Behavior and Nonverbal Communication: What Do Conversational Hand Gestures Tell Us?

Robert M. Krauss, Yihsiu Chen, and Purnima Chawla

CONTRIBUTORS

Numbers in parentheses indicate the pages on which the authors' contributions begin.

SCOTT T. ALLISON (53), Department of Psychology, University of Richmond, Richmond, Virginia 23173

JIM BLASCOVICH (1), Department of Psychology, University of California, Santa Barbara, Santa Barbara, California 93106

C. MIGUEL BRENDL (95), Fachgruppe Psychologie, Universitat Konstanz, D39, 78434 Konstanz, Germany

PURNIMA CHAWLA (389), Department of Psychology, Columbia University, New York, New York 10027

YIHSIU CHEN (389), Department of Psychology, Columbia University, New York, New York 10027

JACQUELYNNE ECCLES (281), Department of Psychology, University of Michigan, Ann Arbor, Michigan 48106

E. TORY HIGGINS (95), Department of Psychology, Columbia University, New York, New York 10027

LEE JUSSIM (281), Department of Psychology, Rutgers University, New Brunswick, New Jersey 08903

ROBERT M. KRAUSS (389), Department of Psychology, Columbia University, New York, New York 10027

DIANE M. MACKIE (53), Department of Psychology, University of California, Santa Barbara, Santa Barbara, California 93106

STEPHANIE MADON (281), Department of Psychology, Rutgers University, New Brunswick, New Jersey 08903

DAVID M. MESSICK (53), Department of Organizational Behavior, Kellogg Graduate School of Management, Northwestern University, Evanston, Illinois 60208

DALE T. MILLER (161), Department of Psychology, Princeton University, Princeton, New Jersey 08544

GORDON B. MOSKOWITZ (211), Department of Psychology, Princeton University, Princeton, New Jersey 08544

LEONARD S. NEWMAN (211), Department of Psychology, University of Illinois at Chicago, Chicago, Illinois 60607

DEBORAH A. PRENTICE (161), Department of Psychology, Princeton University, Princeton, New Jersey 08544

JOE TOMAKA (1), Department of Psychology, University of Texas at El Paso, El Paso, Texas 79968

JAMES S. ULEMAN (211), Department of Psychology, New York University, New York, New York 10003

THE BIOPSYCHOSOCIAL MODEL OF AROUSAL REGULATION

Jim Blascovich

Joe Tomaka

I. Introduction

Since the 1970s, the relationships between psychological activity and autonomic arousal have intrigued me (JB). This curiosity grew as my own perceptions of cardiac responses under varying but mundane situations concretely reinforced the notion of causal relationships between cognitive and physiological responses. For example, while gambling as a young adult, I can recall experiencing my heart pounding as I made (relatively) large bets at the blackjack table or in "friendly" poker games. Many years later, in ancitipation of major abdominal surgery, I experienced my heart pounding as I contemplated potential outcomes. Within both situations, I can remember sometimes associating my interoceptions with positive feelings and sometimes with negative feelings.

As a psychologist, I wanted to examine the relationships between mind and body empirically, mostly in the laboratory. In my case, this was easier said than done. It took several years for me to implement even a fairly simple, relevant experimental study (i.e., Blascovich, Nash, & Ginsburg, 1978), and many more years to become familiar enough with psychophysiological theory and methodology to establish a bona fide social psychophysiology laboratory. Along the way, I received expert tutelage in psychophysiology from such experts as John Cacioppo, Ed Katkin, Bob Kelsey, and Lou Tassinary.[1] Graduate students in my laboratory challenged and sharpened our thinking about arousal regulation. Karen Allen, John Ernst, Diane

[1] The first author benefited immensely as a National Science Foundation Fellow in the Program for Advanced Study and Research in Social Psychophysiology at The Ohio State

ADVANCES IN EXPERIMENTAL
SOCIAL PSYCHOLOGY, VOL. 28

Quinn, John Rousselle, Kristen Salomon, and Daryl Wansink all made important contributions. More than anything else, however, the collaboration between the authors of this chapter has brought this line of investigation into focus and fruition.

A. BACKGROUND ASSUMPTIONS

Over the years, like so many others, we have come to the explicit realization that many important behavioral domains are fundamentally related to physiological responses including emotion (at least at the superordinate levels), motivation, and health. More important, perhaps, we also have come to the conclusion that disciplinarily idiosyncratic approaches to the study of arousal regulation generally limit our understanding and restrict empirical investigations of arousal-related behaviors.

Consequently, we advocate in integrative, interdisciplinary approach because we believe that such an approach best represents the reality of arousal-regulation processes. We doubt, for example, that purely cognitive, biological, dispositional, or social psychological theories even begin to reflect the complex nature of arousal-related domains. However, we believe strongly that more integrated, multidisciplinary theoretical models can and do reflect such processes. Furthermore, we believe that theoretical dilemmas or ambiguities regarding arousal-related behaviors at a single subdisciplinary level of analysis can often be resolved by looking to other levels of analysis. Finally, we believe in the value, and perhaps the necessity, of powerful empirical models of arousal-relevant situations.

B. ILLUSTRATIVE DILEMMA

We can illustrate a major problem created by a unidimensional framework for arousal regulation by looking no further than our own past research. If we limit ourselves to a purely dispositional approach for explaining arousal-related behaviors, our arguments might take the form that certain types of individuals (based on dispositional categories) exhibit more or less autonomic arousal in psychologically relevant situations. We could

---

University during the summer of 1989 under the expert tutelage of Gary Berntson, PhD, John T. Cacioppo, PhD, and Louis G. Tassinary, PhD. Both authors benefited from less structured, but equally important training in psychophysiology, from Edward S. Katkin, PhD, and Robert A. Kelsey, PhD. None of these individuals, however, bear any responsibility for any errors in our own theoretical or methodological psychophysiological thinking.

index such arousal by using subjective (i.e., self- or other report) or objective (i.e., physiological) measures.

1. Competitiveness

For example, we might hypothesize that highly competitive individuals exhibit more arousal in demanding performance situations because they are more motivated than noncompetitive individuals (cf. Brehm & Self, 1989; Wright & Dill, 1993). Self-report measures could provide a test of our hypothesis. However, we could also seek convergent, more "objective" dependent measures. Being true to our dispositionally idiosyncratic approach but naive psychophysiologically (not uncommon, in our opinion, in the dispositional arousal-regulation tradition), we might choose cardiovascular measures such as heart rate or blood pressure changes (i.e., reactivity) to index the arousal associated with motivation—the higher the heart rate or blood pressure, the more motivated and, presumably, the more successful the individual.

Indeed, we have found support for the hypothesized relationship. Specifically, we found that we could predict which male in a dyad would win a fair but competitive zero-sum game[2] on the basis of precompetition but postinstructional physiological arousal as indexed by heart rate (Blascovich et al., (1978). In this study, subjects came into our laboratory in same-gender pairs where experiments wired them for electrocardiogram (ECG) recording. Subsequently, the subjects, placed in separate "player rooms," rested while we obtained baseline physiological recordings. Next, they received instructions pertinent to the upcoming zero-sum experimental game and played a few practice trials. A postinstructional but pretask ECG recording was made, and finally the game commenced while the ECG recording continued for 50 trials. Each dyadic competition produced a winner and a loser (there were no ties). Examination of opposing players' respective significant differences in heart rate changes during the critical periods in the study revealed that male competitors with greater increases in heart rates just before commencement of the game prevailed (Figure 1). Indeed, this was true for 19 of 20 male pairs. Notably, we did not find that heart rate discriminated winners and losers in female dyads.

2. Stressfulness

Taking a dispositional approach, we might also argue that individuals prone to experience stress exhibit more arousal in demanding performance situations as a function of psychological threat. Again, being true to our

---

[2] Zero-sum games are ones in which the outcome expectancies across all competing players is zero (i.e., a friendly poker game).

Male Dyads

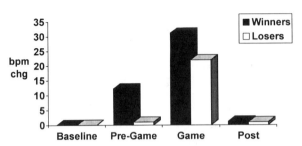

Fig. 1.   Heart rate change data (Blascovich et al., 1978).

dispositional approach and naive psychophysiologically, we might choose a cardiovascular measure such as heart rate or blood pressure changes to index the arousal associated with stress—the higher the heart rate or blood pressure, the more stressed the individual.

We and many others (Blascovich & Katkin, 1993a; Matthews et al., 1986; Turner, Sherwood, & Light, 1993) have found data to support the predicted relationship. Indeed, in one study (reported in Blascovich & Katkin, 1993b), heart rate increased during the performance of a potentially stressful task, but also psychologically driven cardiovascular change itself predicted the extent of coronary artery disease, presumably a disease related to dispositional differences in stress responses (cf. Matthews et al., 1986;Turner et al., 1993).

Data collection took place in a study involving 30 patients undergoing diagnostic evaluation for coronary artery disease. All patients underwent exercise stress testing and "psychological stress testing" (performing a sensorimotor, signal detection task) in counterbalanced order in a clinical ECG laboratory at a large hospital. These patients then went on to coronary angiography, an invasive diagnostic technique used to determine the extent of coronary artery disease. Figure 2 illustrates the results of regression analyses revealing that the cardiovascular measures, including heart rate, recorded during psychological stress testing (entered into the regression model after the cardiovascular measures recorded during exercise stress testing) predicted significantly and substantially more variance in the degree of coronary occlusion in the three major coronary arteries than the traditional cardiological predictors recorded during exercise stress testing.

3. The Apparent Dilemma

Considered together, the separately hypothesized and empirically supported relationships among competitiveness, cardiovascular arousal, and

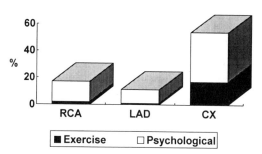

Fig. 2. Occlusion in three major coronary arteries: Right coronary artery (RCA), left anterior descending artery (LAD), and circumplex artery (CX) (Blascovich & Katkin, 1993).

successful performance on the one hand, and among stressfulness, cardio-vascular arousal, and coronary artery disease on the other hand, pose a theoretical and empirical dilemma for arousal-regulation research. How can data indicating that cardiovascular reactivity in potentially stressful performance situations positively indexes both adaptive processes (i.e., appetitive motivation, superior performance) and maladaptive processes (i.e., aversive motivation, stress, disease) be reconciled? In our view, the dilemma cannot be resolved satisfactorily using only a dipositional approach; instead, an interdisciplinary, multilevel approach is required.

C. OVERVIEW

In this chapter, we describe and discuss the results from a multidiscipli-nary, integrative approach to the study of arousal regulation, integrating not only dispositional but also cognitive, physiological, and social dimensions. In doing so, we move from discussion of the concept of *arousal* and the notion of *arousal regulation* to a description of our integrative *theoretical model,* the general *empirial model* we use in our work, and our major *research findings.* We also discuss *implications* of our work and chart *future directions* for empirical endeavors.

II. Arousal and Its Regulation

Arousal plays an important theoretical role in many categories of behav-ior. Intense emotional experiences and expressions such as terror, rage, lust, and ecstasy easily come to mind. Many other behavioral domains amenable to an arousal-based explanation exist including stress and stress management; anxiety disorders such as panic, hypochondriasis, and obsessive-compulsive disorder (cf. Barlow, 1988); and addictions (cf. Cappell & Greeley, 1987). Furthermore, the outcomes of dysfunctional, arousal-based processes include not only the aforementioned psychopathologies, but also medical problems such as coronary heart disease (see Blascovich & Katkin, 1993c, for a review) and immunosuppression (see O'Leary, 1990, for a review).

A. CONCEPTUAL ISSUES

We have discussed the ubiquity of the arousal construct in psychology in considerable detail elsewhere (Blascovich, 1990; Blascovich & Katkin, 1982; Blascovich & Kelsey, 1990). Arousal has generally played the role of a motivational or "emotivational" construct in psychological theories at least since Hull (1943). In social psychology, arousal has been a major motivational construct since the late 1800s. Indeed, in the last half of the twentieth century, arousal-based theories were at the forefront of the subdiscipline for nearly 30 years, until the social cognition perspective became prominent.[3]

Festinger's (1957) work revolutionized the attitude literature by introducing arousal, albeit initially in semidisguised form (e.g., dissonance), as the driving force underlying attitude change. The resulting plethora of consistency theories (Abelson et al., 1969) did not question Festinger's arousal and arousal reduction notions as much as they specified an ever-increasing number of antecedents to arousal. Similarly, Schachter and Singer (1962) revolutionized the conceptual role of arousal in emotion, a role that persisted for at least a quarter of a century. Most critics of Schachter and Singer's approach did not question the arousal component of the neo-Jamesian perspective. Rather they argued against and refined the cognitive aspects of the theory (e.g., Marshall & Zimbardo, 1979; Maslach, 1979). Likewise, classic theories of prosocial (e.g., Piliavin, Piliavin, & Rodin, 1975) and antisocial (e.g., Zillmann, 1978) behavior; social justice (e.g., Walster, Walster, & Berscheid, 1978); interpersonal influence (e.g., Triplett, 1987; Zajonc, 1965); and interpersonal attraction (e.g., Schachter, 1959)

---

[3] One might speculate that the reliance of mainstream theories in social psychology on a fuzzy, affect-related construct such as arousal contributed in at least a small way to the abandonment by many of arousal-based theories in social psychology for the more "rational" cognitive approach.

incorporated arousal as their primary motivational component and generally remained unchallenged in doing so.

Ubiquity, of course, does not guarantee clarity, and arousal remains largely a fuzzy concept, especially in social psychology. Indeed, the fact that the common language definition of arousal, "being stirred up to activity, or excited" (cf. *Oxford English Dictionary*, 1989), appears to be as good as a general psychological definition, speaks volumes to the lack of attention on the part of many social psychological theorists to this central theoretical concept. However, the common language definition of arousal lacks precise scientific meaning. As we have argued previously (Blascovich, 1992), because definitional imprecision typifies the arousal construct in many theories, the scientific meaning of arousal within these theories from its empirical operationalization must be inferred, an often hopeless task.

Two types of arousal constructs pervade psychological theories. Some (cf. Averill, 1974; Harre, 1972) argue that the most common usage is purely hypothetical or symbolic. This type includes all uses and definitions of arousal constructs for which empirical operationalizations and, hence, direct empirical assessments are inherently impossible; for example, notions such as intrapsychic tension, imbalance, or dissonance where the arousal construct serves as a mere metaphor. Use of arousal constructs in a metaphoric sense is often found in psychological theories, such as many of the social psychological theories previously noted, which in the Hullian tradition posit arousal as the primary motivational factor. Prototypically, certain theoretically specified circumstances (e.g., oppositional cognitions, inequity, mere presence) cause increasing levels of arousal (e.g., dissonance, feelings associated with being under- or overbenefited, energization), which the individual is more or less automatically driven to reduce.

The second, but historically less common, usage can be labeled scientific (cf. Harre, 1972). This category includes all uses and definitions of arousal constructs for which empirical assessments are possible. We have argued that the basis for the use of arousal constructs in the scientific sense should necessarily rest on firm physiological theory pertinent to the domains within which the specified arousal construct plays a theoretical role (Blascovich & Kelsey, 1990). Consequently, the use of any sort of general arousal construct, however valuable metaphorically, is not scientific.

B. MEASUREMENT

Two major approaches to the assessment of arousal constructs have pervaded the psychological literature: self-report and physiological. Often, each approach has been used naively. In essence, naive measurement of arousal, whether via self-report or physiological recording, results from the same fundamental problem—a lack of precise specification of the criteria for what constitutes an instance or episode of the arousal construct. The leap from hypothetical (metaphoric) usage of an arousal construct to measurement is always naive. Not surprisingly, an established self-report measure, or even a limited set of self-report measures, of general arousal has failed to take hold in the literature. Furthermore, without precise specification of the biological meaning of arousal, many researchers have used physiological measures, particularly autonomic measures, as though each were an independent and interchangeable measure of arousal.

Recently, theorists and researchers have taken a more precise and sophisticated view of arousal definition. This has resulted in more valid self-report and physiological measures. Notable, in regard to the former, are the efforts of Larsen, Diener, and Emmons (1986) and Shields (1989). The relative success of these more sophisticated self-report measures derives from the more precise specification of a narrower rather than a broader or more general arousal concept. Thus, the self-reported arousal in such theories is more limited and context specific.

Regarding physiological measures, Cacioppo and his colleagues (e.g., Berntson, Cacioppo, & Quigley, 1991; Cacioppo & Tassinary, 1990), as well as Blascovich and Kelsey (1990), have taken a strong position on precise specification of the arousal construct and the measurement of appropriate physiological responses. Hence,

> Valid physiological assessment of arousal requires the provision of a contextually relevant theoretical basis for the arousal construct and the measurement of a corresponding set of physiological responses over time (Blascovich & Kelsey, 1990; Cacioppo & Tassinary, 1990). Resulting patterns of physiological activity enable the investigator to determine the degree to which arousal of a theoretically specified type is present. (Blascovich et al., 1992, p. 165)

C. AROUSAL REGULATION DEFINED

How individuals become aroused and how they reduce, maintain, or enhance such arousal defines the domain of arousal-regulation theories. Such theories and research have appeared, not only within more biologically oriented subdisciplines of psychology such as psychophysiology (e.g., Fowles, 1988), but also within nonbiologically oriented subdisciplines such as personality (e.g., Eysenck, 1967; Stelmack, 1990) and social psychology (e.g., Carver & Scheier, 1990; Cioffi, 1991). Since the mid-1960s, arousal-regulation theories within each of these fields have advanced markedly, reflecting increased theoretical and methodological sophistication. Yet, these advances have occurred relatively independently.

D. SUMMARY

We maintain that the well-worn concept of arousal, although valuable theoretically and symbolically, often fails empirically because without concrete definition the scientific measurement of arousal remains futile. For scientific purposes, we argue that the arousal concept must be specified within an appropriate external (i.e., environmental) and internal (i.e., biological) context. Furthermore, we argue that disciplinarily idiosyncratic approaches to the study of arousal-regulation processes have limited value. We believe that a multidisciplinary biopsychosocial approach represents a much more fruitful approach for understanding arousal regulation.

III. Theory: The Biopsychosocial Model

A. GENERAL COMMENTS

A very primitive version of our arousal-regulation model appeared in the early 1980s (Blascovich & Katkin, 1982), an expanded version (Blascovich, 1990) and a revised version in the early 1990s (Blascovich, 1992), and herein the most recent version. Obviously, theoretical model building is a dynamic enterprise and scientists should expect to continuously expand and refine models over time. We believe the dynamics of our biopsychosocial modeling process provides a constantly advancing conceptual framework for explaining and testing arousal-regulation processes.

Importantly, although we apply the biopsychosocial model within a specific limited context, the model itself is general and does not necessarily depend on any particular concrete specification of arousal and associated arousal measurement strategy. Rather, the model can frame various specific arousal constructs and measurement strategies. For example, the model can frame affect (as a specific arousal construct) regulation exhibited and measured somatically via the facial musculature. It also can frame stress (as a specific arousal construct) regulation exhibited and measured autonomically via the electrodermal and cardiovascular system.

We believe that empirical research derived from our biopsychosocial model of arousal regulation has facilitated understanding of interactions among many of the intrapersonal, interpersonal, and physiological factors involved in arousal-regulation processes. These discoveries have led us to a theoretical account that resolves the apparent dilemma—arousal as beneficial versus arousal as pathological—described earlier.

Because arousal-regulation processes are undoubtedly multiply determined (cf. Cacioppo & Berntson, 1992; Dienstbier, 1989), integration of multiple levels of analysis (e.g., physiological, dispositional, cognitive, social) and methods has the potential to advance our understanding of arousal-regulation processes rapidly. Thus, arousal regulation, as a multiply determined process in the simplest case and as a set of multiply determined processes in the most complex case, requires an interdisciplinary approach. The biopsychosocial framework guiding our research is such an approach.

B. PRIMARY PROCESS

1. Situation-Arousal Component

According to the biopsychosocial (BPS) model (Figure 3), the major or primary arousal-regulation process (illustrated by the black, descending arrows) begins with the perception and subsequent cognitive appraisal of a goal-relevant situation which leads, in turn, to a pattern of physiological arousal associated with situational demands and appraisal outcome. A goal-relevant situation has perceived (real or imagined) consequences for the well-being (psychological or physical) of the individual (Lazarus, 1991). Individuals experience both metabolically demanding (e.g., track and field events) and nonmetabolically demanding (e.g., delivering a lecture, writing a memo) goal-relevant situations throughout their lives. Goal relevancy defines the general domain of the BPS model. Relatively nonmetabolically demanding, goal-relevant situations specify the domain within which we have, for the most part, concentrated our theoretical and empirical efforts.[4]

Nonmetabolically demanding, goal-relevant situations can occur in relatively passive form, such as the presentation of emotionally evocative photographs or news magazine accounts of the economy, attracting the individual's attention but requiring or demanding little or no immediate overt or cognitive action. Similar to Obrist (1981), we label this type of situation a *passive situation.* However, goal-relevant situations may occur in relatively interactive form, such as an academic examination, a speech, or a specific job duty, attracting not only the individual's attention, but also requiring

---

[4] Nonmetabolically demanding performance situations simply do not require the energy requirements of metabolically demanding ones. The latter, involving large muscle movement, represent quite a different domain for the BPS model. Undoubtedly, different patterns of cardiovascular response result from benign and malignant overall appraisals in metabolically demanding situations versus nondemanding situations.

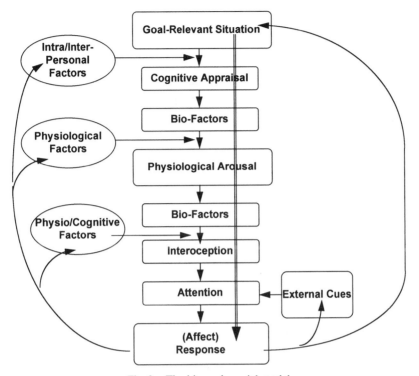

Fig. 3.   The biopsychosocial model.

or demanding immediate overt or cognitive action that can be evaluated by the individual and observers. We call the latter type of situation a *motivated performance situation*. Because both types of goal-relevant situations pervade our lives, both deserve study. However, because goal-relevant passive and motivated performance situations differ fundamentally in behavioral and cognitive demands for action, the type of goal-relevant situation, as it is hoped the reader sees from our data, must not be overlooked when making predictions about and conducting empirical studies of arousal-regulation processes. We mostly focus empirically on the motivated performance or active-coping (cf. Obrist, 1981) type of situation but also have data relevant to more passive kinds of situations.

The BPS model specifies *cognitive appraisal* as the initial mediator in the goal relevant situation-arousal component of the BPS model (see Figure 3). We specify a fairly simple cognitive appraisal process based on the phenomenological comparison of two component appraisals: primary and secondary. *Primary appraisal* refers to the degree of demand, uncertainty, and/or danger in the situation. *Secondary appraisal* refers to the degree of perceived resources or abilities that one brings to bear on the situation. If comparative primary and secondary appraisals result in a perception of demand that cannot be overcome by perceived resources, then *threat* becomes the overall resultant appraisal. If comparative primary and secondary appraisals result in a perception of resources that can overcome the perceived demand, then *challenge* becomes the overall resultant appraisal.

In our view, primary and secondary appraisals drive the resultant overall cognitive appraisals relatively equally in motivated performance situations. In passive situations, however, primary appraisals explain more of the variance in the resultant overall appraisals. Our arguments for this distinction are based on the following rationale. As previously discussed, we assume the goal relevance of both passive and motivated performance situations such that individuals are motivated to remain in and adapt to both types of situations as well as they can. Primary appraisals in both types of situations can vary considerably within individuals. However, the repertoire of resources that can be brought to bear on the two types of situations differs categorically within individuals. Resources appropriate to goal-relevant passive situations are likely to be limited to emotional stamina or endurance, or what Lazarus and Folkman (1984) termed "emotion-focused coping resources." Resources appropriate to goal-relevant motivated performance situations include not only emotion-based abilities but also cognitive and behavioral abilities, with Lazarus and Folkman (1984) termed "problem-focused coping resources." In essence, passive situations limit the range and relevance of secondary appraisals.

Although our notions of cognitive appraisal take root in Lazarus and Folkman's theoretical efforts (Lazarus, 1991; Lazrus & Folkman, 1984), important differences between their conceptions and our conceptions exist. First, the Lazarian concept of primary appraisal is much more inclusive than ours. For example, Lazarus includes goal relevance within the notion of primary appraisal, whereas we do not. Second, his notions of secondary appraisal are less situation specific than ours, as he does not emphasize the distinction that we (and others such as Obrist [1981]) do between passive and active (i.e., motivated performance) kinds of situations. Third, and perhaps most important, Lazarus and Folkman regard challenge as a type of primary appraisal, whereas we believe that challenge, especially in motivated performance situations, cannot be determined on the basis of primary appraisal alone, but must involve consideration of secondary appraisals of coping resources and abilities.

The situation-appraisal link in the BPS model is moderated by both intra- and interpersonal factors (see Figure 3). Intrapersonally, dispositional as well as cognitive and affective factors influence resultant appraisals of goal-relevant situations. We contend that certain personality traits predispose individuals to appraise situations as more or less challenging or threatening. The most important of these include self-esteem, belief in a just world, and a sense of control—traits that, in the proper configuration, can increase an individual's resilience. Certainly, individuals high in self-esteem, high in belief in a just world, and high in degree of perceived control would more likely make overall challenge appraisals compared to individuals low in these traits in motivated performance situations. Thus, we would expect individuals with the former configuration to make much higher secondary appraisals (i.e., of coping abilities) than individuals with the latter configuration. However, in our view, dispositions, although important, do not explain all the variance in overall cognitive appraisals.

Cognitive factors can also moderate the situation-appraisal link intrapersonally. Knowledge, past experiences in similar situations, and even attitudes can affect appraisals. Such factors can influence both primary and secondary appraisals in either a positive or negative direction. Finally, affective states can also moderate the situation-appraisal link intraindividually. Whether they do so directly by influencing appraisals (cf. Salovey & Birnbaum, 1989) or indirectly by stimulating state-congruent memories (cf. Kavanaugh & Bower, 1985) remains open to question and empirical investigation. Few clinicians would argue against the notion that individuals experiencing negative affective states experience more situational threat than individuals experiencing positive affective states.

Interpersonal factors also moderate the situation-appraisal link. Social facilitation theory and research (e.g., Zajonc, 1965) suggests that even the mere presence of others may moderate this link. Relationship nature may also be important (Allen, Blascovich, Tomaka, & Kelsey, 1991). The quality of relationships with others in motivated performance situations undoubtedly influences appraisals. For example, the presence of evaluative others may increase primary appraisal in motivated performance situations. However, the presence of nonevaluative, supportive others may decrease primary appraisal in such situations. Liking and interpersonal attraction may work in similar ways. In addition, group membership and social identity may moderate the situation-appraisal link. Stigma (Crocker & Major, 1989), stereotype vulnerability (Steele, 1992), ingroup and even outgroup characteristics most likely contribute to the nature of appraisals in goal-relevant situations.

Biological factors (see Figure 3) also mediate the goal-relevant, situation-physiological arousal component of the BPS model. Here, genetic, structural, and functional factors undoubtedly play a role. The importance of the role of hereditary factors for appraisal-driven physiological responses can be and certainly has been debated. However, as in all nativist-empiricist debates, extreme positions generally provide little substance for theoretical advancement. But, because biological structures and processes necessarily provide the mechanisms by which phenomenological experiences such as cognitive appraisals result in physiological responses, the mediating role of hereditary and anatomic factors cannot be dismissed.

Most assuredly, physiological influences moderate the biological factors–physiological arousal link in the BPS model (see Figure 3). Any factors that serve to disrupt the normal functioning of relevant neural and endocrine processes would also serve to disrupt normal physiological respones to cognitive appraisals in goal-relevant situations. For example, severe neuro-transmitter depletion might substantially alter somatic and vascular re-sponses. Pathophysiological (i.e., disease) states can substantially alter such responses. Metabolic changes induced by exercise or ingestion of foodstuffs and other substances (e.g., alcohol, caffeine, psychotropic drugs) can also alter such resposnes. Finally, maturational changes (e.g., puberty, senes-cence) can bring about such alterations.

In sum, biological factors (e.g., genetic, anatomic, functional) moderated by physiological processes (e.g., maturation, disease, metabolism) define the dynamic range of physiological arousal systems. Cognitive appraisals, moderated by intrapersonal factors (e.g., personality traits, attitudes, affec-tive states) and interpersonal factors (e.g., presence of others, interpersonal attraction) provide momentum and determine the direction of change or adjustment of the physiological arousal system. Thus, *these mediating and moderating factors account for individual differences in the intensity and polarity of arousal evoked by the same or similar stimuli.*

In passive goal-relevant situations, we believe that distinguishable pat-terns of physiological arousal follow from primary appraisals of demand or danger and are best differentiated somatically via the muscles of facial expression and differentiated to a lesser extent autonomically. In the case of motivated performance situations, we believe that distinguishable pat-terns of physiological arousal follow from the interaction of primary apprais-als of demand or danger and secondary appraisals of ability (i.e., overall challenge or threat appraisals) and can best be differentiated autonomically via myocardial and vascular responses.

2. Physiological Arousal-Response Component

This aspect of the BPS model focuses on the generation of arousal-motivated responses or behaviors. According to the BPS model (see Figure 3), biological factors, interoception, and attention, in turn, mediate the relationship between physiological arousal and resultant behaviors. We propose that biological factors mediate the arousal–interoception link. These factors are similar, and potentially related to, those mediating the link between cognitive appraisal and physiological arousal (e.g., anatomy, genetics). Likewise, physiological factors similar to, and perhaps related to, those moderating the link between biological factors and physiological arousal (e.g., pathophysiology, metabolism, maturation) moderate the biological factors–interoception link.

According to the BPS model, internal (i.e., interoceptive or somesthetic) and external (i.e., environmental) cues of stimuli compete for the individual's attentional capacity.The allocation of attention varies, in part, as a function of the relative influence and strength of these two cue sources. A somesthetically hypersensitive individuals (e.g., a hypochondriac) might fix attention nearly exclusively on internal physiological cues, whereas, a somesthetically hyposensitive individual might fix attention almost exclusively on external or environmental cues.

The importance of the physiological arousal-response component of the BPS model derives from the orthogonality of dispositional physiological response levels (i.e., individual response stereotypy) and dispositional somesthetic sensitivity. Physiologically hyper-reactive individuals are not necessarily somesthetically hypersensitive. Wide individual and group differences exist in this regard (Katkin, Blascovich, & Goldband, 1981; Reed, Harver, & Katkin, 1990; Roberts & Pennebaker, 1995). Thus, except perhaps at extreme levels of physiological arousal, wide variation exists in the somesthetic accuracy of individuals even for relatively specific visceral responses such as heartbeats, respiratory cycles, and intestinal responses (Reed et al., 1990) (Figure 4).

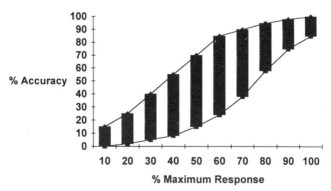

Fig. 4.   Theoretical variability in somesthetic accuracy as a function of intensity of physiological response.

We maintain that phenomenological experiences driven by physiological responses in goal-relevant situations vary as a function of the interoceptive or somesthetic sensitivity of the individual. Furthermore, we maintain that when phenomenological/physiological verdicality occurs, most likely the overall *intensity* of physiological responses is more accurately experienced somesthetically rather than specific patterns necessarily composed of multiple physiological responses. We maintain that the *specificity* of arousal-based phenomenological experiences is mainly a function of the preceding overall cognitive appraisal and the presence of confirming and disconfirming external or environmental cues. Thus, internal physiological cues more likely drive the intensity rather than polarity of emotivational states resulting from overall cognitive appraisals of goal-relevant situations. In the absence of physiological cues, individuals must rely on initial appraisals and concomitant external cues for both the intensity and specificity of emotivational states.

According to the BPS model (see Figure 3), the primary process results in a motivated, multifaceted response. We assume that such a response includes affective, cognitive, and behavioral components, although in our view the affective component orients the others. Specifically, the affective polarity of a response generally determines the arousal-regulation goals of the cognitive or behavioral response components. If the polarity is negative, arousal-reducing cognitive and behavioral responses should predominate. If the polarity is positive, arousal-enhancing cognitive and behavioral responses should predominate.

3. Responses

Affect-relevant, arousal-regulation responses include a raft of possible self-protective and/or self-enhancing behavioral interventions and cognitive strategies. As illustrated by the upward pointing arrow in the far right of Figure 3, some responses (usually behavioral) are intended to alter the goal-relevant situation itself or at least external cues associated with the situation. Although the essential aspects of the goal-relevant situation cannot be changed without altering the goal-relevant nature of the situation itself, certain aspects of these situations relevant to primary appraisal (i.e., demand, uncertainty, danger) may be modified. For example, a doctoral student might arrange that his or her dissertation defense take place in a pleasant physical environment.

Other behavioral responses can influence the moderating factors previously discussed (see Figure 3). For example, our doctoral student might arrange that nonessential, evaluative others (e.g., peers, parents) absent themselves from the oral defense, or, conversely, that nonessential, nonevaluative others appear at the defense. Ingestion of alcohol or other psychotropic drugs might alter moderating physiological factors in ways that can either increase or decrease physiological arousal responses and/or interoception, or that can affect physiological arousal directly. Finally, cognitive strategies including defensive mechanisms, attitude change, self-handicapping strategies, meditation, imagery, and so on, can alter these same moderating factors.

C. SECONDARY PROCESS

The BPS model allows for direct association (i.e., secondary process) between goal-relevant situations and arousal-regulation responses. Specifically, the primary process need not occur in every goal-relevant situation for arousal-regulation to occur. A secondary process can operate (illustrated by the long descending arrow linking the situation and response components in Figure 3). If the association between a goal-relevant situation and arousal-regulation responses becomes well learned, the secondary, associationistic process may operate (cf. Harris & Katkin, 1975). The relative rapidity of an arousal-regulation response once the individual finds him- or herself in a motivated performance situation indicates the likely operation of a secondary process. Thus, to the extent that the goal-relevant situation is familiar, a direct link between the situation and response will facilitate arousal-regulation responses. Conversely, to the extent that the goal-relevant situation is novel, the full primary process will occur.

D. THE ITERATIVE NATURE OF THE PRIMARY PROCESS

Because of the dynamic character of most goal-relevant situations, individuals constantly reappraise them. For example, the fact that an individual endured the first few moments of a horror film (i.e., passive situation) might cause the individual to reduce his or her primary appraisal of it or increase his or her perceptions of ability to emotionally endure the film. Similarly, the fact that an individual survived the first few moments of an important speech (i.e., motivated performance situation) with positive audience feedback might cause the individual to reappraise the situation more positively. Of course, such reappraisals might take a negative turn as well, or even alternate very quickly between positive and negative reappraisals. In addition, once the individual initiates an arousal-regulation response, the situation must be reappraised.

IV. Empirical Model

As previously discussed we believe that the BPS model can help us to understand the nature of arousal-regulation within goal-relevant situations. However, empirical tests of the model require a contextually (i.e., goal-relevant situation) appropriate, theoretically based (i.e., psychophysiologically based) concept of arousal, with valid specified indices of arousal—that is, *an empirical model.*

We have benefited from access to such an empirical model in the same way that biomedical researchers have benefited from access to "animal models" of health and disease. To illustrate, certain strains of mice are predisposed to develop certain types of cancers, whereas other strains are relatively immune to such disease. In the natural course of maturation, individual animals within the susceptible strain will almost certainly develop disease, whereas individual animals from the immune strain will not. By assessing deviations from the natural developmental course of the disease (e.g., among susceptible strains), biomedical researchers are able to examine experimentally potential mediators and moderators of disease outcomes.

Following the same rationale, we have aspired to develop and use standard empirical models in order to investigate the BPS model empirically. In addition to being ecologically and theoretically valid, such models must also be pragmatic, that is, relatively easily incorporated into experiments. Conceptually, the empirical models that we have used in the past and currently employ are short-lived, laboratory-based *motivated performance situations.* Such situations, as previously described are goal relevant to the individual, are presented to the individual in relatively interactive form, and demand relatively immediate overt or cognitive action that can be evaluated by the performer and observers.

Many laboratory situations involving performance tasks qualify as motivated performance situations, not only because they include a task demanding overt or cognitive action on the part of study participants, but also because they engender a meaningful degree of evaluation apprehension (Rosenberg, 1965). That is, participants generally believe that their performance on the laboratory task provides the observer (i.e., experimenter) with valid information about task-relevant skills and abilities that generally reflect on their self-worth. In a psychophysiology laboratory, the attachment of electrophysiological sensors and other transducers reinforces and enhances evaluation apprehension, an argument supported by the rationale of, and data pertinent to the "bogus pipeline" (Jones & Sigall, 1971) and various forms of lie detection. Specific performance tasks that we have used within our laboratory-based motivated performance situation category include mathematical (e.g., serial subtraction, number series problems), analytic (e.g., the Remote Associates Task) (McFarlin & Blascovich, 1981; Mednick, 1962), attitudinal (e.g., pairwise preference judgments), signal detection (e.g., choice-deadline reaction time tasks), and verbal (e.g., speech anticipation and delivery) tasks.

Much of our empirical work actually has been devoted to the explication of cardiovascular response patterns evoked during motivated performance situations. These response patterns have theoretical roots in the pioneering work of Obrist (1981) on active coping and Dienstbier's (1989) work on physiological toughness. According to Obrist, integration of cardiovascular and somatomotor activity via the central nervous system occurs frequently in daily life. Such integration results in what Obrist termed "cardiac-somatic coupling," during which parasympathetic (i.e., vagal) control dominates over sympathetic control of the heart. Cardiac-somatic coupling occurs during activities such as rest and exercise, and during conditions that involve passive receipt of environmental stimulation. According to Obrist, lack of cardiovascular and somatomotor integration, which he termed "cardiac-somatic uncoupling," occurs during situations that require the individual to cope actively. During cardiac-somatic uncoupling, Obrist maintained that sympathetic influences dominate cardiac control.

Functionally, however, it seems unlikely that a unitary pattern of cardio-vascular response (i.e., one indexing cardiac-somatic uncoupling) that is consistently and invariably elicited during active coping (or what we term "motivated performance") exists. Such a unitary pattern would suggest no biological or physiological differentiation between motivated performance situations in which benign, positive appraisals predominate from those motivated performance situations in which malignant, negative appraisals predominate—a situation that is unlikely at best.

More recently, Dienstbier (1989) and others (e.g., Manuck, Kamarck, Kasprowicz, & Waldstein, 1993) have delineated more than one possible pattern of autonomic responses during motivated performances situations. Increased activity of the sympathetic-adrenomedullary (SAM) axis marks a benign pattern. Increased activity of the pituitary-adrenocortical (PAC) axis marks a malignant pattern when such activation occurs alone or in combination with SAM activation. In the context of cardiovascular arousal during motivated performance situations, the benign pattern (i.e., SAM activation) would be expected to be associated with positive cognitive ap-praisals and marked by increasing cardiac or myocardial performance and by decreasing vascular resistance. In contrast, the malignant pattern (i.e., PAC activation or SAM/PAC coactivation) would be expected to be associated with negative cognitive appraisals and increasing cardiac or myocardial performance, but accompanied by stable or increasing vascular resistance.[5]

With regard to neural control, we suspect that the benign pattern of physiological activation is reflected by relatively pure SAM activation, which includes 1) sympathetic neural stimulation of the myocardium that enhances cardiac performance, and 2) adrenal medullary release of epinephrine causing vasodilation in large skeletal muscle beds and bronchi, resulting in an overall decline in systemic vascular resistance, as well as some additional enhancement of cardiac performance. Functionally, this pattern represents the efficient mobilization of energy for coping. Regarding the malignant pattern, as noted, we suspect dual activation of the SAM and PAC axes. In our view, SAM neural stimulation of the myocardium causes elevations of cardiac performance over resting levels. However, accompanying PAC activity inhibits SAM release of epinephrine and norephinephrine from the adrenal medulla. Such inhibition results in moderate elevations in cardiac output without accompanying decreases in systemic vascular resistance. We believe that the inhibitory effect of PAC activity on SAM activity reflects anxiety and uncertainty over options for coping (e.g., flight or avoidance versus task performance). To a certain extent, our hypotheses regardig PAC inhibition are based on neurophysiological work linking anxiety and anxiety-related behavior to brain centers that control PAC activity (e.g., the septo-hippocampal system) (Gray, 1982; McNaughton, 1993).

V. Research

A. BACKGROUND

Prior to our work and the appearance of our BPS model, arousal-relevant physiological coping models, such as Obrist's (1981) model, and cognitive

---

[5] Many authors have noted differences in activation along these two SNS subsystems (Lundberg & Frankenhaeuser, 1980; Mason, 1975), and such differences can be traced to theoretical differences between Cannon and Selye as to how to view stress responses. Contemporary researchers have argued that the SAM is an "effort" system, responsible primarily for energy mobilization to support actual or anticipated behavioral coping. The PAC system, in contrast, is a "distress" system associated with perceptions of actual or potential physical or psychological harm. Relevant to our hypothesis that the PAC system is associated with malignant cognitive appraisals, Mason (1975) and others (Lovallo, Pincomb, Brackett, & Wilson, 1990) have demonstrated convincingly the extreme sensitivity of the PAC system to negative emotional experience. Moreover, regarding the hypothesized relationship of the SAM to benign cognitive appraisals, the SAM system appears sensitive to emotional factors (i.e., positive and negative) only to the extent that they involve energy mobilization (e.g., fear or exhilaration).

appraisal coping models, such as Lazarus and Folkman's (1984), had not been integrated. Psychophysiological and cognitive-appraisal researchers made implicit assumptions regarding the other domain, largely ignoring advances in those domains. For example, for Obrist and many subsequent cardiovascular psychophysiological theorists and researchers (with the notable exception of Dientsbier), all active-coping situations were presumed as stressful or threatening, and resulting cardiovascular responses were used to index the degree of stress or threat. However, for Lazarus, differences in physiological response patterns underlying passive and active situations were largely ignored.

As social psychophysiologists, it seemed to us that laboratory tasks used to explore the nature of cardiovascular reactivity to stress could be used to experimentally test cognitive appraisal notions as well. That is, individuals should show less of a stress response (i.e., less cardiovascular reactivity) if we can intervene and decrease their primary appraisals of demand and danger, increase their secondary appraisals of ability, or both. Of course, such an idea did not develop as clearly and as quickly as the previous couple of sentences imply. Rather, the idea came about as the result of two experiments that we conducted. In addition, it is important to note that our notion regarding stress response and cardiovascular reactivity was naive and not yet as sophisticated as the challenge and threat patterns previously discussed.

B. EARLY STUDIES

1. Self-Deception and Self-Presentation Concern

Numerous investigators have demonstrated differences in cardiovascular arousal during active-coping tasks (i.e., motivated performance situations) as a function of dispositional or personality factors, such as coronary-prone personality, hostility, and so on. Although it is now clear to us that these dispositional factors moderate the situation-appraisal link in the BPS model (see Figure 3), it was not always so apparent. Our early efforts in the area of personality factors focused on dispositional defensiveness. Tomaka, Blascovich, and Kelsey (1992)[6] investigated the relationships between cardiovascular reactivity and dispositional defensiveness constructs, including self-deception and self-presentation concern, using mental arithmetic tasks in a motivated performance situation.

[6] Due to the vagaries of publication, reference dates throughout the article to our empirical work are not indicative of the actual order in which studies were conducted. Studies were conducted in the order explicit or implied in the text of the manuscript.

Subjects arrived at our laboratory by appointment. As is typical in cardio-vascular reactivity studies, they received instructions regarding the upcoming experiment including the nature of the task that they would be performing and the nature of the physiological measures that would be taken. After providing informed consent, subjects entered a recording room where appropriate physiological sensors and transducers were affixed. Subsequently, subjects were allowed to relax and adapt to the recording room environmental before baseline physiological recordings were made. Following the baseline recording period, subjects received instructions regarding the upcoming mental arithmetic task (i.e., serial subtraction) and answered questions designed to ascertain both their primary and secondary appraisals of the ensuing task. After it was clear that participants understood the task instructions, their performance commenced.

For this particular study, subjects had filled out questionnaires during a prior mass testing session designed to measure target disposition. Self-deception and self-presentation concern were assessed via Sackheim and Gur's (1979) self-deception scale and Crowne and Marlowe's (1964) social desirability scale, respectively. In our sample, the correlation between these two variables was positive and significant [$r(63) = .33$, $p < .01$]. For purposes of subsequent analyses, subjects were divided (based on median splits) into high and low groups on each target disposition. These analyses revealed that the high self-deception group made lower primary appraisals of the upcoming task and showed smaller increases in physiological response (i.e., heart rate) during the task (Figure 5) than the low self-deception group. The high compared to the low self-presentation concern group, however, did not differ in appraisals but did differ in physiological response.

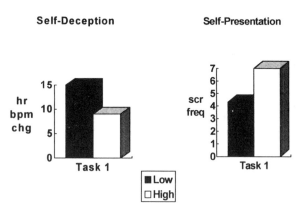

Fig. 5. Autonomic responses as a function of dispositional defensiveness (Adapted from Tomaka et al., 1992).

The former group exhibited greater increases in physiological response (i.e., skin conductance responses) during the task (see Figure 5).

These data intrigued us because they demonstrated that two dispositional constructs, although positively related, were related to different patterns of autonomic response during a motivated performance situation. We reasoned that individuals high in self-deception were less affected by the potentially stressful experimental task than individuals low in self-deception, whereas individuals high in self-presentation concern were more affected by the experimental task than individuals low in self-presentation concern. Because of the key pretask difference in primary appraisal between high and low self-deceivers, we concluded that these dispositions affected the phenomenological experience of the experimental task and that such experience was potentially mediated via cognitive appraisal processes.

2. Human and Canine Friends

At about the same time, we conducted another study varying the presence of others during performance of an active-coping task, again, mental arithmetic. In this study (Allen et al., 1991), we recorded autonomic responses while middle-age women performed mental arithmetic tasks in our laboratory and again 2 weeks later in their homes. The presence manipulations were accomplished in the home setting where the subjects either performed the active-coping tasks "alone" (control condition), in the presence of their best female human friend, or in the presence of their beloved pet dog with the experimenter present in all three conditions.

The presence of the human friend resulted in significantly larger increases in autonomic responses (Figure 6) compared to the presence of just the experimenter (control condition). Conversely, the presence of the pet dog

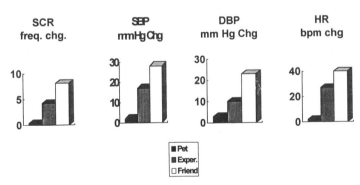

Fig. 6.   Cardiovascular reactivity as a function of the presence of others (Adapted from Allen et al., 1991).

resulted in significantly smaller autonomic increases than the presence of just the experimenter. Futhermore, the presence of a human friend resulted in substantial performance decrements compared to the other conditions. We interpreted the results of this study in terms of the perceived evaluative nature of the human friend. We reasoned that the human friend was more likely to be perceived as evaluative than the canine friend. Hence, in our view, the presence of the friend increased the threat of the situation.

3. Theoretical Impact

These early studies confirmed that intrapersonal (i.e., self-deception and self-presentation concern) and interpersonal (i.e., presence of others) factors could moderate autonomic responses, particularly skin conductance and cardiovascular responses (e.g., blood pressure, heart rate). Furthermore, these studies suggested to us that these factors probably moderate an early stage or link in the situation-arousal component of the BPS model.[7] This link likely involved the perception and interpretation or "cognitive appraisal" of the stimulus situation itself. In the dispositional study (Tomaka et al., 1992) previously described, we hypothesized that denial-based dispositions such as self-deception might alter the cognitive-appraisal process causing individuals high in such traits to make more benign appraisals of potentially stressful events. Indeed, high self-deceivers reported the initial upcoming mental arithmetic task (i.e., after instructions and immediately before performance) as significantly less threatening than low self-deceivers.

The specific physiological responses measured in these studies were primarily chosen naively as more or less interchangeable indices of arousal associated with cardiac-somatic uncoupling and on the basis of available technology. As we show, both the theoretical underpinnings and the specific physiological indices of arousal in motivated performance situations were to change.

C. THE MEDIATING ROLE OF COGNITIVE APPRAISAL

We next undertook a series of studies to examine the possible mediating role of cognitive appraisal within the situation-physiological arousal component of the BPS model. As we conducted these studies, it became apparent to us from both theoretical work (e.g., Dienstbier, 1989, as previously discussed) and empirical work (based on some chapters in Blascovich &

---

[7] At the time this study was conducted, cognitive appraisal was not specified in the BPS model (cf. Blascovich, 1990).

Katkin, 1993a) that there were two discernible patterns of cardiovascular responses or reactivity that could be found in motivated performance situations. Large increases in cardiac responses accompanied by large decreases in systemic vascular resistance marked one pattern, whereas some increase in cardiac responses accompanied by small increases in systemic vascular resistance marked the other pattern. Furthermore, the benign nature of the former pattern and the malignant nature of the latter pattern had been suggested by Dienstbier (1989) and Manuck et al. (1993), respectively.

Cardiac changes could be ascertained using mesures such as pre-ejection period (PEP) (i.e., ventricular contractility), cardiac output (CO) (i.e., the product of stroke volume and heart rate), and heart rate (HR). Systemic vascular changes could be ascertained using a measure of total peripheral resistance (TPR). The availability of impedance cardiographic and continuous blood pressure monitoring equipment, as well as appropriate data acquisition and scoring software that had been previously developed and tested in large part in our laboratory (Kelsey & Guethlein, 1990), faciliated such multidimensional cardiovascular assessment.[8]

We conducted three types of studies designed to determine whether positive or benign cognitive appraisals in motivated performance situations were associated with the benign pattern of cardiovascular responses and whether negative appraisals were associated with the malignant pattern. In the first type of study, subjects freely appraised upcoming tasks in a motivated performance situation. In the second type, we independently manipulated appraisals. In the third, we manipulated patterns of cardiovascular response (i.e., benign versus malignant). As will become apparent, each methodology has distinct implications for the BPS model. For example, if cognitive appraisal mediated the situation-physiological arousal link of the BPS model, we would expect that both free and manipulated appraisals would be associated with the appropriate cardiovascular response patterns, but that the manipulation of the cardiovascular responses themselves would be unrelated to appraisals.

1. Free Appraisal Studies

In our first set of studies (Tomaka, Blascovich, Kelsey, & Leitten, 1993), subjects performed mental arithmetic tasks in a motivated performance situation (i.e., two mental arithmetic tasks in an evaluative context). Before each task but after task instructions, the subjects' primary appraisals (i.e.,

[8] Robert A. Kelsey provided the psychophysiological expertise and conducted beta tests of the software, and William Guethlein provided the programming expertise in this joint effort.

task demands) and secondary appraisals (i.e., available resources) for the upcoming tasks were assessed. Before and during each task, subjects' cardiovascular responses were continuously recorded. In all three experiments, cognitive appraisals were positively related to self-reported stress levels such that the more threatened the individual before the task, the more stress the subject reported experiencing during a task.[9]

Assessments of primary and secondary appraisals were accomplished by means of self-report to queries designed to tap explicitly notions of primary and secondary appraisals as previously described (cf. Lazarus & Folkman, 1984). Primary appraisal was assessed with the question, "How threatening do you expect the upcoming task to be?" Secondary appraisal was assessed with the question, "How able are you to cope with the upcomng task?" Judgments were made on similar seven-point scales. However, in a deviation from previous appraisal research, and based on our belief that challenge appraisals necessarily involve secondary appraisals of coping ability, we chose to distinguish challenged subjects from threatened subjects based on the patterns of primary and secondary appraisal. Subsequently, subjects were classified as challenged if their secondary appraisals of coping ability exceeded their primary appraisals of task threat. Conversely, subjects were classified as threatened if the opposite relationship was true.[10]

In the first study, in which we did not include measures allowing us to assess vascular resistance, we found that overall challenge (i.e., benign) appraisals were associated with greater cardiac and hemodynamic responses during task performance than overall threat (i.e., malignant) appraisals. In the second study, in which we used impedance cardiography together with continuous blood pressure monitoring, groups of subjects with categorically different appraisals, challenge or threat, exhibited reliably different patterns of cardiovascular responses during task performance (Figure 7). Specifically, an overall *challenge appraisal* resulted in relatively strong increases in myocardial performance during performance and an accompanying strong decrease in vascular resistance; whereas an overall *threat appraisal* resulted in somewhat smaller increases in myocardial performance, but also a small increase in vascular resistance during performance. Furthermore, as expected, subjects who made challenge appraisals outperformed subjects who made threat appraisals (Figure 8).

The physiological pattern as well as performance data were replicated for the motivated performance type of situation in a third study, which included type of situation as a between subjects factor. Situation was manip-

---

[9] These task stress self-reports were assessed post hoc immediately following task completion.

[10] This simplistic algorithm is certainly not the only one possible. More complicated, potentially more accurate algorithms are in the offing.

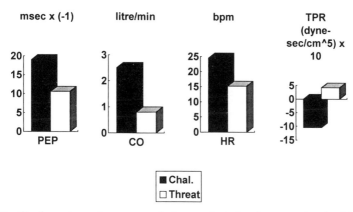

Fig. 7.   Cardiac and vascular responses during a motivated performance situation (Adapted from Tomaka et al., 1993; Study 2).

ulated by requiring either that subjects perform in a psychologically de-manding motivated performance situation (i.e., mental arithmetic) or en-gage in a passive task situation (i.e., view slides of mutilated automobile accident victims, maxillofacial surgery patients).

Figure 9 shows that, as in the prior study, the same patterns of cardiac and vascular reactivity resulted for those making challenge and threat appraisals in the motivated performance situation. For the passive task, however, as Figure 10 depicts, only primary appraisals were relevant and

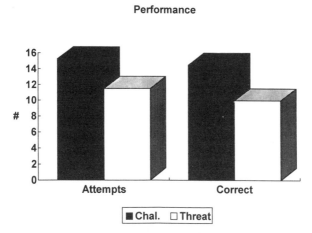

Fig. 8.   Performance data (Adapted from Tomaka et al., 1993; Study 2).

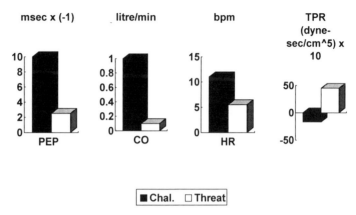

Fig. 9.   Cardiac and vascular responses during a motivated performance situation (Adapted from Tomaka et al., 1993; Study 3).

directly related to the relative intensity of cardiac responses. There were no differences for vascular responses (i.e., TPR). This pattern of relations for passive coping underscores our earlier point that type of goal-relevant situation is critical to the determination of expected appraisal-physiological response linkages.

2. Appraisal Manipulation

At this point, we were certainly aware that the relationships we had demonstrated between cognitive appraisals, as we had operationally defined

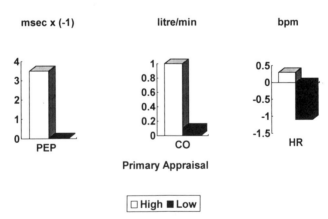

Fig. 10.   Cardiac and vascular responses during a passive situation (Adapted from Tomaka et al., 1993; Study 3).

them, and patterns of cardiac and vascular responses were essentially corre-lational. In addition, these relationships did not verify the direction of causality—from appraisal to physiological response—that we had postu-lated.

In another study (Tomaka & Lovegrove, 1995), we addressed this concern by manipulating an instructional set to encourage challenge or threat ap-praisals in a motivated performance situation involving a mental arithmetic task. The manipulation of the instructional set was within subjects and appropriately counterbalanced. Challenge instructions reflected our request that subjects try their best and think of the task as something to be met and overcome. Threat instructions, in contrast, emphasized that task perfor-mance was mandatory for subjects and that our intention was to evaluate task performance. Results indicated that the instructional sets produced the expected patterns of appraisal (Figure 11) and physiological reactivity (i.e., less cardiac contractility), and an increase in systemic vascular resis-tance (see Figure 11). Challenge instructions resulted in lower stress ap-praisals, greater cardiac reactivity, and a decline in systemic vascular resis-tance. Thus, these data provide compelling support that causality runs from cognition (i.e., appraisals) to physiological response.

3. Arousal Manipulation

It was also incumbent upon us to test the more Jamesian-like notion of causality—from physiological response to appraisal. This involved two studies conducted in our laboratory (Blascovich, Kibler, Ernst, Tomaka, & Vargas, 1994) one in which we independently manipulated the threat pat-tern of cardiovascular response, and one in which we independently manip-ulated the challenge pattern of cardiovascular response prior to engaging

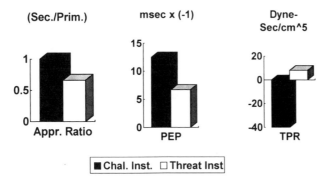

Fig. 11.   Cardiac and vascular responses as a function of instructional set (Adapted from Tomaka & Lovegrove, 1995).

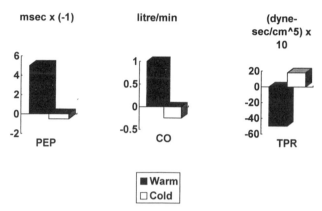

Fig. 12.   Pressor responses (Adapted from Blascovich, Kibler, Ernst, Tomaka, 1994).

subjects in a motivated performance situation involving mental arithmetic. To make a long story short, our physiological manipulations were successful. The use of cold and warm pressors allowed us to reproduce a pattern of cardiovascular responses similar to the prototypical challenge and threat patterns (Figure 12). Similarly, the use of moderate exercise (50 W on a recumbent ergometer) allowed us to reproduce a pattern of cardiovascular response similar to the challenge pattern (Figure 13). The control group in this study simply sat without pedaling the ergometer. Importantly, there were *no* resulting differences (appropriate $F's < 1$) in cognitive appraisal as a function of the manipulated physiological responses. In sum, these

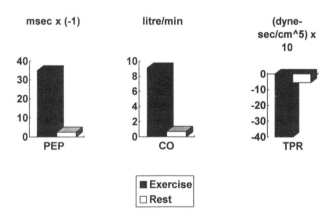

Fig. 13.   Exercise responses (Adapted from Blascovich et al., 1994).

findings, although null, suggest that physiological response patterns do not mediate cognitive appraisal.

4. Summary

Our appraisal studies demonstrated that critically different patterns of cardiovascular responses result from overall challenge and threat appraisals in nonmetabolically demanding, motivated performance situations. Specifically, these patterns held in experiments involving free appraisals and manipulated appraisals. Moreover, independent manipulations of the different patterns of cardiovascular responses themselves were not related to differences in overall cognitive appraisals. Hence, we believe that cognitive appraisal is a critical mediator in the arousal-regulation process (see Figure 3).

D. INTRAPERSONAL MODERATORS OF THE SITUATION-COGNITIVE APPRAISAL LINK

As discussed, the BPS model specifies both intra- and interpersonal moderators of the situation-cognitive appraisal link. We have focused theoretically and empirically on three types of intrapersonal moderators: dispositional, cognitive, and affective. To date, we have completed at least one study within each type or category and have several more in progress. The completed studies demonstrate that these types of intraindividual factors do indeed moderate the situation-appraisal link.

1. Dispositional Moderators: Belief in a Just World

Individuals vary dispositionally in their general beliefs regarding fairness in the world. Some believe that people generally "get what they deserve" from life, whereas others believe that "life is inherently unfair" (Lerner, 1980). According to several theorists (e.g., Lazarus & Folkman, 1984; Lerner, 1980, Lerner & Miller, 1978) dispositional belief in a just world protects individuals, allowing them to adapt better to the demands of everyday life.

We (Tomaka & Blascovich, 1994) conducted a study to determine whether dispositional belief in a just world moderates appraisals in motivated performance situations. Prior to instructions and "hook-up" within a typical motivated performance situation in our laboratory (i.e., serial subtraction), subjects completed the Belief in a Just World (BJW) scale (Rubin & Peplau, 1975). Subsequently, we assessed subjects' cardiovascular responses during a sequence of two rest and task performance periods.

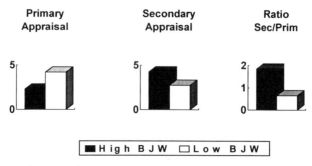

Fig. 14.   Cognitive appraisal as a function of Belief in a Just World (BJW) (Adapted from Tomaka & Blascovich, 1994).

Primary and secondary appraisals were assessed following task instructions. Subjective measures of task stress and performance were assessed immediately following each task performance.

As expected, appraisals of the upcoming tasks differed as a function of BJW. High BJW subjects made significantly lower primary appraisals and more challenging overall appraisals (i.e., ratio of secondary to primary appraisal) of the upcoming tasks (Figure 14). Also, as expected high BJW subjects exhibited the challenge pattern (i.e., strong increases in cardiac performance coupled with strong vasodilation), whereas low BJW subjects exhibited the threat pattern (i.e., increases in cardiac performance coupled with slight vasoconstriction) (Figure 15). Furthermore, regarding perceptions, high BJW subjects perceived the tasks as less stressful and perceived their performance to be better than low BJW subjects (Figure 16). Finally, high BJW subjects performed better than low BJW subjects (Figure 17).

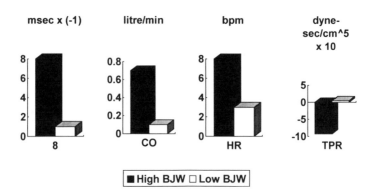

Fig. 15.   Cardiac and vascular responses as a function of Belief in a Just World (BJW) (Adapted from Tomaka & Blascovich, 1994).

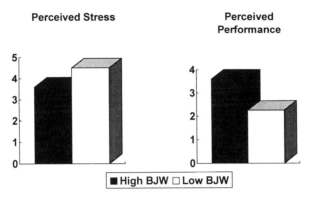

Fig. 16.   Task perceptions as a function of Belief in a Just World (BJW) (Adapted from Tomaka & Blascovich, 1994).

The results of the BJW study confirm that dispositional factors can moderate the situation-appraisal link. Undoubtedly, other dispositional factors also moderate the link. For example, that self-esteem and personal control moderate the same process can easily be justified theoretically and on the basis of nonphysiological research (Becker, 1975; Greenberg, Pyszczynski, & Solomon, 1987; Lazarus, 1983; Lerner, 1980).

2. Cognitive Moderators: Attitudes

Many theorists argue that attitudes function to facilitate decision making, thereby easing one's journey through life (Allport, 1935; Fazio, 1989; Katz, 1960; Smith, Bruner, & White, 1956). Presumably, attitudes provide individ-

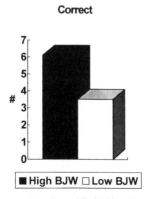

Fig. 17.   Task performance as a function of Belief in a Just World (BJW) (Adapted from Tomaka & Blascovich, 1994).

uals with relatively accessible knowledge that enables them to make easier decisions in demanding situations. From the perspective of the theoretical BPS model, attitudes should serve to decrease primary appraisal by decreasing the perceived uncertainty and demands of the situation and to increase secondary appraisal by increasing the perceived knowledge or abilities that one brings to a motivated performance situation in which attitude objects play a pivotal role. Overall, then, task object-relevant attitudes should increase the likelihood of a challenge rather than a threat appraisal in a motivated performance situation, thereby causing a challenge rather than a threat pattern of cardiovascular activity.

Fazio, Blascovich, and Driscoll (1992) reported a relevant paradigm and some interesting studies suggesting that attitudes toward specific objects could serve to lower blood pressure for individuals during demanding decision-making tasks involving those objects. Although these findings are certainly consistent with a moderating role for attitudes in the situation-appraisal link of the situation-arousal component of the BPS model, they are not specific vis-à-vis the distinctive pattern of cardiovascular responses associated with challenge and threat, respectively.

Although not specifically testing attitudes as a moderator within the situation-arousal component of the BPS model at the time, we (Blascovich et al., 1993; Experiment 2) did conduct a study that, in retrospect, tested this aspect of the model quite nicely. In this study, individuals were brought into the laboratory for a two-phase experiment. In the first phase, subjects developed attitudes toward a set of novel objects, abstract paintings, using an attitude rehearsal procedure developed by Fazio and colleagues (e.g., Fazio, Chen, McDonel, & Sherman, 1982). Half of the subjects rehearsed attitudes toward one subset (15) of the abstract paintings, and the other half rehearsed attitudes toward a mutually exclusive subset (15) of the abstract paintings. In the second phase, a motivated performance situation, subjects made rapid pairwise preference judgments for 34 slides of randomly paired abstract paintings (i.e., attitude objects). Half of each group of subjects expressed preferences within paired abstract paintings selected from the subset toward which they had rehearsed attitudes, whereas the other half were presented pairs from the unfamiliar subset. Throughout the experiment, the subjects' cardiovascular responses were continuously monitored using impedance cardiographic and blood pressure monitoring equipment.

Drawing on the BPS model, we hypothesized that in the pairwise preference situation (i.e., motivated performance situation) for which rehearsed attitudes were relevant (i.e., involving rehearsed, familiar attitude objects), a challenge pattern of cardiovascular arousal should be evident, whereas in the situation for which rehearsed attitudes were irrelevnt, more of a threat pattern should be evident. The data confirm our hypothesis. As Figure 18 shows, subjects in the rehearsed painting condition exhibited increased cardiac response and vasodilation, the challenge pattern, whereas subjects in the novel painting condition exhibited increased cardiac response and vasoconstriction, the threat pattern.

Just as the BJW study confirmed that dispositional factors can moderate the situation-appraisal link and resulting patterns of physiological response, our attitude study confirmed that cognitive factors can also moderate the link and resulting physiological patterns. The nature of these other cognitive factors remains speculative at this point, although we certainly believe that associative learning and memory play an important role. In addition, we believe that cognitive factors may moderate the situation-appraisal link, either positively or negatively. Thus, individuals who find themselves in motivated performance situations similar to those in which they have previously prevailed may be more likely to appraise the new situation as challenging, whereas those who find themselves in situations similar to those in which they have previously failed may be more likely to appraise the new situation as threatening.

3. Affective Moderators: Music and Pain

Theoretical arguments can be mustered to support the notion that affective states such as mood and emotion can moderate the situation-appraisal link in the BPS model. Individuals in positive moods are likely to have lower primary appraisals (i.e., decreased demand and danger) and perhaps higher secondary appraisals (i.e., increased abilities) resulting in overall

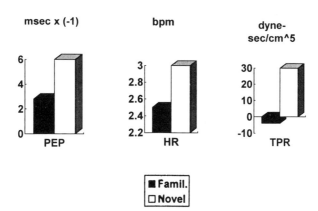

Fig. 18. Cardiac and vascular responses as a function of attitude objects (Adapted from Blascovich et al., 1993).

challenge appraisals in motivated performance situations, whereas individuals in negative moods are likely to have higher primary and lower secondary
appraisals resulting in overall threat appraisals. That depressed individuals
find life in general more threatening than nondepressed individuals appears
likely (cf. Beck, 1967). That joyous individuals find life more challenging
can also be argued. Unfortunately, little data link mood and cognitive
appraisal, and no data exist linking moods differentially to challenge and
threat patterns of cardiovascular response (Ernst, 1994).

Two of our studies suggest, albeit indirectly, that mood affects the motivated performance situation-appraisal link in the BPS model. In one study
(Allen & Blascovich, 1994), we involved surgeons in a motivated performance situation in which they performed three different mental arithmetic
tasks (i.e., serial subtraction). The surgeons listened to music prior to, and
during, two of the mental arithmetic tasks. The particular selections to
which they listened consisted of a standard or control piece, Pachelbel's
Canon in D (a selection often used in commerical "stress-reduction" tapes)
and an idiosyncratic piece—that is, a self-selected piece (one that they
typically played during their surgeries). Because this study was conducted
outside of our own laboratory, we were unable to gather the full range of
cardiovascular measures that enable us to distinguish challenge and threat
patterns definitively. Nevertheless, our results demonstrated that music
did, in fact, affect cardiovascular responses in ways compatible with our
challenge/threat patterns. Significantly lower blood pressure responses
(consistent with vasodilation) in the motivated performance situation occurred during the task with idiosyncratic background music than during the
task with control background music, and significantly lower blood pressure
responses occurred during the task with control background music than
during the task without background music (Figure 19). Assuming that the

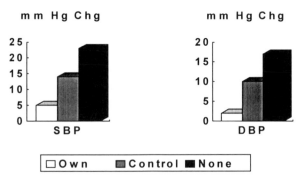

Fig. 19.   Blood pressure responses as a function of music condition. SBP, systolic blood
pressure; DBP, diastolic blood pressure (Adapted from Allen & Blascovich, 1994).

two music conditions elevated mood, with the idiosyncratic music condition elevating mood the most, these data are certainly consistent with the notion that mood moderates the situation-appraisal link. Because music often appears in the literature as a mood induction technique (Martin, 1990), the veracity of the assumption is likely.

Another of our studies, the pressor study (Blascovich et al., 1994), also bears upon the issue of affect as a moderator of the situation-appraisal link. As discussed, the pressor manipulation did not influence appraisal. However, self-reported pain during the pressors did. Specifically, individuals reporting high levels of pain appraised the upcoming task as more threatening than individuals reporting low levels of pain regardless of pressor condition. Because pain is regarded as a psychological phenomenon and because the quality of the objective stimulus (e.g., the cold pressor at 34° F) remained the same, reported pain can be considered a proxy for relative feeling state or affect. This finding provides additional data consistent with the notion that affective state can moderate the situation-appraisal link.

An ad hoc analysis of our physiological data during the cold-pressor task provides even more interesting data in this regard. Grouping subjects by virtue of a median split on self-reported pain, we found significant differences in systemic vascular resistance. As shown in Figure 20, individuals in the cold-pressor condition had similar responses during the first minute (minute 1 in Figure 20) of the 3-min, cold-pressor task. Those in the high pain condition subsequently responded with increased systemic vascular resistance (i.e., vasoconstriction), whereas those in the low pain condition subsequently responded with decreased systemic vascular resistance (i.e., vasodilation), even though subjects in both groups kept their hands immersed in the ice water bath for the same length of time (i.e., through

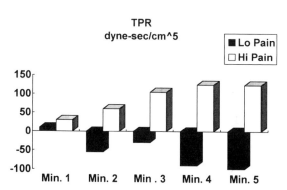

Fig. 20.   Vascular resistance during a cold pressor as a function of perceived pain (Blascovich et al., 1994).

minute 3 in Figure 20). In addition, this difference in vascular reactivity continued through subjects' performances of mental arithmetic (minutes 4 and 5 in Figure 20). These data, together with the pain data described in the preceding paragraph, suggest that an overall challenge cognitive appraisal in a motivated performance situation can overcome the normal vascular response (i.e., vasoconstriction) to a physical stressor. Furthermore, these data support an earlier argument of ours that the pituitary-adrenal-cortical (PAC) axis, which responds to harm and potential harm (i.e., anticipation of pain) (see Mason, 1975), likely contributes to threat-related responses.

Although we realize that these data do not provide the strongest possible basis for inference regarding the effect of affect on cognitive appraisal, we believe that they are strongly suggestive of such an effect. Experiments testing this notion directly are currently underway. We expect that experiments examining ambient mood, specific emotional, and/or feeling states as moderators of the situation-appraisal link will provide important data in this regard.

4. Intraindividual Differences

Intrapersonal factors within the dispositional category moderate the situation-appraisal link; however, this does not rule out within-subject, or intrapersonal, differences in overall cognitive appraisals and accompanying patterns of cardiovascular responses in motivated performance situations. Although dispositional factors may predispose individuals toward either an overall challenge or threat appraisal (recall the BJW study), these factors by no means explain all the variance and could easily be counteracted by cognitive and affective factors. Certainly, individuals may perceive more skill or abilities (i.e., higher secondary appraisal) in one type of motivated performance situation (e.g., giving a speech) than another (e.g., writing an essay), or may be in a better or worse mood in the same type of motivated performance situation at different times. A given individual may well have different appraisals across different motivated performance situations and/ or for the same or very similar motivated performance situations across time.

The data from our within-subjects appraisal manipulation study described in the previous paragraph (Tomaka & Lovegrove, 1995) demonstrate intra-individual differences in challenge and threat appraisals and the associated cardiovascular patterns. We expect the same in free-appraisal situations as well. This latter point was suggested by the first pilot patient in a study in which we have begun to reexamine the relationship between patterns of cardiovascular responses to psychological stress and cardiovascular disease, taking into account our more sophisticated BPS model and physiological measures. This patient appraised and performed consecutive but different tasks in a 20-min motivated performance situation. He freely appraised one task, serial subtraction, as a challenge. He freely appraised the other, a choice-deadline signal detection task, as a threat. As Figure 21 shows, these differential appraisals were accompanied appropriately by the two different response patterns.

The likelihood of intraindividual differences in overall appraisals in motivated performance situations has important empirical, as well as applied, implications. Regarding the former, we believe that the BPS model and our patterns of differential cardiovascular response to the same tasks show strongly that one *cannot* assume that any given task in a motivated performance situation represents a "standard" psychological stressor or challenge for all subjects. Hence, *there can be no standard psychological load in a sense analogous to the standard physical load used in an exercise ECG stress testing.* Our model and data suggest that psychological stress testing in the laboratory for diagnostic and/or predictive purposes should include idiosyncratically stressful tasks.

Regarding applied implications, our work suggests that individual experiences in motivated performance situations can change over time for the better (i.e., toward overall challenge appraisals) or for the worse (i.e., toward overall threat appraisals). This leaves open the possibility of successful intervention and training efforts, as well as dysfunctional ones. To the extent that interventions are successful in reducing primary appraisals and increasing secondary appraisals, individuals will appraise given motivated performance situations more benignly.

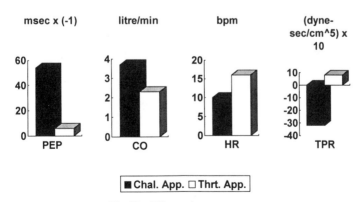

Fig. 21.   Pilot patient responses.

E. INTERPERSONAL MODERATORS OF THE SITUATION-COGNITIVE APPRAISAL LINK

As specified by the BPS model, interpersonal factors may also moderate the situation-appraisal link. We have focused theoretically and empirically on two types of interpersonal moderators: the presence of others and stigma. As with intrapersonal moderators, to date, we have completed at least one study within each type or category and have several more in progress. The completed studies demonstrate that these types of interindividual factors do indeed moderate the situation-appraisal link.

1. The Presence of Others

The pet–human friend study described earlier (Allen et al., 1991) as well as similar work by others (Kamarck, Manuck, & Jennings, 1990; Snydersmith & Cacioppo, 1992), led us to hypothesize that the presence of others moderated the situation-appraisal link in motivated performance situations. Furthermore, data from these studies led us to believe that the possible effects of this moderator are bidirectional—that is, the presence of others can predispose individuals toward challenge or threat appraisals. As we (Allen et al., 1991) reasoned, the perceived evaluative nature of observers influences this direction. The presence of presumably nonevaluative friends (i.e., the pet dogs) and presumably evaluative friends (i.e., the female human friends) led to different appraisals and ultimately different cardiovascular patterns. Alternative explanations, of course, are also possible. For example, Snydersmith and Cacioppo (1992) suggest that liking may play an important role.

Salomon and Blascovich (1995) conducted a motivated performance situation study using a confederate as an observer. In this study, they manipulated the perceived liking of the observer for the subject and the perceived evaluative nature of the observer. They matched the genders of subject and observer in a crossed design. The major analysis of the physiological responses revealed a significant three-way interaction. As Figure 22 depicts, females exhibited a threat pattern of cardiovascular responses in the disliked, evaluative-other condition. Males appeared unaffected by the presence of the observer in any combination of liking and perceived evaluative conditions. Interestingly, the previous relevant studies (i.e., Allen et al., 1991; Kamarck et al., 1990; Snydersmith & Cacioppo, 1992) used female subjects exclusively.

2. Stigma

Stigma is another aspect of interpersonal moderation of the situation-appraisal link that researchers have begun to investigate (Crocker & Major,

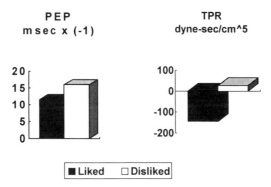

Fig. 22.   Cardiac and vascular responses during the female-evaluative condition (Salomon & Blascovich, 1995).

1989). Stigma occurs when an individual feels denigrated or stigmatized by others on the basis of some physical or other characteristic. Stigma affects many categories of individuals including those judged to be disabled, disfigured, or otherwise unattractive by mainstream society. The initial stigma study (Blascovich, Epstein, Quinn, Kibler, & Ernst, 1995) involved overweight and nonoverweight women. The motivated performance situation in this study involved speech-making, a potentially stressful task (Light, Turner, Hinderliter, & Sherwood, 1993). After receiving instructions and having the appropriate physiological sensors attached, overweight and nonoverweight women received instructions to mentally prepare a speech for 3 min and then spend 3 min delivering the speech. All subjects were told that a group of their peers would evaluate a tape of their speech. Half of the women in each group were told that their speeches would be audiotaped. The other half were told that their speeches would be videotaped. It was hypothesized that the stigma of being overweight would have greater relevance for the individuals who were videotaped compared to those who were audiotaped and would influence cardiovascular responses accordingly. A significant condition by overweight interaction supported the hypothesis. As depicted in Figure 23, neither group showed a threat pattern (no reliable differences in vasodilatory response). However, nonoverweight women in the video condition evidenced more challenge (i.e., significantly increased contractility accompanied by vasodilation). There were no significant differences for those in the audiotape condition.

3. Interpersonally Relevant Organismic Variables

The gender effects of the study examining the presence of others described previously (Salomon & Blascovich, 1995) as well as the stigma

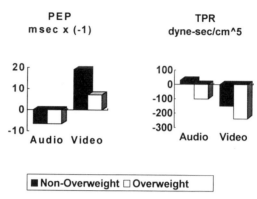

Fig. 23.   Cardiac and vascular responses as a function of weight (Blascovich et al., 1995).

study suggested the notion that socially relevant, physical, or organismic characteristics might moderate the situation-appraisal link of the BPS model. Factors such as race and sex come easily to mind. We believe that such factors moderate the situation-appraisal link, not because of basic biological differences among the sexes or races, but because of socialized or learned differences (cf. Anderson, McNeilly, & Myers, 1993; Deaux & Major, 1987).

We (Tomaka, Blascovich, & Kibler, 1995) found gender differences in appraisals during a standard motivated performance situation involving mental arithmetic tasks and a passive situation involving a slide viewing task. We found accompanying somatic gender differences using electromyographic (EMG) facial measures of affect. Regarding the appraisal differences, women found our motivated performance task more demanding and perceived less ability to cope with it than men did. Women also found the slide-viewing task more threatening. Somatically, women exhibited greater corrugator supercilii activity (indexing negative affect) and lower zygomaticus major activity (indexing positive affect) than men. However, women and men who made overall challenge appraisals evidenced the same challenge-type cardiovascular patterns, and women and men who made overall threat appraisals evidenced the same threat-type cardiovascular pattern.

These data indicate to us that although women may be more threatened by our laboratory-motivated performance situations, the arousal-regulation processes operate in similar fashion for both genders. Moreover, it suggests an explanation for the gender effects in the zero-sum experimental game study discussed at the beginning of this chapter (Blascovich et al., 1978). Specifically, in this early study, because we used heart rate, an ambiguous physiological response (in the sense that it does not allow us to distinguish positive from negative psychological reactions to a situation), and because we did not assess cognitive appraisals, we likely missed the fact that most, if not all, of the women in that study were threatened, whereas there was a better distribution of males over the challenge and threat categories.

Further investigating interpersonally relevant, organismic variables, Blascovich, Steele, and Spencer (1995) have commenced an examination of racial and gender stereotype vulnerability in academically relevant, motivated performance situations. To the extent that members of negatively stereotyped groups believe such stereotypes (e.g., that African Americans perform poorly on academic tasks such as tests; that females perform poorly on advanced mathematics), we expect them to appraise such tasks as threatening and evidence threat patterns of cardiovascular responses in motivated performance situations. At this time, however, the data have not been fully collected.

F. INTEROCEPTION

Admittedly, most of our empirical efforts have been devoted to the investigation of the mediating and moderating factors within the situation-arousal component of the BPS model. However, we have also made at least beginning empirical efforts to examine the mediating and moderating factors within the arousal-response component.

For example, in three separate studies, we (Blascovich et al., 1992) have shown that affect intensity, a general temperamental disposition accounting for individual variability in the regulation of arousal (Larsen & Diener, 1987; Larsen et al., 1986), relates primarily to somesthetic (i.e., interoceptive) sensitivity to cardiovascular response rather than either basal or evoked levels of cardiovascular responses in motivated performance situations. Specifically, as Table I shows,[11] affect intensity is unrelated to either basal or evoked cardiovascular responses but significantly and negatively related to perceived cardiac response. Accordingly, we conclude that individuals high in affect intensity do not derive their tendency to report extreme levels of emotion from extreme levels of physiological arousal. Indeed, they exibit decreased somesthetic sensitivity to such arousal. Earlier work (Eichler, Katkin, Blascovich, & Kelsey, 1987), in which we demonstrated that the degree of negative affect reported during a passive situation (viewing slides of mutilated automobile accident victims) was inversely related to somesthetic sensitivity ($r(19) = -.53$), supports the affect intensity findings.

[11] Somesthetic sensitivity was assessed using a slight modification of our heartbeat detection paradigm (Katkin et al., 1981).

TABLE I
AFFECT INTENSITY—HEART RATE/BEAT CORRELATIONS[a]

	Basal	Evoked	Somesthetic sensitivity
Study 1	ns[b]	ns	−.28 ($p < .04$)
Study 2	ns	ns	−.58 ($p < .001$)
Study 3	ns	ns	−.33 ($p < .01$)

[a] *Source:* Blascovich et al. (1992).
[b] ns = not significant.

G. SUMMARY

To the best of our knowledge, these empirical efforts represent, not only the first examinations of self-reported cognitive appraisal as a mediator of physiological responses within the context of motivated performance situations, but also the first demonstrations of the meaningful differentiation of cardiovascular responses (i.e., cardiac and vascular) as a function of categorically different appraisals (i.e., threat vs. challenge). Furthermore, the results of our examinations of specific intrapersonal and interpersonal moderators of the situation-appraisal link of the BPS model not only demonstrate the important role of these factors in arousal regulation, but also provide evidence converging on the validity of our challenge and threat patterns. We have not found the opposite pattern of what we would expect from well-established social psychological theories and empirical data in any of the cases.

VI. Conclusions and Future Directions

Importantly, our understanding of the biopsychosocial processes involved in arousal regulation helps us to reconcile the illustrative dilemma previously described. That is, the inconsistency in the literature among data demonstrating a benign relationship between cardiovascular responses and motivation in performance studies and data demonstrating a malignant relationship between cardiovascular responses and disease can be resolved, at least for motivated performance situations, by the phenomenological and cardiovascular fractionation inherent in the BPS model.

If the challenge-to-myocardial reactivity and threat-to-vascular reactivity links hold up to replication and further scrutiny, we likely will have not only a better understanding of arousal-regulation processes, one that is truly biopsychosocial, but we also will have discovered an important psychophysiological assessment tool, a kind of real rather than bogus pipeline (Jones & Sigall, 1971). If we can indeed distinguish individuals in threatened states from those in challenged states during motivated performance situations, we will be able to do psychology better. Whatever the purpose and domain of the assessment (i.e., basic theoretical or applied), the identification of physiological patterns associated with threat or challenge states allows us to differentiate those who phenomenologically experience such states (marked by appraisal-physiological consistency) from those who merely report them (marked by appraisal-physiological inconsistency). Theoretically, we should be better able to test a myriad of psychological theories across a number of domains. Clinically, we should be able to develop and test better anxiety and stress-management interventions. In terms of application, we should be better able to optimize person-situation selection procedures.

We believe that our model and data are also quite relevant to the study of emotion. They suggest the importance of a biopsychosocial approach for understanding superordinate dichotomous positive and negative categories of emotion such as challenge and threat, approach and avoidance, flight and fight, and others. Regarding basic level emotions, we have no doubt that cognitive appraisals are often involved in their generation. We have purposively limited our model and interpreted our data in terms of challenge and threat as superordinate categories of emotion. Although it is hotly debated in the literature (Ekman, Levenson, & Friesen, 1983; Stemmler, 1989), we believe that it is entirely within the realm of possibility that more fine-grained analyses of appraisals (perhaps using dimensions based on Smith and Ellsworth's (1985, 1987) appraisal models), along with even more advanced physiological measurement techniques, would allow definitive identification of physiological response patterns, not necessarily but possibly autonomic, associated with basic level emotions. However, we are unlikely to turn to such empirical adventures anytime in the near future as we perceive the utility of our superordinate categorical distinction (i.e., threat and challenge) to be compelling.

Instead, we will turn to further investigations pertinent to the BPS model itself and to important social psychological theories to which it can bring important empirical information to bear. Key aspects of the BPS model of arousal regulation remain unexplored or relatively unexplored. For example, the mediating effects of biological factors and the moderating role of physiological factors within the situation-arousal component hold much interest. The functional utility of various categories of arousal-regulation responses (e.g., self-handicapping strategies) also demands attention. The validity of secondary processes needs empirical investigation. Regarding social psychological theory, our near-term investigations will focus on stereotype vulnerability theory as implied. We also look to explore the utility of our model and the value of our physiological assessments within the domain of leader and situation match (Chemers, 1994).

Finally, it is our hope that more theorists and investigators will test and refine biopsychosocial models of arousal regulation, learn appropriate social psychophysiological measurement methods and techniques, and apply them to their own areas of expertise. We firmly believe that our understanding of traditional topics and issues within social psychology including attitudes, antisocial behaviors, conflict resolution, coping behaviors, emotion, persuasion, relationships, self-protective strategies, social facilitation, and social justice can only improve with such efforts.

Acknowledgments

This work was supported by funds from the National Science Foundation Awards BNS 9010231 and SBR 9310202 to Jim Blascovich. Correspondence concerning this article should be addressed to Jim Blascovich, Department of Psychology, University of California, Santa Barbara, Santa Barbara, CA 93106.

References

Abelson, R. P., Aronson, E., McGuire, W. J., Newcomb, T. M., Rosenberg, M. J., & Tannenbaum, P. H. (Eds.). (1969). *Theories of cognitive consistency: A sourcebook.* Chicago: Rand McNally & Company.

Allen, K., & Blascovich, J. (1994). Surgeons and cardiovascular reactivity: The moderating effects of music. *Journal of the American Medical Association, 272,* 882–884.

Allen, K., Blascovich, J., Tomaka, J., & Kelsey, R. M. (1991). The presence of human friends and pet dogs as moderators of autonomic responses to stress in women. *Journal of Personality and Social Psychology, 61,* 582–589.

Allport, G. W. (1935). Attitudes. In C. Murchison (Ed.), *Handbook of social psychology* (pp. 798–844). Worcester, MA: Clark University Press.

Anderson, N. B., McNeilly, M., & Myers, H. (1993). A biopsychosocial model of race differences in vascular reactivity. In J. Blascovich & E. S. Katkin (Eds.), *Cardiovascular reactivity to psychological stress and disease: An examination of the evidence* (pp. 83–108). Washington, DC: American Psychological Association.

Averill, J. R. (1974). An analysis of psychophysiological symbolism and its influence on emotions. *Journal for the Theory of Social Behaviour, 4,* 147–190.

Barlow, D. H. (1988). Anxiety and its disorders: The nature and treatment of anxiety and panic. New York: Guilford Press.

Beck, A. T. (1967). Depression: Clinical, experimental and theoretical aspects. New York: Hoeber.

Becker, E. (1975). The denial of death. New York: Free Press.

Berntson, G. G., Cacioppo, J. T., & Quigley, K. S. (1991). Autonomic determinism: The modes of autonomic control, the doctrine of autonomic space, and the laws of autonomic constraint. Psychological Review, 98, 459–487.

Blascovich, J. (1990). Individual differences in physiological arousal and perception of arousal: Missing links in Jamesian notions of arousal-based behaviors. Personality and Social Psychology Bulletin, 16, 665–675.

Blascovich, J. (1992). A biopsychosocial approach to arousal regulation. Journal of Social and Clinical Psychology, 11, 213–237.

Blascovich, J., Brennan, K., Tomaka, J., Kelsey, R. M., Hughes, P. H., Coad, M. L., & Adlin, R. (1992). Affect intensity and cardiac arousal. Journal of Personality and Social Psychology, 63, 164–174.

Blascovich, J., Epstein, L. E., Quinn, D., Kibler, J., & Ernst, J. M. (1995). Cardiovascular response patterns as a function of stigma. Unpublished manuscript, State University of New York at Buffalo.

Blascovich, J., Ernst, J. M., Tomaka, J., Kelsey, R. M., Salomon, K. A., & Fazio, R. H. (1993). Attitude as a moderator of autonomic activity. Journal of Personality and Social Psychology, 64, 165–176.

Blascovich, J., & Katkin, E. S. (1982). Arousal-based social behaviors: Do they reflect differences in visceral perception? Review of Personality and Social Psychology, 3, 73–95.

Blascovich, J., & Katkin, E. S. (1993a). (Eds.), Cardiovascular reactivity to psychological stress and disease. Washington, DC: American Psychological Association.

Blascovich, J., & Katkin, E. S. (1993b). Psychological stress testing for coronary heart disease. In J. Blascovich & E. S. Katkin (Eds.), Cardiovascular reactivity to psychological stress and disease (pp. 27–48). Washington, DC: American Psychological Association.

Blascovich, J., & Katkin, E. S. (1993c). Cardiovascular reactivity to psychological stress and disease: Conclusions. In J. Blascovich & E. S. Katkin (Eds.), Cardiovascular reactivity to psychological stress and disease (pp. 225–238). Washington, DC: American Psychological Association.

Blascovich, J., & Kelsey, R. M. (1990). Using electrodermal and cardiovascular measures of arousal in social psychological research. Review of Personality and Social Psychology, 11, 45–73.

Blascovich, J., Kibler, J., Ernst, J. M., Tomaka, J., & Vargas, Y. (1994). Manipulations of cardiac and vascular reactivity: Effects on cognitive appraisal. Psychophysiology, 31, S26.

Blascovich, J., Nash, R. F., & Ginsburg, G. P. (1978). Heart rate and competitive decision making. Personality and Social Psychology Bulletin, 4, 115–118.

Blascovich, J., Steele, C., & Spencer, S. (1995). Stereotype vulnerability, cognitive appraisal, and cardiovascular response patterns. Unpublished manuscript, State University of New York at Buffalo.

Brehm, J. W., & Self, E. (1989). The intensity of motivation. In M. R. Rozenweig & L. W. Porter (Eds.), Annual Review of Psychology (pp. 109–131). Palo Alto, CA: Annual Reviews.

Cacioppo, J. T., & Berntson, G. (1992). Social psychological contributions to the decade of the brain: The doctrine of multilevel analysis. American Psychologist, 47, 1019–1028.

Cacioppo, J. T., & Tassinary, L. G. (1990). Inferring psychological significance from physiological signals. American Psychologist, 45, 16–28.

Cappell, H., & Greeley, J. (1987). Alcohol and tension reduction: An update on research and theory. In H. T. Blane & K. E. Leonard (Eds.), *Psychological theories of drinking and alcoholism* (pp. 15–54). New York: The Guilford Press.

Carver, C. S., & Scheier, M. (1990). Origins and functions of positive and negative affect: A control process view. *Psychological Review, 97,* 19–35.

Chemers, M. M. (1994). *Function and process in effective leadership: A theoretical integration.* Madison, WI: Brown & Benchmark.

Cioffi, D. (1991). Beyond attentional strategies: A cognitive-perceptual model of somatic interpretation. *Psychological Bulletin, 109,* 25–41.

Crocker, J., & Major, B. (1989). Social stigma and self-esteem: The self-protective properties of stigma. *Psychological Review, 96,* 608–630.

Crowne, D., & Marlowe, D. (1964). *The approval motive: Studies in evaluating dependence.* New York: Wiley.

Deaux, K., & Major, B. (1987). Putting gender into context: An interactive model of gender-related behavior. *Psychological Review 94,* 369–389.

Dienstbier, R. A. (1989). Arousal and physiological toughness: Implications for mental and physical health. *Psychological Review, 96,* 84–100.

Eichler, S., Katkin, E. S., Blascovich, J. J., & Kelsey, R. M. (1987). Cardiodynamic factors in heartbeat detection and the experience of emotion. *Psychophysiology, 24,* S587.

Ekman, P., Levenson, R. W., & Friesen, W. V. (1983). Autonomic nervous system activity distinguishes among emotions. *Science, 221,* 1208–1210.

Ernst, J. (1994). *The effect of mood on cognitive appraisal.* Unpublished manuscript, State University of New York at Buffalo.

Eysenck, H. J. (1967). *The biological bases of personality.* Springfield, IL: Charles C Thomas.

Fazio, R. H. (1989). On the power and functionality of attitudes: The role of attitude accessibility. In A. R. Pratkanis, S. J. Breckler, & A. G. Greenwald (Eds.), *Attitude structure and function* (pp. 153–179). Hillsdale, NJ: Lawrence Erlbaum Associates.

Fazio, R. H., Blascovich, J., & Driscoll, D. (1992). On the functional value of attitudes: The influence of accessible attitudes upon the ease and quality of decision making. *Personality and Social Psychology Bulletin, 18,* 388–401.

Fazio, R. H., Chen, J., McDonel, E. C., & Sherman, S. J. (1982). Attitude accessibility, attitude-behavior consistency, and the strength of the object-evaluation association. *Journal of Experimental Social Psychology, 18,* 339–357.

Festinger, L. (1957). *A theory of cognitive dissonance.* Stanford, CA: Stanford University Press.

Fowles, D. C. (1988). Psychophysiology and psychopathology: A motivational approach. *Psychophysiology, 25,* 373–391.

Gray, J. A. (1982). *The neuropsychology of anxiety: An enquiry into the functions of the septo-hippocampal system.* Oxford, England: Oxford University Press.

Greenberg, J., Pyszczynski, T., & Solomon, S. (1987). The causes and consequences of a need for self-esteem: A terror-management theory. In R. F. Baumeister (Ed.), *Public and private selves.* New York: Springer-Verlag.

Harre, R. (1972). *The philosophies of sciences.* Oxford, England: Oxford University Press.

Harris, V. A., & Katkin, E. S. (1975). Primary and secondary emotional behavior: An analysis of the role of autonomic feedback on affect, arousal, and attribution. *Psychological Bulletin, 82,* 904–916.

Hull, C. L. (1943). *Principles of behavior.* New York: Appleton-Century-Crofts.

Jones, E. E., & Sigall, H. (1971). The bogus pipeline: A new paradigm for measuring affect and attitude. *Psychological Bulletin, 76,* 359–364.

Kamarck, T. W., Manuck, S. B., & Jennings, J. R. (1990). Social support reduces cardiovascular reactivity to psychological challenge: A laboratory model. *Psychosomatic Medicine, 54,* 42–58.

Katkin, E. S., Blascovich, J., & Goldband, S. (1981). Empirical assessment of visceral self-perception: Individual and sex differences in the acquisition of heart beat discrimination. *Journal of Personality and Social Psychology, 40,* 1095–1101.

Katz, D. (1960). The functional approach to the study of attitudes. *Public Opinion Quarterly, 24,* 163–204.

Kavanaugh, D. J., & Bower, G. H. (1985). Mood and self efficacy: Impact of joy and sadness on perceived capabilities. *Cognitive Therapy and Research, 9,* 507–509.

Kelsey, R. M., & Guethlein, W. (1990). An evaluation of the ensemble averaged impedance cardiogram. *Psychophysiology, 28,* 24–33.

Larsen, R. J., & Diener, E. (1987). Affect intensity as an individual difference characteristic. *Journal of Research in Personality, 21,* 1–39.

Larsen, R. J., Diener, E., & Emmons, R. A. (1986). Affect intensity and reactions to daily life events. *Journal of Personality and Social Psychology, 51,* 803–814.

Lazarus, R. S. (1983). The costs and benefits of denial. In S. Breznitz (Ed.), *The denial of stress* (pp. 1–30). New York: International Universities Press.

Lazarus, R. S. (1991). *Emotion and adaptation.* New York: Oxford.

Lazarus, R. S., & Folkman, S. (1984). *Stress, appraisal, and coping.* New York: Springer.

Lerner, M. J. (1980). *The belief in a just world: A fundamental delusion.* New York: Plenum Press.

Lerner, M. J., & Miller, D. T. (1978). Just world research and the attribution process: Looking back and ahead. *Psychological Bulletin, 85,* 1030–1051.

Light, K. C., Turner, J. R., Hinderliter, A. L., & Sherwood, A. (1993). Race and gender comparisons: I. Hemodynamic responses to a series of stressors. *Health Psychology, 12,* 354–365.

Lovallo, W. R., Pincomb, G. A., Brackett, D. J., & Wilson, M. F. (1990). Heart rate reactivity as a predictor of neuroendocrine responses to aversive and appetitive challenges. *Psychosomatic Medicine, 52,* 17–26.

Lundberg, U., & Frankenhaeuser, M. (1980). Pituitary-adrenal and sympathetic-adrenal correlates of distress and effort. *Journal of Psychosomatic Research, 24,* 125–130.

Manuck, S. B., Kamarck, T. W., Kasprowicz, A. S., & Waldstein, S. R. (1993). Stability and patterning of behaviorally evoked cardiovascular reactivity. In J. Blascovich & E. S. Katkin (Eds.), *Cardiovascular reactivity to psychological stress and disease: An examination of the evidence* (pp. 83–108). Washington, DC: American Psychological Association.

Marshall, G. D., & Zimbardo, P. G. (1979). Affective consequences of inadequately explained physiological arousal. *Journal of Personality and Social Psychology, 37,* 970–988.

Martin, M. (1990). On the induction of mood. *Clinical Psychology Review, 10,* 669–697.

Maslach, C. (1979). Negative emotional biasing of unexplained arousal. *Journal of Personality and Social Psychology, 37,* 953–969.

Mason, J. W. (1975). A historical view of the stress field. *Journal of Human Stress, 1,* 22–36.

Matthews, K. A., Weiss, S. M., Detre, T., Dembroski, T. N., Falkner, B., Manuck, S. B., & Williams, R. B. (1986). *Handbook of stress, reactivity, and cardiovascular disease.* New York: Wiley & Sons.

McFarlin, D. B., & Blascovich, J. (1981). The effects of self-esteem and performance feedback on affective preferences and cognitive expectations. *Journal of Personality and Social Psychology, 4,* 521–531.

McNaughton, N. (1993). Stress and behavioral inhibition. In S. C. Stanford & P. Salmon (Eds.), *Stress: An integrated approach* (pp. 91–109). New York: Academic Press.

Mednick, S. A. (1962). The associate basis of the creative process. *Psychological Review, 69,* 220–232.

Obrist, P. A. (1981). *Cardiovascular psychophysiology: A perspective.* New York: Plenum.

O'Leary, A. (1990). Stress, emotion, and human immune function. *Psychological Bulletin, 108,* 363–382.

Oxford English Dictionary, 2nd Ed. (1989). New York; Oxford University Press.

Piliavin, I., Piliavin, J. A., & Rodin, J. (1975). Costs, diffusion, and the stigmatized victim. *Journal of Personality and Social Psychology, 32,* 429–438.

Reed, S. D., Harver, A., & Katkin, E. S. (1990). Interoception. In J. T. Cacioppo & L. G. Tassinary (Eds.), *Principles of psychophysiology: Physical, social, inferential elements* (pp. 253–291). Cambridge, England: Cambridge University Press.

Roberts, T-A., & Pennebaker, J. W. (1995). Gender differences in perceiving internal state: Toward a his-and-hers model of perceptual cue use. In M. P. Zanna (Ed.), *Advances in Experimental Social Psychology, 27,* 143–176.

Rosenberg, M. (1965). *Society and the adolescent self image.* Princeton, NJ: Princeton University Press.

Rubin, Z., & Peplau, L. A. (1975). Who believes in a just world? *Journal of Social Issues, 31,* 65–90.

Sackheim, H. A., & Gur, R. C. (1979). Self-deception, other deception, and self-reported psychopathology. *Journal of Consulting and Clinical Psychology, 47,* 213–215.

Salomon, K., & Blascovich, J. (1995). *The presence of others as a moderator of cardiovascular response patterns during motivated performance situations.* Unpublished manuscript, State University of New York at Buffalo.

Salovey, P., & Birnbaum, D. (1989). Influence of mood on health-relevant cognitions. *Journal of Personality and Social Psychology, 57,* 539–551.

Schachter, S. (1959). *Psychology of affection.* Stanford, CA: Stanford University Press.

Schachter, S., & Singer, J. E. (1962). Cognitive, social, and physiological determinants of emotional state. *Psychological Review, 69,* 379–399.

Shields, S. A. (1989). The body awareness questionnaire: Reliability and validity. *Journal of Personality Assessment, 53,* 802–815.

Smith, C. A., & Ellsworth, P. C. (1985). Patterns of cognitive appraisal in emotion. *Journal of Personality and Social Psychology, 48,* 813–838.

Smith, C. A., & Ellsworth, P. C. (1987). Patterns of appraisal and emotion related to taking an exam. *Journal of Personality and Social Psychology, 52,* 475–488.

Smith, M. B., Bruner, J. S., & White, R. W. (1956). *Opinions and personality.* New York: Wiley.

Snydersmith, M. A., & Cacioppo, J. T. (1992). Parsing complex social factors to determine component effects: I. Autonomic activity and reactivity as a function of human association. *Journal of Social and Clinical Psychology, 11,* 263–278.

Steele, C. M. (1992, April). Race and the schooling of black Americans. *The Atlantic Monthly.*

Stelmack, R. M. (1990). Biological bases of extraversion: Psychophysiological evidence. *Journal of Personality, 58,* 293–311.

Stemmler, G. (1989). The autonomic differentiation of emotions revisited: Convergent and discriminant validation. *Psychophysiology, 26,* 617–632.

Tomaka, J., & Blascovich, J. (1994). Effects of justice beliefs on cognitive appraisal of and subjective, physiological, and behavioral responses to potential stress. *Journal of Personality and Social Psychology, 67,* 732–740.

Tomaka, J., Blascovich, J., & Kelsey, R. M. (1992). Effects of self-deception, social desirability, and repressive coping on psychophysiological reactivity to stress. *Personality and Social Psychology Bulletin, 18,* 616–624.

Tomaka, J., Blascovich, J., Kelsey, R. M., & Leitten, C. L. (1993). Subjective, physiological, and behavioral effects of threat and challenge appraisal. *Journal of Personality and Social Psychology, 65,* 248–260.

Tomaka, J., Blascovich, J., & Kibler (1995). *Gender differences in appraisal, somatic, and cardiovascular responses in motivated performance situations and passive situations.* Unpublished manuscript, University of Texas at El Paso.

Tomaka, J., & Lovegrove, A. (1995). *Effects of instructional set on threat and challenge appraisals.* Unpublished manuscript, University of Texas at El Paso.

Triplett, N. (1897). The dynamogenic factors in pacemaking and competition. *American Journal of Psychology, 9,* 591–605.

Turner, J. R., Sherwood, A., & Light, K. C. (Eds.). (1993). *Individual differences in cardiovascular response to stress.* New York: Plenum.

Walster, E., Walster, G. W., & Berscheid, E. (1978). *Equity: Theory and research.* Boston: Allyn & Bacon.

Wright, R. A., & Dill, J. C. (1993). Blood pressure responses and incentive appraisals as a function of perceived ability and objective task demand. *Psychophysiology, 30,* 152–160.

Zajonc, R. (1965). Social facilitation. *Science, 149,* 269–274.

Zillmann, D. (1978). *Hostility and aggression.* Hillsdale, NJ: Erlbaum.

OUTCOME BIASES IN SOCIAL PERCEPTION: IMPLICATIONS FOR DISPOSITIONAL INFERENCE, ATTITUDE CHANGE, STEREOTYPING, AND SOCIAL BEHAVIOR

Scott T. Allison

Diane M. Mackie

David M. Messick

Reagan's triumph was very much . . . a rousing vote of confidence in him and his politics. [*Newsweek,* shortly after Ronald Reagan defeated President Jimmy Carter with 50.7% of the popular vote in 1980 (Goldman, 1980)]

I. Introduction

Behavioral outcomes are pervasive and inescapable features of social life. A marriage proposal is either accepted, or it is declined. A job interview either leads to a job offer or a rejection. A tenure candidate either receives tenure, or he or she is turned down. Indeed, the dichotomous nature of many decision outcomes belies the complexity of their etiology. A winning presidential candidate may garner only 50.7% of voter support, but observers of the election appear more than willing to overlook the diveristy of voter opinion that this percentage of support clearly implies. As *Newsweek*'s coverage of Ronald Reagan's 1980 victory suggests, a common and seemingly reasonable conclusion is that the election outcome reflects the preferences of those who produced it. Perceivers, in short, tend to show an outcome bias in their social judgments, attributing characteristics to people that correspond to the outcomes that those people generate, even when known or available information suggests that there is very little correspon-

ADVANCES IN EXPERIMENTAL
SOCIAL PSYCHOLOGY, VOL. 28

dence (Allison & Messick, 1985, 1987; Allison, Worth, & King, 1990; Beggan & Allison, 1993; Mackie & Allison, 1987; Mackie, Allison, Worth, & Ascuncion, 1992a, 1992b; Mackie, Worth, & Allison, 1990; McHoskey & Miller, 1994; Schroth & Messick, 1994).

II. Historical Roots of Outcome-Biased Inferences

Outcome-biased inferences about groups are but one example of a general class of outcome-bias phenomena that have long pervaded social psychology's empirical landscape. One of the earliest demonstrations of the impact of outcomes was Brehm's (1956) classic investigation of postdecisional shifts in the desirability of chosen and unchosen options. Brehm (1956) opened his paper by noting that social psychologists have been preoccupied "with the phenomena that lead up to [a] choice" at the expense of "what happens after the choice" (p. 384). Operating from a dissonance theory framework, Brehm discovered that an important inferential consequence of choosing between two equally desirable options is that the chosen option tends to be bolstered, whereas the unchosen option tends to be derogated. In short, the outcome of the choice leads to inferences about the choice environment that are clearly outcome biased (see also Gerard & White, 1983).

Festinger's (1957) theoretical formulation spawned numerous hypotheses about outcome biases because it proposed that cognitions about behavioral outcomes are less malleable than other types of cognitions, such as beliefs, attitudes, and preferences. Because outcomes are often public knowledge, they are difficult to ignore, reverse, or deny (Jones, 1985). The power of outcomes in shaping inferences is therefore seen in a variety of dissonance-related phenomena, such as the tendency of people to especially value outcomes for which they have suffered (Aronson & Mills, 1959), the tendency to enhance behavioral outcomes that are produced for little external reward (Festinger & Carlsmith, 1959), and the tendency of outcomes to trigger consensus seeking when they disconfirm one's beliefs (Festinger, Riecken, & Schachter, 1956).

While investigations of dissonance theory proliferated during the 1960s, a second important class of outcome-bias phenomena began to attract the attention of social psychologists. These phenomena were initially concerned with the inferential implications of observing others' choices. Heider's (1958) initial treatise on attributional processes contained the notion of "behavior engulfing the field," which portrayed perceivers of behavioral outcomes as being unduly influenced by those outcomes. Data from Jones and Harris (1967) supported Heider's speculation and opened the flood-gates for investigations of this "fundamental attribution error" (e.g., Harvey & McGlynn, 1982; Jones, 1979; Miller, 1976; Monson & Snyder, 1977; Quattrone, 1982; Ross, 1977; Ross, Amabile, & Steinmetz, 1977). A popular explanation for this outcome bias supported Heider's initial insight by focusing on the greater perceptual salience of behavior relative to its situational causes (McArthur & Post, 1977; Rholes & Pryor, 1982; Ross, 1977; Taylor & Fiske, 1975).

A short time later, attribution theorists began to explore the attributional implications of observing one's own behavioral outcomes. Bem's (1972) self-perception theory proposed that people often rely on their own outcomes as an important source of self-knowledge. Moreover, Ross and his colleagues (Ross, Greene, & House, 1977) discovered that people's own choices have implications for the way they attribute traits and behaviors to others. Specifically, the decision outcomes that people produce lead them to overestimate the frequency with which they are produced by others, a phenomenon known as the false-consensus effect. As with the fundamental attribution error, this outcome-biased consensus judgment was viewed as evidence of the many "shortcomings" inherent in the cognitive functioning of the intuitive psychologist. In fact, during the two decades following Jones and Harris' (1967) initial discovery of attributional outcome biases, it was fashionable for social psychologists to construct theories that portrayed social perceivers as "cognitive misers" whose overattention to behavioral outcomes reflected their inability to process information adequately or rationally. As we shall see, this emphasis on cognitive shortcomings later gave way to a more contextualistic view of humans as "motivated tacticians" (Fiske, 1992) whose level of preoccupation with outcomes depended on the situation.

Empirical work exploring outcome-biased attributions in the 1960s and 1970s did not single-mindedly focus on the dependent variable of attitude or trait inferences. Walster (1966) published a classic study that explored how perceivers of negative behavioral outcomes show an outcome bias in assigning responsibility for those outcomes. Her results suggested that perceivers tend to blame people more for actions that yield extremely negative outcomes than for identical actions that yield only mildly negative outcomes. A number of subsequent studies supported the idea that people tend to view past outcomes as foreseeable, inevitable, and even preventable. For example, Shaver's (1970) studies of defensive attributions, Fischhoff's (1975) work on the hindsight bias, and Lerner and Miller's (1978) concept of a just world all underscore the tendency of people to use outcomes as vehicles for imposing order, control, and justice on a world that is often disorderly, uncontrollable, and unjust.

These outcome-bias studies of the 1970s were particularly impressive because of their discovery of people's insensitivity to the fact that identical intentions and behavior can produce different outcomes. A failed parking brake can cause a car to smash either a person or a tree, and yet perceivers blame the driver more for the mishap when it harms human life than when it harms plant life. Although a faulty parking brake is the cause of both outcomes, the different outcomes lead to markedly different inferences about the performer. Experiments in the 1980s explored outcome biases that occur even when the behavior and known risks associated with varying outcomes were held constant. Baron and Hershey (1988) conducted a series of studies that explored whether people based their evaluations of decisions on the outcomes of those decisions. Subjects read scenarios describing decisions involving risk and uncertainty (e.g., a decision whether to undergo a bypass operation). In some instances, the decisions led to positive outcomes (e.g, the operation was a success); in others, the decisions produced negative outcomes (e.g., the patient died). Although the known risks associated with the decisions were identical in both positive and negative outcome scenarios, subjects rated the decisions as more "clearly correct" and decision makers as "most competent" when the outcomes of the decisions were favorable than when they were unfavorable.

In summary, many social psychological studies since the mid-1940s have revealed numerous ways in which people are sensitive to behavioral outcomes. Outcomes appear to bias our judgments about their origins and causes, influence our evaluations of the individuals who produce them, affect our estimates of how frequently others produce them, bias our assessments about who is responsible for them, influence our estimates of how foreseeable they should have been, affect our beliefs about how likely they are to occur in the future, bias our perceptions of how much they were deserved, influence our beliefs about how controllable and preventable they were, and affect how satisfied we are with them in comparison to other possible outcomes.

III. Outcome-Biased Dispositional Inferences:
Theoretical Underpinnings

A large body of work has emerged in the past decade on outcome-biased dispositional inferences. The theoretical legacy of this work can be traced back to Heider's (1958) naive psychology and to Jones and Davis's (1965) seminal treatment of the conditions that elicit correspondent inferences. The central question asks: How do perceivers of behavioral outcomes draw inferences about the internal characteristics of those who produce them? Inasmuch as theory and research on outcome-biased inferences about individual targets have been reviewed elsewhere (e.g., Fiske & Taylor, 1991; Gilbert, 1989; Jones, 1990; Trope & Higgins, 1993), we limit our discussion in this section to theoretical and empirical work addressing the processes underlying outcome-biased dispositional inferences about group targets.

In one of the first investigations of outcome-biased dispositional inferences about groups, Allison and Messick (1985) proposed that the process of understanding group targets on the basis of group behavior parallels the process of understanding individual targets in terms of individual behavior. Just as perceivers of individual behavior are vulnerable to committing the "fundamental attribution error" by inferring too much correspondence between behavior and underlying dispositions, so perceivers of group behavior were hypothesized to be similarly vulnerable to committing a type of "group attribution error" by assuming too much correspondence between group decision outcomes and group members' dispositional characteristics. To test this idea, Allison and Messick gave subjects a scenario containing information about the outcome of a fictitious Montana recall election, after which subjects inferred the attitudes of Montana's voting citizens. One half of the subjects were informed in the scenario that 43% of the voters supported the recall, whereas the other half read that the recall received 57% support. In addition, subjects were informed of the decision rule used to determine the outcome of the recall (i.e., the minimum percentage of voter support needed for the recall attempt to succeed). Subjects were told that the decision rule was 65%, 50%, or 35%. Thus, when subjects were informed that 57% of the voters supported the recall, they learned that the recall effort had failed when the decision rule was said to be 65%, but that it had succeeded when the rule was said to be either 50% or 35%. Similarly, when subjects were informed that 43% of the voters supported the recall, they learned that the recall effort had succeeded when the rule was said to be 35%, but that it had failed when the rule was said to be either 50% or 65%.

The results showed that subjects judged voters as being more in favor of the recall when the known percentage of voter support exceeded the percentage specified by the decision rule than when this percentage fell short of the decision rule. Specifically, when voter support for the recall was known to be 43%, subjects inferred that voters held stronger prorecall attitudes when the decision rule was 35% (a successful outcome) than when the rule was either 50% or 65% (a failed outcome). The same pattern of outcome bias held true when voter support was known to be 57%. In short, the outcome of a group vote was judged to be diagnostic of voter opinion, even when information contrary to the diagnosis was known and recalled accurately. Allison and Messick (1985) also uncovered evidence that these outcome-biased inferences were stronger when subjects perceived a decision outcome reached by an in-group than when they perceived an outcome reached by an out-group. This finding is suggestive of the mechanisms underlying the outcome bias that we explore in the next section.

A. HEURISTIC PROPERTIES OF
OUTCOME-BIASED INFERENCES

In offering an explanation for outcome biases in people's attitude inferences about groups, Allison and Messick (1987) proposed that the bias reflects the misapplication of a heuristic of the form, "Groups make decisions that are representative of group members' attitudes." From this theoretical perspective, outcome-biased judgments are made "quickly and with little thought," perhaps even "spontaneously and automatically," (p. 138) because they reflect the use of less extensive or heuristic information-processing strategies. Worth, Allison and Messick (1987) investigated this idea by first asking groups of subjects to arrive at a group decision and by then individually measuring subjects' inferences about the attitudes of the group on the decision issue. One half of the groups made a decision that had consequences for the members of the group; these groups were led to believe that they would perform a task if they decided that it was interesting. In contrast, the other half of the groups made a decision that had no consequences for group members; these groups were led to believe that others would perform the task if it was deemed interesting. The results showed that subjects drew outcome-biased inferences about members of their decision-making group, but that they were less likely to do so when the decision outcome had consequences for the group than when it did not. Worth et al. (1987) concluded that "the hedonic relevance of the situation . . . caused the decision makers to engage in a more careful attributional analysis of the outcome than they might do otherwise" (p. 680). In short, the relevance of the decision task to perceivers moderated their heuristic processing strategies.

Additional evidence for the heuristic properties of the outcome bias was uncovered by Allison et al. (1990), who created experimental conditions designed specifically to promote or to inhibit heuristic processing of group decision information. In one study, subjects were provided with a scenario that contained three facts about a community's decision either to pass or to reject a proposed new law. These three facts included the percentage of voting citizens supporting the decision (43%); the decision rule used by the community (either 35% or 50%); and the final group decision outcome (pass or reject), which, of course, was determined by the percentage of group support and the decision rule.

One half of the subjects were given all three pieces of information and were then asked to draw inferences about the attitudes of the group. As predicted, these subjects formed outcome-biased inferences about group members. When the percentage of voter support exceeded the decision rule (the 35% rule condition), this group of subjects inferred strong support for the new law, but when this same percentage of voter support fell short of the rule (the 50% rule condition), the subjects inferred strong opposition to the law.

The other half of the subjects, however, were provided with only the first two facts (the level of group support for the decision and the decision rule) and were compelled to use these facts to ascertain the decision outcome for themselves. Allison et al. (1990) hypothesized that the process of calculating the outcome would induce these subjects to devote attention and cognitive energy to the factors that determined the outcome, thus undermining their default mode of heuristic information processing. As predicted, this group of subjects showed a much smaller outcome bias than did the subjects who had been given the outcome of the community's decision.

In a second study, Allison et al. (1990) manipulated subjects' motivation to process information systematically. The subjects were University of Richmond students who read about their university's decision to increase graduation requirements. One half were told that the increase would take effect immediately (high personal relevance), whereas the other half were informed that the increase in requirements would affect future generations of students (low personal relevance). The results showed that subjects made significantly stronger outcome-biased judgments about members of the decision-making group when the decision was low in personal relevance to subjects than when the decision was high in personal relevance. Moreover, subjects were more likely to make outcome-biased inferences about "the typical member of the group" than about "a group member selected at random." Perceiving a group's "typical member" apparently evokes an abstration-based cognitive representation of the group, whereas perceiving a group's "random member" evokes an instance-based representation (Park & Hastie, 1987). Instance-based representations may portray groups as more complex and heterogeneous than do abstraction-based representations because a consideration of instances—in this case, individual group members—may promote an awareness of a group's many diverse parts in lieu of the group as a monolithic whole. Consequently, drawing inferences about a random member may promote more thorough (and therefore less heuristic) processing of group members' dispositional qualities.

The heuristic properties of the outcome bias were also revealed in a pair of studies conducted by Schroth and Messick (1994). These investigators proposed that the prototypical or schematic action–outcome sequence is one that features an initial action followed by an outcome or consequence of that action. As a result of this prototypical representation, perceivers of outcomes that follow from a behavior should be more likely to process information heuristically than should perceivers of outcomes that follow from a logically equivalent nonbehavior. Moreover, because people experience greater difficulty interpreting nonccurences than they do interpreting occurrences (Ross, 1977), perceivers of passively made outcomes should spend more time and cognitive energy attempting to understand those outcomes than should perceivers of actively made outcomes.

The results of Schroth and Messick's two experiments supported these ideas. Both studies manipulated whether the outcome was produced actively or passively, and whether the status quo was changed or maintained (which unconfounded the effects of action always leading to a change in status quo). In one experiment, subjects were presented with a town's decision either to increase or decrease the percentage of new buildings allowed each year within the city limits. Subjects in the active-outcome condition were informed that the outcome compelled the mayor actively either to increase or decrease the percentage of new buildings. In contrast, subjects in the passive-outcome condition were told that the percentage of increase or decrease would kick in automatically unless the mayor intervened. Schroth and Messick found that subjects' dispositional inferences about group members were significantly more outcome biased when the group decision outcome was made actively than when it was made passively, independent of whether activity or passivity preserved the status quo.

McHoskey and Miller (1994) proposed that outcome-biased dispositional inferences about groups might diminish in magnitude to the extent that perceivers are able to identify external constraints operating to produce group decision outcomes. Subjects read scenarios describing groups that reached decision outcomes, and in addition to drawing dispositional inferences about group members, the subjects were asked to indicate the extent to which the typical member of these groups had an influence on the group outcomes. These influence judgments served as the measure of the perceived constraint operating on the decision-making group. McHoskey and Miller manipulated the level of constraint; some groups reached their decision via a 92% popular vote of group members, some by an elected committee, some by an appointed group leader, and some by an external governing body that made the decision for the group. The results showed that the greater the constraint, the less likely subjects were to form outcome-biased inferences. More importantly, the data indicated that constraint identification is an important mediator of the bias; the more likely subjects were to recognize the constraints acting on the group, the less likely they were to make outcome-biased inferences.

In a second study, McHoskey and Miller (1994) manipulated the salience of the constraints operating on the decision-making groups. After exposure to the group decisions, one half of the subjects were first asked to draw dispositional inferences about group members, a condition expected to encourage heuristic processing. The remaining subjects were first asked to respond to a number of questions that highlighted the constraints placed on the group decision, a condition expected to elicit systematic processing. The results revealed that heuristic processors formed stronger outcome-biased judgments than did systematic processors, but more important, the results showed that systematic processors were better able to identify the constraints operating on the group than were heuristic processors. The investigators highlighted an important reason why outcome biases are stronger under conditions that foster heuristic processing. Heuristic processors make more extreme outcome-biased inferences because they overlook features of the group decision setting (other than group members' preferences) that play a role in producing group outcomes.

Allison, Beggan, Midgley, and Wallace (1995) proposed that forming outcome-biased inferences about groups reflects only one part of the process of acquiring an understanding of groups from their behavioral outcomes. These investigators developed a model of the dispositional inference process that resembles the model developed by Gilbert and his colleagues (Gilbert, Krull, & Pelham, 1988; Gilbert & Osborne, 1989; Gilbert, Pelham, & Krull, 1988; Osborne & Gilbert, 1992). According to Gilbert's model, the process of understanding individual targets consists of an initial characterization stage and a subsequent correction stage. From this theoretical perspective, perceivers first draw outcome-biased character inferences from behavior ("Nellie is a nervous person") and then correct those inferences with information about the context in which the behavioral outcomes occurred ("but given that she is about to give a job talk, she may be a more relaxed person than she seems"). Thus, the first stage of this model may reflect perceivers' uses of the heuristic, "Behavioral outcomes are representative of underlying dispositions," whereas the second stage reflects perceivers' adjustments for the context in which behavioral outcomes occur. Figure 1 illustrates the two stages of Gilbert and Osborne's (1989) process model.

Allison, Beggan, Midgley et al. (1995) proposed that the process of understanding groups from their behavior shares the same "characterization and correction" framework shown in Figure 1, but that perceivers' recognition of unique aspects of group behavior alter the nature of this

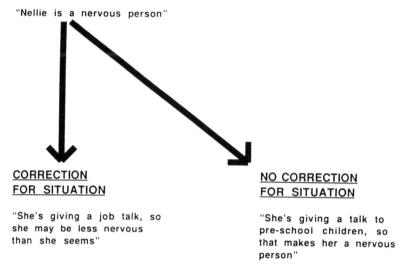

CHARACTERIZATION

"Nellie is a nervous person"

CORRECTION
FOR SITUATION

"She's giving a job talk, so
she may be less nervous
than she seems"

NO CORRECTION
FOR SITUATION

"She's giving a talk to
pre-school children, so
that makes her a nervous
person"

Fig. 1.   A model of outcome-biased dispositional inferences about individual targets.
(Adapted from Gilbert & Osborne, 1989.)

framework. Figure 2 displays the model of Allison and colleagues in which
perceivers are first presumed to characterize groups heuristically in much
the same way that they initially characterize individuals. When a group, as
a unit, produces a decision outcome, perceivers draw the outcome-biased
inference that most or all group members are supportive of the outcome.
Next, perceivers make two corrections that reflect their beliefs about two
unique properties of group decision making. Perceivers first correct for
whether the target group is recognized as inherently unanimous (e.g., juries,
married couples, or religious cults) or as inherently democratic (e.g., large
legislative bodies, states of the United States, or democratic nations).
Groups judged as inherently unanimous require little or no correction
from the initial characterization, whereas group recognized as inherently
democratic require some correction for the group's probable heterogeneity
of opinion. Past research suggests that perceivers estimate that roughly
65% of the members of these democratic groups typically support their
groups' decisions (Beggan & Allison, 1993).

The model in Figure 2 proposes further that under most circumstances,
perceivers of inherently unanimous groups have no need to consider making
any additional corrections— that is, the initial outcome-biased characterization stands. However, perceivers of inherently democratic groups may cor-

CHARACTERIZATION

"The state legislature is supportive of the bill"

"The jury is supportive of a guilty verdict"

CORRECTION FOR TYPE OF GROUP

"The state legislature is inherently democratic, so only about 65% of legislators may support the bill"

NO CORRECTION FOR TYPE OF GROUP

"Juries are inherently unanimous, so all the jurors favor guilt"

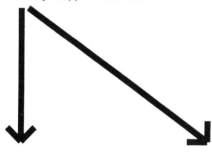

CORRECTION FOR DECISION RULE

"The state legislature uses 2/3 majority rule, so about 85% of the legislators support the bill"

NO CORRECTION FOR DECISION RULE

"The state legislature uses majority rule, so about 65% of the legislators support the bill"

Fig. 2.   A model of outcome-biased dispositional inferences about group targets. (Adapted from Allison, Beggan, Midgley et al., 1995.)

rect for the formal decision rules that such groups often use to transform their members' diverse views into a final decision outcome. Two of the more common decision rules used by democratic groups are simple majority rule and two-thirds majority rule. Clearly, if a two-thirds majority rule is in operation, perceivers must adjust their judgments about group support for the group's decision (to a figure higher than 65%) to account for this more stringent decision criterion. The more stringent the decision rule, the more perceivers' twice-corrected judgments resemble their initial outcome-biased characterization of the group as fully supportive of the decision outcome.

To test this process model of dispositional inferences about groups, Allison, Beggan, Midgley, et al. (1995) conducted two experiments based on Gilbert and Osborne's (1989) assumption that the initial characterization stage requires fewer cognitive resources to implement than does either of the subsequent correction stges. This assumption implies that in the processing of information about a group decision outcome, the addition of another resource-consuming task should impair the correction stages more than the characterization stage of the inference process. In the first study, subjects read a scenario containing a description of a decision reached by either a unanimous group (a jury) or a democratic group (the United Nations). Subjects were placed under high- or low-cognitive load while reading the group decision information and while drawing dispositional inferences. Consistent with the model, perceivers of the jury decision drew outcome-biased inferences while they were under both high- and low-cognitive load. Perceivers of the United Nations' decision, however, were more likely to draw outcome-biased inferences under high-cognitive load (when their ability to correct was impaired) than under low-cognitive load. In the second experiment, subjects were informed of a decision made by an inherently democratic group that used a decision rule of two-thirds majority rule. The results revealed that perceivers inferred greater support for the decision outcome under low-cognitive load (when their ability to correct for the two-thirds majority rule was unimpaired) than under high-cognitive load.

In comparing the model of Gilbert and Pelham (1988) (Figure 1) with the model of Allison, Beggan, Midgley et al. (1995) (Figure 2), it is interesting to note that the former focuses on corrections for forces external to the target individual, whereas the latter is preoccupied with corrections for forces within the target group. Allison and colleagues speculate that this difference between the two models reflects a fundamental difference in perceivers' typical efforts to understand individual versus group targets from their behavioral outcomes. The most salient aspects of person perception are the person's behavior and the situational context of the behavior. Person perceivers are usually less concerned with (and are less aware of) the individual target's ambivalence about action than they are with the action itself and its situational context. Groups, however, are known to be more internally complex social entities. Consequently, a salient aspect of group perception is the group's action (or decision outcome) in relation to its inherent complexity. We know intuitively that democratic groups often struggle to reach decision outcomes, and that even inherently unanimous groups do not become unanimous overnight or effortlessly.

However, it may also be the case that the models portrayed in Figures 1 and 2 overlook important aspects of person perception and group perception, respectively. The model of Gilbert and Pelham (1988) may fail to take into account perceivers' awareness of an individual's internal struggle or ambivalence about action, and the model of Allison, Beggan, Midgley et al. (1995) may overlook perceivers' awareness of the situational forces that affect group actions. Inferences about both individual and group targets may show an extreme outcome bias to the extent that the target is judged (1) as homogeneous rather than complex, (2) as resolute rather than conflicted about its action, and (3) as immune to situational impediments to behavior rather than as slave to them.

B. LONGEVITY OF OUTCOME-BIASED INFERENCES

Several past studies have investigated the longevity of outcome-biased inferences to shed light on the specific heuristic mechanisms that underlie the bias. Allison et al. (1990) provided perceivers with a scenario describing a group decision outcome and then asked them to make attitude inferences about the group immediately as well as 6 weeks later. Subjects inferred a correspondence between the group outcome and group attitudes immediately after reading the scenario, despite recalling accurately that (a) the majority of the group did not approve of the outcome, and (b) the group used a decision rule that was responsible for undermining the correspondence between the group outcome and members' preferences. After 6 weeks, subjects were no longer able to recall accurately the percentage of voter support, nor could they remember correctly the decision rule. However, virtually all of the subjects remembered the group outcome, which made their inferences significantly more outcome biased after 6 weeks than they had been immediately. This pattern emerged for both heuristic and systematic processors, and it added a temporal twist to Festinger's (1957) claim that cognitions about behavioral outcomes are less malleable than other types of cognitions. The durability of outcome information in memory over time suggests that, under most circumstances, outcome-biased judgments will grow stronger through time.

Subsequent research has corroborated this notion. Beggan and Allison (1993) asked residents of Virginia and Kentucky to estimate the magnitude of voter support for the winner of the 1989 Virginia gubernatorial election. The Virginia election was remarkably close, with the victorious candidate,

Douglas Wilder, attracting 50.2% of the popular vote compared to his opponent's 49.8%. Kentucky subjects knew that Wilder had won, but they were entirely unaware of the narrow margin of victory. When asked to indicate the percentage of popular support that Wilder had received from voters, Kentucky residents estimated that Wilder attracted roughly 65% of voter support. Subjects from Virginia, in contrast, were quite aware immediately following the election of the closeness of the popular vote. But 6 months after Wilder's narrow victory, Virginians' estimates of voter support resembled the erroneous estimates of their Kentucky counterparts. In short, as time passed, Virginia subjects tended to forget the narrowness of their own governor's victory margin and drew increasingly outcome-biased inferences about voters' election-day preferences.

In a similar study, Allison, Beggan, McDonald, and Rettew (1995) asked subjects shortly after the November 1992, presidential election to indicate the percentage of the popular vote received on election day by Bill Clinton, George Bush, and Ross Perot. The results showed that Clinton, who actually received less than a majority of voter support (43%), was perceived to have attracted majority support (51.8%). Moreover 7 months after the election, in June of 1993, perceived majority support for Clinton on election day grew stronger (to 56.8%), whereas perceived voter support for Bush and Perot declined. This outcome-biased judgment was made by Clinton supporters as well as by Clinton detractors, and it was surprising for several reasons. First, with the popular vote split among 3 major candidates, one might have expected perceivers to recognize that the odds of the winner receiving majority support are significantly reduced. Second, for a number of weeks following the election, the media dubbed Clinton "the 43% President," and political pundits speculated about how resistant Americans and Congress would be to this nonmajority President's new programs (Fineman, 1992). Third, Clinton's public approval rating dropped precipitously from November of 1992 to June of 1993 (Klein, 1993), leading one to expect, perhaps, a similar decline in retrospective judgments of voter support for Clinton on election day. Despite all of these factors, however, that would seem to highlight and reinforce the absence of majority support for Clinton in November of 1992, subjects were convinced that his victory had been endorsed by the majority of American voters.

The results of the Wilder and Clinton field studies would seem to support the idea that outcome-biased dispositional inferences grow stronger with the passage of time. However, there appear to be limits to the effect. Although Virginians made more extreme outcome-biased inferences over time in their perceptions of Wilder's narrow gubernatorial victory, Kentuckians did not. We can sepculate that Kentucky subjects, who were entirely unaware of Wilder's close call, drew inferences immediately after the election (as well as long after the election) that reflected their intuitive belief about how much voter support the winners of elections typically receive. This belief appears to be roughly 65%, which happens to be the estimate that Virginians were converging toward over time as they forgot the narrowness of Wilder's victory. Thus, it appears that the outcome bias increases over time when perceivers initially believe that fewer than 65% of the members of inherently democratic groups support their decision outcomes. This precondition existed in Allison et al.'s (1990) laboratory study, in the Wilder field study conducted by Beggan and Allison (1993), and in the Clinton field study conducted by Allison, Beggan, McDonald et al. (1995).

If perceivers' inferences about group support for inherently democratic group outcomes converge over time toward 65%, then it follows that inferences should show a reverse outcome bias if perceivers are initially led to believe that group support for an outcome exceeds 65%. Allison, Beggan, Midley et al. (1995) tested precisely this idea. Subjects were informed that Cheyenne, Wyoming had elected a new mayor; one half of the subjects were informed that the mayor had received the unanimous support to Cheyenne's voting citizens, whereas the other half were not informed at all about voter support for the outcome. After reading the scenario, subjects were asked to infer voters' attitudes and to recall (or to estimate) the percentage of the voting citizens who had supported the outcome. After 6 weeks, subjects returned to the laboratory and were asked to make these judgments again. The results showed that perceivers who lacked information about how much Cheyenne voters had supported its decision outcome estimated that roughly 65% had done so, and this estimate did not change 6 weeks later. In contrast, subjects who were informed that the outcome enjoyed unanimous support were able to recall this fact immediately after reading the scenario, but showed a significant change in their beliefs about voter support for the outcome 6 weeks later. Specifically, after admitting that they had forgotten exactly how much the city had supported its outcome, these subjects made estimates of support that approached 65%. As time passes, perceivers appear to rely increasingly on such inferential heuristics, and this heightened reliance can lead to inferences that later become more or less outcome biased depending on perceivers' beliefs about the group (either inherently democratic or unanimous) and on their initial knowledge about the level of group support for the outcome (either below or above 65%).

IV. Outcome-Biased Inferences: Implications for Attitude Change, Stereotyping, and Social Behavior

One index of the importance of outcome-biased inferences is the extent to which they influence a wide range of social phenomena. Outcome-biased inferences have now been studied and found to be involved in a number of domains central to social psychology. These domains include attitude formation, attitude change, social influence, stereotype formation, stereotype change, and social behavior. Research on outcome biases in these domains has added to our theoretical understanding of the mechanisms underlying these biases and other phenomena as well.

A. ATTITUDES AND ATTITUDE CHANGE: PERCEPTIONS OF CHANGE, SOCIAL INFLUENCE, AND PERSUASION

The paradigm used in studying outcome biases involves asking subjects to draw inferences about people's attitudes (Allison & Messick, 1985; Mackie & Allison, 1987; Mackie et al., 1992a, 1992b; Worth et al., 1987). The occurrence of outcome biases in such inferences typically contributes to a view of the social world as stable, predictable, and constant. Outcomes are presumed to reflect enduring dispositions, such as attitudes and traits, rather than fleeting circumstances such as group decision rules. Ironically, however, this very feature—increased perception of stability triggered by outcome-biased inferences—may enhance perceptions of change if outcome-biased inferences change over time.

Just such an effect was demonstrated when Mackie and Allison (1987) induced observers to make consecutive attitude inferences, each biased by a different outcome. In the first of these studies, subjects read that a measure recalling the members of a Boardwalk committee was put to popular vote in a small resort community off the coast of Florida. Subjects were told that approximately 57% of the population voted for the measure (the exact percentage was varied among subjects to reduce demand). Success or failure of the recall depended, however, on election decision rules. Half the subjects were told that 50% of the population had to favor the measure for it to be successful. With this condition, the 57% popular vote meant that the recall had succeeded. The rest of the subjects were informed that a 65% popular vote was necessary for success; these subjects thus read that the recall bid had failed, despite its having attracted 57% of the vote.

After learning the outcome of the first election, subjects were told that a local ordinance required any recall attempt to appear on the ballot in two consecutive elections before the final fate of those being recalled could be decided. Consequently, a second recall election was held approximately 7 months later. Again subjects were told that the measure attracted approximately 57% of the popular vote. Whereas some of the subjects read that the second election was guided by the same rules as the first election, other subjects read that new decision rules were in place. No reason for the change in decision rules was given. Specifically, half of the subjects given the 50% decision rule and half of the subjects given the 65% decision rule in the first election were told that the measure had to be favored by 50% to pass. The rest of the subjects were told that the recall measure had to attract 65% of the vote to be successful. Thus some subjects saw no change in decision rules (50% at both elections or 65% at both elections) and read about consistent outcomes (with 57% of the popular vote the measure passed both times if the decision rule was 50% and failed both times if it was 65%). Other subjects, however, were faced with constant behavior, changing decision rules, and changing outcomes.

After receiving information about both elections, students made inferences about the attitude of the typical citizen toward the recall measure. Their inferences about both the first and second elections were clearly biased by outcomes. When the recall measure passed, subjects thought that popular opinion favored the recall more than when the measure did not pass, regardless of the fact that the measure attracted an almost identical percentage of the vote in both conditions. Follow-up studies indicated that these effects occurred even when the rule change occurring between elections was imposed on, rather than initiated by, the community, and even when subjects made inferences about the first election before knowing the outcome of the second.

The fact that subjects made outcome-biased inferences about each election thus set the stage for assessing perceptions of the stability of the group's attitudes. When asked if the community's views on the issue had changed between the two elections, subjects who had been led to make inferences biased by differing outcomes responded in the affirmative. Subjects were significantly more likely to perceive the group's attitudes as having changed when the election outcome changed than when it did not. Moreover, the greater the difference between attitude inferences made after failed versus successful recall attempts, the more likely subjects were to conclude that the group's attitude had changed. Perceptions of change appeared to depend on a comparison of outcome-biased inferences rather than a comparison of performances or outcomes.

A set of studies in the early 1990s demonstrated the same effect for the correspondence bias when the holder of the attitude was an individual rather than a group. Also, it will be remembered that subjects in the classic Jones and Harris (1967) study believed that a target assigned to write a pro-Castro essay in fact held pro-Castro attitudes. If the same target was later constrained to write an anti-Castro essay, would subjects now infer that he opposed Castro? Moreover, would they in addition believe that the target had undergone a change of heart about Castro?

Allison, Mackie, Muller, and Worth (1993) showed that the answer to both of these questions was "yes." In their studies, subjects read about a target whose instructor assigned him to write a pro-Castro essay at the start of a creative writing class and then an anti-Castro essay at the end of the course, or vice versa. In the first experiment 9 months was said to have elapsed between the writing of the first and second essays; a second study (using different materials and a different attitude object) examined shorter interessay intervals of 2 months and 1 week, respectively. In each case, subjects were asked to estimate the target's own level of support for the relevant issue at the time each essay was written.

Once again, correspondent inferences were made. When the target wrote the assigned pro-Castro essay, subjects believed him to harbor pro-Castro attitudes, whereas when he wrote the assigned anti-Castro essay they attributed anti-Castro sentiments to him. These inferences did not depend on the interessay interval. When asked if the target's attitude toward Castro had changed significantly, subjects indicated that they believed it had—the target was seen as having undergone a significant attitude change, even in the course of a week. The greater the difference between inferences made about each incident of essay writing, the greater the attitude change subjects believed the target had undergone.

These results thus parallel those obtained when the target was a group. Just as subjects thought that two inconsistent actions taken by a group were each diagnostic of the group's attitude, so subjects also thought that two actions performed by an individual were diagnostic of the individual's attitudes, even when the behaviors were completely constrained and even when the two behaviors were completely contradictory. Although inconsistent information often triggers more careful processing (Hastie, 1984; Maheswaran & Chaiken, 1991), the fact that the behaviors were inconsistent apparently made subjects more likely to infer dispositional change than to consider the constraints on the behavior.

Insensitivity to context can thus lead perceivers to make varying attitude inferences about invariant behavior. Outcome biases not only contribute to the attitudes we attribute to other people, but, under the right circumstances, they also contribute to the impression that those attitudes have changed. As Silka (1989) has noted, the mechanisms underlying perceptions of change have been virtually ignored while processes promoting perceptions of stability—as outcome biases often do—have received much greater attention. Our findings suggest that a single mechanism—outcome-biased inferences—can contribute to perceptions of both stability and change.

In the studies discussed so far, subjects' outcome biases facilitated their perception that other people's attitudes had changed. Indeed, several experiments that assessed the impact of outcome biases on subjects' own attitudes produced little evidence of such change. In one study, for example, subjects who participated in a group decision task attributed outcome-consistent attitudes to their fellow group members, but not to themselves (Worth et al., 1987, Experiment 2). This finding is consistent with actor–observer differences found in other inferences showing that internal attributions correspondent with behavior are made about others, but not about the self (Jones & Nisbett, 1972).

Nevertheless, the results of another study in this series did suggest that outcome biases might help produce attitude change under certain conditions (Worth et al., 1987, Experiment 1). In this study, subjects were led to believe that their initial vote in a jury decision-making task either agreed or disagreed with the majority of other votes, and, independently, either agreed or disagreed with the group's final verdict (changes in the decision rule determined whether a majority or minority determined the jury's final decision). Subjects' opinions on the issue were then measured again. When subjects' initial views coincided with the group's verdict, no changes in subjects' attitude were found. But when subjects' initial views disagreed with the group outcome, subjects adopted the group verdict if it had been determined by a majority of votes. That is, subjects' confidence in (and maintenance of) their initial view seemed to be sustained by its consistency with the group outcome (regardless of whether the subject held a majority or minority view), but could not be sustained when they disagreed with an outcome that also represented the majority view of the group. Thus, when initial opinions agreed with the group decision, that outcome appeared to constitute an additional source of social confirmation for the validity of subjects' opinions. When the outcome contradicted initial opinions, it appeared to represent social validity for those holding a minority view, and thus produced an attitude change.

These findings suggest that information about outcomes, similar to information about consensus, can contribute to attitude formation and change. Such information provides evidence of the validity of certain propositions (Mackie & Skelly, 1994) and thus can affect the knowledge upon which attitudes depend. In this sense, outcome biases might become a powerful means of changing beliefs, and thus of changing attitudes.

Consider, for example, a public health campaign that advocated avoiding exposure to the sun in order to reduce the incidence of skin cancer. An individual's attitude toward avoiding the sun is no doubt affected by his or her beliefs about the degree of protection that such a strategy affords. Those beliefs can in turn be influenced by outcome biases. Imagine, for example, learning that 25% of the people who suntan regularly develop skin cancer. How should such information be interpreted? Perhaps suntanning carries a significant risk, but perhaps it does not. Indeed, how significant the risk seems may well depend on a decision rule about where safety ends and risk begins. If the decision rule indicates that a 1 in 4 chance of developing cancer constitutes a serious risk, attitudes may turn against sun exposure. If, however, the decision rule indicates that a 25% chance of contracting cancer is not serious, favorable attitudes toward tanning may be maintained.

To assess the possible role of decision–rule outcomes in attitude change, Allison and Mackie (1995) provided subjects with both a piece of information relevant to an already assessed attitude issue and a decision rule that helped them interpret that information. In one condition, for example, subjects were led to believe that they were reading excerpts from an actual newspaper article reporting that 25% of people who regularly suntan develop skin cancer. Some subjects then read that the Surgeon General had declared that a 1 in 4 incidence of skin cancer was significant enough to warrant avoiding extended exposure to the sun. Other subjects read that the Surgeon General had declared that a 1 in 4 chance of developing cancer was not significant enough to warrant extended avoidance. We then measured beliefs about whether suntanning was likely to cause skin cancer and attitudes about suntanning. The outcome of the Surgeon General's decision rule had a significant impact on both the beliefs and the attitudes of our subjects. Compared to initial beliefs about the dangers of suntanning, postexperimental beliefs became more negative when the decision outcome indicated serious risk and more favorable when it indicated lack of risk. Attitudes changed in parallel, becoming more opposed to suntanning when the decision outcome indicated risk, and more favorable when it did not. In another condition, subjects were first informed that 50% of criminals who do not serve their entire prison term become repeat offenders and were then told whether the Attorney General considered that rate a risk or not. Similar effects on both beliefs and attitudes were obtained. These responses provided evidence for the impact of outcome biases on both beliefs and attitudes.

Thus, outcome biases can influence inferences made about the attitudes held by both individuals and groups; can contribute to perceptions that these attitudes have changed even when behavioral evidence suggests that they have not; and can facilitate attitude change itself, both by altering the social dynamics of influence and by changing beliefs about attitude objects. One of the obvious extensions of this work is to investigate now whether outcome-biased attitudes translate into actual behavioral changes, or whether outcomes can have a direct impact on behavioral intensions and thus behavior.

B. STEREOTYPE FORMATION AND CHANGE

Most of the early work on outcome-biased inferences dealt with inferences about attitudes. Of potentially greater importance is the question of whether outcome biases influence inferences about personality traits. If outcomes trigger biased inferences about personality traits, they may represent contributors to stereotypes. After all, if members of one group fail to gain admittance to colleges and universities, whereas members of another group succeed, outcome-biased inferences would lead to the conclusion that the first group is less intellectually capable than the second. This inference might be drawn even if circumstantial constraints actually accounted for the difference in admission rates.

The potential contribution of outcome biases to stereotype formation was first demonstrated by a study in which subjects made inferences about groups who succeeded or failed in an intellectual endeavor (Mackie et al., 1990). In these experiments, subjects read a vignette about a group of 10 college students attempting to qualify as representatives of their school in a college bowl competition. To screen potential representatives, the college's math department held qualifying rounds in which prospective teams had to solve a series of deductive reasoning problems. To manipulate the trait about which subjects would make inferences, half of the subjects were told that the correct solution of these problems required motivation and the willingness to work hard, whereas the other half were told that successful solution of the problems depended on raw intelligence and superior intellectual ability.

All subjects were then told that the group they read about had solved 70% of the problems in the preliminary round. Qualification success or failure depended, however, on the decision rule the math department was said to be using. Half of the subjects were told that the group needed to complete 65% of the problems correctly to qualify, whereas the rest of the subjects were told that the group needed to score 75% to succeed. When the decision rule was 65%, the group scoring 70% succeeded in qualifying; but when the decision rule was 75%, the group failed to qualify. Our primary concern was with subjects' inferences about the intelligence and motivation of the successful and failing groups. As predicted, subjects in the relevant conditions believed the successful group to be significantly more hardworking or significantly more intelligent than the group that failed, despite the group's objectively identical performances.

Subjects were quite willing to infer enduring traits correspondent with a group's outcomes, even when performance was identical and only the criterion differed. Outcome biases thus constitute a viable mechanism of stereotype formation. In this regard, our results dovetail nicely with other demonstrations of the role that situation-insensitive inferences play in stereotype formation and maintenance. Social roles theory (Eagly, 1987) suggests, for example, that males' and females' differential representations in agentic versus nurturing social roles contribute to gender stereotypes. The traits associated with employee roles—task orientation, assertiveness, and rationality—are attributed to men, whereas women are assumed to have the traits associated with homemaker roles—sensitivity, affection, and gentleness (Eagly & Steffen, 1984). In experimental tests of these ideas, college students have indeed been found to perceive members of fictitious nonhuman groups as nurturing, affectionate, and gentle if they were described as involved in child care, but as competitive and ambitious if they were said to be paid employees (Hoffman & Hurst, 1990). More important, Eagly and her colleagues point out the important part played in this process by environmental constraints: Men and women more often are consigned to roles rather than free to choose them, yet role-correspondent qualities are attributed to them. Similar observations have been made about the stereotypes of other groups that are similarly constrained to particular socioeconomic roles (LeVine & Campbell, 1972; Pettigrew, 1980). Role-insensitive correspondent inferences reflect what people do rather than how they came to do it, just as constraint-insensitive outcome biases reflect people's outcomes rather than how those outcomes were obtained.

Our initial studies thus showed that outcome biases could contribute to the formation of stereotypes of groups about whom little was known. But what of groups about whom stereotypes are already established? Can outcomes bias inferences even when people already harbor firm expectancies about a group's qualities? More significant, can outcomes alter inferences in a stereotype-inconsistent direction? When groups produce outcomes inconsistent with the impressions held about them, do those impressions change?

To find out, we asked subjects to read vignettes in which groups received stereotypic or counterstereotypic outcomes, not because of their behavior but because of a decision rule (Mackie et al., 1992b). In a first experiment, subjects read about either a conservative or a liberal political group (the Young Conservatives or the Young Democrats) that voted on a liberal social measure (the placing of condom vending machines in campus dormitories). According to the scenario, a slight majority (57%) of the group voted for the measure. Whether the measure passed or failed, however, depended on the group's bylaws. When the group required a two-thirds majority, the measure failed (a conservative outcome), whereas when the group required only a simple majority, the measure passed (a liberal outcome). Thus, depending on the condition, subjects read about either a liberal or a conservative group that experienced either a liberal or a conservative outcome.

To assess the impact of outcomes on inferences about the groups, subjects were asked how liberal or conservative the group was.

Subjects' inferences were, in fact, biased by the outcome of the vote. Even though the percentage of group members voting for the measure was identical in every condition, the group was seen as more liberal when the liberal measure passed and more conservative when the liberal measure failed to pass. Importantly, outcomes that were counterstereotypic had just as much impact on inferences as outcomes that were stereotype consistent. That is, the passage of a liberal measure resulted in the conservative group, as well as the liberal group, being seen as more liberal. Similarly, failure of the liberal measure resulted in the liberal group, as well as the conservative group, being perceived as more conservative.

Because attitudes are probably more malleable than other aspects of stereotypes, it was important to demonstrate that outcome biases would also affect inferences about the enduring dispositions relevant to real social stereotypes. To do so, we asked our subjects—all of whom were White Americans—to read slightly modified versions of the vignettes about the group trying to qualify as college bowl representatives of their school. All subjects read that the group was required to solve deductive reasoning problems. To ensure that subjects would draw inferences about dispositional traits, we again made it clear that successful solution of these problems reflected superior intelligence or exceptional motivation, depending on the condition. All subjects were informed that the group correctly solved 70% of the problems, and that the fate of the group depended once again on the decision rule. Half of the subjects were told that the group needed to complete 65% of the problems correctly; in this condition, the group succeeded in qualifying. The other half of the subjects were told that the group had to solve 75% of the problems, and thus the group they read about failed. We modified the vignettes by identifying the group of students attempting to qualify for the college bowl competition. Some subjects read that the group all belonged to the Black American Student Association, whereas others were told that the group were members of the Asian-American Student Association. According to our subjects' stereotypes, successful completion of the deductive reasoning task represented a stereotypic outcome for Asian students and a counterstereotypic outcome for Black students, whereas failure to qualify represented a stereotypic outcome for African-Americans and a counterstereotypic outcome for Asian-Americans.

Subjects were then asked about the intelligence of the group. Outcome information biased inferences about intelligence regardless of whether it was stereotypic or counterstereotypic. When the group was described as having qualified for the college bowl competition, they were thought to be more intelligent and more hardworking than when they failed to qualify. This effect occurred even when the outcomes biased inferences in a counter-stereotypic direction—outcome biases operated as strongly when Blacks succeeded and Asians failed as when the opposite was true—and as strongly for the more stable trait of intelligence as for the more malleable quality of motivation (Mackie et al., 1990). Moreover, outcomes had this effect despite the fact that the group's actual performance was constant across all conditions. Thus, outcomes not only were powerful enough to modify perceptions of traits central to real stereotypes, but also to modify those perceptions in a counterstereotypic fashion. In fact, the impact of outcomes was stronger on counterstereotypic inferences than on stereotypic inferences.

These effects were replicated in a second series of studies in which college professors or janitors either did or did not qualify for a Jeopardy-like trivia contest (Mackie et al., 1992a). Qualifying groups, whether professors or janitors, were seen as smarter than failing groups, again regardless of their occupation. Thus, even when inconsistent with prevailing stereotypes, inferences reflected outcomes.

One of the potential benefits of modifying perceptions about even a few members of a stigmatized group is the possibility that such judgments might generalize to the group as a whole. If judging a small subset of a group to be smart and hardworking generalized to the overall group stereotype, we would have evidence that outcome biases might contribute not only to stereotype formation, but also to stereotype modification. We thus attempted to show that outcome-biased stereotype-relevant judgments made about a small subgroup might generalize to the stereotype of the group as a whole.

We accomplished this by asking subjects their impressions of the intelligence of two occupational groups, custodians and college professors (Mackie et al., 1992a). We then asked subjects to make inferences about a small group of either custodians or professors at a college who participated in a general knowledge "Jeopardy-like" quiz competition. Regardless of which group they read about, subjects were told that the group scored a certain number of points in the competition. Because of the variations in the criterion for winning, however, this performance was either good enough or not good enough to let the group win. After reading about the group's performance, subjects made inferences about the intelligence of the group they read about, and then some time later, about the intelligence of custodians and professors as a whole. With the latter dependent measure, of course, we wished to see whether any biased inferences that occurred about a specific subgroup of custodians and professors would generalize to custodians and professors as a whole.

Subjects made outcome-biased inferences, seeing both the custodians and the professors as more intelligent if they won and less intelligent if they lost, despite their identical scores. When later asked about the population as a whole, subjects reported thinking that professors were smarter overall than custodians. However, their outcome-biased inferences did make a difference. When the subgroup the subjects read about succeeded—leading to outcome-biased inferences of intelligence—the whole group was seen as more intelligent. Similarly, when the subgroup lost the competition, the whole group was seen as less intelligent. These effects were equally strong for janitors and professors and for generalization of stereotypic and counter-stereotypic inferences. Not surprising, the impact of outcome-biased infer-ences on perceptions of the group as a whole was weaker than on inferences about the performing subgroup. Nevertheless, the results clearly showed that inferences biased by outcomes could have a significant impact on general stereotypes.

Some aspects of our experimental procedure may have made such gener-alization easier. There may have been an element of demand in asking for group ratings soon after ratings about the subgroup. In conditions in which inferences were biased by stereotypically inconsistent outcomes, students received only this strongly inconsistent information. Finally, it may be that social stereotypes about occupational groups such as custodians and professors are less strongly held and thus more malleable than other kinds of stereotypes. In a second experiment designed to exclude these possible explanations, we presented subjects with both stereotypically consistent and inconsistent outcomes about strongly stereotyped groups using procedures intended to reduce demand characteristics as much as possible.

In this experiment, subjects were led to make outcome-biased inferences about the intelligence of a small group of African-American or Asian-American college students who either succeeded and then failed, or who failed and then succeeded, on an intellectual task (Mackie et al., 1992a). The fact that each group both succeeded and failed meant that subjects received both stereotype-consistent and stereotype-inconsistent informa-tion about every group (recall that our White American student population thought that Asian-Americans were of higher intelligence than African-Americans). After receiving information about the subgroups' outcomes and after making inferences about their intelligence, subjects attended a lecture on general psychology in which they took notes for approximately 45 minutes. At this time, subjects were approached by a second experimenter posing as a graduate student who needed to collect information about various social groups as part of a research project. After reading a long and detailed cover story, subjects were asked to assess the intelligence (among many other traits) of African-Americans, Asian-Americans, or White Americans in general.

The results showed that the most recent outcome influenced judgments made about the target group as a whole. When subjects had read about an African-American subgroup, African-Americans (but not Asian- or White Americans) were seen as more intelligent when the subgroup finally succeeded than when they finally failed, compared to when subjects had read about a different subgroup. Similarly, when subjects had read about an Asian-American subgroup, Asian-Americans (but not African- or White Americans) were seen as more intelligent when the subgroup succeeded than when they failed, but these results did not reach conventional levels of statistical significance.

To seek further evidence of the role of outcome-biased inferences about a subgroup on evaluations of the group as a whole, we correlated subjects' assessments of the target population's intelligence with estimates of the subgroup's intelligence. These correlations showed that ratings of the intelligence of the African-American subgroup, after their second attempt to qualify, were significantly related to assessments of the intelligence of the African-American population as a whole, but not to ratings of other groups. Ratings of the intelligence of the Asian-American subgroup were also associated with ratings of the intelligence of the Asian-American population as a whole, but not with ratings of other groups. Thus the most recent outcome-biased judgment about a small group influenced (albeit weakly) stereotypic judgments about the larger group.

Finally, these studies demonstrated that outcome-biased inferences produced the perception that stereotypic attributes had changed even when actual behavior did not. As with the perceptions of changes in attitudes, the occurrence of consecutive inferences about stereotypic qualities, biased by different outcomes, created that illusion that the group's stereotypic qualities had changed.

Although the changes in the stereotypes produced in this series of experiments were small, we were able to change stereotypic judgments about groups under quite conservative circumstances. Stereotypes about the intelligence and motivation levels of real social groups such as African-Americans and Asian-Americans are quite firmly held, and our subjects received stereotype-consistent information along with stereotype-inconsistent information. In addition, we went to some lengths to remove obvious demand characteristics from the experimental situation.

Why does the outcome bias produce meaningful changes in stereotypes when other attempts to bring stereotype-inconsistent information to an observer's attention so often fail? One reason might lie in the ease with which the outcome heuristic is used. We have seen that outcome biases are made even by subjects who remember both the actual performance and the decision rule. Thus people may, under normal circumstances, be unaware of the impact that outcomes have on their inferences. Inferences that appear to follow from an outcome ("They succeeded so they must be smart") may be made with little thought, and judgments that appear to follow from a comparison of inferences ("They were smart before, but now they don't seem so smart") may occur the same way.

In fact, several features of outcome-biased inferences may be particularly useful in changing stereotypes. First, we have seen that in experiments in which subjects read about a change in a group's outcomes, the subjects made different inferences about behavior that actually did not change. If stereotypes arise more as the result of biased inferences than of objectively negative behavior on a stigmatized group's part, then changes in stereotypes may require changes in outcomes. Second, because outcomes appear to be more memorable than behavioral or situational information, the impact of outcomes on inferences grows rather than declines over time (Allison et al., 1990; Baron & Hershey, 1988; Mackie & Allison, 1987). Thus changing outcomes may have greater long- than short-term impact on the perception of stereotyped groups.

Our findings also have practical implications for social policy designed to promote positive outcomes for members of currently stigmatized groups. Our research shows that programs that facilitate such outcomes— admissions to universities and graduate programs, for example, or promotion to management positions—have social psychological as well as tangible material benefits. The social psychological benefits come in the form of the more positive perceptions triggered by those outcomes. These positive benefits usually accrue regardless of whether external circumstances facilitate or impede such outcomes. Discrimination that favors members of powerful groups has rarely undermined favorable perceptions of their achievements, any more than discrimination against stigmatized groups has served as an extenuating circumstance for their failures. Our research suggests that both the positive and negative effects of outcomes biases depend on insensitivity to the conditions that contribute to outcomes. When different standards are applied to different groups, they may become salient reasons to discount positive inferences that might be made about success. When social programs draw attention to differences in how members of different groups are treated, some of the consequences of outcome biases may be undermined. This creates a double bind: Advertising the existence of these outcomes evidences good faith efforts to end discrimination, but might undermine the positive perceptions that usually follow positive outcomes.

C. PERCEPTIONS OF IN-GROUPS AND OUT-GROUPS

If outcomes bias the perception of groups' characteristics, do they have an equal impact on the perception of in- and out-group attributes? In one of the first studies demonstrating the group attribution error, Allison and Messick (1985) found that inferences about out-groups were more likely to be outcome biased than inferences about in-groups. In these studies, subjects read that the leader of the United States (the in-group), the Netherlands, or the Soviet Union (two out-groups) had either established or severed diplomatic relations with a small fictitious nation. Relations between the two nations were not described as either positive or negative, and no reason for the action was provided. The main dependent measure was whether subjects would make equally confident inferences about the attitudes of in- and out-group citizens. Given that they knew only the leader's actions, what did subjects believe the attitude of the typical citizen of each country to be?

Subjects made strong inferences about the attitudes of each nation's citizens on the basis of its leader's actions. When the leader decided to establish relations, subjects felt that citizens would hold a more favorable attitude toward the country than when relations were severed. Of even more interest, the strength of this effect depended on the country that subjects read about. The impact of the leader's actions on inferred attitudes was greatest when subjects read about the Soviet Union and least when they read about the United States, with Holland falling between. Although only the inferences made about the Soviet Union and the United States were significantly different, the results indicated that out-group inferences were more influenced by outcomes than in-group inferences.

Such findings are consistent, of course, with other related literatures. First, the presumption of greater coherence of out-group than of in-group attitudes on the basis of a single piece of information is consistent with the out-group homogeneity effect (Quattrone & Jones, 1980). To the extent that in-groups are seen as more variable and differentiated than out-groups, it may be more difficult to attribute a uniform attitude to in-group members than to out-group members. Second, the findings parallel actor–observer differences in attribution: Just as people are less likely to make correspondent inferences about themselves than about others, so too, they are less likely to make these kinds of dispositional inferences about their own as opposed to another group.

There are other reasons to suspect that outcome biases might have less impact on inferences made about in-groups than those made about out-groups. As described earlier, relying on outcomes to make inferences has heuristic properties; outcome biases are more likely when subjects devote less capacity or motivation to the processing task. In-group information is, for the most part, inherently interesting and by definition self-relevant, two factors likely to increase the motivation to process carefully (Chaiken, Liberman, & Eagly, 1989). If subjects processed information about in-group behavior and its consequences more carefully than they did information about out-group behavior and its consequences, outcome-biased inferences about in-groups should be less likely.

Mackie and Ahn (1995) tested this idea in a series of studies in which subjects read about the children from two different elementary schools, who were competing to appear at a local science fair. Subjects read that because the science fair had become so popular, the local school board allowed only schools whose science teams passed a preliminary science test to enter the competition. In the first experiment, White American and Asian-American subjects read about teams attempting to qualify from two different schools, both of which had predominantly White American students, or both of which had predominantly Asian-American students. Students at both schools performed very similarly on the preliminary exam, but only one school qualified for the science fair because the qualification criterion was different for the different schools. Thus, despite the fact that children from both schools performed at about the same level, children from one school entered the science fair and children from the other school did not. Subjects thus read either about in-group or about out-group members, some of whom succeeded and some of whom failed because of differences in a decision rule, not because of differences in performance.

After reading the scenarios, subjects rated the intelligence of the children at each school and how likely they were to succeed in future intellectual pursuits. When subjects read about out-group members, outcome-biased inferences were made. That is, both Asian-American subjects and White American subjects rated the group that succeeded as smarter than the group that failed when they were reading about out-group members. But when they read the same scenarios about in-group members, neither White Americans nor Asian-Americans made outcome-biased inferences: In-group members were judged to be of about equally high intelligence whether they qualified for the science fair or not.

Despite the many reasons to suspect that outcome biases might be made more frequently about out-group than about in-group members, these results are still somewhat surprising. After all, in many of our previous studies, subjects who read about other students or other citizens of the United States shared in-group membership with the targets but nevertheless made outcome-biased inferences about them. In Allison and Messick's (1985) study, for example, in-group inferences were still influenced by outcomes, although less strongly than were outcome inferences. Worth et al. (1987,

Experiment 2) also obtained outcome biases that were as strong for the subjects' in-group as for an out-group. What then might altogether eliminate the impact of outcomes on inferences about the in-group? If careful processing reduces outcome biases, it seems that extremely careful processing could have occurred in the in-group condition. Why might this have been so?

One possibility is that some aspects of the scenario that we gave the subjects reduced outcome biases. For example, subjects in this experiment read about two groups who performed similarly but received startlingly different outcomes. Such inconsistencies could trigger careful processing and might thus reduce heuristic use. Careful processing triggered by informational inconsistency could not alone explain all of our findings because subjects received equally inconsistent information about the out-group, and made outcome-biased inferences about them.

Another possibility is that the context about which subjects received information—differences in educational outcomes accruing to different groups—made subjects particularly sensitive to judgments about the groups. Again, the context alone was not enough to eliminate outcome-biased inferences completely, as evidenced by the fact that subjects made them about the out-group. But perhaps the political sensitivity of the context made subjects particularly wary of making inferential claims about the in-group.

To ascertain whether something about the inconsistency in outcomes or something about the context eliminated outcome-biased inferences about the in-group, Mackie and Ahn (1995) ran a second study. White American and Asian-American subjects read about either two groups of White Americans or two groups of Asian-Americans at different schools. Once again, both groups tried out for the science fair, and once again, their outcomes depended not on their performance alone but on the school board's decision rule. The context about which information was presented was thus identical to that of Experiment 1. In this case, however, subjects read that the groups from the two schools performed very similarly and received the same outcome—that is, the teams from both schools either both succeeded or both failed. Results indicated that subjects' inferences were outcome biased in both cases, regardless of whether they read about in- or out-group members. Thus, even when in-group members were involved, outcome biases were not eliminated unless there was an element of inconsistency or unfairness: Similar performances resulted in different outcomes. Interestingly, this combination was not sufficient to eliminate outcome-biased inferences about the out-group.

This finding fits nicely with other demonstrations showing that notions of what is fair or just apply to members of in-groups compared to out-groups. Just as out-group members seem to benefit less from norms that prohibit aggression and promote altruism (Bond, 1988; Dovidio, Piliavin, Gaertner, Schroeder, & Clark, 1991; Miller & Eisenberg, 1988), so too are out-group members often excluded from the bounds of fair play and humane treatment. Opotow (1990) has labeled this tendency as moral unconcern or moral exclusion. In the context of our study, it may be that a state of affairs that would be intolerably unfair for the in-group would seem less troubling if it impacted only the out-group. As a final demonstration that this was indeed the case, we asked White subjects to read scenarios in which in- and out-group members achieved similar performances but received different outcomes because of disparity in decision rules. The important manipulation here was that these decision rules sometimes favored the in-group and sometimes favored the out-group. Consistent with our expectations, subjects made outcome-biased inferences when the disparity favored the in-group but not when it favored the out-group. In this context at least, outcome-biased inferences seemed to work in the service of moral exclusion.

Thus, independently of the effects of perceptions of reduced out-group variability and of actor–observer differences in attributions, outcome biases about out-groups are influenced by motivational goals. Such motivational goals determine in part when subjects will engage in the extra effort of discounting the impact of any extenuating circumstances (either internal or external to the group).

In addition to motivational concerns triggered by group membership, other goals seem likely to have similar effects at both the group and individual levels. Obvious candidates are goals such as self-efficacy, positive self-regard, and successful social interaction. We might predict that outcome biases promoting important goals are more likely to occur than outcome biases frustrating the achievement of such goals. For example, we might be more vulnerable to outcome-biased inferences suggesting that a group with whom we are to compete is not very intelligent than to biased inferences suggesting that they are extremely bright.

If motivational goals influence outcome biases, then chronic individual differences in goal activation should produce individual differences in vulnerability to outcome biases. For example, individuals high in need of cognition—those who enjoy thinking hard about complex problems (Cacioppo & Petty, 1982; Cohen 1957)—might be systematically less likely to make such errors compared to those low in need of cognition. Because they care about smooth interactions, for example, high self-monitors might be more likely to draw outcome-biased inferences that promote such interactions than ones that do not (Snyder, 1974). Low self-monitors, however, might be more prone to the bias when it allows their "true qualities" to be expressed.

D. OUTCOME-BIASED INFERENCES AND SOCIAL BEHAVIOR

The fact that outcome biases have important consequences for intergroup perception suggests that other goals, relationships, and groups-based social phenomena might also be affected by outcome biases. One such phenomenon has been investigated. Group behavior involves multiple memberships, roles, and goal-related processes. It involves interdependence, as people's outcomes are affected by the behavior of others as well as by their own behavior. In no social context is this interdependence more obvious than when a group is faced with a social dilemma (Messick & Brewer, 1983).

Social dilemmas are situations in which the pursuit of individual self-interest and the interests of the group are at odds. In a public goods dilemma, for example, a particular benefit can only be made available to the group if a certain number of group members contribute to its payment (Messick & Brewer, 1983). Public television is a good example. If there are too few subscribers, the public good cannot be provided, and nobody receives benefits. If a certain level of support is received, the benefits will be available for everyone. The essential tension of the social dilemma lies in this last fact: As long as enough members contribute to its upkeep, the benefit if provided even to those who do not. For each individual, then, the best outcome is to refuse to contribute, but to receive the benefit anyway because others have done so. However, if every individual followed his or her best self-interest by not contributing, the good of the group would be sacrificed; there would be not public benefit.

In most social dilemmas, the individual's interests loom large. When deciding whether to contribute to public television, for example, most people choose to view free of charge, with the subsequent risk that public goods such as high-quality television programming, clean air, unpolluted waters, effective public education systems, and so on, may disappear. For obvious reasons, then, social pyshologists have been concerned with increasing group members' cooperation with and contribution to the group good. Information about the group's past behavior as a predictor of the group's future behavior has been found to be important. Group members who have cooperated in the past provide role models for undecided memebers: They confirm that norms of cooperation are appropriate, reassure nervous members that they will not be exploited, and produce expectations of future cooperative behavior (Caporeal, Dawes, Orbell, & Van de Kragt, 1989; Sattler & Kerr, 1991; Tetlock, 1989). For all these reasons, information about previously cooperative or noncooperative behavior might influence an individual's decisions about cooperation. The goal of the experiments described here, conducted by Allison and Kerr (1994), was to determine if outcomes biases influenced the perception of cooperation, and if so, whether this perception would affect people's own decision to cooperate.

In the experiments, subjects joined a group that had previously either succeeded or failed to provide a public good through membership contributions. Subjects were told the number of people in their group who had contributed to the good and the number of people required to contribute before the good could be provided (the investment quota). The number of members who contributed to the good was held constant but the quota for success was manipulated. When the number of contributors exceeded the quota, the group was successful. If the number of contributors fell short of the investment quota, the group failed to solve the social dilemma, even though the same number of group members cooperated. This meant that the group's success or failure in solving the social dilemma and providing the public benefit depended no so much on the group's prior behavior, which was constant across conditions, but on the criterion level for success.

Nevertheless, subjects' inferences about their groups were expected to be biased by the groups' outcomes. Subjects who believed their group had succeeded in solving the social dilemma saw group members as more self-sacrificing, more willing to take risks, and more likely to cooperate in the future compared to subjects who thought their group had failed. These effects occurred even though the absolute level of cooperative choices for succeeding and failing were constant, and even though subjects knew that their group was unaware of the necessary investment quota. These findings represent the first demonstration that outcome biases arise in actual social dilemma situations, a context far removed from the scenarios previously used in this research.

Allison and Kerr (1994) also evaluated subjects' own behavior in the social dilemma—their decision to invest their own resources or not—to see if it was influenced by the outcome-biased inferences that they had made about their group. Subjects were presented with three public good investment problems, each similar to the one that their group had ostensibly encountered (either successfully or unsuccessfully) earlier. The results showed that when faced with a subsequent public goods dilemma in which the investment quota was either unknown or particularly difficult to meet, subjects' inferences about their group did influence their own behavior. Those who believed that their group had succeeded were more likely to contribute to provision of the good than those who believed otherwise. These judgments were mediated by the outcome-biased inferences that subjects had made about their group members. Only when the investment quota was particularly low and the dilemma easily solved did inferences about previous group outcomes have no impact.

These experiments thus revealed that subjects' outcome-biased inferences about their group's collective efficacy mediated their own behavior in the task. These results extend our understanding of the consequences of outcome-biased inferences in two respects. First, outcome biases influence group behavior, extending previous findings from attitude attribution, impression formation, and stereotyping. Second, outcome biases have behavioral effects. These results suggest that there are many other group contexts in which outcome biases might play a role.

V. Conclusions

We have reviewed research that we and our collaborators have conducted on the ways in which the outcomes of individual or group action influence perceptions of the attitudes and dispositions of the actors and groups that produce the outcomes. We suggest that outcomes play a focal role in the evaluation of people and policies. The simple heuristic that seems to be used is that there is a "fit" among an agent, an action, and its outcome, even in situations where the outcome is palpably caused by external, random, or extraneous factors. The causal role of such contextual factors is either underestimated or ignored. The idea that people deserve their outcomes in life is an intuitive (and incorrect) theory of justice. The idea that good decisions always lead to good outcomes is an intuitive (and incorrect) theory of decision making. The idea that group decision outcomes represent the "will" of the group members is an intuitive (and incorrect) theory of democracy.

Our analysis of the literature suggests that outcome-biased dispositional inferences about groups result largely from a less extensive or heuristic processing strategy employed by social perceivers. A consistent finding is that perceivers who are induced to process information in a heuristic fashion are more likely to draw outcome-biased dispositional inferences about groups than are perceivers who are induced to process information in a more extensive or systematic fashion. As with research on heuristic and systematic processing in the context of attitude change and persuasion (Chaiken et al., 1989), current research on dispositional inference about individual and group targets focuses on the role of both motivation and cognitive capacity in stimulating perceivers to engage in systematic processing. When perceivers are sufficiently invested in the outcome issue, they appear to show little or no evidence of outcome biases in their judgments (Allison et al., 1990; Worth et al., 1987). Moreover, when perceivers are unencumbered by the cognitive demands of the situation, they are similarly less apt to make outcome-biased inferences (Allison et al., 1990; Allison, Beggan, Midgley et al. 1995; Schroth & Messick, 1994).

Table I displays a general framework for understanding the types of variables that are likely to trigger different modes of processing about group outcome information. As Table I shows, there are two primary categories of moderating variables focusing on characteristics of the perceiver and the target of inference. With regard to perceiver characteristics, past research has illuminated both motivational and cognitive factors that determine whether group outcome information will be processed heuristically or systematically. Specifically, perceivers who are highly inspired to process outcome information thoroughly (Allison et al., 1990; Worth et al., 1987) or those who are not cognitively burdened (Allison, Beggan, Midgley et al., 1995) show a lesser tendency to make outcome-biased inferences than do uninspired or cognitively taxed perceivers.

Target characteristics also appear to influence perceivers' motivation and cognitive abilities to process information systematically. If the target group is perceived as an out-group, then the motivation to view the individual members of the group as predictable and controllable may lead to more extreme correspondent inferences than are warranted (Heider, 1958). Moreover, as Mackie and Ahn (1995) have shown, perceivers are more motivated to make outcome-biased inferences when it benefits the in-group than when it benefits the out-group. Out-group targets may also affect the type of cognitive processing in which perceivers engage by eliciting more homogeneous conceptions of out-group members than of in-group targets. The more homogeneous the group is perceived to be, the more likely perceivers will be to make extreme judgments about group members (Linville & Jones, 1980; Park & Rothbart, 1982). Moreover, if the target of inference is a random group member rather than the group as a whole (or the typical member), then perceivers will cognitively engage in more

TABLE I

PERCEIVER AND TARGET VARIABLES THAT MODERATE PERCEIVERS' MOTIVATION AND COGNITIVE CAPACITIES TO PROCESS OUTCOME INFORMATION SYSTEMATICALLY

	Motivation	Cognitive capacity
Perceiver characteristics	Self-relevance (Worth et al., 1987; Allison et al., 1990)	Cognitive load (Allison et al., 1995)
Target characteristics	In-group/out-group (Allison & Messick, 1985)	In-group/out-group (Allison & Messick, 1985)
	Detriment to in-group (Mackie & Ahn, 1995)	Typical/random member (Worth et al., 1987; Allison et al., 1990)

thorough considerations of the group's diversity of opinion. This relatively high level of cognitive engagement precludes the formation of extreme outcome-biased inferences (Allison et al., 1990; Worth et al., 1987).

A number of contextual factors also assume a role in influencing the accessibility of outcome information, thereby affecting the magnitude of outcome-biased inferences. For example, outcomes appear to be more accessible—and outcome biases therefore more prominent—when the group outcome is produced actively rather than passively by group members (Schroth & Messick, 1994), when perceivers are compelled to calculate the outcome on their own from other relevant information (Allison et al., 1990), and when perceivers have fresh, immediate access to relevant group decision information in memory (Allison et al., 1990; Allison, Beggan, McDonald et al., 1995; Allison, Beggan, Midgley, et al., 1995; Beggan & Allison, 1993).

We summarize research that demonstrates the power of outcome-biased judgments in numerous domains. We conclude with some speculations about why this heuristic form of judgment seems to be so pervasive and compelling.

First, and possibly most important, this heuristic reverses a perfectly sensible relationship: Good decisions should lead to good outcomes; good people should achieve good outcomes; and a group's desire should be fulfilled by a group decision. However, these relationships are not perfect. Pure bad luck can cause the best decision to have an unhappy consequence: Cancer can infect the holiest of people, and powerful minorities can derail majority intentions. The outcome biases that we discuss represent a type of inverse fallacy. It is the characteristic of good decisions that on the average, in the long run, they will produce better outcomes than poor decisions. It does not follow, therefore, that good outcomes were produced by good decisions. Bad decisions may have lucky outcomes just as good decisions may result in poor ones. The inverse fallacy makes a type of good form, a simplifying assumption with a good gestalt.

A second reason why outcome biases are compelling is that they may often be self-serving. People may strategically show outcome biases when these biases best serve their own emotional or motivational interests (Mackie & Ahn, 1995). Outcome biases may also serve a self-protective function. Stupid decisions that result in a positive consequence can produce cognitive and emotional ambivalence. It is threatening to those who deem themselves moral creatures to concede that terrible things can happen to them. The belief in a "just world" is comforting, but it implies that people to whom bad things happen deserve misfortune. The self-serving quality of these biases becomes evident with outcomes that have both positive and negative elements. The agents or actors have a stake in highlighting the positive aspects of the outcome, in finding the silver lining, so that both they and the action producing the outcome may be viewed in a positive light. Kramer and Messick (1995) have alluded to people as "intuitive lawyers" to spotlight the extent to which actors claim credit for benefits and create shields against blame.

Finally, people can always find social validation to support the intuition that outcomes are supreme. This validation stems in part from the prevalence of the intuition, and partly from the strategic use of the principle. For every claim that an outcome was the product of good luck, there will be a counterclaim that "it is better to be lucky than to be smart" or something similar, implying that luck can be a personal attribute to which the positive outcome can be attributed instead of intelligence. Thus even lucky outcomes speak to character. Furthermore, it will be said that "one makes his own luck," which seems to amount to the same thing. The claims are particularly prevalent when there is a reason for wanting to credit the lucky person. On the negative side, the assertion that one "should have known" is an effort to assign blame by attributing foreknowledge, in order to link dispositions with outcomes.

Unarguably, the process of inferring a target's dispositional qualities from available information about the target is a pervasive component of human social cognition, but from what type of information are correspondent inferences most likely to be generated? The theoretical progenitors of the "correspondent inference" phenomenon (Jones & Davis, 1965; Jones & Harris, 1967) focused solely on the role of behavior in revealing correspondent dispositions. Since the mid-1960s, the process of gleaning dispositions from behavior has been a dominant research area in social cognition. Our review suggests, however, that the *consequence* of behavior—namely, the behavior's ultimate outcome—can have a more profound impact on dispositional inference than the behavior that produced the outcome. It is not that behavior is uninformative about dispositions, only that it is subordinate to outcomes. Outcomes are the irrevocable bottom line; they imply finality. Behavior may indeed "engulf the field," but outcomes appear to engulf behavior. Outcomes enjoy unsurpassed psychological significance, permitting them to reign supreme in the process of knowing others.

Acknowledgments

Correspondence concerning this chapter should be directed to Scott Allison, Department of Psychology, University of Richmond, Richmond, VA 23173. Electronic mail (E-mail) can be sent to Allison @urvax.urich,edu.

This research was supported by a Faculty Research Grant awarded to Scott Allison from the University of Richmond and by NSF Grant SBR-9209995 awarded to Diane Mackie.

References

Allison, S. T., Beggan, J. K., McDonald, R. A., & Rettew, M. L. (1995). The belief in majority determination of group decision outcomes. *Basic and Applied Social Psychology, 16,* 367–382.

Allison, S. T., Beggan, J. K., Midgley, E., & Wallace, K. (1995). Dispositional and behavioral inferences about inherently democratic and unanimous groups. *Social Cognition, 15,* 105–125.

Allison, S. T., & Kerr, N. L. (1994). Group correspondence biases and the provision of public goods. *Journal of Personality and Social Psychology, 66,* 688–698.

Allison, S. T., & Mackie, D. M. (1995). *Outcome-biased attitude formation and attitude change.* Unpublished manuscript, University of Richmond, Virginia.

Allison, S. T., Mackie, D. M., Muller, M. M., & Worth, L. T. (1993). Sequential correspondence biases and perceptions of change: The Castro studies revisited. *Personality and Social Psychology Bulletin, 19,* 151–157.

Allison, S. T., & Messick, D. M. (1985). The group attribution error. *Journal of Experimental Social Psychology, 21,* 563–579.

Allison, S. T., & Messick, D. M. (1987). From individual inputs to group outputs, and back again: Group processes and inferences about members. In C. Hendrick (Ed.), *Review of personality and social psychology.* (Vol. 8). Beverly Hills: Sage.

Allison, S. T., Worth, L. T., & King, M. W. C. (1990). Group decisions as social inference heuristics. *Journal of Personality and Social Psychology, 58,* 801–811.

Aronson, E., & Mills, J. (1959). The effect of severity of initiation on liking for a group. *Journal of Abnormal and Social Psychology, 59,* 177–181.

Baron, J., & Hershey, J. C. (1988). Outcome bias in decision evaluation. *Journal of Personality and Social Psychology, 54,* 569–579.

Beggan, J. K., & Allison, S. T. (1993). The landslide victory that wasn't: The bias toward consistency in recall of election support. *Journal of Applied Social Psychology, 23,* 669–677.

Bem, D. J. (1972). Self-perception theory. In. L. Berkowitz (Ed.), *Advances in experimental social psychology* (Vol. 6). New York: Academic Press.

Bond, M. H. (1988). *The cross-cultural challenge to psychology.* Newbury Park, CA: Sage Publications.

Brehm, J. W. (1956). Post-decision changes in desirability of alternatives. *Journal of Abnormal and Social Psychology, 52,* 384–389.

Cacioppo, J. T., & Petty, R. E. (1982). The need for cognition. *Journal of Personality and Social Psychology, 42,* 116–131.

Caporael, L. R., Dawes, R. M. Orbell, J. M., & Van de Kragt, A. J. C. (1989). Selfishness examined: Cooperation in the absence of egoistic incentives. *Behavioral and Brain Sciences, 12,* 683–699.

Chaiken, S., Liberman, A., & Eagly, A. H. (1989). Heuristic and systematic information processing within and beyond the persuasion context. In J. S. Uleman & J. A. Bargh (Eds.), *Unintended thought: Limits of awareness, intention, and control.* (pp. 212–252). New York: Guilford.

Cohen, A. (1957). Need for cognition and order of communication as determinants of opinion change. In C. Hovland (Ed.), *The order of presentation in persuasion.* New Haven, CT: Yale University Press.

Dovidio, J. F., Piliavin, J. A., Gaertner, S. L., Schroeder, D. A., & Clark, R. D. (1991). The arousal cost-reward model and the process of intervention: A review of the evidence. In M. S. Clark (Ed.), *Prosocial behavior* (pp. 86–118). Newbury Park, CA: Sage.

Eagly, A. H. (1987). *Sex differences in social behavior: A social-role interpretation.* Hillsdale, NJ: Erlbaum.

Eagly, A. H., & Steffen, V. J. (1984). Gender stereotypes stem from the distribution of women and men into social roles. *Journal of Personality and Social Psychology, 46,* 735–754.

Festinger, L. (1957). *A theory of cognitive dissonance.* Stanford, CA: Stanford University Press.

Festinger, L., & Carlsmith, J. M. (1959). Cognitive consequences of forced compliance. *Journal of Abnormal and Social Psychology, 58,* 203–210.

Festinger, L., Riecken, H., & Schachter, S. (1956). *When prophecy fails.* Minneapolis: University of Minnesota Press.

Fineman, H. (1992, November 16). Knowing when the party's over. *Newsweek, 38,* 38–40.

Fischhoff, B. (1975). Hindsight does not equal foresight: The effect of outcome knowledge on judgment under uncertainty. *Journal of Experimental Psychology, 1,* 288–299.

Fiske, S. T. (1992). Thinking is for doing: Portraits of social cognition from daguerreotype of laserphoto. *Journal of Personality and Social Psychology, 63,* 877–889.

Fiske, S. T., & Taylor, S. E. (1991). *Social cognition.* New York: McGraw-Hill.

Gerard, H. B., & White, G. L. (1983). Post-decisional reevaluation of choice alternatives. *Personality and Social Psychology Bulletin, 9,* 364–369.

Gilbert, D. T. (1989). Thinking lightly about others: Automatic components of the social inference process. In J. S. Uleman & J. A. Bargh (Eds.), *Unintended thought: Limits of awareness, intention, and control* (pp. 189–211). New York: Guilford.

Gilbert, D. T., Krull, D. S., & Pelham, B. W. (1988). Of thoughts unspoken: Social inference and the self-regulation of behavior. *Journal of Personality and Social Psychology, 55,* 685–694.

Gilbert, D. T., & Osborne, R. E. (1989). Thinking backward: Some curable and incurable consequences of cognitive busyness. *Journal of Personality and Social Psychology, 57,* 940–949.

Gilbert, D. T., Pelham, B. W., & Krull, D. S. (1988). On cognitive busyness: When person perceivers meet persons perceived. *Journal of Personality and Social Psychology, 54,* 733–740.

Goldman, P. (1980, November 17). The Republican landslide. *Newsweek, 69,* 27–28.

Harvey, J. H., & McGlynn, R. P. (1982). Matching words to phenomena: The case of the fundamental attribution error. *Journal of Personality and Social Psychology, 43,* 345–346.

Hastie, R. (1984). Causes and effects of causal attribution. *Journal of Personality and Social Psychology, 46,* 44–56.

Heider, F. (1958). *The psychology of interpersonal relations.* New York: Wiley.

Hoffman, C., & Hurst, N. (1990). Gender stereotypes: Perception or rationalization? *Journal of Personality and Social Psychology, 58,* 197–208.

Jones, E. E. (1979). The rocky road from acts to dispositions. *American Psychologist, 34,* 107–117.

Jones, E. E. (1985). Major developments in social psychology during the past five decades. In G. Lendzey & E. Aronson (Eds.), *Handbook of social psychology* (Vol. 1). New York: Random House.

Jones, E. E. (1990). *Interpersonal perception.* New York: W. H. Freeman.

Jones, E. E., & Davis, K. E. (1965). From acts to dispositions: The attribution process in person perception. In L. Berkowitz (Ed.), *Advances in experimental social psychology* (Vol. 2). New York: Academic Press.

Jones, E. E., & Harris, V. A. (1967). The attribution of attitudes. *Journal of Experimental Social Psychology, 3,* 1–24.

Jones, E. E., & Nisbett, R. E. (1972). The actor and observer: Divergent perceptions of the causes of behavior. In E. E. Jones, D. E. Kanouse, H. H. Kelley, R. E. Nisbett, S. Valins, &

B. Weiner (Eds.), *Attribution: Perceiving the causes of behavior* (pp. 79–94). Morristown, NJ: General Learning.

Klein, J. (1993, June 7). What's wrong? *Newsweek*, 16–19.

Kramer, R. M., & Messick, D. M. (1995). Ethical cognition in the framing of organizational dilemmas: Decision makers as intuitive lawyers. In D. Messick (Ed.), *Behavioral research in business ethics* (pp. 131–162). Beverly Hills: Sage.

Lerner, M. J., & Miller, D. T. (1978). Just world research and the attribution process: Looking back and ahead. *Psychological Bulletin, 85,* 1030–1051.

Linville, P. W., & Jones, E. E. (1980). Polarized appraisals of out-group members. *Journal of Personality and Social Psychology, 38,* 689–703.

Mackie, D. M., & Ahn, M. N. (1995). *Outcome-biased inferences about in-groups and out-groups.* Unpublished manuscript, University of California, Santa Barbara.

Mackie, D. M., & Allison, S. T. (1987). Group attribution errors and the illusion of group attitude change. *Journal of Experimental Social Psychology, 23,* 460–480.

Mackie, D. M., Allison, S. T., Worth, L. T., & Asuncion, A. G. (1992a). The generalization of outcome-biased counter-stereotypic inferences. *Journal of Experimental Social Psychology, 28,* 43–64.

Mackie, D. M., Allison, S. T., Worth, L. T., & Asuncion, A. G. (192b). The impact of outcome biases on counter-sterebtypic inferences about groups. *Personality and Social Psychology Bulletin, 18,* 44–51.

Mackie, D. M., & Skelly, J. J. (1994). The social cognition analysis of social influence: Contributions to the understanding of persuasion and conformity. In P. L. Devine, D. L. Hamilton, & T. M. Ostrom (Eds.), *Social cognition: Impact on social psychology* (pp. 259–291). Orlando, FL: Academic Press.

Mackie, D. M., Worth, L. T., & Allison, S. T. (1990). Outcome-biased inferences and the perception of change in groups. *Social Cognition, 8,* 325–342.

Maheswaran, D., & Chaiken, S. (1991). Promoting systematic processing in low motivation settings: Effect of incongruent information on processing and judgment. *Journal of Personality and Social Psychology, 61,* 13–25.

McArthur, L. Z., & Post, D. L. (1977). Figural emphasis and person perception. *Journal of Experimental Social Psychology, 13,* 520–535.

McHoskey, J. W., & Miller, A. G. (1994). Effects of constraint identification, processing, mode, expectancies, and intragroup variability on attributions toward group members. *Personality and Social Psychology Bulletin, 20,* 266–276.

Messick, D. M., & Brewer, M. B. (1983). Solving social dilemmas: A review. In L. Wheeler & P. Shaver (Eds.), *Review of personality and social psychology* (Vol. 4, pp. 11–44), Beverly Hills, CA: Sage.

Miller, A. G. (1976). Constraint and target effects on the attribution of attitudes. *Journal of Experimental Social Psychology, 12,* 325–339.

Miller, P. A., & Eisenberg, N. (1988). The relation of empathy to aggressive and externalizing/antisocial behavior. *Psychological Bulletin, 103,* 324–344.

Monson, T. C., & Snyder, M. (1977). Actors, observers, and the attribution process: Toward a reconceptualization. *Journal of Experimental Social Psychology, 13,* 89–111.

Opotow, S. (1990). Moral exclusion and injustice. *Journal of Social Issues, 46,*(1), 1–20.

Osborne, R. E., & Gilbert, D. T. (1992). The preoccupational hazards of social life. *Journal of Personality and Social Psychology, 62,* 219–228.

Park, B., & Hastie, R. (1987). Perception of variability in category development: Instance versus abstration-based stereotypes. *Journal of Personality and Social Psychology, 53,* 621–635.

Park, B., & Rothbart, M. (1982). Perception of out-group homogeneity and levels of social categorization: Memory for the subordinate attributes of in-group and out-group members. *Journal of Personality and Social Psychology, 42,* 1051–1068.

Pettigrew, T. F. (1980). Race relations: Social and psychological aspects. In D. L. Sills (Ed.), *The international encyclopedia of the social sciences* (Vol. 13, pp. 277–282). New York: Macmillan.

Quattrone, G. A. (1982). Behavioral consequences of attributional bias. *Social Cognition, 1,* 358–378.

Quattrone, G. A., & Jones, E. E. (1980). The perception of variability within in-groups and out-groups: Implications for the law of small numbers. *Journal of Personality and Social Psychology, 38,* 141–152.

Rholes, W. S., & Pryor, J. B. (1982). Cognitive accessibility and causal attributions. *Personality and Social Psychology Bulletin, 8,* 719–727.

Ross, L. (1977). The intuitive psychologist and his shortcomings: Distortions in the attribution process. In L. Berkowitz (Ed.), *Advances in experimental social psychology* (Vol. 10). New York: Academic Press.

Ross, L., Amabile, T. M., & Steinmetz, J. L. (1977). Social roles, social control, and biases in social perception processes. *Journal of Personality and Social Psychology, 35,* 485–494.

Ross, L., Green, D., & House, P. (1977). The false consensus phenomenon: An attributional bias in self-perception and social perception processes. *Journal of Experimental Social Psychology, 13,* 279–301.

Sattler, D. N., & Kerr, N. L. (1991). Might versus morality explored: Motivational versus cognitive bases for social motives. *Journal of Personality and Social Psychology, 60,* 756–765.

Schroth, H. A., & Messick, D. M. (1994). *Attribution of group attitudes from active versus passive decisions.* Unpublished manuscript, Northwestern University, Chicago.

Shaver, K. G. (1970). Defensive attributions: Effects of severity and relevance on the responsibility assigned for an accident. *Journal of Personality and Social Psychology, 14,* 101–113.

Silka, L. (1989). *Intuitive judgments of change.* New York: Springer Verlag.

Snyder, M. (1974). The self-monitoring of expressive behavior. *Journal of Personality and Social Psychology, 30,* 526–537.

Taylor, S. E., & Fiske, S. T. (1975). Point of view and perceptions of causality. *Journal of Personality and Social Psychology, 32,* 439–445.

Tetlock, P. E. (1989). Methodological themes and variations. In P. Tetlock (Ed.), *Behavior, society, and nuclear war.* New York: Oxford University Press.

Trope, Y., & Higgins, E. T. (Eds.). (1993). On inferring personal dispositions from behavior [special issue]. *Personality and Social Psychology Bulletin, 19,* 493–601.

Walster, E. (1966). The assignment of responsibility for an accident. *Journal of Personality and Social Psychology, 3,* 73–79.

Worth, L. T., Allison, S. T., & Messick, D. M. (1987). Impact of a group's decision on perceptions of one's own and others' attitudes. *Journal of Personality and Social Psychology, 53,* 673–683.

PRINCIPLES OF JUDGING VALENCE: WHAT MAKES EVENTS POSITIVE OR NEGATIVE?

C. Miguel Brendl

E. Tory Higgins

I. Introduction

The positivity or negativity of events is a major parameter for theorizing in diverse areas of psychology (e.g., altruism, conflict, attitudes, impression formation, conditioning, memory, decision making). Typically investigators ask what impact the positivity or negativity of an event has on experience and behavior, such as emotional experience or decision behavior. Much less attention has been devoted to factors that initially cause an event to be positive or negative, and investigators often regard it as self-evident that the valence (i.e., the positivity or negativity) of an event is fixed, as if it were an inherent property of the event.

We do not wish to question the fact that there are such events of fixed valence, that is, events that are always perceived as positive or negative between and within individuals. Newborns, for example, perceive sweet solutions as positive and sour solutions as negative (cf. Ganchrow, Steiner, & Daher, 1983). Such perceptions might be wired-in. Further, the fixed valence of some events might be contingent on prior learning not directly related to the event (Hebb, 1949) or on maturation of the nervous system (Gray, 1971). For example, fear of strangers in humans and chimpanzees (Hebb, 1949) or fear of heights in humans (Campos & Sternberg, 1981) has been observed to develop reliably some months after birth without prior negative experiences with these objects of fear. We suspect that the positivity or negativity acquired in direct connection with some events might also vary little between or within individuals when the valences of these events are extremely positive or extremely negative. Nevertheless, an event often is perceived by some people as positive and by others as

95

negative. Moreover, even the same person might find an event positive at one time and negative at another time, such as hearing loud music at a dance versus during sleep. Thus, many types of events, if not most, do not have a fixed perceived valence.

Our primary question in this chapter is how people judge the valence of an event. As a secondary question we examine the nature of the shift from negative to positive valence. In other words, if we could line up a number of events along a dimension from very negative to very positive, where would negative events end and positive events begin? Further, would this shift be discontinuous or would neutral events exist that provide a transition from negative to positive? Rather than provide a comprehensive overview of a particular area of literature, we integrate theorizing and evidence from various areas of psychology.

A. VALENCE

Usually the term *valence* refers to the positivity or negativity of an event. At least linguistically, then, valence is described as a property of the event. It would therefore be fruitless to examine the psychological factors that influence valence. Our position, however, is that valence derives from a person–situation relation. More precisely, it derives from a person processing a situational input. Thus, when we refer to the valence of an event, we are describing the valence that a perceiver ascribes to the event. If something changes in the way a person processes information about an event, the event's valence might change as well. Valence is not inherent to an event, nor does the valence of an event remain constant (Lewin, 1926b, 1935; Roseman, Spindel, & Jose, 1990). The valence of most events is quite variable across situations, across individuals, and over time.

Typically in psychology, the concept of valence is associated with Kurt Lewin (e.g., 1926a, 1926b).[1] He suggested that people experience many objects and events not as neutral, but as demanding an action, and he called such objects or events "valenced".[2]

> The valence of an object usually derives from the fact that the object is a means to the satisfaction of a need, or has indirectly something to do with the satisfaction of a need. The kind (sign) and strength of the valence of an object or event thus

[1] Lewin (1926a, 1926b) is partly translated into English in Lewin (1926/1935) and Lewin (1926/1951b), respectively.

[2] For Lewin (1926b) the "demand of an object" on acting is a crucial characteristic of valence that distinguishes it from the value ("Wert") of the object. This distinction resembles the distinction between "behavioral intentions" and "attitudes toward an object" (Ajzen & Fishbein, 1980; Fishbein, 1979).

depends directly upon the momentary condition of the needs of the individual concerned. . . . One may distinguish two large groups of valences according to the sort of initial behavior they elicit: the positive valences (+), those effecting approach: and the negative (−), or those producing withdrawal or retreat. (Lewin, 1935, pp. 78–81)

Lewin distinguished two aspects of valence: its kind (sign) and its strength. We refer to the kind of valence (i.e., positive vs. negative) as *valence quality*, and to the strength of valence as *valence quantity,* and when both types of valence are meant in general, we simply refer to them as *valence.*

In sum, Lewin's analysis suggests that a current need determines the mentally represented valence of an event, which in turn determines the type of behavior (and motivation) toward the event (approach vs. avoid). In addition, it is often suggested that when an event is represented as positive versus negative, it respectively elicits positive versus negative affect. We suggest not only that the valence of an event can determine affect and motivation, but also that affect or motivation can at times determine the valence of an event. For example, an event causing physical injury might produce immediate pain and result subsequently in a negative evaluation of the event. Throughout this chapter, therefore, the direction of causality between two constructs is changed (e.g., between event valence and affect). We are careful to avoid circularity, however. For example, when valence explains affect, we propose variables other than affect to explain valence. However, this does not preclude that there are other times when affect determines valence. We are examining a mental system that includes cognition (e.g., the mental representation of event valence), motivation (e.g., orientation to approach or avoid an event), and affect (e.g., feeling about an event). We assume that each of these three components can influence the other two. Therefore, it is essential to consider bidirectional causal influences.

B. PRINCIPLES OF JUDGING VALENCE

We focus on four principles that influence judgments of valence: goal supportiveness, membership status, referential status, and response elicitation. These principles are not totally independent, however, and there might be additional ones.

The principle of *goal supportiveness* refers to the degree to which an event is judged to facilitate or impede the satisfaction of a set goal. Facilitation leads to judgments of positive valence quality and impediment to judgments of negative valence quality. For example, an individual with the goal of avoiding burglars should judge the barking of his or her dog as positive in valence quality when it scares off a burglar, but negative in valence quality when he or she is taking a nap and there is no intruder. The principle of goal support-iveness is basically the same as Lewin's (1935) principle of need satisfaction.

The principle of *membership status* refers to the association of an event with a valenced representation. A prime example is conditioning in which a previously neutral event (e.g., a rat "sitting in a box") acquires valence by being associated with another event (e.g., an electric shock) such that future instances of the neutral event are assigned to the representation of a valenced contingency relation (e.g., if condition *x,* then pain *y*). The principle of membership status implies that the event is associated with or assimilated to the valenced representation.

The principle of *referential status* refers to comparing an event with a reference point. For example, a first-year student who compares his exam result of 250 out of 350 points to the scores of his classmates is likely to evaluate it positively when his classmates receive 200 points on the average, but negatively when his classmates receive 300 points on the average.

The principle of *response elicitation* refers to making inferences about the valence of an event based on someone's response (self or other) to the event. You may have experienced sitting down in a public bus and having the person sitting beside you change seats. You might have inferred that sitting next to you had negative valence, at least for this passenger.

II. Hierarchical Organization of Goals

Lewin and his associates systematically examined the influence of goals on valence. One central question of their level of aspiration research (for reviews see Lewin, 1951a; Lewin, Dembo, Festinger, & Sears, 1944) asked what factors determine the experiences of "success" and "failure." The valence quality of a "success" event was considered positive, and the valence quality of a "failure" event was considered negative (Lewin et al., 1944). In this research paradigm, participants were typically observed in a multitrial achievement task that allowed for variation in task difficulty (e.g., dart throwing). The level of aspiration was defined as the whole of one's expecta-tions, goals, and aspirations for one's prospective performance (Hoppe, 1931) and was usually operationalized by asking participants to state their goal on the next trial. Hoppe assumed that the experience of success and failure was not dependent on the objective results of an action, but on whether or not the level of aspiration was reached for that particular action. Thus, a goal is assumed to separate positively valenced events from nega-tively valenced events, or an area of success from an area of failure, with the former being approached and the latter being avoided (Lewin et al.,

1944). Lewin (1926b) assumed that the intention of reaching a goal creates a quasi need. Events that satisfy the goal are then a means for satisfying the quasi need and should have positive valence quality.

Some modern cognitive theories of emotion also assume that reaching versus frustrating a goal concept (Lazarus, 1993; Ortony, Clore, & Collins, 1988) or a motive (Roseman, 1984) is experienced positively versus negatively, respectively. In sum, goal-based theories suggest that if a goal for an action is set (see Gollwitzer, 1990, 1993, for the significance of actually setting the goal), it is the event specified by the goal (i.e., the end state of the goal) that lies near the threshold between positive and negative valence quality. For example, if the goal is to finish writing a paper before a self-imposed date, then finishing it before the date is good, but not finishing it before the date is bad. It follows that events clearly satisfying the goal are positively valenced, and events clearly impeding the goal are negatively valenced.

To better understand the effects of goals on valence, we first discuss hierarchical goal systems and then base our discussion of valence on the properties of such systems. Cybernetic theories (Carver & Scheier, 1990a; Miller, Galanter, & Pribram, 1960; Powers, 1973; Schank & Abelson, 1977; Vallacher & Wegner, 1985) conceptualize behavior regulation in terms of feedback loops that include two important elements: a reference value and movement of the organism toward (i.e., approach) or away from (i.e., avoidance) the reference value. Approach is regulated by negative feedback loops because they decrease the distance to a postively valenced reference value, and avoidance is regulated by positive feedback loops because they increase the distance from a negatively valenced reference value (Carver & Scheier, 1990b). In our definition of the term *goal* we include both the direction of movement (i.e., approach or avoidance) and the reference value that we call the *end state* of the goal. For example, the goal of a woman who wants to get pregnant would include two elements: the end state of being pregnant and the movement direction of approach. For a woman who does not want to be pregnant, the goal would have the same end state (i.e., pregnancy), but the directional movement would be avoidance. As with cybernetic theories, we refer to end states in a general way, subsuming, for example, specific events (e.g., "an open door"), physiological needs (e.g., hunger), and general values (e.g., fairness) as desired or undesired end states.

There are a number of approaches that assume that planned action is controlled by a hierarchical system of reference values such as goals (Carver & Scheier, 1990a; Hoppe, 1931; Miller et al., 1960; Ortony et al., 1988; Powers, 1973; Schank & Abelson, 1977; Vallacher & Wegner, 1985). The theory of action identification (Vallacher & Wegner, 1985, 1987) argues that higher levels of action identification reflect the reason "why" one engages in an action, and lower levels of action identification reflect "how" one engages in an action. Bower, Black, and Turner (1979) suggest that "why questions" can be answered by moving one level up in the goal hierarchy, and "how questions" can be answered by moving one level down. In other words, superordinate goals provide significance for subordinate goals, and subordinate goals provide the instructions for what must be done to achieve that significance. For our current purposes we can simplify a multilevel goal hierarchy to three levels: high-identity goals at the top (the why level), low-identity goals in the middle (a how level), and strategic goals at the bottom (another how level).

A. HIGH-IDENTITY GOALS

High-identity goals, such as maintaining self-esteem, are attained by reaching subordinate goals (e.g., being praised or outperforming competitors). Subordinate goals, therefore, are in the service of superordinate goals (Schank & Abelson, 1977; Vallacher & Wegner, 1985). Further, high-identity goals are applicable to events across many contexts. Note that such high-identity goals as maintaining self-esteem cannot be reached by any single event, unless the event has extreme implications for the high-identity goal. This would be the case when any possibility of ever reaching the high-identity goal is wiped out by a single event, as when the goal is to "be loved by mother" and the mother dies. Usually, however, the end states of high-identity goals are subordinate goals rather than specific events. Because high-identity goals usually supply meaning to events across many different contexts, rather than specifying particular events as end states, they are abstract goals. In order to relate high-identity goals to specific events, subordinate goals (i.e., low-identity goals) must exist.

High-identity goals are considered abstract because they lend significance (i.e., meaning) to *many* events. There is evidence in cognition that abstract representations in general lend meaning to events. Bransford and Johnson (1972) report that participants found a series of events that they read as more comprehensible when an appropriate context was provided. Moreover, applying a different abstract context to the same event can change the perceived meaning of the event. For example, participants read a passage that to most people would describe a prisoner. However, when the participants were student wrestlers in a physical education class, they categorized the same described person as a wrestler instead of a prisoner (Anderson, Reynold, Shallert, & Goetz, cited in Anderson, 1977, p. 426). In a similar vein, Asch (1952) found that when the statement, "I hold it that a little rebellion, now and then, is a good thing" (p. 421), was introduced as authored by Lenin versus Jefferson to his presumably American participants, they interpreted the meaning of the word rebellion to be revolution versus peaceful transition, respectively. This evidence demonstrates that abstract concepts, such as high-identity goals, lend meaning to events.

B. LOW-IDENTITY GOALS AND STRATEGIC GOALS

We define low-identity goals (i.e., our middle level of identity) as serving higher identity goals in terms of a "how to" relation and of having a level of abstraction sufficiently low to specify single events as end states. Low-identity goals are applicable to single events (e.g., winning a specific tennis match) and thus to a small number of contexts. Low-identity goals specify the event that must follow an action in order to achieve the goal. Thus, it is possible to infer whether a low-identity goal has been achieved by knowing the experienced outcome of a single activity. Low-identity goals can be satisfied or frustrated by a single event in an all-or-nothing fashion (i.e., total support or impediment). Strategic goals are subordinate to low-identity goals and specify how to achieve the event specified by the low-identity goal. Thus, strategic goals are also specific enough to refer to events. However, they can be so specific that they do not relate to the whole event specified by the low-identity goal (e.g., rush the net, do not double fault when serving versus winning the match).

The notion of subordinate goals bearing "how to" information for superordinate goals is supported by evidence that shows that when tasks are difficult or individuals have little experience with a task, they move to lower levels of action identification (Vallacher & Wegner, 1987). Further, there is evidence showing that people actually represent actions on several levels of identity (Vallacher, Wegner, Bordieri, & Wenzlaff, 1981, cited in Vallacher & Wegner, 1985).

III. The Principle of Goal Supportiveness

The previous section suggests that, principally, an event should be judged positive versus negative when it fulfills versus impedes a goal, respectively. We have also distinguished goals according to their level of identity (high vs. low). Do high- and low-identity goals have different functions when used to judge the valence of an event?

A. HIGH-IDENTITY GOALS ORDER EVENTS IN
TERMS OF VALENCE

We suggest that the valence of an event can be derived from the event's meaning to an individual. Because high-identity goals lend meaning to an event, the relation of the event to a high-identity goal should be relevant for the valence of the event. More specifically, we suggest that the more supportive an event is of a high-identity goal, the more positive will be the event's valence, and the more it impedes a high-identity goal, the more negative will be the event's valence. Thus, high-identity goals can serve as criteria to order events along a single dimension of goal supportiveness.

Because most single events are not sufficient in themselves to satisfy or frustrate a high-identity goal in an all-or-nothing fashion, it is usually not possible to derive from a high-identity goal whether a single event is goal supportive or goal impeding in absolute terms. For example, a college student could infer from the goal of maintaining self-esteem that a grade of B on a specific exam is *more* goal supportive (or less goal impeding) than a grade of C. Nevertheless, he or she could not infer whether a B is goal supportive or goal impeding per se. Thus, the student could not infer whether a B is positive or negative in valence quality. More information would be needed to make such a judgment.

If events are so extreme that they support or frustrate a high-identity goal in an all-or-nothing fashion, then they can be judged as positive or negative in valence quality, respectively. This might sometimes be the case, and such extreme events would then constitute the endpoints of a valenced event dimension. However, the most extreme events imaginable in a specific situation are not necessarily extreme enough to be clearly positive or clearly negative in valence quality. Even when our student fails the exam, it would not necessarily mean that his or her goal of maintaining self-esteem had been violated. The exam might be so difficult that just taking the exam is evaluated positively, regardless of the result. This might be the case, for example, for a "part-time" Olympic athlete for whom merely competing with the athletic elite is positively valenced, even if he or she places last in the competition.

To summarize, high-identity goals serve to set up an ordinal dimension of goal supportiveness, which, in turn, determines a valenced dimension of events. Further, high-identity goals can sometimes determine absolute valence when an event is extremely supportive or impeding. The events in the midrange of goal supportiveness cannot be categorized as positive or negative, however, by means only of the high-identity goal. The high-identity goal determines how these events ordinally relate to each other in terms of their valence without making reference to an absolutely positive or negative valence quality.

B. LOW-IDENTITY GOALS DIVIDE AN ORDERED EVENT DIMENSION INTO POSITIVE VERSUS NEGATIVE VALENCE QUALITY

Our discussion of high-identity goals and level of aspiration research suggests that high-identity goals order potential events along a dimension of goal supportiveness, but it is not clear how a person can divide such a dimension into positive and negative segments. Could low-identity goals serve such a function?

The level of aspiration research (for reviews see Lewin et al., 1944; Rotter, 1942) typically examined low-identity goals, such as a performance goal, on the next trial of dart throwing. The Lewin group assumed that there was such a single-performance goal on each trial and called it an "action goal" (Dembo, 1931; Hoppe, 1931) or "real goal" (Lewin et al., 1944). It was found that the action goal shifted from trial to trial, and it was assumed that it separated an area of success from an area of failure for each trial.

This research suggests that the setting of a low-identity goal on an ordered event dimension could separate this dimension into a positively and a negatively valenced area. Siegel (1957) extended the level of aspiration research to decision making in general and assumed that on a utility scale, the points on and above the level of aspiration have positive utility, and that the points below the level of aspiration have negative utility. According to Siegel, the utility function of an individual should be steepest between the level of aspiration and the first negatively valenced event. For example, for a student whose level of aspiration is the grade C, the largest utility difference between any two grades should be between C and D. Siegel observed a high correlation between the estimates of level of aspiration derived from the individual utility functions and those derived in interviews. He also found that when all of the participants ($N = 20$) "won" a C in a course and were offered the possibility to improve the grade if they waited until the course instructor returned from a long-distance call, each participant who left before 1 hour had passed ($N = 4$) had an aspiration level of C. This suggests that C already had positive valence quality for the participants who left. (The levels of aspiration of the participants who waited were not reported.)

Note that low-identity goals are sufficient only to separate positive from negative valence quality, and high-identity goals are sufficient only to infer degrees of valence quantity within positive and negative valence quality, respectively. When both a B and a B+ support low-identity goals, our student needs to know from a high-identity goal that a B+ is more goal supportive than a B in order to infer that a B+ is more positive than a B. Let us turn now to an additional complexity regarding low-identity goals.

C. MINIMAL AND MAXIMAL GOALS AS TYPES OF LOW-IDENTITY GOALS

The participants in Gould's (1939) level of aspiration research reported in qualitative interviews that they had set their action goals (i.e., low-identity goals) in various ways. Sometimes, they set their goals in terms of the minimal expected performance that they were trying to overreach. Alternatively, they set their goals in terms of the maximal performance that they hoped to approximate, but did not necessarily expect to reach. Gould (1939) interpreted her interview data in terms of minimal levels sometimes serving as a protection against failure and maximal levels sometimes serving as an incentive.

These observations stimulated research (Preston & Bayton, 1941) that explicitly asked participants to give several levels of aspiration on each trial of tasks such as adding numbers. Participants provided aspired performance scores for a minimal level below which they did not expect to fall, an actual level that they felt they would actually make, and the maximal level that they could possibly make. The results suggest that when people have to report all three types of levels, three different events (i.e., performance scores) are specified for the three levels.[3] For example, in the addition task each participant received performance feedback ranging between 95 and 131 points. The authors reported that for this task that participants' actual levels of aspiration were typically much closer to their estimate of their maximal level (median of difference = 13) than to their estimate of their minimal level (median of difference = 30). We suggest that it is useful to distinguish two different types of low-identity goals: *minimal goals* and *maximal goals*. Both types serve high-identity goals, but minimal goals specify a region in which events that impede the minimal goal are represented as impeding the high-identity goal, whereas maximal goals specify a region in which events that support the maximal goal are represented as supporting the high-identity goal. Consistent with our definition, Rotter (1954/1982a, 1970/1982b) defines a minimal goal as one almost involving punishment (i.e., if the goal is not met), and as the lowest goal whose end state will still produce satisfaction. He points out that minimal goals can exist in any domain, such as the moral, ethical, achievement, sexual, or affectional domain (Rotter, 1970/1982b) (see Figures 1A and 1B).

It follows that an assumption of only one goal serving as the dividing line between positive and negative valence quality might not be sufficient.

---

[3] Note that Preston and Bayton (1941) operationalized levels of aspiration as an expectancy concept. In contrast, for other investigators (Lewin et al., 1944; Rotter, 1942), including ourselves, a level of aspiration refers to the valence of an outcome. However, as we discuss later, valence and expectancy need not be independent (e.g., Atkinson, 1957, Escalona, 1940).

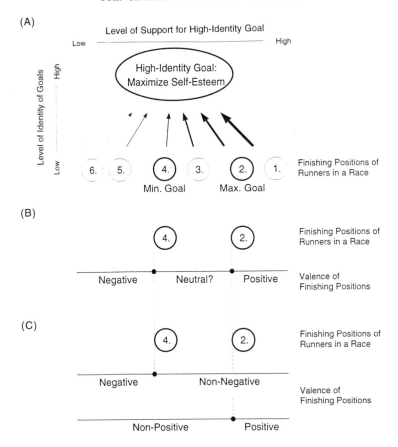

Fig. 1.   (A) A minimal goal of finishing fourth in a race and a maximal goal of finishing second for a hypothetical runner. Bolder arrows represent more support (or less impediment) of a finishing position for the high-identity goal. (B) Valence of finishing positions that do not meet both the minimal and maximal goals or that do meet both the minimal and maximal goals. (C) Valence of all finishing positions in relation to the minimal or the maximal goal.

We propose that minimal goals serve to separate a negative region from a nonnegative region and that maximal goals separate a positive region from a nonpositive region (Figure 1C). In other words, the end states of the low-identity goals defining positive versus negative events might be different for minimal versus maximal goals.

There is some evidence consistent with the idea that minimal goals establish a negatively valenced region. Norem and Cantor (1986a, 1986b) distinguished two types of individuals whose high achievement behavior is consistent with setting maximal versus minimal goals. Specifically, Norem and Cantor (1986b) showed that before an exam, optimists focused on doing well, and defensive pessimists focused on doing poorly. The authors described the prototypic defensive pessimists as the "straight-A students who have never failed a test in their lives but repeatedly insist that they are, without question, going to 'bomb' an upcoming exam" (p. 1209). Defensive pessimists showed higher degrees of anxiety in an achievement situation and set lower performance goals than did optimists, despite their performing as well on the experimental task. Defensive pessimists seem to be motivated to avoid failure.

A comparable effect was found in the study by Preston and Bayton (1941). They found that African-American college students lowered their minimal levels of aspiration (i.e., minimal goals) when comparing their performance with a Caucasian group of college students. In general, the African-American students did not lower their minimal levels of aspiration when the comparison group was African-American, nor did they change their maximal levels of aspiration as a result of any social comparison. Because the study was conducted in 1941, it is likely that the African-American students were threatened by the stereotype that African-Americans perform worse than Caucasians. They might have reduced their chances of failing by lowering their minimal goals. There is also evidence that people tend to lower their goals after failure (Hoppe, 1931; Jucknat, 1938). The fact that the African-American participants lowered only their minimal goals is consistent with the notion that minimal goals define failure.

D. MINIMAL AND MAXIMAL GOALS AS BOUNDARIES BETWEEN NEGATIVE AND POSITIVE VALENCE QUALITY

1. Valence Quality of Events

Previously we suggested that minimal goals divide negative events from nonnegative events and that maximal goals divide positive events from nonpositive events (see Figure 1C). That is, events that fail to satisfy a minimal goal are negatively valenced, and events that satisfy a maximal goal are positively valenced.

What valence quality do events have that satisfy minimal goals but do not satisfy maximal goals? There are two possibilities. One possibility is that these events are neutral. Then the area of neutral events would be defined as existing between a minimal and a maximal goal (see Figure 1B). Thus, a minimal goal and a maximal goal would jointly separate areas of negative, neutral, and positive valence quality. Alternatively, achieving a minimal goal could be positive, and impeding a maximal goal could be negative. Then each goal type by itself would separate an area of negative valence quality (i.e., impeding that goal) and positive valence quality (i.e., supporting that goal) (see Figure 1C). This implies the existence of an area that could have either positive or negative valence quality depending on whether a minimal or maximal goal is emphasized.

To decide on one of these two possibilities, we need to know whether a nonnegative event has positive valence quality and whether a nonpositive event has negative valence quality. In an excellent review of the animal learning literature, Gray (1971) reported several sources of evidence showing that nonpunishment shares the rewarding properties of reward and that nonreward shares the aversive properties of punishment. For example, Lawler (1965) trained rats to escape electric shock into a distinctive escape box in the first stage of the experiment. This same escape box acted as a secondary reward in the second stage of the experiment in which no shocks were given. Animals that had at first been shocked preferred to run into the distinctive escape box more often than controls that had not been shocked. Thus, the escape box associated with nonpunishment acted like a reward. Adelman and Maatsch (1956) showed that rats previously rewarded in the goal box of an alley but now not rewarded (nonreward group) jumped out of their goal box faster than rats that had never been rewarded (control group). In addition, nonreward animals jumped out even faster than those specifically rewarded for jumping out. Thus, nonreward acted as negative reinforcement. In summary, the evidence reviewed by Gray (1971) strongly suggests that nonpositive events are negatively valenced and that nonnegative events are positively valenced (see also Mowrer, 1960).

This conclusion is corroborated by further evidence. In a classical conditioning study with humans, Zanna, Kiesler, and Pilkonis (1970) found that words were evaluated more positively when they had previously been paired with the offset rather than the onset of an electric shock. Solomon and Corbit (1974) reviewed an impressive collection of various phenomena demonstrating that an affective reaction to a stimulus is followed by an affective reaction of opposite valence quality after the stimulus is terminated. Consistent with these observations are Roseman's findings (1984; 1991; Roseman et al., 1990) that the presence of punishments and the absence of rewards are experienced as negative emotions and that the presence of rewards and the absence of punishments are experienced as positive emotions (see also Lazarus, 1968; Stein & Jewett, 1986). Thus, minimal goals and maximal goals should each separate an area of positively and negatively valenced events, resulting in two types of positive valence quality and two types of negative valence quality of events. It follows that an event between the end states of a minimal and a maximal goal can be either positive or negative depending on which goal is activated. Indeed, the event could even be experienced as both positive and negative if both goals are activated (see Figure 1C).

How is it possible that the area between a set minimal goal and a set maximal goal is both positively and negatively valenced? This is possible because valence is not an absolute property of an event. Valence is defined relative to a goal that is impeded or satisfied, and there can be more than one goal. "Mixed" valence would be perceived, however, only when both a minimal and a maximal goal are activated or have actually been set (cf. Gollwitzer, 1990, 1993). We do not know how such "mixed" valence would be experienced phenomenologically. It might be perceived as ambivalence, as confusion, or simply as the experience of multiple emotions. However, it would not be experienced as neutral (compare Figures 1B and 1C).

We next have to make the distinction between minimal and maximal goals beyond negative versus positive valence quality if we want to use these concepts as sources of valence quality. In the following we first discuss such additional distinctions, and then we elaborate on what factors might determine whether a minimal or a maximal goal is set.

2. Direction of Motivated Movement on the Strategic Goal Level

Minimal and maximal goals specify positively valenced end states as events to be approached. However, we suggest that these goals differ on the strategic goal level (i.e., in terms of the goal levels subordinate to them). The strategic level subordinate to minimal goals can be described by a positive feedback loop (i.e., by an avoidance movement that increases the distance from an end state). For example, a mountain climber might have the minimal goal of staying at least at a 15-ft safety distance from dangerous crevasses. Finding him- or herself 10 ft from a crevasse, the mountain climber is going to move toward the positively valenced 15-ft safety distance until it is reached. The mountain climber could either regulate this movement by increasing the distance from the crevasse or by decreasing the distance to the security zone. Note that the security zone is defined in reference to the dangerous crevasse. Thus, we suggest that the mountain climber regulates his or her movement toward the security zone by increasing the distance to the crevasse (i.e., avoidance) until having reached the security zone. This can be conceptualized by embedding the positive feedback loop (i.e., avoidance) on the subordinate strategic level in a negative feedback loop (i.e., approach) on the superordinate low-identity level. In summary, both approach and avoidance are taking place, approach on the low-identity goal level and avoidance on the subordinate strategic goal level.

Assume a specific situation in which moving away from the crevasse is *not* caused by a prior evaluation of a crevasse. For example, a novice mountain climber may have no prior knowledge about the danger of crevasses but is told by a teacher to keep a minimum distance from them. The teacher has thus communicated a minimal goal by specifying an end state (the minimum distance) and by implying the strategic means (avoidance of the crevasse). The novice would not have to be told about the negative valence of the crevasse to infer that being too close to a crevasse is a negative event. In this case, the event receives its negative valance because it is the end state of a minimal goal. In other situations something else could assign valence quality to an event, and the type of goal would be set because the event has this certain valence quality. For example, the teacher might say that crevasses are dangerous, which would typically be understood as a negative evaluation. Because of this negative evaluation the novice might apply the minimal goal of keeping a safety distance. Thus, in this situation, we have a pattern of bidirectional causality: Either a given negative valence quality results in a minimal goal that produces avoidance of the event at the strategic level, or a given strategic avoidance produces a minimal goal that results in a negative evaluation of the event. We next discuss other sources of minimal versus maximal goal setting.

The strategic level subordinate to maximal goals can be described by a negative feedback loop (i.e., by an approach movement toward a positively valenced end state). This can be conceptualized by embedding a negative feedback loop (i.e., approach) on the subordinate strategic level in a negative feedback loop on the superordinate low-identity level. For example, the mountain climber with the maximal goal of finding as many water sources as possible would be regulating his or her movement toward a rivulet by decreasing the distance to the rivulet.

In conclusion, minimal and maximal goals are alike in that they both specify positively valenced events as end states. They differ, however, in terms of specifying nonnegative versus positive events as end states, respectively, and in terms of the subordinate avoidance versus approach strategy, respectively, by which the goal is reached. The nonnegative end state of a minimal goal is reached by avoiding negative events. In contrast, the positive end state of a maximal goal is reached by approaching positive events.

3. Two Psychological Situations for Each Valence Quality

Minimal goals separate negative from nonnegative events. In keeping with previously used terminology (see Higgins, 1987; Higgins, Roney, Crowe, & Hymes, 1994; Higgins & Tykocinski, 1992), we refer to these two types of events as two psychological situations: the presence of a negative outcome and the absence of a negative outcome. Maximal goals separate positive from nonpositive events. We refer to these two types of events as two additional psychological situations: the presence of a positive outcome and the absence of a positive outcome. Thus, two types of psychological situations are positively valenced, and two types are negatively valenced.

An event that meets either type of goal has positive valence quality, and an event that impedes either type of goal has negative valence quality. Within individuals, the end state of a minimal goal is usually less goal supportive of a high-identity goal than is the end state of a maximal goal (see Figure 1A). Take, for example, a marathon runner whose minimal goal is to finish at least fourth, whereas his or her maximal goal is to finish second. Finishing second is more supportive of the high-identity goal of maximizing self-esteem than finishing fourth. When the end state of the minimal goal is less supportive of a high-identity goal than that of a maximal goal, the presence of a positive outcome would likely have more positive *valence quantity* than would the absence of a negative outcome. In our example, finishing fourth (i.e., the absence of the negative outcome of finishing less than fourth) has less positive valence quantity than does finishing second (the presence of a positive outcome). Of course, this comparison is only valid when keeping a constant discrepancy from each of the two types of low-identity goals (e.g., exactly meeting the low-identity goals by finishing fourth or second, or overreaching them each to the same degree by finishing third or first). Thus, it is not only the support of an event for the low-identity goal that results in positive valence quantity, but also the extent to which meeting the low-identity goal supports the high-identity goal. Although finishing fourth and second each satisfies a low-identity goal, finishing second is more positive because it supports the high-identity self-esteem goal to a greater extent. By the same token, the presence of a negative outcome would likely have more negative valence quantity than the absence of a positive outcome (keeping the discrepancy from each type of low-identity goal constant). For example, finishing fifth (the presence of a negative outcome) is more damaging for self-esteem than finishing third (the absence of a positive outcome).

Given the previous arguments, one might want to conclude that holding maximal goals has emotional advantages over holding minimal goals. However, these advantages are countered by the fact that the proportion of positively valenced to negatively valenced events is larger for minimal goals than for maximal goals, because minimal goals usually need less high-identity goal supportiveness to be attained. In our example, holding the minimal goal offered four positively valenced finishing positions (i.e., fourth, third, second, first), whereas holding the maximal goal offered only two (second and first).

Thus, finishing third has positive valence quality when the minimal goal is held but negative valence quality when the maximal goal is held. As discussed later, however, minimal versus maximal goals do not refer to absolute degrees of high-identity goal supportiveness. For example, an individual's minimal goal at one time may very well be more high-identity goal supportive than the same individual's maximal goal at another time. It is within individuals at one point in time that we predict the high-identity goal supportiveness of a minimal goal to be lower than or equal to that of a maximal goal.

4. Summary

Our main question was "how do people judge the valence of an event?" The previous sections provide some initial answers. The effect of high-identity goals is to order events along a dimension of goal supportiveness and thus to provide an ordinal dimension of valence. The effect of low-identity goals is to separate areas of negative and positive valence quality. Our second question concerned the nature of the transition from negative to positive valence quality. We conclude that valence quality changes with shifts in regions defined by the support or impediment of activated low-identity goals. The type of psychological situation for each valence quality depends on the type of goal: minimal or maximal.

E. INFLUENCES ON SETTING MINIMAL VERSUS MAXIMAL GOALS

As previously mentioned, it is meaningful to conceive of a minimal or a maximal goal as determining valence quality only if factors other than valence quality determine the goal type as minimal versus maximal at the time of judgment. Next, we discuss factors that may influence whether a goal is represented as minimal or maximal.

1. Chronic Outcome Focus[3a]

Higgins (in press-a, in press-b) has identified individual differences in chronic outcome focus. People with a chronic positive outcome focus are chronically oriented to maximize the presence of positive outcomes (e.g., gains) and to minimize the absence of positive outcomes (e.g., nongains). People with a chronic negative outcome focus are chronically oriented to

---

[3a] After we completed this chapter, Higgins has used the term regulatory focus instead of outcome focus, promotion focus instead of positive outcome focus, and prevention focus instead of negative outcome focus.

maximize the absence of negative outcomes (e.g., nonlosses) and to minimize the presence of negative outcomes (e.g., losses). Thus difference in outcome focus is nicely illustrated in the metaphor of viewing one's glass as half full or half empty (Higgins, in press-b). To draw the analogy further, people with a positive outcome focus would perceive a glass on a fullness dimension (e.g., almost full, not at all full), and people with a negative outcome focus would perceive a glass on an emptiness dimension (e.g., not at all empty, almost empty). Differences in chronic outcome focus should be revealed especially for events that are moderate in their support for high-identity goals (e.g., a half-full or half-empty glass) rather than extreme (e.g., a totally full or totally empty glass). People with a chronic negative outcome focus should set more minimal goals than people with a chronic positive outcome focus, whereas people with a chronic positive outcome focus should set more maximal goals than people with a chronic negative outcome focus. Is there evidence then for individual differences in chronic outcome focus?

We have already reported some evidence that suggests chronic individual differences in outcome focus. Before an achievement situation, defensive pessimists focus more on failure than do optimists, whereas the reverse is true for focusing on success (Norem & Cantor, 1986a, 1986b). Self-discrepancy theory distinguishes individuals with a chronic negative outcome focus (predominantly ought-discrepant individuals) from individuals with a chronic positive outcome focus (predominantly ideal-discrepant individuals) (for a review see Higgins, in press-b).[4] In a study by Higgins et al. (1994, Study 3), for example, strategies to maintain friendship were elicited from participants that represented either avoidance movement on a strategic goal level (e.g., avoid being a poor friend) or approach movement on a strategic goal level (e.g., approach being a good friend). Participants from a second sample were either asked, "When you think about strategies for not being a poor friend in your close relationship, which three of the following would you choose?" (p. 283), or they were asked to choose strategies for being a good friend. Participants chose more avoidance strategies when asked how to avoid failure as a friend, whereas they chose more approach strategies when asked how to succeed as a friend, corroborating the assumption that the strategies really represented avoidance versus approach inclinations. In the critical third sample, participants were all given the same neutral task and were therefore asked, "When you think about

---

[4] *Ought discrepancies* are chronic differences between how individuals think they actually are and how they (or others, they believe) think it is their duty or obligation to be. *Ideal discrepancies* are chronic differences between how individuals think they actually are and how they (or others, they believe) hope or wish they would be. People with predominant ought discrepancies have high ought but low ideal discrepancies, whereas people with predominant ideal discrepancies have high ideal but low ought discrepancies.

strategies for friendship, which of the following would you choose?" Participants with a chronic negative outcome focus (predominantly ought-discrepant persons) selected avoidance strategies for maintaining friendships more often than participants with a chronic positive outcome focus (predominantly ideal-discrepant persons). For example, they selected the avoidance strategy, "Stay in touch. Don't lose contact with friends" more than the approach strategy "Be generous and willing to give of yourself" (Higgins et al., 1994, p. 283). This relation was reversed for approach strategies.

These findings suggest that chronic outcome focus as indicated by self-discrepancies might determine people's inclination for approach versus avoidance movements on the strategic goal level (i.e., subordinate to low-identity goals), and thus determine their preference for minimal versus maximal goals. For example, two runners with the low-identity goal of finishing the race in fourth position could infer that finishing fourth has positive valence quality, whereas finishing fifth has negative valence quality. With a chronic negative outcome focus, one runner would have a tendency to represent the low-identity goal as minimal and consequently infer that finishing fifth is the presence of a negative outcome. In contrast, the runner with a chronic positive outcome focus and a low-identity goal of finishing fourth would have a tendency to represent the goal as maximal and consequently infer that finishing fifth is the absence of a positive outcome (cf. Figure 1C).

If individual differences in chronic outcome focus predict the preferences of people in setting minimal versus maximal goals, it is important to consider the sources of chronic outcome focus. According to self-discrepancy theory (Higgins, 1987, in press-a), a chronic positive outcome focus develops from a history in which a child's caregiver provides and withdraws positive events (e.g., love, nurturance), and a chronic negative outcome focus develops from a history in which a caregiver administers or refrains from administering negative events (e.g., criticism, physical punishment).

This theory presupposes that infants are equipped to feel pleasure and pain, and evidence to that effect exists (see Lazarus, 1991). Evidence for pleasure comes from the fact that the behaviors of newborns can be reinforced (for a review see Rovee-Collier, 1987), for example, by using rewards such as sucking (Siqueland, 1968), moving a mobile (Rovee-Collier & Hayne, 1987; Watson, 1972), their mother's voice (DeCasper & Fifer, 1980), human heartbeats (DeCasper & Sigafoos, 1983), or even a specific piece of prose repeatedly read aloud by their mothers during pregnancy (DeCasper & Spence, 1986). There is also evidence for aversive reinforcers (DeCasper & Sigafoos, 1983; DeCasper & Spence, 1986), and aversive everyday experiences are discussed by Lipsitt (1990). Further, a newborn's hedonic reactions to tasting solutions are positive for sweet solutions and negative for sour solutions (Ganchrow et al., 1983; for a review see Cowart, 1981). Given that infants can feel pleasure and pain, chronic orientations in outcome focus could be produced by the parents' mode of responding to the child.

2. Previous Success or Failure

If persons experience a positive event at time t_0, they might subsequently set a different type of low-identity goal at time t_1 than if they experience a negative event at t_0. There is evidence in achievement settings that positive and negative prior experiences affect the level of aspiration in a following task. In achievement settings people raise their goals most often after success, and they lower or maintain their goals most often after failure (Escalona, 1940; Hoppe, 1931; Jucknat, 1938) (e.g., increasing the difficulty level of a computer game after success but decreasing it after failure.)

These typical shifts in levels of aspiration have been explained by assuming that success or failure at a task changes the likelihood of success at the same task (Atkinson, 1964; Atkinson & Birch, 1970). For example, if the expected likelihood of success is $p = .50$ at difficulty level 10 of a computer game, then success on a present trial might raise the expectation for success on a subsequent trial to $p = .60$, but failure might lower it to $p = .40$. The theory of achievement motivation assumes that people with a motive to succeed choose tasks with an expected likelihood of success of $p = .50$. Thus, after success the difficulty level 11 (i.e., more difficult than 10) might have the expected likelihood of success of $p = .50$, but after failure it might be difficulty level 9. Recall that the level of aspired difficulty marks the lowest difficulty level that still has positive valence quality. Thus, as the aspired level of difficulty changes, the valence quality of some difficulty levels changes. In summary, this explanation for the typical shifts in chosen task difficulty implies that a single goal separating success and failure shifts up and down along the dimension of task difficulty, depending on the expected likelihood of success.

We would like to note the possibility that shifts in chosen task difficulty might additionally reflect a change in the type of goal. One can speculate that people might set minimal goals most often after failure and maximal goals most often after success. Lowering the level of aspiration (e.g., from difficulty level 10 to level 9) after failure would involve setting a minimal goal, and thus evaluating the outcome of the next trial as the presence of a negative outcome when having failed, and as the absence of a negative outcome when having succeeded. In contrast, raising the level of aspiration after success (e.g., from difficulty level 10 to level 11) would involve setting a maximal goal and thus evaluating the outcome of the next trial as the absence of a positive outcome when having failed and as the presence of a positive outcome when having succeeded. Note, however, that these considerations implicitly assume a situation in which a person has no choice to leave the field (cf. Lewin, 1935). Thus, success or failure might serve as a recent context that could affect the setting of minimal versus maximal goals as well as determine the difficulty level at which these goals are set. The difficulty level separates positive from negative events, and the type of goal (maximal vs. minimal) determines the type of psychological situation involved (e.g., the presence of a positive outcome vs. the absence of a negative outcome). Thus, the causal chain in this example would be that success or failure on a previous trial determines the type of goal set on the next trial, which in turn determines the valence of the next event.

3. Valenced Reference Points as the Result of Prior Evaluations of Events

One of our assumptions is that the type of low-identity goal is directly related to the interpretation of the event. We assume, for example, that an event supporting a goal is always positive, that an event meeting a maximal goal always represents the presence of a positive outcome, and that, likewise, an event meeting a minimal goal always represents the absence of a negative outcome. Thus, we assume consistency between goals and event evaluations. In the previous section, we explain that the evaluation of an event depends on the type of goal set before the evaluation takes place. For example, setting a maximal goal at time t_0 results in interpreting the possible events as showing the presence versus the absence of a positive outcome at time t_1. If there is consistency, however, it should also be possible that an evaluation first takes place at t_0, and then the type of goal is determined at t_1, in which case an evaluation would determine a goal type, and not vice versa. One simple way in which such a previous evaluation can take effect is by one person communicating it to another.

For example, when supervisors describe the success of an employee on a sales project as the presence of a positive outcome (e.g., "you did well") versus the absence of a negative outcome (e.g., "you did not do badly"), they communicate a prior evaluation of the type of positive event. Communicating "you did well" versus "you did not do badly" should lead to setting maximal versus minimal goals, respectively, on the next sales project. Similarly, describing failure as the absence of a positive outcome (e.g., "you did not do well") versus the presence of a negative outcome (e.g., "you did badly") should also lead to setting maximal versus minimal goals, respectively, the next time. Roney, Higgins, and Shah (in press, Study 2) had all their participants ultimately fail a preset goal on an anagrams task. When feedback for the failure trials was expressed as the absence of a positive outcome (e.g., "you didn't get that one right"), persistence and performance was better than when feedback was expressed as the presence of a negative outcome (e.g., "no, you missed that one"). This result is consistent with the notion of a communicated evaluation influencing the type of goal set. If a "framing" in terms of the presence of a negative outcome promotes setting minimal goals, and if a "framing" in terms of the absence of a positive outcome promotes setting maximal goals, and also if individuals' minimal goals are usually set at a lower performance level than their maximal goals (cf. Figure 1A), then power persistence and lower performance should result from framing failure in terms of the presence of a negative outcome versus the absence of a positive outcome.

More generally, when the psychological situation of an event that serves as a reference point is communicated explicitly, such as in the previous supervisor example, a valenced reference point is created. When a supervisor says that an employee did not do badly, he or she explicitly labels the employee's performance as not bad and a lower performance as bad (i.e., he points out absence versus presence of badness). Because it is difficult to mentally represent information about the absence of features (see Nisbett & Ross, 1980), we suggest that the employee would typically use the bad performance as a valenced reference point for subsequent evaluations. More generally, the presence of a valenced outcome (i.e., the presence of a negative outcome or the presence of a positive outcome) should typically serve as a valenced reference point because people have difficulty representing the absence of events (see Nisbett & Ross, 1980).

Let us elaborate more on the technique of message "framing" pioneered by Tversky and Kahneman (1981). Framing manipulations are commonly used in marketing (e.g., when juice is advertised as having 90% natural flavors instead of 10% artificial flavors). A problem with framing techniques for a priori predictions is that there is no unanimous agreement among people as to the valence quality of the reference event. For example, although many Americans might represent the drinking of natural juices as the presence of a positive outcome (e.g., healthy food), some might represent it as the presence of a negative outcome (e.g., poor taste). Thus, clear predictions from framing techniques should be possible only if one knows how an event or its consequence are experienced by most individuals of a population. For some events or their consequences (e.g., physical pain, death) such knowledge might be straightforward, but for others, ideographic pretesting is unavoidable. Understanding the processes by which the framing of an event at time t_0 influences judgments of valence at time t_1 allows prediction for t_1 only when we know a person's perception of the frame at

t_0. Because we usually do not have access to a person's history before time t_0, pretesting at t_0 is often unavoidable.

In another way, an evaluation can precede and thus determine goal setting when a person knows, for example, that frustrating a goal will lead to punishment. Punishment should usually be experienced as the presence of a negative outcome and thus should result in setting a minimal goal (again assuming consistency between evaluation and goal). One example can be seen in culturally institutionalized punishment contingencies. Rotter (1954/1982a) explained that cultures provide inflexible presumptions for certain situations in which violation is severely punished. Such cultural prescriptions cover a wide range of domains (e.g., table manners, religious commandments). Meeting such prescriptions is rarely rewarded, but violating them is punished. Thus, most people should represent violating such prescriptions as the presence of a negative outcome, and meeting them as the absence of a negative outcome. If people set a low-identity goal to meet a prescription, then it should be a minimal goal.[5] For example, in Western culture most job applicants know that because of cultural prescriptions, eating noisily and talking with a full mouth during a job interview luncheon could cost them the job, whereas displaying perfect table manners will not usually get them the job. Thus, they should have a minimal goal for good table manners, such as, "display good table manners" implemented by an avoidance strategy such as "never speak with your mouth full." Good table manners have a minimal character. They are necessary for getting the job, but certainly not sufficient.

In summary, we suggest that at the time when an event is evaluated, previously established evaluations of reference events can come to mind and serve as valenced reference points. To maintain consistency between the type of event and the type of goal, the setting of a minimal versus a maximal goal would then be determined by the valenced reference point.

The evaluation of the event results from comparing the event to the reference event, that is, comparing the event to a reference event that typically represents the presence of a negative outcome or the presence of a positive outcome. The evaluation results either in the presence of the reference event's valence quality (i.e., the presence of either a positive or a negative outcome) or in the absence of the reference event's valence quality (i.e., the absence of either a positive or a negative outcome). If people take into account not only whether an event is more or less goal

[5] Note that such cultural prescriptions are often quite behavior specific, that is, represented on a low-identity level. However, there are positively valenced high-identity goal representations that are served by meeting the cultural prescriptions. For example, mastering such prescriptions as table manners is supportive of a potential high-level goal of being respected by others.

supportive (i.e., the event's valence), but also whether the reference point is present or absent, then systematic differences between presence representations and absence representations should be detectable. Consistent with this idea, we found systematic differences in how sensitively people discriminate between different money amounts framed as presence events (i.e., gains, losses) versus absence events (nonlosses, nongains) (Brendl, Higgins, & Lemm, in press). More specifically, participants indicated how much larger or smaller a certain monetary net gain (or net loss) was than a $50 net gain (or net loss) by scaling the intensity of their emotions toward the net gain (or net loss). For example, a participant might have indicated that he or she felt more pleased about gaining $150 as compared to $50. Participants discriminated more sensitively when the event was framed as a presence event instead of an absence event. For example, they indicated a larger increase in positive affect about the same increase in a monetary gain when the gain was framed as the presence of a gain rather than as the absence of a loss.

4. Summary

Individuals can operate in terms of predominantly minimal goals or predominantly maximal goals. In either case the goal can be very high or very low in absolute terms on a dimension of superordinate goal supportiveness. That is, minimal and maximal goals do *not* refer to absolute outcomes. Two students, for example, might both identify high grades as their high-identity goal and also have the same low-identity performance goal (A−), but one student might have a positive outcome focus regarding the low-identity goal ("I hope to get A− or better in all my courses"), whereas the other student might have a negative outcome focus regarding the low-identity goal ("I must get no less than A− in all my courses"). The tendency to use one goal type can be due to chronic individual differences (e.g., a chronic negative outcome focus), to previous successes or failures, or to evaluating events prior to setting a goal (e.g., framing a message in a particular way).

When an individual holds both a minimal and a maximal goal concurrently, the minimal goal would typically be lower in terms of superordinate goal supportiveness than the maximal goal. When the minimal goal is set lower than the maximal goal, valence quality changes at two points on the event dimension, once at the minimal goal and once at the maximal goal.[6] Three types of valenced events can then be distinguished. Events that fall short of both goals have only negative valence quality; events that exceed

---

[6] Minimal goals can be set unrealistically high, that is, higher than participants expect to achieve (see Wright & Mischel, 1982).

both goals have only positive valence quality, and events that exceed the minimal goal but fall short of the maximal goal have ambiguous or mixed valence quality whose nature (i.e., the absence of a negative outcome or the absence of a positive outcome) varies depending on the relative accessibility of the two goals (see Figure 1C).

IV. The Principle of Membership Status

The principle of membership status is also necessary for understanding judgments of valence. We discuss three cases of the principle of membership status: contingency relations, category membership, and part–whole relations. In all three cases an event receives its valence by being "assigned" to a representation that is itself valenced. Thus the event takes on the valence of the representation. The event can be an instance of a condition in a represented contingency relation (e.g., conditioning); the event (e.g., a social behavior) can be an instance of a categorical representation (e.g., a valenced trait), and the event (e.g., a downward curving lip) can be an instance of a represented part in a whole (e.g., a frown). Of course, the principle of membership status cannot be the first link in a causal chain explaining valence because it presupposes a valenced representation. Nevertheless, we believe that it is an important factor in determining the valence of events.

A. CONTINGENCY RELATIONS

One form of membership status that an event can have is a contingency relation to a valenced representation. When an event has a close contingency relation to a valenced representation, the event should acquire the valence of the representation.

1. Conditioning

One example of spatial-temporal contingency relations is the well-supported phenomenon in which a neutral type of event acquires aversive or pleasurable properties through classical conditioning. In classical conditioning a neutral type of event (CS) is put into spatial-temporal contingency with a valenced type of event (UCS), and this association is learned so that the formerly neutral event takes on the valence of the UCS as if it were assigned to the UCS. Eagly and Chaiken (1993) review evidence that people can acquire attitudes toward objects (e.g., nonsense words) through pairing them with valenced events (e.g., a loud noise, a pleasant picture). The results are generally consistent with a classical conditioning interpretation, although more evidence is necessary to rule out some alternative interpretations.

In reinforcement, a behavior is brought into a contingency relation with a subsequent event that is valenced (i.e., the reinforcer). If one assumes that reinforcement changes the valence of the behavior, then reinforcement can also be regarded as a cause of valence. There is also some evidence for the influence of reinforcement on attitudes, but alternative interpretations have not been ruled out (see Eagly and Chaiken, 1993).

2. Representativeness

We learned earlier that for low-identity goals, an event can be clearly supportive or unsupportive. It is less clear whether an event supports a high-identity goal. Many different degrees of supportiveness are conceivable (see Figure 1A). One of our major propositions was that high-identity goals order events along a dimension of goal supportiveness. How might individuals draw such inferences when the events that satisfy the goal are not specified as clearly supportive?

People might use the representativeness heuristic (e.g., Kahneman, Slovic, & Tversky, 1982; Kahneman & Tversky, 1972, 1973; Nisbett & Ross, 1980; Tversky & Kahneman, 1974, 1982) to judge the degree of goal supportiveness an event has for a high-identity goal.

> Representativeness is a relation between a process or a model, M, and some instance or event, X, associated with that model. Representativeness, like similarity, can be assessed empirically, for example, by asking people to judge which of two events, X_1 or X_2, is more representative of some model, M, or whether an event, X, is more representative of M_1 or of M_2. (Tversky & Kahneman, 1982, p. 85)

Let us temporarily suggest that when an event X_1 is judged as more representative of M than a second event X_2, then X_1 is judged as more goal supportive of M. Later, we elaborate this hypothesis. Support from a recent field experiment (Brendl & Higgins, 1995) exemplifes our suggestion. In a between-participants study we asked university students on campus how much they would pay for a lottery ticket with which they could win a prize of $1000. In one condition we asked students who were lining up at the bursar to pay their university bills. For these students, presumably, the goal of paying their bills was highly activated. Those to whom we offered the $1000 prize as a bill waiver versus as a cash award indicated that they would pay more for the lottery ticket. Note that a bill waiver is more representative than a cash award for the goal of paying a bill. It is thus more goal supportive and consequently more positive in valence quantity, making it consistent with paying more money for a lottery ticket that could win it. In contrast, when the goal is to win cash rather than a bill waiver, people should pay more for a lottery ticket that can win a cash award instead of a bill waiver. This was, in fact, the case for a control group in a cafeteria where the goal of accumulating cash was presumably more activated than the goal of paying a university bill.

We earlier defined a goal in terms of an end state (e.g., a paid bill) and a direction of movement (e.g., approach). With this in mind, we can elaborate our representativeness hypothesis. In the Brendl and Higgins (1995) study, both events (i.e., winning cash and winning a bill waiver) enabled approach movement toward the end states of a paid bill or accumulated cash. Therefore, the directions of movement in reference to the end states embodied by the events and by the goals are congruent, and thus both events are goal supportive. The events simply vary in their representativeness of the end states. For example, when the end state is a paid bill, the event that is more representative of the paid bill is judged more goal supportive (i.e., winning a bill waiver is judged to be more goal supportive). How would our analysis change if the direction of movement specified by the goal was inconsistent with the direction of movement embodied by the event as when the goal, for example, is paying a bill, but the event is the losing of a bill waiver or the losing of an equivalent cash amount? In principle, for an object that is positively valued when won, the event of losing the object should be negatively valued. We suggest that when an event embodies inconsistent movement in respect to a goal, it should be evaluated on a dimension of goal impedingness. The more representative a goal-impeding event is of an end state, the more negatively the event should be evaluated. Thus, when the goal is to approach the end state of a paid bill, losing a bill waiver should be judged as worse than losing an equivalent cash amount because a bill waiver is more representative of a paid bill than cash.

A study by Brendl, Markman, and Higgins (1995) supports this elaborated representativeness hypothesis and provides more specific evidence for representativeness as a mediating variable. Participants rated a cash voucher as more similar to cash than a gambling chip. Participants read about three college students who visited a gambling casino: Each one had won $25 in an initial gamble. However, one student had won the $25 as a gambling chip, one as a cash voucher, and one as cash. Participants then rated the likelihood that each student would risk his previous $25 winning (i.e., gambling chip, cash voucher, or cash, respectively) as a stake in a subsequent gamble. If we assume that our participants regarded the students' high-identity goal as that of maximizing their cash assets (i.e., leaving the casino with as much cash as possible), then they should have regarded the loss of any type of money as goal impeding. In addition, losing cash should have been the most goal impeding, and thus the most negative, because cash (as a loss in a specific gamble) is the most representative of cash (as part of the high-identity end state). Losing a chip should have been the least goal impeding because a chip is the least representative of cash. Finally, losing a cash voucher should have been intermediate in its goal impedingness because a cash voucher falls somewhere between cash and a chip in its representativeness of cash. Consistent with this analysis, the student who risked cash was judged to be least likely to gamble; the student who risked a chip was judged to be most likely to gamble; and the student who risked a cash voucher fell somewhere between.

The representativeness hypothesis predicts the way events can be ordered along a dimension of valence quantity. However, it does not predict the polarity of that dimension, that is, whether events are ordered in terms of goal supportiveness or goal impedingness. At this point the best hypothesis that we can offer for predicting polarity is a comparison of the directions of movements embodied by the goal and by the event. If both embody the same direction, higher representativeness predicts more goal supportiveness, and if the directions are inconsistent, higher representativeness predicts more goal impedingness. In both cases higher representativeness predicts greater valence quantity.

B. CATEGORY MEMBERSHIP

When an event is judged to be an instance of a valenced category, the event should acquire the same valence as the category. How can people judge the status of an event as a member of a valenced category?

1. Ease of Categorization

It might be fairly easy to generate exemplars or prototypes of events that are supportive of goals. Such prototypically goal-supportive events could serve as models for judging the goal supportiveness of actual events. The closer the association of the judged event to a goal-supportive model, the more goal supportive the event should be judged to be. Thus, people might infer goal supportiveness from judgments of closeness. People could employ the availability heuristic (Tversky & Kahneman, 1973) for such judgments of the closeness of an event to a goal-supportive model.

When using the availability heuristic, people use the subjective feeling of the ease of carrying out a mental operation as information in subsequent judgments (cf. Schwarz et al., 1991), or they may just assess how difficult the mental operation would be if they were to carry it out (Tversky & Kahneman, 1973). Such effects on judgment have been demonstrated using the ease of retrieving instances from memory (Kahneman & Miller, 1986; Schwartz et al., 1991; Stepper & Strack, 1993; Tversky & Kahneman, 1973) and the ease of mentally simulating an event (Kahneman & Miller, 1986; Kahneman & Tversky, 1982b; Miller, Turnbull, & McFarland, 1989; Tversky & Kahneman, 1973). We propose that the easier it is to categorize an event as an instance of a prototypically goal-supportive event, the more goal supportive the event will be judged to be. Similarly, the easier it is to categorize an event as an instance of a prototypically goal-impeding event, the more goal impeding the event will be judged to be.

Evidence reported by Schwarz et al. (1991) is consistent with this ease of categorization hypothesis. These authors determined in a pretest that it was difficult for their participants to recall 12 examples of a time when they had previously behaved either assertively or unassertively, but that it was easy for them to recall 6 such examples. The actual experiments employed a between-participants manipulation, such that participants recalled either 6 or 12 assertive behaviors or 6 or 12 unassertive behaviors. In a subsequent task, participants rated their own assertiveness. If ease of categorization is used a heuristic for judging goal supportiveness or goal impedingness, then the feeling of how easily assertive or unassertive behaviors come to mind should affect judgments of assertiveness. Consistent with the ease of categorization hypothesis, ease of recall did, in fact, polarize judgments. Specifically, when it was easier to recall assertive behaviors, participants judged themselves to be more assertive (presumably a more positive judgment). In contrast, when it was easier to recall unassertive behaviors participants judged themselves to be less assertive (presumably a more negative judgment). Note that for participants who recalled 12 examples of either assertive or unassertive behaviors there were more such behaviors available in memory. Still, the subjective ease of recall had a larger impact on judgments of assertiveness than did the number of available instances. When the informational value of ease of recall was discredited by a misattribution manipulation, however, recalling more assertive behaviors resulted in judgments of higher assertiveness, and recalling more unassertive behaviors resulted in judgments of lower assertiveness, independent of the ease of recall. This supports the hypothesis that the subjective feeling of the ease of recall was used as information for judgments when there was no misattribution manipulation. In summary, these results (also Stepper & Strack's, 1993) suggest that the experienced ease of categorizing an event as goal supportive or goal impeding can serve as information for judging the degree of the event's goal supportiveness or goal impedingness, respectively.

2. Category Accessibility

It is well documented that an event can be perceived as an instance of either a positively valenced category or a negatively valenced category depending on category accessibility (for reviews see Higgins, in press-c; Srull & Wyer, 1989). For example, it has been shown that the same behavior (e.g., crossing the Atlantic in a sailboat) is categorized as either positive (e.g., adventurous) or as negative (e.g., reckless) depending on whether the category of adventurous or reckless is more accessible in memory at the time of encoding (Higgins, Rholes, & Jones, 1977). Thus, when an event is identified as a member of a positively instead of a negatively valenced category, it is appraised as being positively valenced rather than negatively valenced. Indeed, this valenced appraisal is evident as well in subsequent judgments of liking the target person. As another example, consider Trope's (1986a, Experiment 1) participants who judged the emotional valence quality of an ambiguous facial expression as positive versus negative depending on whether the facial expression was associated with a positive situation (e.g., "the horse that he bet on is about to win the race," p. 245) versus a negative situation (e.g., "a coach, whose team is losing," p. 245), respectively.

C. PART–WHOLE MEMBERSHIP

Category membership implies that an event categorized as an instance of a category receives category properties, including the category's valence. Alternatively, an event can receive its valence by being "part" of a valenced "whole." In a part–whole membership the event does not only receive its valence from the whole (e.g., the category); it also is part of what makes the whole valenced. Although we are not aware of research directly pertaining to the valence quality of events in part–whole relations, there is closely related research.

In Asch's (1946) classic studies on impression formation, participants were told to form impressions of an imaginary target person who was described by a series of traits. Asch discovered that there are "central" traits (e.g., warm vs. cold) that influence the overall impression both in terms of its valence quality and its content. At the same time, the meaning and valence quality of the single traits are affected by the surrounding traits. Asch presented some evidence showing that even the central traits themselves are influenced by the surrounding traits. He concluded as follows:

> The single trait possesses the property of a part in a whole. A change in a single trait may alter not that aspect alone, but many others, at times all. As soon as we

isolate a trait we not only lose the distinctive organization of the person; the trait itself becomes abstract. The trait develops its full content and weight only when it finds its place within the whole impression. (p. 284)

Higgins and Rholes (1976) showed that an adjective (e.g., green) that is evaluated at one polarity of valence quality (e.g., positive) in isolation can be part of an oppositely valenced whole (e.g., "green bread"), which is evaluated negatively. Thus, as part of that whole, the adjective should be evaluated negatively (i.e., as "moldy" would be) instead of positively. Thus, green is evaluated negatively as a result of being associated with bread, but it also influences the valence of the whole (i.e., green bread). In Schachter and Singer's (1962) famous study, participants attributed physiological arousal either to a positive or to a negative situation, respectively, and evaluated their state as positive or negative. On the one hand, participants' experience of arousal defined part of a larger situation, and on the other hand, the event of experiencing arousal received the valence of that larger situation. The distinction between part–whole membership and category membership is subtle but useful.

V. The Principle of Referential Status: The Case of Neutral Reference Points

There is substantial evidence that valenced appraisals of an object or an event are affected by reference points, frames of reference, or standards of comparison (e.g., Herr, Sherman, & Fazio, 1983; Houston, Sherman, & Baker, 1989; Strack, Schwarz, Chassein, Kern, & Wagner, 1990; Tverskey & Kahneman, 1974). The principle of *referential status* refers to inferring the valence of an event from comparing it to a reference point (for a review on types of reference points see Higgins, 1990; Higgins, Strauman, & Klein, 1986). The reference point itself can be neutral or valenced.

We previously chose to discuss valenced reference points in the context of goal supportiveness, because low-identity goals can have the function of valenced reference points. The current section is devoted to neutral reference points, which is the usual concern with reference points in the social psychological literature.

We proposed earlier that high-identity goals order events along a dimension of goal supportiveness and that people can use low-identity goals (i.e., minimal and maximal goals) as valenced reference points to divide the dimension into areas of positive and negative valence quality. We also discussed how valenced reference points can be the result of prior evaluations, as when messages are positively or negatively framed. Given an event dimension ordered in terms of goal supportiveness and the absence of low-identity goals, however, individual events can also receive their valence quality by their relationship to a neutral event. This possibility is especially appealing because it does not require a predictor variable that already carries information about valence quality.

When an event dimension of ordered goal supportiveness is related to a neutral reference point, up to three potential areas can be distinguished: the neutral reference point itself, and two areas of events that deviate from it on each side (Figure 2A). A neutral reference point at the extreme end of the event dimension has just one deviating area. The area of events for

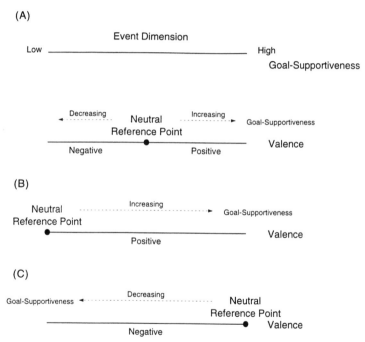

Fig. 2. (A) Representativeness of an event dimension ordered along degrees of goal supportiveness. Decreasing goal supportiveness from a neutral reference point determines negative valence quality. Increasing goal supportiveness from a neutral reference point determines positive valence quality. (B) A neutral reference point at the least goal-supportive extreme of the event dimension results in one nonneutral area with increasing goal supportiveness, which is therefore positively valenced. (C) A neutral reference point at the most goal-supportive extreme of the event dimension results in one nonneutral area with decreasing goal supportiveness, which is therefore negatively valenced.

which goal supportiveness increases with distance from the reference point has positive valence quality (Figure 2B), and the area of events for which goal supportiveness decreases with distance from the reference point has negative valence quality (Figure 2C). We do not make specific assumptions about the nature of the neutral reference point. It may be a single (not necessarily existing) point (cf. Helson, 1971); it may be like a reference area if composed of more than a single event (cf. Parducci, 1965, 1968), and it may have fuzzy boundaries (cf. Rosch, 1978).

A. THEORIES SUGGESTING NEUTRAL REFERENCE POINTS

In adaptation-level theory, Helson (1948, 1964, 1971) describes the establishment of a reference point for judgments in general. An adaptation level is defined as a geometric mean of previous stimulations; that is, each new stimulation shifts the adaptation level in its own direction. In an experiment of judging the heaviness of weights, for example, the adaptation level is defined as the geometric mean of the previously lifted weights. As another example, being exposed to many tall buildings should shift the adaptation level for the height of buildings toward a larger height. For a single attribute dimension, it is assumed that the adaptation level establishes a neutral reference point on that dimension. Stimuli that deviate in opposite directions from the adaptation level are assumed to elicit opposite reactions, such as the perception of pleasantness or approach behavior as opposed to the perception of unpleasantness or avoidance behavior. At the adaptation level, responses are assumed to be neutral, such as the perception of affective neutrality. For example, in a weight-judging experiment participants judged stimuli that were lighter than the adaptation level as light, and stimuli that were heavier than the adaptation level as heavy (Helson, 1948). Thus, the adaptation level is a neutral reference point that adapts to previous stimulations. New Yorkers, for example, might judge a 5-story building as short because it is below their adaptation level for the height of buildings, whereas inhabitants of a town with low buildings might judge the same building as tall.

Adaptation predicts a neutralizing effect when either positive or negative events are experienced frequently. For example, if a person's adaptation level for a salary is $2500 a month, and a new job pays a salary of $3500 a month, he or she should evaluate that salary as positive. Frequent experiences of receiving this new salary will follow. However, after a long time on the job, receiving the monthly salary of $3500 would raise the adaptation level closer to $3500. Then $3500 should slowly become neutral. If in addition, the person is exposed to other salaries that are even higher, his or her adaptation level might rise to $4500 and make $3500 appear to be a poor salary (cf. Brickman & Campbell, 1971; Frijda, 1988).

In summary, adaptation-level theory assumes that an adaptation level exists that constitutes a neutrally valenced area separating a positively from a negatively valenced area. We can derive from the theory that the neutral reference point shifts toward events that have been experienced frequently.

Prospect theory (Kahneman & Tversky, 1979) also assumes the existence of neutral reference points. It assumes that people encode monetary prospects in relation to a neutral reference point. Specifically, monetary transactions tend to be encoded as gains or losses, which are defined in relation to neutral reference points. People are assumed to calculate gains and losses for separate, fairly narrowly defined mental accounts (Tversky & Kahneman, 1981) rather than to relate changes in wealth to assets. Both prospect theory (Kahneman & Tversky, 1979) and adaptation level theory (Helson, 1964), however, are silent on how an individual determines whether an event that mismatches the neutral reference point is positively or negatively valenced.

There is evidence that it is the abnormality of conditions that gives them their status of being a cause for an event (Einhorn & Hogarth, 1986; Hilton & Slugoski, 1986; Miller, Taylor, & Buck, 1991; see also Weiner, 1985 and Wells & Gavanski, 1989). We assume that events are evaluated positively if they are regarded as a cause of fulfilling a goal, and that they are evaluated negatively if they are regarded as a cause of goal impediment. For example, imagine a host who wants to impress his or her guests with an exquisite dinner. If, for example, preparing spinach is regarded as the cause for the success of the dinner party, he or she should evaluate preparing spinach as positive. However, if preparing spinach is regarded as the cause of the failure of the party, it should be evaluated negatively. The causal relation of event and goal is essentially a contingency relation; that is, it is an instance of the principle of membership status.

Applied to the idea of goal fulfillment as a causal relation of event to goal, it follows that abnormal events should be regarded as causes for reaching or not reaching goals and should therefore be evaluated as positive or negative, respectively. However, normal events should not be perceived as causal, and should therefore be neither supportive nor unsupportive of a goal; that is, they should be appraised as neutral in valence quality. Next, we discuss a possible way in which people can make judgments of the normality of an event.

B. EASE OF CONSTRUCTING A MENTAL MODEL[7]

Consider the following example. You start as a cabdriver in a foreign country. You do not know how large a "neutral" tip is, that is, a tip that is neither good nor bad. Most people would probably evaluate as neutral the tip that is normal for the country. You would probably evaluate as positive tips that exceed that normal amount and as negative tips that fall short of that normal amount. In other words, abnormal tips would have either positive or negative valence quality. After you have transported a number of customers, you may establish a feeling for the size tip that is normal (e.g., 10% of the fare). You would find a tip of 1% or 20% to be abnormal, and evaluate it as negative or positive, respectively.

How could an individual make the judgments described in the cab driver example? The goal would usually be to get a tip as large as possible, so the smallest tip would be least goal supportive and the largest tip most goal supportive. From that goal, however, you cannot infer whether a 20% tip is actually positive or just less negative than a 1% tip, so you would need to calculate the normal event or, according to adaptation-level theory, the central tendency of the distribution of tips. People may use a simple heuristic for such judgments; that is, they may infer an event's normality from the subjective feeling of the ease of constructing a mental model of the event. From a distribution of events, those events for which a mental model is easiest to construct would be judged as normal (e.g., a 10% tip). Those events for which constructing a mental model is experienced as more difficult would be judged as deviating from the norm (e.g., a 1% and a 30% tip). They would be judged as positively or negatively valenced depending on whether their goal supportiveness increased or decreased, respectively, with deviation from the normal event (see Figure 2A). In summary, ease of constructing a mental model would be the basis for the judgment of normality (cf. Tversky & Kahneman, 1973).

We suggest this hypothesis on the basis of the availability heuristic (Tversky & Kahneman, 1973) in general and the norm theory in particular (Kahneman & Miller, 1986). Norm theory suggests that the most typical event in a distribution of events is computed by using ease of constructing a mental model as a heuristic. The event experienced as easiest to construct is considered the normal event, operationalized as the most typical, least-surprising event. Norm theory also suggests that people use ease of constructing a mental model to make judgments of surprise or typicality. We

[7] We thank Fritz Strack for suggesting the label "ease of constructing a mental model" as a substitute for a previous label.

further suggest that people can use ease of constructing a mental model to make judgments of neutrality.

There is evidence that people use ease of constructing a mental model to make judgments related to surprise or typicality, such as judgments of frequency (Tversky & Kahneman, 1973), suspiciousness (Kahneman & Miller, 1986), or personality traits (Schwarz et al., 1991; Stepper & Strack, 1993). Thus, the experience of ease of constructing a mental model is a heuristic that people employ for various types of judgments based on distributions of attributes. When we earlier reported research by Schwarz et al. (1991), we suggested that people use the availability heuristic to make judgments of how goal supportive or goal impeding an event is. Here we suggest that people can also use the availability heuristic to make judgments of how neutral an event is. A study by Ostrom (cited in Ostrom & Upshaw, 1968) is consistent with the idea that people can use ease of constructing a mental model for inferring both neutral and valenced reference points. Participants were asked to write down one specific content belief for different levels of an attitude rating scale, and they rated how easy or difficult it was for them to construct each belief. Ease of constructing a belief was highest for the neutral scale midpoint (and for the extreme scale endpoints). This is consistent with the idea that ease of generating a mental model might sometimes be used to infer a neutral reference point and sometimes to judge the goal supportiveness or the goal impedingness of events.

There are further findings consistent with the claim that the event for which it is easiest to construct a mental model can serve as a neutral reference point. It follows from adaptation-level theory that the event that happens most frequently should have the largest impact on moving the neutral adaptation level in its direction. In accordance with this prediction, it has been shown that stimuli with longer exposure times have stronger effects on moving the adaptation level in their direction (Helson & Kozaki, 1968, cited in Helson, 1971, p. 9). In addition, there is evidence that stimuli that have been activated frequently, and thus have been activated for longer time periods, are especially accessible in memory (for a review see Higgins, in press-c). It should feel easy to retrieve highly accessible representations from memory. Thus, frequent events coincide with the shifting of the neutrally valenced area in their direction and with the feeling of ease in mentally representing them. Also, accessibility allows for adaptation, that is, for shifts in the adaptation level due to frequent or recent stimulation.

Finally, it should be pointed out that the ease of constructing a mental model for judgments of neutrality is not only consistent with computing the central tendency of a distribution as a reference point for judgments, but also with taking into account the range of a distribution as a reference frame (cf. Ostrom & Upshaw, 1968; Parducci, 1965, 1968). Ease of representing a mental model does not confine the neutral reference point to a single event. In fact, most of the distribution could be easy to construct and thus be evaluated neutrally.

C. LIKELIHOOD CONCEPTS AND VALENCE

We suggested earlier that in the absence of low-identity goals, events that comprise the central tendency of a distribution of degrees of goal supportiveness are evaluated neutrally. The distribution of goal supportiveness may be correlated with other distributions. Of special interest are likelihood distributions because of their status in expectancy-value theories. For example, in achievement contexts, the subjective likelihood of success is associated with the valence of an event (Atkinson, 1957; Escalona, 1940; Feather, 1982a; Festinger, 1942; Heckhausen, 1977; Kuhl, 1978; Lewin et al., 1944) because the subjective likelihood of success is diagnostic for self-esteem (Trope, 1986b). Thus, if the goal is to enhance self-esteem, then the less likely a success (i.e., the more difficult the task), the more positive the evaluation of a success (Trope, 1986b). Note that the likelihood of success is a specific type of outcome expectancy and that there should also be types of outcome expectancies that are not correlated with valence (cf. Crozier, 1979). For example, if one would like to borrow a book from the library supposing that it is available, then borrowing this book has positive valence. The likelihood that one will be able to borrow the book is usually undiagnostic of the valence of borrowing it. Note that one might not set a goal to borrow the book after all if one does not expect it to be available. (Of course, there might also be cases in which the valence of borrowing the book would be lowered because it seems unlikely to be available, reintroducing a correlation of outcome expectancy and valence.)

Although we were inspired by norm theory (Kahneman & Miller, 1986) to derive our predictions about the influence of ease of constructing a mental model from judgments of neutral valence, it is important to note that in norm theory ease of constructing a mental model predicts a likelihood concept—specifically, surprise. The less likely an event seems after it has happened, the more surprising it is. Thus, the judgment of surprise is affected by a posteriori computed likelihood distribution, although a priori expectations affect surprise as well. In contrast, our predictions for valence are based on a distribution of goal supportiveness. Thus, in our model and in norm theory the same type of judgment process (i.e., ease of constructing a mental model) is applied to different objects (i.e., distributions of goal supportiveness vs. likelihood, respectively).

A correlation of a likelihood concept with the valence of events should not be confused with the influence of likelihood concepts on related variables, such as emotion or motivation. Our conception of the valence of an event is not the same as the emotions we feel about an event or our motivation to act toward an event. In the language of expectancy-value models (e.g., Feather, 1982b), our use of valence describes the value term of the equation. Emotion and motivation would additionally be influenced by a likelihood concept corresponding to the expectancy term of the equation. For example, surprise (i.e., a likelihood concept) has been shown to amplify affect (Johnson, 1986; Kahneman & Miller, 1986; Kahneman & Tversky, 1982b; Landman, 1987; Miller & McFarland, 1987; Miller, 1984 cited in Miller, Turnbull, & McFarland, 1990) and outcome expectancy can influence choice behavior independent of valence (cf. Crozier, 1979).

Thus, if an event involves an action, we conceive of the event's valence as if the event actually occurs. This is different from the valence of an action that could (i.e., with uncertainty) lead to the event. For example, winning a large prize in a lottery has very positive valence for many people, but few people are motivated to participate in such lotteries because the likelihood of winning is low. Similarly, in our book-borrowing example one might not be motivated to make the trip to the library because it is unlikely that the desired book is available, even though borrowing the book might have very positive valence. Thus, likelihood affects motivation, but not valence as we define it here. Similarly, consider the well-known vignette in which two airplane passengers arrive 30 minutes late at the airport (Kahneman & Tversky, 1982b): Mr. Tees who misses his delayed flight by only 5 min is more upset than Mr. Crane who misses his flight by 30 min. Presumably, Mr. Tees's negative emotions are amplified by the surprise of barely missing the plane (c.f., Kahneman & Miller, 1986). However, this does not necessarily imply that missing the plane per se has more negative valence for Mr. Tees than for Mr. Crane. This notion is consistent with the theory of reasoned action (Ajzen & Fishbein, 1980; Fishbein, 1979) that finds that attitudes toward an object and attitudes toward a behavior are different. For example, college students' attitudes toward Jaguar and Mercedes cars were hardly related to their attitudes toward buying one of these cars (Ajzen & Fishbein, 1980, p. 161).

D. SUMMARY

We examine how the valence of an event can be conceptualized as goal supportive deviation from one or more neutral events. While a goal can serve to create a distribution of events in terms of their goal supportiveness, "the ease of constructing a mental model" of events can serve to determine the neutral area of such a distribution. The ease of constructing a mental model could also account for adaptation effects that would shift the neutral area as a function of the frequent or recent experience of events.

We expect ease of constructing a mental model to influence the valence of events, especially when the events are not extremely goal supportive or goal unsupportive. Thus, this heuristic should be especially important for our question of where the boundary between positive and negative valence quality is situated. Further, factors suggested elsewhere to promote heuristic information processing (Chaiken, Liberman, & Eagly, 1989; Sherman & Corty, 1984) should also promote heuristic information processing here, that is, factors such as limited cognitive capacity or low involvement. Finally, we expect ease of constructing a mental model to influence the valence of events when a judgment of valence could reasonably be based on a frequency distribution, such as in our cabdriver example (given that minimal or maximal goals are not active and that prototypically goal supportive or goal impeding events are not highly accessible).

It should be noted that there are means of generating valence that can be regarded as a transition case between the principle of membership status and the principle of referential status. Higgins and King (1981), for example, distinguish the concepts of "identification as" and "identification with." *Identification* of an event *as* belonging to a valenced construct would clearly be an instance of the principle of membership status. However, *identification* of an event *with* a construct would refer to drawing an analogy with the construct, for example, as in saying that a trip was like a nightmare. On the one hand, the trip is associated with a nightmare; on the other hand, it is not categorized as an actual nightmare but as being related to a nightmare in some key respects, including its valence.

VI. The Principle of Response Elicitation

In this section we suggest that individuals sometimes observe other peoples' responses or their own external or internal responses to an event and infer the valence of the event from these responses. In other words, people's implicit or explicit theories about responses include the valence of events as causes for responses. Moreover, people at times infer the valence of an event from observing a response to the event. The principle of response elicitation, then, is clearly attributional in character.

A. OBSERVATION OF OTHERS' BEHAVIORS

We include in others' behaviors both direct communication as well as behaviors that were not intended as communications. People often infer the valence quality of events from being told by others that an event elicits a certain response or by being told directly about the valence quality of the events. Persuasion (e.g., Chaiken et al., 1989; Petty & Cacioppo, 1986) is one instance of this means of generating valence. The importance of persuasion as a specific case of intentionally communicating valence is underscored by the fact that many people spend a substantial amount of time trying to persuade others.

How do people infer valence quality from observing response that are not intended to communicate valence quality to them? We suggest that people have implicit or explicit theories of behavior according to which positive events should cause approach motivation and which negative events should cause avoidance motivation, motivations which in turn are associated with approach and avoidance *behavior*, respectively. Under limited conditions observers try to infer valence quality from the direction of movement; that is, they try to infer a cause from an observed effect.

Directional movement toward (i.e., approach) or away (i.e., avoidance) can only take place in relation to a reference point. Observers have access only to the movement itself, not to the reference point, so they must assume a reference point and infer from the relation of the movement to the assumed reference point whether the movement involves approach or avoidance. Thus, the accuracy of inference about the direction of the movement depends on whether observers "guess" correctly the reference point used by the target. For example, is a rat that is running from a start box to a goal box approaching the goal box or avoiding the start box? The problem is that the observer has to infer cause from effect in a situation where there are several potential causes for an observed action. The movement from start box to goal box could have been caused by the rat approaching one reference point or by it avoiding another. Because there are usually more than just two potential reference points, the problem is even more severe. Assume that without the knowledge of the observer, our rat has been fed in the goal box but has been mildly shocked by touching a red plate that has to be crossed in order to reach the goal box, and that the animal is currently moving again toward the red plate. The observer could come to the wrong conclusion that the red plate is positively valenced, when in fact, it is negatively valenced and the rat is only approaching it to reach the goal box.

Nevertheless, we suggest that when cues about valence quality are weak or ambiguous (i.e., when valence is uncertain), observers use a *movement heuristic* to infer valence quality from a movement that is observed in relation to an assumed reference point. According to this heuristic, when a reference point is approached, positive valence quality is inferred, and when a reference point is avoided, negative valence quality is inferred.

When approach and avoidance are inconsistent over time, a boundary region between positive and negative valence quality is inferred. The movement heuristic has a high potential for erroneous conclusions because it favors a single cause for an effect where other causes could be at work (cf. Beebe-Center, 1932). This type of weakness has been identified for other heuristics as well (Nisbett & Ross, 1980).

Different individuals might have differently elaborated movement heuristics. For example, in addition to the movement direction, some may take acceleration into account. They may take into account how the movement changes over time; that is, if our rat only avoids the start box, it should slow down over time, and if it only approaches the goal box, it should speed up over time (cf. Miller, 1959). Thus, the observer might infer from a decelerated movement that the rat is avoiding the start box because the box has negative valence quality. In this case the same problem of inferring a cause from an effect arises, however. Although decelerated movement could have been caused by the increasing distance from a negatively valenced start box, other factors could have caused the decelerated movement, such as not overshooting an approached goal,[8] or trying to avoid the red, electrifying plate on the way to the goal box.[9] In summary, we suggest that when information is weak or ambiguous, people sometimes use a movement heuristic to infer valence quality, even though such inferences have a potential for error.

B. SELF-OBSERVATION OF ACTUAL BEHAVIOR

Bem's (1972) self-perception theory (1972) suggests the following:

> Individuals come to "know" their own attitudes, emotions, and other internal states partially by inferring them from observations of their own overt behavior and/or the circumstances in which this behavior occurs. Thus, to the extent that internal cues are weak, ambiguous, or uninterpretable, the individual is functionally in the same position as an outside observer, an observer who must necessarily rely upon those same external cues to infer the individual's inner states. (p. 2)

Consistent with Bem, we suggest that when internal cues are weak, ambiguous, or uninterpretable (i.e., when direct information about valence

---

[8] We are grateful to Charles Wright for bringing to our attention the issue of "overshooting" in the context of control systems.

[9] The information that can be deduced from acceleration bear an interesting similarity to Carver and Scheier's (1990a) suggestions concerning acceleration. They suggest that accelerated movement toward a reference point (i.e., approach) leads to exhilaration, and that decelerated progress toward a reference point leads to "deexhilaration." Exhilaration has positive valence quality and "deexhilaration" has negative valence quality.

is unavailable or when information from which valence could be inferred is undiagnostic), individuals may draw inferences about valence quality from observing their own (psychological and physical) movements. When an individual does not know whether to enter a certain restaurant, he or she might infer from his or her hesitation that the last visit to the restaurant was not pleasurable. Likewise, as someone is moving away from a conversation at a party, he or she might infer from that action that he or she does not enjoy the conversation, forgetting that originally he or she wanted to have a look out the window. Evidence in the area of attitudes supports the assumption that the influence of self-perception is limited to cases when people hold very weak prior attitudes or none at all (Fazio, 1987). Our previous conclusions about drawing inferences from approach and avoidance behavior for observing others also apply for observing oneself, including the possibility of erroneous inferences.

In their analysis of action slips, Heckhausen and Beckmann (1990) provide anecdotal evidence about persons carrying out actions for which they cannot retrieve the goal that originally prompted the action, and about situations in which actions are started by one goal but are then changed to other actions before goal completion, all without awareness of the initiating goal. For example, a professor goes to his bedroom to change his tie for dinner, but then goes to bed instead. Both actions share the initial act of removing the tie. However, losing awareness of the goal that started an action could produce such action slips. Assuming incorrect reference points should be less common, though, when observing self instead of others. Indeed, Heckhausen and Beckmann point out that action slips are often accompanied by a feeling that something is amiss.

C. SELF-OBSERVATION OF SIMULATED BEHAVIOR

Andersen's (1984) data suggest that people not only make inferences from their own behavior but also from their thoughts and feelings. Elaborating this notion, it might not be necessary for people to observe their actual behaviors. They might make use of a simulation heuristic (Kahneman & Tversky, 1982b) in which they construct a model of an event and infer that the model requiring the least effort (i.e., the easiest) to construct reflects their most likely behavior. Thus, a potential restaurant patron might just sit at home and infer from having less difficulty constructing a model of entering the restaurant than of not entering it that she likes the restaurant. If the model easiest to construct is one in which she hesitates when entering the restaurant, she should infer that the restaurant is neutral or slightly negative in valence quality. Heckhausen and Beckmann (1990) also provide examples of action slips caused by a person only thinking about an action.

D. SELF-OBSERVATION OF MOTIVATIONAL ORIENTATION

Just as directional movement needs a reference point, so does motivational orientation. A reference point evaluated negatively should produce avoidance motivation (ie., a motivation to increase the distance to the reference point), and a reference point evaluated positively should produce approach motivation (i.e., a motivation to decrease the distance to the reference point) (cf. Carver & Scheier, 1990b). Thus, it is not necessary for individuals to observe their actual movements. They might use introspections of their motivations to approach or avoid. For example, standing in front of the restaurant and feeling an urge to go inside should be enough for concluding that the restaurant has positive valence quality, at least at that point in time.

The motivation to approach or avoid an event could at times precede the evaluation of the event. Such an effect might occur when a motivation to approach or avoid is carried over from an unfinished attempt to satisfy a now forgotten goal. If the active motivation is associated with a new reference point, the valence quality of that reference point might be erroneously inferred from the active motivation, provided that other cues for the valence quality of the reference point are weak.

Evidence supports the idea that motivation to achieve a goal remains active until the goal is acheived, even when the person is not involved in any goal-directed activities (Kuhl, 1986; Lewin, 1935). When people are interrupted at a task before they can reach a goal, they will spontaneously resume the task at a later time unless they have completed another task with substitution value (Ovsiankina, 1928). Zeigarnik (1927) also showed that recall for interrupted activities is better than for completed activities. Intentions to carry out an activity also have effects on memory accessibility (see Gollwitzer, 1993). There is some evidence that a motivation aroused in one task can be carried over into a very different task. Participants with a predominant hope for success were interrupted before they could solve an achievement-related "mastermind" problem designed to activate an achievement motivation. In a subsequent target-shooting game, they performed better than a "hope for success" control group that had been interrupted at reading a story. This difference was not observed for participants with a predominant fear of failure (Kuhl & Koch, 1984).

Self-observations of one's emotions might also be informative about the valence of events in the same way as self-observations of one's motivational orientation. Again we point out that the emotion (or the motivation) could be caused by something totally unrelated to the event at hand. As long as a person perceives the emotion or motivation as a result of the event, he or she will find the emotion or motivation diagnostic for the valence of the event. In this specific case it would not be circular to explain the judged valence of the event in terms of the felt emotion, because the emotion would not actually have been caused by the event.

E. SUMMARY

According to the principle of response elicitation people assume that the valence quality of an event acts as a cause for a response, and then they infer from their responses to events the valence quality of the events. We identified two basic ways of making such inferences, namely, communicating about valence and using a movement heuristic. When employing a movement heuristic people must assume a reference point for the response, and to infer the event's valence quality, they might observe someone else's responses, their own actual responses, their own simulated responses, their own motivational orientation, or their own emotional responses.

VII. Implications

A. RELATIONS AMONG THE PRINCIPLES OF JUDGING VALENCE

In our discussion we have mainly examined the sources of perceived valence of an event. As a secondary issue we have paid attention to the nature of the transition from negative to positive valence quality. We have identified four principles of generating valence: goal supportiveness, membership status, referential status, and response elicitation. We have also examined the way in which people might actually implement these principles.

Goal supportiveness of events for high-identity goals orders events continuously in terms of valence without categorizing them according to positive or negative valence quality. Thus, the principle of goal supportiveness is relevant to solving an ordering problem. The principle of membership status is relevant to the actual judgment of goal supportiveness, such as through representativeness or ease of categorization.

To determine the valence quality of an event, a reference point is needed that separates the ordered event dimensions into areas of positive and negative valence quality. Thus a reference point problem has to be solved. A perceiver, for example, could infer a neutral reference point by means of the ease of constructing a mental model of events. However, this means for separating positive from negative valence quality presupposes that the ordering problem has been solved. Only after both the ordering problem and the reference point problem have been solved are inferences about the valence quantity of an event possible. The greater the distance of an event on the dimension of goal supportiveness from the reference point separating valence qualities, the larger the valence quantity.

Most judgments of valence require the principle of goal supportiveness along with other principles. Classical conditioning, as one of the principles of membership status, might be one exception because it can associate an initially neutral event with an unconditioned stimulus that has "wired-in valence." Thus, neither of these two stimuli need to receive their valence through the principle of goal supportiveness. Another possible exception might be cases using the principle of response elicitation, such as observing one's own motivational orientation to approach or avoid.

B. ANOTHER LOOK AT AVOIDANCE MOTIVATION

Carver and Scheier (1981, 1990a) identify two potential problems that occur in isolated positive feedback loops. In the following, we examine how these problems are circumvented in our model by not viewing positive feedback loops in isolation (cf. Carver, in press) but rather by embedding them in a system of high-identity goals, low-identity goals, and strategic goals.

1. The Potential Problem of Lacking a Stop Rule

As Carver and Scheier (1990a) explained from a cybernetic perspective, approach motivation can be thought of as a negative feedback loop because it reduces the distance to an aspired reference value. In contrast, avoidance motivation can be thought of as a positive feedback loop because it increases the distance to a nonaspired reference value. We conceptualized the strategic goals that are subordinate to minimal versus maximal goals as involving positive versus negative feedback loops, respectively. So far we have not explicitly discussed the important assumption for minimal goals that positive feedback loops at the strategic level are usually subordinate to negative feedback loops at the superordinate level (cf. Carver, in press). Because of this assumption, in our model positive feedback loops occur only on the strategic goal level subordinate to minimal goals. For example, a person with the high-identity goal of being friendly could have a minimal goal of carrying on conversations for at least 2 mins. The minimal goal would have a negative feedback loop because it would aim at reducing any discrepancy between the length of a conversation and the valued end state of lasting at least 2 mins. In turn, a minimal goal would be implemented by subordinate strategic goals that avoid events incompatible with the minimal goal. Such a strategic goal could be to "avoid speech acts that cut off conversations." This goal can be conceived of as a positive feedback loop because it aims at increasing the discrepancy between the current style of conversation and speech acts that cut off conversations. Once the 2 min have passed, the minimal goal has been reached, the subordinate strategic goal of avoiding incompatible acts is stopped, and the person is free to move on.

Carver and Scheier (1981) hypothesized that positive feedback loops are potentially unadaptive because they do not have a criterion that stops increasing the distance to the reference value with the resulting possibility of an endless cycle. Therefore, as the authors suggest, positive feedback loops would have to be embedded in negative feedback loops that stop the positive loop at some point. Although we are silent on how the stop-rule problem is generally solved, we suggest on the basis of these hypotheses that the positive feedback loops on the strategic goal level of minimal goals are constrained by a stop rule provided by the superordinate level of minimal goals. Recall that our mountain climber increased the distance to the dangerous crevasse (i.e., positive feedback loop) until he or she reached the minimal safety distance (i.e., stop rule provided by the minimal goal), thus ensuring that he or she does not run away from the crevasse forever.

It should also be noted that high-identity goals, despite the involvment of negative feedback loops, also lack a stop rule. This is so because there is no final attainment of such abstract goals. For example, to support the goal of "being a fair person" one must constantly display goal-supportive behavior. There is no stop rule indicating when one has reached the goal of being a fair person. This is why our model needs a minimum of three levels of identity in the goal hierarchy. The high-identity level does not provide a stop rule for subordinate levels. Because we assume that avoidance motivation exists, but also that it has to be constrained by a stop rule, there is need for an intermediate level (i.e., the low-identity level) that provides a stop rule for positive feedback loops at the lowest level (i.e., the strategic level).

2. The Potential Problem of Lacking Direction

Carver and Scheier further point out that a positive feedback system "by itself is not very adaptive in the longer term, because it doesn't guide behavior anywhere (unless the dimension in question is clearly defined and bipolar). It just creates increasing deviations in whatever direction the present state happens to be leaning. . . ." (Carver & Scheier, 1981, p. 164; see also Powers, 1973, p. 45). This lack-of-direction argument is quite similar to Lewin's (1935) discussion about punishment of the child in which he claims that punishment leads to leaving the field unless preventive measures are taken. To solve the lack of direction problem, Carver (in press) suggested that a positive feedback system is usually bounded by a negative feedback system, which does guide behavior into a specific direction. Consistent with this argument the positive feedback loops in our model are subordinate to higher level goals (minimal and high identity goals), they are not an isolated positive feedback system. Thus, the lack-of-direction argument does not apply. The potentially nondirectional influence of positive feedback loops on behavior should be "funneled" by superordinate goals (e.g., high-identity levels). The direction of movement should be a result of both the positive feedback loops and the superordinate negative feedback loops. For example, our mountain climber should not avoid the crevasse by running in any direction but rather by increasing his distance from it in a way that minimizes his distance to the top of the mountain. In addition, the stop rule ensures that if a direction of movement is unsupportive of superordinate goals, a supportive direction is resumed as soon as the positive feedback loop is stopped.

It is possible that several directions of avoidance movement are equally supportive of a superordinate goal. Even then the direction of avoidance movements can be further funneled by psychological barriers. A barrier can be set up by internalized superordinate goals for which certain directions of avoidance movements are unsupportive. Such superordinate goals can be moral values or social standards, for example, a parent's saying, "Remember you are a good girl," or a playmate's saying, "Boys don't do this" (Lewin, 1935). Thus, if movement toward one specific superordinate goal can be achieved by several directions of avoidance on the strategic level of identity, other superordinate goals can set up barriers that limit the direction of avoidance movements. Because leaving the field impedes superordinate goals, it is often so negatively valenced that it is not even considered as an avoidance alternative.

3. Costs and Benefits of Avoidance Motivation

A benefit of avoidance motivation is highlighted when one conceptualizes self-regulation in field theoretical terms (Lewin, 1935, 1951a). It becomes clear that feedback loops must deal with barriers in the life space. Keeping a distance from a barrier must be coordinated with decreasing the distance to the original goal. We illustrate this with our example of the mountain climber who wants to reach the top without falling into crevasses. In Lewinian terms, approach and avoidance vectors would add up to a resultant vector that would get the climber closer to the top while circumventing the crevasses. We believe that the real world is full of crevasses around which people have to navigate constantly in order to arrive at their aspired destinations, and that minimal goals with their subordinate positive feedback loops could serve exactly that function. A list of everyday crevasses could include being overrun by a car, breaking a law, contracting a disease, failing an exam, or hurting someone's feelings. We reported previously that defensive pessimists are motivated by avoiding failure (Norem & Cantor, 1986b). However, their strategy to avoid failure is in the service of a superordinate goal that they want to obtain (i.e., approach), such as being a top student.

Although we have described how avoidance motivation can be beneficial in terms of guiding behavior around obstacles, we should point out that it can also be maladaptive because the emotions it produces (e.g., fear) can disrupt other goal-directed activities. This might be especially the case when a lot of psychological barriers exist that serve as multiple sources of fear. Lewin (1935) identifies two maladaptive effects of barriers: leaving the field by flying into unreality (e.g., daydreaming) and suicide as the last resort. In summary, minimal goals and their subordinate positive feedback loops can be adaptive because they allow circumvention of barriers, but they can also be maladaptive because their effects can disrupt behavior related to other goals. The fear associated with minimal goals can motivate behavior compatible with superordinate goals, but it can also disrupt such behavior if a person cannot cope with the fear.

C. IMPLICATIONS FOR ATTITUDES

Definitions of attitudes vary widely (for a review, e.g., Zanna & Rempel, 1988), but all definitions seem to incorporate the notion of an evaluative judgment (see also Eagly & Chaiken, 1993). How might some existing models of attitude formation and change relate to our four principles of judging valence (see also Sections III to VI)?

1. The Principle of Goal-Supportiveness as a Source of Attitudes

Rosenberg's (1956) principle of instrumentality (i.e., beliefs that an attitude object facilitates or blocks the attainment of important values) is similar to the principle of goal supportiveness. Rather than proposing that instrumentality can be a source for attitudes, however, Rosenberg focuses on how attitudes toward objects are correlated with instrumentality. Thus, he does not examine cause and effect relationships between attitudes and instrumentality. It might be fruitful to examine more systematically the role of goal supportiveness as a source of attitudes.

2. The Principle of Membership Status as a Source of Attitudes

Theories of attitudes have made use of the principle of membership status. As we discussed earlier, investigators have explained attitude formation in terms of classical conditioning (for a review Eagly & Chaiken, 1993). Attitudes have been described in terms of an association between a given object and a given evaluative category (Fazio, Jeaw-Mei, McDonel, & Sherman, 1982a). The strength of this association determines the accessibility of the attitude. The stronger the membership of an object in an evaluative category, the stronger the attitude. This is revealed, for example, in the finding that repeated expression of the evaluation of an object increases attitude accessibility (Fazio et al., 1982a). In contrast to classical conditioning, however, this model makes use of the principle of membership status to define an attitude rather than to explain the source of an attitude, and attitude strength is not the same as the positivity or negativity of the attitude.

We are not aware of any attitude models that make explicit use of two other cases of the principle of membership status, namely, representativeness and ease of categorization.

3. The Principle of Referential Status as a Source of Attitudes

The principle of referential status is reflected in Ostrom and Upshaw's (1968) perspective model for attitudes. This model predicts attitude ratings as a function of so-called "upper and lower perspective end anchors" that correspond to valued reference points at the extreme ends of the attitude continuum. For example, prison charges were judged more sternly when the maximum length of a sentence that participants considered was 5 instead of 30 years.

Eiser and Stroebe's (1972; see also Eiser & van der Pligt, 1988) accentuation theory approach to social judgment can also be viewed as an instance of the principle of referential status. The approach explains how individuals make evaluative judgments of statements about a certain topic, for example, drug use. The judgments are made in terms of an attribute dimension. For example, participants might rate the statement, "all drugs should be legal," along the attribute dimension of permissiveness. The accentuation theory approach suggests that individuals not only relate a specific statement about drug use to the attribute dimension (e.g., permissiveness), but that they also relate the statement to two additional reference dimensions, one being the valence of the judged attribute itself (e.g., whether high permissiveness has positive or negative valence quality for the participant) and one being the acceptableness of the particular statement to the participant (e.g., whether legalizing all drugs has positive or negative valence quality for the participant).

Thus, two reference scales are superimposed on the attribute scale. These two reference scales can be either evaluatively congruent or incongruent. For example, for a judge who positively values legalization of drugs as well as permissiveness, both scales are congruent. However, for a judge who positively values permissiveness but negatively values legalization of drugs, these two scales are incongruent. The model predicts that when several statements (e.g., "all drug use should be punished") are rated along the same dimension, such as permissiveness, differences between the statements a judge accepts and rejects will be accentuated when the two reference scales are congruent. For incongruent dimensions, however, this accentuation should not take place. Thus, our first judge who agrees with drug legalization should rate the two statements as more different in terms of the permissiveness that they express than our second judge. The reasoning is that if two reference scales are congruent, they are positively correlated cues that, because of their "agreement," provide additional information about the difference between the two statements. In summary, the referential status of statements in relation to the valence quality of two valenced reference points (as part of the two superimposed reference scales) influences evaluative judgments of these statements.

Whereas both of these models employ referential status regarding valenced reference points, we are not aware of attitude models that make use of referential status regarding neutral reference points.

4. The Principle of Response Elicitation as a Source of Attitudes

As mentioned previously, the principle of response elicitation is reflected in the extensive research on persuasion (e.g., Chaiken et al., 1989; Petty & Cacioppo, 1986) and, especially, on self-perception theory (Bem, 1972; Fazio, 1987). Persuasion focuses on the impact of communications about attitude objects on attitude formation and attitude change, and self-perception theory is concerned with the impact of individuals' own responses (including verbal statements) on their attitudes. To our knowledge, the observation of another person's noncommunicative behavior, the self-observation of simulated behavior, or the self-observaton of motivational orientation have not been considered as sources of attitudes.

5. Exploring Conditions of Attitude Formation

It might be useful for investigators to examine when and how principles of judging valence act together to form an attitude. For example, self-perception theory has been found to be applicable when weak or no prior attitudes exist (Fazio, 1987). We stress that it would be useful to know more about the interrelatedness of the principles of judging valence in order to predict when specific principles will influence judgments of valence. For example, if a person is committed to a specific low-identity goal and is currently planning the implementation of this goal (see Gollwitzer, 1990), then we would expect this low-identity goal to be a prime candidate as a source of valence. In contrast, a heuristic for computing a neutral reference point is unlikely to be used once a low-identity goal has been set because the low-identity goal leaves little room for neutral events. On the other hand, the use of a neutral reference point can precede the setting of a low-identity goal. Let us reconsider the example in which you are a cabdriver and have determined by means of ease of generating a mental model that a 10% tip is neutral. As a consequence you might set the minimal goal of getting at least a 10% tip from the customers who are about to enter your cab. On the other hand, consider the student whose minimal goal is to get an A. She won't have much interest in determining the central tendency of the grade distribution. Even if she knew that A- was above the central tendency, she would still regard it as a negative grade. In conclusion, assuming that different avenues to attitude formation are interdependent, progress can be made in predicting the conditions of attitude formation.

If different principles of attitude formation lead to different attitudes, and if people have some control over the process of attitude formation, then people might influence their attitudes in order to satisfy high-identity goals. A student before an exam could increase the negativity of failing or the positivity of doing well in order to study harder. People could also change their attitudes in order to cope with stressful events. This is consistent with suggestions that unrealistically positive views of oneself and the world can boost well-being (Taylor & Brown, 1988).

D. IMPLICATIONS FOR EMOTIONS

Some of the factors for judging valence that we identified might be useful in predicting the type and intensity of experienced emotions. Our basic assumption is that experiencing an event as valenced causes an emotional experience. This does not preclude situations where an emotion is produced without awareness of valence, and then the emotion's valence influences the experienced valence of the event such as in the case of "sense-feelings" (cf. Reisenzein & Schönpflug, 1992). In addition, emotional experiences influence motivation and action. We basically agree with the hedonic principle that people are motivated to experience positive emotional states and to avoid experiencing negative emotional states (cf. Lopes, 1987, but see Parrott, 1993). Thus, emotional consequences can provide an individual with the motivation to carry out an action. However, emotions can also interfere with actions, such as when unsuccessful coping with fear interferes with current activities. Note that resources for savoring positive emotions are limited (Linville & Fischer, 1991), just as resources for coping with negative emotions are limited. Thus, positive emotions can also be disruptive, such as when happiness about a positive event is so intense that it is not possible to concentrate on anything else.

1. Breaking the Circular Reasoning about the Valence of Emotions and the Valence of Events

It is quite common to define a positive or negative emotion such as pleasure or pain, respectively, as one caused by a positively or negatively valenced event. It is also common to define a positively or negatively valenced event as one that causes positive or negative emotions. If both views are used concurrently, we are faced with circular reasoning. For example, once we explain the pleasure that a cabdriver feels from the positive valence quality of receiving a 20% tip, we cannot argue that the tip has positive valence quality because the cab driver feels happy about receiving it. By describing the valence quality of an event independent of its effect on emotions, we could avoid this circularity. The principles of judging valence identified in this paper allow an independent description of the valence quality of an event by identifying its sources independent of its relation to emotions. For example, the positive versus negative valence quality of an event can be described in terms of violating or achieving a low-identity goal, of membership with a valenced representation, of being related to a neutral or valenced reference point, or as being judged as eliciting an approach or avoidance response. We could argue, for example, that as a cabdriver you have determined the positiveness of the 20% tip by relating it to the neutral reference point of a 10% tip determined via ease of generating a mental model. We could then argue that your emotions are positive as a result of the positive valence of receiving the 20% tip. In this way, the valence quality of an emotion can be described in terms of the valence quality of an emotion-eliciting event (cf. Ortony et al., 1988) in which the source of the event's valence quality is independent of the emotion. Of course, we need to further investigate the sources of our emotion-eliciting conditions. For example, we need to ask, as some investigators have done (e.g., Atkinson & Birch, 1970; Bargh, 1990; Lewin et al., 1944), what the sources of goal setting are.

2. Categorization Variables for Emotions

Ortony et al. (1988) defined types of emotions by considering the eliciting conditions they share independent of the emotion words that describe each of the emotions. Ortony et al. explicitly excluded variables that influence the intensity of the emotion as distinguishing criteria for emotion categories. By taking principles of judging valence into account, the valence quality of an event can be used without circularity as a categorization variable for positive versus negative emotions. In addition, it has been suggested (Higgins, in press-a) that the type of psychological situation within each valence quality (e.g., for positive valence quality, the presence of a positive outcome or the absence of a negative outcome) can serve as a categorization variable for emotions. Although Roseman and colleagues (Roseman 1984, 1991; Roseman et al., 1990) use a different terminology, their research suggests and provides some evidence for this viewpoint. In their studies, the experienced emotions[10] associated with the two positively valenced psychological situations are "joy" for the presence of a positive outcome and "relief" for the absence of a negative outcome. The emotions associated with the two negatively valenced psychological situations are "distress" for the presence of a negative outcome and "sorrow" for the absence of a positive outcome. In a similar fashion, Feather (1963) argued that discon-firmed hope motivation leads to disappointment (i.e., negative affect) and that disconfirmed fear motivation leads to relief (i.e., positive affect). Further, there is evidence that self-discrepancies representing the presence of a negative outcome are associated with negative agitation emotions, such as tension, and that self-discrepancies representing the absence of a positive outcome are associated with negative dejection emotions, such as sadness (for reviews Higgins, 1987, 1989, in press-a). In summary, evidence supports the importance of both valence quality and the type of psychological situation within valence quality as categorization variables for emotions.

The resulting four psychological situations include another factor, namely, the presence versus the absence of a valenced outcome, as seen, for example, in the presence versus the absence of a positive outcome. Thus, one can distinguish *presence emotions* from *absence emotions.* We have already reported behavioral evidence that the absence of a valenced outcome is of opposite valence quality than its presence (Adelman & Maatsch 1956; Gray, 1971; Lawler, 1965). Similarly, for the same valenced reference event, presence emotions are of opposite valence quality than absence emotions. For the presence of a positive outcome as a reference event, for example, joy (i.e., presence emotion) has a valence quality oppo-

---

[10] We refer here to only the group of emotions that Roseman (1984) might call "certainty emotions," or which Stern (1935) would call "retrospective" emotions (see later).

site from that of sadness (i.e., an absence emotion), and for the presence of a negative outcome as a reference event, tension (i.e., a presence emotion) has a valence quality opposite from that of relief (i.e., an absence emotion).

The existence of absence emotions resolves apparently paradoxical phenomena. For example, a person who gets a free draw in a lottery and does not win has not really lost anything in relation to the beginning of the episode, so one might assume that he or she should feel no emotion. Johnson's (1986) data, however, suggest that this person would feel negative emotions. According to our model, winning the lottery has positive valence for the individual, perhaps because of inferences from response elicitation or because of a set goal. Thus, not winning is the absence of a positive outcome and should produce a negative affect (e.g., disappointment). In summary, the valence quality of an event, its type of psychological situation within valence quality, and the representation of the event as the presence versus the absence of a valenced outcome can serve as categorization variables for emotions. It is possible that some emotions are caused by fewer eliciting factors than other emotions. "Contentment," for example, might be elicited by the positive valence quality of an event so that both "calmness" and "satisfaction" resulting from the absence of a negative outcome and the presence of a positive outcome, respectively, share the simultaneous experience of contentment. In addition, there are certainly other eliciting conditions of emotions that result in further dividing our emotion categories (cf. Ortony et al., 1988; Roseman, 1984). For example, the absence of a negative outcome, such as the healing of an illness, would cause relief when attributed to situational circumstances, liking when attributed to another person, and maybe pride or self-satisfaction when attributed to oneself.

3. Intensity Variables for Emotions

Some of the principles for judging valence also have implications for the intensity of experienced affect. The larger the valence quantity of an event, the more intense the experienced emotions should be.

We assume that high-identity goals will have different degrees of importance for the individual. The importance of the high-identity goals should be passed on to the specific goals. Schank and Abelson (1977) point out the case in which priorities of abstract goals change and lead to changes also in the implementation of more specific goals; that is, the importance of high-identity goals is passed on to subordinate levels. Thus, we hypothesize that a particular outcome will elicit stronger affect when the associated superordinate goals are of higher importance to the individual.

We would like to revive a forgotten categorization of emotions, namely the distinction between *prospective* emotions and *retrospective* emotions (Stern 1935), that is, emotions that refer to future events (e.g., hope, fear) versus past events (e.g., joy, annoyance). According to Roseman (1984) the difference between hope and joy, for example, lies in their reference to an uncertain versus a certain event, respectively. Although prospective emotions usually refer to uncertain events, they can sometimes refer to certain events. For example, when your flight is delayed and you are told that you will make the connecting flight because the plane will wait, you feel relief in respect to a future event that is now certain. Similarly, retrospective emotions usually refer to certain events, but they can at times refer to events that are uncertain (e.g., the fear of parents who do not know whether their child was involved in an accident that took place). The concept of certainty is relevant here because certainty is a likelihood concept, and likelihood has an important influence on the intensity of emotions.

We suggest that the subjective likelihood that a specific outcome is (or was) going to take place will influence the intensity of the experienced emotions. The more likely an uncertain prospective event seems subjectively, the more intense the experienced emotion. For example, the higher an individual perceives the likelihood to be that the dentist will pull a tooth, the more he or she should be afraid, yet the negative valence of a tooth being pulled should not vary.

For retrospective events that are certain, the emotional amplification hypothesis of norm theory (Kahneman & Miller, 1986) should apply. According to this hypothesis, the more surprising (i.e., abnormal) an event, the more intense the experienced emotion (cf. Kahneman & Miller, 1986; Miller et al., 1990). According to norm theory, however, surprise is not just a disconfirmed a priori expectation. In addition to disconfirmed a priori expectations, computations that take place after the event has happened can influence surprise (Kahneman & Miller, 1986). We conceive of these a posteriori computations as an a posteriori likelihood concept, that is, a likelihood computed after the event has happened. The more likely an event seems a priori, the less surprising it is if it takes place (i.e., it produces less intense presence emotions), and the more surprising it is, if it does not take place (i.e., it produces more intense absence emotions). Imagine that the airplane you want to board is overbooked by just one seat, and you have volunteered to give up your seat to wait for the next flight. If your seat is needed, you will receive a flight certificate worth $2000. You would like to be selected for this bonus, but it is not clear yet whether your seat will be needed because with a few minutes left before takeoff, either 1 passenger or 20 passengers with reserved seats have not yet checked in. When the number of passengers not yet checked in is 20 instead of only

1, you are less likely to be selected, because the likelihood is higher than 1 of 20 passengers will not show up (to eliminate the 1 overbooked seat). Probably, you would be less surprised if you were selected when being selected is more likely (i.e., when 1 passenger instead of 20 passengers is missing), and you would feel less pleased about actually being selected. On the other hand, you probably would be more surprised about *not* being selected when 1 passenger instead of 20 is missing, and you would feel more disappointed about actually not being selected.

Similarly, the more likely an event seems a posteriori, the less surprising it is if it took place (i.e., less intense presence emotions), and the more surprising it is if it did not take place (i.e., more intense absence emotions). Imagine that before takeoff you did not know how many passengers were still missing. After you are told that you are selected, you are also told that either only 1 passenger was missing or that there were 20 missing. You would probably react as in the a priori example. When selection is more likely in hindsight (i.e., you are less surprised to be selected), you would probably feel less pleased to be selected. However, it would be more surprising *not* to be selected and consequently more disappointing.

The emotional amplification hypothesis (i.e., "surprise amplifies affect") is well supported for retrospective events that are certain by vignette-type studies (Johnson, 1986; Kahneman & Miller, 1986; Kahneman & Tversky, 1982b; Landman, 1987; Miller, 1984 cited in Miller et al., 1990; Miller & McFarland, 1987). Further, for an achievement task Feather (1969) reported that the less confident the participants were before the task that they would succeed, the more satisfied they were after having succeeded (i.e., surprise amplified satisfaction).

It has been found that among individuals who chronically aspire to possess more positive traits than they believe they actually possess, those who expect to possess those aspired traits in the future suffer more than those who do not have such an optimistic expectation (Higgins, Tykocinski, & Vookles, 1990). At first sight, this seems to contradict the proposed relation between likelihood and emotional intensity. Should not the individuals who expect to live up to their ideals feel better than their counterparts without this expectation? First, one has to determine whether the suffering of these individuals involves emotions concerning events that are certain or uncertain. Higgins et al. (1990) point out that the psychological situation as a whole for the individuals with the higher outcome expectancies is one of "chronically unfulfilled hopes." This is the case because they *chronically* do not meet their ideals. In contrast, the individuals with low outcome expectancies have "chronically unfulfilled wishes." A hope and a wish are the same type of emotion, but a hope is felt more intensely because the expectation is higher.[11] Chronically unfulfilled wishes or hopes refer to events that are certain; that is, it is certain that the hopes or wishes were not fulfilled in the past. Consistent with our model, people with chronically unfulfilled hopes suffer more than people with chronically unfulfilled wishes because it is more surprising for the former that they do not live up to their aspired traits (i.e., they feel more intense absence emotions).

There is considerable evidence that information has less impact on people and animals when it is represented as the absence of a feature rather than as the presence of a feature (Allison & Messick, 1988; Fazio, Sherman, & Herr, 1982b; Hearst, 1988; Higgins, 1976; Hovland & Weiss, 1953; Jenkins & Sainsburry, 1969, 1970; Miller, McDougall, & Zolman, 1988; Newman, Wolff, & Hearst, 1980; Smedslund, 1963; Ward & Jenkins, 1965; Wason & Johnson-Laird, 1972; for reviews Nisbett & Ross, 1980; Ross, 1977). Brendl et al. (in press) found that the rate of increasing emotional intensity as a function of increasing valence quantity was higher for presence emotions than for absence emotions. Although we did not measure the absolute degree of emotional intensity, it appears reasonable to propose on the basis of these findings that, everything else being equal, presence emotions are felt more intensely than absence emotions, except for those with extreme valence quantities (cf. Kahneman & Tversky, 1982a).

In summary, several variables have implications for the experienced intensity of emotions, namely, the valence quantity of an event, the importance of high-identity goals, the likelihood of an event, and the representation of an event as the presence versus the absence of a feature.

VIII. Final Comment

It was our goal to convince the reader that the valence of an event cannot be taken for granted and that, consequently, it is useful to explore what principles guide judgments of valence. Considering that valence (or hedonic value, or utility) is one of the most central variables in psychology, it is surprising how little attention has been devoted to the sources of valence. We hope that this discussion will stimulate interest in the question of why, as Lewin (1926b) put it, people perceive events as demanding approach or avoidance.

---

[11] Note that different emotion words apply to different intensities of the same type of emotion (Ortony et al., 1988), for example, terror, fear and apprehension.

Acknowledgments

We thank Ellen Crowe, Carol Dweck, Curtis Hardin, Kristi Lemm, Dale Miller, Fritz Strack, and Yaacov Trope for their helpful comments on previous drafts of this article. Correspondence concerning this article should be addressed to C. Miguel Brendl who is now at the Universität Konstanz, Fachgruppe Psychologie, Postfach 5560 D39, 78434 Konstanz, Germany; or to E. Tory Higgins, Department of Psychology, 406 Schermerhorn Hall, Columbia University, New York, NY 10027.

References

Adelman, H. M., & Maatsch, J. L. (1956). Learning and extinction based upon frustration, food reward, and exploratory tendency. *Journal of Experimental Psychology, 52,* 311–315.

Ajzen, I., & Fishbein, M. (1980). *Understanding attitudes and predicting social behavior.* Englewood Cliffs, NJ: Prentice Hall.

Allison, S. T., & Messick, D. M. (1988). The feature-positive effect, attitude strength, and degree of perceived consensus. *Personality and Social Psychology Bulletin, 14,* 231–241.

Anderson, R. N. (1977). The notion of schemata and the educational enterprise: General discussion of the conference. In R. C. Anderson, R. J. Spiro, & W. E. Montague (Eds.), *Schooling and the acquisition of knowledge* (pp. 415–431). Hillsdale, NJ: Wiley.

Andersen, S. M. (1984). Self-knowledge and social inference: II. The diagnosticity of cognitive/ affective and behavioral data. *Journal of Personality and Social Psychology, 46,* 294–307.

Asch, S. E. (1946). Forming impressions of personality. *Journal of Abnormal and Social Psychology, 41,* 258–290.

Asch, S. E. (1952). *Social psychology.* New York: Prentice Hall.

Atkinson, J. W. (1957). Motivational determinants of risk taking behavior. *Psychological Review, 64,* 359–372.

Atkinson, J. W. (1964). *An introduction to motivation.* Princeton, NJ: van Nostrand.

Atkinson, J. W., & Birch, D. (1970). *The dynamics of action.* New York: Wiley.

Bargh, J. A. (1990). Auto-motives: Preconscious determinants of social interaction. In E. T. Higgins & R. M. Sorrentino (Eds.), *Handbook of motivation and cognition. Foundations of social behavior* (Vol. 2, pp. 93–130). New York: Guilford.

Beebe-Center, J. G. (1932). *The psychology of pleasantness and unpleasantness.* New York: van Nostrand.

Bem, D. J. (1972). Self-perception theory. In L. Berkowitz (Ed.), *Advances in experimental social psychology* (Vol. 6, pp. 1–62). New York: Academic Press.

Bower, G. H., Black, J. B., & Turner, T. J. (1979). Scripts in memory for text. *Cognitive Psychology, 11,* 177–220.

Bransford, J. D., & Johnson, M. K. (1972). Contextual prerequisites for understanding: Some investigations of comprehension and recall. *Journal of Verbal Learning and Verbal Behavior, 11,* 717–726.

Brendl, C. M., & Higgins, E. T. (1995, March) *Heuristic decision making: Representativeness of means to ends.* Poster presented at the annual meeting of the Eastern Psychological Association, Boston, MA.

Brendl, C. M., Higgins, E. T., & Lemm, K. M. (1995). Sensitivity to varying gains and losses: The role of self-discrepancies and event framing. *Journal of Personality and Social Psychology, 69,* 1028–1051.

Brendl, C. M., Markman, A. B., & Higgins, E. T. (1995). *Unpublished research data.*

Brickman, P., & Campbell, D. T. (1971). Hedonic relativism and planning the good society. In M. H. Appley (Ed.), *Adaptation-level theory* (pp. 287–302). New York: Academic Press.

Campos, J. J., & Sternberg, C. R. (1981). Perception, appraisal and emotion: The onset of social referencing. In M. E. Lamb & L. R. Sherrod (Eds.), *Infant social cognition: Empirical and theoretical considerations* (pp. 273–314). Hillsdale, NJ: Erlbaum.

Carver, C. S. (in press). Some ways in which goals differ and some implications of those differences. In P. M. Gollwitzer & J. A. Bargh (Eds.), *The psychology of action: Linking cognition and motivation.* New York: Guilford.

Carver, C. S., & Scheier, M. F. (1981). *Attention and self-regulation: A control-theory approach to human behavior.* New York: Springer-Verlag.

Carver, C. S., & Scheier, M. F. (1990a). Origins and functions of positive and negative affect: A control-process view. *Psychological Review, 97,* 19–35.

Carver, S. C., & Schier, M. F. (1990b). Principles of self-regulation: Action and emotion. In E. T. Higgins & R. M. Sorrentino (Eds.), *Handbook of motivation and cognition. Foundations of social behavior* (Vol. 2, pp. 3–52). New York: Guilford.

Chaiken, S., Liberman, A., & Eagly, A. E. (1989). Heuristic and systematic information processing within and beyond the persuasion context. In J. S. Uleman & J. A. Bargh (Eds.), *Unintended thought* (pp. 212–252). New York: Guilford.

Cowart, B. J. (1981). Development of taste perception in humans: Sensitivity and preference throughout the life span. *Psychological Bulletin, 90,* 43–73.

Crozier, W. R. (1979). The interaction of value and subjective probability in risky decision-making. *British Journal of Psychology, 70,* 489–495.

DeCasper, A. J., & Fifer, W. P. (1980). Of human bonding: Newborns prefer their mothers' voices. *Science, 208,* 1174–1176.

DeCasper, A. J., & Sigafoos, A. D. (1983). The intrauterine heartbeat: A potent reinforcer for newborns. *Infant Behavior and Development, 6,* 19–25.

DeCasper, A. J., & Spence, M. J. (1986). Prenatal maternal speech influences newborns' perception of speech sounds. *Infant Behavior and Development, 9,* 133–150.

Dembo, T. (1931). Der Ärger als dynamisches Problem [Anger as dynamic problem]. *Psychologische Forschung, 15,* 1–144.

Eagly, A. H., & Chaiken, S. (1993). *The psychology of attitudes.* Fort Worth, TX: Harcourt Brace Jovanovich.

Einhorn, H. J., & Hogarth, R. M. (1986). Judging probable cause. *Psychological Bulletin, 99,* 3–19.

Eiser, J. R., & Stroebe, W. (1972). *Categorization and social judgement.* London: Academic Press.

Eiser, J. R., & van der Pligt, J. (1988). *Attitudes and decisions.* London: Routledge.

Escalona, S. K. (1940). The effect of success and failure upon the level of aspiration and behavior in manic-depressive psychoses. *University of Iowa Studies in Child Welfare, 16,* 199–302.

Fazio, R. H. (1987). Self-perception theory: A current perspective. In M. P. Zanna, J. M. Olson, & C. P. Herman (Eds.), *Social influence: The Ontario symposium* (Vol. 5, pp. 129–150). Hillsdale, NJ: Erlbaum.

Fazio, R. H., Jeaw-Mei, C., McDonel, E. C., & Sherman, S. J. (1982a). Attitude accessibility, attitude-behavior consistency, and the strength of the object-evaluation association. *Journal of Experimental Social Psychology, 18,* 339–357.

Fazio, R. H., Sherman, S. J., & Herr, P. M. (1982b). The feature-positive effect in the self-perception process: Does not doing matter as much as doing? *Journal of Personality and Social Psychology, 42,* 404–411.

Feather, N. T. (1963). Mowrer's revised two-factor theory and the motive-expectancy-value model. *Psychological Review, 70,* 500–515.

Feather, N. T. (1969). Attribution of responsibility and valence of success and failure in relation to initial confidence and task performance. *Journal of Personality and Social Psychology, 13,* 129–144.

Feather, N. T. (1982a). Actions in relation to expected consequences: An overview of a research program. In N. T. Feather (Ed.), *Expectations and actions: Expectancy-value models in psychology* (pp. 53–95). Hillsdale, NJ: Erlbaum.

Feather, N. T. (Ed.). (1982b). *Expectations and actions: Expectancy-value models in psychology.* Hillsdale, NJ: Erlbaum.

Festinger, L. (1942). Wish, expectation, and group standards as factors influencing level of aspiration. *Journal of Abnormal and Social Psychology, 37,* 184–200.

Fishbein, M. (1979). A theory of reasoned action: Some implications and applications. In H. E. Howe & M. M. Page (Eds.), *Nebraska Symposium on Motivation, 27* (pp. 65–116). Lincoln: University of Nebraska Press.

Frijda, N. H. (1988). The laws of emotion. *American Psychologist, 43,* 349–358.

Ganchrow, J. R., Steiner, J. E., & Daher, M. (1983). Neonatal facial expressions in response to different qualities and intensities of gustatory stimuli. *Infant Behavior and Development, 6,* 189–200.

Gollwitzer, P. M. (1990). Action phases and mind-sets. In E. T. Higgins & R. M. Sorrentino (Eds.), *Handbook of motivation and cognition. Foundations of social behavior* (Vol. 2, pp. 53–92). New York: Guilford.

Gollwitzer, P. M. (1993). Goal achievement: The role of intentions. *European Review of Social Psychology, 4,* 141–185.

Gould, R. (1939). An experimental analysis of "level of aspiration." *Genetic Psychology Monographs, 21,* 3–115.

Gray, J. (1971). *The psychology of fear and stress.* New York: McGraw-Hill.

Hearst, E. (1988). The feature-positive effect in pigeons: Conditionality, overall predictiveness, and type of feature. *Bulletin of the Psychonomic Society, 26,* 73–76.

Hebb, D. O. (1949). *The organization of behavior: A neuropsychological theory.* New York: Wiley.

Heckhausen, H. (1977). Achievement motivation and its constructs: A cognitive model. *Motivation and Emotion. 1,* 283–329.

Heckhausen, H., & Beckmann, J. (1990). Intentional action and action slips. *Psychological Review, 97,* 36–48.

Helson, H. (1948). Adaptation-level as a basis for a quantitative theory of frames of reference. *Psychological Review, 55,* 297–313.

Helson, H. (1964). *Adaptation-level theory.* New York: Harper & Row.

Helson, H. (1971). Adaptation-level theory: 1970 and after. In M. H. Appley (Ed.), *Adaptation-level theory* (pp. 5–17). New York: Academic Press.

Helson, H., S. Kozaki, (1968).

Herr, P. M., Sherman, S. J., & Fazio, R. H. (1983). On the consequences of priming: Assimilation and contrast effects. *Journal of Experimental Social Pscyhology, 19,* 323–340.

Higgins, E. T. (1976). Effects of presupposition on deductive reasoning. *Journal of Verbal Learning and Verbal Behavior, 15,* 419–430.

Higgins, E. T. (1987). Self-discrepancy: A theory relating self and affect. *Psychological Review, 94,* 319–340.

Higgins, E. T. (1989). Knowledge accessibility and activation: Subjectivity and suffering from unconscious sources. In J. S. Uleman & J. A. Bargh (Eds.), *Unintended thought* (pp. 75–123). New York: Guilford.

Higgins, E. T. (1990). Personality, social psychology, and person-situation relations: Standards and knowledge activation as a common language. In L. A. Peruvian (Ed.), *Handbook of personality: Theory and research* (pp. 301–338). New York: Guilford.

Higgins, E. T. (in press-a). Emotional experiences: The pains and pleasures of distinct regulatory systems. In R. D. Kavanaugh, B. Z. Glick, & S. Fein (Eds.), *Emotion: The G. Stanley Hall Symposium.* Hillsdale, NJ: Erlbaum.

Higgins, E. T. (in press-b). Ideals, oughts, and regulatory outcome focus: Relating affect and motivation to distinct pains and pleasures. In P. M. Gollwitzer & J. A. Bargh (Eds.), *The psychology of action: Linking motivation and cognition to behavior.* New York: Guilford.

Higgins, E. T. (in press-c). Knowledge activation: Accessibility, applicability, and salience. In E. T. Higgins & A. W. Kruglanski (Eds.), *Social psychology: Handbook of basic principles.* New York: Guilford.

Higgins, E. T., & King, G. (1981). Accessibility of social constructs: Information-processing consequences of individual and contextual variability. In N. Cantor & J. F. Kihlstrom (Eds.), *Personality, cognition, and social interaction* (pp. 69–121). Hillsdale, NJ: Erlbaum.

Higgins, E. T., & Rholes, W. S. (1976). Impression formation and role fulfillment: A "holistic reference" approach. *Journal of Experimental Social Psychology, 12,* 422–435.

Higgins, E. T., Rholes, W. S., & Jones, C. R. (1977). Category accessibility and impression formation. *Journal of Experimental Social Psychology, 13,* 141–154.

Higgins, E. T., Roney, C., Crowe, E., & Hymes, C. (1994). Ideal versus ought predilections for approach and avoidance: Distinct self-regulatory systems. *Journal of Personality and Social Psychology, 66,* 276–286.

Higgins, E. T., Strauman, T., & Klein, R. (1986). Standards and the process of self-evaluation. Multiple affects from multiple stages. In R. M. Sorrentino & E. T. Higgins (Eds.), *Handbook of motivation and cognition: Foundations of social behavior* (pp. 23–63). New York: Guilford.

Higgins, E. T., & Tykocinski, O. (1992). Self-discrepancies and biographical memory: Personality and cognition at the level of psychological situation. *Personality and Social Psychology Bulletin, 18,* 527–535.

Higgins, E. T., Tykocinski, O., & Vookles, J. (1990). Patterns of self-beliefs: The psychological significance of relations among the actual, ideal, ought, can, and future selves. In J. M. Olson & M. P. Zanna (Eds.), *Self-inference processes: The Ontario symposium* (Vol. 6, pp. 153–190). Hillsdale, NJ: Erlbaum.

Hilton, D. J., & Slugoski, B. R. (1986). Knowledge-based causal attribution: The abnormal conditions focus model. *Psychological Review, 93,* 75–88.

Hoppe, F. (1931). Erfolg und Mißerfolg [Success and failure]. *Psychologische Forschung, 14,* 1–62.

Houston, D. A., Sherman, S. J., & Baker, S. M. (1989). The influence of unique features and direction of comparison on preferences. *Journal of Experimental Social Psychology, 25,* 121–141.

Hovland, C. I., & Weiss, W. (1953). Transmission of information concerning concepts through positive and negative instances. *Journal of Experimental Psychology, 45,* 175–182.

Jenkins, H. M., & Sainsbury, R. S. (1969). The development of stimulus control through differential reinforcement. In N. J. Mackintosh & W. K. Honig (Eds.), *Fundamental issues in associative learning. Proceedings of a symposium held at Dalhousie University, Halifax* (pp. 123–161). Halifax: Dalhousie University Press.

Jenkins, H. M., & Sainsbury, R. S. (1970). Discrimination learning with the distinctive feature on positive or negative trials. In D. I. Mostofsky (Ed.), *Attention: Contemporary theory and analysis* (pp. 239–273). New York: Meredith.

Johnson, J. T. (1986). The knowledge of what might have been: Affective and attributional consequences of near outcomes. *Personality and Social Psychology Bulletin, 12*, 51–62.

Jucknat, M. (1938). Leistung, Anspruchsniveau und Selbstbewußtsein [Achievement, level of aspiration, and self-esteem]. *Psychologische Forschung, 22*, 89–179.

Kahneman, D., & Miller, D. T. (1986). Norm theory: Comparing reality to its alternatives. *Psychological Review, 93*, 136–153.

Kahneman, D., Slovic, P., & Tversky, A. (Eds.). (1982). *Judgment and uncertainty: Heuristics and biases.* Cambridge: Cambridge University Press.

Kahneman, D., & Tversky, A. (1972). Subjective probability: A judgment of representativeness. *Cognitive Psychology, 3*, 430–454.

Kahneman, D., & Tversky, A. (1973). On the psychology of prediction. *Psychological Review, 80*, 237–251.

Kahneman, D., & Tversky, A. (1979). Prospect theory: An analysis of decision under risk. *Econometrica, 47*, 263–291.

Kahneman, D., & Tversky, A. (1982a). The psychology of preferences. *Scientific American, 246*, 160–173.

Kahneman, D., & Tversky, A. (1982b). The simulation heuristic. In D. Kahneman, P. Slovic, & A. Tversky (Eds.), *Judgment and uncertainty: Heuristics and biases* (pp. 201–208). Cambridge: Cambridge University Press.

Kuhl, J. (1978). Standard setting and risk preference: An elaboration of the theory of achievement motivation and an empirical test. *Psychological Review, 85*, 239–248.

Kuhl, J. (1986). Motivation and information processing: A new look at decision making, dynamic change, and action control. In R. M. Sorrentino & E. T. Higgins (Eds.), *Handbook of motivation and cognition: Foundations of social behavior* (pp. 404–434). New York: Guilford.

Kuhl, J., & Koch, B. (1984). Motivational determinants of motor performance: The hidden second task. *Psychological Research, 46*, 143–153.

Landman, J. (1987). Regret and elation following action and inaction: Affective responses to positive versus negative outcomes. *Personality and Social Psychology Bulletin, 13*, 524–536.

Lawler, E. E. (1965). Secondary reinforcement value of stimuli associated with shock reduction. *The Quarterly Journal of Experimental Psychology, 17*, 57–62.

Lazarus, A. A. (1968). Learning theory and the treatment of depression. *Behaviour Research and Therapy, 6*, 83–89.

Lazarus, R. S. (1991). Cognition and motivation in emotion. 98th annual convention of the American Psychological Association distinguished scientific contributions award address (1990, Boston, Massachusetts). *American Psychologist, 46*, 352–367.

Lazarus, R. S. (1993). From psychological stress to the emotions: A history of changing outlooks. *Annual Review of Psychology, 44*, 1–21.

Lewin, K. (1926a). Vorbemerkungen über die psychischen Kräfte und Energien und über die Struktur der Seele [Preliminary remarks about the psychic forces and energies, and about the structure of the mind]. *Psychologische Forschung, 7*, 294–329.

Lewin, K. (1926b). Vorsatz, Wille und Bedürfnis [Intention, will, and need]. *Psychologische Forschung, 7*, 330–385.

Lewin, K. (1935). *A dynamic theory of personality.* New York: McGraw-Hill.

Lewin, K. (1951a). Field theory in social science. In D. Cartwright (Ed.), *Field theory in social science.* Chicago: The University of Chicago Press.

Lewin, K. (1951b). Intention, will and need. In D. Rapaport (Ed.), *Organization and pathology of thought: Selected sources* (pp. 95–153). New York: Columbia University Press. (Original work published 1926.)

Lewin, K., Dembo, T., Festinger, L., & Sears, P. S. (1944). Level of aspiration. In J. M. Hunt (Ed.), *Personality and the behavior disorders* (Vol. 1, pp. 333–378). New York: Ronald Press.

Linville, P. W., & Fischer, G. W. (1991). Preferences for separating or combining events. *Journal of Personality and Social Psychology, 60,* 5–23.

Lipsitt, L. P. (1990). Learning and memory in infants. *Merrill Palmer Quarterly, 36,* 53–66.

Lopes, L. L. (1987). Between hope and fear: The psychology of risk. In L. Berkowitz (Ed.), *Advances in experimental social psychology* (Vol. 20, pp. 255–295). San Diego: Academic Press.

Miller, D. T., & McFarland, C. (1987). Counterfactual thinking and victim compensation: A test of norm theory. *Personality and Social Psychology Bulletin, 12,* 513–519.

Miller, D. T., Taylor, B., & Buck, M. L. (1991). Gender gaps: Who needs to be explained? *Journal of Personality and Social Psychology, 61,* 5–12.

Miller, D. T., Turnbull, W., & McFarland, C. (1989). When a coincidence is suspicious: The role of mental simulation. *Journal of Personality and Social Psychology, 57,* 581–589.

Miller, D. T., Turnbull, W., & McFarland, C. (1990). Counterfactual thinking and social perception: Thinking about what might have been. In M. P. Zanna (Ed.), *Advances in experimental social psychology* (Vol. 23, pp. 305–331). Orlando, FL: Academic Press.

Miller, G. A., Galanter, E., & Pribram, K. H. (1960). *Plans and the structure of behavior.* New York: Adams-Bannister-Cox.

Miller, J. S., McDougall, S. A., & Zolman, J. F. (1988). The ontogeny of the feature-positive effect in young chicks. *Animal Learning and Behavior, 16,* 195–198.

Miller, N. E. (1959). Liberalization of basic S-R concepts: Extensions to conflict behavior, motivation and social learning. In S. Koch (Ed.), *Psychology: A study of a science. General and systematic formulations, learning, and special processes* (Vol. 2, pp. 196–292). New York: McGraw-Hill.

Mowrer, O. H. (1960). *Learning theory and behavior.* New York: Wiley.

Newman, J. P., Wolff, W. T., & Hearst, E. (1980). The feature-positive effect in adult human subjects. *Journal of Experimental Psychology Human Learning and Memory, 6,* 630–650.

Nisbett, R., & Ross, L. (1980). *Human inference: Strategies and shortcomings of social judgment.* Englewood Cliffs, NJ: Prentice Hall.

Norem, J. K., & Cantor, N. (1986a). Anticipatory and post hoc cushioning strategies: Optimism and defensive pessimism in "risky" situations. *Cognitive Therapy and Research, 10,* 347–362.

Norem, J. K., & Cantor, N. (1986b). Defensive pessimism: Harnessing anxiety as motivation. *Journal of Personality and Social Psychology, 51,* 1208–1217.

Ortony, A., Clore, G. L., & Collins, A. (1988). *The cognitive structure of emotions.* Cambridge: Cambridge University Press.

Ostrom, T. M., & Upshaw, H. S. (1968). Psychological perspective and attitude change. In A. G. Greenwald, T. C. Brock, & T. M. Ostrom (Eds.), *Psychological foundations of attitudes* (pp. 217–242). New York: Academic Press.

Ovsiankina, M. (1928). Die Wiederaufnahme unterbrochener Handlungen [The resumption of interrupted tasks]. *Psychologische Forschung, 11,* 302–379.

Parducci, A. (1965). Category judgment: A range-frequency model. *Psychological Review, 72,* 407–418.

Parducci, A. (1968). The relativism of absolute judgments. *Scientific American, 219,* 84–90.

Parrott, W. G. (1993). Beyond hedonism: Motives for inhibiting good moods and for maintaining bad moods. In D. M. Wegner & J. W. Pennebaker (Eds.), *Handbook of mental control* (pp. 278–305). Englewood Cliffs, NJ: Prentice Hall.

Petty, R. E., & Cacioppo, J. T. (1986). The elaboration likelihood model of persuasion. In L. Berkowitz (Ed.), *Advances in experimental social psychology* (Vol. 19, pp. 123–205). San Diego: Academic Press.

Powers, W. T. (1973). *Behavior: The control of perception.* Chicago: Aldine.

Preston, M. G., & Bayton, J. A. (1941). Differential effect of a social variable upon three levels of aspiration. *Journal of Experimental Psychology, 29*, 351–369.

Reisenzein, R., & Schönpflug, W. (1992). Stumpf's cognitive-evaluative theory of emotion. *American Psychologist, 47*, 34–45.

Roney, C. J. R., Higgins, E. T., & Shah, J. (in press). Goals and framing: How outcome focus influences motivation and emotion. *Personality and Social Psychology Bulletin.*

Rosch, E. (1978). Principles of categorization. In E. Rosch & B. B. Lloyd (Eds.), *Cognition and categorization* (pp. 27–48). Hillsdale, NJ: Erlbaum.

Roseman, I. J. (1984). Cognitive determinants of emotion. A structural theory. In P. Shaver (Ed.), *Review of personality and social psychology, Vol. 5. Relationships, and health* (pp. 11–36). Beverly Hills, CA: Sage.

Roseman, I. J. (1991). Appraisal determinants of discrete emotions. *Cognition and Emotion, 5*, 161–200.

Roseman, I. J., Spindel, M. S., & Jose, P. E. (1990). Appraisals of emotion-eliciting events: Testing a theory of discrete emotions. *Journal of Personality and Social Psychology, 59*, 899–915.

Rosenberg, M. J. (1956). Cognitive structure and attitudinal affect. *Journal of Abnormal and Social Psychology, 53*, 367–372.

Ross, L. (1977). The intuitive psychologist and his shortcomings: Distortions in the attribution process. In L. Berkowitz (Ed.), *Advances in experimental social psychology* (Vol. 10, pp. 174–221). New York: Academic Press.

Rotter, J. B. (1942). Level of aspiration as a method of studying personality: I. A critical review of methodology. *Psychological Review, 49*, 463–474.

Rotter, J. B. (1982a). Social learning and clinical psychology: Basic concepts. In J. B. Rotter (Ed.), *The development and applications of social learning theory* (pp. 49–143). New York: CBS Educational and Professional Publishing. (Original work published in 1954.)

Rotter, J. B. (1982b). Some implications of a social learning theory for the practice of psychotherapy. In J. B. Rotter (Ed.), *The development and applications of social learning theory* (pp. 237–262). New York: CBS Educational and Professional Publishing. (Original work published in 1954.)

Rovee-Collier, C. (1987). Learning and memory in infancy. In J. D. Osofsky (Ed.), *Handbook of infant development* (*2nd ed.*), [Wiley series on personality processes] (pp. 98–148). New York: Wiley.

Rovee-Collier, C., & Hayne, H. (1987). Reactivation of infant memory: Implications for cognitive development. In H. W. Reese (Ed.), *Advances in child development and behavior* (Vol. 20, pp. 185–238). Orlando, FL: Academic Press.

Schachter, S., & Singer, J. E. (1962). Cognitive, social, and physiological determinants of emotional state. *Psychological Review, 69*, 379–399.

Schank, R. C., & Abelson, R. P. (1977). *Scripts, plans, goals, and understanding: An inquiry into human knowledge structures.* Hillsdale, NJ: Erlbaum.

Schwarz, N., Bless, H., Strack, F., Klumpp, G., Rittenauer-Schatka, H., & Simons, A. (1991). Ease of retrieval as information: Another look at the availability heuristic. *Journal of Personality and Social Psychology, 61*, 195–202.

Sherman, S. J., & Corty, E. (1984). Cognitive heuristics. In R. S. Wyer & T. K. Srull (Eds.), *Handbook of social cognition* (Vol. 1, pp. 189–286). Hillsdale, NJ: Erlbaum.

Siegel, S. (1957). Level of aspiration and decision making. *Psychological Review, 64*, 253–262.

Siqueland, E. R. (1968). Reinforcement patterns and extinction in human newborns. *Journal of Experimental Child Psychology, 6*, 431–442.

Smedslund, J. (1963). The concept of correlation in adults. *Scandinavian Journal of Psychology, 4*, 165–173.

Solomon, R. L., & Corbit, J. D. (1974). An opponent-process theory of motivation: I. Temporal dynamics of affect. *Psychological Review, 81*, 119–145.

Srull, T. K., & Wyer, R. S. (1989). Person memory and judgment. *Psychological Review, 96*, 58–83.

Stein, N. L., & Jewett, J. L. (1986). A conceptual analysis of the meaning of negative emotions: implications for a theory of development. In C. Izard & P. Read (Eds.), *Measuring emotions in infants and children* (Vol. II, pp. 238–267). Cambridge: Cambridge University Press.

Stepper, S., & Strack, F. (1993). Proprioceptive determinants of emotional an nonemotional feelings. *Journal of Personality and Social Psychology, 64*, 211–220.

Stern, W. (1935). *Allgemeine Psychologie auf personalistischer Grundlage* [*General psychology on a personalistic basis*]. Haag, The Netherlands: Martinus Nijhoff.

Strack, F., Schwarz, N., Chassein, B., Kern, D., & Wagner, D. (1990). Salience of comparison standards and the activation of social norms: Consequences for judgments of happiness and their communication. *British Journal of Social Psychology, 29*, 303–314.

Taylor, S. E., & Brown, J. D. (1988). Illusion and well-being: A social psychological perspective on mental health. *Psychological Bulletin, 103*, 193–210.

Trope, Y. (1986a). Identification and inferential processes in dispositional attribution. *Psychological Review, 93*, 239–257.

Trope, Y. (1986b). Self-enhancement and self-assessment in achievement behavior. In R. M. Sorrentino & E. T. Higgins (Eds.), *Handbook of motivation and cognition: Foundations of social behavior* (pp. 350–378). New York: Guilford.

Tversky, A., & Kahneman, D. (1973). Availability: A heuristic for judging frequency and probability. *Cognitive Psychology, 5*, 207–232.

Tversky, A., & Kahneman, D. (1974). Judgment under uncertainty: Heuristics and biases. *Science, 185*, 1124–1131.

Tversky, A., & Kahneman, D. (1981). The framing of decisions and the psychology of choice. *Science, 211*, 453–458.

Tversky, A., & Kahneman, D. (1982). Judgments of and by representativeness. In D. Kahneman, P. Slovic, & A. Tversky (Eds.), *Judgment under uncertainty: Heuristics and biases* (pp. 84–98). Cambridge: Cambridge University Press.

Vallacher, R. R., & Wegner, D. M. (1985). *A theory of action identification.* Hillsdale, NJ: Erlbaum.

Vallacher, R. R., & Wegner, D. M. (1987). What do people think they're doing? Action identification and human behavior. *Psychological Review, 94*, 3–15.

Ward, W. C., & Jenkins, H. M. (1965). The display of information and the judgment of contingency. *Canadian Journal of Psychology, 19*, 231–241.

Wason, P. C., & Johnson-Laird, P. N. (1972). *Psychology of reasoning. Structure and content.* Cambridge, MA: Harvard University Press.

Watson, J. S. (1972). Smiling, cooing, and "the game." *Merill-Palmer-Quarterly, 18*, 323–339.

Wegner, S. Vallacher, (1986).

Weiner, B. (1985). "Spontaneous" causal thinking. *Psychological Bulletin, 97*, 74–84.

Wells, G. L., & Gavanski, I. (1989). Mental stimulation of causality. *Journal of Personality and Social Psychology, 56*, 161–169.

Wright, J., & Mischel, W. (1982). Influence of affect on cognitive social learning person variables. *Journal of Personality and Social Psychology, 43*, 901–914.

Zanna, M. P., Kiesler, C. A., & Pilkonis, P. A. (1970). Positive and negative attitudinal affect established by classical conditioning. *Journal of Personality and Social Psychology, 14*, 321–328.

Zanna, M. P., & Rempel, J. K. (1988). Attitudes: a new look at an old concept. In D. Bar-Tal & A. W. Kruglanski (Eds.), *The social psychology of knowledge* (pp. 315–334). Cambridge: Cambridge University Press.

Zeigarnik, B. (1927). Das Behalten erledigter und unerledigter Handlungen [The retention of completed and uncompleted actions]. *Psychologische Forschung, 9*, 1–85.

PLURALISTIC IGNORANCE AND THE PERPETUATION OF SOCIAL NORMS BY UNWITTING ACTORS

Deborah A. Prentice
Dale T. Miller

I. Introduction

Social life often requires us to form judgments and take action on the basis of imperfect information. When we decide to express an opinion, ask for clarification, order another drink, or overlook an inappropriate remark, we do so in light of what we believe other people are thinking and feeling. We believe that they will embrace our opinion, or at least respect it; that they will not find our question stupid or intrusive; that they will take our drinking as a positive social activity; and that the remark we considered inappropriate they considered amusing or simply unremarkable. If we believed otherwise, we would almost certainly act differently. But how reliable are these beliefs on which we predicate so much of our social behavior? How keen is our social understanding? In this chapter, we offer a skeptical view, focusing on the phenomenon of pluralistic ignorance.

Pluralistic ignorance describes the case in which virtually every member of a group or society privately rejects a belief, opinion, or practice, yet believes that virtually every other member privately accepts it. The term pluralistic ignorance is something of a misnomer, for in these cases, group members are not, in fact, ignorant of one another's private sentiments; rather, they think they know, but are mistaken. Nor is the so-called ignorance truly pluralistic: It is an error that each individual makes in judging the sentiments of the plurality. Nevertheless, Floyd Allport (1933) coined the term pluralistic ignorance more than 60 years ago, and we continue to use it. In doing so, we are simply conceding the well-known social fact that it is much easier to abide by an established convention than to change it.

ADVANCES IN EXPERIMENTAL
SOCIAL PSYCHOLOGY, VOL. 28

Moreover, it is precisely this concession that often gives rise to pluralistic ignorance.

Pluralistic ignorance begins with a discrepancy between public actions and private sentiments, typically produced by widespread behavioral adherence to a social norm. The norm may be a general, largely implicit prescription regarding appropriate social behavior, or it may be a more specific and explicit prescription regarding how to act as a member of a particular group. Whatever its content, the norm simply must be powerful enough to induce people to act in ways that do not correspond to their private thoughts and feelings. Under such circumstances, a curious divergence between self- and social perception is often revealed: Individuals recognize that their own norm-congruent behavior is at variance with their true sentiments, but they do not assume a similar discrepancy in others. Instead, their social perception is guided by what they observe: They infer that the actions of others reflect accurately the way they are thinking and feeling.

Pluralistic ignorance is a pervasive feature of social life: It has been found to characterize the dynamics of social situations (e.g., emergencies, classroom lectures), social groups (e.g., nurses, prison guards, gangs), and social movements (e.g., the civil rights movement, the sexual revolution) (see Miller & McFarland, 1991; Miller & Prentice, 1994, for reviews). The first of these areas has been of special interest to experimental social psychologists, who have invoked pluralistic ignorance to explain anomalous behavior in a number of real-world situations. For example, Latané and Darley (1970) linked pluralistic ignorance to the failure of bystanders to intervene in emergency situations. According to their analysis, bystanders to emergencies are initially afraid of embarrassing themselves by overreacting, and thus attempt to remain calm, cool, and collected while they figure out if there is cause for concern. They interpret their own nonchalant demeanor and inaction correctly. But they infer from the similar behavior of other bystanders that these individuals are genuinely unconcerned, and that there is probably nothing to worry about. Similarly, Miller and McFarland (1987) invoked pluralistic ignorance to explain a classroom dynamic familiar to any lecturer: students' reluctance to ask questions during class. According to Miller and McFarland, bewildered students often hesitate to accept a lecturer's encouragement to request clarification of material because they fear asking a stupid or ill-formed question. However, they infer from the fact that other students do not raise their hands that these individuals genuinely understand the material. They assume that they alone are confused.

Although these two examples of pluralistic ignorance occur under very different circumstances, they have a similar underlying structure. In both, behavior is guided by the norm that prohibits making a fool of oneself in public. Bystanders do not intervene and students do not raise their hands because they do not want to embarrass themselves, and it is this motivation that individuals are better able to appreciate in themselves than in others (see Miller & McFarland, 1991). But fear of embarrassment does not underlie all cases of pluralistic ignorance. Consider, for example, Matza's (1964) demonstration of pluralistic ignorance among members of juvenile gangs. He found, in private interviews, that individual gang members expressed considerable discomfort with their own antisocial behavior. Yet because they were unwilling to express their reservations publicly, they each appeared to the others as fully committed to, and comfortable with, the group's delinquency. Their facade of toughness appeared authentic to their peers. But what motivated their facade? Fear of embarrassment seems an unlikely candidate. Instead, their public behavior appears to have been driven by their desire to behave in accordance with the norms of the gang (a valued social group) and to be accepted as good gang members. It was their failure to recognize the power of this motive to influence the behavior of others that caused the pluralistic ignorance.

We believe that group identification is the root cause for many cases of pluralistic ignorance—that individuals often act out of a desire to be good group members but interpret others' similarly motivated behavior as reflecting personal beliefs and opinions. Two such cases of pluralistic ignorance are presented in this chapter.

II. Methodological Considerations

Traditionally, when experimental social psychologists have wanted to investigate a phenomenon such as pluralistic ignorance, they have sought to capture it in the laboratory. This approach is predicated on the belief that the best way to ensure a true understanding of what causes a phenomenon is to demonstrate that it can be produced reliably in the lab. Moreover, once this step is achieved, the investigator can examine the moderators, mediators, and limiting conditions of the phenomenon by varying specific aspects of the experimental paradigm. All of these features make the laboratory approach enormously attractive. However, this approach has its limitations as well. In particular, the laboratory experiment is best suited for studying phenomena that arise in response to immediate situational contingencies and are quickly dissipated. In the ideal case, the experimenter brings in willing participants, exposes them to conditions that produce the phenomenon of interest, allows it some behavioral expression, and then sends participants home unchanged. The phenomenon is caused by and contained within the situation constructed in the laboratory. Of course, not all social psychological phenomena are so temporally and situationally bounded, and those that are not are less suited to the laboratory approach.

These methodological considerations clearly show why social psychologists have focused their attempts to understand pluralistic ignorance on cases driven by fear of embarrassment: Such a case is contained within a single situation. Fear of embarrassment is a motivational state closely linked to situational contingencies: The appropriate set of circumstances will produce it in most of the people most of the time. As a result, pluralistic ignorance arising from fear of embarrassment is highly suited to laboratory investigation. All an experimenter needs to do is expose subjects to public conditions that leave them embarrassed to act on their private beliefs and feelings. For example, the experimenter can introduce ominous smoke into a room where some subjects are completing a questionnaire (see Latané & Darley, 1968), or offer each subject the opportunity to make a public request for help on an incomprehensible assignment (see Miller & McFarland, 1987). These conditions will reliably produce fear of embarrassment in the would-be actors, leading to behavioral inhibition and the erroneous social inferences that characterize pluralistic ignorance.

Of course, some version of group identification can also be created in the laboratory. An experimenter can divide subjects into groups and thereby create ingroup–outgroup differentiation (see Tajfel, 1981). Further, the experimenter can place the groups in competition with each other, give the members of each group a common goal, or employ any of the various manipulations that have been shown to strengthen group identification. These laboratory methods will create sufficient identification to produce in-group favoritism, conformity, and many other group phenomena (see Asch, 1951; Tajfel, 1981; Turner, Hogg, Oakes, Reicher, & Wetherell, 1987). Moreover, it may be enough to produce pluralistic ignorance as well. In domains governed by group norms, members of ad hoc laboratory groups may assume that norm-congruent behavior reveals more private acceptance of the norms by their fellow members than they are feeling themselves. Indeed, there are hints of this dynamic in several studies of minority influence, in which subjects' perception that others are not as persuaded by the dissident as they are appears to inhibit them from publicly acknowledging their private conversion (see Moscovici & Lage, 1976; Moscovici & Neve, 1972).

However, the laboratory approach to studying group-based pluralistic ignorance is unsatisfactory in several respects. First, group identification cannot be rendered authentic in the laboratory. Unlike fear of embarrassment, it is not simply a response to situational contingencies but actually develops and endures over time. Thus, pluralistic ignorance in laboratory groups cannot have the strong psychological impact of its real-world counterpart: The motivation to exhibit norm-congruent behavior, the discomfort of behaving inauthentically, and the pain of feeling deviant from one's peers will all be much stronger in groups that are valued by their members. Second, many of the consequences of pluralistic ignorance within groups occur over time. Pluralistic ignorance can wax and wane, depending on events both inside and outside the group; it can lead individuals to change their personal beliefs and opinions; and it can lead to immediate or gradual changes in group norms. Understanding these developments is key to understanding the phenomenon, and they cannot be captured in the laboratory. Finally, the laboratory approach eliminates one of the most interesting aspects of group-based pluralistic ignorance: the particulars of the groups and communities in which it arises. Cases of pluralistic ignorance offer us insight into more than just the psychology of individuals. Such cases highlight the psychology of social life. From this perspective, the particulars of the group are of interest. Therefore, Matza's (1964) discovery of pluralistic ignorance among members of juvenile gangs is important, not simply because it provides yet another example of the phenomenon, but also because it helps us to understand the psychology of juvenile gangs. A laboratory demonstration of the same dynamics within ad hoc groups would not have nearly so much value.

In light of these considerations, we have opted to investigate pluralistic ignorance outside of the laboratory, forsaking the control that it affords in exchange for the opportunity to study real-world groups. Admittedly, we have retreated to the lab from time to time in an effort to understand some causes of the phenomenon. But the consequences, and even the mechanisms that underlie it, we have tried to capture in the field. Our investigations have focused on two cases of pluralistic ignorance, one concerning the attitudes of college students toward alcohol use on campus, and the other concerning the gender stereotypes held by elementary school children.

III. Pluralistic Ignorance and Alcohol Use on Campus

Alcohol use by college undergraduates has become a major concern of university administrators and public health officials across the United States (Berkowitz & Perkins, 1986; Maddox, 1970; Straus & Bacon, 1953). Surveys of college students estimate that more than 90% have tried alcohol, and approximately 20% to 25% exhibit symptoms of problem drinking (cf. Meilman, Stone, Gaylor, & Turco, 1990; Perkins & Berkowitz, 1989; Thorner, 1986; see Berkowitz & Perkins, 1986, for a review). Alcohol and alcohol-related events are the number one cause of death among young people in the United States, primarily because of alcohol-related car accidents and the role that alcohol plays in suicide (Thorner, 1986). In addition, heavy drinking among college students is associated with low academic performance, a high rate of getting into trouble with authorities, disruptions in personal relationships, and, for male students, a high risk of fighting or of damaging property (see Berkowitz & Perkins, 1986).

There is now considerable evidence to suggest that social influence processes play a powerful role in promoting drinking among college students. In particular, numerous studies have shown that one of the most consistent predictors of alcohol use is a student's perception of alcohol use by his or her peers (see, e.g., Graham, Marks, & Hansen, 1991; Kandel, 1980; Perkins, 1985; Stein, Newcomb, & Bentler, 1987). In a review of the literature on alcohol and other drug use, Kandel (1980) found that the extent of perceived drug use in the peer group, self-reported drug use by peers, and perceived tolerance for use were all strong predictors of an adolescent's own drug use (see also Orford, 1985). Similarly, Grube, Morgan, and Seff (1989) found that, among Irish adolescents, the perceived level of peer drinking was the single best predictor of alcohol use by the individual, with parental disapproval showing a much smaller effect (see also Perkins, 1985). Stein et al. (1987) found correlations between the individual's own drug use and his or her perceptions of peer drug use to range upward of .70. These and many similar findings have been taken as evidence that perceptions of peers exert a considerable influence on the drinking behavior of adolescents, even though not many of the studies have directly addressed the question of causality (see Kandel, 1980).

Peer influence alone is not sufficient to explain why college students tend toward excessive alcohol consumption. Presumably, peers could as easily encourage moderation as excess. However, on most college campuses, peer influence is directed by norms that promote comfort with alcohol use. Indeed, drinking sometimes to excess is central to the social identity of many college students and is an important part of social life on most campuses. Thus, it is not surprising that going to college produces an increase in alcohol consumption, both in terms of the percentage of students who drink and in the amount consumed by those who were already drinkers (Friend & Koushki, 1984; Hill & Bugen, 1979; Wechsler & McFadden, 1979). In addition, the influence of liberal campus drinking norms appears to increase with time spent in the campus environment (Perkins, 1985). These findings support the view that students' alcohol use is driven by normative pressure. They reflect a trend toward increasingly uniform, norm-consistent behavior over time (for similar examples in other domains, see Crandall, 1988; Festinger, Schachter, & Back, 1950; Newcomb, 1943).

The private sentiments of students toward alcohol use are subject to very different sources of influence. Within their first few months at college, students are typically exposed to vivid and irrefutable evidence of the negative consequences of excessive alcohol consumption: They nurse sick roommates, overlook inappropriate behavior and memory losses, and hear about serious injuries and even deaths that result from drinking. They may have negative experiences with alcohol themselves and notice its effects on their academic performance. This accumulating evidence of alcohol's ill effects is likely to cause students considerable anxiety about their own and others' drinking, anxiety that runs contrary to the dictates of campus norms. Although their public behavior may signal comfort and ease with excessive alcohol consumption, their private attitudes are likely to be much more conservative.

In short, students' beliefs about alcohol use on campus may be characterized by pluralistic ignorance: They may assume that their own private attitudes and judgments are more conservative than those of other students, even though their public behavior is identical. If this conjecture is valid, we should find a systematic discrepancy between students' ratings of their own comfort with campus drinking practices and their estimates of the comfort of the average student: Students should express less comfort themselves than they attribute to others. We should also find evidence for an illusion of universality in student estimates of peer attitudes. If students infer the attitudes of others from their uniformly norm-congruent behavior, then they will perceive little variability in these sentiments. As a result, they will believe that there is more uniform support for the liberal drinking norm than actually exists.

A. DEMONSTRATIONS

We began our empirical research with the goal of documenting the existence of pluralistic ignorance in students' attitudes toward drinking on campus (Prentice & Miller, 1993, Study 1). In our first study, we asked a cross section of male and female Princeton undergraduates to indicate their own comfort with the alcohol drinking habits of their fellow students and to estimate the comfort of the average Princeton undergraduate. Mean comfort ratings for the two targets are shown in Figure 1. As expected, students rated themselves as significantly less comfortable with campus drinking practices than they estimated the average student to be. This

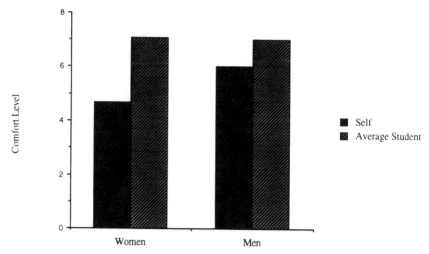

Fig. 1.   Mean ratings by male and female students of own comfort and the comfort of the average student with alcohol use on campus.

difference was larger for women than for men, but was significant for both genders.

We also asked students to estimate the variability of peer attitudes. After they had indicated the comfort of the average student, they were instructed to bracket the lower and upper scale values between which the attitudes of 50% of students fall. Median estimates of the two bound-aries of the interquartile range were 5 and 9, respectively. Thus, students estimated the distribution of attitudes toward drinking on campus to have a mean of approximately 7, with an interquartile range from 5 to 9. In fact, the actual distribution of attitudes, as reflected by students' own comfort ratings, had a mean of 5.33, with an interquartile range from 3 to 8. These distributions demonstrate the two defining features of pluralistic ignorance: a divergence of self- and other-ratings and an illusion of universality.

We have replicated the self–other difference in students' comfort with alcohol use with a number of other-student targets. These studies have shown that students rate themselves as less comfortable, on average, than they perceive the typical student, most students, and even their own friends to be (see Claire & Prentice, 1995; Prentice & Miller, 1993, Study 2).

Moreover, we are not alone in documenting this discrepancy between the student's own attitudes toward drinking and their perceptions of peer attitudes. Perkins and Berkowitz (1986) asked more than 1,000 undergraduates to indicate which of the following statements best represented their own attitude, and which represented "the general campus attitude toward drinking alcohol beverages" (p. 964):

1. Drinking is never a good thing to do.
2. Drinking is alright, but a student should never get "smashed."
3. An occasional "drunk" is okay, as long as it doesn't interfere with grades or responsibilities.
4. An occasional "drunk" is okay, even if it does occasionally interfere with grades or responsibilities.
5. A frequent "drunk" is okay, if that's what the individual wants to do.

Almost two-thirds of their sample endorsed the moderate statement, "An occasional 'drunk' is okay, as long as it doesn't interfere with grades or responsibilities," as representing their own attitude toward drinking, and less than 20% endorsed the two more permissive statements. By contrast, more than 60% selected one of these two more permissive statements as representing the general campus attitude toward drinking.

In summary, we have considerable evidence that college students see themselves as less comfortable with alcohol use on campus than they believe other students are. In addition, students appear to underestimate the variability of their peers' attitudes, seeing others as uniformly more comfortable with students' alcohol use than they are. These findings provide strong support for our claim that students' attitudes toward drinking on campus are characterized by pluralistic ignorance. However, there are a number of alternative explanations for these results: Students might simply be trying to present themselves in a favorable light to faculty researchers, for example. Or they might be making accurate inferences about the attitudes of a biased sample of the campus population. To establish that this pattern of results represents pluralistic ignorance, we needed more definitive evidence for the mechanism underlying it.

B. MECHANISM

In the next study, we examined more closely students' public presentations, private attitudes, and inferences about others' attitudes toward drinking on campus (Prentice & Miller, 1995). Our goal was to test more directly the claim that students' attitudes are characterized by pluralistic ignorance. In particular, we sought evidence for two critical assumptions of our analysis: 1) Students present themselves publicly as more comfortable with alcohol use than they actually are, and 2) they infer the private views of others from their public presentations.

To test these predictions, we brought groups of female undergraduates into the laboratory to participate in what they were told was a study of focus groups. There were two to four women in each group, all from the same class but previously unacquainted with each other. (We chose women for this study because we wanted to control for gender, and because women typically show a larger self–other discrepancy in comfort with drinking than do men.) Each participant began by completing a brief questionnaire in which she indicated both her own comfort with the alcohol drinking habits of students at Princeton and the comfort of the average female student.

After collecting these questionnaires, the experimenter told the group that the purpose of the study was to evaluate the effectiveness of focus groups as a means of assessing public opinion. She explained, "We are bringing in groups of students to discuss various campus issues, taping the discussions, and then giving the tapes to trained coders who will assess the opinions expressed and try to estimate the general opinions of the campus. Those estimates will then be compared to the results of campus-wide surveys." She went on to say, "The issue we would like you to discuss today is the role of alcohol in campus life. On the board you will see a series of general questions—these are meant to provide some structure for your discussion. We would like you to discuss the issue of alcohol use on campus for about 10 minutes. We are not interested in the particulars of your personal experiences, and we would also prefer that you didn't mention any particular student by name in your discussion." On the black-board were five general questions asking participants about campus alcohol practices, their feelings about student drinking, and their own experiences with alcohol. The experimenter turned on the tape recorder and let them discuss for 10 min.

After the discussion, each student completed a second questionnaire in which she rated the comfort with alcohol of each other member of her discussion group; how comfortable the other members believe her to be; how similar her opinions are to theirs; and, in groups with three or more participants, how similar their opinions are to those of each other.

Means of the students' prediscussion ratings of their own comfort and the comfort of the average female student are shown on the left side of Figure 2. These ratings replicated the self–other discrepancy that we found in earlier studies, with students expressing less comfort themselves than they attributed to the average student of their gender. We were interested in the relation of these prediscussion comfort ratings to the comfort the students expressed in the group discussion. In particular, we expected students to express more comfort publicly than they felt privately. Their ratings of how other group members would rate their comfort supported this expectation. As shown in Figure 2, students indicated after the discussion

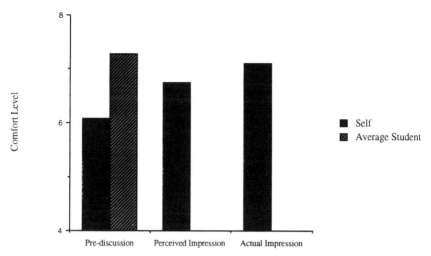

Fig. 2. Means of students' prediscussion ratings of their own comfort with alcohol use and the comfort of the average female student, and postdiscussion ratings by each participant of the comfort she believed she conveyed to others, and by the other group members of the comfort she actually conveyed in the group discussion.

that other group members would believe them to be significantly more comfortable with campus drinking habits than their own prediscussion ratings suggested. Indeed, their ratings of the comfort they conveyed to others were closer to (and statistically indistinguishable from) the comfort they attributed to the average female student than they were to their own private views.

Our second hypothesis concerned the relation of students' public presentations to the way they were perceived by other group members. In particular, we were interested in whether they convinced each other with their public displays of comfort. Again, the data suggest that they did: As shown in Figure 2, group members' ratings of each others' comfort were in line with their ratings of the impressions they conveyed to each other, and were significantly higher than their prediscussion comfort ratings. In addition, a regression analysis predicting others' ratings of a target person's comfort showed a strong effect of the comfort that target person claimed to have conveyed in the discussion and no effect of either the private comfort of the target or the private comfort of the rater.

These results provide convincing evidence for pluralistic ignorance in students' comfort with alcohol use. Their tendency to express opinions publicly that are more consistent with liberal drinking norms than their private views leads them to see more support for those norms than actually exists. This process can account for both their assumption that they are less comfortable with alcohol use than the average student and their overestimation of the uniformity of others' comfort.

One additional finding provided further support for this analysis. We found a significant correlation of −.28 between own comfort ratings and ratings of the homogeneity of other group members' opinions. Thus, the less comfortable students were with alcohol use, and therefore the more discrepant they believed themselves to be from their peers, the more homogeneous they estimated others' opinions about alcohol to be. This link between seeing oneself as less comfortable than the average and perceiving others to be homogeneous in their (greater) comfort is completely consistent with our claim that pluralistic ignorance is at work.

C. CONSEQUENCES

Armed with this evidence for pluralistic ignorance, we set out to document the psychological consequences of the phenomenon. In particular, we were interested in exploring two ways that students might respond to the belief that their attitudes toward alcohol use on campus are different from those of their peers. One possibility is that they would gradually change their attitudes in the direction of the average student's attitude either because they were persuaded by the group's position or because they internalized the sentiments that they originally expressed inauthentically. This prediction has considerable precedent in the social influence literature, which has always placed a heavy emphasis on conformity as a means of resolving self–group discrepancies (see Moscovici, 1985). However, in the case of alcohol use on campus, irrefutable evidence of the ill effects of excessive drinking may make it very difficult for students to change their attitudes in the direction of greater comfort. An alternative possibility is that they would be alienated from the drinking situation on campus and from the university in general. This prediction also has precedent in the literature exploring the consequences of real deviance (e.g., Festinger et al., 1950). Whether a similar phenomenology characterizes the illusory deviance produced by pluralistic ignorance was one of the questions we sought to address.

1. Internalization of Perceived Peer Opinion

In the next study, we tested the hypothesis that students over the course of the semester would increasingly adopt the position toward alcohol use on campus that they attributed to the average student (Prentice & Miller,

1993, Study 3). We surveyed a random sample of Princeton sophomores by telephone at two time points: initially, in September, when they had just returned from summer vacation and had had little recent exposure to college drinking norms, and then again, in December, after they had spent several months as active members of the campus community. (We chose second-year students for this study because we assumed that they would be familiar with student culture and, in particular, with norms for drinking, but that they would still be new enough at the university to be concerned about fitting in.) In each interview, we asked the students how comfortable they felt with students' drinking habits, how comfortable the average Princeton undergraduate felt with students' drinking habits, and two questions about their own alcohol consumption—how many alcoholic drinks they had consumed in the last week, and how many alcoholic drinks they have in a typical week during the semester.

We predicted that students would respond to pluralistic ignorance by changing their own attitudes in the direction of the average student's attitude, and thus would show greater comfort over time. Students' ratings of their own comfort and the comfort of the average student at each time point are shown for men in Figure 3 and for women in Figure 4. As these figures indicate, there was support for our prediction among male, but not among female, students. Male students rated themselves as significantly less comfortable with alcohol drinking than the average Princeton under-

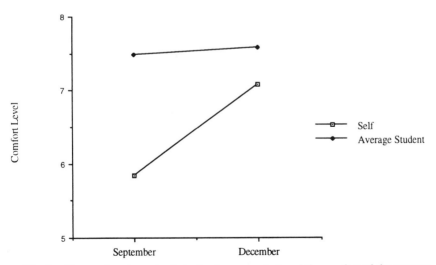

Fig. 3.   Mean ratings by male students of own comfort and the comfort of the average student in both September and December.

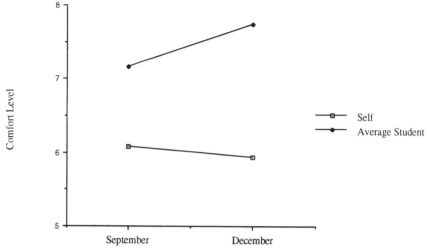

Fig. 4.   Means ratings by female students of own comfort and the comfort of the average student in September and December.

graduate at the first interview; at the second interview, that difference was eliminated. Female students, however, rated themselves as less comfortable than the average student in both interviews.

Correlational analyses provided further evidence of internalization among male but not among female students. If students respond to perceived deviance by bringing their private views on alcohol into line with their perceptions of peer views, we would expect the correlation between ratings of own comfort and the comfort of the average student to increase over time. Male students showed just such an increase. The correlation between own comfort and average-student comfort increased from .34 in the first interview to .76 in the second among male respondents. Female respondents showed a substantial decrease in the correlation, from .60 in the first interview to −.08 in the second.

We also examined the relation of comfort ratings for self and for the average student to drinking behavior. Students' estimates of the number of drinks they had consumed in the past week and the number of drinks they had consumed in a typical week were highly correlated, so we averaged them to form a single index of drinking behavior at each interview. We then correlated this index with comfort ratings separately at each time point. For women, both sets of correlations remained fairly stable over time. The own comfort-behavior correlation was approximately .5 at both interviews, and the average-student comfort-behavior correlation was not significantly different from zero at either time point. For men, by contrast, the correlations of behavior with both comfort ratings increased over the course of the semester: The own comfort-behavior correlation went from .28 at the first interview to .59 at the second, and the average-student comfort-behavior correlation went from −.11 at the first interview to .34 at the second. These results for men are completely consistent with the operation of conformity pressures to bring personal attitudes and behavior into line with the perceived dictates of the group.

One final set of analyses lent further support to this conclusion. We performed separate multiple-regression analyses for men and women within interviews to predict both own comfort with drinking behavior and perceived average student comfort. For women, this model provided a very good prediction at the start of the term ($R = .75$ at the first interview), which grew substantially worse over time ($R = .36$ at the second interview). For men, the opposite was true: Their alcohol drinking habits and their estimates of others' comfort with drinking provided a relatively poor prediction of their own comfort at the start of the term ($R = .44$ at the first interview), but that prediction became much better over time ($R = .85$ at the second interview).

These results provide clear evidence for internalization on the part of men and alienation on the part of women. The obvious question that follows is why men and women respond to pluralistic ignorance so differently. Because we did not predict these gender differences, we can only speculate on their basis. Two general explanations seem especially worthy of consideration.

First, it is possible that the difference is specific to the issue and context of this study. In particular, alcohol consumption may be more central or integral aspect of male social life than of female social life on campus. Surveys of college students' drinking behavior consistently find higher levels of alcohol consumption among male students than among female students (see Kandel, 1980, for a review); in the present study, male respondents reported an alcohol consumption rate more than double that reported by female respondents (see Prentice & Miller, 1993, Study 3). If alcohol use is a more defining issue for men than for women, then men might very well experience greater pressure to become comfortable with alcohol. Women, and especially women at historically male institutions such as Princeton, may be accustomed to finding themselves out of step with their peers on the drinking issue and, as a result, may experience less pressure to bring their private sentiments into line.

A second possibility is that men are simply more inclined to react to perceived deviance with conformity, whereas women react with alienation. Although this suggestion runs contrary to previous theorizing about gender differences in susceptibility to influence (see Eagly, 1978), there is some support for it in the literature on ego defenses. Considerable research suggests that in the face of ego threat, men react with externalizing defenses, such as projection and displacement, whereas women react with internalizing defenses, such as repression and reaction formation (Cramer, 1987; Levit, 1991). In cases of pluralistic ignorance, these differences in ego defenses may lead women to turn against themselves for being deviant and men to internalize what they perceive to be the normative position in order to avoid feeling deviant.

One final point deserves consideration. Although men appear able to resolve pluralistic ignorance through internalization, it is important to note that in college, at the beginning of their second year both men and women were experiencing pluralistic ignorance in equal measure. Furthermore, our initial demonstrations provided evidence of pluralistic ignorance in a cross section of the male student population, including upperclass as well as underclass students. Thus, internalization of the perceived campus sentiment appears to provide, at best, a temporary resolution of the self–other discrepancy in comfort with alcohol. When social pressures are less immediate (e.g., during school breaks) or when they assume less importance (e.g., as they do during students' third and fourth years at Princeton when academic and career concerns become paramount), men may experience recurring concerns about students' excessive drinking habits.

2. Alienation

The foregoing results suggest that, although some students respond to pluralistic ignorance by internalizing the position that they believe other students hold, this response is neither universal nor entirely effective. Thus, in the next study, we explored an alternative response to perceived deviance: alienation and disidentification from the university (Prentice & Miller, 1993, Study 4). We were interested in testing Noelle-Neumann's (1984) contention that people are unwilling to express opinions publicly that they believe to be deviant, even if that belief is in error. We were also interested in whether a mistaken belief in the deviance of their opinions might produce more general symptoms of alienation and disidentification from the campus community.

To test these hypotheses, we needed a case of pluralistic ignorance in which the attitude in question had a clearly available means of public expression. Such an issue arose in the fall of 1991 when Princeton University instituted a campus-wide policy banning kegs of beer. The keg ban was imposed unilaterally by the president of Princeton, who saw it as a largely symbolic act designed to demonstrate the university's concern about drinking on campus. The policy was immediately unpopular: Editorials appeared in the student newspaper and other publications, and there was even protest from alumni groups (who would no longer be able to have kegs at reunions).

Despite the apparent consensus around a negative attitude toward the keg ban, we suspected that private sentiments were not nearly so negative. It was a time of great concern about alcohol use on campus, and many students privately expressed approval that the president of the university was willing to take action on the issue. Also, because the ban affected only kegs, students would still be free to drink bottled beer and other forms of alcohol if they wished. In short, the keg ban was a well-motivated, if somewhat ill-conceived, policy that was unlikely to have dire consequences for social life at Princeton.

Thus, the keg ban provided the perfect issue for our investigation of the behavioral manifestations of alienation because, unlike general comfort with alcohol, attitudes toward the keg ban had a clear means of public expression: We could ask students how willing they were to participate in social actions designed to protest the ban. We expected that we would find evidence of pluralistic ignorance in attitudes toward the keg ban, with students' own private views being much less negative than the views they attributed to the average student. In addition, we expected that, regardless of how negatively they felt toward the ban, feeling deviant from their peers would inhibit students from taking any action in protest and might produce more general symptoms of alienation and disidentification from the university as well.

Approximately a month and a half after the keg ban was instituted, we asked a cross section of male and female students to indicate how they felt about the university's new policy banning kegs on campus, and compared to them, how the average Princeton undergraduate felt about the keg ban. As we expected, the majority of students indicated that they were more positive about the keg ban than the average student: Forty of 52 women and 29 of 42 men indicated that the average student was either somewhat more negative or much more negative about the keg ban than they were. Eleven women and 11 men indicated that the average student felt about the same as they did. Only 1 woman and 2 men indicated that the average student was more positive than they were. This distribution of responses confirmed that students' attitudes toward the keg ban, like their general comfort with alcohol, were characterized by pluralistic ignorance: Students showed a systematic tendency to believe that the average student felt more negatively about the keg ban than they did.

We also asked students several questions about their willingness to take public action related to the keg ban and about their identification with the university in general. First, students were asked to indicate how many signatures they would be willing to collect in protest of the ban and how much of their time they would be willing to spend discussing ways to protest the ban. Then they were asked what percentage of reunions they expected to attend after graduation and how likely they were to donate money to Princeton after graduation. We expected students who believed their attitudes toward the keg ban to be more positive than the average student's to be less willing to take action and less connected to the university than students who believed their attitudes to be the same as the average student's, irrespective of the actual valence of those attitudes. To test this prediction, we divided respondents into two groups: Those who indicated that the average student held a more negative attitude than they did, and those who indicated that the average student held the same attitude they did. (The few students who indicated that the average student held a more positive attitude than they did were excluded from this analysis.) Not surprisingly, students' own attitudes toward the ban corresponded to their comparative ratings of others' attitudes: Students who indicated that the average student was more negative expressed more favorable attitudes toward the ban than did those who indicated that the average student's attitude was the same as their own. But controlling for this difference in private attitudes, students who indicated that their attitude was different from that of the average student were still less likely to take public action and less identified with the university. Mean responses of the two groups to each question, adjusted for their private attitudes toward the ban, are shown in Figure 5. Analyses of covariance indicated that the difference between the others-more-negative and the others-the-same groups was significant for all but the donations question and was consistent across male and female respondents.

Taken together, the results of this and the previous study provide an interesting picture of the consequences of pluralistic ignorance regarding alcohol use on campus. For men, the pattern of results followed quite closely the predictions of the social influence literature: When they perceived their attitudes to be different from those of their peers, men showed symptoms of alienation and responded by changing their attitudes in the direction of perceived peer opinion. For women, the pattern of results was more anomalous: They also showed symptoms of alienation when they perceived their attitudes to be deviant, but did not respond by moving closer to perceived peer opinion. Indeed, if anything, they appeared to grow more alienated over time.

We believe that the most parsimonious account for these results focuses on the different relations of men and women to both the behavioral norm and the institution in question. As we discussed earlier, alcohol use is likely

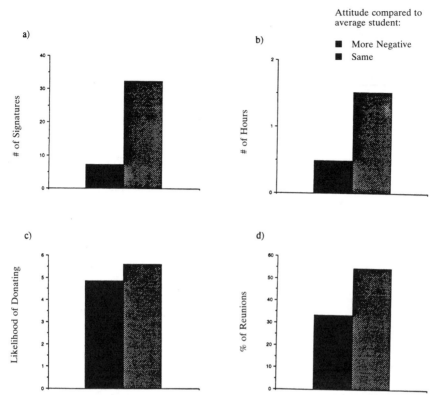

Fig. 5.   Mean responses of students who believed that others held more negative attitudes toward the keg ban than they did and of students who believed that others held the same attitude they did to questions about a) the number of signatures they were willing to collect, b) the number of hours they were willing to spend, c) their likelihood of donating money to Princeton, and d) the percentage of reunions they expected to attend after graduation, controlling for their own attitudes toward the ban.

to be more central and defining for men than for women. Likewise, fitting in at the university may be more critical for men than for women. Even though Princeton has admitted women for a quarter of a century, at the time this research was conducted, male students were still both the statistical and the psychological norm. (Many of the university's institutions and traditions were developed when it was an all-male school.) Thus, whereas Princeton men are likely to experience strong conformity pressures, Princeton women may not expect to be comfortable with the norms of the university. They may see some degree of deviance and alienation as inherent in their position within a historically male institution. Of course, this explanation is speculative, but it is consistent with previous theorizing about social influence and with the present set of results.

D. DISPELLING PLURALISTIC IGNORANCE

These studies of the consequences of pluralistic ignorance highlight its very negative role in campus social life, demonstrating the ways in which it perpetuates dysfunctional drinking norms and engenders alienation within the campus community. But pluralistic ignorance also has a more positive side: It offers a clear route to behavior change. If students' excessive drinking habits are fostered, or at least maintained, by the erroneous perception that other students are more pro-alcohol than they are, then correcting this misperception should lower their alcohol consumption.

Most attempts to promote responsible drinking on college campuses have taken the form of informational programs, designed to convey legal and pharmacological information about the effects of alcohol (Berkowitz & Perkins, 1987). More sophisticated programs have sought to teach individual students to make responsible decisions about alcohol and alcohol consumption in drinking situations (e.g., Meacci, 1990). Yet with few exceptions (e.g., Hansen & Graham, 1991), these attempts at alcohol intervention have focused on changing the attitudes of individual students and have ignored the social context in which most drinking on college campuses takes place.

Our analysis suggests that a more effective way to change students' drinking behavior would focus instead on revealing their erroneous assumptions about the attitudes of their peers toward alcohol. Numerous demonstrations of pluralistic ignorance have revealed that the majority of students already hold the moderate attitudes towards drinking that informational campaigns and individual counseling sessions seek to foster. What students need, in addition, is to understand that those attitudes are shared. If they are made aware that their estimates of other students' attitudes are too liberal—that is, if they are exposed to the concept of pluralistic ignorance in a group setting—then they should experience much less social pressure to consume excessive amounts of alcohol. As a result, they should drink less and be more comfortable with their drinking behavior.

There are at least two ways in which dispelling pluralistic ignorance could lead to a reduction in drinking behavior. First, it could change the level of drinking that students perceive to be condoned by their peers. Given the news that their peers are not as comfortable with current drinking practices as they had thought, students might construct a new, more conservative norm for drinking, one that corresponds to true campus sentiment. This change in the level of drinking prescribed by the norm would produce changes in drinking behavior. Students would still experience social pressure to drink, but the level of drinking they felt pressured to achieve would be lower, more in line with their private sentiments, and would have much less deleterious consequences.

Alternatively, or perhaps additionally, dispelling pluralistic ignorance could change drinking behavior by changing the prescriptive strength of the norm. Social norms derive much of their prescriptive force from their perceived universality (Turner, 1991); indeed, the presence of even one deviant within a group sharply reduces the power of the group norm to induce conformity (e.g., Asch, 1951). Providing students with evidence of pluralistic ignorance regarding alcohol use would certainly indicate to them that support for the drinking norm was not universal, and thus should weaken the norm's prescriptive power. This change in the strength of the drinking norm would produce changes in drinking behavior. Students would no longer experience the same degree of social pressure to bring their own alcohol use into line with the campus standard.

Our next study was designed to test these hypotheses regarding the behavioral and psychological consequences of correcting students' misperceptions of their peers' attitudes toward drinking (Schroeder & Prentice, 1995). Entering students were randomly assigned to participate in one of two types of discussion sessions about alcohol use during their first week at Princeton. The structure of all sessions was identical: Students first completed a brief questionnaire, then watched a 7-minute video that portrayed several alcohol-related social scenes in a university setting, afterward took part in a 20-minute discussion about drinking on campus, and finally completed another questionnaire. The two types of sessions differed in the content of the 20-minute discussion.

In the *peer-oriented condition,* the discussion centered on pluralistic ignorance and its implications. The facilitator began by describing to students the finding of a self–other discrepancy in comfort with drinking on campus and by briefly explaining the phenomenon of pluralistic ignorance. Students were encouraged to talk about how and why these misperceptions of peer opinion might have developed. They were also asked to reflect on how misperceiving each others' attitudes toward drinking might affect social life on campus.

In the *individual-oriented condition,* the discussion centered on the individual and how he or she makes responsible decisions about alcohol consumption. Students were encouraged to reflect on the types of situations in which they might encounter alcohol at the university, to explore their options in those situations, and to consider the personal and social consequences of various courses of action. They also talked about the effects of alcohol and how it might interfere with their decision-making abilities. The individual-oriented condition was included as a control from which to evaluate the effects of the peer-oriented discussion; it was chosen as the comparison because it is respresentative of many existing programs designed to change drinking behavior.

Four to 6 months after the discussions, students in both conditions completed self-report measures of their alcohol consumption, their involvement in campus groups, and their feelings of comfort and belonging on campus. We expected to find lower levels of reported alcohol consumption and less evidence of alcohol-related alienation among students in the peer-oriented condition than among students in the individual-oriented condition.

In addition to demonstrating the effects of correcting misperceptions of the drinking norm, we were interested in understanding the psychological mechanisms underlying these effects. Thus, we included several additional measures designed to shed some light on *why* exposure to evidence of pluralistic ignorance might reduce students' alcohol consumption. First, we asked all participants to rate both their own comfort with alcohol use and the comfort of the average student, directly before the discussion sessions and also at the time of the follow-up. If dispelling pluralistic ignorance reduces drinking by changing the level of drinking prescribed by the norm, then students in the peer-oriented condition should rate the average student as less comfortable at the follow-up than did students in the individual-oriented condition, and they should drink less as a result of this difference. Second, immediately following the discussion sessions, we asked all participants to complete the short form of Watson and Friend's (1969) Fear of Negative Evaluation Scale (Leary, 1983). This scale assesses the extent to which people are characteristically anxious about others' evaluations of them and fearful of losing social approval. (For example, items include: "When I am talking to someone, I worry about what they may be thinking of me," and "If I know someone is judging me, it has little effect on me.") We intended this scale to serve as a measure of the extent to which students are sensitive to normative social influence. If dispelling pluralistic ignorance reduces drinking by reducing the strength of the norm, then the effects of this manipulation should be greatest for those students who are most sensitive to, and therefore most influenced by, social pressure. Thus, we expected fear of negative evaluation (FNE) to moderate differences between the individual- and peer-oriented conditions.

1. Behavioral Consequences

Did dispelling pluralistic ignorance reduce students' drinking behavior? We averaged their estimates of the number of drinks they had consumed in the past week and in the typical week to create a single index of alcohol consumption. Means on that index for male and female students in each condition are shown in Figure 6. As we predicted, students in the peer-oriented condition consumed significantly fewer drinks each week than did students in the individual-oriented condition. This difference was consistent across gender and was not attributable to differences in rates of abstinence, as there was no effect of condition on the percentage of participants who did not drink during the semester. Thus, it appears that the peer-oriented condition reduced alcohol consumption relative to the individual-oriented condition among students who actually drank alcohol.

We next sought to determine more precisely the mechanism underlying this condition difference. We first considered the possibility that students in the peer-oriented condition drank less because they used the information on peer (dis)comfort to construct a new, more conservative norm. In this case, at the follow-up assessment, students in the peer-oriented condition should rate the average student as less comfortable with campus drinking practices than do students in the individual-oriented condition, and than they themselves did before participating in the discussion sessions. Moreover, this condition difference in average-student comfort ratings should account for the difference in drinking behavior. To evaluate this possibility, we examined students' ratings of their own comfort and the average student's comfort with drinking immediately before the discussion session and at the follow-up assessment several months later. These ratings showed a

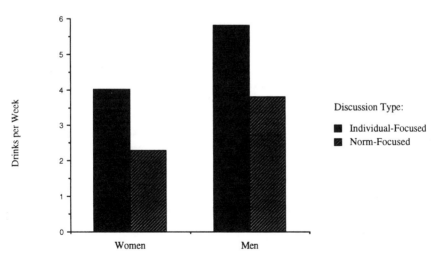

Fig. 6.   Mean number of drinks reported by male and female students in the individual-oriented and peer-oriented conditions at the follow-up assessment.

significant discrepancy between own comfort and average-student comfort at the beginning of the school year and a reduction in this discrepancy by the time of the follow-up. This reduction in pluralistic ignorance was larger for men than for women, replicating our earlier finding of gender differences (see Figures 3 and 4), but it did not vary by condition. None of the interactions of condition with target or time was significant. Thus, it appears that the behavioral effects of dispelling pluralistic ignorance did not result from a reconstruction of the drinking norm. Because students in *both* conditions attributed less comfort to the average student over time, this effect cannot account for the condition difference in drinking.

Therefore, we turned our attention to the possibility that the discussion of pluralistic ignorance in the peer-oriented condition reduced the level of perceived support for the norm and thus its prescriptive strength. We reasoned as follows: In a situation with strong, consensual social norms, individuals will be guided in their behavior both by what they believe those norms to prescribe and by how much they fear the negative evaluations of their peers. Individuals who are highly fearful of negative evaluation should show a stronger relation between their estimates of the norm and their behavior than individuals who are less fearful. In a situation with weak social norms, there should be no relation between FNE and behavioral conformity, because individuals will have no reason to fear social censure for displaying counternormative behavior. Therefore, if educating students about pluralistic ignorance reduces the prescriptive strength of the drinking norm, we should find a difference across conditions in the relations between FNE, estimates of the average student's comfort, and drinking behavior.

To test these predictions, we conducted a regression analysis in which students' scores on the drinking index were predicted from condition, FNE, and estimates of the average student's comfort with alcohol. We expected to find a three-way interaction between these variables: Students should drink in accordance with their perceptions of the average student to the extent that they are fearful of negative evaluation, but only in the individual-oriented condition. Students in the peer-oriented condition, who were informed about pluralistic ignorance, should show no such pattern of results. In addition, we included own comfort level and gender in the analysis because of their strong associations with alcohol consumption.

The results yielded support for our proposed mechanism. In particular, there was a significant interaction between fear of negative evaluation and average-student comfort, which was qualified by the predicted three-way interaction with condition. The form of this three-way interaction is shown in Figure 7. (Note that these results control for own comfort, and thus average-student comfort is calibrated in relative terms. High average-

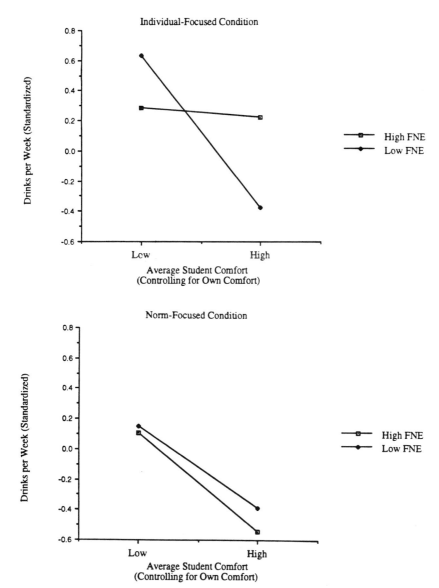

Fig. 7.   Predicted level of drinking behavior for students one standard deviation above and below the mean on fear of negative evaluation (FNE) and perceptions of others' comfort by condition.

student comfort means rating the average student as comfortable relative to oneself; low average-student comfort means rating the average student as uncomfortable relative to oneself. This accounts for the inverse relation between average student comfort and drinking.) The relation between perceptions of the average student and drinking behavior depended on FNE, but only for students in the individual-oriented condition. In this condition, high FNE students drank less than low FNE students when they perceived average-student comfort to be low and more when they perceived average-student comfort to be high. This pattern of results appears to reflect behavioral conformity in response to social pressure. In the peer-oriented condition, there was no such pattern: Indeed, the results for all students mirrored the results for low FNE students in the individual-oriented condition.

These results support the claim that the observed differences in drinking across conditions were due, at least in part, to differences in the prescriptive strength of the drinking norms. It appears that informing students in the peer-oriented condition about pluralistic ignorance reduced perceived support for the norm and thereby lessened the social pressure to drink excessively. As a consequence, these students drank less and showed less evidence of social influences on their alcohol use than did students in the individual-oriented condition.

2. Psychological Consequences

We were also interested in the effects of dispelling pluralistic ignorance on students' involvement and comfort on campus. There were seven questions on the follow-up questionnaire that assessed involvement in campus groups, feelings of comfort and satisfaction at the university, and the importance of fitting in. Our previous studies (e.g., Prentice & Miller, 1993, Study 4) suggested that we would find an association between perceiving the average student to be more comfortable with alcohol than oneself and each of these measures of discomfort at the university. However, if educating students about pluralistic ignorance reduced the preciptive strength of the drinking norm, then it should eliminate this relation. Thus, we should find significant correlations of perceived deviance with social involvement and comfort only for students in the individual-oriented condition. Students in the peer-oriented condition should regard deviance on the alcohol issue as relatively unimportant, and as a result it should not be linked to other aspects of their social life on campus.

We conducted an initial set of analyses to test for differences across conditions in the average levels of involvement, comfort, and the importance of fitting in reported by students. There were no significant effects, although students in the peer-oriented condition rated fitting in as marginally less important than did students in the individual-oriented condtion (Ms = 4.29 and 4.75, respectively). But correlational analyses provided support for our predictions. We computed correlations between perceived deviance (average-student comfort minus own comfort) and each of the social involvement and comfort measures separately by condition. For students in the individual-oriented condition, all of these correlations were significant: Perceived deviance was associated with greater involvement in campus groups (r = .24), less comfort at the university (r = −.31), and less importance placed on fitting in (r = −.28). For students in the peer-oriented condition, none of the correlations was even close to significant.

We interpret these results as evidence for differences in the importance of the drinking norm in the social life of the two groups. Students in the individual-oriented condition, like students in our earlier studies, seemed to take quite seriously what they perceived to be the relation of their own attitudes toward drinking to the attitudes of their peers. Numerous aspects of their social life on campus depended on the extent to which they perceived themselves to be deviant on the alcohol issue. By contrast, students in the peer-oriented condition showed no relation of perceived deviance on alcohol to social involvement and comfort on campus. Again, these findings are consistent with the claim that dispelling pluralistic ignorance serves to reduce the prescriptive strength of the drinking norm.

E. SUMMARY

These investigations of alcohol use on campus have taught us a considerable amount about the causes and consequences of pluralistic ignorance. We obtained evidence tht pluralistic ignorance does, in fact, begin with public expressions and behaviors that misrepresent private sentiments. We maintain that these misrepresentations arise not out of a fear of embarrassment, as previous investigations have emphasized (e.g., Miller & McFarland, 1987, 1991), but rather out of identification with the student body. Students express more positive views about alcohol than they actually hold because they believe those views to be consensual within an enormously valued group. Of course, as they act on that erroneous belief, their public behavior provides further evidence for its validity. Thus, we see the self-perpetuating cycle of erroneous inferences that characterizes pluralistic ignorance.

In addition, our investigations revealed that students' erroneous perceptions of each other's attitudes have real consequences for their own attitudes, their behaviors, and their attachment to the university. Although for most students, their deviance on the alcohol issue is illusory, they apparently experience it as quite real: They react with some combination of behavioral conformity, internalization of perceived peer opinion, and disidentification from the institution. Moreover, our final study provided evidence for the basis of this prescriptive power: the perception that the norm has universal support.

Although we have made considerable progress in our understanding of pluralistic ignorance and comfort with drinking on campus, many unanswered questions remain. Two of these seem particularly noteworthy. First, why are men more likely than women to show a reduction in pluralistic ignorance over time? This finding may be specific to the issue of alcohol use, or it may reflect more pervasive gender differences in reactions to perceived deviance. Additional research is needed to disentangle these possibilities. Second, how precisely does dispelling pluralistic ignorance change drinking behavior? Although we know that students who were educated about pluralistic ignorance drank less than students not so educated, we do not know how this difference was manifest in their day-to-day behavior. It is possible, for example, that students who knew about pluralistic ignorance were less likely to binge drink, drank slightly less alcohol at each party, or attended fewer events each week at which alcohol was available. A more precise understanding of how dispelling pluralistic ignorance changed their patterns of drinking might provide further insight into the psychological processes underlying these behavioral effects.

IV. Pluralistic Ignorance and Sex-Typing in Children

We now turn to a second case of pluralistic ignorance, one that is also driven by group identification: children's beliefs about gender stereotypes. Like the other examples of pluralistic ignorance that we have described, this one also begins with widespread behavioral adherence to social norms—in this case, the norms prescribing appropriate behavior for boys and girls. Children learn these norms at a very young age: By the time they reach elementary school, they are aware of the toys and activities considered most appropriate for each gender (Blakemore, LaRue, & Olejnik, 1979; Carter & Patterson, 1982; Levy & Carter, 1989; see Huston, 1983, for a review). They know which trait adjectives typically describe girls and which typically describe boys (Best et al., 1977; Williams, Bennett, & Best, 1975). They perceive achievement in school subjects as gender-related (Archer & McCrae, 1991) and know which occupations are traditionally held by men and which by women (Garrett, Ein, & Tremaine, 1977; O'Keefe & Hyde,

1983). In short, elementary school children are well aware of the norms governing gender-appropriate behavior.

Moreover, it appears that they act on this awareness. Numerous studies have shown that children behave in a sex-typed fashion, preferring toys and activities considered appropriate for their gender and actively avoiding those considered appropriate for the opposite gender (O'Brien & Huston, 1985; Ruble, Balaban, & Cooper, 1981; see Huston, 1983, for a review). Children's preferences for stereotype-consistent behaviors extend to their future aspirations as well. When asked to indicate which jobs they would most like to hold, girls typically choose traditionally female occupations, and boys choose traditionally male occupations (Eccles & Hoffman, 1984; Farmer & Sidney, 1985; O'Keefe & Hyde, 1983). In their public behaviors and preferences, children display marked conformity to gender-role norms.

Of course, public adherence to social norms is not in itself sufficient to produce pluralistic ignorance: It must occur in the absence of private endorsement of those norms. At least two studies have provided indirect evidence that children may not believe in gender stereotypes as strongly as their behavior suggests. First, Bacon and Lerner (1975) surveyed second-fourth-, and sixth-grade girls about their mother's occupational status, their beliefs about women's employment opportunities, and their own occupational aspirations. They found that daughters of working mothers held quite egalitarian beliefs about the kinds of jobs men and women can do, and this egalitarianism increased with the age of the sample. Yet, the girls uniformly indicated that they themselves would still choose traditional female occupations. In a similar vein, Carter and Patterson (1982) surveyed boys and girls in kindergarten through the eighth grade about their knowledge of and beliefs about gender stereotypes. They found that children became increasingly knowledgeable about the stereotypes as they got older, but were less and less willing to endorse stereotypical beliefs. These findings suggest that children may conform to gender stereotypes without believing in them. In children as young as second-graders, we see evidence of a disjunction between private beliefs and public behaviors that appears to increase with age.

If this analysis is correct, then we would expect to find pluralistic ignorance in children's beliefs about gender stereotypes. Children will hold their own egalitarian beliefs independent of their norm-congruent behavior. Indeed, they will recognize the behavior for what it is: an attempt to act the way a girl or a boy is supposed to act. However, they are unlikely to have similar insight into the causes of other children's norm-congruent behavior. Instead, they will infer their peers' private beliefs directly from what they observe: They will assume that all the other kids actually endorse the gender stereotypes.

A. DEMONSTRATIONS

The first demonstration that children attribute more stereotypical beliefs to their peers than to themselves was provided by Girgus and Gellman (1995). They asked third- and fourth-grade children to indicate their own beliefs about what toys and activities girls and boys like, what jobs women and men can do, and what traits best describe females and males. They also asked the children to indicate how their peers would respond to the same questions. For example, in the toys and activities domain, children were asked, "Who likes to climb trees? What do *you* think?" and were given the options of circling *boys, girls,* or *both.* Then, in a later section of the questionnaire, they were asked, "Who likes to climb trees? What do *other* kids think?" and were again given the options of circling *boys, girls,* or *both.*

The results showed that children attributed significantly more sex-typed beliefs to other children than to themselves. In the tree-climbing example, the prototypical subject indicated that he or she thought that both boys and girls liked to climb trees, but that other kids thought only boys liked to climb trees. This self–other discrepancy was larger for girls than for boys and also varied across domains, with questions about occupations showing the largest discrepancy, questions about activities showing less discrepancy, and questions about traits showing the least discrepancy. Still, the tendency to attribute more sex-typed beliefs to other children than to the self was significant for children of both genders across all three content categories. Thus, there was some preliminary evidence showing that children believe other children endorse gender stereotypes more strongly than they themselves do.

This finding was in keeping with our analysis but was also open to a number of alternative explanations. For example, children could simply be trying to present themselves well to grown-ups, whom they perceive to hold (or at least to endorse) egalitarian views. Perhaps more likely, though, their estimates of the beliefs of their peers may be overly influenced by a vocal minority of children who hold sex-typed beliefs. That is, children who endorse gender stereotypes, believing that they are in the majority, may be quite outspoken about their opinions, whereas children with more egalitarian views may be reluctant to express those views publicly. A number of cases of pluralistic ignorance have been traced to the influence of a vocal minority (e.g., Katz & Schanck, 1938; Korte, 1972; see Miller & Prentice, 1994, for a review). In the present case, this minority might very well consist of boys, who tend to endorse and to adhere to gender-role prescriptions more strongly than do girls (see, e.g., Carter & McCloskey, 1983; O'Keefe & Hyde, 1983). If children base their estimates of the beliefs of other children on boys alone, they will exaggerate support for gender stereotypes. Indeed, this process could explain why Girgus and Gellman (1995) found a larger self–other discrepancy for girls than for boys.

Our goal, therefore, was to establish more conclusively that the self–other difference in endorsement of gender stereotypes was due to erroneous inferences about the causes of norm-congruent behavior. We also sought to strengthen our case for pluralistic ignorance by documenting some consequences of children's misperceptions of their peers. Thus, we conducted a study among third-, fourth-, and fifth-grade boys and girls to test two hypotheses: 1) Children would express less sex-typed beliefs themselves than they would attribute to other children, even when they were asked specifically about children of their own gender; and 2) children would experience pressure to conform to what they perceived to be other children's views (Prentice, Miller, & Girgus, 1995). The design of the study also allowed us to test for a gender difference and an age trend in the magnitude of the self–other discrepancy, which previous studies suggested we might find.

B. GENERAL VERSUS GENDER-SPECIFIC OTHERS

We began with the goal of demonstrating that girls think they hold less sex-typed beliefs than other girls, and boys think they hold less sex-typed beliefs than other boys. All children were first asked to complete a questionnaire, in which they expressed their own beliefs about whether boys, girls, or both boys and girls like each of 30 toys and activities. We chose to focus on toys and activities rather than on traits or occupations, because children have ample opportunity to observe their peers playing with toys and participating in activities. The availability of these observational data is critical to our analysis, for we maintain that they serve as the basis for the erroneous inferences about others' private views that characterize pluralistic ignorance. The 30 items were taken from Perry, Perry, and Hynes's (1990) Toy and Activities Preferences Questionnaire and included 10 masculine, 10 feminine, and 10 neutral toys and activities.

Next, children completed a second questionnaire, in which they answered the same 30 questions as in the first questionnaire but this time they indicated how they thought other children would respond. We varied the composition of the group of other children about whom they were asked. Some of the children were asked the general question about "other kids" that Girgus and Gellman (1995) used. Other children were asked about children of their own gender: Girls were asked to indicate what "other girls" think, and boys were asked to indicate what "other boys" think. Children were randomly assigned to one of these two other target conditions by classroom. We expected that children would express less sex-typed beliefs than they attributed either to other children in general or to other children of their own gender. Our measure of sex-typed beliefs was the number of times children circled *both* (out of 30 possible). Thus, higher numbers indicate less sex-typed responding. Means on this measure by gender, target, and condition, are shown in Figure 8. As expected, children expressed more egalitarian beliefs when responding for themselves rather than for other children, regardless of the composition of the other children group. Thus, we can be fairly certain that they were not simply basing their estimates of other children on a highly sex-typed and unrepresentative sample. Indeed, children showed considerable sensitivity to the particular other children about whom they were asked. As shown in Figure 8, there was a three-way interaction between gender, target, and condition: Girls showed a larger self–other discrepancy when they were asked about other children in general than when they were asked about other girls; boys showed the reverse pattern. We believe that this interaction stems from observable differences between boys and girls in their public adherence to gender–role norms. Boys behave in a more sex-typed fashion than do girls (see, e.g., Carter & McCloskey, 1983; O'Keefe & Hyde, 1983). If children are basing

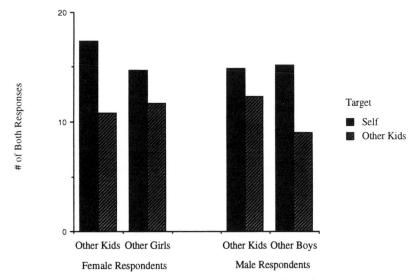

Fig. 8. Mean numbers of *both* responses attributed to self and others by gender and specificity of other-target.

their inferences about other children's beliefs on observable behavior, then they should attribute more sex-typed beliefs to an all male group than to a mixed-gender group and more sex-typed beliefs to a mixed-gender group than to an all female group. This is precisely the pattern of results we obtained.

The results also revealed an increase in the self–other discrepancy with age. Mean numbers of *both* responses to self and other questions for children in each grade are shown in Figure 9. As previous research has suggested, the gap between children's own beliefs and the beliefs they attributed to their peers was larger for older children than for younger children. This increasing discrepancy held for both boys and girls across all other targets.

C. CONSEQUENCES

A second goal of this study was to demonstrate that children's misperceptions of their peers' beliefs about gender stereotypes have psychological consequences. More specifically, we sought evidence that children experience pressure to conform to what they perceive to be other children's views. In our studies of comfort with alcohol use on campus, we tested that hypothesis in two different ways: by examining changes in attitudes and behaviors over time (Prentice & Miller, 1993, Study 3) and by testing for

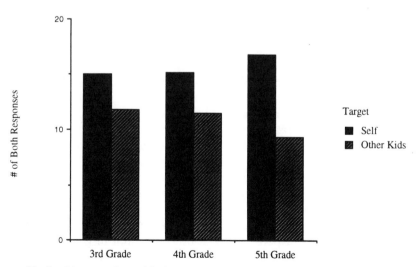

Fig. 9.   Mean numbers of *both* responses attributed to self and others by grade.

moderating effects of fear of negative evaluation (FNE) on the relation between perceptions of others and behavior (Schroeder & Prentice, 1995). The difficulty with the first of these methods in the present context was that we had reason to expect children's beliefs to show developmental changes over time, and it would be very difficult to disentangle developmental trends from the effects of social influence processes. Thus, we opted for the second method. We predicted that FNE would moderate the link between children's perceptions of their peers' beliefs and their own levels of sex-typing: Girls high in FNE would be more feminine and less masculine to the extent that they believed other children held sex-typed views, and boys high in FNE would be more masculine and less feminine to the extent that they believed other children held sex-typed views. We expected children low in FNE to show a much weaker relation between perceptions of others' beliefs and sex-typing. Moreover, we expected to find this pattern of results more strongly among children judging a gender-specific other target than among those judging a general other target, because children of their own gender should serve as a much stronger reference group for our 8- to 10-year-old respondents.

After children had completed the questionnaires assessing their own beliefs about gender stereotypes and the beliefs they attributed to their peers, they completed a final questionnaire that included standardized measures of FNE and sex-typing. The former was a modified version of the short form of the Fear of Negative Evaluation Scale (Leary 1983), with changes designed to make it appropriate for 8- to 10-year-old children (e.g., items were changed to read, "I worry what kids will think of me even when I know it doesn't matter," and "I am not worried even if I know kids might see me in a bad way"). The latter was the short form of the Children's Sex Role Inventory (Boldizar, 1991), which provided a masculinity score and a femininity score for each child.

We conducted regression analyses in which we predicted masculinity and femininity scores from gender, FNE, and estimates of other children's beliefs. The analyses were done separately for respondents who judged other children in general and respondents who judged other children of their gender. We expected to find a three-way interaction between these variables: Both boys and girls should be more sex-typed to the extent that they believe other children hold sex-typed views, especially if they are high in FNE. We also included own beliefs about gender stereotypes in the equation as a control variable.

The results yielded partial but encouraging support for our prediction. We found no effects of perceptions of other children in general on sex-typing, but we did find the expected three-way interaction between gender, FNE, and gender-specific estimates of others on masculinity scores. The form of this three-way interaction is shown in Figure 10. (Note that for estimates of others, higher numbers indicate more egalitarian beliefs.) The relation between perceptions of other children's beliefs and masculinity depended on FNE for both boys and girls, but the pattern of the interaction was reversed in the two cases. For high FNE boys, masculinity decreased as others' beliefs became more egalitarian, whereas for low FNE boys, there was no such trend. For high FNE girls, masculinity increased as others' beliefs became more egalitarian, whereas for low FNE girls, it tended to decrease. The pattern was much stronger for girls than for boys, perhaps because boys showed significantly less variability in their masculinity scores than did girls.

Taken together, the results of this study support our contention that children's beliefs about gender stereotypes are characterized by pluralistic ignorance. We found consistent evidence that children estimate other children's beliefs to be more sex-typed than their own. This difference held across several other targets but varied in its magnitude: Both boys and girls showed a larger discrepancy as more boys were included in the other target group. This pattern is precisely what one would expect if children were relying heavily on observable behavior to estimate their peers' beliefs. Moreover, the children clearly believed in the validity of their estimates. They showed evidence of experiencing pressure to conform to what they perceived to be other children's views. All of these findings are consistent with our pluralistic ignorance account.

D. FUTURE DIRECTIONS

Having established that children's beliefs about gender stereotypes represent a case of pluralistic ignorance, we plan, in future work, to explore some of the causes and consequences of the phenomenon. On the cause side, we would like to examine more closely children's understandings of their own behavior and how those relate to their understandings of their peers' behavior. Although we have assumed that children are aware that their own public behavior does not reflect their private beliefs, this may not be the case: Children may fail to realize just how sex-typed they act in public. They may think that their behavior provides an accurate reflection of their private views, just as they assume that the behavior of others does. Or, as an alternative account, children may realize that they do not act on their beliefs, but assume that others can discern their true beliefs anyway: They may not realize how much their own inferences about others, and others' inferences about them, are driven by public behavior. We hope to

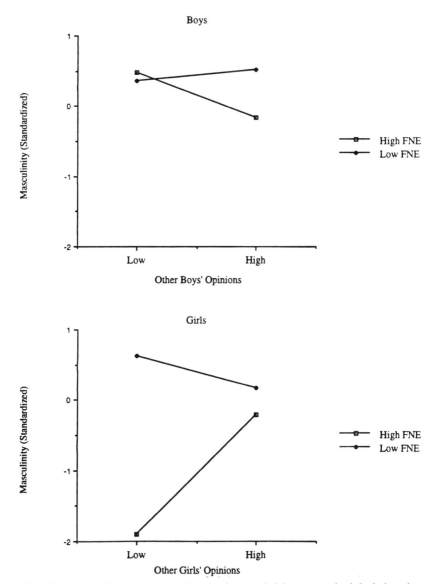

Fig. 10. Predicted level of masculinity for boys and girls one standard deviation above and below the mean on fear of negative evaluation and perceptions of others' beliefs.

disentangle these and other possible causes of the self–other difference in laboratory studies.

On the consequence side, we plan to examine the implications of pluralistic ignorance for efforts to reduce sex-typing in children. Previous attempts to promote gender equity have tended to focus on changing the beliefs of individual children, rather than on changing the social dynamics that foster sex-typing within the peer group. In line with our alcohol work, we believe that programs aimed at dispelling pluralistic ignorance may prove more effective at reducing sex-typing. How best to dispel pluralistic ignorance with children is unclear. The group discussion method we used in our alcohol research may require kinds of reasoning abilities that are not well developed in this age group. Instead, it may be necessary to change children's behavior directly, so that correspondent inferences will map better onto their private beliefs. We will experiment with a number of different techniques for dispelling pluralistic ignorance in future studies.

V. Theoretical Integration

We have presented empirical evidence for two cases of pluralistic ignorance, one concerning college students' attitudes toward alcohol use on campus, and the other concerning gender stereotypes held by elementary-school children. Although these two cases differ in many respects, their underlying motivational structure is quite similar. In both, participants are motivated to behave in norm-congruent ways by a desire to be good and appropriate members of a valued social group. College students drink to excess in part to behave as college students are supposed to behave. Similarly, little boys play with trucks and girls play with dolls because those activities help to define what it means to be a boy or a girl. Pluralistic ignorance arises because children of all ages have enormous difficulty recognizing the motive force of group identification in their fellow group members. Either they fail to realize just how much their own behavior is influenced by their identification with their group, or they fail to entertain the notion that others' norm-congruent behavior is also socially motivated. Whatever the case, they clearly see social motives as more potent causes of their own behavior than that of others.

A. CAUSES OF PLURALISTIC IGNORANCE

In an earlier review paper, we offered two accounts for this self–other difference in the perceived power of social motives (Miller & Prentice,

1994). One traced the difference to the availability of cues that signal social motivation in oneself and in others (Miller & McFarland, 1987). According to this argument, social motives (e.g., fear of embarrassment) are defined primarily by internal, unobservable cues to which people have more access in themselves than in others. As a result, individuals develop a general and enduring belief that they experience these social motives more strongly or more often than others do. Consistent with this account, Miller and McFarland (1987) provided evidence that people rate themselves as more extreme than the average person on traits pertaining to social inhibition as well as other states defined by internal cues (see also McFarland & Miller, 1990).

This explanation was offered specifically to account for cases of pluralistic ignorance driven by fear of embarrassment (see Miller & McFarland, 1987, 1991); however, it may provide a partial account for the type of cases we have studied as well. That is, it seems quite plausible that the feelings of belonging, social anxiety, and alienation that arise from group identification are also largely internal and unobservable. Thus, people may hold an enduring belief that they experience these states more strongly or more often than others do.

A second possibility, suggested by Miller and Prentice (1994), is that our cultural beliefs about human motivation tend to underestimate the power of social motives to influence behavior. According to this argument, individuals base their assessment of their own motivation on past and present experience, which, for most people, turns up considerable evidence that they act to maintain their social identity and social standing. By contrast, they base their inferences about the motivation of others on collective representations of the relative power of different motives. These representations lead them to overestimate the extent to which others are acting on their private beliefs and attitudes and to underestimate the extent to which they are acting to establish their social identity and to maintain their relations with their peers. When behavior is socially motivated, as is true in cases of pluralistic ignorance, these different methods of assessing self and others produce a *motivational inversion:* People's actions are dominated by a motive that their cultural theories of motivational potency suggest is not as influential in determining the actions of other people (Miller & Prentice, 1994).

These two explanations for pluralistic ignorance, one based on differential access to internal cues and the other on misleading collective representations, both offer reasonable accounts for most of the results we have described. At the same time, our data suggest two elaborations to the simple picture of pluralistic ignorance they provide.

First, we actually know very little about the attributions people make about their own norm-congruent behavior. Throughout this discussion, we have assumed that individuals recognize the true causes of their own behavior: They know that they act in accordance with social norms, and know further that they do so in order to fit in. In fact, we have no empirical evidence to support this assumption. Individuals may not realize how norm-congruent their own behavior is, and they may not reflect much on why they act the way they do. They may simply know how they feel, and infer from observable behavior that others feel differently. This simpler set of inferences would be sufficient to produce pluralistic ignorance.

Second, although both explanations provide reasonable accounts for the self–other difference associated with pluralistic ignorance, neither fully explains when and why perceptions of others' sentiments have prescriptive power. Our studies highlighted two conditions that appear to be necessary for the perceived descriptive difference between self and others to have prescriptive force:

1. The others in question must serve as a reference group. In our study of sex-typing, we found that children felt pressure to conform to the views of other children of their own gender but not to the views of other children in general (Prentice, Miller & Girgus, 1995). It appears that, among 8- to 10-year-old children, the others that matter are other boys for boys and other girls for girls.

2. The others in question must be seen as uniform in their opinions. The importance of this criterion was revealed quite clearly when we educated students about pluralistic ignorance (Schroeder & Prentice, 1995). Specifi-cally, we found that informing students of pluralistic ignorance regarding campus drinking practices did not affect the magnitude of the self–other difference in comfort with those practices, but it did reduce the prescriptive strength of peer opinion, as measured by its links to drinking behavior and to other aspects of social life on campus. We interpreted these results to indicate that educating students about pluralistic ignorance served to reduce the perceived uniformity of support for the norm, to make students aware that there was diversity of opinion about the alcohol issue on campus. The comfort of the average student may have remained the same, but the perceived variability of opinion was increased.

The point that both of these findings illustrate is that the consequences of pluralistic ignorance do not follow directly from the perceived self–other difference: It is also necessary that the others represent an important refer-ence group and that they be perceived as uniform in their sentiments. Of course, in cases of pluralistic ignorance, these additional criteria are typically met: Pluralistic ignorance begins with widespread conformity to social norms, which is typically driven by the (perceived) opinions of an important reference group and, in turn, produces the uniformity of behavior from which uniformity of sentiment is inferred. Nevertheless, it is important to delineate these additional steps in the process. Norm-congruent behavior is critical, not simply for producing the self–other discrepancy, but also for giving that discrepancy its psychological impact. Neither of the explanations that we have offered fully specifies these influence processes.

B. RELATION TO OTHER SOCIAL PSYCHOLOGICAL PHENOMENA

Pluralistic ignorance is a member of the family of psychological states that reveal themselves in perceived similarities and differences between self and others. In this section, we highlight its distinctive features by describing its relation to other members of the family.

1. False Consensus

False consensus refers to the well-documented tendency to estimate more support for one's own position than do people holding the opposite position (see Marks & Miller, 1987; Ross, Greene, & House, 1977). This tendency leads one to overestimate the degree of similarity between self and others, and thus would seem to be inconsistent with, and indeed contrary to, pluralistic ignorance. In fact, however, the two processes appear to be largely independent. For example, most field studies of pluralistic ignorance turn up evidence of false consensus as well (e.g., Fields & Schuman, 1976; Prentice & Miller, 1993). That is, the results typically demonstrate an over-estimation of support for the (mis)perceived public norm, and also a system-atic discrepancy between respondents' own views and their estimates of others' views. The latter relation may be, in part, a measurement artifact (see Judd, Kenny, & Krosnick, 1983), but it almost certainly reflects false consensus as well. In estimating social distributions, it appears that people take into account both their own position and the positions they infer, from observable behavior, that others hold. The combination of these sources of knowledge can produce both false consensus and pluralistic ignorance (see Nisbett & Kunda, 1985, for a similar account).

2. False Uniqueness

A second phenomenon that is superficially more similar to pluralistic ignorance is known as the false uniqueness effect: the tendency to overesti-mate the degree of dissimilarity between self and others because of a need to feel unique or superior (Campbell, 1986; Goethals, 1986; Marks, 1984;

Snyder & Fromkin, 1980; Suls & Wan, 1987). For some self–other differ-ences, this motivational explanation seems compelling. For example, Goe-thals (1986) asked students to indicate whether or not they were willing to donate blood and then to estimate the percentage of other students who would act similarly. Those students who volunteered were in the majority (making up 60%), but they predicted that they would be in the minority (making up less than 40%). Goethals argued that the perceptions of those students who agreed to volunteer were motivated by their desire to enhance their self-esteem. The plausibility of this account is strengthened by the estimates of those who refused to volunteer (presumably a socially undesir-able act). These students overestimated the percentage of others who would act as they did by almost 25%.

Because a uniqueness motive also manifests itself in an exaggeration of self–other differences, it stands as an alternative explanation for all pluralis-tic ignorance effects. However, we do not find the alternative compelling in either of the cases we have examined. First, when the uniqueness effect is found, it is typically in judgments of abilities and accomplishments and not in judgments of opinions and attitudes, areas in which thinking one is unique presumably carries the threatening implication that one also is deviant (Kernis, 1984; Marks, 1984). Second, even if one assumed that children might feel good about holding more egalitarian beliefs than their peers, it is difficult to see how a uniqueness motive could explain why girls and boys rated gender-specific other targets so differently or why they felt pressure to conform to the beliefs of these gender-specific others. Similarly, if college students reported holding more conservative attitudes about drinking than their peers because of a desire to feel unique or superior (a conjecture we find farfetched), why would they show symptoms of alienation and internalize others' sentiments?

3. Actor–Observer Bias

The actor–observer bias refers to the tendency to make dispositional attributions for others' actions and situational attributions for one's own (Jones & Nisbett, 1971). It is similar to pluralistic ignorance in that it too represents a divergence of self- and other-perception, but the divergence is sharply different in the two cases. The actor–observer bias is manifest when perceivers make correspondent inferences to explain another person's behavior and situational attributions to explain their own. Pluralistic igno-rance is manifest when perceivers make correspondent inferences to explain another person's behavior and a different kind of dispositional attribution to explain their own, one that links the behavior to a social motive. Thus, the actor–observer bias would produce this attributional discrepancy: "He drinks because he likes the taste of alcohol: I drink because alcohol is a relaxant." Pluralistic ignorance, on the other hand, would produce this discrepancy: "He drinks because he likes the taste of alcohol; I drink because I want to fit in." Further, the fact that one attributes one's own behavior to something about the stimulus or the situation, and the behavior of others to something about them, would not be expected to produce the consequences (e.g., feelings of alienation and deviance) that attend pluralistic ignorance. The belief that other students chose to major in psychology because of something about them, whereas you did so because of something about psychology (Nisbett, Caputo, Legant, & Maracek, 1973), will not lead you to assume that they are more committed to psychology than you are or that they enjoy their psychology classes more than you do. However, these inferences would be expected to follow from the belief that others' decisions to major in psychology reflected their genuine interest in psychology, whereas your similar decision reflected your desire to fit in with a valued social group.

4. Spiral of Silence

Finally, the phenomenon that shares the most in common with pluralistic ignorance is the spiral of silence (Noelle-Neumann, 1984). The spiral of silence is a social dynamic that arises in the expression of public opinion. It stems from two interrelated features of human psychology: First, individuals are sensitive to the opinions of those around them and are inhibited from expressing views they believe that others will not support. Second, they gauge others' views primarily on the basis of observable indicators, including public expressions by particular individuals and reports of the media. As a result, public opinion is vulnerable to a spiral of silence: Individuals who perceive their position to be unsupported—even if they, in fact, constitute a majority—will fall silent, thereby creating the appearance of even less support for the position. Thus, the spiral of silence, like pluralistic ignorance, results from the tendency to overestimate the diagnosticity of public acts: In cases of pluralistic ignorance, perceivers overestimate the degree to which public behavior reflects a corresponding disposition of the actor; in cases of the spiral of silence, perceivers overestimate the degree to which the public expressions of a sample of others reflect the distribution of private opinions within the population.

C. CONSEQUENCES OF PLURALISTIC IGNORANCE

Our field studies of pluralistic ignorance revealed many, but not all, of the psychological and behavioral consequences that have been ascribed to the phenomenon. Perhaps the most notable exception was our failure to find any evidence that pluralistic ignorance left its victims feeling bad about themselves. Previous reviews have speculated that one consequence of pluralistic ignorance might be a reduction in self-esteem (Miller & McFarland, 1991; Miller & Prentice, 1994). Indeed, this consequence has considerable intuitive appeal in cases of pluralistic ignorance driven by fear of embarrassment. In those cases, participants fail to act because they believe that they are more uncertain and confused than everyone else. This belief can hardly leave them feeling good about themselves.

In cases of pluralistic ignorance driven by group identification, however, the intuition is less clear. Do college students feel good or bad about themselves for holding more conservative attitudes about drinking than their peers? Do children feel good or bad about themselves for exceeding their peers in egalitarianism? One obvious way to find out is simply to include measures of self-esteem in studies of these phenomena. We did so (Prentice, Miller, & Girgus, 1995; Schroeder & Prentice, 1995) and found no relation of self-esteem to perceived deviation from peer opinion. Still, we hesitate to conclude from these initial attempts that group-based pluralistic ignorance does not have consequences for self-esteem. Instead, we believe that its consequences depend on the value that individuals privately attach to the attitudes in question. If college students value permissive attitudes toward excessive drinking, then their failure to hold these attitudes may leave them feeling unsophisticated and uptight. However, if they value conservative attitudes toward drinking, then their own views may leave them feeling sensible and mature. Similarly, if children place a positive value on gender stereotypes, then their failure to see the world in those terms may leave them feeling naive and confused. However, if they value egalitarianism, then their views may leave them feeling enlightened and progressive.

Although our studies did not support the claim that pluralistic ignorance would reduce self-esteem, they did document several of its other deleterious consequences. In particular, we found considerable evidence among both children and college students for the role of pluralistic ignorance in perpetuating unpopular social norms and practices. This outcome appears to stem from two separate effects. First, public opinion is quite resistant to change, much more resistant than private attitudes. Individuals tend to assume that everybody feels the way they have always felt, even in cases in which their own views have changed. This conservative lag characterized both of the domains we studied: Indeed, efforts to raise consciousness about alcohol use and gender equality may have affected private attitudes, but they appear to have left public attitudes, and therefore social norms, relatively untouched. Second, pluralistic ignorance carries with it some degree of social pressure to conform to the norm. We found moderating effects of FNE on the relation of perceived peer beliefs to drinking behavior (Schroeder & Prentice, 1995) and to sex-typing (Prentice, Miller, & Girgus, 1995). In both cases, individuals who were most sensitive to social pressure showed the strongest influence of estimated others' views on their behavior—an effect that attests to the presence of conformity pressures. Many, if not most, cases of pluralistic ignorance involve both a conservative lag and conformity pressures. The conjunction of these two processes clearly has the potential to serve as a powerful inhibitor of social change.

In light of the many punishing consequences of pluralistic ignorance—its role in perpetuating dysfunctional social practices and existing inequalities between groups—one might expect individuals to defy their group and violate its norms. Consistent with this expectation, we found some evidence that pluralistic ignorance was associated with disidentification from the group: Students who believed their attitudes toward the keg ban to be deviant showed less willingness to take action and less attachment to the university (Prentice & Miller, 1993, Study 4). Rejection of the group and its norms might seem an obvious way to resolve pluralistic ignorance: After all, if everyone simply withdrew their public support for the norms, the self-perpetuating cycle of pluralistic ignorance would be broken. But this straightforward solution to one dilemma would very likely produce another: It would leave the group and its members without an identity. The latter circumstance may well be as painful as pluralistic ignorance itself.

To illustrate this point, we return to the examples of pluralistic ignorance that we examined in this chapter. Consider first the case of alcohol use by Princeton students. Suppose that the majority of students agreed that drinking did more harm than good and that all drinking traditions and alcohol-driven events should be discontinued. This action might very well accord with students' private sentiments. But what would they do instead? What would define social life at Princeton if it were not for social drinking? What would differentiate Princeton undergraduates from undergraduates at Columbia or Penn, or from Princeton faculty and administrators? The case of children's gender stereotypes is even clearer in this regard. Suppose it were possible to eliminate all manifestations of sex-typing, such that girls and boys were socialized to be exactly the same. Then what would it mean to be a girl or a boy? How would a child show that she was the former and not the latter?

This discussion returns us to the point at which we began: People value their membership in social groups and are motivated to express identification with these groups by behaving in accordance with group norms. Sometimes the norms prescribe behaviors that violate their private sentiments, and under these circumstances, individuals experience alienation from their group and its members. Eliminating the norms may reduce this sense of alienation, but will often replace it with a different kind of alienation—that associated with not having a group identity. One implication of this argument is that attempts to dispell pluralistic ignorance should be accompanied by efforts to develop new and more widely supported norms. It should be much easier to accept the loss of one group identity if it is quickly replaced by another.

VI. Conclusions

We have studied pluralistic ignorance as it is manifested in two real-world settings. This case-based approach raises the question of what general conclusions we can draw from our studies about the psychology of pluralistic ignorance. We believe there are several. First, we chose to study college students' attitudes toward drinking on campus and elementary school children's endorsement of gender stereotypes because we saw both as stemming from a failure to appreciate the power of group identification to influence others' behavior. Our studies supported this assumption and revealed a number of additional similarities: We found consistent evidence for a self–other difference in ratings of private sentiments across all other targets, but predictable selectivity in the other targets whose views had a psychological impact. In addition, we found consistent evidence that pluralistic ignorance produces pressures to conform to social norms, but no evidence that it impacts on individuals' self-esteem. These commonalities across cases allow us to make some tentative generalizations about pluralistic ignorance as it occurs within social groups, although perhaps not as confidently as laboratory studies would allow.

At the same time, we would caution against losing sight of the particulars of these two cases, because they are important both to the clarity of our conceptual analysis and to our understanding of the real world. Because we chose to conduct studies of pluralistic ignorance in field contexts, our operationalizations of the independent and dependent variables derive their meaning from those contexts. Comfort with alcohol means something different to Princeton undergraduates than it does to members of other populations: It has normative force at Princeton and plays a critical role in social life. Similarly, gender stereotypes mean something different to boys than to girls and to elementary-school children than to college students. These details are critical to understanding the results of our studies and to drawing inferences from them about the psychology of pluralistic ignorance. But conceptual clarity is not the only reason for taking an interest in the particulars of our two cases: Each represents a topic of interest in its own right. Alcohol use among college undergraduates and sex-typing among elementary-school children are social problems of considerable significance, ones that have proven very difficult to eradicate. We believe that the potential of social psychological theory to help us understand these problems is at least as promising, and also as valuable, as the potential of the problems to serve as domains in which to test theory. There is no reason why researchers cannot pursue both of these agendas.

Acknowledgments

Preparation of this chapter was supported by National Institute of Mental Health Grant MH44069. We thank Mark Zanna for his helpful comments on an earlier draft of this chapter.

References

Allport, F. H. (1933). *Institutional behavior.* Chapel Hill: University of North Carolina Press.

Archer, J., & McCrae, M. (1991). Gender-perceptions of school subjects among 10- and 11-year-olds. *British Journal of Educational Psychology, 61,* 99–103.

Asch, S. E. (1951). Effects of group pressure upon the modification and distortion of judgments. In H. Guetzkow (Ed.), *Group leadership and men* (pp. 177–190). Pittsburgh, PA: Carnegie Press.

Bacon, C., & Lerner, R. M. (1975). Effects of maternal employment status on the development of vocational-role perception in females. *The Journal of Genetic Psychology, 126,* 187–193.

Berkowitz, A. D., & Perkins, H. W. (1986). Problem drinking among college students: A review of recent research. *Journal of American College Health, 35,* 21–28.

Berkowitz, A. D., & Perkins, H. W. (1987). Current issues in effective alcohol education programming. In J. S. Sherwood (Ed.), *Alcohol policies and practices on college and university campuses* (Vol. 7, pp. 69–85). National Association of Student Personnel Administrators Monograph Series.

Best, D. L., Williams, J. E., Cloud, J. M., Davis, S. W., Robertson, L. S., Edwards, J. R., Giles, H., & Fowles, J. (1977). The development of sex-trait stereotypes among children in the United States, England, and Ireland. *Child Development, 48,* 1375–1384.

Blakemore, J. E. O., LaRue, A. A., & Olejnik, A. B. (1979). Sex-appropriate toy preference and the ability to recognize toys as sex-role related. *Developmental Psychology, 15,* 339–340.

Boldizar, J. P. (1991). Assessing sex typing and androgyny in children: The Children's Sex Role Inventory. *Developmental Psychology, 27,* 505–515.

Campbell, J. D. (1986). Similarity and uniqueness: The effects of attribute type, relevance, and individual differences in self-esteem and depression. *Journal of Personality and Social Psychology, 50,* 281–294.

Carter, D. B., & McCloskey, L. A. (1983). Peers and the maintenance of sex-typed behavior. The development of children's concepts of cross-gender behavior in peers. *Social Cognition, 2,* 294–314.

Carter, D. B., & Patterson, C. J. (1982). Sex roles as social convention: The development of children's conception of sex-role stereotypes. *Developmental Psychology, 18,* 812–824.

Claire, T. V., & Prentice, D. A. (1995). *Conceptual and methodological issues in the estimation of peer opinion.* Unpublished manuscript, Princeton University, Princeton, NJ.

Cramer, P. (1987). The development of defenses. *Journal of Personality, 51,* 79–94.

Crandall, C. S. (1988). Social contagion of binge eating. *Journal of Personality and Social Psychology, 55,* 588–598.

Eagly, A. H. (1978). Sex differences in influenceability. *Psychological Bulletin. 85,* 86–116.

Eccles, J., & Hoffman, L. (1984). Sex roles, socialization, and occupational behavior. In H. W. Stevenson & A. E. Siegel (Eds.), *Research in child development and social policy* (Vol. 1, pp. 367–420). Chicago: University of Chicago Press.

Farmer, H., & Sidney, J. S. (1985). Sex equity in career and vocational education. In S. Klein (Ed.), *Handbook for achieving sex equity through education* (pp. 338–364). Baltimore: Johns Hopkins University Press.

Festinger, L., Schachter, S., & Back, K. (1950). *Social pressures in informal groups.* New York: Harper & Row.

Fields, J. M., & Schuman, H. (1976). Public beliefs and the beliefs of the public. *Public Opinion Quarterly, 40,* 427–448.

Friend, K. E., & Koushki, P. A. (1984). Student substance abuse: Stability and change across college years. *International Journal of the Addictions, 19,* 571–575.

Garrett, C. S., Ein, P. L., & Tremaine, L. (1977). The development of gender stereotyping of adult occupations in elementary school children. *Child Development, 48,* 507–512.

Girgus, J. S., & Gellman, V. A. (1995). *Pluralistic ignorance and children's sex-role stereotypes.* Unpublished manuscript, Princeton University, Princeton, NJ.

Goethals, G. R. (1986). Fabricating and ignoring social reality: Self-serving estimates of consensus. In J. Olson, C. P. Herman, & M. P. Zanna (Eds.), *Relative deprivation and social comparison: The Ontario Symposium on Social Cognition* (Vol. 4, pp. 137–157). Hillsdale, NJ: Erlbaum.

Graham, J. W., Marks, G., & Hansen, W. B. (1991). Social influence processes affecting adolescent substance use. *Journal of Applied Psychology, 76,* 291–298.

Grube, J. W., Morgan, M., & Seff, M. (1988). Drinking beliefs and behaviors among Irish adolescents. *International Journal of the Addictions, 24,* 101–112.

Hansen, W. B., & Graham, J. W. (1991). Preventing alcohol, marijuana, and cigarette use among adolescents: Peer pressure resistance training versus establishing conservative norms. *Preventive Medicine, 20,* 414–430.

Hill, F. E., & Bugen, L. A. (1979). A survey of drinking behavior among college students. *Journal of College Student Personnel, 20,* 236–243.

Huston, A. C. (1983). Sex-typing. In M. Hetherington (Ed.), *Handbook of child psychology: Vol. 4 Socialization, personality, and social development* (pp. 387–467). New York: Wiley.

Jones, E. E., & Nisbett, R. E. (1971). *The actor and the observer: Divergent perceptions of the causes of behavior.* Morristown, NJ: General Learning Press.

Judd, C. M., Kenny, D. A., & Krosnick, J. A. (1983). Judging the positions of political candidates: Models of assimilation and contrast. *Journal of Personality and Social Psychology, 44,* 952–963.

Kandel, D. B. (1980). Drug and drinking behavior among youth. *Annual Review of Sociology, 6,* 235–285.

Katz, D., & Schanck, R. L. (1938). *Social psychology.* New York: Wiley.

Kernis, M. H. (1984). Need for uniqueness, self-schemas, and thought as moderators of the false consensus effect. *Journal of Experimental Social Psychology, 20,* 350–362.

Korte, C. (1972). Pluralistic ignorance about student radicalism. *Sociometry, 35,* 576–587.

Latané, B., & Darley, J. M. (1968). Group inhibition of bystander intervention. *Journal of Personality and Social Psychology, 10,* 215–221.

Latané, B., & Darley, J. M. (1970). *The unresponsive bystander: Why doesn't he help?* New York: Appleton-Century Crofts.

Leary, M. R. (1983). A brief version of the fear of negative evaluation scale. *Personality and Social Psychology Bulletin, 9,* 371–375.

Levit, D. B. (1991). Gender differences in ego defenses in adolescence: Sex roles as one way to understand the differences. *Journal of Personality and Social Psychology, 61,* 992–999.

Levy, G. D., & Carter, D. B. (1989). Gender schema, gender constancy, and gender-role knowledge: The roles of cognitive factors in preschoolers' gender-role stereotype attribution. *Developmental Psychology, 25,* 444–449.

Maddox, G. L. (Ed.). (1970). *The domesticated drug: Drinking among collegians:* New Haven, CT: College and University Press.

Marks, G. (1984). Thinking one's abilities are unique and one's opinions are common. *Personality and Social Psychology Bulletin, 10,* 203–208.

Marks, G., & Miller, N. (1987). Ten years of research on the false consensus effect: An empirical and theoretical review. *Psychological Bulletin, 102,* 72–90.

Matza, D. (1964). *Delinquency and drift.* New York: Wiley.

McFarland, C., & Miller, D. T. (1990). Judgments of self-other similarity: Just like other people, only more so. *Personality and Social Psychology Bulletin, 16,* 475–484.

Meacci, W. G. (1990). An evaluation of the effects of college alcohol education on the prevention of negative consequences. *Journal of Alcohol and Drug Education, 35,* 66–72.

Meilman, P. W., Stone, J. E., Gaylor, M. S., & Turco, J. H. (1990). Alcohol consumption by college undergraduates: Current use and 10-year trends. *Journal of Studies on Alcohol, 51,* 389–395.

Miller, D. T., & McFarland, C. (1987). Pluralistic ignorance: When similarity is interpreted as dissimilarity. *Journal of Personality and Social Psychology 53,* 298–305.

Miller, D. T., & McFarland, C. (1991). When social comparison goes awry: The case of pluralistic ignorance. In J. Suls & T. Wills (Eds.). *Social comparison: Contemporary theory and research* (pp. 287–313). Hillsdale, NJ: Erlbaum.

Miller, D. T., & Prentice, D. A. (1994). Collective errors and errors about the collective. *Personality and Social Psychology Bulletin, 20,* 541–550.

Moscovici, S. (1985). Social influence and conformity. In G. Lindzey & Aronson (Eds.), *The handbook of social psychology* (3rd ed., Vol. 2, pp. 347–412). New York: Random House.

Moscovici, S., & Lage, E. (1976). Studies in social influence: III. Majority and minority influence in a group. *European Journal of Social Pscyhology, 6,* 149–174.

Moscovici, S., & Neve, P. (1972). Studies in social influence: I. Those absent are in the right; convergence and polarization of answers in the course of social interaction. *European Journal of Social Psychology, 2,* 201–214.

Newcomb, T. M. (1943). *Personality and social change.* New York: Holt, Rinehart & Winston.

Nisbett, R. E., Caputo, C., Legant, P., & Maracek, J. (1973). Behavior as seen by the actor and as seen by the observer. *Journal of Personality and Social Psychology, 27,* 154–164.

Nisbett, R. E., & Kunda, Z. (1985). Perceptions of social distributions. *Journal of Personality and Social Pscyhology, 48,* 297–311.

Noelle-Neumann, E. (1984). *The spiral of silence.* Chicago: University of Chicago Press.

O'Brien, M., & Huston, A. C. (1985). Development of sex-typed play behavior in toddlers. *Developmental Psychology, 21,* 866–871.

O'Keefe, E. S. C., & Hyde, J. S. (1983). The development of occupational sex-role stereotypes: The effects of gender stability and age. *Sex Roles, 9,* 481–492.

Orford, J. (1985). *Excessive appetites: A psychological view of addictions.* Chicester, England: Wiley.

Perkins, H. W. (1985). Religious traditions, parents, and peers as determinants of alcohol and drug use among college students. *Review of Religious Research, 27,* 15–31.

Perkins, H. W., & Berkowitz, A. D. (1986). Perceiving the community norms of alcohol use among students: Some research implications for campus alcohol education programming. *International Journal of the Addictions, 21,* 961–976.

Perkins, H. W., & Berkowitz, A. D. (1989). Stability and contradiction in college students' drinking following a drinking-age law change. *Journal of Alcohol and Drug Education, 35,* 60–77.

Perry, L. C., Perry, D. G., & Hynes, J. (1990). *The relation of sex-typing to the outcomes children expect for sex-typed behavior.* Unpublished manuscript, Florida Atlantic University, Boca Raton.

Prentice, D. A., & Miller, D. T. (1993). Pluralistic ignorance and alcohol use on campus: Some consequences of misperceiving the social norm. *Journal of Personality and Social Psychology, 64,* 243–256.

Prentice, D. A., & Miller, D. T. (1995). Unpublished data, Princeton University, Princeton, NJ.

Prentice, D. A., Miller, D. T., & Girgus, J. S. (1995). Unpublished data, Princeton University, Princeton, NJ.

Ross, L., Greene, D., & House, P. (1977). The "false consensus effect": An egocentric bias in the social perception and attribution process. *Journal of Experimental Social Psychology, 13,* 279–301.

Ruble, D. N., Balaban, T., & Cooper, J. (1981). Gender constancy and the effects of sex-typed televised toy commercials. *Child Development, 52,* 667–673.

Schroeder, C. M., & Prentice, D. A. (1995). *Pluralistic ignorance and alcohol use on campus II: Correcting misperceptions of peer opinion:* Unpublished manuscript, Princeton University, Princeton, NJ.

Snyder, C. R., & Fromkin, H. L. (1980). *Uniqueness: The human pursuit of difference.* New York: Plenum Press.

Stein, J. A., Newcomb, M. D., & Bentler, P. M. (1987). An 8-year study of multiple influences on drug use and drug use consequences. *Journal of Personality and Social Psychology, 53,* 1094–1105.

Straus, R., & Bacon, J. M. (1953). *Drinking in college.* New Haven, CT: Yale University Press.

Suls, J., & Wan, C. K. (1987). In search of the false uniqueness phenomenon: Fear and estimates of social consensus. *Journal of Personality and Social Psychology, 52,* 211–217.

Tajfel, H. (1981). *Human groups and social categories: Studies in social psychology.* London: Cambridge University Press.

Thorner, G. (1986). A review of the literature on alcohol abuse and college students and the alcohol awareness program at SUNYAB. *Journal of Alcohol and Drug Education, 31,* 41–53.

Turner, J. C. (1991). *Social influence.* Pacific Grove, CA: Brooks Cole.

Turner, J. C., Hogg, M., Oakes, P., Reicher, S., & Wetherell, M. (1987). *Rediscovering the social group: A self-categorization theory.* Oxford, UK: Basil Blackwell.

Watson, D., & Friend, R. (1969). Measurement of social-evaluative anxiety. *Journal of Consulting and Clinical Psychology, 33,* 448–457.

Wechsler, H., & McFadden, M. (1979). Drinking among college students in New England. *Journal of Studies on Alcohol, 40,* 969–996.

Williams, J. E., Bennett, J. M., & Best, D. L. (1975). Awareness and expression of sex stereotypes in young children. *Developmental Psychology, 11,* 635–642.

PEOPLE AS FLEXIBLE INTERPRETERS: EVIDENCE AND ISSUES FROM SPONTANEOUS TRAIT INFERENCE

James S. Uleman
Leonard S. Newman
Gordon B. Moskowitz

I. Introduction

Social psychologists have labored long to explicate the ways in which knowledge, attitudes, beliefs, and meaning are actively constructed. The models that they have developed, however, typically emphasize the effortful nature of the cognitive processes that people use to manipulate and process information. At the very least, it is almost universally assumed that the use of prior cognitive structures and even simple decision rules require an explicit intention to interpret a person, behavior, or event. This way of thinking leaves little room for the possibility that inferences about our social worlds occur effortlessly, and even unintentionally. But do we routinely and habitually impose meaning on the events around us, even when we have no immediate purpose in doing so? Or do we engage in the quest for comprehension only selectively, using concepts to categorize and infer only for an immediate purpose, or when we are confronted by unusual and mysterious events? In this chapter, we attempt to make the case for the first possibility—that the meaning of many social events is constructed routinely, habitually, and unintentionally (i.e., spontaneously). We do this primarily by summarizing the research since 1984 on spontaneous trait inferences (STIs), and by discussing some of its implications for related literatures.

"Spontaneous trait inferences" are said to occur when attending to another person's behavior produces a trait inference in the absence of our explicit intention to infer traits or form an impression of that person. We

ADVANCES IN EXPERIMENTAL
SOCIAL PSYCHOLOGY, VOL. 28

make inferences "spontaneously" when we form them "in accordance with or resulting from [our] natural feeling, temperament, or disposition, or from a native internal proneness, readiness, or tendency, without compulsion, constraint, or premeditation" (*Webster's New Universal Unabridged Dictionary,* 1983, p. 1756). For example, if you were at a wedding and happened to see a man stepping on his girlfriend's feet while the two of them were trying to dance, you might infer that he is *clumsy.* Also, if you read that "John returned the lost wallet with all the money in it," you might imagine that John is *honest.* The research on STI indicates that people make such inferences not only in the absence of explicit goals to form trait inferences, but also without even being aware that they have made them. We effortlessly extract meaning from the environment (or construct meanings to fit it), with no proximate goal for doing so. We are inveterate interpreters, habitually and routinely scanning the world around us and reading its meanings as naturally as we extract oxygen from the air.

STIs are inferences in the sense that they require the perceiver to combine behavioral information and extract or construct some meaning. In some sense, this describes all of perception and cognition. Bruner (1957) described perception as acts of categorization. However, we have a more specific meaning in mind, first because we have relied exclusively on trait inferences from behavior, and second because we rely on text rather than film to present behavior. Our focus has been on the level of cognitive processes that makes sentence and story comprehension possible. These processes are more complex than those producing the "direct" construct activation that characterizes word comprehension and underlies semantic and repetition priming. They involve combining the meanings of many words, and selecting among the many meanings of each word, to arrive at an emergent meaning that cannot be attributed to any one of the sentence parts. The inference rules that permit text comprehension (which are not completely understood, to say the least; see Balota, d'Arcais, & Rayner, 1990; Graesser & Bower, 1990) have been our prototypes in thinking about inference processes. Despite our exclusive focus on inferences drawn from text, we assume that observing actual behaviors has similar consequences, and that people have analogous procedures for parsing the stream of behavior, disambiguating its parts, and extracting its meaning(s).

If the activation of single concepts through priming marks the lower bound of the inference processes we have in mind, then the upper bound is marked by deliberate, effortful reasoning and problem solving. For the fluent reader, comprehension of simple text proceeds with relatively little effort because we have become "experts" (Chi, Glaser, & Farr, 1988). It is only when these procedures fail to yield intelligible results that more reflective, deliberate, and effortful reasoning occurs. At that point, the processes are no longer spontaneous.

Thus, we began by accepting the commonly held proposition that "perception is a constructive process," even though our phenomenology provides little or no evidence of this. One of the authors remembers being amazed at Hebb's (1949) summary of Senden's (1932) account of the visual experience of patients who had their congenital cataracts removed as adults. They could not "see" even the simplest shapes. They had to look for corners to distinguish circles from triangles, rather than "perceive" the shapes directly as we do.

> A patient was trained to discriminate square from triangle over a period of 13 days, and had learned so little in this time "that he could not report their form without counting corners one after another . . . ." (Hebb, 1949, p. 32, from Senden, 1932, p. 160)

Today, congenital cataracts are removed shortly after birth. However, a similar perceptual problem arises with profoundly hearing-disabled candidates for cochlear implants. Adults who have been unable to hear since birth benefit the least and are least likely to learn to understand spoken language. Developing the constructive processes that produce the phenomenologically "simplest" perceptions requires extensive learning or experience, which is denied to those who experience hearing or visual disability from birth. However, if you are fluent with spoken language, even word meanings can capture your attention when you are not attending to their source, as demonstrated by the well-known "cocktail party effect" (Cherry, 1953). Most of us experience the shape of triangles or the meanings of words in the auditory speech stream quite routinely and habitually without any apparent effort or particular processing goals. These complex perceptual processes occur "spontaneously."

Our research asks whether interpretive processes that are more cognitive and less perceptual (whatever this distinction might mean) also occur spontaneously. Are social categories such as traits used spontaneously in the same way that object categories are?

One might imagine that using person categories (such as traits) accurately requires more observations over a longer period of time than using object categories. Srull and Wyer (1979) suggested that single observations of discrete behaviors are not sufficient to trigger trait inferences without an explicit intent to extract an inference from the behavior. Although extended observation is required for some person categories (and some object categories as well), Ambady and Rosenthal (1992) found that "thin slices" of behavior are remarkably informative. They performed a meta-analysis of research on the objective accuracy[1] of behavioral predictions made from very brief observations of people and their behavior. They concluded that "predictions based on observations under ½ min in length did not differ significantly from predictions based on 4- and 5-min observations" (Ambady & Rosenthal, 1992, p. 256). It, therefore, is possible to judge some traits very quickly and accurately, although this may depend on the extent to which the behavioral evidence is infused with meaning (e.g., Heider, 1958; McArthur & Baron, 1983; Moskowitz & Roman, 1992). People can also be quick to make trait inferences of questionable validity. For example, there is a large body of research supporting the immediacy of stereotype activation and judgments (e.g., Berry & McArthur, 1986; Brewer, 1988; Fiske & Neuberg, 1990).

One might also imagine that social perception is less "basic" than object perception, in the sense that it depends less directly on innate capacities, and hence is less likely to be spontaneous. However, there is a growing body of opinion suggesting that many kinds of social perception depend on innate capacities. We seem to be "hard wired" for the perception of faces (Johnson & Morton, 1991) and for interpreting emotions from facial expressions (e.g., Ekman, 1972; cf. Russell, 1994). Language is clearly central to social life and perception, and its acquisition seems to depend on inborn neurological structures (e.g., Pinker, 1990). We may even be innately prepared to use such abstract social concepts as cheating in social exchanges (Cosmides, 1989), or to develop theories of others' beliefs, desires, and intentions (Leslie, 1987; Premack, 1990). Therefore, neither evolutionary nor neuroscientific reductionism provide clear bases for believing that person perception is less basic, and hence less spontaneous than object perception.

However, there are some differences between social categories such as traits and object categories such as triangles and squares. Most object categories are fuzzy, typically having a graded structure organized around a central prototype (Posner & Keele, 1968; Rosch, Mervis, Gray, Johnson, & Boyes-Braem, 1976), whereas trait concepts are probably even fuzzier (e.g., Cantor & Mischel, 1979), and may be based more on theory. (Borkenau, 1990; Uleman, in press). There are more profound differences between social perception and object perception. Kenny (1994), who is particularly interested in person perception processes embedded in social interaction, lists four differences (that he then accommodates in his elegant formal models).

[1] Person perception is reciprocal. . . . The two-sided nature of person perception means that people are simultaneously "checking each other out." . . . [2] When I

---

[1] Objective criteria included experts' ratings and the presence of deception.

encounter another person, not only is the other person perceiving me; I also know that the other is doing so, and I wonder how he or she sees me. . . . [3] Person perception is directly tied to self-perception, whereas in object perception, self-perception is much less important. . . . [4] People change much more than physical objects do. . . . An individual's behavior changes when he or she is with different interaction partners. (pp. 1–2)

This last point is reminiscent of Heider's (1944) observation that because others change from moment to moment, we seek stable features that give us coherent knowledge on which to base predictions of their future behavior. Trait inference provides this sense of predictive veridicality (Bruner, 1957). These considerations suggest that social perception is more complex than much object perception.

A priori arguments can therefore be generated for or against the possibility of spontaneous social inferences because social perception resembles or differs from object perception. Our intuition was that spontaneous inferences occur, and in this we were not alone.

We look at a person and immediately a certain impression of his character forms itself in us. A glance, a few spoken words are sufficient to tell us a story about a highly complex matter. We know that such impressions form with remarkable rapidity and great ease. Subsequent observations may enrich or upset our first view, but we can no more prevent its rapid growth than we can avoid perceiving a given visual object or hearing a melody. (Asch, 1946, p. 258)

Our program of research supports this intuition and demonstrates the existence of STIs. However, it has also generated many challenging questions that are just beginning to receive attention. What conditions are necessary and sufficient for spontaneous inferences to occur? When (if ever) do we become aware that we are making spontaneous inferences or become conscious of their content? When inferences occur spontaneously (i.e., without the goal of categorizing something), do these activated concepts refer to anything, and if so, in what sense? Are these inferences about people or just descriptions of their behaviors? What are the consequences of STIs? Are there individual or cultural differences in the proclivity to make STIs? Moreover, is there anything unique about trait categories and inferences, or do the STI results generalize to the other categories we use to give events meaning? In this chapter, we describe the research that gave rise to these questions and the initial answers it suggests.

II. Evidence for STI

We are not the first to investigate the issue of how readily inferences about others occur when inferences are not the focal task. However, most prior research was on spontaneous causal inferences, and it used more reactive paradigms than those described in the following discussion (see Hastie, 1984; Kanazawa, 1992; Weiner, 1985). People were asked to think aloud and report their "spontaneous" thoughts about others. It is likely that such instructions prompt more elaborate processing than would otherwise occur, and such procedures cannot reveal nonconscious inferences.

Smith and Miller (1983) developed a less reactive method for investigating which attributions occur when trait-implying behaviors are encountered. Participants in their studies were given trait-implying sentences to read, followed by one of eight possible questions (Study 1) on a computer screen. Response times (RTs) were analyzed to compare attributions. The shortest RTs were for the actor's gender, whether the person intended the action, and whether a particular trait described the actor. Smith and Miller concluded that "sentences are processed during their comprehension in a way that . . . involves tentative-schema-based judgments related to causality, in particular the inference of whether or not the event is intended and what traits the actor might possess to cause the event. This causal material is stored in memory along with a representation of the sentence itself" (p. 504). Participants in this study could not anticipate which one of the eight questions they would be asked after each sentence, because these occurred randomly. However, pretraining and practice trials made it clear that one of eight questions would follow each sentence. This procedure, therefore, cannot address the question of whether trait inferences from behaviors occur spontaneously when trait questions are not anticipated.

All of the evidence for STI comes from experiments in which people attend to descriptions of others' behaviors. These descriptions are as concrete as possible, and avoid interpreting the behaviors' meanings. They employ predominantly what Semin and Fiedler (1992) call "descriptive action verbs," rather than "interpretive action verbs" or "state verbs." Participants are asked to read these descriptions under a variety of instructions, but they are never asked to form impressions or infer traits. (Impression-formation or trait-inference instructions make any trait inferences nonspontaneous, by definition, because they provide the proximate goal of inferring traits.)

To date, seven different paradigms have been employed to detect and investigate spontaneous trait inference: (1) cued recall under memory instructions (and other nonimpression goals); (2) cued recall of distractors; (3) recognition probe; (4) lexical decision; (5) delayed recognition; (6) word stem completion; and (7) relearning. A description of the basic evidence for STI from each paradigm follows.

A. CUED RECALL UNDER MEMORY INSTRUCTIONS

The cued recall paradigms are based on Tulving's principle of encoding specificity, which states that "specific encoding operations performed on what is perceived determine what is stored, and what is stored determines what retrieval cues are effective in providing access to what is stored" (Tulving & Thomson, 1973, p. 369). This principle stresses "the importance of encoding events at the time of input as the primary determinant of the storage format and retrievability of information . . ." (Tulving, 1972, p. 392). This means that if people study focal information for a subsequent memory test, and it is accompanied by secondary information that gets incidentally encoded along with focal information, this secondary information will provide effective retrieval cues. Cue effectiveness is "the probability of recall of the target item in the presence of a discrete retrieval cue" (Tulving & Thomson, 1973, p. 354), relative to noncued or free recall. Thomson and Tulving (1970) demonstrated encoding specificity by pairing focal words (e.g., CHAIR) with weak semantic associates (e.g., GLUE) in a list that participants studied with the expectation of being tested on the focal words. Recall of the focal words was best when the secondary information (e.g., GLUE) was provided as cues. It was significantly better than noncued recall, and most remarkably, it was better than recall cued by strong semantic associates (e.g., TABLE).

Winter and Uleman (1984) reasoned that if people study sentences that imply traits, and they spontaneously infer these traits at the time of encoding, the traits will be encoded into memory with the sentences and subsequently serve as effective retrieval cues. This procedure was similar to Thomson and Tulving's (1970) except that the secondary information was never explicitly presented. Its "presentation" was implicit and depended on participants' inferences.

Participants carefully studied a series of 18 trait-implying sentences, for about 8 s each, in preparation for a memory test. Many of these sentences were from Smith and Miller (1983) (e.g., "The reporter steps on his girlfriend's feet during the foxtrot."). Trait implications had been carefully established in a series of pretests, and sentence actors were designated by occupational roles unrelated to the traits. (See Table I for more examples. The "action gist cues" are discussed in Section VIII,A.) After a 2-min anagrams distractor task to clear short-term memory, participants completed a cued recall test of memory for the sentences. Some sentences were cued with the trait implied by that sentence (e.g., CLUMSY); others were cued by strong semantic associates of the sentence actor (e.g., NEWSPAPER), and others had no cue. Winter and Uleman predicted that traits would be more effective than no cues, and would be at least as effective

TABLE I
ILLUSTRATIVE TRAIT-IMPLYING SENTENCES AND THEIR RECALL CUES
(From Winter et al., 1985)

Sentence	Semantic	Action gist	Trait
The child tells his mother that he ate the chocolates.	Toys	Confessing	Honest
The decorator tells the dentist all about her neighbor's habits.	Interior	Talk	Nosy
The mailman picks his teeth during dinner at the fancy restaurant.	Letters	Eating	Ill-mannered
The minister gets his poem published in the *New Yorker*.	Church	Writing	Talented
The receptionist steps in front of the old man in line.	Telephone	Cutting in front	Rude
The secretary solves the mystery halfway through the book.	Typewriter	Reading	Clever
The tailor carries the old woman's groceries across the street.	Clothes	Assisting	Helpful

as strong semantic cues. The semantically cued condition controlled for the possibility of undetected but weak semantic associations between the trait cues and sentence words. If trait cues are at least as effective as strong semantic associates, but are not strong semantic associates themselves, then their association with the sentences must have been established at encoding.

Results confirmed Winter and Uleman's prediction. Trait-cued sentence recall was as high as semantic-cued recall, and was higher than noncued recall. In a second experiment, they used strong semantic associates of the sentence verbs rather than the actors (e.g., OUCH was the associate of "steps on feet"). Trait-cued recall was higher than both semantic-cued and noncued recall. The authors concluded that participants had spontaneously inferred traits during comprehension.

The sentences used by Winter and Uleman (in this and subsequent studies) had a consistent four-part structure. Each was composed of an actor, a verb, a direct or indirect object, and a prepositional phrase (e.g., The plumber / slips / an extra $50 / into his wife's purse). Therefore, cued recall could be analyzed as a function of sentence part. In practice, however, recall for the three sentence parts making up the predicate (i.e., the verbs, objects, prepositional phrases) tends to be very similar. Therefore, sentence part analyses have typically compared actor recall to predicate recall. Such analysis allows one to compare the trait-cued recall of the identities of people performing the behaviors with the trait-cued recall of the behaviors themselves.

Thus Winter and Uleman analyzed the recall of actors and of predicates separately, providing additional information on the links in memory between semantic cues, spontaneously inferred traits, and actors and behaviors. Trait-cued recall of behaviors was higher than trait-cued recall of actors in both studies. This is not surprising because the traits were implied by the behaviors but not the actors. However, it raises the question (to which we return next) of whether spontaneous trait inferences are about the actor or merely about the behavior.

In Winter and Uleman, semantic cues were associates of the actors (Experiment 1) or of the verbs (Experiment 2). Trait-cued recall of behaviors in both studies confirmed the pattern predicted from encoding specificity, but this was not true for recall of actors. In Experiment 1, when the semantic cues were associates of the actors' semantic-cued recall of actors exceeded trait-cued recall, which exceeded noncued recall. This is not surprising because the cues were associates of the actors, but this result does not support the prediction from encoding specificity that trait inferences would be encoded with the actors and be *at least as effective* in retrieving actors as are strong semantic associates. In Experiment 2, when the semantic cues were associates of the verbs, actor recall did not differ among the three cuing conditions. Thus, the evidence for STI in these studies really came from recall of the behaviors. Trait-cued recall of behaviors exceeded semantic-cued and noncued recall, regardless of whether the semantic cues were associates of the actor or the behavior.

In all subsequent studies, the semantic cues have been associates of the actors rather than the verbs for two reasons. First, Winter and Uleman's Experiment 2 showed that trait-cued recall of behaviors exceeds semantic-cued recall under conditions that provide the strongest test of the spontaneous inference hypothesis: when the semantic cues are associates of behavior-description words themselves. This point, therefore, has generally been regarded as established. Second, researchers have continued to think of trait inferences as referring to actors as well as behaviors. Therefore, semantic associates of actors have been seen both as generally appropriate semantic cues, and as providing an informative comparison condition for the trait-cued recall of actors.

The basic result—that trait-cued recall of behaviors is at least as high as semantic-cued recall, and exceeds noncued recall—has been replicated in four subsequent studies. Uleman, Winborne, Winter and Shechter (1986) asked participants to study a set of 12 sentences and then administered a memory test. Trait-cued and semantic-cued recall were similar, and both exceeded noncued recall. Claeys (1990) asked Dutch undergraduates to study a set of 18 trait-implying behaviors for a memory test. Trait-cued recall exceeded semantic-cued recall, indicating that STI occurred. Delmas (1992, July; Experiment 1) used French translations of 20 sentences from Winter and Uleman (1984) and Winter, Uleman, and Cunniff (1985). French undergraduates studied each sentence for 8 s for a memory test. After the 2-min anagrams distractor task, trait-cued recall of behaviors exceeded semantic-cued and noncued recall of behaviors, again indicating STI. Finally, Uleman and Moskowitz (1994, Experiment 1) had participants study 18 sentences for a memory test, then place a check on a sheet of paper each time they silently rehearsed each sentence. Trait-cued recall of the behaviors exceeded semantic-cued recall, indicating STI. But there was only a weak tendency ($p < .11$) for trait-cued recall to exceed noncued recall. In another condition of this study, participants had the same task but were also asked to ignore sentence meanings during rehearsal (to see whether this would inhibit STI). Trait-cued recall of behaviors was nonsignificantly higher than semantic-cued recall, and significantly higher than noncued recall, replicating the predicted pattern.

In summary, the basic pattern predicted from the principle of encoding specificity—that trait-cued recall of behaviors would be at least as high as semantic-cued recall, and exceed noncued recall—has been found in five studies done in three languages. In addition, the relatively poor trait-cued recall of actors in these studies highlighted an important issue: Do STIs reflect the categorization of behavior into trait-relevant categories rather than the attribution of traits to the people performing those behaviors? We return to this subtle distinction in Section IV later.

B. CUED RECALL OF DISTRACTORS

The defining feature of spontaneous inferences is that they occur unintentionally. Thus trait inferences made in the course of studying behavior descriptions for a memory test fit this definition. However, the meaning and structure of goals are complex (see Section III), and this makes the cued recall evidence given earlier more ambiguous than it seems at first. Pursuing one goal may entail pursuing other goals because goals may be nested as well as mutually exclusive. There are a variety of ways to memorize something, and one very effective way is elaboration. In the aforementioned studies, the sentences that participants memorized implied traits, so intentional elaboration easily could have produced trait inferences, albeit "unintentionally." Does STI occur if participants do not expect to have their memory tested, and are therefore presumably less likely to use elaboration as a strategy for processing the sentences?

Winter et al. (1985) devised a way to study this question by presenting the trait-implying sentences as distractors. Participants learned that their primary task was to memorize strings of digits. Each trial consisted of 1) the presentation of a string of digits to memorize, 2) the presentation of a "distractor sentence" to read aloud and then repeat from memory, and 3) recall of the digits. After 16 such trials and a 2-min anagrams task, participants were surprised by a cued recall test of their memory for the sentences. Trait-cued recall of the behaviors exceeded semantic-cued and noncued recall, indicating STI. Lupfer, Clark, and Hutcherson (1990; no information condition) and Uleman, Newman, and Winter (1992) have replicated these results. Thus STI does not depend on an elaboration strategy for memorizing trait-implying sentences. They occur even when they are attended to briefly and treated as distractors.

Cued recall has been used for some time to investigate inferences made during text comprehension, but it is not without its ambiguities. Anderson and Ortony (1975) used it to investigate context effects on the elaborative meanings given to words. For example, they found that recall of "nurses are often beautiful" is more effectively cued by ACTRESS than by DOCTOR, whereas "nurses have to licensed" is more effectively cued by DOCTOR than by ACTRESS. Paris and Lindauer (1976) showed that implicit instruments (e.g., SCISSORS for "The athlete cut out an article for his friend") cue retrieval as effectively as explicit instruments (when the sentence includes "cut out an article with scissors"). However, their encoding interpretation was effectively challenged by Corbett and Dosher (1978) and Singer (1979), who offered an alternative explanation that credited the results to processes occuring at retrieval rather than at encoding.

Winter and Uleman (1984) attempted to rule out retrieval explanations through extensive pretesting, but their efforts did not convince all of their critics. For example, referring to the sentence, "The reporter steps on his girlfriend's feet during the foxtrot," and the cue, CLUMSY, Wyer and Srull (1989) argued that

> when subjects were asked to recall the behaviors but could not remember them, they used the trait cues they were given to generate typical behaviors that exemplified the concept, hoping that characteristics of these more general behaviors would remind them of the specific behavior that had actually been presented. (Thus, a subject who is given the cue "clumsy" may think of typical clumsy behaviors, such as "bumps into people on the dance floor,". . .) These *behavioral* features may then cue the recall of the stimulus behavior even if the behavior had not been encoded in trait terms at the time it was read. (p. 146)

Although a retrieval explanation of the basic cued recall results (presented earlier) has some plausibility, more complex cued recall results cannot be explained solely in terms of retrieval. For example, several studies have shown that manipulating encoding conditions affects the effectiveness of trait cues (presumably established at encoding) more than that of semantic cues (which depends on a priori associations). Uleman et al. (1992), using a procedure similar to the one developed by Winter et al. (1985), manipulated the availability of cognitive resources at encoding. They did this by varying the difficulty of the digit recall task participants engaged in while they read the behavioral descriptions. The cognitive load manipulation was successful (as revealed by a probe reaction time measure), and the most difficult digit recall task selectively depressed trait-cued recall; recall aided by semantic cues was unaffected. These results indicated that the link in memory between trait cues and behaviors typically found in studies using this experimental procedure depends on inferential activity occurring at encoding. (See also Uleman and Moskowitz (1994) for conceptually similar findings involving the manipulation of processing goals.) The results of Newman and Uleman's (1990) study (discussed in more detail in Section III, C) also argue against an exclusive retrieval interpretation of cued-recall studies. Newman and Uleman used evaluatively ambiguous sentences (e.g., "Molly would not take no for an answer") and found that the trait primes that participants were exposed to before reading the sentences determined the effectiveness of alternative retrieval cues (e.g., DETERMINED or PUSHY). The STIs that participants made depended on the traits that were most accessible to them.

Nevertheless, STI evidence from another paradigm that detects inferences made during comprehension but minimizes the role of strategic retrieval from long-term memory would be informative.

C. RECOGNITION PROBE

McKoon and Ratcliff (1986, Experiment 1) used a recognition probe procedure to investigate "predicting inferences," that is, events that one might predict while reading text. Participants read paragraphs on a cathode ray tube (CRT) screen, one sentence at a time (e.g., "After locating the cavity, the dentist told John to open his mouth"). After each paragraph, a probe word (e.g., DRILL) appeared on the screen and participants indicated, as quickly and accurately as possible, whether the word had literally been in that paragraph. The occurrence of the probes could not be anticipated because paragraph lengths varied randomly. McKoon and Ratcliff reasoned that when a paragraph predicted the event described by the probe, error rates would be greater or RTs would be longer because the event's representation had been activated. Such concept activation makes it harder to reject the recognition probes quickly and accurately. This is exactly what they found when they compared error rates and RTs after predicting versus control paragraphs. (Control paragraphs contain the major words of the predicting paragraphs, but do not imply the probe concept. The control sentence in the last example was, "John opened his mouth for the dentist, but there were no cavities.") Note that in this paradigm, inferences interfere with optimal performance, thus pitting intentional and unintentional processes against each other and thereby providing strong evidence that inferring the probe concepts is unintended.

Newman (1991, Experiment 2) adapted this paradigm to study STI among fifth-graders and college students by having a tape recorder present the paragraphs over headphones and by manually triggering the computer that presented recognition probes on a CRT screen. College students' RTs for predicting paragraphs resembled those reported by McKoon and Ratcliff: 902 ms for predicting paragraphs and 862 ms for control paragraphs. However, no parallel results were obtained with trait-implying paragraphs. For example, RTs to the probe word NEAT were no slower following the paragraph, "Jennifer told her friends to wait until she picked up the mess she had made in her room, even though they asked her to hurry up because they wanted to go outside," than they were following the paragraph, "In her room, Jennifer got ready in a hurry because her friends told her they wanted to go mess around outside, and she had asked them to wait until she was done." Part of the problem seemed to be that the control paragraphs were significantly harder to comprehend than the trait-implying paragraphs (as rated by college students), which increased control RTs. Newman (1993, Experiment 2) used a procedure closer to McKoon and Ratcliff's (1986), but failed again to find the predicted main effect with trait-implying paragraphs. (However, he did find important interactions between trait RTs and other variables, which are discussed in Section VII,B.)

Uleman, Hon, Roman, and Moskowitz (in press) reported three studies with this paradigm that did show the expected main effect; STI interfered with responding to the probes quickly and accurately. Study 1 replicated McKoon and Ratcliff's procedure exactly but substituted trait-implying sentences for predicting sentences. There were more errors to trait probes following trait-implying sentences than to those following control sentences (and no RT differences, thus ruling out a speed-accuracy trade off). However, RTs were considerably longer than those in McKoon and Ratcliff's study, suggesting that participants were insufficiently motivated to respond quickly. To increase motivation, Study 2 replicated Study 1 with the addition of feedback on each trial. RTs dropped to the range reported by McKoon and Ratcliff, and were longer for trait probes after trait-implying sentences than after controls. Study 3 replicated Study 2, but included both trait-implying and predicting sentences. The expected RT difference was found for both trait and predicting inferences, and there was no difference between them. Thus, Study 3 replicated McKoon and Ratcliff's findings for predicting inferences, and showed that trait inferences have the same effect.

Lupfer, Clark, Church, DePaola, and McDonald (1995, Experiment 2) asked participants, on each of 27 trials, to memorize digits (as in Section B above) and perform a recognition probe task as a "distractor" during digit rehearsal. They used three types of distractor sentences: trait-implying, situational-cause-implying, and ambiguous. Four recognition probes followed each sentence: one trait, one situational cause, and two words that had actually appeared in the text. Participants made more errors on trait probes following trait-implying sentences and on situation probes following situation-implying sentences than in any other conditions. Interestingly, RTs did not differ among conditions, and were about as long as in the Uleman et al. study (in press, Experiment 1).

Thus four studies (Lupfer et al., 1995; Uleman et al., in press) have produced evidence of STI with this paradigm. Although it precludes the kind of strategic retrieval processes posited by Wyer and Srull (1989) for cued recall paradigms, this paradigm is not without its ambiguities. Critics such as Keenan, Potts, Golding, and Jennings (1990) have argued that "a recognition test of inferences does not allow one to distinguish between: 1) inferences occurring while reading, 2) inferences occurring during testing, or 3) compatibility matching processes occurring at the time of test" (p. 389). Therefore, they prefer activation measures such as lexical decision (see next section). McKoon and Ratcliff (1990) have countered by insisting that a speeded recognition probe procedure can rule out the last two possibilities. A speeded procedure requires participants to respond within 300 ms, giving them insufficient time for postprobe inferences or compatibility matching. Although this procedure has not yet been used to test for STI online, it has demonstrated predicting inferences (McKoon & Ratcliff, 1986, Experiment 4). The fact that Study 3 by Uleman et al. (in press) found no difference between predicting and trait inferences, using an unspeeded recognition probe procedure, suggests that the speeded procedure would show similar results for STIs.

D. LEXICAL DECISION

In a lexical decision task, participants decide as quickly and accurately as possible whether a string of letters is a word (e.g., BUTTER) or not (e.g., BUTHER). Typically, the letter string is presented on a CRT screen, and participants respond YES or NO with the press of a key. Lexical decision RTs are usually interpreted as measures of the time it takes to access the word in the lexicon. If the word has been activated (primed) before its presentation (e.g., by the reading of BREAD), the RT is shorter. Thus if reading about trait-implying behaviors activates traits, lexical decision RTs for trait words should be shorter than those following control sentences. Three studies have sought evidence of STI with lexical decisions, and all have found it.

Lupfer et al. (1995, Experiment 3) asked participants, on each of 32 trials, to memorize digits (as in Section B) and perform a distractor task during digit rehearsal. The distractor task consisted of two parts on each trial: reading sentences and making lexical decisions. Sentences were either trait-implying, situational-cause-implying, or fillers. In order to ensure attention to the sentences, participants were told that they would be asked questions about them later. Lexical decisions for trait words following trait-implying sentences were both faster (710 ms) and more accurate (95.8% correct) than they were following situation-implying sentences (740 ms and 92.8%).

Lea (1995) asked participants to read short stories and make lexical decisions after each one. The critical stories ended with trait-implying sentences. Some of these sentences were in story contexts that supported the trait implication, and some were in contexts that undermined it (similar to those in Lupfer et al., 1990). Lexical decisions to trait words were faster (1312 ms) when the preceding context supported the trait implication than when it did not (1430 ms).[2]

Finally, Zárate and Uleman (1994) successfully used lexical decisions to detect STI. That study is described later in Section VII,B.

E. DELAYED RECOGNITION

Delayed recognition, like immediate recognition, has been used to study inferences in text comprehension. It has similar but more severe ambiguities than immediate recognition does because of the greater time lapse between study and test, the typically longer RTs, and the greater opportunity for strategic inferences at retrieval. All this makes it more difficult to pinpoint which inferences occurred at encoding rather than later. Nevertheless, delayed recognition has occasionally been used to study STI. The paradigm calls for the comparison of false-positive error rates as well as RTs. One predicts more errors and longer RTs in recognizing "new" items implied

[2] The unusual length of these RTs is probably due to both a very low, 1% error rate, and to using multisyllabic and multiword targets (e.g., ILL MANNERED).

by the behavior but not present than in recognizing "new" items that were not implied. Thus as with recognition probes, STI should increase errors and RTs.

Lupfer et al. (1995, Experiment 3) asked participants to memorize digits and perform a distractor task during digit rehearsal. The distractor consisted of reading sentences and making lexical decisions, as described earlier. The critical sentences implied either traits or situational causes, and participants expected to answer questions about them later. Following the last digit memory trial, recognition memory for traits and situational causes was tested by the presentation of 16 words, one-at-a-time, half of them "old" and half "new." For half of the participants, the new words represented trait or situational inferences that they might have made; for the other participants, they did not. Error rates were higher, and latencies were longer for rejecting new trait words when they were implied by earlier sentences than when they were not. This is consistent with STI at encoding. (It also suggests spontaneous situation inferences; see Section VIII,B.)

D'Agostino (1991) reported two studies of STI with delayed recognition measures. Both employed 24 trait-implying sentences, half of which also explicitly included the trait. Half of the participants studied the sentences for a memory test, and half read them to form impressions of the actors. All recognition items were traits—either explicit old, implicit new, or unrelated new—and they were primed with relevant actor cues to increase the measure's sensitivity. In both studies, error rates were higher for implicit new traits than for explicit old traits. (Unfortunately, this comparison of false-positive with false-negative rates is not ideal. Error rates for unrelated new traits were not reported, so we do not know whether they were lower than the error rates for implicit new traits.) More interesting, in Experiment 1 there was no difference in error rates between memory and impression participants. This suggests that participants inferred traits as much under memory as under impression instructions. In Experiment 2, half of the participants were subliminally primed with relevant trait words during the study period. For the other nonprimed participants, there was again no difference between memory and impression conditions.[3] Thus these two studies seem to provide some evidence for STI.

In sum, there are three studies using delayed recognition that are consistent with the occurrence of STI, with the Lupfer et al. (1995) Experiment 3 yielding the clearest results.

[3] Our interpretations of D'Agostino's data differ markedly from his interpretation. Diligent readers should consult the original source. We have ignored the "inference" condition in Experiment 1 because most evidence indicates that people are unaware of making spontaneous trait inferences. This readily accounts for the data in this condition. In Experiment 2, errors were higher for impression than memory subjects, suggesting that intentional trait inferences may be more sensitive to subliminal priming. See Newman and Uleman (1990) for evidence of superliminal priming of STI.

F. WORD STEM COMPLETION

All of the paradigms described previously (except for the lexical decision paradigm) use explicit memory measures that ask participants to explicitly refer to a prior event. Implicit memory measures, by contrast, do not. Instead, they detect the effects of prior events without any explicit reference to them. The next two paradigms employ such implicit memory measures.

Whitney and Williams-Whitney (1990) used constrained word stems (CWSs) to obtain evidence of online trait inferences. Participants read brief trait-implying and control paragraphs, and completed two CWSs and a comprehension question after each paragraph. For critical paragraphs, the first CWS could be completed with the implied trait (e.g., CL __ __ __ __ could be CLUMSY). Participants were told to complete each word stem "with the first word that comes to mind and fits properly into the blanks." Results for the control paragraphs showed that 10% of the CWSs were completed with the relevant trait, whereas results rose to 31% for the trait-implying paragraphs. This approaches the 38% rate at which pretest participants said that the paragraphs implied the traits. The authors concluded that STI occurs online.

Whitney, Waring, and Zingmark (1992, Experiment 2) showed that CWS completions are more sensitive to inferences made online than are word fragment (WF) completions (e.g., T __ __ A __ O for Tomato). (CWS completions are a subset of WF completions in which all of the fragments provided are initial and adjacent letters. They thus suggest a simpler, more homogeneous retrieval route into the lexicon.) Although the precise basis for this difference is unclear, it may nevertheless shed some light on findings reported by Bassili and Smith (1986). Using a WF task, they failed to find evidence for STI after presenting subjects with a series of trait-implying sentences for memorization. The findings of Whitney et al. suggest that because CWS completions are a more sensitive task, they might have detected STI.

G. RELEARNING

In a relearning paradigm, participants memorize stimuli at Time 1 and then memorize them again at Time 2. Typically, at Time 2 it takes less time or fewer trials to reach the same learning criterion, or the old material is learned more easily than new material. Such savings effects are attributed to implicit memory because they do not require explicit reference by participants to Time 1 stimuli. Carlston and Skowronski (1994) used a relearning paradigm to study STI.

In the first study, participants at Time 1 encountered photographs of 29 people paired with self-descriptive statements that implied traits. (e.g., *cruel* was implied by "I hate animals. Today I was walking to the pool hall and I saw this puppy. So I kicked it out of my way.") They were asked to either "think of a specific trait word that would describe each stimulus person's personality," "form an impression of the personality of each person;" or "familiarize [themselves] with materials to be used later in the experiment, . . . simply look at the photos and the accompanying information." Then at Time 2, they attempted to learn photo-trait pairs. Some photos were paired with traits implied by the previous self-descriptive behaviors, creating "relearning" pairs. Finally, participants viewed these photos and tried to recall the paired traits. The savings effect was estimated from this Time 2 paired-associates learning task by comparing trait recall for relearning pairs with that for novel pairs. They found large savings effects that did not differ by instruction, indicating that the familiarization group had inferred traits spontaneously.

In three subsequent experiments, a recognition task was added to the end of this procedure to assess whether explicit memory for the self-descriptive behaviors at Time 1 mediated the savings effect. Results showed clearly that it did not. Savings were unaffected by whether or not participants recognized which self-descriptive behaviors had been paired with a photo. These studies provide strong support for STI, which occurred when participants spent less than 4 min looking through a booklet with 29 pairs of photos and self-descriptions, merely to familiarize themselves with it. Carlston, Skowronski, and Sparks (1995) have extended this series of studies with five more, all of which demonstrate STI with this paradigm. These studies are discussed in Section IV,A.

Not all implicit memory measures are alike. Specifically, Roediger (e.g., Roediger, Weldon, & Challis, 1989) distinguished between data-driven and conceptually driven processes and tests of implicit memory. Data-driven (or perceptual) tests depend heavily on the match between the perceptual features of the stimuli at study and at test. Conceptually-driven tests depend more on the match between conceptual processing at study and at test. Word fragment completion is strongly data-driven in that completions are sharply reduced by changes in perceptual features such as modality or type font. Because STI does not generate any "perceptual features" that could match the stimuli presented for word fragment or word stem completions, such completions probably provide less sensitive measures of STI than does the relearning paradigm.

The relearning paradigm has an additional important advantage. It is sensitive to the establishment of associations between concepts, not merely to prior exposure to concepts. Therefore, it can be used both to study prior activation of concepts and to determine what other features or stimuli became associated with these concepts. This advantage has led to the important findings reviewed in Section IV,A on the referents of STIs.

H. SUMMARY

Researchers studying social inference processes typically present people with descriptions or depictions of behavior, asking them to carefully attend to the information, so they can make the best judgments possible. Such an approach is inappropriate for research on spontaneous processes. It prevents the researcher from learning about the kinds of effortless inferences people make without intentions or awareness. A variety of complications arise even when someone tries to interpret the results of studies in which participants make intentional and controlled judgments; people do not always do what they say or say what they do (Nisbett & Wilson, 1977). It is not surprising then that documenting spontaneous processes is arguably even more difficult, because the chain of inference required to connect dependent variables to the phenomenon of interest is inevitably more tenuous.

None of the measures of STI discussed so far have yielded findings completely immune to alternative explanations, and we have looked at the complications involved with each technique. When no one measure or method can be relied on to yield unambiguous evidence for some phenomenon, a strategy of converging operations is called for. We believe that the research reviewed in Section II represents the successful execution of such a strategy. The earliest kind of evidence for STIs (Winter & Uleman, 1984) involved presenting participants with descriptions of behavior and asking participants to memorize them. High levels of trait-cued recall indicated that STIs had occurred, but the possibility remained that subjects had intentionally formed impressions to enhance the memorability of the behaviors (see Hamilton, 1981). Presenting sentences to subjects as distractors in the context of some other task (e.g., Winter et al., 1985) controls for this problem. In both kinds of studies, however, a great deal of time elapses between the hypothesized spontaneous inference process and the recall measures used to detect it. This feature of these studies leaves their results open to alternative explanations involving processes that could occur during the intervening time period (e.g., the retrieval-based explanation of the cued recall studies). Lexical decision and word stem completion tasks (e.g., Lupfer et al. 1995, Whitney et al., 1992) do not suffer from this problem. Unfortunately, in experiments using these methods, successfully completing what subjects believe is their primary task is facilitated by making trait inferences that put the spontaneous status of the trait inference processes in jeopardy. The recognition probe paradigm (Uleman et al., in press) does not have this drawback. Thinking about the trait implications of behaviors actually works against optimal performance on the recognition task. However, as discussed earlier, the recognition probe technique is not without its own ambiguities. For example, the trait-implying behaviors are still in short-term memory when the key dependent variable (RT) is measured. This leaves open the possibility that the inference sometimes occurs only after the recognition probe appears. Fortunately, this is not an issue with the original cued recall procedure for documenting STIs.

No one technique for studying STI is flawless, but the strength of one paradigm tends to compensate for the weakness of another. Thus, STIs have been documented in multiple studies by many investigators from several different laboratories, using seven different paradigms. A few other paradigms that provide evidence for STI (e.g., Marsman, 1994) are mentioned later.

III. What Are the Necessary Conditions for STI?

What are the motivational, informational, and cognitive conditions required for STI? We discuss motivational conditions primarily in terms of goals (although "motivation" has a much broader purview), dividing them into proximal and distal goals. Proximal goals describe immediate objectives that are sought in the short term, whereas distal goals concern the long-range future. Proximal goals are usually conscious, explicit, specific, and often instigated through instructions to participants in experiments. Distal goals are more global and chronic, providing general direction and producing persistence in the face of obstacles to more specific proximal goals (Gollwitzer & Moskowitz, in press). For reasons of parsimony and theoretical clarity, we prefer to regard distal goals as also (at least potentially) conscious and explicit (Uleman, 1996). Both kinds of goals affect STI, although proximal goals have been studied most and are more open to experimental manipulation.

Our discussion of informational conditions reviews how the trait-relevant information presented in STI studies has been systematically varied, and what its effects have been. Our treatment of cognitive conditions focuses on the efficiency of STI and its minimal demands on cognitive capacity.

A. PROXIMAL GOALS

1. The Absence of Trait Inference Goals

The defining feature of STIs is that people make them *without* any intention to infer traits or form impressions. The evidence reviewed earlier demonstrates, in multiple ways, that STIs occur without such goals. In most cued recall studies, participants expected a memory test and were not instructed to form impressions. In five of them (Lupfer et al., 1990, 1995, Experiments 2 and 3; Uleman et al., 1992; Winter et al., 1985), the trait-implying sentences were "distractors." Even so, results provided clear evidence of STI. Other paradigms illustrate the point in other ways.

Although this finding may not be surprising, it either contradicts or complements theories of social inference that posit the necessity of specific inference goals. Perhaps the best known example is Wyer and Srull's (1989) model, which is admirably explicit on this issue.

> Postulate 4.3. Semantic concepts are not applied to input information by the Comprehender unless they are necessary to understand the denotative meaning of this information. . . . Overt behaviors are generally interpretable in terms of action and noun concepts, and personality traits are higher level attribute concepts that are applied only after comprehension at a lower level has occurred. Consequently, Postulate 4.3 implies that *behaviors will typically not be spontaneously encoded in terms of trait (attribute) concepts unless more detailed processing objectives require it.* (pp. 57–58; emphasis in original)

In support of this, Wyer and Srull cite two representative papers. Hamilton, Katz, and Leirer (1980) found that when participants read a list of behaviors under impression formation instructions, the behaviors were clustered in free recall according to their trait implications, but no such clustering occurred under memory instructions. Hamilton et al. concluded that this clustering reflected organization at encoding and, therefore, that memory instructions did not produce trait inferences. Wyer and Gordon (1982) asked participants to read lists of traits and related behaviors. They found that the recall of traits cued recall of related behaviors under impression instructions, but not under memory instructions, so they also concluded that memory instructions do not produce trait inferences at encoding.

However, Klein and Loftus (1990) showed that clustering in such paradigms primarily reflects retrieval strategies rather than inferences and organization at encoding. Impression formation instructions do make trait elaborations of each behavior more likely at encoding so that free recall is higher and traits can serve more readily to organize retrieval. However, impression formation instructions do not produce links at encoding between behaviors that imply the same trait, and need not even produce clustering at recall. Experiment 2 showed that free recall was higher under impression instructions than under memory instructions, but clustering did not exceed chance levels under either set of instructions. The evidence from Klein and Loftus's three studies favors an elaboration rather than an organization explanation of the effects of impression instructions on encoding, "in which behaviors exemplifying the same trait are stored independent of one another in memory" (p. 400). Thus the absence of clustering in free recall under memory instructions provides no evidence against STI.

Notice that the claim that STI occurs without the intention to infer traits does *not* mean that this intention cannot increase trait inferences or make them more likely. It is perfectly possible, even likely, that an intention to infer traits will make trait inferences more likely or frequent. Our claim is only that STI occurs to some extent, not necessarily to the maximum extent. This claim has not always been clear and has produced some misunderstandings, in which we have claimed that "the glass is half full" while others have argued that, "on the contrary, the glass is half empty." For example, when Bassili and Smith (1986) found that impression formation instructions produced higher trait-cued recall than did memory instructions, they interpreted this as evidence against STI.

If someone intends to form impressions or infer traits, then, by definition, the trait inferences are not "spontaneous." However, intentional processes may proceed in parallel with, or depend on spontaneous processes. Gilbert's (1989) research on trait inferences may illustrate this. His participants were always asked to form an impression of the target person. He and his students have demonstrated that it is relatively easy to reduce the impact of situational information by putting participants under a concurrent cognitive load. However, the trait inference itself resembles a spontaneous inference, in that it is relatively difficult to disrupt (see Section D later).

In summary, STI, by definition, occurs without intentions to infer traits. Previous evidence on clustering in recall that seemed to contradict the occurrence of STI is actually more consistent with a model that accounts for that clustering in terms of retrieval processes. Moreover, STI can apparently be augmented by, or operate in parallel with, intentional trait inference processes.

2. Effects of Other Processing Goals

At a minimum, STI requires attention to trait-implying stimuli. Additional intentions are unnecessary, but they can affect STI, either increasing or decreasing it relative to what is found under memory instructions. Uleman and Moskowitz (1994, Experiment 3) asked some participants to judge how similar they were to the actors in trait-implying sentences, or how likely they would be to perform the behaviors described. Traits were just as effective in cuing sentence recall as when participants made intentional trait inferences, indicating a very high level of STI. Furthermore, trait cues were more effective after these social judgments than when the same sentences were simply read for a memory test, even though the social judgments need not have entailed trait inferences. However, the effectiveness of trait cues declined when participants examined these sentences to look for isolated features, such as phonemes or pronoun genders (Experiment 2). Even so, these feature detection instructions still produced cued recall evidence of some STI.

STI, therefore, does not even depend on an intention to comprehend the sentences. STI occurred even when participants searched for isolated sentence features. Only when they searched the sentences for a particular letter (grapheme) was there no cued recall evidence of STI. The fact that STI does not depend on intentions to comprehend the sentences, and that some level of comprehension occurs incidentally, is an important point that has been missed by some of the most eminent investigators in the field (e.g., Bargh, 1990, p. 95, commenting on an earlier version of Uleman & Moskowitz, 1994). Moreover, it suggests that Wyer and Srull's (1989) Comprehender must operate at some level, even without explicit goals or intentions.

Whitney et al. (1992) also varied participants' intentions in reading trait-implying paragraphs, but they used constrained word stem (CWS) completions to detect STI. Each paragraph was followed by a CWS that participants completed as a distractor from the primary task of either verbatim recall or comprehension of the paragraph. Each participant's comprehension questions requested either factual details, nontrait inferences, or impressions of the actor. CWS completions were higher in both the inference and impression tasks than in the verbatim or factual memory tasks. This demonstrates that STI occurs when people have the goal of making nontrait inferences. (The failure to find evidence of STI for the goals of verbatim recall and factual comprehension suggests that CWS completion may be a less sensitive indicator of STI than cued recall, as noted earlier at the end of Section II,G. Some null results may also be due to low statistical power; there were only 12 participants per task.)

STIs may produce intentions to inhibit them when they interfere with task performance. In the Uleman et al. (in press) recognition probe studies described previously, STIs interfered with participants' performance by slowing them down or introducing errors. In Experiments 2 and 3, which included speed and accuracy feedback after each trial, participants somehow learned to inhibit STI by the last half of the trials, so that probe RTs after the trait-implying sentences were no longer slower than after the control sentences. Unfortunately, participants were not interviewed afterward about their intentions or possible control strategies, so we do not know whether these were conscious. They may not have been, because people can acquire and modify procedural knowledge without declarative knowledge of those procedures (Lewicki, 1986; Reber, 1993). Participants may have known only that they intended to "respond as quickly and accurately as possible," without knowing that the inhibition of STIs would advance that goal.

As we have already noted, Uleman and Moskowitz (1994) showed that goals such as detecting sentence features can reduce STI, even without an explicit inhibitory intent. (See also Newman, Uleman, & Lipsitt, 1988.) Participants in these studies were unaware of STIs, so unlike those in the study of Uleman et al. (in press) who got RT feedback on each trial, they could not have developed intentional control over them. Nevertheless, the participants had the possibility of control, which they could have exercised intentionally if they had known of their goals' effects. That is, they could have intentionally focused on isolated features of the sentences in order to reduce STI and avoid the sentences' overall meanings, in much the same way that some of Milgram's (1974) participants focused on the minute technical details of their task, apparently to avoid the broader meanings of their obedience. Thus STI is controllable, but usually uncontrolled. Future research should address the possibility that STI can be intentionally inhibited (cf. Wegner, 1994). This possibility is particularly important to explore for trait inferences facilitated by stereotypes. Devine (1989) has suggested that nonprejudiced people are only able to inhibit the use of stereotypes when making judgments about others, but that they cannot inhibit stereotype activation. The results of Uleman et al. (in press) suggest that nonprejudiced people may even be able to inhibit unintended social inferences, such as stereotype-based STIs.

In summary, the likelihood of STI can be increased or decreased by other goals, relative to the level of STI found under memory instructions. This occurs even though participants are unaware of STI. Recent evidence suggests that people can inhibit STI if it interferes with a focal task that gives them clear feedback. Whether they can intentionally inhibit particular STIs remains a question for future research.

B. DISTAL GOALS

As part of the process of constructing social knowledge and deriving meaning from the social world, STI may serve as the foundation from which subsequent adjustments and corrections produce conscious inferences, impressions, judgments, and attributions (e.g., Gilbert, 1989; Moskowitz, 1993b; Park, 1989; Trope & Liberman, 1993). Trait inference categorizes behavior, and in so doing attributes meaning to it, as any act of categorization does (Bruner, 1957). By recognizing the ability of STI to give meaning to events, we can begin to address a question that we skirted in the previous section: If proximal goals that explicitly lead people to intend to form inferences are not required for producing STI, then why does it occur at all?

Gollwitzer and Moskowitz (in press) suggested that even when proximal goals do not call for trait inferences, more distal goals exist that can be fulfilled by forming them. Thus, just as the intention to act on a goal can be somewhat automatically triggered by the presence of goal-relevant cues in the environment (Gollwitzer, 1993), so the presence of another's trait relevant behavior may serve to trigger the STI process in the service of distal goal pursuit (see also Bargh's discussions of auto-motives, 1990, and with Barndollar, 1995). The key here is not that trait inference will always occur, but that when there is a link between a stimulus in the environment and one's distal goals (a link that varies in strength, which Lewin termed "valence"), then that stimulus can speak to the goal and draw out an appropriate goal-directed response. From this perspective it is clear how the interpretation of both the situation and the actions of others within the situation depend on several factors. These include situational press, objective qualities of stimuli in the environment, objective links between stimuli and an individual's needs, responses of the sensory organs to the properties and qualities of the stimuli (autochthonous factors), and such qualities of the perceiver as accessible constructs, mood, values, chronic goals, needs, and motives.[4]

From the pragmatist perspective, a fundamental, distal goal that motivates much of human psychological functioning is the search for meaning, understanding, or certainty in belief (Dewey, 1929; Peirce, 1877). This goal is reflected in a variety of attribution models, beginning with what Heider (1958) refers to when describing balance and cognitive consistency, and continuing through what Kruglanski (1990) refers to when describing an epistemic process driven by a search for closure and structure. What unites such theories is the proposition that experiencing doubt—a sense that one's beliefs are invalid, or a lack of confidence in one's social judgments—is an aversive state that people attempt to reduce by restoring belief, certainty, and meaning. Categorizing can deliver such meaning, but is there anything fundamental about dispositional categorization?

---

[4] Much of this could be restated in the language of production systems and the conditions that trigger their operation (J. R. Anderson, 1983; Smith, 1984). However, this would give a rather different heuristic thrust to these considerations.

According to Heider (1944), dispositional categories are both parsimonious and powerful explanations for the behavior of others. People's actions produce changes—disturbances in the equilibrium that once permitted their mastery over events in the environment. The behaviors of others create unexplained occurrences. If those behaviors are understood and categorized, then behavioral disruptions in one's understanding of the social environment can be reversed. "Persons, as absolute causal origins, transform irreversible changes into reversible ones. . . . The person can represent the disturbing change in its entirety" (Heider, 1944, p. 361). Another reason why dispositional categorization is pervasive stems from its ability to facilitate the attainment of several goals related to the desire for meaning, closure, and certainty—the desires to control, maintain effective interactions with, and predict with some degree of veridicality one's future interactions with the social world.

According to Bruner's (1957) discussion of predictive veridicality, one function of categorization is to provide individuals with expectancies and allow them to anticipate others' responses. Bruner regarded categorization as particularly useful in "perceiving the states of other people, their characteristics, intentions and so forth. . . . The ability to use minimal cues quickly in categorizing the events of the environment is what gives the organism its lead time in adjusting to events" (p. 142).

Related to the goal of prediction is the goal of control. Heider (1958) (see also Anderson & Deuser, 1993; Jones, 1979; Pittman & Heller, 1987) believed that trait inference aided the individual in controlling the environment. Such control enables one to achieve a sense of power over an object in a stimulus array that would otherwise be overly complex and overwhelming. He states, "in Lewin's (1936) terms, an unstructured region, that is, a region whose properties are not known to the person, can be considered a barrier which makes action and therefore control difficult if not impossible. Perception helps to structure the region and to remove this barrier" (p. 71). White (1959) labeled this the effectance motive, which has the goal of maintaining control over the environment through effective interactions.

More recent empirical work seems to corroborate this position. Newman (1991) provided evidence of a correspondence between the likelihood of forming STIs and the use of traits as stable personality dispositions from which to predict events. He found that 10- to 11-year-old participants were more likely than college students to rely on dispositional (as opposed to contextual) information in predicting people's future behavior. This age difference was paralleled in a second study, in which the younger participants were also more likely than adults to spontaneously infer traits from behavior. Moskowitz (1993a) also linked the control motive to attributional activity by showing that STIs are more likely among people with a high personal need for structure. He stated that because of this link to such a fundamental motive state, social inferences become highly practiced and routinized.

Finally, Gollwitzer and Moskowitz (in press) suggested that the operation of STI is linked to the context within which goals operate. The control motive will not lead individuals to infer traits in the presence of every behavior. The behavior must acquire valence (be goal-related) and facilitate goal achievement, which trait inference itself does when it pursues the goals of prediction, effectance, and attaining meaning. These goals, however, will not be served by behaviors that are not diagnostic of traits; such behaviors have no valence. For this reason, perhaps, person memory studies often fail to find evidence of trait inference when individuals are not given explicit impression formation goals (e.g., Srull & Brand, 1983); they utilize stimuli that have no valence. As Gollwitzer and Moskowitz (in press, p. 58) stated: "Simply put, it is not functional, unless specifically asked to attempt to do so, to draw an inference about disposition based on information that does not imply traits. . . . Given an impression set one could, however, generate inferences that satisfy the proximal goal." For this reason, we should not always expect to find trait inference (cf. Gilbert, 1989).

Although fundamental in some respects, trait inference is also dependent on the presence of valenced stimuli [see also McArthur & Baron's (1983) discussion of dynamic stimulus displays and Moskowitz & Roman's (1992) discussion of stimulus behaviors infused with meaning], on a distal goal facilitated by trait inference, and on the absence of goals that inhibit trait inference (e.g., Krull, 1993; Quattrone, 1982; Uleman & Moskowitz, 1994). Most STI research to date has simply assumed that these conditions were satisfied and did not manipulate or measure them in any way.

C. TRAIT-RELEVANT INFORMATION

Describing the behavioral bases for trait inferences has been an important focus of attribution theory and research since the mid-1960s (Jones & Davis, 1965), and it continues to be vigorously pursued (e.g., Trope & Higgins, 1993). STI researchers have not attempted to formally characterize the kind of information that supports trait inferences, but have relied instead on pretesting to develop stimuli that "work." Most STI research to date has used vignettes to describe behaviors at a relatively basic, uninterpreted level. This choice of stimulus materials was based on the ease of preparing, pretesting, and presenting text; the availability of well-developed ways of describing text and understanding how it is processed; and the recognition that the flexibility and versatility of language permits the presentation of almost any situation and behavior. Syntax, semantics, and pragmatics can be more clearly identified in text than in behavior, although we assume that they exist there as well. However, as a result of this research strategy, both vocal and nonverbal information that might imply traits has been completely ignored. Research by Ambady and Rosenthal (1992), Brewer (1988), McArthur and Baron (1983), and others, though, indicates the importance of such information in trait inference.

To date, five STI studies have systematically manipulated trait-relevant information. Newman and Uleman (1990) primed relevant trait concepts before trait-implying sentences were read, to see whether this would influence STI. Participants completed "two unrelated studies," following the paradigm of Higgins, Rholes, and Jones (1977). In the first study, the positive or negative pole of four trait constructs was primed. In a second "unrelated memory study," participants read ambiguous sentences that could be interpreted in terms of either the positive or the negative pole of a trait dimension (e.g., "Molly would not take no for an answer" can imply that she is either *determined* or *pushy*). Trait-cued recall of the sentences was then obtained, followed by a surprise recall test for the primes from the "first study."

Predictions were based on Lombardi, Higgins, and Bargh (1987), who found that participants who recalled primes from a "first study" (actually the priming procedure) showed contrast effects on a subsequent "unrelated" impression formation task, whereas those who did not recall the primes showed assimilation effects. Lombardi et al. (1987) suggested that the re-called primes were likely to be those that participants were aware of during impression formation. These primed concepts could have functioned as extreme reference points used in judging the target person (cf. Martin & Achee, 1992). Therefore, it was argued that being aware of a trait prime (e.g., BULLHEADED) while interpreting a behavior ("Only rarely does he change his mind") has the effect of reducing the perceived fit between the primed concept and the behavior.

Newman and Uleman found a parallel effect for *spontaneous* trait infer-ences. The effectiveness of traits for cuing the recall of a behavior was an interactive effect of the primes and the participants' recall of those primes. When participants recalled a prime (e.g., PERSISTENT or STUBBORN), a cue with the opposite valence (e.g., PUSHY or DETERMINED, respec-tively) was most effective, demonstrating a contrast effect for STI. When participants did not recall a prime, then a cue that was synonymous with the prime was most effective, thus demonstrating an assimilation effect. Therefore, trait concepts that are primed before encoding affect STI.

Lupfer et al. (1990) investigated whether preceding contextual informa-tion would affect STI. They used the cued recall of distractors paradigm, and presented a trait-implying sentence on each trial along with information that supported either a trait or a situational inference about the focal event. For example, "The businessman steps on his girlfriend's feet during the foxtrot" (which implies *clumsy*) was preceded by "The businessman and his girlfriend plan a 'night on the town.' He spills a drink on her dress.", or "The businessman and his girlfriend are trying to dance on a very crowded dance floor. Everyone is bumping into others." On each trial, participants read the "distractor" information and then repeated the focal sentence aloud from memory before recalling the digits. Compared with a control condition in which only focal sentences were presented, STI was more likely with trait information and was unaffected by situational information. Variations in the difficulty of the digit memory task also had no effect. These two latter results were interpreted as supporting Gilbert, Pelham, and Krull's (1988) three-stage model of person perception (see Section D later).

Lea (1995) also investigated effects of preceding context on STI. He asked participants to read short stories and make lexical decisions after each one. As in Lupfer et al. (1990), the critical stories ended with a trait-implying sentence. Some stories supported the trait implication and some did not.[5] For example, "The minister gets his poem published in the *New Yorker*" (which implies *talented*) ended a story titled either "An Unusual Hobby" or "The Printing Errors." The first story began as follows: "The minister's hobby is writing poems. Last year a published book of his poems won a prize. This year he has written, he thinks, his best poem." The second story began this way: "The minister writes a poem for the church newsletter. A couple of printing errors occur. His poem becomes something so hilarious that the national press is alerted." Lexical decisions for trait words were faster when the context supported the trait implication, replicating aspects of the study by Lupfer et al. (1990).

Although both of these studies suggest that preceding contextual information can promote STI, they are ambiguous because the contextual information itself also seems to imply the relevant traits: The clumsy businessman with big feet also spilled a drink on his companion; the talented minister who got his poem published had already won a prize. Therefore, it is not clear whether these studies merely show that two trait activations are better than one, with activations summing, or that contextual information is integrated with the focal sentences in more complex ways under these relatively incidental reading conditions.

Lupfer et al. (1995) studied effects of contextual information that follows focal, trait-implying sentences. They developed three sets of focal sentences:

[5] These stories were actually filler items in a study designed for other purposes. That design precluded having a "no information" condition comparable to the control condition of Lupfer et al. (1990).

1) trait implying, 2) ambiguous with traits and situations that were equally likely explanations, and 3) situation implying. For some participants, these focal sentences were followed by consensus and distinctiveness covariation information (Kelley, 1967) that supported trait inferences, and for others the information following the sentences supported situational inferences. Experiment 2 used the recognition probe paradigm, with four probes following each paragraph: the trait implication, the situation implication, and two words that were presented. Error rates for trait probes showed that STI was most likely following trait-implying sentences, regardless of the covariation information. Experiment 3 used a lexical decision paradigm and omitted ambiguous sentences. Error rates and latencies for trait probes again showed that STI was most likely following trait-implying sentences, regardless of the covariation information. (Remember that the tasks in both Experiments 2 and 3 were presented as distractors from the focal task of digit memory.) Thus both studies indicate that subsequent covariation information—which does affect intentional trait attributions, as established in Experiment 1—does not affect STI when it is included with trait-implying information in a distractor task.

In short, these results suggest that STI is affected by prior activation (priming) of trait concepts, but is unaffected by subsequent information that does affect intentional inferences.

D. COGNITIVE CAPACITY AND EFFICIENCY

Automatic processes were once considered the opposite of strategic, controllable, intentional processes (Posner & Snyder, 1975; Shiffrin & Schneider, 1977). It is now clear that all characteristics of automatic processes do not always covary. A process may be "automatic" in some respects, but not in others (e.g., Bargh, 1989; Uleman, 1989). In addition, most cognitive processes of interest to social psychologists, including STI, are so complex that they probably include both automatic and strategic components. Bargh (1994) has summarized social cognition research on the four central characteristics of automatic processes: awareness, intentions, cognitive efficiency, and control. It is instructive to consider the evidence for the role that each of these plays in STI. We find later that STIs occur without awareness (Section V,A). We have already described the way that STIs proceed without trait inference intentions and are typically controllable but uncontrolled. In this section, we review evidence showing that STI is very cognitively efficient, requiring little (but some) cognitive capacity.

This research was prompted by the question of whether STI is automatic (Winter et al., 1985). This was a misguided question because the answer depends upon which aspects of automaticity are considered and how stringent the criteria are. Bargh (1989) has characterized STI as a goal-dependent automatic process because it depends on the goal of sustained attention to trait-implying stimuli, is affected by other goals, but is largely automatic in other respects. Thus, although STI has some aspects of automatic processes, it lacks others. This is why we prefer to characterize STI as "spontaneous" and then elaborate the meaning of that term through future research.

The efficiency of a cognitive process can be assessed by observing how easily it can be disrupted with concurrent tasks that impose a "cognitive load." (Efficiency can also be defined in terms of response speedup; see Section VI,A on Proceduralization.) For example, Gilbert et al. (1988) asked participants to keep digits in memory while they formed an impression of a person being interviewed on silent videotape about personal sexual fantasies. They proposed that intentional impression formation proceeds in three stages: *categorizing* the behavior in trait terms, *characterizing* the person in those terms, and *correcting* this characterization to take situational factors into account. They showed that the concurrent digit memory load interferes most with taking situational factors into account, producing the correspondence bias (Jones, 1979) of neglecting situational causes. Participants under the digit memory load rated the target as more anxious, and gave insufficient weight to the interview topic (sexual fantasies) as an alternative, situational cause of the target's anxious behavior.

In the early 1990s Krull (1993) demonstrated parallel effects for situational inferences. His participants were asked to form an impression of the situation, which could be corrected with person information. The "correction stage" was less efficient than the first two stages in that the cognitive load reduced the impact of the person information. Although this research tells us that cognitive load reduces the impact of information that is not directly about the intended focal target (i.e., in Gilbert's terms, that categorization and characterization are more efficient than correction), it does not address the efficiency of categorization and characterization. Direct evidence for the relatively efficient nature of trait inference is provided by several STI studies.

Winter et al. (1985) investigated STI's efficiency, in this sense of its immunity to disruption by concurrent load. Remember that participants in this study thought that their primary task was to remember strings of digits while they read trait-implying sentences as "distractors." Some participants had digit strings that were much more difficult to remember than those of other participants. Yet this load difference did not affect STI. Lupfer et al. found the same thing with cued recall (1990), recognition probes (1995, Experiment 2), and lexical decisions (1995, Experiment 3), suggesting that

STI is quite efficient. However, Uleman et al. (1992) added a probe reaction time task to the participants' other two tasks to get a direct measure of the amount of available cognitive capacity under each load condition. They found some interference with STI at the highest load levels. This suggests that STI, though highly efficient, is not impervious to interference by concurrent task demands.

E. SUMMARY

Research on the conditions affecting STIs reveals that certain information processing goals can interfere with them, whereas some can make them more likely. There is evidence that STIs can be intentionally inhibited. It also can be shown that STIs can be made more probable by the presence of prior trait-relevant contextual information. Finally, severe cognitive loads can reduce them.

It seems safe to conclude that STIs do not inevitably occur when we observe or interact with others. They do seem to occur, however, when people are exposed to trait-relevant behaviors, when they do not necessarily have a goal to make trait inferences, when they actually have other information processing goals involving nontrait features of behavior, and when multiple task demands leave little cognitive capacity for any kind of complex social information processing. In summary, the conditions in which STIs occur resemble the conditions we typically experience during most of our waking hours.

IV. To What Do STIs Refer?

The aforementioned research leaves little doubt that trait concepts are activated by attending to behaviors that imply the corresponding traits, even when the attention is incidental to another task, or occurs in the course of a search for other information (Uleman & Moskowitz, 1994, Experiment 2). But what do these STIs represent? To Heider (1944), "not the doing only, but the doer" is "susceptible to a value judgment" (p. 365). Thus traits can refer not only to behaviors, but also to the people who are the source of these behaviors. Winter and Uleman (1984), following Smith and Miller's (1979, 1983) interest in causal attributions, simply assumed that an STI refers to 1) the actor, 2) the behavior (selected through pretesting to imply the trait), and 3) the cause of the actor's behavior. Trait terms are used in all three ways. But do STIs simultaneously refer to all three, or only to one or two of these referents? The desirability of distinguishing between 1) and 2) was raised by Higgins and Bargh (1987, pp. 377–378), has been elaborated by Bassili (1989a, 1989b; see also Newman & Uleman, 1993), and is central to Trope's (1986) model of dispositional attribution. The distinction between 1) and 3) has been developed by Hamilton (1988) and Newman and Uleman (1989) (see also Hilton, Smith, & Kim, 1995). We consider each of these distinctions in turn.

A. DO STIs REFER TO ACTORS OR MERELY TO BEHAVIORS?

This question arises naturally from the fact that trait-cued recall of actors is typically lower than trait-cued recall of behaviors (e.g., Winter & Uleman, 1984). If STIs refer to actors, why is recall of the actors so poor? Although in some studies, trait-cued recall of actors has exceeded noncued recall (Uleman et al., 1986; Winter & Uleman, 1984, Experiment 1), it has not always done so under memory instructions (Delmas, 1992, Experiment 1; Uleman & Moskowitz, 1994, Experiment 1; Winter & Uleman, 1984, Experiment 2), and it has never done so with cued recall of distractors (Uleman et al., 1992; Winter et al., 1985).

There are several potential reasons for the poor recall of actors. First, actor identities in the studies were chosen for their irrelevance to the action in the sentences. For example, mailmen are not known for being ill-mannered, and secretaries are not known for being clever (see Table 1). Given the rapidity and complexity of the task (up to 20 sentences presented with no more than 8 seconds for each), participants may ignore information perceived to be less relevant to performing the task. Anecdotal evidence in real life shows us that people are notorious for ignoring or forgetting names, even in less cognitively demanding situations than STI studies. The irrelevance of actors in the studies not only makes them instantly forgettable, but it creates an impoverished encoding environment. Thus, whether STIs refer to actors cannot be decided by citing the poor recall of actors in these studies. Instead, we should ask a more informative question: *When* are actors referred to, and when they are, what type of reference is made?

There are several ways in which traits can refer to actors. Uleman, Moskowitz, Roman, and Rhee (1993) introduced a distinction among intentional, manifest, and tacit references. Intentional reference occurs when a speaker deliberately points to a particular thing. In such a case, the reference is usually clear to others and certainly clear to the speaker. However, when a construct is activated spontaneously, what is its referent? How can we tell what it is "about," or if it is about anything at all? One might say that its referent is whatever activated it. In that sense, STIs refer to behaviors, pretested and selected for their trait implications. But that is dull and trivial. "Manifest" and "tacit" references refer to more interesting cases.

> Spontaneous trait inferences "manifestly" refer to the actors if there are direct links in explicit memory from traits to actors. They "tacitly" refer to the actors if trait-irrelevant features of the actor influence their frequency. (Uleman et al., 1993, p. 321)

In other words, STIs manifestly refer to an actor if they cue a recall of that actor. They tacitly refer to an actor if features such as the actor's charisma, vividness, or sex appeal make STIs more likely—STIs that are unrelated to charisma, vividness, or sex appeal per se. By definition, tacit reference results from features that do *not* imply the particular trait inferences that are made, but that may increase the target's general interest value.

Trait-relevant features of the actor may influence the frequency of STIs. Because this phenomenon is best illustrated by features implying traits that are stereotypic for the actor, we call it "stereotypic reference." Carlston and Skowronski (1994) introduced the additional possibility of implicit memory links between traits and actors. We, therefore, have four interesting kinds of reference to consider.

1. Manifest Reference

The finding that trait-cued recall of actors sometimes exceeds noncued recall might seem to be evidence of manifest reference (i.e., a direct link in explicit memory from the trait to the actor). However, such findings may also reflect indirect links (e.g., from trait to behavior to actor). Such indirect links must be ruled out to obtain clear tests of manifest reference. One way to do this is to covary out trait-cued recall of behaviors from trait-cued recall of actors. Moskowitz (1993a) did this and found evidence that STIs manifestly refer to actors, but only among participants with a high personal need for structure (PNS) (Thompson, Naccarato, Parker, & Moskowitz, 1993). Such people are more likely to engage in social categorization. (PNS was unrelated to both noncued recall of actors and trait-cued recall of behaviors, controlling for recall of the actors.) Thus among some individuals, direct links do occur in memory between STIs and actors.

Uleman and Moskowitz (1994) used another method to detect manifest reference. Instead of covarying out trait-cued recall of behaviors, they analyzed recall of actors within that subset of sentences (for each participant) in which the behavior had been recalled. Such a conditional analysis of actor recall rendered the indirect links through behaviors irrelevant, because behavior recall is constant and given. Participants read trait-implying sentences under a variety of goals. When they formed impressions of the actors in trait terms, there was clear evidence of manifest reference (as one would expect). More important, when participants were under memory instructions, as in many previous studies, there was no evidence of manifest reference. Recall of actors was no higher with trait cues than with no cues among sentences where behavior was recalled. (A reanalysis of data from Winter and Uleman's (1984) Experiment 1 in which trait-cued recall exceeded noncued recall of actors under memory instructions also failed to show manifest reference.) When participants had the goal of judging how similar they were to each actor, there was also no evidence of manifest reference. Only when the participants' goal was to judge their own likelihood of doing what the actor had done did conditional trait-cued recall of actors tend to support the existence of manifest reference.

Uleman et al. (1993) sought to increase the likelihood of manifest reference by presenting more complex and lifelike representations of the actors. Some trait-implying sentences were paired with color photos of the actor, whereas others were paired with photos of scenes or patterns. Participants in Experiment 1 read trait-implying sentences for a memory study. Their conditional trait-cued recall of actors showed no evidence of manifest reference. Predictably, when the same sentence and photo pairs were presented as distractors in Experiment 2, there was also no evidence of manifest reference. Surprisingly, though, when participants were asked to visualize the events in the sentences and photos as vividly as possible, a surprise cued recall test also failed to produce any evidence of manifest reference.

In Newman and Uleman's (1990) studies, actors were named rather than identified by occupational roles. Not surprisingly, recall of actors' names was poor (Experiment 1). However, participants always designated actors' genders in some way in their recall protocols. When behaviors were correctly recalled but actors were not, actors' genders were correct 94% of the time. This suggests either some degree of manifest reference, or that behavioral encodings included gender information in some other way.

Moskowitz (1993b) used a different design and stimulus array to see whether STIs are manifestly about actors. Rather than relying directly on recall of actors' identities, the design provides indirect evidence that their identities are used in an explicit memory task. Set size effects reveal how information is organized in memory. If all of the items in a set are category exemplars connected with only their category labels, then a negative set size effect results; more exemplars make each one in the set harder to recall. If there are many connections among exemplars, this effect can be neutralized or even reversed to produce a positive set size effect (i.e., a positive relation between the size of the memory set and the amount recalled). Analogous results can be expected if behaviors (exemplars) are organized by actor (category) in memory (see Gordon & Wyer, 1987). Moskowitz (1993b) kept the total number of behaviors presented to participants constant, but manipulated the number of behaviors associated with each actor. Behaviors were otherwise unrelated to each other, thus minimizing interitem connections. If sentences are organized in memory according to actors, then manipulating the number of behaviors each actor performed should yield negative set size effects. If sentences are not organized by actor, then recall should not vary as a function of this manipulation. Results showed that participants formed STIs, and that person organization was being used, despite the fact that recall for these actors was poor. A negative set size effect occurred. Thus, increasing the amount of behavioral information to be remembered about a person may affect whether direct links to the person are established in memory.

The studies show that evidence of manifest reference—direct links in explicit memory from traits to actors—is mixed. The clearest evidence came from Moskowitz's (1993a) participants who had high personal need for structure, and from participants who memorized several behaviors performed by each actor (Moskowitz, 1993b). Weaker evidence came from Uleman and Moskowitz's (1994) participants who made self-relevant judgments about actors' behaviors, and from Newman and Uleman (1990), who looked at participants' accuracy in recalling actors' genders. Other studies (Uleman & Moskowitz, 1994; Uleman et al., 1993; Winter & Uleman, 1984) have found no evidence of manifest reference.

2. Stereotypic Reference

Stereotypic reference occurs when trait-relevant features of the actor influence the likelihood of STI. In most STI studies, actor identities are unrelated to the traits of interest. However, in one study, stereotypic reference was investigated and found. Delmas (1992, Experiment 2) used memory instructions and French translations of the sentences from Winter and Uleman (1984), in which actors were identified by occupations. In his choice of actor identities, half of the occupations were strongly suggested by the traits and half were irrelevant. For example, being *talented* suggested *professor* but not *social worker,* and being *ill-mannered* suggested *truck driver* and not *trader*. Associated occupations facilitated STI, as indicated by trait-cued recall of behaviors. It is likely that such facilitation occurs because actor stereotypes prime relevant trait concepts.

3. Tacit Reference

Tacit reference occurs when trait-irrelevant features or aspects of the actor influence the likelihood of STI. Therefore, no a priori associations between actor identities and the traits, stereotypic or otherwise, should be available to account for these effects. Uleman et al. (1993) sought evidence of tacit reference with the paired photos described earlier and obtained it. Possible relevance of the photos to traits was controlled for by couterbalancing photo-sentence pairings. Under memory instructions (Experiment 1), trait-cued recall of behaviors was higher when the sentences had been paired at encoding with person photos instead of scene or pattern photos. Tacit reference also occurred when participants visualized the sentence-photo pairs and then completed a surprise memory test (Experiment 3). It only failed to occur when the sentence-photo pairs were presented as distractors (Experiment 2).

There is good evidence then that STIs can tacitly refer to actors. To date, STIs seem to occur when actors are more realistically presented. Perhaps more realistic stimuli invoke more of the distal goals on which trait inferences depend or instantiate more of the initial conditions associated with trait inference procedures (see Section VI,A on Proceduralization later). However one conceptualizes these results, STIs are less likely to occur with the relatively impoverished actor stimuli that have been used in much STI research.

4. Implicit Reference

Implicit reference to an actor is evident when information about the actor influences subsequent responses to him or her, independent of explicit memory for that information. Carlston and Skowronski (1994) demonstrated this with the relearning paradigm (see earlier discussion). There was a significant savings effect in learning pairs of actor photos and traits at Time 2 when these matched pairs of actor photos and behaviors from Time 1. This savings effect was independent of participants' ability to recognize the behaviors from Time 1, thus making the reference largely implicit.

Carlston et al. (1995, Experiments 1 and 2) further explored the bases for this effect by asking some participants "to write down a trait word to describe the person in the photo" at Time 1. Two days later, they participated in the relearning task. Savings were largely restricted to those photo-trait pairs that matched the traits generated at Time 1. Another study (Experiment 5) showed that this trait specificity of the savings effect was not mediated by recall of the trait generated at Time 1. Participants followed the same procedures except that at Time 2, 2 days after generating traits to photo-behavior pairs, they listed "up to three trait words that came to mind when looking at each photo." There was very little overlap between traits generated at Times 1 and 2, providing fairly clear evidence that the savings effect is primarily based on implicit rather than explicit memory of implied traits and behaviors from Time 1.

Note that in this paradigm, there is a clear intentional reference between the actors and the trait-implying behaviors at Time 1; the behaviors are presented and worded as self-descriptions. Carlston et al. (1995, Experiment 4) examined whether such intentional reference at Time 1 is necessary for implicit reference. They did this by telling participants that the descriptions given by the people in the photos were descriptions of *other people.* Some participants were asked to simply familiarize themselves with the materials (as in previous studies), and others were asked to form impressions of either the person in the photo or the person being described. The savings effect occurred in the familiarization condition but not in the impression formation conditions. This shows that the implicit link between photo and STI does *not* require an intentional reference between photo and behavior; mere association is sufficient. (However, the effects were not as large with mere association as with self-descriptions.) It also shows that when people intentionally form impressions, potentially misleading implicit links are prevented or overridden.

Marsman (1994, Experiments 4 and 5) argued that STIs refer to actors, not merely behaviors, on the grounds that different verb types have parallel effects on dispositional inferences and free recall of sentence parts. She constructed 12 sentence pairs that were equally meaningful with action verbs (HELP) or state verbs (LOVE) (e.g., "The fashion designer helps/ loves the model, who is dressed in a red evening gown."). (All of the sentences had actors as both verb subjects and objects. Subordinate clause referents were counterbalanced.) Participants read these sentences under either memory or impression formation instructions. After a 2-min distractor task, they freely recalled the sentences. Finally, they rated "the degree to which they could say something about the personality make-up or traits of the two persons in each sentence" (p. 69). As predicted from prior research on the implicit event instigation and implicit dispositional implications in verbs (Semin & Marsman, 1994), action verbs produced stronger dispositional attributions to sentence subjects than did state verbs. On this basis, Marsman predicted that participants in the memory condition would process subject actors more elaborately with action verbs than with state verbs, so that free recall of subject actors would be higher with action verbs than with state verbs. In contrast she noted that if STIs are primarily about behaviors, free recall should be higher for verbs than for actors.

Results clearly supported the first hypothesis. Subject actors with action verbs were recalled better (36%) than those with state verbs (30%); object actor recall did not differ by verb type (25%); and verbs were recalled the most poorly (16%). Thus, verb type (action versus state) influenced free recall of actors, and explicit memory for verbs was poor. Although this study included no evidence of STI per se, it is very likely that trait-implying sentences with action and state verbs would show similar effects. We classified these effects as implicit reference because prior exposure to particular verb types affected subsequent responses to (explicit free recall of) the actors, even though explicit recall of the behaviors (verbs) was low.

There is one other study that concerns implicit reference. No evidence for it was found, but there are reasons to question the study's premise. Whitney, Davis, and Waring (1994) asked participants to read four-sentence stories in which the last sentence implied a trait. Information in the first sentence was either neutral, consistent, or inconsistent with this trait implication. Participants anticipated answering either factual or impression formation questions. Whitney et al. (1994) reasoned that if STIs occur during comprehension, and if they refer to the actor, not merely the behavior, then all participants should take longer to read the last sentence when it is inconsistent with initial information. Results showed longer reading times only for impression formation readers. Therefore, Whitney et al. concluded that "traits activated spontaneously when subjects are not deliberately forming impressions represent categorizations of behavior" (p. 19). However, Carlston and Skowronski (1994) pointed out that because "implicit trait inferences seem unlikely to precipitate explicit efforts at reconciliation, it isn't clear that the failure to find longer processing times for incongruent stimuli provides evidence against such inferences" (p. 842).

In short, there is good evidence for implicit reference. The relearning paradigm provides the clearest evidence. Recent results with it show that implicit reference does not depend on intentional reference, and that mere association can produce it. This points to an important difference between STI and intentional impression formation processes. When STIs are formed, they may become associated with whoever is around. Marsman's free recall paradigm provides another kind of evidence for implicit reference and a promising method for further research.

The four types of reference above—Stereotypic, Tacit, Implicit, and Manifest (STIM)—have some relationships to each other. Stereotypic and tacit reference concern effects of actors' features on the nature and likelihood of STIs, respectively. These are depicted in Figure 1 as influences on how the behavior is interpreted (S) and on the likelihood of the STI process (T). Implicit and manifest reference concern associative links between STI and actor in memory. Implicit reference (I) involves an implicit memory

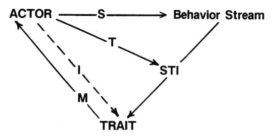

Fig. 1.   Reference relations among ACTOR and TRAIT concepts and the Behavior Stream. Spontaneous Trait Inferences (STIs) are made from Behavior to TRAIT. Stereotypic (S) features of the ACTOR may influence interpretation of the Behavior Stream, and other features may influence the likelihood of STI through tacit (T) reference. ACTOR may be linked in implicit (I) memory to TRAIT. TRAIT may have a direct, manifest (M) link in explicit memory to ACTOR.

link between STI and actor (and apparently anyone associated with the behavior), which facilitates intentionally learning associations between the person and the trait in the future. Manifest reference (M) involves an explicit memory link from trait to actor, as in cued recall.

Note that Figure 1 depicts a mixture of influences (S and T), inferences (STI), and associative links (I and M), but most of the lines are *not* associative links. That is, the connecting lines do not depict paths that conduct spreading activation. Instead, they depict conceptual relations among types of reference. In addition, ACTOR and TRAIT represent unitary concepts, whereas the Behavior Stream is a temporal sequence of features and events with a meaning that must be inferred. Finally, Figure 1 does not show all possible relations among these elements; it only shows those that have been demonstrated in STI research.

B. DO STIs DESCRIBE ACTORS OR THE CAUSES OF BEHAVIOR WITHIN ACTORS?

Hamilton (1988) has presented a strong case for distinguishing between trait inferences and causal attributions. He pointed out that trait inferences have traditionally been equated with causal attributions, at least since Jones and Davis (1965) asked how we infer traits from behaviors. Moreover, traits certainly can be appropriate answers to causal questions. In the traditional view, "correspondent" trait inferences are a consequence of making causal attributions. However, Hamilton (1988) and Reeder's (1985) alternative view is that traits can also serve as summary descriptions of another's behavior and personality, without always resulting from a causal analysis.

If I observe a person's outgoing and gregarious behavior at a party and infer that she is friendly, I am not attempting to explain why she mingled and chatted with others but am simply summarizing a pattern of behavior and inferring a trait characteristic from it. In making the inference I have implicitly assumed that her behavior is at least somewhat representative of her personality. (Hamilton, 1988, p. 377)

Causal attribution may produce trait inferences, but not all trait inferences arise from attribution processes. Furthermore, although "the trait inference is not itself an attribution, [once it has] been made, it becomes the basis for an attribution when one is needed" (Hamilton, 1988, p. 376). In this view, then, whether or not a trait is a cause depends on the process used to infer it, not on the use to which it may subsequently be put.

Hamilton offers two lines of evidence for preferring this more differentiated view of traits. First, there is a lot of evidence that information consistent with prior expectations is processed differently from information that is inconsistent. When it is consistent with prior expectations, or when there are no prior expectations, processing is likely to produce a summary trait description, as in the previous example. When it is inconsistent, processing takes longer, more elaorative links are formed among items, and trait explanations (causes) are more likely. People seem to respond to inconsistencies by spontaneously asking the causal attribution question "Why?" (Clary & Tesser, 1983; Hastie, 1984; Weiner, 1985). In other words, implicit "What?" and "Why?" questions are prompted by different kinds of information and lead to different kinds of processes. Causal questions prompt more extensive processing that includes attempts to establish coherence or consistency among multiple items of information.

The second line of evidence shows that after reading trait-relevant passages, participants are quicker to answer questions about actors' traits and intentions than questions about whether the cause was "something about the person" or "something about the situation" (Hamilton, 1988, pp. 371–373; Smith & Miller, 1983). If Kelley's (1967) model of causal attributions is accepted as a process model, then participants should first decide on the causal locus (personal or situational), and afterward identify the particular cause (e.g., trait or intention). If they make causal attributions in the course of reading the passages, then they should be faster, not slower, to answer locus questions. Hence, these results indicate that the participants made trait but not causal attributions.

Recent research on "implicit causality in verbs" supports the distinction between causal and dispositional inferences on completely different grounds. As noted previously, in subject-verb-object sentences with interpersonal verbs, action verbs (e.g., "Paul HELPS David") imply that the subject caused the event, but state verbs (e.g., "Paul LIKES David") imply that the object caused the event. Semin and Marsman (1994) argued that prior research on this topic has confounded event instigation (causation) with dispositional inference by asking participants how much they agree with statements such as "Paul is the type of person [dispositional inferences] who helps people [event instigation]" (p. 843). When the researchers measured instigation and disposition separately, they found that implicit event instigation was a function of verb type (action versus state) and valence. Implicit dispositions were unaffected by valence, but they were a function of verb type and whether the verbs have object referent adjectives (e.g., LIKEABLE) and, secondarily, whether they have subject referent adjectives (e.g., HELPFUL). Thus, implicit causality and implicit dispositions are distinct in being determined by different properties of verbs.[6]

All of this suggests that STIs are best regarded as descriptions of actors rather than causes within them, although they may be used in subsequent causal explanations once they occur.

C. SUMMARY

We posed two questions to organize this section, and found the simplest answer for the second question: Do STIs describe actors or the causes of behavior within actors? The studies show that STIs describe actors rather than causes within actors, although this distinction may be lost in subsequent processing and trait use.

The answer to the first question—Do STIs refer to actors or merely to behaviors?—depends on what one means by "refer to." By definition, STIs do not intentionally refer to anything. The criteria differ for answering this question in terms of the other reference types depicted in Figure 1 and our acronym STIM: stereotypic, tacit, implicit, and manifest references. There is some clear evidence for stereotypic reference; stereotypic features of actors make stereotypic STIs more likely. There is good evidence for tacit reference; more vivid and life-like actors make STIs more likely. There is very good evidence of implicit reference. Prior exposure to trait-implying behaviors by an actor makes it easier to learn the same trait–actor associations later. The relearning paradigm to date has demonstrated this in more

---

[6] It is worth noting that "causality" is a complex concept with multiple meanings. The grounds, therefore, for distinguishing between trait and causal inferences depend on which meaning of causality is adopted. The work cited here seems to regard causes as initiators of unexpected events (see also Hewstone, 1989, pp. 72–93; Hilton & Slugoski, 1986). Other research traditions view causes as elements of a narrative sequence that give it coherence and focus (e.g., Graesser & Clark, 1985; Kintsch, 1988; Trabasso & Sperry, 1985) and assert that analyses of causality in this sense are an intrinsic part of comprehending ordinary as well as unexpected events.

than 10 studies and many more conditions. In addition, this paradigm has demonstrated implicit reference to the source of the behavior description, even when that person is not the actor. Prior exposure to trait-implying behaviors also affects free recall of the actor. Finally, there is mixed evidence on manifest reference; not all conditions produce direct memory links from traits to actors. Manifest reference is more likely among people with high personal need for structure and when the same actor performs several behaviors. It may occur when some kinds of social judgments are made, but it does not occur with simple memory instructions or goals.

V. What Are the Consequences of STI?

This question of STI consequences has not received as much attention as it deserves. We describe four topics on which there are findings, and then suggest some other possibilities.

A. AWARENESS

Because STI proceeds without any intention to infer traits, people may be unaware of the stimuli (as in subliminal priming), the way the stimuli are interpreted or categorized, or the effects of categorization on subsequent judgments (Nisbett & Wilson, 1977). There is no evidence of the first kind for STIs. Trait-implying sentences must be presented long enough for comprehension, and this cannot occur at subliminal exposure speeds (e.g., 15 ms). It is possible that other kinds of stimuli containing trait information, such as facial expressions or postures, could be processed that quickly. But this has not been investigated and remains a topic for future research.

It is clear that people are usually unaware of the process of making STIs, the STIs themselves and, therefore, their effects on subsequent processing. Winter and Uleman (1984) found that participants were unaware not only of making STIs, but also of finding them useful in recall. Participants were questioned after cued recall of the sentences. Traits or personality inferences were rarely mentioned in responses to open-ended questions and were judged on rating scales to be relatively infrequent. Furthermore, the few claims of making trait inferences were uncorrelated with the actual effectiveness of trait cues for recall. Similar findings have been reported in other cued recall studies (Uleman et al., 1986), even when the awareness questions occurred right after participants read the last sentence (Lupfer et al., 1990; Moskowitz, 1993a; Uleman & Moskowitz, 1994; Uleman et al., 1992; Uleman et al., 1993; Winter et al., 1985).

B. PRIMING

Several studies have demonstrated that STIs can serve as primes and affect subsequent impressions of other targets. Moskowitz and Roman (1992) told participants that they were participating in two unrelated studies. In the "first study," they read trait-implying sentences under either memory or impression instructions. This created two groups: those making STIs who were thereby subtly primed and unaware of the activated trait concepts, and those who were aware of their trait inferences. In the "second study," everyone rated the ambiguous Donald (from Higgins et al., 1977), a character acting in a way that was relevant to the traits that had just been either spontaneously or explicitly inferred. As predicted, those who were unaware of the STI primes showed assimilation effects, so that ambiguous descriptions of Donald were interpreted in accord with the primes. Also as predicted, the blatant primes in the impression group produced contrast effects, so that Donald was rated toward the opposite pole of the primed dimension. This research provides an ecologically valid extension of the priming literature because the constructs that guided subsequent judgment were made accessible, not through the presentation of trait words, but through self-generated inferences that subjects spontaneously formed.

Although Moskowitz and Roman (1992) credited awareness of the primes with creating contrast effects (as had Lombardi et al., 1987; and Newman & Uleman, 1990; see Section III,C), Stapel, Koomen, and van der Pligt (1996) argued that contrast occurs when an activated trait concept refers to a specific person, whereas assimilation occurs when it remains an abstract concept. Two studies provide good support for this formulation.

In the first study, participants in the "impersonal" condition first read simple trait-implying sentences (e.g., "He knew he could handle most problems that would come up."), either for a subsequent memory test or to form an impression of the actor. The trait implications were either positive (*confident* and *persistent*), negative (*conceited* and *stubborn*), or irrelevant to the second task. Then in a second task, participants formed an impression of the ambiguous Donald ("Erik" in Dutch) from Higgins et al. (1977). Results replicated the study by Moskowitz and Roman (1992) in that memory instructions on the first task produced assimilation effects, whereas impression instructions produced contrast effects. Additional participants in a "personal" condition were first asked to study and memorize a page of passport photos with names and ages. Then they went through the previous procedure, except that sentence actors were now designated by the names they had just studied, rather than by pronouns. This produced contrast effects for both memory and impression formation conditions, apparently because the personal condition gave the traits specific referents rather than allowing them to remain abstract.

In the second study, these same trait-implying sentences with named actors were read under either memory or impression formation instructions. The sentences were followed by consensus and distinctiveness information that implied either a situation attribution or a person attribution (Kelley, 1967), or the information was irrelevant to attributions. The two covariation contexts were designed to activate abstract trait categories or concrete actor references, respectively. This was followed by the task of forming an impression of Erik. As predicted, the situation-attribution context produced assimilation effects on the impression of Erik, regardless of whether sentences were read under memory or under impression instructions. Similarly, the person-attribution context produced contrast effects, regardless of instructions. The attribution-irrelevant context replicated Moskowitz and Roman (1992), in that memory instructions produced assimilation, and impression formation instructions produced contrast. Stapel et al. (1996) argued from this as well as other evidence that when activated concepts are abstract and "in the background," they serve as interpretive frameworks and, consequently, assimilation occurs. When they are concrete, with specific references and "in the foreground," they are more likely to serve as standards and produce contrast effects. Schwarz and Bless's (1992) inclusion–exclusion model of assimilation and contrast effects is quite consistent with this view.

The range of concrete, specific references that can produce contrast effects is unknown. Intentional reference, from the impression formation conditions, has this effect. However, it is unclear whether the passport photo manipulation of Experiment 1 and the covariation information of Experiment 2 produced manifest or implicit reference, or both, in the memory conditions. This question is worth exploring in future research that seeks to clarify the range of reference types that produce contrast effects.

It is also interesting to note that in the memory condition of Experiment 2, covariation information influenced the nature of STIs, but it had no such effect in Lupfer et al. (1995) (see Section III,C). Although there are many differences between these studies that could account for this (number and nature of sentences, dependent variables), the most important may be that Lupfer's participants read the sentences as distractors rather than for a memory test, which gave them little opportunity or incentive to engage in the kind of elaborative processing that could alter inferences from the focal behaviors.

To summarize, STIs can function as primes and thereby affect subsequent impressions of others. Whether they produce assimilation or contrast depends on a variety of factors, many of which are described by the inclusion–exclusion model of Schwarz and Bless (1982).

C. PREDICTION

STIs may be used to predict actors' future behaviors. Very little relevant research has been done on this, but Newman (1991) provided some suggestive indirect evidence. In Experiment 1, he asked fifth graders and college students to read trait-diagnostic information about others and then predict whether trait-consistent (but different) behaviors would occur in new situations. Fifth graders were more likely to make trait-consistent predictions and less likely to provide interactionist explanations. In Experiment 2, the recognition probe paradigm revealed that fifth graders were more likely to make STIs than were college students. Thus, making STIs and using traits to predict future behaviors reflect parallel developmental courses, suggesting that they rely on the same knowledge structures. In addition, Hamilton's (1988) analysis and our discussion of distal goals (earlier) are consistent with using STI for prediction.

In contrast, Carlston et al. (1995, Experiment 5) found that participants do not recall the STIs they made from behaviors with photos, even when a savings effect showed that STIs had occurred. These findings may not be inconsistent with each other. Perhaps implicit knowledge of actors can influence predictions without any explicit recall of either the behaviors or prior trait inferences. That research has not yet been done. However, such results would be interesting because implicit memory effects would be particularly hard to modify or correct. Such results would suggest expanding Hastie and Park's (1986) distinction between online and memory-based judgments to include and distinguish between explicit and implicit memory-based effects.

D. CORRESPONDENCE BIAS

The correspondence bias is "the tendency to see behavior as caused by a stable personal disposition of the actor when it can be just as easily explained as a natural response to more than adequate situational pressures" (Jones, 1990, p. 138). Watson's (1982) review of the empirical literature shows that this bias is well documented and robust, to the extent that Ross (1977) dubbed it the "fundamental attribution error." In virtually all of the research on this bias, participants intentionally form impressions of others' traits or attitudes, so their impressions are not spontaneous. Nevertheless, STI may be an important foundation for the correspondence bias, because, relatively speaking, it activates trait concepts effortlessly, uncritically, and ubiquitously. These activated concepts can then come readily to mind when observers attempt to form impressions of others. Thus STIs may be important inputs for processes that produce the correspondence bias.

Inferring traits comprises only the first part of the correspondence bias; ignoring situational pressures is the second part. STI research addresses the first part by providing some of the most compelling evidence available on how readily trait concepts are inferred. There are two prominent approaches to the second part of understanding the role that situational information plays in the making of trait inferences: those of Gilbert et al. (1988) and Trope (1986).

Gilbert et al. (1988) posited three stages of impression formation (as noted above in Section III,D): *categorizing* the behavior in trait terms, *characterizing* the person in those terms, and *correcting* this characterization to take situational factors into account. Numerous studies (e.g., Gilbert, 1989) showing that a concurrent cognitive load increases the correspondence bias have been interpreted as evidence that situational correction is the last, and the least automatic stage in a relatively invariant sequence. Trope (1986), in contrast, gives situational information an important role of initially *identifying* behaviors in trait terms and later in moderating dispositional *inferences.* Trope and Alfieri (1993, August) have recently shown that situational information can affect this first stage of behavior identification, regardless of concurrent cognitive load.

Although attempting to reconcile these two models goes well beyond the purposes of this chapter, four STI findings seem to have some relevance. First (as described in Section III,C), Lupfer et al. (1990) found that situational information that precedes trait-implying behaviors and that reduces intentional trait inferences does not affect STIs. Second, according to Lupfer et al. (1995), covariation information favoring trait or situational attributions and following trait-implying information has no effect on STIs. Apparently more intentional inference processes are necessary to integrate such situational information with trait-implying information. It is possible that more concise situational information could be integrated spontaneously, but investigating this awaits future research. In any case these results suggest that STIs exhibit the correspondence bias, although these studies were not designed with this in mind.

In contrast, Stapel et al. (1996) found that situational information did affect STI (Section B earlier). In addition (as described in Section VIII,B later), there is some evidence that people make spontaneous situational inferences (SSIs) just as they make STIs. This evidence, along with Krull's (1993) recent demonstration that the effects of concurrent cognitive loads on intentional *situational* inferences parallel their effects on intentional dispositional inferences, suggests that the activation of trait concepts is not invariably primary or privileged, as implied by Gilbert et al. (1988).

Thus, there are several possible roles for spontaneous processes in producing the correspondence bias. The most obvious is the role of activating trait concepts in the first place. STI research demonstrates more clearly than any other how easily this occurs when people attend, however incidentally, to trait-implying behaviors. In addition, the fact that SSIs occur suggests that situational information could affect STIs, although research at present has not shown their relevance to the correspondence bias. It remains for future research to clarify how spontaneous and intentional processes interact to produce the correspondence bias, whether it occurs spontaneously as well as intentionally, and whether or when SSIs are relevant.

E. SOME OTHER POSSIBILITIES

Newman and Uleman (1989, pp. 171–178) described several phenomena in which STI may be implicated. Subsequent research has not developed these, so they remain ripe for future investigation. We note some of them briefly.

Changes in self-perceptions may be mediated by STI. Fazio, Effrein, and Falender (1981) induced changes in self-perception by interviewing participants with leading questions that presumed introversion or extraversion (e.g., "What things do you dislike about loud parties?"). Subsequent self-ratings and interactions with a confederate were biased in the direction presumed by the interview. Most interestingly, the bias in self-ratings did not account for the bias in the interactions. This suggests the unconscious activation of traits (STIs) that biased both self-ratings and behavior.

Perseverence of beliefs may also be mediated by STI. In the original work on this phenomenon (Lepper, Ross, & Lau, 1986; Ross, Lepper, & Hubbard, 1975), participants received feedback indicating that they had high math aptitude or were good at discriminating genuine suicide notes from fake ones, respectively. The resulting changes in self-perceptions perseverated in the face of subsequently learning that the feedback was bogus. C. A. Anderson (1983) (see also Anderson, New, & Speer, 1985) has shown that perseverence of beliefs is mediated by participants' spontaneous causal analyses. Most of this research presents participants with surprising events that apparently prompt spontaneous causal analyses. It is possible that less surprising events, which would prompt STI rather than causal analyses, could produce similar effects. Only future research will tell.

Self-fulfilling prophecies are based on a series of trait inferences from behaviors. The prominent theories of this process (e.g., Deaux & Major, 1987; Miller & Turnbull, 1986) have not explicitly addressed the role of intentions or awareness, either in making the inferences or in mediating their effects (even though self-fulfilling prophecies depend upon some degree of perceiver ignorance of critical links in this sequence). The paradigms for detecting STI could be used to detect the inferences presumed to underlie self-fulfilling prophecies.

The maintenance of stereotypes may be supported by STI. Two lines of evidence suggest different ways in which this could happen. Slusher and Anderson (1987) have demonstrated what they call "imaginal confirmation" of stereotypes. This occurs when people mistake their inferences for actual occurrences, and consequently overestimate the actual cooccurrence of feature pairings. In the experiments, participants read about members of occupational groups who performed trait-implying behaviors. Some of the accounts contained the traits explicitly, whereas others only implied them. Participants later overestimated the cooccurrence of occupations and explicit traits, confusing traits that had actually been expressed with those they had merely inferred. In other words, their inferences were transformed into evidence that confirmed those very inferences. The participants had no intentions to form impressions or infer traits, so these inferences seem to be STIs.

In a well-known study, Darley and Gross (1983) asked participants to evaluate a filmed child's academic abilities. Hannah's performance on academic tasks was uninformative, but it was preceded by a 6-minute clip of her playing in either a poor neighborhood or an affluent neighborhood. Evaluations after the initial 6-minute clip were the same for both groups, and only diverged after viewing the academic task clip. The authors presented considerable evidence to show that the participants developed expectancies from the first clip and used these to seek confirming evidence from the second clip, without awareness of either their initial hypotheses or their biased interpretation of the identical performance information. If such initial inferences had occurred without an evaluative intention, they would have been STIs. Thus stereotype-consistent STIs may bias the interpretation of subsequent information that is actually uninformative and lead to erroneous confirmation and perpetuation of the stereotype.

VI. How Does STI Develop?

A. PROCEDURALIZATION

How are the cognitive procedures that underlie STI acquired? The basic answer seems to be quite simple: by practice. But the evidence on how long such practice effects persist, and on how well they transfer to new tasks, reveals several interesting phenomena. (For a general discussion, see Smith, 1994.) Smith and Lerner (1986) showed that people get reliably faster on a variety of social judgment tasks in just 10 to 100 practice trials. On each trial, participants judged a different stimulus person in terms of the same criterion. They decided whether 1) persons, each described by different traits, were qualified for a particular job (e.g., librarian); 2) persons, each described by different policy positions, had a particular ideology (e.g., liberal); or 3) persons, each with a different first name, were male. Response speedup—indicating increased proceduralization of aspects of the judgment process—occurred only when the criterion (librarian or liberal or male) was the same on each successive trial. If the criterion changed from trial to trial (e.g., librarian then waitress then male), no speedup occurred. Moreover, after such judgments became relatively efficient, they were more impervious to disruption by a concurrent cognitive load, a fact that clearly links these two measures of efficiency. Finally, after these judgment processes had become relatively efficient, they transferred to other judgment criteria (e.g., from judging librarian to judging waitress) within the same task domain (e.g., judging occupational suitability).

Smith (1989) showed that the speedup of both general and specific procedures for behavior-trait judgments persists over 24 hours with no detectable decrease. Smith, Stewart, and Buttram (1992) further showed that efficiency gains from highly specific procedures (from judging the same behavior-trait pair on only one previous trial) were undiminished for at least 7 days! These effects are much longer lasting than the accessibility effects produced by semantic or repetition priming, and are independent of any memory of prior judgments.

More efficient procedures can dominate less efficient ones. After a series of judgment trials, Smith (1989) asked participants to judge the likability of people who performed intelligent but unfriendly behaviors ("won the political argument with his roommate") or unintelligent but friendly behaviors ("tried to fix his friend's refrigerator but ended up making it worse"). Those who had practiced judging intelligence evaluated the people primarily in terms of intelligence, and those who judged friendliness evaluated primarily in terms of friendliness.

Bassili (1993) demonstrated that consistently practicing trait judgments of behaviors increases STI. When either the judged behavior or the trait criterion was consistent across trials, the likelihood of STI for other behaviors increased, as measured by cued recall. Bassili concluded "that procedural efficiency is clearly implicated in the tendency to make spontaneous trait inferences and that participants' pre-practice levels of efficiency are far from the levels they can ultimately achieve" (p. 204).

In short, STI seems to develop by the inference of traits from behaviors intentionally, repeatedly, and consistently. Such practice establishes a nested hierarchy of cognitive procedures. These include procedures for 1) generally inferring traits from behaviors, 2) inferring particular traits from many behaviors, 3) inferring many traits from particular behaviors, and 4) inferring particular traits from particular behaviors. The first three procedures can be acquired in 10 to 100 consecutive trials of consistent training; the last procedure is significantly strengthened by a single trial. All of these procedures have relatively long-term effects on how behaviors are interpreted and how impressions are formed. Moreover, people are often unaware that these procedures are operating.

B. DEVELOPMENTAL CHANGES

As noted earlier, Newman (1991) studied the developmental course of STI, comparing fifth graders and college students. The developmental literature contains several lines of evidence suggesting that fifth graders are particularly rigid and simple trait theorists. Very young children do not have a clear conception of the internal characteristics that govern behavior in a variety of otherwise unrelated situations (i.e., traits), whereas older children understand that situations interact with traits to determine behavior (see Rholes, Newman, & Ruble, 1990; Ruble & Dweck, 1995). In Experiment 1, Newman asked first graders, fifth graders, and college students to read trait-diagnostic information about others and then predict trait-consistent behaviors for new situations. Fifth graders were most likely to make trait-consistent predictions, and less likely to provide interactionist explanations than were college students. In Experiment 2, fifth graders were more likely than college students to make STIs, suggesting that making STI and using traits to predict have parallel courses of development. The developmental evidence is thus consistent with the idea that the cognitive procedures underlying STI develop as a function of the frequency with which traits are consistently inferred from behavior.

VII. Are There Individual and Cultural Differences in STI?

Yes, there are differences in STI. We first describe individual differences that have not been linked to cultural differences, then those that have.

A. INDIVIDUAL DIFFERENCES

Because people differ in their histories of concept acquisition and use, there should be stable, long-term differences between people in which concepts are chronically accessible and which ones are not cognitively available at all. This is central to Kelly's (1955) psychology of personal constructs. Higgins, King, and Mavin (1982) refined Kelly's measure of construct accessibility and demonstrated the importance of chronicity differences in intentional impression formation. Behaviors associated with chronically accessible constructs were better remembered and had a larger impact on impressions, both after a brief delay and two weeks later. Bargh and Thein (1985) showed that under cognitive overload, people can process behaviors more thoroughly if those behaviors imply chronically accessible traits. Participants were presented with a rapid presentation of 24 behaviors, half of which implied *honesty*. Only those participants with high chronicity for *honesty* could generate impressions online (during the presentation) that reflected the actual proportion of honest behaviors presented. Nonchronic participants could not process the trait implications of the behaviors rapidly enough to do this, so their impressions reflected the proportion of honest behaviors that they recalled afterward rather than the proportion actually presented. Thus, individual differences in the chronic accessibility of traits affect which behavioral information is more heavily weighted and better recalled (Higgins et al., 1982), or processed more easily under information overload (Bargh & Thein, 1985) during intentional impression formation.

What about individual differences in STI derived from behavioral information? Unfortunately, there are no studies of STI and trait chronicity. However, Uleman et al., (1986) reasoned that conventional personality measures related to forming different impressions of others would also predict different STIs. Using the cued recall paradigm, they confirmed this with participants who were either high or low on authoritarianism. Sentences were developed that had different trait implications for each group. For example, "The architect loved the excitement of military parades" implied the trait *patriotic* to people high in authoritarianism. Among those low in authoritarianism, there was much less consensus about the architect. In contrast, when people with low authoritarianism learned that "The reporter slapped his daughter several times whenever she left her clothes on the floor," they inferred that the reporter was *harsh* or *abusive*. Those high in authoritarianism did not. When the participants read these sentences "for a memory study," the trait cues that were most effective for participants low in authoritarianism (e.g., HARSH) were not as effective for those high in authoritarianism. Thus Uleman et al. concluded that there are individual differences in STIs that occur at encoding.

Zelli, Huesmann, and Cervone (1995) also found individual differences in STIs related to participants' aggressiveness. Participants read sentences that can, but need not, be interpreted in terms of hostility (e.g., "The electrician looks at his younger brother and starts laughing."), with the goal of either memorizing them or understanding why the actors did what they did. Then recall was cued with semantic or hostile trait cues. Participants were classified as high or low in aggressiveness on the basis of the self-reported frequency of aggressive behaviors (slapping others, threatening, etc.). Among those with a memory goal (the spontaneous inference condition), hostile traits were more effective than semantic cues for aggressive participants, whereas semantic cues were twice as effective as hostile trait cues for nonaggressive participants. Even more interestingly, there were no differences among participants who had a deliberate inference goal. This suggests that STIs reflect people's most accessible schema, rather than their full range of potential inferences.

Moskowitz (1993a) found that participants with a high personal need for structure (PNS) are more likely to make STIs. PNS reflects a desire for certainty and clarity, and an aversion to ambiguity (Thompson et al., 1993). It is similar to the situationally manipulated state labeled "need for structure" in Kruglanski's (1989) theory of lay epistemics. Those who chronically desire structure are presumably more interested in and practiced at inferring traits from behavior, than they are in suspending judgment or forming more complex impressions that include situational factors.

There is evidence, therefore, of stable individual differences in both the kinds of STIs people generate from the same information (Uleman et al., 1986; Zelli et al., 1995), and in their likelihood of making STIs at all (Moskowitz, 1993a). Differences in idiocentrism also affect STI; these are described later.

B. STIs AND INDIVIDUALISM AND COLLECTIVISM

There is considerable evidence of cultural differences in the way personality traits are used to explain events and describe both oneself and others. These differences are usually described in terms of individualism—

collectivism (Triandis, 1989, 1990) or independence–interdependence (Markus & Kitayama, 1991). In individualistic cultures, the uniqueness and autonomy of the individual is emphasized. People are viewed as separate from their social roles, and self-expression is valued. In collectivistic cultures, the relatedness and interdependence of individuals is emphasized. Occupying one's proper place in the social scheme and self-restraint are valued. Euramerican culture is individualistic; Asian and Latino cultures are more collectivistic (Hofstede, 1980). As a result, attributions of causality and responsibility are couched in terms of traits more in individualistic than in collectivistic cultures (Cha & Nam, 1985, cited by Zebrowitz, 1990, pp. 169–170; Hamilton et al., 1983; Miller, 1984). Euramericans also use more traits, and with fewer qualifiers than Asians or Latinos when describing other people (Shweder & Bourne, 1984) and themselves (Cousins, 1989; Rhee, Uleman, Lee, & Roman, 1995).

The finding that trait inferences become proceduralized only with consistent practice suggests that STI will be more likely in cultures that frequently and consistently use trait terms (i.e., in individualistic cultures). Two lines of research support this idea. The first (and least developed) compares STI in individualistic and collectivistic cultures. The second compares STI among Americans who differ on idiocentrism (individualism at the level of persons rather than cultures).

1. Cultural Differences

As described earlier, Newman (1991) studied STI with the recognition probe paradigm. He predicted that both STIs and the use of traits to predict future behavior would be higher among fifth graders than among college students. Results from a largely Euramerican, suburban fifth-grade sample supported this prediction. However, results were quite different with a fifth-grade urban sample from a largely Puerto Rican neighborhood. Puerto Ricans "were less likely to assume that behavior would be trait-consistent, and were more sensitive to the effects of situational constraints when predicting the future behavior of other people" (Newman, 1993, p. 249). This sample also showed no evidence of STI. Newman speculated that cultural differences might be at work.

Zárate and Uleman (1994) have gathered preliminary data to test this speculation directly. Anglo and Chicano students taking introductory psychology at the University of Texas at El Paso participated in a lexical decision study described as a study of "how people can do two things at the same time, such as studying for an exam while watching TV. For example, does turning your attention to the TV only when you hear a laugh from the audience reduce recall for just-learned material?" Participants read a series of sentences on a computer screen. Then they were given a recall test that simulated "an exam." During the series of sentences, they were interrupted unpredictably by letter strings on the screen. They had to decide, as quickly and accurately as possible, whether each string was a word. Among Anglos, RTs to trait words were shorter following trait-implying sentences than RTs following control sentences, indicating that STIs had occurred. However, there was absolutely no evidence of STI among the Chicano students, even though there was adequate statistical power (with almost 2.5 times as many Chicano as Anglo students) and the intentional inferences of Anglo and Chicano students were very similar.

2. Individual Differences

There are several measures of individualism and collectivism at the individual rather than the cultural level, where these constructs are better termed idiocentrism and allocentrism, respectively. Newman (1993) reported two studies using the measure of idiocentrism developed by Triandis, Bontempo, Villareal, Asai, and Lucca (1988). In Experiment 1, participants read trait-implying sentences for a subsequent memory test. After a brief distractor, they recalled the sentences, half of which had trait cues, and half of which had none. Then they completed the idiocentrism scale. Analyses revealed an idiocentrism × sex × cuing interaction. The expected effect of idiocentrism appeared only among men: Trait cues were more effective than no cues for idiocentric men, but this did not hold for nonidiocentric men.

In Experiment 2, using the recognition probe paradigm, participants read trait-implying sentences, or their scrambled control versions. As usual, the prediction was that if the probe word was not in the preceding text but merely implied there, participants would take longer to respond. Participants then completed the idiocentrism measure. As predicted, there were larger increases in RTs to trait-implying sentences among participants higher on idiocentrism. There were no sex differences.

More recently, Duff, Newman, and Wolsko (1995, May) showed that idiocentric participants are more likely to make STIs and less likely to make spontaneous situational inferences. Participants read 12 sentences (e.g., "On her lunch break, the receptionist steps in front of another person in line"; "The photographer complains about the service in the new restaurant.") for a subsequent memory test. Each sentence had both a dispositional interpretation (e.g., *rude* and *picky,* respectively) and a situational interpretation (e.g., *in a hurry* and *slow,* respectively). After a brief distractor, half of the sentences were cued with trait cues and half with situational cues. Idiocentrism correlated positively with 1) the amount of sentence recall that was trait-cued, negatively with 2) the amount that was situation-cued, and positively with the difference, 1) − 2). In addition, there was a sex difference reminiscent of Newman (1993). Idiocentrism and trait-cued recall correlated positively among men but not women. The fact that sex differences occurred for the delayed cued recall measure in both studies, but not for the immediate recognition probe measure, warrants further investigation.[7]

C. SUMMARY

Some people are more likely than others to spontaneously infer traits, and people vary in terms of the specific traits they readily infer from behavior. But rather than memorizing a list of such individual differences, the reader would profit more from considering how all of them can be understood with reference to our earlier discussion of the way STIs develop.

As noted above, the development of STIs can be understood in terms of the proceduralization of judgment processes. Smith's (1989) work indicates that the cognitive procedures likely to become spontaneous through practice have both general and specific components. Hence, some people, such as those high in idiocentrism and the need for structure, may become more adept at generally inferring traits from behaviors without intentions or awareness. There is also evidence that the trait inference process is more generally proceduralized among people in certain developmental stages, or among those who have been socialized in particular cultural contexts.

Other research on individual differences highlights the proceduralization of more specific trait inference processes, such as those involved in the inferring of particular traits from behavior. Research by Uleman et al. (1986) and Zelli et al. (1995) shows that some people, due to the contingencies in their environments or their histories of concept acquisition, will be more practiced at inferring specific trait concepts. Previous research on differences in chronic accessibility revealed that people process particular trait concepts more efficiently and are more likely to rely on those concepts when intentionally judging others. It also seems probable that people differ in the traits that they are likely to infer spontaneously.

Thus, the cognitive procedures that underlie STI are acquired through practice. Some people practice more than others, in both general and specific ways.

[7] Triandis (1990) observed that behavioral and attitudinal differences between individualists and collectivists often correspond to differences between males and females in individualist societies (see also Josephs, Markus, & Tafarodi, 1992). Note, however that the sex differences we report here are more complex than a difference in mean levels of idiocentrism (although we consistently find modest differences of this sort, with males scoring higher). Instead, the construct itself seems to predict different kinds of spontaneous inferences within each group.

VIII. Are Other Social Categories Inferred Spontaneously?

Traits are not the only frequently used social category that might become highly proceduralized. People can also be described in terms of types, goals, roles, and ethnic or other social groups. Behaviors can be described in ways unrelated to traits, and some situational categories are also of chronic interest. None of the factors governing the proceduralization of trait inferences seem to be unique to traits, so other social inferences may also occur spontaneously. The paradigms reviewed earlier provide some evidence for two kinds of spontaneous social inferences besides STIs: behavioral gists and situational causes.

A. SPONTANEOUS BEHAVIORAL GIST INFERENCES

"Behavioral gists" in the STI literature describe behavior in ways that are not directly relevant to traits. "The child tells his mother that he ate the chocolates" implies *honest,* but the behavior can also be categorized as *confessing* (see Table 1 for other examples of "action gists"). Note that because behavioral gists are not relevant to trait attributions, by definition, they do not contribute to STI. In Trope's (1986) model, dispositional inferences depend upon the identification of the current behavior. In the model of Gilbert et al (1988), behavior is categorized before the person is characterized. However, both of these models assume "that identification processes represent the incoming stimulus information in terms of attribution-relevant categories (e.g., friendly or unfriendly behavior, friendly or unfriendly situation). The results of these processes serve as input for dispositional inference." (Trope, 1986, p. 239). However, behavioral gist inferences are *not* trait attribution-relevant categories, so they cannot serve as direct input for dispositional inferences.

Winter et al. (1985) were the first to use gist cues along with trait cues in the cued recall of distractors paradigm. Gist cues were just as effective as trait cues in retrieving the sentences. Most recently, Uleman and Moskowitz (1994) used gist cues in studying the effects of goals on spontaneous inferences. Gist cues were at least as effective as trait cues in these studies, too. Three other findings are noteworthy.

First, contrary to the expectation that spontaneous trait and gist inferences would compete for processing capacity or procedures so that they would be mutually exclusive and their effectiveness as cues would be negatively correlated, Uleman and Moskowitz (1994) found that their effectiveness was positively correlated. These correlations reached significance in some conditions but not in others (with Ns about 35), but they were always positive. Thus, spontaneous trait and gist inferences tend to co-occur and not be mutually exclusive.

Second, goals had a different effect on the likelihood of trait inferences than they did on the likelihood of gist inferences. In Experiment 2, participants read trait-implying sentences with one of three feature detection goals: detecting graphemes, detecting phonemes, or determining the gender of pronouns. Trait-cued recall showed a significant linear increase across these three goal conditions. In contrast, gist-cued recall showed a significant linear decrease across these same conditions. That is, processing goals had different effects on STI versus spontaneous gist inference. Therefore, although goals had unintended effects on both kinds of unintended inferences, these effects were quite distinct, suggesting that different processes or procedures are involved in STI compared to gist inference.

Third, conditional analyses of actor recall (that held behavior recall constant) revealed that when participants had the goals of judging their own similarity to actors or events in the sentences (Experiment 3), there was clear evidence of direct memory links between gists and actors (although not between traits and actors as noted earlier in Section IV,A on manifest reference). This suggests that, "at least with the current measures and goals, people are more likely to remember the gist of what the actor did than its trait implications" (Uleman & Moskowitz, 1994, p. 499).

B. SPONTANEOUS SITUATIONAL INFERENCES

Do people infer situational causes spontaneously? The evidence shows that they do. As noted earlier, Lupfer et al. (1990) used the cued recall of distractors paradigm to investigate both STIs and spontaneous situational inferences (SSIs). Participants read distractor paragraphs containing information that supported trait inferences, information that supported situational inferences, or no information besides the focal sentence. Trait-implying sentences from previous studies served as the focal sentences, so the stimulus materials favored trait inference. Without accompanying information, situational cues (e.g., NOT ENOUGH ROOM for "The businessman steps on his girlfriend's feet during the foxtrot") were no more effective than no cues for recalling focal sentences, and were less effective than trait (e.g., CLUMSY) or gist (e.g., DANCING) cues. Thus, SSIs did not occur for these trait-implying sentences. But when they were preceded by information supporting SSIs (e.g., "A businessman and his girlfriend are trying to dance on a very crowded dance floor. Everyone is bumping into others."), situational cues became more effective than no cues. Participants showed no awareness of making SSIs. Interestingly, information supporting SSIs did not affect the effectiveness of either trait or gist cues, and information supporting STIs did not affect the effectiveness of either situational or gist cues. Therefore, STI and SSI are independent of each other in the same way that STI and gist inferences are.

Lupfer et al. (1995) used several paradigms with sentences that were trait-implying, situational-cause-implying, or ambiguous. These sentences were followed by no information or by covariation information that supported trait or situation inferences. In Experiment 2, the recognition probe paradigm was modified so that these paragraphs were read as distractors and followed by trait, situational, and other probes. Regardless of accompanying information, participants made more errors on situational probes following situational sentences than on other sentences, and more than on trait probes following situational sentences. In Experiment 3, these same paragraphs were presented as distractors in a lexical decision task, with participants expecting to answer questions about the paragraphs at the end of the study. Lexical decision target strings included the same traits and situational causes as in Experiment 2. Participants were faster and more accurate in identifying situational causes as words when they followed situational paragraphs rather than trait-implying paragraphs, again regardless of accompanying information. All of these results indicate that SSI occurred and were not affected by subsequent covariation information.

As noted earlier, Duff et al. (1995) predicted that people high on a scale of idiocentrism are less likely to make SSI. This is precisely what they found, and as noted above, there was a sex difference that replicated Newman's findings (1993). Idiocentrism and disposition-cued recall correlated positively among men but not among women. The opposite pattern obtained for situation-cued recall. It correlate negatively with idiocentrism among women but not among men.

In short, there is evidence that SSI does occur, suggesting that STI and SSI may be similar when all other things are equal (as they seldom are). This is reminiscent of Krull's (1993) finding that intentional situational inferences are less likely to be influenced by competing dispositional information under cognitive load than under no load, just as intentional dispositional inferences are less likely to be influenced by competing situational information under load than no load (Gilbert, 1989).

IX. Conclusion

Fiske and Taylor (1991) noted: "As the cognitive miser viewpoint has matured, the importance of motivations and emotions has again become evident. . . . The emerging view of the social perceiver, then, might best be termed the *motivated tactician,* a fully engaged thinker who has multiple cognitive strategies available and chooses among them based on goals, motives and needs" (p. 13).

We would alter this persepctive somewhat and advocate viewing people as flexible interpreters. "Motivated tactician" is as one-sided as the term "cognitive miser," implying that people are always driven by explicit cognitive goals, constantly deliberating and deliberate. But they are not. People interpret the meaning of events spontaneously as well as tactically, and go beyond not only the information given, but also beyond the immediate demands of their proximal goals. They also daydream, engage in cognitive play, and are struck by ideas from out of the blue. Our cognitive processes are not merely instrumental. They also have a spontaneous life of their own. People are flexible interpreters and have at their disposal a whole repertoire of cognitive procedures that they can deliberately deploy or "put on automatic." In some distal sense, all of this is motivated. Spontaneous, as well as tactical processes, are affected by goals, motives, and needs, and these may not be explicit. The sources, limits, and mechanisms behind this flexibility are important topics for research, but the flexibility itself is fundamental. Hence our preference for emphasizing the flexibility of social cognitions.

Acknowledgments

Preparation of this chapter was supported by NSF Grant SBR-9319611 to the first author. We would like to thank Craig Anderson, Douglas Krull, Michael Lupfer, Gooitske Marsman, John Skowronski, and Yaacov Trope for their thoughtful comments and suggestions on an earlier draft. Of course, the conclusions are our own, and they should not be blamed for any conclusions that you dislike.

Correspondence can be directed to any of the authors:

Professor James S. Uleman, Department of Psychology, New York University, 6 Washington Place, Room 753, New York, NY 10003; e-mail JimU@Psych.NYU.EDU.

Professor Leonard S. Newman, Department of Psychology (MIC 285), 1009 Behavioral Sciences Building, University of Illinois at Chicago, 1007 West Harrison Street, Chicago, IL 60607-7137; e-mail LNewman@UIC.EDU.

Professor Gordon B. Moskowitz, Department of Psychology, Green Hall, Princeton University, Princeton, NJ 08544-1010; e-mail GordonMo@PUCC.PRINCETON.EDU.

References

Ambady, N., & Rosenthal, R. (1992). Thin slices of expressive behavior as predictors of interpersonal consequences: A meta-analysis. *Psychological Bulletin, 111,* 256–274.

Anderson, C. A. (1983). Abstract and concrete data in the perseverance of social theories: When weak data lead to unshakable beliefs. *Journal of Experimental Social Psychology, 19*, 93–108.

Anderson, C. A., & Deuser, W. E. (1993). The primacy of control in causal thinking and attributional style: An attributional functionalism perspective. In G. Weary, F. Gleicher, & K. L. Marsh (Eds.), *Control motivation and social cognition* (pp. 94–121). New York: Springer-Verlag.

Anderson, C. A., New, B. L., & Speer, J. R. (1985). Argument availability as a mediator of social theory perseverance. *Social Cognition, 3*, 235–249.

Anderson, J. R. (1983). *The architecture of cognition.* Cambridge, MA: Harvard University Press.

Anderson, R. C., & Ortony, A. (1975). On putting apples into bottles—A problem of polysemy. *Cogntiive Psychology, 7*, 167–180.

Asch, S. E. (1946). Forming impressions of personality. *Journal of Abnormal and Social Psychology, 41*, 258–290.

Balota, D. A., d'Arcais, G. B. F., & Rayner, K. (Eds.). (1990). *Comprehension processes in reading.* Hillsdale, NJ: Erlbaum.

Bargh, J. A. (1989). Conditional automaticity: Varieties of automatic influence in social perception and cognition. In J. S. Uleman & J. A. Bargh (Eds.), *Unintended thought* (pp. 3–51). New York: Guilford.

Bargh, J. A. (1990). Auto-motives: Preconscious determinants of social interaction. In E. T. Higgins & R. M. Sorrentino (Eds.), *Handbook of motivation and cognition: Foundations of social behavior* (Vol. 2, pp. 93–130). New York: Guilford.

Bargh, J. A. (1994). The four horsemen of automaticity: Awareness, intention, efficiency, and control in social cognition. In R. S. Wyer, Jr., & T. K. Srull (Eds.), *Handbook of social cognition: Vol. 1, Basic processes* (2nd ed., pp. 1–40). Hillsdale, NJ: Erlbaum.

Bargh, J. A., & Barndollar, K. (1995). Automaticity in action: The unconscious as repository of chronic goals and motives. In P. M. Gollwitzer & J. A. Bargh (Eds.), *The psychology of action.* New York: Guilford.

Bargh, J. A., & Thein, R. D. (1985). Individual construct accessibility, person memory, and the recall-judgment link: The case of information overload. *Journal of Personality and Social Psychology, 49*, 1129–1146.

Bassili, J. N. (1989a). Trait encoding in behavior identification and dispositional inference. *Personality and Social Psychology Bulletin, 15*, 285–296.

Bassili, J. N. (1989b). Traits as action categories versus traits as person attributes in social cognition. In J. N. Bassili (Ed.), *On-line cognition in person perception* (pp. 61–89). Hillsdale, NJ: Erlbaum.

Bassili, J. N. (1993). Procedural efficiency and the spontaneity of trait inference. *Personality and Social Psychology Bulletin, 19*, 200–205.

Bassili, J. N., & Smith, M. C. (1986). On the spontaneity of trait attributions: Converging evidence for the role of cognitive strategy. *Journal of Personality and Social Psychology, 50*, 239–246.

Berry, D. S., & McArthur, L. Z. (1986). Perceiving character in faces: The impact of age-related craniofacial changes on social perception. *Psychological Bulletin, 100*, 3–18.

Borkenau, P. (1990). Traits as ideal-based and goal-derived social categories. *Journal of Personality and Social Psychology, 58*, 381–396.

Brewer, M. B. (1988). A dual process model of impression formation. In T. K. Srull & R. S. Wyer, Jr. (Eds.), *Advances in social cognition* (Vol. I, pp. 1–36). Hillsdale, NJ: Erlbaum.

Bruner, J. S. (1957). On perceptual readiness. *Psychological Review, 64*, 123–152.

Cantor, N., & Mischel, W. (1979). Prototypes in person perception. In L. Berkowitz (Ed.), *Advances in experimental social psychology* (Vol. 12, pp. 3–52). New York: Academic Press.

Carlston, D. E., & Skowronski, J. J. (1994). Savings in the relearning of trait information as evidence for spontaneous inference generation. *Journal of Personality and Social Psychology, 66,* 840–856.

Carlston, D. E., Skowronski, J. J., & Sparks, C. (1995). Savings in relearning: II. On the formation of behavior-based trait associations and inferences. *Journal of Personality and Social Psychology, 69,* 420–436.

Cha, J.-H., & Nam, K.-D. (1985). A test of Kelley's cube theory of attribution: A cross-cultural replication of McArthur's study. *Korean Social Science Journal, 12,* 151–180.

Cherry, E. C. (1953). On the recognition of speech with one, and with two ears. *Journal of the Acoustical Society of America, 25,* 975–979.

Chi, M. T. H., Glaser, R., & Farr, M. (1988). *The nature of expertise.* Hillsdale, NJ: Erlbaum.

Claeys, W. (1990). On the spontaneity of behavior categorization and its implications for personality measurement. *European Journal of Social Pscyhology, 4,* 173–186.

Clary, E. G., & Tesser, A. (1983). Reactions to unexpected events: The naive scientist and interpretive activity. *Personality and Social Psychology Bulletin, 9,* 609–620.

Corbett, A. T., & Dosher, B. A. (1978). Instrument inferences in sentence encoding. *Journal of Verbal Learning and Verbal Behavior, 17,* 479–491.

Cosmides, L. (1989). The logic of social exchange: Has natural selection shaped how humans reason? Studies with the Wason selection task. *Cognition, 31,* 187–276.

Cousins, S. D. (1989). Culture and selfhood in Japan and the US. *Journal of Personality and Social Psychology, 56,* 124–131.

D'Agostino, P. R. (1991). Spontaneous trait inferences: Effects of recognition instructions and subliminal priming on recognition performance. *Personality and Social Psychology Bulletin, 17,* 70–77.

Darley, J. M., & Gross, P. H. (1983). A hypothesis-confirming bias in labeling effects. *Journal of Personality and Social Psychology, 44,* 20–33.

Deaux, K., & Major, B. (1987). Putting gender into context: An interactive model of gender-related behavior. *Psychological Review, 94,* 369–389.

Delmas, F. (1992, July). *Impact of target's category membership on spontaneous trait inference.* Poster presented at the XXV International Congress of Psychology, Brussels, Belgium.

Devine, P. G. (1989). Stereotypes and prejudice: Their automatic and controlled components. *Journal of Personality and Social Psychology, 56,* 5–18.

Dewey, J. (1929). *The quest for certainty.* New York: Minton, Balch & Company.

Duff, K. J., Newman, L. S., & Wolsko, C. (1995, May). *Culture and spontaneous inferences.* Paper presented at the annual meeting of the Midwestern Psychological Association, Chicago, IL.

Ekman, P. (1972). Universals and cultural differences in facial expressions of emotion. In J. Cole (Ed.), *Nebraska symposium on motivation, 1971* (pp. 207–283). Lincoln: University of Nebraska Press.

Fazio, R. H., Effrein, E. A., & Falender, V. J. (1981). Self-perceptions following social interaction. *Journal of Personality and Social Psychology, 50,* 1152–1160.

Fiske, S. T., & Neuberg, S. L. (1990). A continuum of impression formation, from category-based to individuating processes: Influences of information and motivation on attention and interpretation. In M. P. Zanna (Ed.), *Advances in experimental social psychology* (Vol. 23, pp. 1–74). New York: Academic Press.

Fiske, S. T., & Taylor, S. E. (1991). *Social cognition* (2nd ed.). New York: McGraw-Hill.

Gilbert, D. T. (1989). Thinking lightly about others: Automatic components of the social inference process. In J. S. Uleman & J. A. Bargh (Eds.), *Unintended thought* (pp. 189–211). New York: Guilford.

Gilbert, D. T., Pelham, B. W., & Krull, D. S. (1988). On cognitive busyness: When person perceivers meet persons perceived. *Journal of Personality and Social Psychology, 54,* 733–740.

Gollwitzer, P. M. (1993). Goal achievement: The role of intentions. In W. Stroebe & M. Hewstone (Eds.), *European review of social psychology* (Vol. 4, pp. 141–185). Chichester, UK: Wiley.

Gollwitzer, P. M., & Moskowitz, G. B. (in press). Goal effects on thought and behavior. In E. T. Higgins & A. W. Kruglanski (Eds.), *Social psychology: Handbook of basic principles.* New York: Guilford.

Gordon, S., & Wyer, R. S., Jr. (1987). Person memory: Category-set-size effects on the recall of a person's behavior. *Journal of Personality and Social Psychology, 53,* 648–662.

Graesser, A. C., & Bower, G. H. (Eds.). (1990). *The psychology of learning and motivation, Vol. 25: Inferences and text comprehension.* New York: Academic Press.

Graesser, A. C., & Clark, L. F. (1985). *The structures and procedures of implicit knowledge.* Norwood, NJ: Ablex.

Hamilton, D. L. (1981). Cognitive representations of persons. In E. T. Higgins, C. P. Herman, & M. P. Zanna (Eds.), *Social cognition: The Ontario symposium* (Vol. 1, pp. 135–159). Hillsdale, NJ: Erlbaum.

Hamilton, D. L. (1988). Causal attribution viewed from an information-processing perspective. In D. Bar-Tal & A. W. Kruglanski (Eds.), *The social psychology of knowledge* (pp. 359–385). Cambridge, UK: Cambridge University Press.

Hamilton, D. L., Katz, L. B., & Leirer, V. O. (1980). Cognitive representation of personality impressions: Organizational processes in first impression formation. *Journal of Personality and Social Psychology, 39,* 1050–1063.

Hamilton, V. L., Sanders, J., Hosoi, Y., Ishimura, Z., Matsubara, N., Nishimura, H., Tomita, N., & Tokoro, K. (1983). Universals in judging wrongdoing: Japanese and Americans compared. *American Sociological Review, 48,* 199–211.

Hastie, R. (1984). Causes and effects of causal attribution. *Journal of Personality and Social Psychology, 46,* 44–56.

Hastie, R., & Park, B. (1986). The relationship between memory and judgment depends on whether the judgment task is memory-based or on-line. *Psychological Review, 93,* 258–268.

Hebb, D. O. (1949). *The organization of behavior: A neuropsychological theory.* New York: Wiley.

Heider, F. (1944). Social perception and phenomenal causality. *Psychological Review, 51,* 358–374.

Heider, F. (1958). *The psychology of interpersonal relations.* New York: Wiley.

Hewstone, M. (1989). *Causal attribution: From cognitive processes to collective beliefs.* Oxford, UK: Basil Blackwell.

Higgins, E. T., & Bargh, J. A. (1987). Social cognition and social perception. *Annual Review of Psychology, 38,* 369–425.

Higgins, E. T., King, G. A., & Mavin, G. H. (1982). Individual construct accessibility and subjective impressions and recall. *Journal of Personality and Social Psychology, 43,* 35–47.

Higgins, E. T., Rholes, W. S., & Jones, C. R. (1977). Category accessibility and impression formation. *Journal of Experimental Social Psychology, 13,* 141–154.

Hilton, D. J., & Slugoski, B. R. (1986). Knowledge-based causal attribution: The Abnormal Conditions Focus model. *Psychological Review, 93,* 75–88.

Hilton, D. J., Smith, R. H., & Kim, S. H. (1995). Processes of causal explanation and dispositional attribution. *Journal of Personality and Social Psychology, 68,* 377–387.

Hofstede, G. (1980). *Culture's consequences: International differences in work-related values.* Beverly Hills, CA: Sage.

Johnson, M. H., & Morton, J. (1991). *Biology and cognitive development: The case of face recogntion.* Oxford: Blackwell.

Jones, E. E. (1979). The rocky road from acts to dispositions. *American Psychologist, 34,* 107–117.

Jones, E. E. (1990). *Interpersonal perception.* New York: W. H. Freeman.

Jones, E. E., & Davis, K. E. (1965). From acts to dispositions: The attribution process in person perception. In L. Berkowitz (Ed.), *Advances in experimental social psychology* (Vol. 2, pp. 220–266). New York: Academic Press.

Josephs, R. A., Markus, H. R., & Tafarodi, R. W. (1992). Gender and self-esteem. *Journal of Personality and Social Psychology, 63,* 391–402.

Kanazawa, S. (1992). Outcome or expectancy: Antecedent of spontaneous causal attribution. *Personality and Social Psychology Bulletin, 18,* 659–668.

Keenan, J. M., Potts, G. R., Golding, J. M., & Jennings, T. M. (1990). Which elaborative inferences are drawn during reading? A question of methodologies. In D. A. Balota, G. B. F. d'Arcais, & K. Rayner (Eds.), *Comprehension processes in reading* (pp. 377–402). Hillsdale, NJ: Erlbaum.

Kelley, H. H. (1967). Attribution theory in social psychology. In D. Levine (Ed.), *Nebraska symposium on motivation* (pp. 192–241). Lincoln: University of Nebraska Press.

Kelly, G. A. (1955). *The psychology of personal constructs* (Vols. 1 and 2). New York: W. W. Norton.

Kenny, D. A. (1994). *Interpersonal perception: A social relations analysis.* New York: Guilford.

Kintsch, W. (1988). The role of knowledge is discourse comprehension: A construction-integration model. *Psychological Review, 95,* 163–182.

Klein, S. B., & Loftus, J. (1990). Rethinking the role of organization in person memory: An independent trace storage model. *Journal of Personality and Social Psychology, 59,* 400–410.

Kruglanski, A. W. (1989). *Lay epistemics and human knowledge: Cognitive and motivational bases.* New York: Plenum.

Kruglanski, A. W. (1990). Motivations for judging and knowing: Implications for causal attribution. In E. T. Higgins & R. M. Sorrentino (Eds.), *Handbook of motivation and cognition: Foundations of social behavior: Vol. II* (pp. 333–368). New York: Guilford.

Krull, D. S. (1993). Does the grist change the mill? The effect of the perceiver's inferential goal on the process of social inference. *Personality and Social Psychology Bulletin, 19,* 340–348.

Lea, B. (1995). *Lexical decision evidence for spontaneous trait inference.* Unpublished raw data.

Lepper, M. R., Ross, L., & Lau, R. R. (1986). Persistence of inaccurate beliefs about the self: Perseverance effects in the classroom. *Journal of Personality and Social Psychology, 50,* 482–491.

Leslie, A. M. (1987). Pretense and representation: The origins of "theory of mind." *Psychological Review, 94,* 412–426.

Lewicki, P. (1986). *Nonconscious social information processing.* Orlando, FL: Academic Press.

Lewin, K. (1936). *Principles of topological psychology.* New York: McGraw-Hill.

Lombardi, W. J., Higgins, E. T., & Bargh, J. A. (1987). The role of consciousness in priming effects on categorization. *Personality and Social Psychology Bulletin, 13,* 411–429.

Lupfer, M. B., Clark, L. F., Church, M., DePaola, S. J., & McDonald, C. D. (1995). *Do people make situational as well as trait inferences spontaneously?* Unpublished manuscript, University of Memphis.

Lupfer, M. B., Clark, L. F., & Hutcherson, H. W. (1990). Impact of context on spontaneous trait and situational attributions. *Journal of Personality and Social Psychology, 58,* 239–249.

Markus, H. R., & Kitayama, S. (1991). Culture and the self: Implications for cognition, emotion, and motivation. *Psychological Review, 98,* 224–253.

Marsman, J. G. (1994). *The influence of interpersonal verbs on cognitive inferences and memory.* Unpublished doctoral dissertation, Free University of Amsterdam.

Martin, L. L., & Achee, J. W. (1992). Beyond accessibility: The role of processing objectives in judgment. In L. L. Martin & A. Tesser (Eds.), *The construction of social judgments* (pp. 195–216). Hillsdale, NJ: Erlbaum.

McArthur, L. Z., & Baron, R. (1983). Toward an ecological theory of social perception. *Psychological Review, 90,* 215–238.

McKoon, G., & Ratcliff, R. (1986). Inferences about predictable events. *Journal of Experimental Psychology: Learning, Memory and Cognition, 15,* 326–338.

McKoon, G., & Ratcliff, R. (1990). Textual inferences: Models and measures. In D. A. Balota, G. B. F. d'Arcais, & K. Rayner (Eds.), *Comprehension processes in reading* (pp. 403–421). Hillsdale, NJ: Erlbaum.

Milgram, S. (1974). *Obedience to authority.* New York: Harper.

Miller, D. T., & Turnbull, W. (1986). Expectancies and interpersonal processes. *Annual Review of Psychology, 37,* 233–256.

Miller, J. G. (1984). Culture and the development of everyday social explanation. *Journal of Personality and Social Psychology, 46,* 961–978.

Moskowitz, G. B. (1993a). Individual differences in social categorization: The effects of personal need for structure on spontaneous trait inferences. *Journal of Personality and Social Psychology, 65,* 132–142.

Moskowitz, G. B. (1993b). Person organization with a memory set: Are spontaneous trait inferences personality characterizations or behavior labels? *European Journal of Personality, 7,* 195–208.

Moskowitz, G. B., & Roman, R. J. (1992). Spontaneous trait inferences as self-generated primes: Implications for conscious social judgment. *Journal of Personality and Social Psychology, 62,* 728–738.

Newman, L. S. (1991). Why are traits inferred spontaneously? A developmental approach. *Social Cognition, 9,* 221–253.

Newman, L. S. (1993). How individualists interpret behavior: Idiocentrism and spontaneous trait inference. *Social Cognition, 11,* 243–269.

Newman, L. S., & Uleman, J. S. (1989). Spontaneous trait inferences. In J. S. Uleman & J. A. Bargh (Eds.), *Unintended thought* (pp. 155–188). New York: Guilford.

Newman, L. S., & Uleman, J. S. (1990). Assimilation and contrast effects in spontaneous trait inferences. *Personality and Social Psychology Bulletin, 16,* 224–240.

Newman, L. S., & Uleman, J. S. (1993). When are you what you did? Behavior identification and dispositional inference in person memory, attribution, and social judgment. *Personality and Social Psychology Bulletin, 19,* 513–525.

Newman, L. S., Uleman, J. S., & Lipsitt, N. (1988). Limits on the spontaneity of trait inference. *Representative Research in Social Psychology, 18,* 15–39.

Nisbett, R. E., & Wilson, T. D. (1977). Telling more than we can know: Verbal reports on mental processes. *Psychological Review, 84,* 231–259.

Paris, S. G., & Lindauer, B. K. (1976). The role of inference in children's comprehension and memory for sentences. *Cognitive Psychology, 8,* 217–227.

Park, B. (1989). Trait attributes as on-line organizers in person impressions. In J. N. Bassili (Ed.), *On-line cognition in person perception* (pp. 39–60). Hillsdale, NJ: Erlbaum.

Peirce, C. (1877). The fixation of belief. *Popular Science Monthly.*

Pinker, S. (1990). Language acquisition. In D. N. Osherson & H. Lasnik (Eds.), *An invitation to cognitive science: Vol. 1. Language* (pp. 199–241). Cambridge, MA: MIT Press.

Pittman, T. S., & Heller, J. F. (1987). Social motivation. *Annual review of psychology, 38,* 461–489.

Posner, M. I., & Keele, S. W. (1968). On the genesis of abstract ideas. *Journal of Experimental Psychology, 73,* 28–38.

Posner, M. I., & Snyder, C. R. R. (1975). Attention and cognitive control. In R. L. Solso (Ed.), *Information processing and cognition: The Loyola symposium* (pp. 55–85). Hillsdale, NJ: Erlbaum.

Premack, D. (1990). The infant's theory of self-propelled objects. *Cognition, 36,* 1–16.

Quattrone, G. A. (1982). Overattribution and unit formation: When behavior engulfs the person. *Journal of Personality and Social Psychology, 42,* 593–607.

Reber, A. S. (1993). *Implicit learning and tacit knowledge: An essay on the cognitive unconscious.* New York: Oxford University Press.

Reeder, G. D. (1985). Implicit relations between dispositions and behaviors: Effects on dispositional attribution. In J. H. Harvey & G. Weary (Eds.), *Attribution: Basic issues and applications* (pp. 87–116). Orlando, FL: Academic Press.

Rhee, E., Uleman, J. S., Lee, H. K., & Roman, R. J. (1995). Spontaneous self-descriptions and ethnic identities in individualistic and collectivistic cultures. *Journal of Personality and Social Psychology, 69,* 142–152.

Rholes, W. S., Newman, L. S., & Ruble, D. N. (1990). Understanding self and other: Developmental and motivational aspects of perceiving people in terms of invariant dispositions. In E. T. Higgins & R. Sorrentino (Eds.), *Handbook of motivation and cognition: Foundations of social behavior: Vol. II* (pp. 369–407). New York: Guilford.

Roediger, R. L., III, Weldon, M. S., & Challis, B. H. (1989). Explaining dissociations between implicit and explicit measures of retention: A processing account. In H. L. Roediger, III, & F. I. M. Craik (Eds.), *Varieties of memory and consciousness: Essays in honour of Endel Tulving.* Hillsdale, NJ: Erlbaum.

Rosch, E., Mervis, C. B., Gray, W., Johnson, D., & Boyes-Braem, P. (1976). Basic objects in natural categories. *Cognitive Psychology, 8,* 382–439.

Ross, L. D. (1977). The intuitive psychologist and his shortcomings: Distortions in the attribution process. In L. Berkowitz (Ed.), *Advances in experimental social psychology* (Vol. 10, pp. 174–221). New York: Academic Press.

Ross, L. D., Lepper, M. R., & Hubbard, M. (1975). Perseverance in self-perception and social perception: Biased attributional processes in the debriefing paradigm. *Journal of Personality and Social Psychology, 32,* 880–892.

Ruble, D. N., & Dweck, C. S. (1995). Self-conceptions, person conceptions, and their development. In N. Eisenberg (Ed.), *Review of personality and social psychology: Vol. 15. Social Development* (pp. 109–139). Thousand Oaks, CA: Sage.

Russell, J. A. (1994). Is there universal recognition of emotion from facial expression? A review of the cross-cultural studies. *Psychological Bulletin, 115,* 102–141.

Schwarz, N., & Bless, H. (1992). Constructing reality and its alternatives: An inclusion/exclusion model of assimilation and contrast effects in social judgments. In L. L. Martin & A. Tesser (Eds.), *The construction of social judgments* (pp. 217–245). Hillsdale, NJ: Erlbaum.

Semin, G. R., & Fiedler, K. (1992). The inferential properties of interpersonal verbs. In G. R. Semin & K. Fiedler (Eds.), *Language, interaction and social cognition* (pp. 58–78). London: Sage.

Semin, G. R., & Marsman, J. G. (1994). "Multiple inference-inviting properties" of interpersonal verbs: Event instigation, dispositional inference, and implicit causality. *Journal of Personality and Social Psychology, 67,* 836–849.

Senden, M. v. (1932). *Raum- und Gestaltauffassung bei operierten blindgeborenen vor und nach der operation.* Leipzig: Barth.

Shiffrin, R. M., & Schneider, W. (1977). Controlled and automatic human information processing: II. Perceptual learning, automatic attending, and a general theory. *Psychological Review, 84,* 127–190.

Shweder, R. A., & Bourne, E. J. (1984). Does the concept of the person vary cross-culturally? In R. A. Shweder & R. A. LeVine (Eds.), *Culture theory: Essays on mind, self, and emotion* (pp. 158–199). Cambridge, UK: Cambridge University Press.

Singer, M. (1979). Processes of inference during sentence encoding. *Memory and Cognition, 7*, 192–200.

Slusher, M. P., & Anderson, C. A. (1987). When reality monitoring fails: The role of imagination in stereotype maintenance. *Journal of Personality and Social Psychology, 52*, 653–662.

Smith, E. R. (1984). Model of social inference processes. *Psychological Review, 91*, 392–413.

Smith, E. R. (1989). Procedural efficiency: General and specific components and effects on social judgment. *Journal of Experimental Social Psychology, 25*, 500–523.

Smith, E. R. (1994). Procedural knowledge and processing strategies in social cognition. In R. S. Wyer, Jr., & T. K. Srull (Eds.), *Handbook of social cognition: Vol. 1, Basic processes* (2nd ed., pp. 99–151). Hillsdale, NJ: Erlbaum.

Smith, E. R., & Lerner, M. (1986). Development of automatism of social judgments. *Journal of Personality and Social Psychology, 50*, 246–259.

Smith, E. R., & Miller, F. D. (1979). Salience and the cognitive mediation of attribution. *Journal of Personality and Social Psychology, 37*, 2240–2252.

Smith, E. R., & Miller, F. D. (1983). Mediation among attributional inferences and comprehension processes: Initial findings and a general method. *Journal of Personality and Social Psychology, 44*, 492–505.

Smith, E. R., Stewart, T. L., & Buttram, R. T. (1992). Inferring a trait from a behavior has long-term, highly specific effects. *Journal of Personality and Social Psychology, 62*, 753–759.

Srull, T. K., & Brand, J. F. (1983). Memory for information about persons: The effect of encoding operations on subsequent retrieval. *Journal of Verbal Learning and Verbal Behavior, 22*, 219–230.

Srull, T. K., & Wyer, R. S., Jr. (1979). The role of category accessibility in the interpretation of information about persons: Some determinants and implications. *Journal of Personality and Social Psychology, 37*, 1660–1672.

Stapel, D. A., Koomen, W., & van der Pligt, J. (1996). *The referents of trait inferences: The impact of trait concepts versus actor-trait links on subsequent judgments. Journal of Personality and Social Psychology, 70.*

Thompson, M. M., Naccarato, M. E., Parker, K. E., & Moskowitz, G. B. (1993). *Measuring cognitive needs: The development and validation of the personal need for structure and personal fear of invalidity scales.* Manuscript submitted for publication.

Thomson, D., & Tulving, E. (1970). Associative encoding and retrieval: Weak and strong cues. *Journal of Experimental Psychology, 86*, 255–262.

Trabasso, T., & Sperry, L. L. (1985). Causal relatedness and importance of story events. *Journal of Memory and Language, 24*, 595–611.

Triandis, H. C. (1989). The self and social behavior in differing cultural contexts. *Psychological Review, 96*, 506–520.

Triandis, H. C. (1990). Cross-cultural studies of individualism and collectivism. In J. Berman (Ed.), *Nebraska Symposium on Motivation, 1989* (pp. 41–133). Lincoln: University of Nebraska Press.

Triandis, H. C., Bontempo, R., Villareal, M. J., Asai, M., & Lucca, N. (1988). Individualism and collectivism: Cross-cultural perspectives on self-ingroup relationships. *Journal of Personality and Social Psychology, 54*, 323–338.

Trope, Y. (1986). Identification and inferential processes in dispositional attribution. *Psychological Review, 93*, 239–257.

Trope, Y., & Alfieri, T. (1993, August). *Comparing the ease of the processes involved in dispositional attribution.* Poster presented at the annual meeting of the American Psychological Association, Toronto, Canada.

Trope, Y., & Higgins, E. T. (Eds.). (1993). On inferring personal dispositions from behavior [Special issue]. *Personality and Social Psychology Bulletin, 19,* 553–562.

Trope, Y., & Liberman, A. (1993). The use of trait conceptions to identify other people's behavior and to draw inferences about their personalities. *Personality and Social Psychology Bulletin, 19,* 553–562.

Tulving, E. (1972). Episodic and semantic memory. In E. Tulving & W. Donaldson (Eds.), *Organization of memory* (pp. 381–403). New York: Academic Press.

Tulving, E., & Thomson, D. M. (1973). Encoding specificity and retrieval processes in episodic memory. *Psychological Review, 80,* 352–373.

Uleman, J. S. (1989). The self-control of thoughts: A framework for thinking about unintended thought. In J. S. Uleman & J. A. Bargh (Eds.), *Unintended thought* (pp. 425–449). New York: Guilford.

Uleman, J. S. (in press). Toward a view of personality traits as experience-near, theory-based, language- and culture-bound concepts. In K. Fiedler & G. Semin (Eds.), *Language, Social Psychology, and Culture.* London: Sage Publications.

Uleman, J. S. (1996). When do unconscious goals cloud our minds? A commentary on Martin and Tesser's ruminations. In R. S. Wyer, Jr. (Ed.), *Advances in social cognition,* (Vol. 8, pp. 165–176). Hillsdale, NJ: Erlbaum.

Uleman, J. S., Hon, A., Roman, R., & Moskowitz, G. B. (in press). On-line evidence for spontaneous trait inferences at encoding. *Personality and Social Psychology Bulletin.*

Uleman, J. S., & Moskowitz, G. B. (1994). Unintended effects of goals on unintended inferences. *Journal of Personality and Social Psychology, 66,* 490–501.

Uleman, J. S., Moskowitz, G. B., Roman, R. J., & Rhee, E. (1993). Tacit, manifest, and intentional reference: How spontaneous trait inferences refer to persons. *Social Cognition, 11,* 321–351.

Uleman, J. S., Newman, L., & Winter, L. (1992). Can personality traits be inferred automatically? Spontaneous inferences require cognitive capacity at encoding. *Consciousness and Cognition, 1,* 77–90.

Uleman, J. S., Winborne, W. C., Winter, L., & Shechter, D. (1986). Personality differences in spontaneous personality inferences at encoding. *Journal of Personality and Social Psychology, 51,* 396–403.

Watson, D. (1982). The actor and the observer: How are their perceptions of causality divergent? *Psychological Bulletin, 92,* 682–700.

Webster's new universal unabridged dictionary (2nd ed.) (1983). New York: Dorset & Baber.

Wegner, D. M. (1994). Ironic processes of mental control. *Psychological Review, 101,* 34–52.

Weiner, B. (1985). "Spontaneous" causal thinking. *Psychological Bulletin, 97,* 74–84.

White, R. W. (1959). Motivation reconsidered: The concept of competence. *Psychological Review, 66,* 296–333.

Whitney, P., Davis, P. A., & Waring, D. A. (1994). Task effects on trait inference: Distinguishing categorization from characterization. *Social Cognition, 12,* 19–35.

Whitney, P., Waring, D. A., & Zingmark, B. (1992). Task effects on the spontaneous activation of trait concepts. *Social Cognition, 10,* 377–396.

Whitney, P., & Williams-Whitney, D. L. (1990). Toward a contextualist view of elaborative inferences. In A. C. Graesser & G. H. Bower (Eds.), *The psychology of learning and motivation* (Vol. 25, pp. 279–293). New York: Academic Press.

Winter, L., & Uleman, J. S. (1984). When are social judgments made? Evidence for the spontaneousness of trait inferences. *Journal of Personality and Social Psychology, 47,* 237–252. Also see correction in *Journal of Personality and Social Psychology* (1986), *50,* 355.

Winter, L., Uleman, J. S., & Cunniff, C. (1985). How automatic are social judgments? *Journal of Personality and Social Psychology, 49,* 904–917. Also see correction in *Journal of Personality and Social Psychology* (1986), *50,* 381.

Wyer, R. S., & Gordon, S. E. (1982). The recall of information about persons and groups. *Journal of Experimental Social Psychology, 18,* 128–164.

Wyer, R. S., Jr., & Srull, T. K. (1989). *Memory and cognition in its social context.* Hillsdale, NJ: Erlbaum.

Zárate, M. A., & Uleman, J. S. (1994). *Lexical decision evidence that Anglos do, and Chicanos do not make spontaneous trait inferences.* Unpublished manuscript, University of Texas at El Paso.

Zebrowitz, L. A. (1990). *Social perception.* Pacific Grove, CA: Brooks/Cole.

Zelli, A., Huesmann, L. R., & Cervone, D. (1995). Social inference and individual differences in aggression: Evidence for spontaneous judgments of hostility. *Aggressive Behavior, 21,* 405–417.

SOCIAL PERCEPTION, SOCIAL STEREOTYPES, AND TEACHER EXPECTATIONS: ACCURACY AND THE QUEST FOR THE POWERFUL SELF-FULFILLING PROPHECY

Lee Jussim

Jacquelynne Eccles

Stephanie Madon

I. Introduction

How are social perception and social reality related? Social psychology has long emphasized the power of beliefs to create reality, and the power of interpersonal expectancies to create social problems (e.g., Gage & Cronbach, 1955; Jones, 1986, 1990; Merton, 1948; Miller & Turnbull, 1986; Snyder, 1984). Social scientists have a longstanding interest in one particular source of expectations—stereotypes—largely because stereotypes may contribute to social inequalities and injustices. But are people so malleable that they readily fulfill others' inaccurate expectations? How accurate are interpersonal expectations? To what extent do stereotypes bias person perception and lead to self-fulfilling prophecies? Who is most vulnerable to self-fulfilling prophecies?

In this article, we address these questions as follows. First, we present a brief overview of research on accuracy, error, bias, and self-fulfilling prophecies. Second, we review our own research showing that teacher expectations predict student achievement mainly because they are accurate, although they do lead to small self-fulfilling prophecies and biases.

We subsequently embark on a quest to identify conditions under which self-fulfilling prophecies might be considerably more powerful. Third, therefore, we report the results of new research showing that teacher expectancy effects are more powerful among girls, students from lower socioeconomic status (SES) backgrounds or African-Americans.

ADVANCES IN EXPERIMENTAL
SOCIAL PSYCHOLOGY, VOL. 28

Social psychological research on stereotypes suggested a possible explanation for this pattern: Teachers rely on stereotypes in developing expectations for students from stigmatized groups, and because such expectations will often be inaccurate, they are also more likely to be self-fulfilling. Therefore, we review the general literature on the role of stereotypes in creating self-fulfilling prophecies and on issues of accuracy and inaccuracy in stereotypes more generally.

We then address some of these issues empirically in two studies that examined whether teacher perceptions of differences among students belonging to different demographic groups (boys or girls, middle class or poor, African-American or White) were biased or accurate. Although these studies provided some evidence of bias (surprisingly, these biases were usually in favor of students from culturally stigmatized groups), they also showed that, in general, differences in teachers' perceptions of students from the differing groups corresponded well to actual differences between those same groups of students.

Although we found such results particularly interesting in light of the social sciences' emphasis on inaccuracy of stereotypes, they left us still unable to explain why self-fulfilling prophecies were stronger among students from stigmatized groups. We therefore speculate that students who feel devalued in school will be particularly susceptible to confirming teachers' expectations. Although we cannot test this idea directly, we summarize another new study that provides indirectly supportive evidence by showing that students with low self-concepts of ability or with previous records of low achievement were, much like students from stigmatized groups, considerably more vulnerable to self-fulfilling prophecies. We conclude this chapter by reviewing other moderators of expectancy effects, discussing the evidence showing whether self-fulfilling prophecies accumulate or dissipate over time, and making recommendations for future research on self-fulfilling prophecies.

II. Accuracy, Error, Bias, and Self-Fulfilling Prophecy

A. A BRIEF OVERVIEW

Research on accuracy, error, bias, and self-fulfilling prophecy have long traditions in social psychology. Error and bias research dates back at least to the emphasis in the 1930s on the inaccuracy, irrationality, and rigidity of social stereotypes (e.g., Katz & Braly, 1933; LaPiere, 1936). The idea that many social injustices and inequalities reflect self-fulfilling prophecies was first suggested in the 1940s (Merton, 1948). There was lively interest in accuracy through the 1950s (e.g., Taft, 1955; Vernon, 1933), which came to an abrupt and premature end after Cronbach identified many seemingly difficult statistical and methodological problems involved in assessing certain types of accuracy (Cronbach, 1955; Gage & Cronbach, 1955). At the same time, the New Look in Perception, which emphasized a myriad of ways in which perceivers' goals, needs, fears, and motives could influence and undermine the veridicality of perception, initiated a revolution in approaches to perception, at least in social and personality psychology (e.g., Allport, 1955; Bruner, 1957).

Subsequently, from the 1960s through much of the 1980s, social and personality psychology emphasized a host of errors and biases in social perception (e.g., Kahneman & Tversky, 1973; Miller & Turnbull, 1986; Nisbett & Ross, 1980). Central to this effort was the work by Rosenthal demonstrating that experimenters and teachers can evoke expectancy-confirming behavior from both animals and people (see Rosenthal, 1974, for a review; Rosenthal & Jacobson, 1968; see Rosenthal & Rubin, 1978, for a meta-analysis). Numerous researchers then followed up this work with studies of the potentially self-fulfilling effects from expectancies of all sorts in and out of the laboratory (see reviews by Jones, 1977; Jussim, 1986; Snyder, 1984).

Although a few researchers did attempt to keep the study of accuracy alive after the 1950s (Archer & Akert, 1977; McCauley & Stitt, 1978), they were rare voices barely heard above the din of the zeitgeist emphasizing error, bias, and self-fulfilling prophecy. In the 1980s, however, four articles sparked the beginning of a renaissance of interest in accuracy. McArthur and Baron (1983) presented the first coherent theoretical alternative to the constructivist zeitgeist that had dominated thinking about social perception for 30 odd years. They took the ecological approach, which was originally developed to study object perception (Gibson, 1979), and applied it to social perception. This theory emphasized the information in the stimulus, which was in sharp contrast to the social cognitive emphasis on the categories, prototypes, schemas, and assorted cognitive structures existing in the perceiver's mind.

Next, Swann (1984) presented a broad and sweeping review of research on accuracy. Perhaps most influential was his discussion of "circumscribed" accuracy. Swann (1984) argued that perceivers often have no interest in predicting the behavior of targets across all situations and for all time. Thus, it is inappropriate to hold them to this standard. Instead, he suggested that people are usually content to understand and predict others' behavior only when they interact with those others. In terms of this more circumscribed notion of accuracy, Swann (1984) speculated that people might be considerably more accurate than had previously been recognized.

Next, Funder (1987) presented a conceptual and empirical assault on what he believed was social psychology's misplaced emphasis on error and bias. He made two main points: 1) Social psychology's knowledge base regarding error and bias stemmed almost exclusively from studies that were originally designed to assess social perceptual processes, and 2) the studies assessing process did not address the accuracy of outcomes produced by such processes. Funder drew a parallel between the laboratory social cognitive work on illusions, biases, and errors, and the laboratory vision research on illusions. Researchers used controlled visual illusions to probe the dynamics of visual information processing; they never assumed that these illusions reflected deficiencies likely to occur in vision under natural conditions. This, Funder argued, was also the most appropriate interpretation for research on human judgment. For Funder, accuracy was an issue of content, not of process. He also presented data documenting people's moderate to strong accuracy in perceiving others' personalities.

At about the same time, Kenny was publishing numerous articles describing his social relations model (See Kenny, 1994 for a review.). In one of the most influential of these early articles, Kenny and Albright (1987) 1) explained how the social relations model could be used to isolate error and accuracy in social perception; 2) pointed out the similarity between the accuracy components assessed by the social relations model and Cronbach's components of accuracy; and 3) showed how, when applied to social interaction, the model empirically documented considerable accuracy in social perception.

By 1990, the accuracy djinni was most of the way out of the bottle. One more paper popped the cork completely. A main bastion of the scholarly emphasis on error and bias was the expectancy effects literature, especially the literature on social stereotypes [see, e.g., the strong emphasis on the power of expectations to create reality in reviews by Jones (1990), Miller & Turnbull (1986), and Snyder (1984)]. In contrast, Jussim (1991) argued on both theoretical and empirical grounds that this emphasis was misplaced. He presented a model showing how people's beliefs could be in touch with reality most of the time, and yet still sometimes produce biases in person perception leading to self-fulfilling prophecies. This model was then used to interpret previous research on the effects of interpersonal expectancies. Jussim concluded that 1) interpersonal expectancies can lead to biases and self-fufilling prophecies, but these effects tend to be quite small; 2) perceivers' predictions of targets' future behavior and their impressions of targets' past behavior tend to be reasonably accurate; and 3) the evidence on the accuracy of social stereotypes is quite mixed (some accuracy, some inaccuracy). Jussim also showed that much of what looked like expectancy-induced bias in experimental laboratory studies could actually enhance person perception accuracy under some naturally occurring conditions.

The revival in interest in accuracy has, however, with a few exceptions, occurred in parallel with continued interest in error and bias. Many researchers still study and emphasize error, bias, or self-fulfilling prophecy (e.g., Gilbert & Malone, 1995; Snyder, 1992; Stangor, 1995); others focus primarily on accuracy (e.g., Ambady & Rosenthal, 1992; Borkenau & Liebler, 1992; Funder & Colvin, 1988; Levesque & Kenny, 1993). Although several researchers have attempted to integrate accuracy and bias (e.g., Brewer, 1988; Fiske & Neuberg, 1990; Higgins & Bargh, 1987; Kunda, 1990), most have relied primarily on experimental laboratory studies (see Kenny, 1994, for a review of partial exceptions—nonexperimental laboratory studies of accuracy and bias). These attempts, therefore, suffer from the conceptual problem first identified by Funder (1987): Because they focus on process instead of content, and because their relevance to naturalistic situations is unclear, they provide little empirical evidence on accuracy, error, bias, and self-fulfilling prophecy in daily life. (Even some hardcore experimental social psychologists have expressed sympathy with the view that the relevance of laboratory studies to daily life is an unanswered, open, empirical question.) (See Gilbert & Malone, 1995, p. 35.)

Although some researchers have argued that one can only generate logical arguments to show why results from laboratory studies would be applicable in many real-life situations (e.g., Fiske & Neuberg, 1990), we respectfully disagree with this pessimistic sentiment. We do agree that lab experiments alone can never reveal how much the discovered processes actually occur under naturalistic conditions. We would be left to speculate.

Although claims about ecological or external validity are not necessarily a crucial component of all studies (e.g., Mook, 1983), they are essential for generalizing one's findings to the natural world. Moreover, many social psychologists actually suggest, either explicitly or implicitly, that the phenomena under study do indeed occur with considerable frequency outside the social psychological laboratory (see, e.g., Jussim, 1991 for a review of such claims). One of the best examples of such claims is the 1991 American Psychological Association (APA) brief to the U.S. Supreme Court in the case of Hopkins versus Price-Waterhouse. Drawing primarily (although not exclusively) on the results of experimental laboratory studies, the APA brief argued that we know quite a lot about stereotypes, including both the processes by which they lead to bias and discrimination, and the conditions that either facilitate or undermine their tendency to lead to bias and discrimination.

The APA brief was true to the spirit and content of many, if not most, perspectives on social stereotypes current at the time of the case (e.g., Brewer, 1979, 1988; Fiske & Taylor, 1984; Hamilton, Sherman, & Ruvolo, 1990; Jones, 1986; Snyder, 1984; and subsequently, e.g., Greenwald & Banaji, 1995; Stangor, 1995; Von Hippel, Sekaquaptewa, & Vargas, 1995), all of which assume that laboratory studies of bias, error, and self-fulfilling prophecy have good enough ecological validity to justify generalizing the findings to real-world settings. Whether this assumption is warranted, however, is an empirical question. Moreover, if we plan to make policy recommendations and expect our findings to be relevant to legal decisions, then it behooves us to find out what people are actually like in their natural habitats despite the difficulties involved in doing naturalistic research.

Understanding the nature and extent of accuracy, error, bias, and self-fulfilling prophecy under naturalistic conditions is the focus of our own studies on the relations between teacher expectations and student achievement. Because these studies examine teachers and students in sixth-grade public school math classes, they suffer none of the ecological validity problems of laboratory experiments. We believe that these studies provide a wealth of evidence regarding naturally occurring social perception and interaction, evidence that bears directly on long-standing issues in social psychology regarding the prevalence of accuracy, bias, and self-fulfilling prophecy in daily life. We begin by identifying three separate ways in which targets may confirm perceivers' expectancies.

B. THREE SOURCES OF EXPECTANCY CONFIRMATION

Perceivers' expectations may be confirmed for any of at least three reasons—two that involve influences of expectations on behavior or perceptions and one that does not. First, perceivers' expectations sometimes produce *self-fulfilling prophecies:* Their initially erroneous expectations may cause targets to act in ways consistent with those expectations (Cooper, 1979; Darley & Fazio, 1980; Jussim, 1986; Rosenthal & Jacobson, 1968). Second, expectations may lead to *perceptual biases:* perceivers may interpret, remember, and/or explain targets' behavior in ways consistent with their expectations. This type of expectancy confirmation exists in the mind of the perceiver rather than in the behavior of the target (Darley & Fazio, 1980; Eccles & Jacobs, 1986; Jussim, 1991; Miller & Turnbull, 1986). Self-fulfilling prophecies and perceptual biases both represent perceiver expectations creating (or "constructing") social reality, either creating an objective social reality (when self-fulfilling prophecies change targets' actual behavior) or a subjective social reality (when perceptual biases influence perceivers' evaluations of target behavior). Finally, in contrast, expectations also may accurately reflect or predict social reality without infuencing either objective target behavior or even subjective perceptions of that behavior (Brophy, 1983; Jussim, 1991).

Although these three expectancy phenomena are conceptually distinct, they are not mutually exclusive. Any combination of the three (or none at all) can characterize relations between perceiver expectations and student achievement (Jussim, 1989, 1991; Jussim & Eccles, 1992). Consider a teacher who believes a student is especially bright. The teacher may be (largely) accurate—this student may indeed have a stronger academic background than most others. Furthermore, highly positive interactions with the teacher may lead this student to achieve even more highly—thus, demonstrating a self-fulfilling prophecy. Finally, perceptual biases may lead the teacher to evaluate the student even more favorably than is warranted by the student's objective performance.

Although expectations may lead to many combinations of self-fulfilling prophecy, perceptual bias, and accuracy, they may also lead to none; expectations can be both inaccurate and noninfluential. For example, a teacher may expect a student to be a low achiever. Nevertheless, this student may successfully complete most homework assignments in a timely and thorough manner and go on to perform above average on a highly credible standardized achievement test and receive mostly "As" on in-class tests. The teacher may simply acknowledge the error (i.e., the original expectation was erroneous, but there is no perceptual bias), and the student may continue to perform highly (no self-fulfilling prophecy).

Although this article focuses exclusively on relations between teacher expectations and student achievement, expectancy effects undoubtedly occur in many other relationships: employer–employee, therapist–client, and parent–child. Consequently, as we analyze ways to distinguish among self-fulfilling prophecies, perceptual biases, and accuracy, and examine processes underlying expectancy-related phenomena, our discoveries may have some relevance and applicability to many other relationships beyond teachers and students (see also Eccles et al., 1993; Eccles & Hoffman, 1984; Jacobs & Eccles, 1992; Jussim, 1990, 1991; Jussim & Eccles, 1995; Jussim & Fleming, in press).

III. Teacher Expectations

There are few contexts more important for investigating self-fulfilling prophecies than teachers' expectations for their students. Ever since Rosenthal and Jacobson's (1968) seminal and controversial (e.g., Elashoff & Snow,

1971) Pygmalion study, writers in both scholarly journals and the popular press have implicated teacher expectations as a major perpetrator of injustices and inequalities based on ethnicity,[1] social class, and gender (see Wineburg, 1987, for a review). In this article, we present evidence suggesting that such claims present an oversimplified and exaggerated picture of the role of teacher expectations in perpetuating social inequalities. This evidence will convey two main points. First, we briefly review our own and others' research documenting that naturally occurring teacher expectations generally lead to only small self-fulfilling prophecies and perceptual biases. This research also shows that teacher expectations predict student achievement primarily because they are accurate.

Even though teacher expectation effects are generally small, under some conditions or among particular groups, such effects may be considerably larger than usual. Second, therefore, we report the results from some of our efforts to discover instances of more powerful self-fulfilling prophecy effects.

A. ACCURACY MORE THAN SELF-FULFILLING PROPHECY

Through the 1980s and early 1990s, social psychology abounded with testimonies to the power of expectancies to create social reality (e.g., Fiske & Taylor, 1984; Hamilton et al., 1990; Jones, 1986, 1990; Snyder, 1984; see Jussim, 1991, for a review). In contrast, most educational and developmental psychologists argued that expectancy effects were generally minimal (e.g., Brophy, 1983; Brophy & Good, 1974; Cooper, 1979; Eccles & Blumenfeld, 1985; Eccles & Wigfield, 1985; West & Anderson, 1976). Evidence from naturalistic studies consistently failed to support the strong claims of social psychologists, and instead confirmed the perspective of the educational and developmental psychologists, rarely uncovering expectancy effects larger than .1 to .2 in terms of standardized regression coefficients (see Jussim, 1991; Jussim & Eccles, 1995, for reviews). Furthermore, research in educational settings has repeatedly shown that teacher expectations predict student achievement mainly because they are accurate (see Brophy, 1983; Jussim, 1991; Jussim & Eccles, 1995, for reviews). Because two of our studies provided some of the clearest evidence of teacher accu-

[1] Throughout this chapter, the term "ethnicity" primarily refers to African-Americans and Whites. Although the term "race" is used far more widely in reference to these groups, it has little clear scientific meaning (e.g., Marger, 1994; Yee, Fairchild, Weizmann, & Wyatt, 1993). Ethnicity is also a fuzzy concept, although it generally includes physical appearance, similar geographical roots, a unique culture, sense of community, and ascribed membership (Marger, 1994). The term "ethnicity" has a considerably less controversial history and we therefore consider it preferable.

racy to date (Jussim, 1989; Jussim & Eccles, 1992), we describe them as follows in some detail.

B. THE JUSSIM (1989) AND JUSSIM AND ECCLES (1992) STUDIES

1. The Data

All studies described in this chapter are based on the Michigan Study of Adolescent Life Transitions (MSALT), which assessed a variety of social, psychological, demographic, and achievement-related variables in a sample that included more than 200 teachers and 3000 students in the sixth and seventh grades (see Eccles et al., 1989; Midgley, Feldlaufer, & Eccles, 1989; Wigfield, Eccles, MacIver, Reuman, & Midgley, 1991, for more details about this project). A total of about 100 teachers and 1700 students in sixth-grade math classes were the focus of the two studies we summarize here. Both studies tested the hypotheses that 1) teacher expectations early in the year are based on students' previous achievement and motivation and that 2) teacher expectations, student motivation, and students' previous achievement influence students' subsequent achievement (for detailed descriptions of the models and analyses, see Jussim, 1989; Jussim & Eccles, 1992).

Three sixth-grade teacher expectation variables were assessed in early October: perceptions of students' performance, talent, and effort at math. We assumed that teachers inferred students' effort and talent, in part, from their own perceptions of students' performance. Measures included student motivation self-concept of math ability, intrinsic and extrinsic value of math, and self-reports of effort and time spent on math homework. Fall and spring assessments of these motivational variables were included in Jussim (1989); only fall assessments were included in Jussim and Eccles (1992).

There were two measures of previous achievement: final marks in fifth-grade math classes and scores on standardized achievement tests taken in late fifth or early sixth grade. There were two outcome measures of achievement: Final grades in sixth-grade math classes and scores on the math section of the Michigan Educational Assessment Program (MEAP), a standardized test administered to students in Michigan early in seventh grade. All measures were reliable and valid (for more detail, see Eccles (Parsons), Adler, & Meece, 1984; Eccles-Parsons, Kaczala, & Meece, 1982; Jussim, 1987, 1989; Jussim & Eccles, 1992; Parsons, 1980).

2. Results

Because results reported here are from two studies, they are presented in pairs as follows. The first refers to Jussim (1989) and the second refers to Jussim and Eccles (1992). Although the main analyses were performed using the LISREL VI program, all *betas* reported below are interpretable as standardized regression coefficients.

These two studies were the first to explicitly assess and compare self-fulfilling prophecy, perceptual bias, and accuracy. Both studies assessed models that were more complex versions of the model presented in Figure 1. In brief, we assessed whether teacher perceptions early in the school year predicted changes in achievement (by controlling for previous achievement) over and above changes accounted for by motivation (self-concept of ability, valued placed on math, effort, etc.). Table I summarizes the major results from both studies.

Consistent with the self-fulfilling prophecy hypothesis, teacher perceptions of students' math performance in October of the sixth grade significantly related to students' final grades in sixth-grade math (betas = .21, .34) and students' seventh-grade MEAP scores (betas = .10, .15). In Jussim's (1989) study 1) teacher perceptions of talent significantly related to both sixth-grade math grades (beta = .12) and seventh-grade MEAP scores (beta = .17); and 2) teacher perceptions of performance significantly predicted changes in students' self-concept of math ability across the sixth-grade school year (beta = .11).

Results consistent with the perceptual bias hypothesis showed that teacher perceptions of students' effort significantly predicted sixth-grade math grades (betas = .19, .19) to a larger extent than they predicted seventh-

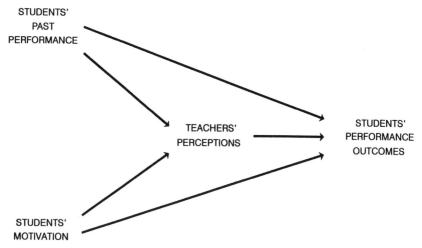

Fig. 1. Conceptual model of relationships between teacher perceptions and student achievement.

TABLE I
CONSTRUCTION AND REFLECTION OF STUDENT ACHIEVEMENT

	Teachers' perceptions of students' performance	Teachers' perceptions of students' talent	Teachers' perceptions of students' effort	All three
Correlation with grades	.54, .71	.57, .64	.50, .63	.63, .73
Effect on grades	.21, .34	.12, .04	.19, .19	.21, .29
Correlation with MEAP scores	.46, .54	.57, .49	.34, .36	.57, .55
Effect on MEAP scores	.10, .15	.17, −.02	.00, −.07	.13, .12

Effects refer to standardized total effects (see Jussim, 1989, and Jussim & Eccles, 1992, for more detail about the models). The first entry within each column is for Jussim (1989, N = 429), the second entry is for Jussim & Eccles (1992, N = 1288). All coefficients greater than .03 are significant at $p < .05$. The difference between correlations and path coefficients is an index of predictive accuracy (see text for explanation). The column titled "All three" reports the multiple correlation of all three teacher perception variables with grades and MEAP scores in the "Correlation" rows and reports the multiple semipartial correlation (controlling for the student background variables) with grades and MEAP scores in the "Effect" rows. (Reprinted with permission from *Journal of Personality.*)

grade MEAP scores (betas = 0, −.07). Teachers assigned higher grades to students whom they believed had exerted more effort. This hypothetically could have represented accuracy—if teachers were rewarding students who actually were working harder. Instead, however, as the results suggest, teachers simply assumed that higher achievers were working harder, whereas we found no evidence that the students who received the higher grades actually worked any harder than their peers. In fact, the students who received low grades reported spending more time on homework than the other students (Jussim, 1989; Jussim & Eccles, 1992). Because effort is difficult to observe directly, we speculated that teachers, perhaps influenced by a belief in a just world (Lerner, 1980) or by the protestant work ethic (Schuman, Walsh, Olson, & Etheridge, 1985; Weber, 1930), simply assumed that "hard work pays off." Therefore, high achievers "must" have been working harder. A consequence, however, is that the academically "rich" (the high achievers) get richer (teachers assign them grades that are even higher than they deserve).

There was both accuracy and inaccuracy in teacher perceptions. Teacher perceptions were largely accurate because they were most strongly linked to appropriate factors: previous grades, standardized test scores, teacher perceptions of in-class performance, and student motivation (the multiple correlation of these factors with teacher expectation variables ranged from about .6 to .8). The results also provide evidence of a small but consistent pattern of gender bias in teacher perceptions, but we discuss this issue in detail later in the chapter.

Results from both studies also provided considerable evidence of predictive accuracy. The zero-order correlation between teacher expectations early in the year and student achievement late in the year equals expectancy effects (influences of teacher expectations on student achievement) plus predictive accuracy (teachers basing their expectations on factors that influence student achievement). Therefore, one index of predictive accuracy is the difference between the zero-order correlation and the size of the expectancy effects (see Jussim, 1989, 1991, 1993; Jussim & Eccles, 1992 for more detailed explanations).

The zero-order correlations of teacher perceptions with seventh-grade MEAP scores ranged from .34 to .57, and the path coefficients ranged from −.07 to .17. The path coefficients relating teacher perceptions to MEAP scores accounted for about 20–30% of the zero-order correlations between initial teacher perceptions and subsequent MEAP scores; the remaining 70–80% represented predictive validity without influence (i.e., accuracy). There was a similar pattern for final grades in sixth-grade math. Zero-order correlations of initial teacher perceptions with year-end grades ranged from .50 to .71. Path coefficients ranged from .04 to .34. The path coefficients relating teacher perceptions to grades accounted for about 30–40% of the zero-order correlations between initial teacher perceptions and subsequent grades; the remaining 60–70% represented accuracy.

Are these results anomalous? Not at all: Research consistently shows that the zero-order correlations between teacher expectations and student achievement generally range from about .4 to .8, and that path coefficients representing effects of teacher expectations on student achievement are generally about .1 to .2 (see Brophy, 1983; Brophy & Good, 1974; Jussim, 1991; Jussim & Eccles, 1995, for reviews).

3. Limitations

The correlational nature of this research leaves open some alternative explanations for the relation between teacher expectancies and student achievement. However, because this study used longitudinal data, reverse causal influences are not possible. Students' achievement at the end of the sixth grade could not have caused teacher expectations at the beginning of the sixth grade.

The main limitation involves omitted variables. Path coefficients only reflect causal effects when all relevant causes of student achievement have been included in the model. If teacher expectations and student achievement are both caused by a third variable that has been omitted from the model, then the model may yield inflated path coefficients relating teacher expectations to student achievement (a "spurious" relation). Unfortunately, no matter how many potential sources of spuriousness are assessed, it is impossible to know if all such sources have been included.

Although this problem can never be completely overcome, it can be minimized with the inclusion of extensive control variables. Few naturalistic studies have included more controls (previous achievement test scores *and* grades, self-concept, and several motivational variables) than we have (Jussim, 1989; Jussim & Eccles, 1992). Thus, these findings provide some of the clearest evidence to date that teacher expectations influence the achievement of some students. Such a conclusion will warrant revision when future research demonstrates empirically that there are important sources of accuracy in teacher perceptions other than those assessed in this study.

It is also important to understand the nature of this limitation. Suppose we omitted important variables that cause both student achievement and teacher expectations. This has a very specific implication—that teachers are even more accurate than we have suggested [i.e., that teacher perceptions predict student achievement less because of their causal influence than because both teacher perceptions and student achievement are based on a third (set of) variables(s)]. Conceptually, of course, this "critique" strengthens our conclusion that teacher expectations predict student achievement more because they are accurate than because they create self-fulfilling prophecies. Nevertheless, it is important to keep these limitations in mind throughout the rest of this chapter. The potential for an omitted variable problem is always present in naturalistic research.

IV. In Search of the Powerful Self-Fulfilling Prophecy

We found our results showing small expectancy effects and high accuracy very surprising. Not only did the social psychological zeitgeist of the 1970s and 1980s emphasize error and bias in judgment and perception, but also accuracy was an all but taboo subject (see, e.g., Funder, 1987; Jussim, 1991; Kenny, 1994, for reviews). Similarly, the social psychological literature had for so long emphasized the power of self-fulfilling prophecies (Darley & Fazio, 1980; Jones, 1986; Merton, 1948; Miller & Turnbull,

1986; Rosenthal & Jacobson, 1968; Snyder, 1984) that we expected to find effects considerably larger than .1 and .2. Although one of us has taken the lead in arguing that such effects are small (Jussim, 1989, 1990, 1991, 1993; Jussim & Eccles, 1992), this position was based on the empirical data base, not on any preconceived notions that such effects always are, or must be, small. In fact, all the authors of this chapter became interested in self-fulfilling prophecies because of their potential to further understanding social injustice and the construction of social reality. We have, however, challenged researchers to empirically identify naturally occurring conditions under which self-fulfilling prophecy effects are large (Jussim, 1989, 1991, 1993; Jussim & Eccles, 1992). Nonetheless, although expectancy effects may be generally small, we strongly suspected that there were conditions under which expectancy effects were substantially larger. Thus, we embarked on a quest to identify more powerful self-fulfilling prophecies. As the next section shows, we have had some success.

A. STUDENT DEMOGRAPHICS AND SUSCEPTIBILITY TO SELF-FULFILLING PROPHECIES

Understanding the role of demographics in educational and occupational attainment has been a major goal of many of the social sciences for a long time. Research on sources of demographic differences is almost always controversial and highly politicized—regardless of whether it is research arguing for genetic explanations of group difference (e.g., Herrnstein & Murray, 1994) or research contending that schools oppress girls [American Association of University Women (AAUW), 1992)]. Still, clarion calls and pleas for social psychological research directly addressing issues of race, class, or gender periodically appear in the literature (e.g., Carlson, 1984; Fine & Gordon, 1989; Graham, 1992). The two phenomena (politicization and lack of research) are probably related: The potential for controversy and outright vilification is so strong that it may deter many scholars from vigorously pursuing research programs into these issues. Yet laboratory researchers often imply or explicitly insist that bias detected by highly artificial procedures or under highly unusual conditions provides insights into biases against African-Americans, women, and people from lower SES backgrounds in naturally occurring social interactions (e.g., Devine, 1989; Greenwald & Banaji, 1995; Von Hippel et al., 1995).

At the minimum there seems to be a broad consensus that issues of race, class, and gender are extremely important. Research on the role of student demographics in moderating teacher expectation effects appears to be particularly important. Such research goes to the heart of the question of whether, how, and how much teacher expectations contribute to social problems and inequality. This alone would be sufficient to justify the exploration of the extent to which student demographics moderate teacher expectation effects.

In addition, however, there were several theoretical arguments leading us to suspect that students from stigmatized groups would be more susceptible to self-fulfilling prophecies than students in general. Abundant evidence suggests that school is often an unfriendly place for many African-American and lower SES students (e.g., Lareau, 1987; Steele, 1992). Although school can be difficult places for both boys and girls, though usually in different ways (e.g., Bye, 1994; Jussim & Eccles, 1995), math and science classes are often less supportive places for high achieving girls than for high achieving boys (Eccles & Blumfeld, 1985; Eccles & Hoffman, 1984; Eccles-Parsons et al., 1982; AAUW, 1992). When school is consistently a difficult place, students may often "disidentify" with achievement by devaluing the importance of school or the particular subjects in which they feel devalued (e.g., Eccles (Parsons), 1984; Eccles (Parsons) et al., 1983; Eccles & Harold, 1992; Jussim, 1986; Meece, Eccles-Parsons, Kaczala, Goff, & Futterman, 1982; Steele, 1992). Such responses may render them more readily influenced by teacher expectations in several ways.

When students with a history of negative school experiences find themselves faced with a supportive, encouraging teacher who also insists on high performance, they may feel as if they have caught a breath of fresh air. Such a teacher may inspire previously low achievers to new heights. This perspective may not be as unrealistic as it sounds. In his influential article on Black disidentification with school, Steele (1992) described academic programs in which previously low-performing students [e.g., some with Scholastic Aptitude Test (SAT) in the 300s] took on difficult honors-level work and came to outperform their White and Asian classmates. Steele's (1992) description of these programs implies that teachers often engage in behaviors much like those that lead to beneficial self-fulfilling prophecies in the classroom and workplace: They are challenging and supportive (e.g., Brophy & Good, 1974; Cooper, 1979; Eccles & Wigfield, 1985; Eden, 1984, 1986; Harris & Rosenthal, 1985; Jussim, 1986; Rosenthal, 1989).

However, these same underprivileged students may also be more susceptible to harmful self-fulfilling prophecies. Steele (1992) has articulately argued that students who feel undervalued and "marked" by stigma have fewer defenses against failure. Therefore, even if students do not fail more frequently than students in general, they are more likely to be psychologically devastated by such failures, leading them to "disidentify" with school and achievement. Although Steele's (1992) analysis focused primarily on the plight of African-American students, he speculated that his observations might also be applicable to girls and students from lower-class social backgrounds.

Although negative teacher expectations are not identical to failure, we speculated that such expectations could readily produce effects analogous to those associated with failure. That is, if students must bear the brunt of inappropriately low teacher expectations, and if they belong to a stigmatized group, their enhanced vulnerability to negative school events may render them more susceptible to self-fulfilling prophecies. Social class and sex (at least in math and science classes) may be at least somewhat similarly stigmatizing. Poor students are frequently seen as inferior to their middle-class peers (Dusek & Joseph, 1983; Rist, 1970), and girls are often viewed as less skilled at math than are boys (Eccles & Hoffman, 1984; Eccles & Jacobs, 1986; Jacobs & Eccles, 1992; Meece et al., 1982; Yee & Eccles, 1988). It is widely believed in our culture that females have less ability in math than males (see Eccles, et al., 1983; Jacobs & Eccles, 1985, 1992). To the extent that females themselves have incorporated this stereotype into their own view of mathematics, they may be especially vulnerable to any behavioral indicators from others that are consistent with the stereotype. For example, Jacobs and Eccles (1985) found that mothers were more likely than fathers to lower their view of their daughters' math ability after being exposed to a media campaign reporting innate gender differences in math ability. These results suggested that females (in this case mothers) are more personally influenced than males by messages consistent with gender-role stereotypes.

There is another very different reason to suspect that students from stigmatized groups may be more strongly affected by teacher expectations. Social psychology has a long history of research suggesting that stereotypes of stigmatized groups are often inaccurate (e.g., G. Allport, 1954; Hamilton et al., 1990; Jones, 1986, 1990; Miller & Turnbull, 1986). By definition, the more inaccurate an expectation, the greater its potential to create self-fulfilling prophecies. Therefore, because students from stigmatized groups are perhaps more likely to be viewed inaccurately, they may be more strongly influenced by teachers' expectations.

B. CONCEPTUAL MODEL

Figure 2 presents the conceptual model underlying the following research. The model assumes that student backgrounds (previous grades and test scores, motivation, self-concept, etc.) influence both teacher perceptions and students' future performance outcomes. The model further assumes that teacher perceptions may also influence student performance outcomes;

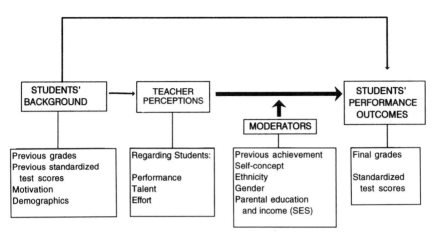

Fig. 2.   Conceptual model of relationships between teacher perceptions and student achievement.

this is captured by the thick, horizontal arrow. Conceptually, this arrow represents self-fulfilling prophecies. The thick, vertical arrow represents the idea that various proposed moderators may increase or decrease the self-fulfilling influence of teacher expectations on student achievement.

The short thin arrow represents the possible influence of various aspects of student backgrounds on teacher perceptions. The long thin arrow represents the controls we have included in assessing relationships between teacher perceptions and students' future performance. The relationships represented by these thin arrows are not discussed in this section (although those relationships are precisely the focus of another series of studies reported later).

C. DATA ANALYTIC STRATEGY

Three separate sets of models were estimated: One set focused on student sex, a second on student social class, and a third on student ethnicity. Our analyses first assessed a baseline model, which assumed that the control variables (students' fifth-grade final math grades, scores on standardized tests taken in fifth or early sixth grade, self-concept of math ability, effort spent on math, time spent on math homework, and intrinsic and extrinsic value placed on math) and the three teacher perception variables (performance, talent, and effort) predict sixth-grade final grades and seventh-grade

MEAP scores (see Eccles, 1988; Jussim, 1989; Jussim & Eccles, 1992, for more information about these variables). The results for these baseline models are similar to those summarized earlier from Jussim (1989) and Jussim and Eccles (1992) because these analyses are based on students in the same sample.

Next, we assessed the moderation hypotheses. Specifically, we estimated a new model that added three product terms to the original model, terms representing the product of the student demographic category with each of the three teacher perception variables (performance, talent, and effort). The hypothesis that a particular student demographic characteristic moderated teacher expectation effects could be confirmed if either the block of three product terms or any of the individual predictors significantly predicted achievement outcomes. However, since the three product terms were highly correlated with each other,[2] testing all three simultaneously could artificially reduce the size and significance of all the product terms (e.g., Gordon, 1968), thereby substantially underestimating the role of any one moderator.[3] Consequently, if at least one of the predictors or the block of three moderators significantly increased the R^2 at $p \leq .10$ level, we examined the individual moderators in three steps.

In step one, we examined a model that added only the product term that most strongly predicted the outcome to the base model. This product term significantly predicted the outcome in each of the analyses that we performed. In step two, we added the other two product terms to the model. If this yielded no significant results (neither the R^2 increment, nor the individual coefficients were significant), the final model included the base model plus the first significant product term. However, if step two yielded significant results (either the R^2 increment or one of the individual coefficients were significant), we included a third step that essentially repeated step one. In step three, we added the stronger of the remaining two product terms to the final model. In this case, the final model included only the base model plus the two significant product terms. No models ever produced three significant product terms. These procedures reduced underestimation of moderator effects due to collinearity among the product terms. Finally, in order to fully explicate the significant moderator effects, we plotted the predicted relations separately for the two different demographic groups in each analysis (see, e.g., Judd & McClelland, 1989).

[2] The three product terms were correlated with each other for two reasons: 1) each teacher perception variable was multiplied by the same potential moderator, and 2) the teacher perception variables themselves were moderately to highly intercorrelated (approximately .5 to .8).

[3] This procedure is "artificial" because it estimates each individual coefficient after controlling for *all* other variables in the model. This includes not only the real control variables but the other teaacher perception-moderator product terms as well—in essence, potentially controlling "out" much of the very moderational relationship we are attempting to assess.

Except where noted, the N's for these analyses were 1765 for sex, 1020 to 1060 for social class, and 1609 to 1663 for ethnicity. Variations in sample size reflected different patterns of missing data, primarily with regard to family income and parent education. All analyses reported below were multiple regressions in which the student was the unit of analyses. Because teachers rated all of the students in their classrooms, teacher perceptions are not independent of one another. However, all analyses included classrooms (coded as dummy variables) as predictors of final grades in sixth-grade math and MEAP scores, thereby rendering all other relationships independent of teachers.

D. STUDENT SEX

Were girls more susceptible to self-fulfilling prophecies than were boys? Although student sex did not significantly interact with teacher perceptions to predict MEAP scores, the interaction did significantly predict final sixth-grade marks. The block of three interaction terms predicted final marks within our significance criterion ($F_{(3,1637)} = 2.32$, $p < .08$). The only statistically significant product term was Talent*Sex (Talent refers to teacher perceptions of talent). We then reestimated the model using only the one Talent*Sex product term, which significantly ($p < .05$) predicted grades. The results from this final analysis for predicting grades are presented in Table II.

The regression analysis yielded the following simplified prediction equation:

$$\text{grades} = 10.58 + .23(\text{Talent}) + .39(\text{Sex}) - .11(\text{Talent*Sex})$$

We refer to this as a "simplified" prediction equation because it contains *only* those coefficients and variables directly relevant to understanding how student sex moderates teacher expectation effects.[4]

[4] In creating this simplified prediction equation, we have assumed that all other variables (i.e., other than those in the simplified prediction equation) are at their mean. With this assumption, all other variables yield a constant. The constant in the simplified prediction equation equals the constant from the full regression equation plus the product of each variable's coefficient and its mean (each variable *except* for Talent, Sex, and the Talent*Sex terms, which are shown explicitly in the simplified prediction equation). Consider the following oversimplified example:
If grades = 1 + .1(Standardized test scores) + .5(Previous grades) + 2(Talent) + 2(Sex) + .5(Talent*Sex), if the mean standardized test score is 50 (50th percentile), and if the mean grade is 10 (translating letter grades to a numerical scale), then the simplified prediction equation becomes:

$$\text{grades} = 11 + 2(\text{Talent}) + 2(\text{Sex}) + .5(\text{Talent*Sex})$$

The new constant of 11 = (the original constant) + .1(standardized test score mean) + .5(previous grades mean) = 1 + .1(50) + .5(10) = 11.

TABLE II

DESCRIPTIVE STATISTICS AND REGRESSION RESULTS FROM STUDENT SEX MODERATION ANALYSIS: FINAL MODEL PREDICTING GRADES

Dependent variable	Mean	SD	Total R^2	$F(1)$	$df(1)$	Model R^2	$F(2)$	$df(2)$
Final marks (sixth grade)[1]	11.47	2.60	.75	40.00****	125,1639	.49	269.96****	12,1639
Predictors	**Mean**	**SD**		**b**			**t**	**beta**
Talent*Sex	—	—		-.11			2.30*	-.14
Teacher perceptions of								
Performance[2]	3.42	1.13		.50			8.08****	.22
Talent[3]	4.86	1.33		.23			2.68****	.12
Effort[3]	5.09	1.39		.28			7.29****	.15
Student background								
Sex[4]	1.47	.50		.39			1.57	.08
Standardized test scores[5]	61.06	25.67		.02			9.42****	.19
Fifth-grade final grades[1]	11.43	2.49		.29			15.07****	.28
Self-concept of ability[6]	10.15	2.46		.08			4.43****	.07
Effort at math[3]	5.73	1.31		.06			2.13*	.03
Time spent on homework[7]	2.46	.87		-.06			1.54	-.02
Intrinsic value of math[6]	9.47	3.44		.03			2.14*	.03
Extrinsic value of math[8]	18.36	3.12		.00			.06	.00

$*p < .05.$
$****p < .0001.$

b = unstandardized regression coefficients. $beta$ = standardized regression coefficient. Total R^2, $F(1)$, and $df(1)$ refer to the full analysis including all dummy variables controlling for individual classrooms. Model R^2, $F(2)$ and $df(2)$ refer to the R^2 increment when the predictor variables shown in this table are added to a model that included only the classroom dummy variables.

[1] Grades were coded such that 16 represented an A+, 15 represented an A, 14 represented an A−, etc., down to 3, which represented an F. A mean of 11.47, therefore, is between a B− and a B. [2] 1 to 5 scale. [3] 1 to 7 scale. [4] Girls = 1, boys = 2. [5] Percentile ranks based on national norms. [6] 2 to 14 scale. [7] 1 to 4 scale. [8] 3 to 21 scale.

In our data, girls were coded as "1" and boys as "2." Therefore, the simplified prediction equation showed that the equations relating teacher perceptions of talent to grades for girls and boys were:

$$\text{girls: Grades} = 10.97 + .12(\text{Talent})$$

$$\text{boys: Grades} = 11.36 + .01(\text{Talent})$$

These equations were obtained by simply entering the values for student sex into the simplified prediction equations (e.g., Judd & McClelland, 1989). For example, for girls:

$$10.58 + .39(\text{sex}) + .23(\text{Talent}) - .11(\text{Talent*Sex})$$
$$= 10.58 + .39(1) + .23(\text{Talent}) - .11(\text{Talent*1})$$
$$= 10.58 + .39 + .12(\text{Talent})$$
$$= 10.97 + .12(\text{Talent}).$$

This equation shows that the slope for girls (.12) is steeper than the slope for boys (.01) (and the test of the product term has already shown that this difference is statistically significant). Figure 3 displays the relationship between teacher perceptions and grades separately for boys and girls. It clearly shows that boys' grades are virtually unaffected by teacher perceptions of talent, whereas girls' grades are affected. Even for girls, though, Figure 3 shows the effect to be quite small. The whole range of teacher

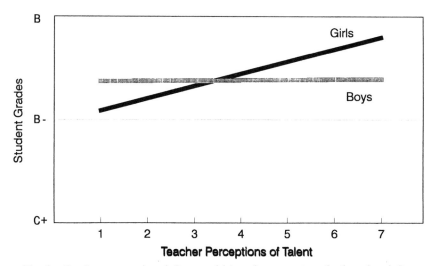

Fig. 3. Teacher expectations influence girls' grades more strongly than they influence boys' grades.

perceptions is barely enough to make a difference of one unit in student grades (e.g., B to B+).

Results reported thus far have been unstandardized. Although unstandardized coefficients are often preferable to the standardized coefficients (see Judd & McClelland, 1989; Pedhazur, 1982), standardized coefficients have one major advantage: They render results from different studies comparable. For example, as discussed previously, effect sizes (in terms of correlation coefficients or standardized regression coefficients) of teacher expectations on student achievement are typically .1 to .3. How do the separate coefficients for boys and girls compare to this general pattern? The standardized coefficient relating talent to grades for girls was .06, and for boys was .01. Thus, even for girls, for whom the effect is strongest, it is still quite small.

E. SOCIAL CLASS

Were students from lower SES backgrounds more vulnerable to self-fulfilling prophecies? Because there were two measures of social class (family income and education[5]), we made one modification to our data analytic approach. Instead of three product terms, six product terms were added to the equations predicting MEAP scores and final grades. Three product terms were created by multiplying each of the three teacher perception variables by mothers' education; three more terms were created by multiplying each of the three teacher perception variables by family income.

Although adding these six terms led to a significant R^2 increment ($F_{(6,1020)} = 3.57$, $p < .01$) in the prediction of MEAP scores, none of the coefficients relating the individual product terms to MEAP scores were statistically significant. This reflects collinearity among the product terms. Consequently, we used procedures like those described earlier to identify the most parsimonious subset of the significant predictive product terms: In this case, the product terms for teacher perceptions of effort*income and teacher perceptions of performance*education, each predicted MEAP scores (p's < .05). The results from this analysis are displayed in Table III. As with our student sex analyses, we obtained a simplified prediction equation by setting all variables that were not involved in the significant product terms at their mean. This yielded the following simplified prediction equation:

---

[5] Income was coded: 1 = less than $10,000/yr; 2 = $10,000–20,000/yr; 3 = $20,000–30,000/yr; 4 = $30,000–40,000/yr; 5 = more than $40,000/yr. Education ranged from 1 (never attended high school) through 9 (doctorate—MD, PhD, etc.). For 98% of the students, this was their mothers' education.

TABLE III
Descriptive Statistics and Regression Results from Student Social Class Moderation Analysis: Final Model Predicting MEAP Scores

Dependent variable	Mean	SD	Total R^2	$F(1)$	$df(1)$	Model R^2	$F(2)$	$df(2)$
MEAP scores[1]	23.45	4.39	.65	13.40****	126, 894	.38	70.48****	14, 1020

Predictors	Mean	SD	b	t	*beta*
Effort*income	—	—	-.13	2.16*	-.25
Performance*education	—	—	-.22	3.46***	-.39
Teacher perceptions of					
Performance[2]	3.55	1.10	1.43	4.70****	.36
Talent[3]	5.02	1.29	.19	1.40	.06
Effort[3]	5.22	1.36	.30	1.23	.09
Student background					
Education[4]	3.99	1.47	.91	3.51***	.31
Income[4]	3.66	1.23	.72	2.30*	.20
Standardized test scores[5]	64.58	24.93	.08	13.72****	.47
Fifth-grade final grades[1]	11.76	2.36	.26	4.70****	.14
Self-concept of ability[6]	10.33	2.38	.06	1.15	.03
Effort at math[3]	5.76	1.28	.01	.09	.00
Time spent on homework[7]	2.42	.86	-.15	1.30	-.03
Intrinsic value of math[6]	9.56	3.33	.04	1.16	.03
Extrinsic value of math[8]	18.47	3.07	.01	.26	.01

*p < .05.
***p < .001.
****p < .0001.

b = unstandardized regression coefficients. *beta* = standardized regression coefficient. Total R^2, $F(1)$, and $df(1)$ refer to the full analysis including all dummy variables controlling for individual classrooms. Model R^2, $F(2)$, and $df(2)$ refer to the R^2 increment when the predictor variables shown in this table are added to a model that included only the classroom dummy variables.

[1]MEAP scores ranged from 3 to 28 (a score of 0 is theoretically possible). [2]1 to 5 scale. [3]1 to 7 scale. [4]Education was on a 1 to 9 scale; income was on a 1 to 5 scale (see text for more details). [5]Percentile ranks based on national norms. [6]2 to 14 scale. [7]1 to 4 scale. [8]3 to 21 scale.

$$\text{MEAP} = 16.14 + .30(\text{Effort}) + 1.43(\text{Performance})$$
$$+ .91(\text{education}) + .72(\text{income})$$
$$- .13(\text{Effort*income}) - .22(\text{Performance*education}),$$

where Effort refers to teacher perceptions of students' effort and Performance refers to teacher percepetions of students' performance.

Among students whose parents had a lower education (some high school, coded as 2), the unstandardized relationship of teacher perceptions of performance to MEAP scores was .99 (.25, standardized). Among students whose parents had a higher education (having completed college, coded as 6), the unstandardized relation was .11 (.03, standardized). Among students from lower income families (family income of $10,000–$20,000/yr, coded as 2), the unstandaridzed relationship of teacher perceptions of effort to MEAP scores was .04 (.01, standardized). Among students from higher income families (greater than $40,000/yr, coded as 5), the unstandardized relationship of teacher perceptions of effort to MEAP scores was actually −.48 (−.15 standardized).

Figure 4 depicts the relationships of teacher perceptions of performance and effort to MEAP scores separately for students from lower and higher

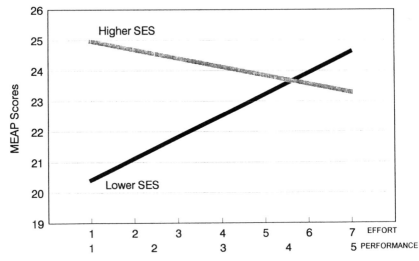

Fig. 4. Teacher expectations influence the standardized test scores of students from lower SES backgrounds more strongly than they influence the standardized test scores of students from higher SES backgrounds. Effort refers to teacher perceptions of effort. Performance refers to teacher perceptions of performance. Because product terms for teacher perceptions of performance with education and teacher perceptions of effort with income both predicted MEAP scores, both are shown here. Lower SES refers to an income of $10,000–20,000 and education of some high school. Higher SES refers to an income of greater than $40,000/yr. and having completed a college B.A.

SES backgrounds. Students from lower social class backgrounds were dramatically more vulnerable to self-fulfilling prophecies than were their more well-off classmates. As shown in Figure 4, the entire range of teacher perceptions makes about a 4-point difference on the MEAP. In terms of sample percentiles, going from 18 to 22 on the MEAP means going from the 17th percentile to the 38th; going from 21 to 25 means going from the 31st percentile to the 66th; and going from 24 to 28 means going from the 55th percentile to the 99th.

The negative relationship of teacher perceptions of effort to MEAP scores for upper class students completely accounts for the declining slope in Figure 4. Although unusual, attribution theory does provide one possible reason for why this negative relationship emerged among high SES students. Performance is often assumed to be influenced in a compensatory way by both effort and ability. If one has high ability, then less effort is needed to achieve the same performance level as that for someone with less ability (Covington & Omelich, 1979). This compensatory relationship may suggest the reason why attributing one's child's or one's students' successes to diligent effort might lead to both lowered ability self-concepts in the child or student and lowered perceptions of one's child's or students' abilities (Yee & Eccles, 1988). To the extent that a teacher is rating a high SES student as working very hard in his or her class, the teacher may also be conveying the indirect message that the student has lower ability. This message could then undermine the student's motivation or increase the student's anxiety such that the student performs more poorly in a standardized testing situation.

Alternatively, the teacher's view that the student is working hard may really mean that student does work harder than other students to compensate for lower ability. If so, then this lower ability level could explain why the student does not do as well as his or her peers in a timed standardized testing situation, in which there is insufficient time for greater effort to compensate for lower ability in determining final performance level.

A similar pattern was obtained for final grades. Although the R^2 increment associated with adding all six product terms approached significance ($F_{(6,926)} = 1.71, p = .12$) only when entered alone, the teacher perceptions of performance by income product term did significantly predict grades ($p < .01$). The final model, then, included only this one product term. These results are summarized in Table IV. This analysis yielded the following simplified prediction equation:

$$\text{Grades} = 8.54 + .88(\text{Performance}) + .33(\text{income})$$
$$- .09 \ (\text{Performance*income}),$$

where Performance refers to teacher perceptions of performance.

TABLE IV
DESCRIPTIVE STATISTICS AND REGRESSION RESULTS FROM STUDENT SOCIAL CLASS MODERATION ANALYSIS: FINAL MODEL PREDICTING GRADES

Dependent variable	Mean	SD	Total R^2	$F(1)$	$df(1)$	Model R^2	$F(2)$	$df(2)$
Sixth grade Final grades[1]	11.72	2.53	.77	24.88****	125, 931	.49	153.77****	13, 931

Predictors	Mean	SD		b		t		beta
Performance*income	—	—		−.09		2.74**		−.14
Teacher perceptions of								
Performance[2]	3.52	1.11		.88		6.29****		.22
Talent[3]	4.99	1.31		.05		.75		.03
Effort[3]	5.20	1.37		.27		5.36****		.15
Student background								
Education[4]	3.96	1.47		−.02		.52		−.01
Income[4]	3.65	1.23		.33		2.90**		.16
Standardized test scores[5]	63.85	25.39		.02		6.97****		.19
Fifth-grade final grades[1]	11.69	2.41		.30		11.76****		.29
Self-concept of ability[6]	10.30	2.38		.06		2.83**		.06
Effort at math[3]	5.76	1.28		.02		.61		.01
Time spent on homework[7]	2.42	.86		−.03		.48		−.01
Intrinsic value of math[6]	9.55	3.34		.04		2.34*		.05
Extrinsic value of math[8]	18.45	3.06		.00		.25		.00

*$p < .05$.
**$p < .01$.
****$p < .0001$.

b = unstandardized regression coefficient. *beta* = standardized regression coefficient. Total R^2, $F(1)$, and $df(1)$ refer to the full analysis including all dummy variables controlling for individual classrooms. Model R^2, $F(2)$ and $df(2)$ refer to the R^2 increment when the predictor variables shown in this table are added to a model that included only the classroom dummy variables.

[1]Grades were coded such that 16 represented an A+, 15 represented an A, 14 represented an A−, etc., down to a 3, which represented an A−. A mean of 11.47, therefore, is between a B− and a B. [2]1 to 5 scale. [3]1 to 7 scale. [4]Education was on a 1 to 9 scale; income was on a 1 to 5 scale (see text for more details).
[5]Percentile ranks based on national norms. [6]2 to 14 scale. [7]1 to 4 scale. [8]3 to 21 scale.

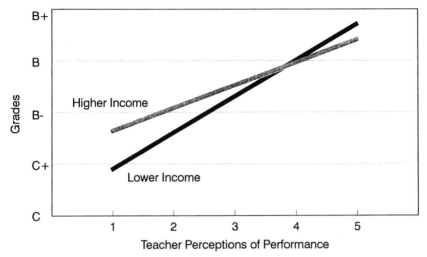

Fig. 5. Teacher expectations influence the grades of students' from lower SES backgrounds more strongly than they influence the grades of students from higher SES backgrounds. Lower income refers to an income of $10,000–20,000. Higher income refers to an income of greater than $40,000/yr.

The relationship of teacher perceptions of performance to grades for students from low income backgrounds (family income of $10,000–$20,000/yr) was .88 (unstandardized) and .31 (standardized). The relationship of teacher perceptions of performance to grades for students from higher income backgrounds was .43 (unstandardized) and .19 (standardized). These results, displayed in Figure 5, clearly show that teacher perceptions influenced the grades of lower income students more strongly than they influenced the grades of upper income students. Comparing these results to those displayed in Figure 4, however, shows that the difference is less dramatic for grades than for MEAP scores. Across the entire range of grades, the teacher expectation effect made a difference of about 2 grade levels[6] for upper income students (e.g., C+ to B) and three grade levels for lower income students (e.g., C+ to B+).

F. ETHNICITY

Were African-American students more susceptible to self-fulfilling prophecies than White students? To answer this question, three ethnic-

---

[6] Grades were coded on a scale going from 3 (F) to 16 (A+), with each unit representing the next grade level: grade 4 was F+; grade 5 was D−; grade 6 was D; grade 7 was D+, and so on.

ity by teacher perception product terms were added to the equations predicting MEAP scores and final grades. The analysis on MEAP scores was based on the 1536 White students and 72 African-American students who had valid data on all variables. Results are summarized in Table V.

The final analysis yielded a significant ethnicity by teacher perception of performance product term ($\beta = -.14$; $t = 2.79$, $p < .01$).[7] The simplified prediction equation was:

$$MEAP = 24.18 - 3.24(\text{ethnicity}) - .35(\text{Performance})$$
$$+ .94(\text{Performance*ethnicity})$$

Ethnicity was coded as 1 for White students and 2 for African-American students. The relationship of teacher perceptions of performance to MEAP scores was .59 (unstandardized) and .14 (standardized) for White students and 1.53 (unstandardized) and .37 (standardized) for African-American students. Figure 6 displays these relations and clearly shows the dramatically greater expectancy effects for African-American students. For White students, the entire range of teacher perceptions of performance makes about a 2.5-point difference score on the MEAP, whereas for African-American students, that range makes about a 6-point difference.

To make this finding more concrete, consider a two- or three-point difference in MEAP scores (the magnitude of the largest changes associated with teacher perceptions among White students). Scores going from 19 to 22 would mean going from the 21st to the 38th percentile, and going from 24 to 26 would mean going from the 55th to the 78th percentile. Now consider a six-point difference (the magnitude of the largest possible changes associated with teacher perceptions among African-American students). Going from 17 to 23 would mean going from the 14th to the 45th percentile, and going from 21 to 27 would mean going from the 31st to the 89th percentile.

Analyses examining predictors of final grades, which included 76 African-American students and 1587 White students, showed a similar pattern. Adding the three product terms significantly increased the R^2 increment ($F(3,1535) = 6.91$, $p < .0001$). In the final model, however, only the ethnic-

---

[7] If added to this model, the ethnicity by teacher perceptions of effort product term was also statistically significant ($p < .05$). However, 1) its coefficient was negative; 2) the unstandardized coefficient for the ethnicity by performance interaction doubled, going from about .9 in the analysis reported in the main text to 1.8; and 3) the coefficient for ethnicity by effort was −.9. Therefore, the net effect of teacher perceptions on achievement was still highly positive, and almost identical to the effect reported in the main text. Because the analysis with only one product term is simpler to present and interpret, and provides essentially the same information as the analysis with two product terms, the main text reports the analysis with the one product term.

TABLE V

DESCRIPTIVE STATISTICS AND REGRESSION RESULTS FROM STUDENT ETHNICITY MODERATION ANALYSIS: FINAL MODEL PREDICTING MEAP

Dependent variable	Mean	SD	Total R^2	F(1)	df(1)	Model R^2	F(2)	df(2)
MEAP scores[1]	23.00	4.63	.77	17.63****	125, 1483	.36	112.10****	12, 1483

Predictors	Mean	SD	b	t	beta
Performance*ethnicity	—	—	.94	2.79**	-.14
Teacher perceptions of					
Performance[2]	3.48	1.11	-.35	.90	-.08
Talent[3]	4.91	1.31	.00	.04	.00
Effort[3]	5.13	1.36	-.04	.40	-.01
Student background					
Ethnicity[4]	3.96	.21	-3.24	2.31*	-.14
Standardized test scores[5]	1.04	25.23	.09	18.03****	.49
Fifth-grade final grades[1]	11.53	2.44	.23	5.07****	.12
Self-concept of ability[6]	10.20	2.44	-.01	.19	.00
Effort at math[3]	5.73	1.30	.00	.06	.00
Time spent on homework[7]	2.44	.87	-.04	.41	-.01
Intrinsic value of math[6]	9.50	3.43	.06	2.14*	.05
Extrinsic value of math[8]	18.44	3.04	.04	1.36	.03

*$p < .05$.
**$p < .01$.
****$p < .0001$.

b = unstandardized regression coefficients. $beta$ = standardized regression coefficient. Total R^2, F(1), and df(1) refer to the full analysis including all dummy variables controlling for individual classrooms. Model R^2, F(2), and df(2) refer to the R^2 increment when the predictor variables shown in this table are added to a model that included only the classroom dummy variables.

[1]MEAP scores ranged from 3 to 28 (a score of 0 is theoretically possible). [2]1 to 5 scale. [3]1 to 7 scale. [4]Whites = 1, African-Americans = 2. [5]Percentile ranks based on national norms. [6]2 to 14 scale. [7]1 to 4 scale. [8]3 to 21 scale.

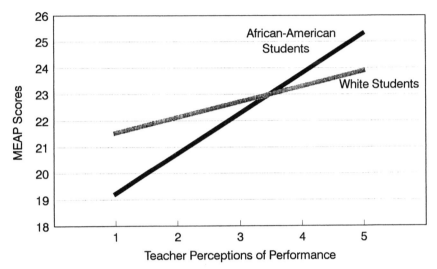

Fig. 6.   Teacher expectations influence the standardized test scores of African-American students more strongly than they influence the standardized test scores of White students.

ity by teacher perceptions of performance product term was significant (adding the other two terms, individually or together, yielded no additional significant individual coefficients and no significant R^2 increments). These results are summarized in Table VI. The simplified prediction equation was:

$$\text{Grades} = 12.05 - .18(\text{Performance}) - 2.11(\text{ethnicity})$$
$$+ .64(\text{Performance*ethnicity}).$$

The results (displayed in Figure 7), are consistent with the prediction that teacher expectation effects are stronger among African-American students than among White students. For White students, the relationship of teacher perceptions of performance to final grades was .46 (unstandardized) and .20 (standardized), and for African-American students, the relationship as 1.28 (unstandardized) and .56 (standardized). Figure 7 shows that, all other variables being held equal, going from the lowest to the highest teacher perceptions predicted a 4-unit change in grades (e.g., going from C to B+) among African-American students, but only a 2-unit change in grades (e.g., going from C+ to B) among White students.

We were concerned about two limitations to our ethnicity study. First, the sample of African-American students was quite small. Because attrition came mainly from students moving in and out of the district during the 3-year span covered by the analyses (fifth through seventh grades), we were able to increase the sample size by omitting some presixth-grade data. We

TABLE VI
Descriptive Statistics and Regression Results from Student Ethnicity Moderation Analysis: Final Model Predicting Grades

Dependent variable	Mean	SD	Total R^2	$F(1)$	$df(1)$	Model R^2	$F(2)$	$df(2)$
Final grades[1]	11.52	2.57	.87	37.06****	125, 1537	.49	251.88****	12, 1537

Predictors	Mean	SD	b	t	beta
Performance*ethnicity	—	—	.64	4.51**	.34
Teacher perceptions of					
Performance[2]	3.45	1.12	-.18	1.12	-.08
Talent[3]	4.89	1.33	.04	.80	.02
Effort[3]	5.12	1.37	.30	7.65****	.16
Student background					
Ethnicity[4]	1.05	.21	-2.11	3.51***	-.17
Standardized test scores[5]	61.51	25.55	.02	9.23****	.20
Fifth-grade final grades[1]	11.47	2.48	.30	15.18****	.29
Self-concept of ability[6]	10.17	2.45	.08	4.49****	.08
Effort at math[3]	5.73	1.30	.04	1.26	.02
Time spent on homework[7]	2.45	.87	-.04	.94	-.01
Intrinsic value of math[6]	9.48	3.44	.03	2.18*	.04
Extrinsic value of math[8]	18.41	3.04	.00	.32	.00

$*p < .05.$
$**p < .01.$
$***p < .001.$
$****p < .0001.$

b = unstandardized regression coefficients. beta = standardized regression coefficient. Total R^2, $F(1)$, and $df(1)$ refer to the full analysis including all dummy variables controlling for individual classrooms. Model R^2, $F(2)$, and $df(2)$ refer to the R^2 increment when the predictor variables shown in this table are added to a model that included only the classroom dummy variables.

[1] Grades were coded such that 16 represented an A+, 15 represented an A, 14 represented an A-, etc., down to a 3, which represented an F. A mean of 11.47, therefore, is between a B- and a B. [2] 1 to 5 scale. [3] 1 to 7 scale. [4] Whites = 1, African-Americans = 2. [5] Percentile ranks based on national norms. [6] 2 to 14 scale. [7] 1 to 4 scale. [8] 3 to 21 scale.

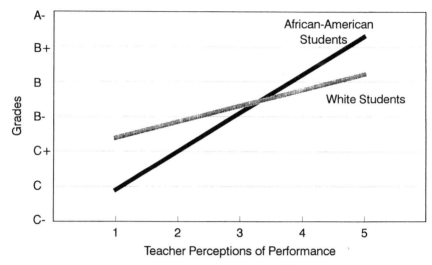

Fig. 7.   Teacher expectations influence the grades of African-American students more strongly than they influence the standardized test scores of White students.

ran one set of additional models that did not require fifth-grade final grades, and another set that did not require previous standardized tests. For the analyses predicting seventh-grade MEAP scores and sixth-grade final grades, these analyses increased the African-American Ns from 72 and 76, to 90 and 121, respectively. The results were virtually identical: Stronger expectancy effects emerged among the African-American students than among the White students.

Second, we were concerned about ethnic heterogeneity in our school districts. Specifically, in one district 97% of the students were African-American; another district had a more even distribution (63% White, 34% African-American, and 3% other). The other 10 districts were predominantly White (95% on the average). We tested for district differences in the pattern of expectancy effects in several ways. Because the students in the ethnically mixed district did not take a standardized test in fifth or early sixth grade, they were excluded from the main analysis, but were included in the analysis that did not use standardized tests as a predictor. These analyses yielded results similar to those already reported.

We also ran the main set of models a second time (i.e., the models depicted in Tables II through VI) excluding the students in the predominantly African-American district. Again, the results were similar to those already reported. Last, we ran a set of models in which we coded the type of district (predominantly White or African-American) as a dummy variable, created product terms representing the interaction of the district with teacher perceptions, and then ran the main models again. None of these interaction terms significantly predicted either student grades or MEAP scores. Therefore, we found no evidence that the patterns we observed varied greatly in districts with considerably different ethnic mixes.

G. UNCONFOUNDING THE EFFECTS OF ETHNICITY AND SOCIAL CLASS

A common problem in research on ethnicity and social class is assessing their separate roles in social phenomena. This is a problem because, on the average, Whites are from higher SES backgrounds than many minorities. However, this was not a major problem in the current study. Ethnicity was uncorrelated with parental education ($r = -.01$, ns), and only weakly related to income ($r = -.18, p < .001$). Nonetheless, several additional analyses further probed this issue. First, we reran the main social class analyses (see Tables III & IV) excluding all African-American students. The results were virtually identical to those reported in Tables III and IV, indicating that results regarding social class do not derive primarily from the African-American students.

Second, despite some important limitations, we ran an additional set of analyses adding both the ethnicity and SES product terms (together) to the models predicting grades and MEAP scores. One limitation is that, because family income and education information was available for only slightly more than half of the sample, the number of African-American students was reduced even further—to 27. Nonetheless, the results for the analysis predicting MEAP scores were striking: All three two-way product terms (involving education, income, and ethnicity) significantly ($p < .05$) predicted MEAP scores, and the regression coefficients were nearly identical to those reported in Tables III and IV.

Results for the model predicting grades were similar but weaker. Here, colinearity was a nuisance. Adding the performance by income and performance by ethnicity terms to the base model significantly increased the R^2 increment ($F(2, 897) = 4.35, p < .02$). However, neither product term, individually, reached statistical significance. The performance by income coefficient was similar to the term shown in Table IV ($-.09$ in the table versus $-.07$ in the current analysis, $p < .06$), but the ethnicity by performance coefficient was lower (.64 in the table versus .32 in the current analysis, $p < .12$).

These results, despite their limitations, were similar to those obtained in the analyses that addressed ethnicity and social class separately. It seems, therefore, that the higher expectancy effects among lower SES students are not due to the greater proportion of African-American students from lower SES backgrounds. It is also unlikely that the greater expectancy effects among African-American students are due to their lower SES backgrounds.

H. MULTIPLE VULNERABILITIES

These analyses, however, raise a more general question: Are students who are members of more than one vulnerable group more susceptible to expectancy effects than other students? For example, are lower SES African-American students most susceptible? Are lower SES girls also doubly vulnerable? Are African-American girls and lower SES, African-American girls also especially vulnerable? The results just reported suggest that the greater vulnerability of lower SES students is largely independent of the greater vulnerability of African-American students. Put differently, they suggest that these effects are additive, which implies that, because SES and ethnicity are both powerful moderators, lower class African-American students would be the most vulnerable of all to teacher expectation effects.

Hypothetically, these questions could be answered by adding the requisite three-way product terms. Unfortunately, however, because African-American students with parental SES information are relatively few in number, the results from a model including three-way product terms combining ethnicity, SES, and teacher perceptions would not have been meaningful. Because we are presently unable to include these three-way product terms, direct assessment of this question must await future research.

We did, however, assess whether lower SES girls and African-American girls were particularly susceptible by assessing models including three-way product terms (between student sex, teacher perceptions, and either SES or ethnicity). Because these models are very complex (base model, plus two-way product terms for all combinations of sex by the three teacher perception variables by either the two SES variables or by ethnicity, plus three-way product terms) we can only summarize our analyses here.

There were four main analyses (Two outcomes by two separate tests of three-way interactions: teacher perceptions by student sex by student SES predicting grades and MEAP; and teacher perceptions by student sex by student ethnicity predicting grades and MEAP). Each analysis was performed in two steps. The first step included the base model, plus all lower-order two-way product terms. Previously obtained significant two-way product terms remained significant in all of these models. In the second step, we added the three-way product terms. For three of the four models, none of the three-way product terms significantly predicted student outcomes.

Even the fourth did not qualify our previous conclusions: It showed that, for MEAP scores, lower SES girls were slightly more susceptible to expectancy effects than were other groups.

These results mean that lower SES girls and African-American girls are more susceptible to expectancy effects than are students who belong to only one vulnerable group (i.e., the two interaction effects were generally additive). These results are consistent with our general conclusions that girls are slightly more susceptible than boys, that lower SES students are considerably more susceptible than upper SES students, and that being a lower SES or African-American girl is a double vulnerability.

V. Stereotypes and Self-Fulfilling Prophecies

Teacher stereotypes would appear to be a likely explanation for why expectancy effects are more powerful among students from stigmatized or disadvantaged social groups. Both the evidence regarding the self-fulfilling effects of social stereotypes and the limitations to that evidence are discussed next.

Many social psychological perspectives and reviews claim or assume that stereotypes are often inaccurate and could likely lead to self-fulfilling prophecies (Hamilton et al. 1990; Jacobs & Eccles, 1992; Miller & Turnbull, 1986; Snyder, 1984; von Hippel et al., 1995). The role of stereotypes in creating self-fulfilling prophecies that contribute to inequalities between ethnic and socio-economic groups and between the sexes may seem "obvious." The dominant group (White men) hold negative stereotypes about other groups. White men treat members of these groups less favorably than they treat other White men, so that members of these other groups receive lower quality education (and lower paying jobs, too).

Undoubtedly, this sequence sometimes occurs. Although the claim that social stereotypes are self-fulfilling appears straightforward, it is considerably more complex than it seems for several empirical and conceptual reasons. Although any stereotype, hypothetically, may be self-fulfilling, most research to date has focused on four particular stereotypes: ethnicity, social class, gender, and physical attractiveness. This research literature is reviewed next, after which we address basic theoretical issues involved in understanding the extent to which stereotypes create social injustices through self-fulfilling prophecies.

A. ETHNIC STEREOTYPES

We are aware of only one study that comes close to documenting self-fulfilling prophecies produced by an ethnic stereotype. In the first classic experiment of Word, Zanna, and Cooper (1974), White Princeton students (perceivers) interviewed targets for a job. In fact, however, targets were confederates who had been carefully trained to engage in the same set of behaviors with each subject. Half of the confederate targets were African-American and half were White. The main dependent variables were interviewers' nonverbal behavior. Consistent with a self-fulfilling prophecy, the perceivers were colder to African-American targets than to White targets. In comparison to White targets, interviewers sat farther away from African-American targets, had more speech dysfluencies when talking to them, and conducted a shorter interview.

In their second experiment, Word et al. (1974) showed that this treatment undermined the performance of interviewees. Confederates were trained to interview subject–applicants in either of two ways: 1) the cold style comparable to that received by the African-American interviewees in Study 1, or 2) the warm style comparable to that received by the White interviewees in Study 2. All subject–applicants in this study were White. Results showed that the applicants treated coldly (as were the African-American applicants in Study 1) actually performed more poorly in the interview (as rated by independent judges) than did the applicants who were treated warmly. The type of treatment accorded African-American applicants in Study 1 undermined the actual interview performance of White applicants in Study 2.

Word et al. (1974) was an important landmark because it was the first experimental attempt to examine the potentially self-fulfilling effects of a social stereotype. However, even in this study, ethnic stereotypes were never measured. Perhaps the self-fulfilling prophecy was triggered, not by perceivers' stereotypes, but by their prejudice (disliking) of African-Americans. In fact, Word et al. (1974) ran a pilot study which documented that other Princeton students were indeed prejudiced against African-Americans. Further, a recent study (Jussim, Nelson, Manis, & Soffin, 1995) found that prejudice toward (disliking of) a group was often a more potent source of biases in person perception than were stereotypes (beliefs about the groups). Alternatively, the source of the self-fulfilling prophecy may be neither stereotypes nor prejudice. It may be anxiety. People often feel anxious when interacting with members of a different ethnic group, especially when the groups have a long history of conflict (e.g., Stephan & Stephan, 1985). Clearly, the source of the self-fulfilling prophecy in this study remains to be pinned down more convincingly.

Regardless of the source, however, the basic finding requires replication. Would the same pattern of results hold up today, in colleges other than Princeton (where the study was conducted) and among nonstudent samples? Would African-American interviewees respond to the differential treatment received by interviewees in Word et al.'s (1974) second study in the same self-fulfilling manner as did the White interviewees? In addition, we cannot help but wonder whether other ethnic stereotypes are self-fulfilling. The answers to these questions are currently unknown.

B. SOCIAL CLASS STEREOTYPES

Abundant evidence shows that people hold higher expectations for individuals from middle class backgrounds than for those from lower class backgrounds (Dusek & Joseph, 1983; Jussim, Coleman, & Lerch, 1987). Nonetheless, we are aware of only two studies that have examined whether these expectations are self-fulfilling.

Perhaps the most dramatic and well-known study of social class-based self-fulfilling prophecies was performed by Rist (1970). Rist observed that by the eighth day of school, a kindergarten teacher had divided her class into three groups: students supposedly smart, average, or dumb. Each group sat at its own table (Tables A, B, and C, respectively). However, the main difference between the students was not intelligence—it was social class. Compared to the others, the students at Table A came from homes that had greater incomes, were less likely to be suppored by welfare, and were more likely to have both parents present; the children themselves were cleaner and more likely to dress appropriately. There were comparable differences between the students at Tables B and C. Table A was positioned closest to the teacher, and she proceeded to direct nearly all of her time and attention to those students. In addition, she was generally friendlier and warmer to the students at Table A. Consequently, Rist (1970) interpreted his study as documenting strong self-fulfilling prophecies.

The differences Rist (1970) observed in teacher treatment of middle class versus poor students would be inappropriate and unjustified, even if there were real differences in the intelligence of the children at the different tables. Nonetheless, despite Rist's (1970) conclusions, the study provided no evidence of self-fulfilling prophecy. Although Rist provided a wealth of observations concerning teacher treatment, he provided few regarding student performance. The differential treatment alone is not evidence of self-fulfilling prophecies. Differences in student outcome measures are also needed. The one student outcome measure that Rist (1970) provided was student IQ scores. In contrast to the self-fulfilling prophecy hypothesis, there were no IQ differences between the students at the different tables at the end of the school year. Thus, although the teacher may have held very different expectations for middle versus lower class students, and even though the teacher may have treated students from different backgrounds very differently, the students' IQ scores were not affected (see Jussim & Eccles, 1995, for a more detailed critique of this case study).

A naturalistic study that included more than 10,000 high school students (Williams, 1976) provided a much more rigorous analysis of the role of social class in educational self-fulfilling prophecies. Williams (1976) used path analytic techniques to assess relationships between teacher expectations and students' previous and future achievement and social class. Consistent with most studies examining social class, Williams (1976) found that teachers held higher expectations for students from upper socioeconomic backgrounds. However, differences in teacher expectations for middle- and lower-class students evaporated after Williams controlled for students' previous levels of performance. This means that, rather than student social class biasing teacher expectations, teachers accurately perceive genuine differences in achievement among students from differing socioeconomic backgrounds. Of course, accurate expectations do not create self-fulfilling prophecies.

A colleague once described the Rist (1970) article as "a real tear-jerker," and we cannot help but agree. Nonetheless, the less well-known Williams (1976) study is much stronger than Rist's (1970) study on almost all important scientific grounds: Rist relied primarily on his own subjective and potentially biased observations, whereas Williams relied on school records and questionnaires; Rist focused on 30 students, whereas Williams focused on more than 10,000 students; Rist claimed to provide strong evidence of self-fulfilling prophecy but actually provided none, whereas Williams (1976) rigorously tested for self-fulfilling prophecies and failed to find any. Although social class may sometimes lead to self-fulfilling prophecies, in terms of drawing scientific conclusions based on evidence, Williams (1976) deserves dramatically more weight than Rist (1970).

C. GENDER STEREOTYPES

Converging evidence from experimental and naturalistic studies shows that gender stereotypes create self-fulfilling prophecies. One series of experiments showed that when women believed they would be interviewed by more sexist or traditional men, they arrived wearing more traditionally feminine clothing (e.g., more make-up and accessories); and, if they believed that he was attractive, they expressed more traditional gender-role attitudes on questionnaires and actually performed worse on an anagrams test (von Baeyer, Sherk, & Zanna, 1981; Zanna & Pack, 1975). Another experiment showed that when targets (who were in a room isolated from perceivers and communicating only by using an electronic signaling system) were labeled as male (all were actually females), they took on more masculine and fewer feminine tasks than when they were labeled as female (Skyrpnek & Snyder, 1982).

Naturalistic studies, too, often find evidence of gender stereotypes leading to self-fulfilling prophecies. When first-grade teachers believe girls are smarter than boys, girls actually achieve more highly (Doyle, Hancock, & Kifer, 1972; Palardy, 1969). Another naturalistic study focused on the self-fulfilling effects of more than 1000 mothers' gender stereotypes on their children's self-perception of their ability in math, sports, and social activities (Jacobs & Eccles, 1992). This study showed that the children's sex interacted with their mothers' gender stereotypes. The children felt that they had more ability when their sex corresponded to the sex that their mother believed was generally superior. For example, among mothers who believed that boys were better at math, boys evaluated their math ability more highly than girls evaluated their own math ability. (This pattern was reversed among the minority of mothers who felt that girls were better at math.) These effects held even after the study controlled for prior achievement levels.

D. PHYSICAL ATTRACTIVENESS STEREOTYPES

Snyder, Tanke, and Berscheid (1977) showed that erroneous beliefs about another person's attractiveness may be self-fulfilling. Men and women were located in different rooms and communicated via telephone. Women believed to be attractive (a variable manipulated by photographs presented to the male perceivers) were treated more warmly than women believed to be unattractive. The women believed to be more attractive also responded with more friendliness.

A subsequent study, however, failed to replicate Snyder et al.'s (1977) findings, although it did yield highly qualified support for an attractiveness-based self-fulfilling prophecy. Andersen and Bem (1981) had androgenous or sex-typed men and women perceivers interact with men and women targets. In contrast to the Snyder et al. (1977) study, Andersen and Bem (1981) did not find that male perceivers influenced women whom they believed were attractive to respond in more pleasant and socially skilled ways.

Some allegedly attractive targets did respond more warmly than allegedly unattractive targets—but only when perceivers were sex-typed women. In contrast, androgenous female perceivers created a "boomerang" effect: Unattractive targets interacting with them were actually rated more favorably than were the attractive targets! These two experiments (Andersen & Bem, 1981; Snyder et al., 1977) do not seem to provide a particularly strong basis for broad statements about the self-fulfilling power of the physical attractiveness stereotype.

One naturalistic study showed that sometimes more attractive MBAs earn more income than their less attractive peers (Frieze, Olson, & Russell, 1991). Although this study was interpreted as showing self-fulfilling effects of the attractiveness stereotype, such an interpretation seems premature. Research consistently shows that physically attractive adults are more so-cially skilled than less attractive adults (e.g., Goldman & Lewis, 1977; see a meta-analysis by Feingold, 1992). It seems likely that more socially skilled MBAs would deserve and actually receive higher salaries than less socially skilled MBAs. Thus, attractiveness may predict MBAs' income because it is a proxy for social skill, rather than because of self-fulfilling prophecies (see Jussim & Eccles, 1995, for a more detailed critique).

Although the development of individual differences in social skill is beyond the scope of this paper, one may wonder where these differences originate. Is it not possible that self-fulfilling prophecies created a difference where none previously existed? However, but the mere existence of social skill differences provides neither empirical evidence nor logical justification for supporting a self-fulfilling prophecy explanation (or any other explana-tion). There are many plausible alternative ways to explain why social skill differences between the attractive and unattractive exist. Furthermore, current evidence indicates that the expectancy explanation is one of the weakest explanations for those differences at any one point in time (see Feingold's [1992] meta-analysis).

E. STEREOTYPE-BASED SELF-FULFILLING PROPHECIES AS EXPLANATIONS FOR SOCIAL INEQUALITIES

As we see it, the evidence that stereotypes lead to self-fulfilling prophecies that exacerbate or perpetuate social inequalities is currently extremely weak. To begin with, except for gender stereotypes, there just is not much evidence of any type—lab or naturalistic—showing that stereotypes actu-ally do lead to self-fulfilling prophecies. Second, most of the studies showing stereotype-based self-fulfilling prophecies are experiments, which only dem-onstrate that stereotypes *may* be self-fulfilling. They provide no evidence that stereotypes actually *are* self-fulfilling in daily life. Only naturalistic studies are capable of documenting that stereotypes actually do create self-fulfilling prophecies. Except for gender studies, there are very few such studies that are well controlled (see reviews by Jussim & Eccles, 1995; Jussim & Fleming, in press).

The existence of social and economic inequalities is a phenomenon to be explained, but their existence does not provide prima facie evidence that all, or even most, ethnic or social class differences result from self-fulfilling prophecies. Social scientists seem to be committing at least one of two errors when they interpret the existence of inequalities as reflecting the effects of self-fulfilling prophecies (Snyder, 1984; Stangor, 1995; von Hippel et al., 1995).

The first error can be illustrated with a faulty syllogism. Premise 1: If minorities are genetically inferior to Whites intellectually, then minorities should, on the average, have lower educational and occupational achievement. Premise 2: Minorities have lower educational and occupational achievment than do Whites. Conclusion: Therefore, minorities are genetically inferior. Clearly, despite the currently popular claims in the *Bell Curve* (Herrnstein & Murray, 1994), this conclusion is unfounded. But the logic is no less inappropriate when the preferred explanation for inequality is a social one, such as self-fulfilling prophecy, rather than a biological one. Premise 1: If stereotypes are self-fulfilling, then one should find stereotype-consistent differences between various groups. Premise 2: There are stereotype-consistent differences between some groups. Conclusion: Therefore, stereotypes are self-fulfilling. Both premises are clearly true. The conclusion, however, does not follow from these premises and is an example of the classic error in logic known as "affirming the consequent."

The second error involves a tendency to generalize too readily from artificial experimental laboratory studies to daily life. Laboratory experiments are extremely well-suited for testing theoretically driven hypotheses, identifying causality, and assessing conditions under which phenomena such as self-fulfilling prophecies are most likely to occur. However, lab experiments can only suggest *possible* explanations for real-life social phenomena. Whether such explanations hold true under naturalistic conditions is itself an empirical question that cannot possibly be addressed by experimental laboratory research. Thus, we agree that the experimental laboratory research does suggest that self-fulfilling prophecies *might* contribute to some social inequalities. However, in the absence of converging evidence from naturalistic studies, we also believe that it is premature and unjustified to conclude that self-fulfilling prophecies actually do make a major contribution to social inequalities.

The claim that stereotypes are self-fulfilling includes an occasionally explicit, but more often implicit, assumption: that stereotypes are, at least initially, inaccurate. This is so because self-fulfilling prophecies, by definition, refer to erroneous expectations leading to their own fulfillment. Before empirically assessing the extent to which stereotypes bias teacher perceptions, we must first evaluate the validity of the assumption that stereotypes are generally inaccurate.

VI. Are Stereotypes Inaccurate?

A long tradition of social scientific research has assumed that stereotypes are generally inaccurate (see, e.g., Allport, 1954; LaPiere, 1936; Marger, 1991; Miller & Turnbull, 1986; Ottati & Lee, 1995; Snyder, 1984; Stangor, 1995). In this section, we examine some of the conceptual and empirical underpinnings of this assumption. First, we address the accuracy issue regarding people's beliefs about groups; second, we address the role of stereotypes in leading to biases and errors in person perception.

A. BELIEFS ABOUT GROUPS

An assumption or definition requiring stereotypes to be inaccurate quickly becomes mired in a swamp of conceptual and empirical troubles. Such a definition creates an undue burden on researchers interested in stereotypes: They must first document inaccuracy before they can consider a belief to be a stereotype. Unfortunately, there rarely is enough research to determine the accuracy of most stereotypic beliefs. Consider the belief that librarians are introverted. If the definition of a stereotype requires it to be inaccurate, then this belief could not be construed as a stereotype. Because there have been no studies assessing the introversion of librarians, we are in no position to evaluate the validity of this stereotype.

A definition of stereotypes as inaccurate would also prevent researchers from considering demonstrably valid beliefs about groups as stereotypes. For example, stereotype researchers could not study people who believe that girls do better in school than boys, that Asians are wealthier than most other ethnic groups, or that the majority of people on welfare are ethnic minorities. All of these beliefs are true (Deparle, 1994; Kimball, 1989; Marger, 1991), and, therefore, would not qualify as stereotypes if stereotypes are, by definition, inaccurate.

The assumption that stereotypes are inaccurate is also empirically problematic, at least if stereotypes are defined as people's perceptions of the attributes of social groups (e.g., Ashmore & Del Boca, 1981). Most reviews of stereotyping conclude that there is very little scientific evidence regarding the validity or invalidity of many beliefs about groups. Moreover, the little empirical evidence that does exist provides a decidedly mixed picture (e.g., Brigham, 1971; Judd & Park, 1993; Jussim, 1990; Jussim, McCauley, & Lee, 1995; McCauley, Stitt, & Segal, 1980; Ottati & Lee, 1995). Of course, validity is not just an issue of mean differences between groups; it also involves perceptions of the distributions of group members (e.g., Judd & Park, 1993; McCauley, 1995). However, the accuracy of people's beliefs about the distribution of social groups on particular attributes has also been assessed rarely (see Lee & Ottati, 1993, for an exception). Because we know so little about whether perceptions of distributions are accurate or inaccurate, we are in no position to assume that stereotypes as perceived distributions are necessarily inaccurate.

There is also a peculiar irony in the claim the stereotypes are both inaccurate and self-fulfilling. If stereotypes are inaccurate (i.e., if people's beliefs about social groups do not correspond to the attributes of members of those groups), then we know that stereotypes are *not* self-fulfilling). If they were, the beliefs would be accurate (in that they would correspond to group members' attributes). Thus, as broad sweeping generalizations, claims that stereotypes are both inaccurate and self-fulfilling are mutually exclusive.

Of course, stereotypes may be inaccurate originally, and through self-fulfilling prophecies become "accurate," which would create both social and conceptual problems. On the social problems side, it means that, even when two groups have similar distributions of skills, interests, motivation, and so forth, self-fulfilling prophecies may lead members of one group to excel (e.g., in school, on jobs, etc.) while undermining the motivation, skills, and performance of other groups. Oblivious to the social bases of such group differences, people can then point to the "objective" differences between groups as justification for maintaining pernicious stereotypes.

Conceptually, as described articulately by Snyder (1984), such processes seriously cloud the meaning of "accuracy." The "validity" of group differences created by perceivers themselves would be a very specious sort of "accuracy."

However, there are at least two conditions necessary for demonstrating that this possibility actually occurs: 1) The perceivers' stereotype must be shown not to correspond to some criterion at some Time 1; and 2) the perceivers' stereotypes must be shown to correspond to the criterion at Time 2. To our knowledge no one has published such data. Eccles and her colleagues are currently trying to get at this issue through longitudinal developmental studies of the socialization of gender differences in abilities, self-concepts, performance, interests, and participation. Among early elementary school-age children, they have assessed individual differences (and gender differences) in sports, instrumental music, math, reading, and peer relations. They have asked the parents and teachers of these children to rate how well the children perform, how interested the children are, and how hard the children are trying to improve in each domain. They also have given the children standardized measures of their current competence in each of these domains. This research shows that there are larger gender differences between the children's sport self-perceptions and the parents' perceptions of their children in the sports domain than in the standardized sport competence measures (Eccles & Harold, 1991). The researchers will use the longitudinal data to model the extent to which the parents' perceptions lead to sex-differentiated socialization practices, which in turn, lead to increases in the gender differences in actual competence. In our opinion, it will take longitudinal, field-based studies like this one to really address the question of whether stereotypes begin as inaccurate, and then, through self-fulfilling prophecies, become "accurate."

B. STEREOTYPES AND PERSON PERCEPTION

Presumably, however, erroneous stereotypes are a social problem primarily if they lead to biases and discrimination. (If some people hold inaccurate social beliefs, but do not act any differently than others who hold accurate social beliefs, inaccuracy would not appear to be a major problem.) Inaccuracy becomes a problem when perceivers treat or evaluate members of one group differently than members of another group. Furthermore, even when a particular stereotype is accurate as a broad generalization, many members of the target group will not fit the stereotype. Therefore, even a generally accurate stereotype may lead to false expectations for many targets. Thus, one of the most important aspects of accuracy and inaccuracy in stereotypes involves their role in person perception.

In this area, too, social psychological theoretical perspectives have emphasized error and bias (e.g., Devine, 1989; Greenwald & Banaji, 1995; Jones, 1986; Miller & Turnbull, 1986). Consequently, stereotypes are frequently accused of being the cognitive culprits in prejudice and discrimination (e.g., Fiske & Taylor, 1990; Hamilton et al., 1990; Stangor, 1995). Others, however, have argued that the empirical evidence supporting the conclusion that stereotypes are generally inaccurate (by any criteria: perceived mean differences, distributions, or correlations) and lead to biases and discrimination is actually sparse, weak, and equivocal (see reviews by Jussim, 1990, 1991; Jussim et al., 1995; McCauley, 1995; McCauley, Stitt, & Segal, 1980; Oakes, Haslam, & Turner, 1994). Even the link between stereotypes and prejudice itself is often quite weak (Eagly & Mladinic, 1989; Haddock, Zanna, & Esses, 1993; McCauley & Thangavelu, 1991), and recent research has shown that, at least sometimes, prejudice is a more potent source of bias in person perception than are stereotypes (Jussim et al., 1995).

Again, however, most social psychological research on the role of stereotypes in person perception has been done in experimental laboratory studies. Lab research probably dominates perspectives on stereotypes for several reasons. First, lab research has several important merits. Tightly controlled studies are particularly well-suited for identifying some of the social and psychological processes relating stereotypes to person perception (e.g., Bodenhausen, 1988; Darley & Gross, 1983; Fiske & Neuberg, 1990; Krueger & Rothbart, 1988; Linville, 1982; Locksley, Borgida, Brekke, & Hepburn, 1980). Furthermore, experiments provide a stronger basis for drawing causal inferences than do naturalistic studies.

However, we suspect that there is also a second class of reasons for performing experiments that have questionable scientific merit. Laboratory studies of stereotypes and person perception often are easier to conduct than naturalistic studies. Researchers can create artificial targets on paper, slides, or videotapes to test any hypothesis. In general, laboratory researchers intentionallly create targets from different groups who have identical personal attributes or engage in identical behaviors. Thus, any mean differences in judgments regarding targets from differing groups must represent bias because of this context.

If experimental studies are by no means easy, then imagine a naturalistic study of stereotypes and person perception in contexts where discrimination is a major social issue. The researcher must first gain the cooperation of an organization (school, workplace, etc.) and the individuals in that organization. The researcher must then arrange to survey perceivers' (teachers, managers, admissions or hiring personnel, etc.) judgments about targets (students, employees, applicants, etc.). Of course, those targets must actually vary on stereotype–category relevant dimensions (ethnicity, social class, sex, attractiveness, etc.). The researcher must then obtain two types of information from targets: their social group membership and their relevant personal attributes (e.g., school or job performance). Demonstrating bias then requires showing that perceivers see greater differences than really exist between individuals from the differing groups. Given the various obstacles and logistic difficulties, it is understandable that such research is daunting to so many social psychologists.

However, even this brief analysis highlights a political difference between lab and naturalistic research that examines whether stereotypes bias person perception. Because lab researchers have typically "operationalized away" differences between groups, they successfully avoided the political fallout that may accompany identification of real differences. In contrast, naturalistic research requires comparing perceivers' judgments to some criterion. Doing so always leaves open the possibility that the groups may really differ on that criterion. Identification of real differences (e.g., between men and women, between middle class and poor, or between ethnic groups) is almost always a delicate situation (e.g., Eagly, 1995; Graham, 1992; Jussim et al., 1995)—perhaps sufficiently delicate to intimidate many researchers away from dealing with such differences at all.

However, the failure of experimental research to examine the role of stereotypes in person perception when social groups really do differ is not just politically more palatable. It represents a major substantive limitation to all existing experimental studies of stereotypes and person perception. Such studies do show that perceivers sometimes see differences between individuals and differing groups when none exist. However, they are completely mute on the issue of how well perceivers judge individuals from groups that really do differ on the attribute being judged. This is unfortunate considering that groups often differ in many ways (see, e.g., Eagly, 1995; Marger, 1994; McCauley et al., 1980; Steele, 1992; Swim, 1994; or the data on education, income, and family status available on various racial, gender, or geographic groups in any U.S. Census report).

Failure to study stereotypes and person perception when the groups really differ characterizes every experimental study of which we are aware (e.g., Beckett & Park, 1995; Darley & Gross, 1983; Duncan, 1976; Krueger & Rothbart, 1988; Linville, 1982; Linville & Jones, 1980; Locksley et al. 1980; Locksley, Hepburn, & Ortiz, 1982), including our own (Jussim, 1993; Jussim et al., 1987, 1995). This means that social psychology actually provides little information about, for example, bias and accuracy in people's perceptions of individual men and women's assertiveness, the academic achievement of individual African-American and White students, or the social skill of individual attractive or unattractive targets (these groups really do differ on these attributes).

Furthermore, operationalizing away real differences prevents studies from assessing perceivers' sensitivity to existing differences between groups. Because bias and accuracy are not mutually exclusive (see, e.g., Jussim, 1989, 1991; Jussim & Eccles, 1992), the finding of bias in lab studies provides little or no information whatsoever about perceivers' accuracy in detecting real differences. Thus, experimental laboratory studies that operationalize away real differences between groups probably underestimate social perceptual accuracy. Fiske and Neuberg (1990) have argued that, because naturalistic research is often so difficult, and because it is almost always impossible to obtain representative samples of relevant situations (job interviews, college admissions evaluations, etc.), all one can do is perform laboratory studies and generate logical arguments for how and when results from laboratory studies might be applicable to real-life situations. We have done just that. We conclude that the laboratory research is restricted to a situation that may rarely occur in the real world—one in which there are no differences between groups.

Of course, there is no theoretical or practical obstacle to conducting research on accuracy and bias in perceptions of individuals from groups that really do differ. If researchers can intentionally construct artificial targets who do not differ, they can just as readily construct targets who *do* systematically differ by their social group membership. Researchers can still avoid political fallout ("Why did you assume that Group X was superior to Group Y? Are you some sort of group-ist?") by counterbalancing the differences within a single study or by performing a second study in which the differences are reversed. In one set of conditions targets from Group X may be somewhat superior to Group Y; in another set, Group Y can be somewhat superior to Group X. Such a design could get at both bias (perhaps perceivers see a huge difference between the groups when X is better than Y, but no difference when Y is really better than X) and accuracy (perhaps the perceived differences covary with the actual differences). Degree of difference can be set to either match real, known differences (see, e.g., Eagly, 1995; McCauley & Stitt, 1978; Swim, 1994) or set "arbitrarily" as needed to test theoretically based hypotheses (Mook, 1983). Especially if objective data (standardized test scores, wins and losses in competitive games, grade point average (GPA), sales figures, words typed per minute, likelihood of having a college degree, etc.) were used as targets' personal characteristics (in current parlance, *individuating information*), assessing accuracy and bias would be straightforward.

Even for more fuzzy attributes (laziness, extravertedness, ambition, etc.), one could scale the differences between targets through the use of independent judges rating the behaviors (without any group label). We can only speculate that the political and academic zeitgeist since the mid-1960s (see also Brigham, 1971; Eagly, 1995; Jussim, 1991; Jussim et al., 1995; Mackie, 1973; Ottati & Lee, 1995; Wineburg, 1987) has created an intellectual environment that facilitated the field's failure to "notice" this glaring gap in research on stereotypes and person peception.

Of course, this type of research is not without its own limitations. Processes contributing to social inequality may take more time to surface than is available in most experiments. Nonetheless, this research would still be valuable, and we conclude that there is no serious obstacle preventing it.

The lab studies also suffer one more extremely important conceptual limitation: They focus exclusively on identifying social-cognitive *processes* involved in stereotyping. However, even if processes are high in experimental realism, they are completely incapable of drawing inferences about the accuracy of the *content* of stereotypes. This requires comparing judgments to real targets, not to laboratory stimuli (see Funder, 1987, 1995; Judd & Park, 1993; McCauley, Jussim, & Lee, 1995).

Because of unknown external validity and important conceptual limitations, we are compelled to conclude that the implications of much of social psychology's knowledge base for understanding the role of social stereotypes in naturally occurring person perception is not clear. Note, however, we are *not* claiming that the experiments are useless or trivial. Experiments have provided a great deal of knowledge about the social psychological processes leading to biases in judgments of similar targets and about the conditions under which such biases are most likely to occur.

However, if we are to address the practical issues involving prejudice, discrimination, and sources of inequality, then identifying accuracy or inaccuracy in the content and use of social stereotypes will require at least some research that meets three conditions. First, it should examine perceivers' judgments regarding targets who are real people with real attributes (as opposed to artificially created social stimuli). Second, there must be some means of measuring targets' attributes (a criterion). Third, perceivers' judgments must be compared to the criterion. In the next section, therefore, we describe two studies that meet these conditions as they analyze the role of stereotypes in biasing teachers' perceptions of students.

VII. Are Teacher Expectations Biased by Students' Sex, Social Class, or Ethnicity?

We now return to the question that sparked our conceptual analysis of self-fulfilling prophecies and stereotypes—why were teacher expectation effects stronger among girls, African-American students, and students from lower SES backgrounds? Classic social psychology suggests that stereotypes, because they are inaccurate and lead to biased perceptions of targets, would lead teachers to develop erroneous expectations for these students, which would then create self-fulfilling prophecies. However, the previous discussion also pointed out that this perspective is based almost entirely on experimental laboratory studies of unknown ecological validity using a conceptually limited paradigm.

Two studies were performed to help redress this limitation by examining naturally occurring person perception and by comparing those perceptions to criteria (Jussim & Eccles, 1995). The first study addressed accuracy by comparing teacher perceptions of achievement and motivation differences among students from differing sex, socioeconomic, or ethnic groups to actual differences among those students. Thus, this first study focused on the *content* of teacher perceptions. The second study examined the *processes* leading to accuracy and inaccuracy in teachers' perceptions of students from differing groups.

A. THE CONTENT STUDY

1. Main Research Questions

The study of content addressed three main questions: 1) Do teachers perceive sex, social class, or ethnic differences in achievement and motivation? 2) How accurate are these perceived differences (or lack of differences)? and 3) Are teachers' perceptions of individual students biased by teachers' own sex, social class, and ethnic stereotypes?

We use the term *bias* to refer to teachers systematically evaluating two groups as differing on some criterion more or less than they really do differ. For example, if banks approve more loan applications for Whites than for equally qualified minorities, the banks would be biased. However, if there are real income differences between ethnic groups, overall loan approval rates may differ among differing groups, even if banking officials are completely unbiased. Of course, if the difference in loan approval rates exceeds what would be predicted on the basis of income differences, the banks are still being biased.

We think that such a response represents one of the most common and critical forms of bias. In the teacher–student situation, it means that teachers see more (or fewer) differences between students from differing groups than really exist. In the MSALT data, higher SES students, on the average, perform better than lower SES students (this is discussed later in detail). Therefore, if teacher perceptions are biased against lower SES students relative to higher SES students, we should find that teachers perceive a greater social class difference, for example, in talent, than actually shows up in students' standardized test scores. Operationally, this means that SES should correlate more strongly with teacher perceptions than with students' actual performance.

Alternatively, there are at least two patterns that show teachers to be biased in favor of lower SES students relative to higher SES students. First, teachers might perceive that high SES students perform better than low SES students, but the perceived difference might be smaller than the real difference in previous achievement. Operationally, this means that the correlation between teacher perceptions and student SES would be smaller than the correlation between previous achievement and student SES. Second, teachers would be biased if they reversed the direction of the difference (i.e., if they viewed the performance of lower SES students more favorably than that of higher SES students). Operationally, this means that the correlation between teacher perceptions and student SES would be in the opposite direction (have the opposite sign) as the correlation between student SES and student achievement.

Again we used the MSALT data set (described earlier) to explore accuracy and bias in teacher perceptions of students from differing demographic backgrounds. We first determined whether teachers perceived achievement and motivation differences among students from the different demographic groups by correlating teachers' ratings of students' performance, talent, and effort with students' demographic characteristics. Teachers were asked to rate each student in their classes. These ratings, therefore, were person perception measures. They were not teachers' beliefs about the differing groups in general (which were not assessed). These correlations indicated the extent to which teachers judged students from one group (e.g., boys) more favorably on the average than they judged students from another group (e.g., girls).

The content study did not address the accuracy of teacher perceptions of individual students *within* each demographic group. This question is conceptually like seeking to discover in an experiment whether perceivers rely on individuating information more when judging targets belonging to one group (e.g., men) than when judging targets belonging to another group (e.g., women). Although this is an interesting and important issue, it is largely irrelevant to the issue of whether perceivers are biased for or against individuals from different groups. Showing, for example, that perceivers are more accurate when judging men than when judging women would provide no information at all about whether perceivers view men or women more favorably. In this example, perceivers' less accurate judgments of women could be, on the average, more favorable or less favorable, than their more accurate judgments of men. Accuracy of perceptions within groups is uninformative with respect to identifying whether there is a general bias or tendency to favor one group over the other. Obviously, however, the accuracy of teacher perceptions (and social perception more generally) within demographic groups is an important issue that should be addressed in future research.

Assessing whether teachers perceived differences between differing demographic groups of students, and whether those perceptions are accurate or biased is the focus of the content study. This involves determining whether teacher perceptions of individual students, aggregated across all students in each of two groups, correspond to the actual aggregated differences among the students in those groups. For example, this research addresses whether the differences teachers perceive between boys' and girls' performances (if any) overestimate, underestimate, or correspond to the real differences (if any) in boys' and girls' performances.

We compared the differing groups on measures of achievement and motivation. Final grades in fifth-grade math classes were used as the criterion for teacher perceptions of performance. Scores on standardized tests taken in fifth grade or early sixth grade were used as the criterion for teacher perceptions of talent. Three student motivation variables were used as criteria for teacher perceptions of student effort: self-concept of ability, self-perceptions of effort, and time spent on homework. These measures were reliable and valid (for more detail about the measures, see Eccles, 1988; Eccles (Parsons), Adler, & Meece, 1984; Jussim, 1987, 1989; Jussim & Eccles, 1992; Parsons, 1980; for a more detailed discussion of the use of these variables as criteria, see Jussim & Eccles, 1995). We considered self-concept of ability to be a motivational variable because it leads to effort and persistence according to many motivational theories (e.g., Bandura, 1977; Eccles et al., 1983; Eccles & Wigfield, 1985; Weiner, 1979). Consistent with this perspective, our data shows the correlation of self-concept of math ability with self-perceptions of effort to be .28 ($p < .0001$).

We concluded that teachers were accurate when the size of the difference they perceived approximately corresponded to the size of the actual difference among students. Teachers' perceptions were *inaccurate* when the differences they perceived between different groups of students substantially deviated from the actual differences. They could be inaccurate in either of two directions: 1) They might overestimate differences between groups (in the extreme, they might see a difference where none existed); or 2) they might underestimate differences between groups (in the extreme, they might perceive no difference, when one existed).[8]

2. Sex

These analyses were based on 942 girls (coded as 1) and 847 boys (coded as 2) from the MSALT study. This was the subsample with valid data on all

[8] These analyses did not control for classroom for several reasons. The criteria, student grades, standardized test scores, and motivation, were obtained from separate individuals, and did not suffer the same nonindependence problem associated with teacher perceptions. Although we could have controlled for classroom in identifying student grades, standardized test scores, and motivation, doing so would have unnecessarily complicated our results. Simple correlations (e.g., between student sex and grades), indicate which sex has received higher grades. This is what we need to know. For example, some schools track by ability, and whole classrooms might achieve at different levels from one another. If a disproportionate number of lower-class or African-American students were in low track classrooms, and we controlled for classroom, results would tend to underestimate the actual demographic difference in grades or standardized test scores. To be comparable to these criteria, therefore, analyses using demographic, motivation, and achievement variables to predict teacher perceptions also did not control for classroom.

variables. Teachers perceived girls as performing slightly better ($r = -.08$, $p < .001$) and as trying harder ($r = -.16$, $p < .001$) than boys. They perceived no difference in boys' and girls' talents ($r = .02$).

Were these perceptions accurate? For the most part, they were. Girls received slightly higher final grades than did boys in fifth-grade math classes ($r = -.07$, $p < .01$), a real difference that corresponds closely to the small perceived difference in performance. There also was no sex difference in standardized test scores ($r = .00$), which corresponds with teachers' perceptions of no difference in talent.

However, there was no evidence that teacher perceptions of sex differences in effort were accurate. Boys and girls reported exerting the same amounts of effort ($r = .00$) and spending the same amount of time on homework ($r = -.03$, ns). Furthermore, boys had higher self-concepts of math ability than did girls ($r = .09$, $p < .001$).

Were teachers biased by students' sex? For performance and talent, the answer is no; for effort, the answer is yes. Teachers evaluated girls as trying harder than boys, even though boys and girls reported working equally hard, and even though boys had higher self-concepts of ability. Were teachers biased for or against girls? Because high effort is generally viewed positively by teachers and others (Covington & Omelich, 1979; Schuman et al., 1985), and because teachers rewarded supposedly harder-working students with higher grades (Jussim, 1989; Jussim & Eccles, 1992), this bias seems to favor girls. Alternatively, however, according to compensatory attributional perspectives [as one attribution goes up, others must go down (e.g., Covington & Omelich, 1979)], this result could be construed as a bias against girls because it implies lower teacher perceptions of girls' math ability. However, our results showing that teachers viewed girls and boys as having similar levels of talent strongly argues against this interpretation. Of course, whether this influences girls favorably in the long run depends on the psychological consequences of perceived effort for students' learning and motivation.

3. Social Class

These analyses were based on 1066 students. The multiple correlation of parental education and family income with each of the three teacher perception variables (all r's reported in this section are multiple r's) assessed whether teachers perceived differences between students from differing socioeconomic backgrounds. Teachers perceived students from higher SES backgrounds as performing better ($R = .21$) and as more talented ($R = .26$, both p's $< .01$). There also were real social class differences in achievement. Family income and education correlated with fifth-grade final grades

($R = .27$) and previous standardized achievement test scores ($R = .31$, both p's $< .001$). Thus, the size of the perceived social class differences closely corresponded to the size of the actual differences.

Teachers also perceived social class differences in effort. They viewed students from higher SES backgrounds as trying harder ($R = .18, p < .01$). Were there real SES differences in effort? Although there were no SES differences in self-reported effort or time spent on homework (both Rs $< .05$, ns), students from higher SES backgrounds had higher self-concepts of math ability ($R = .15, p < .01$). Teacher perceptions of student effort corresponded reasonably well with student SES differences in self-concept of ability, but not with the student reports of effort. Therefore, results for effort provided mixed evidence regarding accuracy and bias.

Overall, there was little evidence that students' social class biased teachers' perceptions. There was no evidence at all that teachers' perceptions of talent or performance were biased against students from lower socioeconomic backgrounds, although the results regarding teacher perceptions of effort were mixed.

4. Ethnicity

Analyses of ethnicity focused on teacher perceptions of African-American and White students. Did teachers perceive differences between African-American and White students? Answering this question turned out to be more difficult than it may seem because of the continuing patterns of school segregation apparent in this study. Owing to the ethnic differences between districts, we performed two sets of analyses. The first analysis examined teacher perceptions in the ethnically homogeneous districts. The second analysis examined teacher perceptions in the ethnically mixed district.

5. The Homogeneous Districts

Three groups were compared: 1) White students in the predominantly White districts; 2) African-American students in the predominantly White districts; and 3) African-American students in the predominantly African-American district. In each of these districts, none of the differences in teachers' perceptions of African-American versus White students were statistically significant (all F's < 2.5, all p's $> .05$). Teachers perceived no differences in the performance, talent, and effort of African-American and White students.

Were the lack of perceived differences in performance or talent accurate? Table VII presents the mean previous grades and standardized test scores for students in these districts, and shows that teacher perceptions were

TABLE VII
Homogeneous Districts: Were Teacher Perceptions of No Differences Justified?

	White students in the White districts	African-American students in the White districts	African-American students in the African-American district
Standardized test scores (percentile ranks)	60 ($n = 2064$)	52 ($n = 39$)	38 ($n = 95$)
Fifth-grade final grades	B−/B ($n = 2040$)	C+/B− ($n = 27$)	C+ ($n = 61$)

In both analyses, the difference between African-American students in the predominantly African-American district and White students is statistically significant (p < .001).

In both analyses, the difference between African-American students and White students in the predominantly White district is not statistically significant.

(From Jussim, L., McCauley, C. R., & Lee Y. T. (1995). Why study stereotype accuracy and inaccuracy? In Y. T. Lee, L. Jussim, & C. R. McCauley (Eds.), *Stereotype accuracy: Toward appreciating group differences.* (pp. 3–27). Copyright © 1995 by the American Psychological Association. Adapted with permission.)

partially justified. In the predominantly White districts, neither the standardized test score differences nor the grade differences were statistically significant (all t's < 1.4, all p's > .1). Therefore, these teachers were justified in perceiving no differences between African-American and White students. In contrast, as Table VII shows, students in the predominantly African-American district performed significantly more poorly according to both standardized test scores and previous grades than did White students in the predominantly White districts (both t's > 3, both p's < .01). Therefore, teachers were not justified in giving equivalent ratings for the performance of these African-American and White students.

Teachers were also mostly justified in perceiving little difference in the effort exerted by the different groups of students. The differences among students on three motivation variables reached statistical significance for time spent on homework ($F_{(2,2383)} = 4.68$, $p < .01$) and self-concept of math ability ($F_{(2,2383)} = 4.58$, $p < .02$), and marginal significance for self-perceptions of effort ($F_{(2,2388)} = 2.81$, $p < .07$). However, only one of the post-hoc comparisons were significant—African-American students in the predominantly African-American district had higher self-concepts of math ability than the White students had in the predominantly White district ($t = 2.11$, $p < .05$). Furthermore, all of the *eta*s were below .07, indicating that although statistically significant, the differences were minor.

6. The Ethnically Mixed District

Did teachers perceive the 22 African-American students differently than they perceived the 40 White students in the ethnically mixed district? They did. Teachers perceived White students as performing better ($r = -.27$, $p < .05$), as more talented ($r = -.26, p < .05$) and as trying harder, although this last difference did not reach statistical significance ($r = -.20, p = .12$).

Were these perceptions justified? The African-American students did have lower grades than White students in this district (C/C+ vs. B−, $r = -.21$). However, this difference was based on only 32 White students and 14 African-American students (not all students attended this district in fifth grade), and it was not statistically significant ($p = .16$). The difference was, however, of about the same magnitude as the differences teachers perceived. Unfortunately, no standardized test was given to fifth-graders in this district.

Did teacher perceptions of effort differences correspond to ethnic differences in the motivation variables? African-American and White students in this district all claimed to be exerting about the same amount of effort, spending about the same amount of time on homework; all reported similar self-concepts of ability (all r's $< .07$, all p's $> .6$). Thus, the nonsignificant ethnic difference that teachers perceived in effort corresponded reasonably well to the lack of difference in the student effort and motivation variables.

B. TEACHER EXPECTATIONS AND STEREOTYPES: PRELIMINARY CONCLUSIONS

Some answers to the questions guiding the content study are now available. Teachers did often (but not always) perceive differences between boys and girls, middle- and lower-class students, and African-American and White students. These perceptions were mostly accurate. For all three demographic groupings, teacher perceptions of the performance or talent of students belonging to different groups generally corresponded closely to the actual differences or similarities in these groups' previous grades and standardized test scores. There was only one exception to this pattern: Teachers rated African-American students in the predominantly African-American district as favorably as other students, even though both their grades and standardized test scores were not as high as those of other students.

The pattern for teacher perceptions of effort was more mixed, providing evidence of both accuracy and inaccuracy. Teachers believed that girls tried harder than boys, but there was no difference between the sexes on the effort measures, and boys felt that they had more math ability than girls felt they had. Thus, there was a small bias in favor of girls. Teachers believed that middle-class students tried harder than lower-class students, which did not correspond to the lack of social class differences in students' reports of their effort or time spent on homework, but did correspond closely to student social-class differences in self-concept of math ability. In both the ethnically mixed and homogeneous school districts, the teachers perceived few differences in the effort of African-American versus White students. These perceptions were reasonably accurate—few differences emerged on either the effort measures or on self-concept of ability.

C. WHY WAS THERE SO LITTLE EVIDENCE OF BIAS?

1. Teachers Held No Stereotypes

The simplest explanation is that teachers held no negative stereotypes about girls, students from lower social-class backgrounds, or African-American students. Iif they held no stereotype, then there would be no stereotype to bias their perceptions. Unfortunately, this possibility cannot be tested directly, because teachers' beliefs about groups were not assessed as part of the MSALT study.

However, this explanation that teachers held no negative stereotypes seems highly implausible. If even a substantial minority held the stereotypes and relied on them, we still should have obtained some evidence of bias. Furthermore, abundant research in the social sciences attests to the widespread existence and importance of these stereotypes (e.g., APA Brief, 1991; Darley & Gross, 1983; Dusek & Joseph, 1983; Fiske & Taylor, 1991; Jones, 1990; Marger, 1991). Thus, the likelihood that this sample of teachers is so unique that virtually none held stereotypes seems slight.

Second, some researchers have argued that one does not need to subscribe to a stereotype for that stereotype to influence social perception (Devine, 1989; Sedikedes & Skowronski, 1991). Knowledge of cultural stereotypes (regardless of whether one accepts them), they argue, is sometimes sufficient to produce biases. For this type of analysis to explain our results, nearly our entire sample of teachers would need to be oblivious to the prevailing cultural stereotypes regarding girls, lower SES people, and African-Americans. This, too, seems highly implausible.

2. Teachers Held Stereotypes But Did Not Use Them

A second explanation is that teachers did hold stereotypes regarding these groups, but did not use them in evaluating students. Research in education and social psychology suggests considerable plausibility for this explanation. Earlier in this chapter we reviewed our own research that shows considerable accuracy in teacher perceptions of students (see also Brophy, 1983; Brophy & Good, 1974; Jussim, 1991, 1993, for reviews). In addition, abundant research shows that, whether individual targets are men and women, African-Americans and Whites, or upper class and lower class, perceivers generally judge them far more on the basis of their personal characteristics than on their membership in these social groups. This occurs both in laboratory studies and in naturalistic studies (see Jussim, 1990, 1993; Jussim, Madon, & Chatman, 1994, for reviews). Thus, even if teachers subscribed to social stereotypes, they probably judged students primarily on their academic performance rather than on their own stereotypes.

3. Teachers Used Valid Stereotypes

A third explanation is that teachers do hold stereotypes regarding these groups, and that they did, at least partially, rely on those stereotypes when judging students. Then why was there so little evidence of bias? If teachers relied on valid stereotypes when judging students, they would justifiably favor one group of students over another. They would have no tendency to exaggerate differences between the groups of students (this issue is addressed in more detail later in this chapter; see also Jussim, 1991).

D. WERE TEACHER PERCEPTIONS INFLUENCED BY ACCURATE OR INACCURATE STEREOTYPES?

The content study showed that teachers' perceptions of differences between students in the various groups mostly coincided with actual differences between the groups on comparable indicators. A follow-up study more deeply probed the processes by which teachers arrived at their judgments regarding students. We first developed a simple conceptual model for identifying whether teachers were relying on accurate stereotypes, inaccurate stereotypes, or no stereotypes when evaluating individual students. Additional analyses using the same MSALT data were performed to address the following two questions: 1) Did relying on an accurate stereotype facilitate accuracy in teacher perceptions? and 2) When teachers were inaccurate, did they inappropriately rely on their stereotype? To address these questions, two subquestions were examined: a) Did teachers rely on stereotypes when judging students? and b) If so, did relying on stereotypes enhance or undermine their accuracy? Thus, whereas the previous study focused exclusively on issues of content (e.g., did teacher perceptions of students from different groups coincide with real group differences), the next study focused on issues of process.

How can one discover whether teachers relied on stereotypes if stereotypes were not assessed? One can do so indirectly by using the methods first developed in experimental social psychological laboratory studies of stereotypes and person perception. Studies in this area typically include no assessment of stereotypes. Instead, social psychologists typically manipulate targets' social group membership, manipulate information about targets' personal characteristics or hold them constant, then assess whether perceivers judge targets from one group differently than targets from another group (e.g., Beckett & Park, 1995; Bodenhausen, 1988; Darley & Gross, 1983; Duncan, 1976; Krueger & Rothbart, 1988; Linville, 1982; Locksley et al., 1980; see reviews by Fiske & Neuberg, 1990; Fiske & Taylor, 1991; Hamilton et al., 1990; Jussim, 1990; Jussim et al., 1994). If perceivers do judge targets from different groups differently (holding targets' behavior or attributes constant), then perceivers are assumed to be relying on their group stereotypes when they are judging individual targets.

This is the strategy we used to determine whether teachers relied on stereotypes in evaluating their students. Analyses assessed whether teachers perceived differences based on student sex, social class, or ethnicity while students' achievement and motivation were held constant. Specifically, we performed a series of regressions in which students' performance and motivation, as well as their social group memberships, predicted teacher perceptions. Operationally, therefore, the "relied on stereotypes" hypothesis was that teacher perceptions would be based on student group membership, even after we controlled for student performance and motivation. First, however, we present a general conceptual model of the relationships between targets' attributes, targets' group memberships, and perceivers' judgments of targets.

E. MODELS OF THE ROLE OF STEREOTYPES IN ACCURACY AND INACCURACY IN PERSON PERCEPTION

The Basic Model in Figure 8 captures the main aspects of our approach to identifying the role of stereotypes in person perception. This model is a variation on the reflection–construction model proposed by Jussim (1991) as a general framework for identifying relations between social perception and social reality. The Basic Model is a flexible tool that can be used with experimental or naturalistic data to address one of the major theoretical issues concerning stereotypes and person perception: Are perceivers' judgments of the differences between individuals belonging to differing groups biased? This has been a paramount question since Locksley's (et al., 1980) controversial studies showing no bias in perceivers' judgments of assertive male and female targets. In Locksley's studies, and much subsequent research (e.g., Baron, Malloy, & Albright, 1995; Beckett & Park, 1995; Dar-

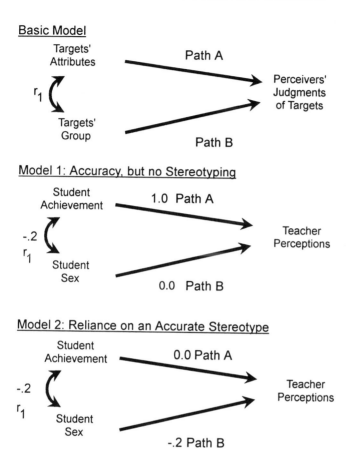

Fig. 8.   Hypothetical models of accuracy in teacher perceptions of differences between boys and girls. Teacher perceptions of sex differences are accurate when the size of the perceived difference between boys and girls equals the actual difference between boys and girls. The perceived difference (r2, not shown) is the correlation between teacher perceptions and student sex, which equals Path B + ($-.2 \times$ Path A). The actual sex differences equals $-.2$ (the correlation between student sex and student achievement).

ley & Gross, 1983; Jussim et al., 1987, 1995; Krueger & Rothbart, 1988; Linville, 1982; Linville & Jones, 1980), researchers have sought to discover whether and when perceivers' a priori beliefs about group differences bias their judgments regarding individual targets. Bias, in this research, refers to seeing targets from different groups as different, even when their personal attributes (individuating information) are identical.

The Basic Model incorporates the main ideas of this experimental laboratory paradigm, but also goes beyond them to allow for assessment of bias
even when the groups really are different. The model has three main
components: 1) the correlation between targets' attributes and their group
membership (r_1); 2) the influence of targets' attributes (i.e., individuating
information) on perceivers' judgments (Path A); 3) and the influence of
targets' group membership (i.e., perceivers' stereotype) on perceivers' judgments (Path B). For simplicity, we assume that Path A and B are standardized.

This Basic Model can be used to determine whether perceivers' reliance
on a stereotype enhances versus undermines the accuracy of their judgments
regarding differences between targets belonging to different groups. Assume that r_2 (not shown in the figure) is the correlation between perceivers'
judgments and targets' group membership. In this model, perceivers see a
difference that corresponds to the actual group difference when $r_2 = r_1$.

In all experimental laboratory research on stereotypes and person perception of which we are aware, r_1 is intentionally rendered zero. In this situation,
if perceivers think that groups really differ, and rely on their stereotype
when judging targets (i.e., if Path B > 0), then they will judge targets from
differing groups differently, even though they are, on the average, the same.
For example, they may judge a man as more assertive than a woman, even
though both targets engage in identical behaviors (Beckett & Park, 1995;
Krueger & Rothbart, 1988). In such cases (i.e., when Path B > 0), perceivers
"see" a difference between a particular man and a particular woman that
does not exist (i.e., $r_2 > 0$, even though $r_1 = 0$).

This model goes beyond the experimental laboratory research because
it shows that the comparison of r_2 to r_1 is a more general index of bias.
Even if there is a real difference between groups (i.e., $r_1 \neq 0$), the model
shows that bias occurs whenever $r_2 > r_1$. For example, even if men are, on
the average, more assertive than women (Swim, 1994), if perceivers judge
the difference between individual men and women targets to exceed the
real difference, their judgments are biased.

This model also shows that there are two separate routes to accuracy in
perceiving the differences between targets from differing groups. With a
few exceptions (Funder, 1995; Jussim, 1991) social psychology has, thus
far, only emphasized one route—judging targets on their personal attributes
(i.e., Path A). The experimental lab paradigm shows no difference between
groups, and perceivers will accurately perceive no difference if they judge
targets solely on their personal attributes. In terms of the Basic Model,
this is true because

$$r_2 = \text{Path B} + r_1 \,(\text{Path A}).$$

"Judging solely on their attributes" means that Path B (the stereotype effect) is zero, and that Path A is high. However, because r_1 (the real difference) is zero, r_2 (the perceived difference) will also be zero, meaning that perceivers see no difference between targets from differing groups. This "judging targets solely on their attributes" (Path A) route will also lead to accurate perceptions of group differences when the groups really do differ (i.e., $r_1 > 0$). Even if there is no stereotype effect (Path B is zero), r_2 (the perceived difference) approaches r_1 (the actual difference) as Path A becomes larger (see preceding equation). Sometimes, perceivers may accurately detect a difference between groups because there really is a difference between individuals from differing groups, not because perceivers are stereotyping.

The second and less well-known route to accuracy in perceptions of group differences is through Path B. Conceptually, Path B represents perceivers relying on a stereotype. How can relying on a stereotype lead to accurate perceptions of group differences? If Path A is zero (i.e., perceivers are oblivious to targets' personal attributes), and if Path B = r_1 (i.e., perceivers stereotype the groups as differing to the same extent that they actually differ), then $r_2 = r_1$ (i.e., the perceived difference corresponds to the actual difference; see preceding equation). This simple model shows that perceivers who rely on a valid stereotype will accurately judge the difference between targets from different groups, even if they completely ignore the targets' individual, personal characteristics. To put it somewhat differently, perceivers relying on an accurate stereotype could make numerous errors in judgments of individuals, yet still arrive at judgments that, when aggregated across the individuals in each group, correspond to the actual difference between the groups. Perceivers' judgments would be *influenced* by the stereotype without them being led to a bias for or against either group because they would see no greater differences between the individuals of differing groups than really exists.

1. Hypothetical Examples

Models 1 through 5 in Figures 8 and 9 present some hypothetical examples involving teacher perceptions and student sex in order to illustrate how the Basic Model can be used to distinguish between different aspects of accuracy and inaccuracy. Models 1 through 4 assume that there is a real difference between the achievement of boys and girls of $-.2$ (coding girls as 1 and boys as 2 results in a negative coefficient when girls perform better than boys, as they did on our grades measure). In these models r_2 = Path B $- .2$(Path A), where r_2 is the correlation of teacher perceptions with student sex.

Model 3: Inaccuracy -- The Stereotype is in the Wrong Direction

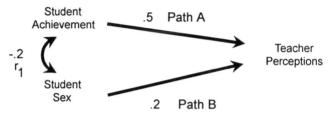

Model 4: Inaccuracy -- The Stereotype Exaggerates Differences

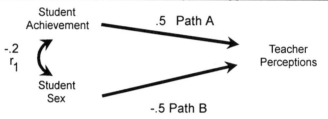

Model 5: Inaccuracy -- The Stereotype Assumes a Difference Where None Exists

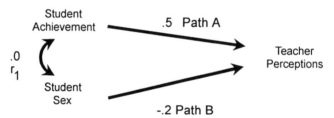

Fig. 9. Hypothetical models of inaccuracy in teacher perceptions of differences between boys and girls. Teacher perceptions of sex differences are inaccurate when the size of the perceived difference between boys and girls does not equal the actual difference between boys and girls. The perceived difference (r2, not shown) equals the correlation between teacher perceptions and student sex, which equals Path B + ([r{student sex, student achievement}] × Path A).

These models show that there are two ways for teachers to perceive an achievement difference between boys and girls that corresponds to the actual achievement difference. The first is shown as Model 1 in Figure 8. If teachers do not stereotype at all, but instead rely completely on achievement, then their perceptions will correlate $-.2$ with student sex. In Model 1, Path B = 0 (indicating no stereotyping at all) and Path A = 1.0 (indicating complete reliance on achievement information), so that

r_2 (the correlation of teacher perceptions with student sex)
$$= 0 - .2 \, (1.0) = -.2.$$

A second route to correspondence, however, is displayed in Model 2 of Figure 8. Even if teachers are oblivious to individual differences in student achievement, if they stereotype girls as performing better than boys (to an extent of $-.2$), then they may perceive a sex difference that corresponds in size to the actual sex difference. In Model 2, Path A = $\emptyset$ (indicating teacher obliviousness to achievement information) and Path B = $-.2$ (indicating a stereotype effect), so that

r_2(the correlation of teacher perceptions with student sex)
$$= -.2 - .2(0) = -.2.$$

Figure 9 displays three models showing how this approach can also identify teachers' reliance on an inaccurate stereotype. In Model 3, the stereotype is in the wrong direction (Path B is positive rather than negative). In this model, Path A = .5, and Path B = .2, so that

r_2(the correlation of teacher perceptions with student sex)
$$= .2 + (-2 \times .5) = .1.$$

In other words, teachers' stereotypes lead them to judge boys as performing better than girls, which is clearly incorrect because, in this example, girls perform better than boys.

In Model 4, teachers' stereotypes lead them to exaggerate real differences between the groups. In this model, Path A = .5, and Path B = $-.5$, so that

$$r_2 = -.5 + (-.2 \times .5) = -.6.$$

The perceived difference between boys and girls ($r_2 = -.6$) greatly exceeds the actual difference ($r_1 = -.2$). In Model 5, the stereotype involves perceiving a difference (Path A is $-.2$) when none exists (the correlation of achievement with sex, r_1, is zero):

$$r_2 = -.2 + 0(.5) = -.2$$

Although these models are quite simple, involving only three variables, the same principles apply when correlations are decomposed in more complex models (e.g., Alwin & Hauser, 1975). Similarly, although we chose to focus on student sex in these examples, identical principles and processes hold for other groups. Obviously, these models could also be used to assess conditions under which bias is more likely to occur, either by including product–interaction terms, or by estimating the models separately in each different condition.

2. A Surprising Implication

These models inexorably lead to an implication that runs counter to an assumption implicit in much published research on stereotypes (e.g., Beckett & Park, 1995; Bodenhausen, 1988; Darley & Gross, 1983; Krueger & Rothbart, 1988) showing that the influence of stereotypes on perceivers' judgments regarding targets is sufficient to demonstrate bias for or against a group. The models displayed in Figures 8 and 9, however, show that this is necessary but not sufficient to demonstrate bias. An influence of stereotypes on judgments of individual targets is systematic group bias when that influence leads perceivers to over- or underestimate the differences between individuals belonging to different groups (or when it leads perceivers to over- or underestimate how much individuals from differing groups vary, but this is an issue beyond the scope of the current paper).

Laboratory studies skirt this problem by holding targets' behavior constant or by rendering it orthogonal to group membership, which forces the correlation between group membership and behavior to be zero. However, as discussed previously, the correlation between group membership and individual behavior often is not zero in real life. For example, studies of the role of sex stereotypes in person perception (e.g., Beckett & Park, 1995; Krueger & Rothbart, 1988) have rendered aggressiveness orthogonal to target sex. Of course, on the average, men really are more aggressive than women (Eagly 1995; Swim, 1994). In terms of the models shown in Figures 8 and 9, in the experimental studies, r_1 is artificially rendered zero. However, with regard to sex and aggressiveness under naturalistic conditions, $r_1 \neq 0$.

Consider the implication when this finding is combined with another frequent finding in the stereotype and person perception area. Virtually every study that manipulates targets' group memberships and individuating information finds that individuating information influences judgments more powerfully than does group membership (see, e.g., Jussim, 1990, 1991; Jussim, Madon, & Chatman, 1994, for reviews). Consider the following hypothetical situation: 1) there is a real sex difference (e.g., $r_1 = .2$); 2) targets' behavior influences judgments (e.g., Path A = .5); and 3) sex directly influences judgments to a small extent (e.g., Path B = .1). In this example, equation 1 is:

$$r_2 = .1 + .2(.5) = .2.$$

Does the effect of sex on judgments represent bias in this situation? Holding all other aspects of this situation constant, would perceivers' judgments about the differences between boys and girls be more accurate if they did not use sex as a small basis of judgment? The answer to both questions, in this hypothetical situation, is no. The real sex difference is .2, and the perceived difference is .2. If perceivers did not use sex as a basis for judgment (i.e., if Path B was 0), the perceived difference would be only .1, which, of course, underestimates the real difference.

We hope to avoid being misinterpreted here. We are not claiming that stereotypes are generally accurate or that beliefs of unknown validity should influence social judgment. Furthermore, we doubt that there are any accurate stereotypes that are applicable to all members of the stereotyped group. Reliance on group membership, even when it correlates with target individuals' behavior and attributes, will always lead to less accurate impressions of individuals than will judging targets solely on the basis of their behavior or attributes if those behaviors or attributes are completely diagnostic of the characteristic being judged. Even when behavior or attributes are not perfectly diagnostic, relying on targets' category will usually produce many errors in judging individual targets.

However, error and bias are not always the same phenomenon. For example, perceivers may see some boys as more aggressive than they really are, and some girls as less aggressive than they really are. These are clearly errors. Of course, perceivers also may see some boys as less aggressive than they really are, and some girls as more aggressive than they really are. If perceivers' errors are systematic—if they are more likely to overestimate boys' aggressiveness and underestimate girls' aggressiveness—we would consider this to be a bias. However, if they are no more likely to overestimate than to underestimate boys' and girls' aggressiveness, there is no bias for or against either group (even if there are many within-group errors). This whole analysis requires comparison of perceivers' judgments to some criterion—in the absence of a criterion, there can be no determination about the existence of systematic bias for or against a group. Once one has criteria, though, there will be a possibility that the groups will actually differ in some ways. With these principles in mind, the process study examined the role of stereotypes in enhancing or undermining teachers' perceptions of students from the different demographic groups.

F. THE PROCESS STUDY

The content study showed that teachers' perceptions of students belonging to different demographic groups generally corresponded well with the real differences and similarities between those groups, although teachers' perceptions were sometimes biased. The process study went a step further, and examined *how* teachers came to judge students from differing groups as being similar or different.

Did teachers rely on students' demographic group memberships when judging them? If so, did such reliance influence the extent to which teacher perceptions of differences corresponded to the actual differences between the groups? These questions were addressed in a series of analyses assessing the influence of student sex, social class, and ethnicity on teacher perceptions. Except where otherwise stated, all analyses used students' previous grades and standardized test scores, self-concept of math ability, time spent on homework, and self-perceptions of effort to predict teacher perceptions (intrinsic and extrinsic value were also used in preliminary analyses but were almost completely unrelated to teacher perceptions). In addition, each analysis also included students' sex, social class, or ethnicity as predictors.

1. When Teacher Perceptions Were Biased

First, we consider the interpretations of the process analyses when the content study showed that teacher perceptions were biased. Teacher perceptions of effort favored girls, even though there was no evidence of sex differences in effort. Therefore, teachers could not have based their perceptions on individuating information. If teachers were basing their perceptions on stereotypes, the process study would have yielded a path coefficient similar in magnitude to, and of the same sign as, the zero-order correlation between teacher perceptions of effort and student sex.

Teachers also perceived the performance and talent of students in the predominantly African-American school district as favorably as they did those of other students, even though those other students received higher grades and higher standardized test scores. The process analyses should also have yielded small positive path coefficients linking student ethnicity to teacher perceptions of performance and talent. They should have been small because previous analyses showed bias only among a subset of African-American students (those in the predominantly African-American district). Moreover, the path coefficients should have been positive because African-American students were coded as 2, and Whites as 1. Positive coefficients mean that, given their performance, African-American students were viewed more favorably than others.

2. When Teacher Perceptions Were Accurate

Results from the content study have shown that many of the teachers' perceptions of the differences between students belonging to the differing groups were accurate. This held true for teachers' perceptions of boys' and girls' performance and talent; teachers' perceptions of SES differences in performance and talent; and teachers' perceptions of ethnic differences in performance, talent, and effort in the predominantly White districts.

The process study is not intended to reassess the accuracy of these perceptions—accuracy is an issue of content, not process, and has already been demonstrated. Drawing on the models in Figures 8 and 9, the process study is intended to assess how and why teacher perceptions became accurate. One possibility is that teachers relied on an accurate stereotype (a belief that groups differed to about the same extent that they actually differed). This possibility would be reflected in a path coefficient linking the student demographic variable to teacher perceptions that is similar in both sign and magnitude to the zero-order correlation between that demographic variable and teacher perceptions. Such a path coefficient would show that teachers by judging students according to their group membership had arrived at a perception of group differences that corresponded to existing actual group differences (of course, such a result is mute on the issue of accuracy and error within groups).

A second possibility is that teachers arrived at accurate perceptions of differences between students belonging to different demographic groups without relying on stereotypes. Instead, they may have relied exclusively on students' personal characteristics and accomplishments (individuating information). Because the groups really did differ on some of these variables, teacher perceptions of the groups would also differ if teachers used the individuating information. This possibility would be reflected in near-zero path coefficients linking student demographics to teacher perceptions, and high coefficients linking other student variables (grades, standardized test scores, effort, etc.) to teacher perceptions.

3. Gender Stereotypes

The main questions here were: 1) Would student sex predict teacher perceptions, independent of the other variables? and 2) If so, did the student sex effect enhance or undermine the accuracy of the teachers' perceptions of differences between boys and girls? Table VIII summarizes the results from these analyses. The results showed that teachers seemed to be relying on an accurate stereotype when judging students' performance. The *beta* relating student sex to teacher perceptions of performance was −.09, which closely corresponded to the sex differences in grades of −.07 (found in the content study). Although teachers did judge students on the basis of their performance, doing so was not the main source of the correlation between teacher perceptions and student sex, despite the fact that girls did get better grades than boys. The small independent effect of student sex on teacher perceptions accounted for most of the small correlation between sex and

TABLE VIII
DID TEACHERS RELY ON STUDENTS' SEX, INDEPENDENT OF STUDENTS'
ACHIEVEMENT AND MOTIVATION?

	Betas relating to teacher perceptions of:		
Predictors	Performance $R^2 = .47*$	Talent $R^2 = .47*$	Effort $R^2 = .32*$
Student sex	−.09*	.02	−.16*
Fifth-grade final marks	.23*	.21*	.22*
Standardized test scores	.36*	.42*	.25*
Self-concept of math ability	.22*	.18*	.15*
Effort self-perceptions	.05*	.00	.11*
Time spent on homework	−.06*	−.05*	−.02

$*p < .01$.
$N = 1789$ (942 girls and 847 boys).
Betas are standardized regression coefficients.
(From Jussim, L., McCauley, C. R., & Lee, Y. T. (1995). Why study stereotype accuracy and inaccuracy? In Y. T. Lee, L. Jussim, & C. R. McCauley (Eds.), *Stereotype accuracy: Toward appreciating group differences*. (pp. 3–27). Copyright © 1995 by the American Psychological Association. Reprinted with permission.)

teacher perceptions. This means that teachers apparently stereotyped girls as performing slightly higher than boys, independent of the actual slight sex differences in performance. However, the extent to which teachers did so corresponded reasonably well with the small sex difference in performance. In other words, teachers perceptions of differences between boys and girls were accurate because teachers relied on an accurate stereotype.

Results for teacher perceptions of talent provided no evidence of teachers relying on a stereotype. The *beta* relating student sex to teacher perceptions of talent was .02 (*ns*), corresponding closely to the 0.0 correlation of student sex with standardized test scores.[9]

[9] The lack of a perceived difference for talent may seem to conflict with our previous research (Jussim, 1989; Jussim & Eccles, 1992) showing that student gender significantly predicts teacher perceptions of talent. However, there is no real conflict. The current analyses differ from others that we have reported previously in one crucial way. The older studies also allowed teacher perceptions of performance to predict teacher perceptions of talent and effort, whereas the current analyses do not. For example, in Jussim and Eccles (1992), the effect of gender on teacher perceptions of talent was .08; the effect of gender on teacher perceptions of performance was −.10; and the effect of teacher perceptions of performance on teacher perceptions of talent was .64. The total effect of gender on teacher perceptions of performance in Jussim and Eccles (1992), therefore, was .08 + (−.10*.64) = .02, which corresponds exactly to the result reported here.

Results for teacher perceptions of effort suggested reliance on an inaccurate stereotype. The *beta* relating student sex to teacher perceptions of effort was $-.16$ ($p < .001$), even though the correlations of student sex with self-concept of ability, time spent on homework, and self-perceptions of effort were .09, $-.03$, and 0.0, respectively. Teachers apparently erroneously stereotyped girls as trying harder, despite the similarities between boys' and girls' actual effort, and despite boys' higher self-concept of ability.

4. Social Class Stereotypes

Analyses were identical to those examining teachers' sex stereotypes, except that instead of student sex, these analyses included parental education and income in the equations predicting teacher perceptions of performance, talent, and effort. Results are presented in Table IX.

These analyses provided no evidence that teachers relied on social class stereotypes. The R^2 increment associated with adding family income and education to the regression equations never exceeded .002 and was never statistically significant (all F's < 2.3, all p's $> .1$). Of the six possible individ-

TABLE IX

DID TEACHERS RELY ON STUDENTS' SOCIAL CLASS, INDEPENDENT OF STUDENTS' ACHIEVEMENT AND MOTIVATION?

	Betas relating to teacher perceptions of:		
Predictors	Performance $R^2 = .48**$	Talent $R^2 = .48**$	Effort $R^2 = .30**$
Parental income	$-.02$	.00	.00
Parental education	.02	.05*	.02
Fifth-grade final marks	.26**	.21**	.27**
Standardized test scores	.35**	.42**	.21**
Self-concept of math ability	.20**	.16**	.11**
Effort Self-perceptions	.09**	.03	.13**
Time spent on homework	$-.06*$	$-.05*$	$-.03$

*$p < .05$.
**$p < .01$.
$N = 1066$.
Betas are standardized regression coefficients.
(From Jussim, L., McCauley, C. R., & Lee, Y. T. (1995). Why study stereotype accuracy and inaccuracy? In Y. T. Lee, L. Jussim, & C. R. McCauley (Eds.), *Stereotype accuracy: Toward appreciating group differences.* (pp. 3–27). Copyright © 1995 by the American Psychological Association. Reprinted with permission.)

ual relations between income and education and the three teacher perception variables, only one was statistically significant (education predicted teacher perceptions of talent, $p < .05$) but the *beta* was trivially small (.05). Apparently, the accuracy of teacher perceptions of social class differences in performance, talent, and effort occurred because teachers evaluated students on the basis of their achievement and motivation—factors which correlated with social class.

5. Ethnic Stereotypes

The main analysis included 1588 White students and 76 African-American students. (Again, because we used previous standardized test scores as a control, and because students in the ethnically mixed district did not take a standardized test in fifth or early sixth grade, they were not included in this analysis.) For this group, the correlations of ethnicity with grades and standardized test scores were $-.12$ and $-.14$, respectively (both p's $< .001$). Ethnicity was coded Whites $= 1$ and African-Americans $= 2$, so these small negative correlations mean that, overall, White students had somewhat (but not dramatically) higher grades and standardized test scores than did African-American students.

Table X presents the results of the regression analysis predicting teacher perceptions. These results consistently show small but *positive* relations

TABLE X
DID TEACHERS RELY ON STUDENTS' ETHNICITY, INDEPENDENT OF STUDENTS' ACHIEVEMENT
AND MOTIVATION?

Predictors	Betas relating to teacher perceptions of:		
	Performance $R^2 = .46$****	Talent $R^2 = .48$****	Effort $R^2 = .29$*****
Student ethnicity	.05**	.11****	.10***
Fifth-grade final marks	.24****	.21****	.24****
Standardized test scores	.32****	.44****	.26****
Self-concept of math ability	.20****	.17****	.10****
Effort self-perceptions	.03	.02	.10****
Time spent on homework	−.06**	−.05**	−.03

*$p < .05$.
**$p < .01$.
***$p < .001$.
****$p < .0001$.
$N = 1664$ (1588 White students and 76 African-American students).
Betas are standardized regression coefficients.

between ethnicity and teacher perceptions (.05, .11, and .10, respectively, for teacher perceptions of performance, talent, and effort, all p's < .01). This means that teachers perceived African-American students slightly more favorably than they perceived White students with similar achievement histories and motivational patterns.

These results, however, do not necessarily represent bias in the sense of teachers evaluating the African-American students in their classes more favorably than similar White students. It seemed likely that this pattern largely reflected differences between the predominantly African-American district and the other districts. To test this possibility, we ran another set of regressions. These were identical to the first with one exception: They excluded the 53 students in the predominantly African-American district. Although there were only 23 African-American students remaining, this analysis directly tested whether teachers were biased in favor of African-American students over White students. In this analysis, all three *beta*s relating ethnicity to teacher perceptions were reduced to .04 (although with the large overall *N,* they were still statistically significant or marginally significant). These results provide little evidence of bias in favor of African-American students over White students. Instead, they show that the main source of the apparent positive bias was the teachers in the predominantly African-American district (who evaluated their students as favorably as the other students, despite poorer performance).

To increase the number of African-American students, we performed one additional analysis. Still excluding the predominantly African-American school district, we did not use standardized test scores that had been used before as predictors of teacher perceptions. This allowed us to include the students in the ethnically mixed district. These analyses, which included 1873 White students and 37 African-American students, also yielded no evidence that teachers relied on ethnicity. The three *beta*s relating ethnicity to teacher perceptions were all below .03, and none were even marginally significant.

G. ACCURACY IN TEACHER PERCEPTIONS OF STUDENTS FROM DIFFERING DEMOGRAPHIC GROUPS: CONTENT AND PROCESS

The process study provided some clear insights into the reasons why the results of the content study showed such minimal evidence of bias. With a few notable exceptions, teachers based their perceptions of students on those students' actual performance and motivation. Student social class did not influence teacher perceptions, after controls were used for students' actual achievement and motivation. Nor did ethnicity, except for the slightly favorably biased ratings that teachers gave to the African-American students in the predominantly African-American district. Similarly, student sex had no influence on teacher perceptions of talent, after controls were used for students' actual achievement and motivation (although student sex did influence teacher perceptions of performance and effort—which we discuss later). These results clearly show that teachers did not rely on stereotypes to arrive at these judgments of students. Teachers were either oblivious to sex, class, and ethnic stereotypes, or they did not apply their stereotypes when evaluating their students.

Teachers probably were not oblivious to three of the major stereotypes in American culture. The cumulative wisdom of years of social psychological research on stereotypes instead points to the second explanation—that teachers did not apply their stereotypes in their evaluations of students. Thus, our results are consistent with abundant laboratory and field research showing that perceivers evaluate targets far more on the basis of targets' personal characteristics, than on targets' membership in social groups (e.g., Krueger & Rothbart, 1988; Linville, 1982; Locksley et al., 1980; see Fiske & Neuberg, 1990; Jussim, 1990, 1991, 1993, for reviews). In general, the more individuating information perceivers have, the less they rely on stereotypes (Eagly et al., 1991; Krueger & Rothbart, 1988; Locksley et al., 1980). Of course, teachers interacting with students over the first month of the school year generally have considerably more (and probably more objective) individuating information about students than do subjects in even the most ecologically valid laboratory experiment. Therefore, perhaps it should come as no surprise that, in general, these teachers did not rely much on their stereotypes when evaluating students.

There were a few exceptions to this pattern. In the case of student sex, teachers did seem to rely on their stereotypes regarding performance. They apparently evaluated students' performance based on their sex, independent of their actual achievement. However, the extent to which they did so yielded a relationship between student sex and teachers' perceptions that corresponded well with actual prior sex differences in achievement. It is important to highlight just what this means. Because even a valid stereotype does not apply equally well to all members of the stereotyped group, teachers probably misperceived some boys and girls. However, it also means that there was no tendency to systematically over- or underestimate the performance of girls as compared to boys.

In contrast, however, teachers seemed to be relying on an inaccurate stereotype in evaluating boys' and girls' effort. Teachers' more favorable impressions of girls' effort probably occurred because, on the average, girls are more cooperative and pleasant than boys, and because teachers prefer more cooperative and pleasant students (e.g., Brophy & Good, 1974; Bye,

1994; Wentzel, 1989). This is consistent with a growing body of literature showing that school is often a hostile place for low-achieving boys. For example, at least some teachers believe that boys suffer from inferior verbal skills, and this belief may become self-fulfilling (Palardy, 1969). Similarly, boys are referred for psychological evaluations far more often than girls, even when the teachers themselves do not rate boys as any more aggressive or in need of psychological services than girls (Bye, 1994). Similarly, one usually finds far more boys than girls in "special education" classes (Bye, 1994). Moreover, boys often receive lower grades than girls, even when their performance on standardized achievement tests are similar (Kimball, 1989).

In fact, this discussion highlights the possibility that affect, rather than or in addition to stereotypes, was driving the effort bias in favor of girls. Recent research on stereotypes and expectancies has suggested a more important role for affect (liking or disliking groups or individuals) in the occurrence of biased judgments and self-fulfilling prophecies (Esses, Haddock, & Zanna, 1993; Jussim et al., 1995; Rosenthal, 1989). Thus, if, on average, girls are more pleasant and cooperative than boys, teachers may come to like girls more than boys (on the average), and this may at least partially contribute to teachers' favorable views of girls' effort.

Teachers' reliance on an inaccurate sex stereotype regarding effort may also reflect attributional biases. Adults often are more likely to attribute females' math achievement to their effort than to their high ability (Yee & Eccles, 1988). Because teachers rated girls' performance slightly higher than that of the boys, but rated their talent the same, teachers may have needed to see girls as trying harder than boys to explain girls' higher performance level.

VIII. If the Cause Was Not Stereotype Bias, Then Why Were Expectancy Effects More Powerful Among Lower-SES and African-American Students, and Girls?

The previous section had two purposes. Our broader purpose was to provide some empirical evidence on the extent to which stereotypes bias person perception. A narrower purpose, which we hope did not get lost in the broader one, was to examine teacher stereotypes as a possible source of the greater expectancy effects among girls, lower SES students, and African-American students. However, we found so little evidence of stereotype-based biases that inaccurate stereotypes did not seem to be a particularly viable explanation for the pattern of differential expectancy effects. Thus, the question remained: Why are expectancy effects more powerful among some stigmatized demographic groups?

The next sections address this issue. First, we examine (and rule out) the possibility that teachers develop less accurate perceptions of students from stigmatized social groups. Second, we discuss another study showing that students with low self-concepts of ability or histories of low achievement in math, much the same as students from stigmatized groups, are considerably more vulnerable to self-fulfilling prophecies—a finding broadly consistent with Steele's (1992) perspective on African-Americans' disidentification with school and with research on students' vulnerability to school transition effects (Midgley et al., 1989).

A. WERE TEACHERS' PERCEPTIONS OF STUDENTS FROM STIGMATIZED GROUPS LESS ACCURATE?

One possibility is that, even if teachers were not particularly biased against these groups, they could still be less accurate in perceiving them. Thus, they may not systematically over- or underestimate the ability and performance of students from differing backgrounds. However, their errors, both positive and negative, might be larger for girls, low SES students, and African-American students. This may explain the pattern of differential expectancy effects because more inaccurate expectations have the potential to create larger self-fulfilling prophecies than more accurate expectations.

We performed another series of analyses to test this possibility. Specifically, we used the variables in the Base Model (except the teacher perceptions), plus one of the demographic characteristics, to predict the three teacher perception variables. We then examined the absolute value of the residuals produced by such an analysis. The residuals indicate whether teachers overestimate (positive residuals) or underestimate (negative residuals) particular students' performance, talent, and effort. Of course, because the demographic variable is controlled, its correlation with the raw residuals will be zero. Nonetheless, there still may be group differences in the absolute values of the residuals. For example, residuals of $+8$ and -8 for two girls, and $+4$ and -4 for two boys, will be uncorrelated with student sex. Obviously, however, in this hypothetical example, teachers are more accurate in perceiving boys than in perceiving girls.

For student sex, however, these analyses (Base Model, plus student sex predicting teacher perceptions of performance, talent, and effort) yielded no evidence that teachers were less accurate in perceiving girls. The correlations of student sex with the absolute value of the residuals were .03, $-.01$, and .09 for performance, talent, and effort, respectively (p's = $ns, ns,$ and .001), indicating that teachers were slightly less accurate in perceiving boys (girls and boys were coded as 1 and 2, respectively). This, therefore, cannot possibly account for the larger teacher exepctancy effect on grades among girls.

A similar pattern emerged for social class. The multiple correlations of income and education with the absolute value of the residuals from the models predicting teacher perceptions (Base Model plus income and education) were .05, .02, .07, for teacher perceptions of performance, talent, and effort, respectively, (all p's = $>$ .05). Thus, there was no evidence that teachers held more erroneous perceptions regarding lower SES students.

The results for ethnicity showed that teachers did hold slightly more inaccurate perceptions of African-American students than of White students. The correlations of ethnicity with the absolute values of the residuals from the models predicting teacher perceptions were .06, ($p <$ .05), .07 ($p <$ .05), and $-$.02 (ns) for performance, talent, and effort, respectively. Although greater error may have contributed to the stronger expectancy effects among African-American students, these differences are so small that they probably represent only a small or minor contribution.

B. MORE ON WHY: SELF AND PREVIOUS ACHIEVEMENT AS MODERATORS

The aforementioned findings indicate that teachers are about as accurate in perceiving girls as boys, lower SES as upper SES students, and African-American as White students. Therefore, greater inaccuracy cannot explain much, if any, of the greater expectancy effects among these students.

Then what does explain these greater expectancy effects? Perhaps something about these students (rather than something about their teachers) renders them more susceptible to expectancy effects. Perhaps students from stigmatized groups have fewer social and psychological resources for resisting teacher expectations. Their families may be less involved in their education (see, e.g., Lareau, 1987, regarding social class), rendering them more susceptible to the influence of other adult figures (such as teachers). The stresses associated with poverty and low income (single parent households, neighborhood crime and drug abuse, etc.) may reduce psychological resistance to teachers' influence. Students who face a relentless barrage of negative teacher expectations may "disidentify" with school (Steele, 1992) and may even take a certain pleasure in confirming teachers' negative expectations (Jussim, 1986). Perhaps a supportive teacher who holds students to higher standards may be seen as such a breadth of fresh air that many students are inspired to achieve more highly.

Although direct measures of students' social and psychological resources were not available, we did test these ideas indirectly. If lower SES and

African-American students (and to a lesser extent, girls) were more susceptible to expectancy effects because they had fewer resources to resist such
expectations, then other students with fewer resources should also be more
susceptible to expectancy effects. Who might such students be? Those who
lack confidence and have histories of low achievement.

1. Self-Concept

Working with the same MSALT data and using essentially the same
Base Model and procedures much like those described earlier for assessing
moderation, we examined whether students' self-concepts moderated expectancy effects (Madon, Jussim, & Eccles, 1995). Using procedures much
the same as those reported here, we found that the self-fulfilling effects of
teacher perceptions were considerably stronger among students with lower
self-concepts of math ability than among student with higher self-concepts
of math ability. For example, for students whose self-concept was one
standard deviation below the sample mean, the standardized coefficient
relating teacher perceptions of performance to MEAP scores was .24,
whereas it was only .10 for students whose self-concept was one standard
deviation above the sample mean.

2. Previous Achievement

In much the same way, students with a history of low achievement might
also be more susceptible to expectancy effects. For example, Midgley et
al. (1989) examined the self-concepts and self-expectations for both low-
and high-achieving adolescents as they made the transition from elementary
school-based sixth grades to junior high school-based seventh grades. About
40% of the students moved from sixth-grade teachers with a high sense of
efficacy for their own teaching ability to seventh-grade teachers who had
doubts about their ability to teach low-skill students. Another 20% moved
in the opposite direction—from sixth-grade teachers who doubted their
ability to teach low-skill students to seventh-grade teachers who were confident in their ability to teach students of all ability levels. The pattern of
change in self-perceptions of the high-achieving students was not affected
by which type of teacher transition they experienced. In contrast, the pattern
of change in the low-achieving students' self-perceptions were significantly
linked to the type of change they experienced in their teachers' expectations.
If they moved to a high-expectancy teacher, their own self-perceptions
increased in the seventh grade. In contrast, if they moved to a low-expectancy teacher, their own self-perceptions decreased.

Why might low-achieving students be more susceptible to teacher expectancy effects? One possibility is that because low-achieving students feel less positive about their academic competence and are less certain of their future success than high-achieving students, these students may be more extrinsically motivated (Harter & Connell, 1984). Students who are more extrinsically motivated are likely to rely more on the teacher for motivation and for interpreting evaluative feedback, which makes these students more susceptible to teacher expectancy effects.

The work by Steele (1992) provides another possible explanation. When students "disidentify" with school, a history of low academic achievement may not be strongly reflected in their global self-esteem (Steele, 1992). Students seem most likely to disidentify with school when school becomes a painful place (either because of failure or cultural devaluation; see Steele, 1992). Disidentification means, in part, investing less energy in school work, which consequently leads to lower academic performance. It also means devaluing the importance of school achievement to one's self-worth. Thus, such students can maintain high self-esteem in the face of difficulties in school. This, in part, may help to explain why African-American students, despite lower levels of academic achievement, do not score lower on self-esteem measures than do White students (Crocker & Major, 1989).

Students with a history of low achievement may respond much the same as students with low self-esteem. Their motivation may be readily undermined by failure (or low teacher expectations), but be dramatically enhanced by a supportive and demanding teacher. We (Madon et al., 1995) have confirmed the hypothesis that self-fulfilling prophecies are stronger among low achievers than among high achievers. In this study, low achievement was operationalized as scores one standard deviation below the sample mean on standardized tests or previous grades and high achievement was operationalized as scores one standard deviation above the sample mean on standardized tests or previous grades. The standardized regression coefficient relating teacher perceptions of performance to MEAP scores was .28 for low achievers and .04 for high achievers. Similarly, the standardized regression coefficient relating teacher perceptions of performance to sixth-grade final marks was .24 for low achievers and .16 for high achievers.

3. Multiple Vulnerabilities

We also performed a series of follow-up analyses to determine whether the self-concept and achievement moderation effects we observed were independent of one another, and independent of the demographic moderation we described previously in this chapter. Because these analyses were quite complex, we only summarize our main findings here.

First, we assessed the independence of moderation by self-concept and by previous achievement. A set of analyses including both sets of moderators (self-concept by teacher perceptions, and previous achievement by teacher perceptions) showed that only the achievement moderators significantly predicted MEAP scores and sixth-grade final grades. The self-concept by teacher perception product terms did not significantly predict either students' future grades or MEAP scores in models that also included the previous achievement by teacher perception product terms.

Overall, therefore, these results indicate that achievement rather than self-concept is an active moderator of expectancy effects. Nonetheless, these results do not undermine the conclusion that students with lower self-concepts are more vulnerable to expectancy effects. They do help to explain why. Self-concept of ability is substantially correlated with actual performance (.41 with previous standardized test scores and .45 with previous grades). Students with records of lower previous achievement, who are the most vulnerable, are more likely also to have lower self-concepts of ability.

We also considered whether the moderating effects of achievement were similar for some of the differing demographic groups of students. However, because of the small number of African-American students, models with three-way product terms for ethnicity by previous achievement by teacher perceptions would not have yielded meaningful results. We did, however, examine whether the overall patterns of achievement moderation were similar for girls and boys, and for students from different SES backgrounds.

First, we created three-way product terms combining achievement, sex, and teacher perceptions and added these to the Base Model plus all lower-order two-way product terms. Neither the block of three-way terms nor any of the individual three-way terms significantly predicted either final grades or MEAP scores. These results indicated that the pattern of achievement moderation was similar for boys and girls.

Next, we examined whether the pattern of achievement moderation was similar for groups of students from different socioeconomic backgrounds. Again, we created three-way product terms combining achievement, SES, and teacher perceptions and added them to the Base Model plus all lower-order two-way product terms. None of the three-way terms (individually or as a block) significantly predicted grades, indicating that the pattern of achievement moderation was similar for groups of students from differing SES backgrounds.

However, the three-way product term combining parental education, students' previous standardized test scores, and teacher perceptions of performance did significantly ($p < .01$) predict MEAP scores. Examination of the regression coefficients showed that the relation of teacher perceptions of performance to MEAP scores was much higher (2.46 unstandardized, .62 standardized) for students with a history of lower achievement and with parents who did not complete high school than for any other combination of SES and previous achievement (coefficients ranging from .50 to 1.08, unstandardized, and .13 to .27 standardized).[10] The .62 standardized coefficient for low-achieving students from lower SES backgrounds, like the coefficients we observed relating teacher perceptions to achievement among African-American students, is one of the most powerful expectancy effects yet observed.

Overall, therefore, these results showed that low math achievers (who also tend to have lower self-concepts of math ability), much the same as low SES and African-American students, were more susceptible to self-fulfilling prophecies. Moreover, our results also showed that students with multiple vulnerabilities are more susceptible to self-fulfilling prophecies than are students with only one vulnerability.

IX. Other Moderators

Our quest for identifying conditions under which expectancy effects are large has only just begun. Undoubtedly, researchers will discover many conditions other than student demographics, self-concept, and previous achievement. Next, therefore, we discuss three classes of factors that may influence expectancy effect sizes: 1) characteristic of the perceiver; 2) characteristics of the target; and 3) situational factors.

A. PERCEIVER CHARACTERISTICS

1. Goals

Perceivers' goals may moderate the influence of their expectations on targets (Hilton & Darley, 1991). Self-fulfilling prophecies are more likely to occur when perceivers desire to arrive at a stable and predictable impression of a target (Snyder, 1992), when perceivers are more confident in the

---

[10] These coefficients were derived in the same way that the coefficients were derived in the earlier section on demographic moderation (see footnote 4). To obtain the coefficients reported here, we operationalized low parental education as "some high school," and high education as having completed a college BA. Low achievement was operationalized as performing at the 10th percentile of our sample, and high achievement was operationalized as performing at the 90th percentile of our sample. The coefficients for each of the four combinations of SES and previous achievement reported in the text were based on the results of the full model, which included the Base Model, the significant three-way product term, and all lower-order two-way product terms.

validity of their expectations (Jussim, 1986; Swann & Ely, 1984), and when they have an incentive for confirming their beliefs (Cooper & Hazelrigg, 1988). Self-fulfilling prophecies and perceptual biases are less likely when perceivers are motivated to develop an accurate impression of a target (Neuberg, 1989), when perceivers' outcomes depend on the target (Neuberg, 1994), and when perceivers' main goal is to get along in a friendly manner with targets (Snyder, 1992). Perceptual biases are more likely when perceivers strive to rapidly reach a particular conclusion (Kunda, 1990; Neuberg, 1994; Pyszczynski & Greenberg, 1987). These findings raise the following question: When are perceivers likely to be motivated by accuracy or a desire to get along in a friendly manner, and when are they likely to be overconfident in their beliefs or motivated by desires to reach a particular conclusion?

2. Prejudice, Cognitive Rigidity, and Belief Certainty

Prejudiced individuals seem especially unlikely to be motivated by either accuracy concerns or the desire to get along with members of the group they dislike. Instead, they seem likely to desire to reach the particular conclusion that members of the stigmatized group have negative, enduring attributes (Pettigrew, 1979). People high in cognitive rigidity or belief certainty also may not be motivated to consider different viewpoints. Cognitive rigidity, which is usually construed as an individual difference factor (e.g., Adorno, Frenkel-Brunswick, Levinson, & Sanford, 1950; Allport, 1954; Harris, 1989), and belief certainty, which is usually construed as a situational factor (Jussim, 1986; Swann & Ely, 1984), are both similar in that they describe people who may be unlikely to alter their beliefs when confronted with disconfirming evidence. Whether the source is prejudice, cognitive rigidity, or belief certainty (which may tend to co-occur with individuals; see Adorno et al., 1950), people overly confident in their expectations may be most likely to maintain biased perceptions of individuals and to create self-fulfilling prophecies (Babad, Inbar, & Rosenthal, 1982; Harris, 1989; Swann & Ely, 1984).

3. Other Individual Differences

Experienced perceivers may be less likely to create self-fulfilling prophecies. We use the term "experienced" here in two different but related senses. One aspect of experience refers to time on the job or in one's role. Thus, for example, more experienced teachers, therapists, doctors, and so forth have probably developed considerably more competence and expertise at appraising people such as students, clients, and patients. If so, then their impressions may be more accurate. The second sense in which we use "experience" involves perceivers' experience with targets. When perceivers have greater information and more opportunities to interact with targets, they have greater opportunity to develop accurate beliefs. Thus, perceivers who have had more information about or experience with particular targets are also likely to be more accurate. Of course, accuracy reduces the potential for self-fulfilling prophecies.

Another such moderator may be professional efficacy. In general, efficacy refers to beliefs concerning one's ability to engage in the behaviors necessary for accomplishing a particular goal (Bandura, 1977). Professional efficacy, therefore, refers to beliefs regarding one's ability to engage in the behaviors necessary for accomplishing the essential work of one's profession. For example, teaching efficacy would refer to beliefs regarding one's ability to teach. When teachers are less confident in their teaching ability (low teaching efficacy), they may be more likely to create expectancy effects. Teachers low in teaching efficacy may feel less able to improve the skills of low-expectancy students; consequently, they may spend less time and effort with such students than do teachers high in teaching efficacy (Midgley et al., 1989). By virtue of spending less time with low-expectancy students (and perhaps more time with high-expectancy students), teachers low in teaching efficacy may exacerbate differences between high- and low-expectancy students to a greater extent than do teachers high in teaching efficacy (Midgley et al., 1989). A similar analysis could be readily applied to other professions (e.g., clinicians, managers, etc.).

A need to control others may also moderate expectancy effects. For example, the more that teachers strive to control students, the more likely it may be that their expectancies will be self-fulfilling and biasing. A high emphasis on control may include a particularly strong preference for having one's expectations confirmed. Control implies predictability, so unpredictable situations (or students) may be perceived as implying a lack of control. When students disconfirm expectations, therefore, teachers who emphasize control may feel threatened. These teachers may be most motivated to "ensure" that students confirm their expectations. This analysis is consistent with a less well-known finding of the original Rosenthal and Jacobson (1968) study: Some teachers responded especially negatively to the successes of students not specifically designated as late-bloomers.

B. TARGET CHARACTERISTICS

1. Goals

Targets may become more or less susceptible to self-fulfilling prophecies, depending on their goals. When perceivers' have something targets want (such as a job), and when targets are aware of the perceiver's beliefs, they often confirm those beliefs in order to create a favorable impression (von Baeyer et al., 1981; Zanna & Pack, 1975). Similarly, when targets desire to facilitate smooth social interactions, they are also more likely to confirm perceivers' expectations (Snyder, 1992). In contrast, when targets believe that perceivers hold a negative belief about them, they often act to discomfirm that belief (Hilton & Darley, 1985). Similarly, when their main goal is to defend a threatened identity, or to express their personal attributes, targets are also likely to disconfirm perceivers' inaccurate expectations (Snyder, 1992).

2. Age

Self-fulfilling prophecies were strongest among the youngest students in the original Rosenthal and Jacobson (1968) study, suggesting that younger children may be more malleable than older children and adults. However, a meta-analysis has shown that the strongest teacher expectation effects occurred in the first, second, and *seventh* grades (Raudenbush, 1984). Further, the largest self-fulfilling prophecy effects yet reported were obtained in a study of adult Israeli military trainees (Eden & Shani, 1982). Although these findings do not deny a moderating role for age, they do suggest that situational factors may also influence targets' susceptibility to self-fulfilling prophecies.

C. SITUATIONAL FACTORS

1. New Situations

People may be more susceptible to confirming others' expectations when they enter new situations. Whenever people engage in major life transitions, such as entering a new school or starting a new job, they may be less clear and confident in their self-perceptions. Unclear self-perceptions render targets more susceptible to confirming perceivers' expectations.

This analysis may help to explain the seemingly inconsistent findings regarding age. Students in the first, second, and seventh grades, and new military inductees, are all in relatively unfamiliar situations. Therefore, all may be more susceptible to self-fulfilling prophecies.

2. Class Size and Resources

Expectancy effects may be more likely in classrooms with large numbers of students than they are in smaller classrooms. People are more susceptible to biases when more of their "cognitive capacity" is being used—when they are trying to do several things at once (Gilbert & Osborne, 1989). The more students in a class, the more "cognitively busy" the teacher is likely to be, and, therefore, the more susceptible to biases and expectancy effects.

A related moderator may be class and school resources. Not only do resources (access to books, computers, laboratories, indoor and outdoor athletic facilities, fine arts, etc.) create a more generally pleasant learning environment; they probably make it easier for teachers to manage the students in their classes. Consequently, they, too, may be less likely to be cognitively overloaded, and, therefore, less suceptible to self-fulfilling prophecies.

At least one study (Finn, 1972) found results consistent with this perspective on class size and resources. Finn (1972) found that teacher expectations influenced the grades they assigned, but only in urban schools (not in suburban schools). Although urban and suburban schools differ in many dimensions, two differences often are class size (suburban schools often have smaller class sizes) and resources (suburban schools are often wealthier).

3. Tracking

School tracking refers to the policy of segregating students into different classes according to their ability. For example, smart students may be assigned to one class, average students to another, and slow students to a third. Tracking may be intended as a prosocial intervention. By putting students with similar capacities together, teachers have the opportunity to tailor their lessons in a way that maximizes those students' learning and achievement.

However, tracking may also moderate expectancy effects. Tracking represents institutional justification for believing that some students are smart and others are not. Due to our cultural beliefs regarding the meaning of low ability, particularly in math and science, tracking essentially provides students and teachers with an explanation for the students' low skill level that absolves both the student and the teacher of responsibility for continued learning. Thus, it may lead to the type of rigid teacher expectations that are most likely to evoke self-fulfilling prophecies and perceptual biases (Eccles & Wigfield, 1985; Jussim, 1986, 1990).

In addition, poor quality instruction may occur in at least some low-tracked courses. In part, this is a consequence of student characteristics. These classes are harder to manage, and traditional teaching techniques are not likely to be successful. However, teachers' expectations can also exacerbate the poor environment. If teachers think that low-skill children cannot learn, or do not want to learn, they may reduce their teaching efforts (Allington, 1980; Evertson, 1982)—exactly the behavior that often leads to self-fulfilling prophecies (Harris & Rosenthal, 1985).

This situation is indeed unfortunate, considering the somewhat arbitrary nature of student placement in tracks, particularly for students of color and students from lower social class backgrounds (Dornbusch, 1994). In addition, when low-skill students were moved up in their track placement, both teacher expectations and students' actual performance on standardized tests improved (Tuckman & Bierman, 1971). In addition, the teachers in this study recommended that most of the students remain in the higher track the following year. These results suggest that long-term differences in the performance level of students in different tracks may reflect expectancy effects as well as ability differences. More field-based studies are needed to test this hypothesis.

X. Accumulation

Even if expectancy effects are small within a single school year, if such effects accumulate over several years, they may produce dramatic differences among students. Consider two students starting the sixth grade with identical IQs of 100. Nevertheless, the sixth-grade teacher believes that one student is bright and the other is dull. Assume that teacher expectations have an effect (in terms of standardized regression coefficients) of only .2 on student achievement. Further assume that the student believed to be bright by her sixth-grade teacher is believed to be bright by teachers in subsequent years, and that the student believed to be dull by her sixth-grade teacher is believed to be dull by her subsequent teachers.

An effect of .2 is equivalent to 1/5 of a standard deviation, and the standard deviation of IQ tests is 15. If a self-fulfilling prophecy increases the IQ of the high-expectancy student by only three points per year, and decreases the IQ of the low-expectancy student by only three points per year, by the end of high school, the "bright" student will have an IQ of 115, the "dull" student an IQ of 85. This is the power of "small" effects that accumulate!

The assumption that small effects accumulate lies at the heart of many strong claims regarding the power of expectations to create social reality. Such claims are usually based on experimental laboratory studies (see reviews by Jones, 1986; Snyder, 1984), even though they involve a single, brief interaction among strangers (e.g., Snyder et al., 1977; see Jussim, 1991, for a review of these claims). The accumulation issue is particularly relevant to social stereotypes. Widely shared social stereotypes may lead many different perceivers to hold similar expectations for targets who are "marked" by some sort of stigma (race, handicap, institutional labels). Consequently, even if the self-fulfilling effects of perceivers' expectations are small within a single interaction, such effects may accumulate over many years and become a major source of individual differences.

However, do expectancy effects actually accumulate? Instead, perhaps they dissipate over time. Even if a teacher does create a 6-point IQ difference between two students, perhaps the next year that difference will tend to lessen or disappear completely. We know of only four studies that have empirically assessed the accumulation of expectancy effects. These are discussed next.

A. ROSENTHAL AND JACOBSON (1968)

Rosenthal and Jacobson (1968) manipulated teachers' expectations in the first year by randomly selecting students and designating them as "late bloomers." However, in the second year, teachers developed expectations without direct intervention by the experimenters. The accumulation hypothesis predicts that there would be greater differences between "late bloomers" and controls in the second year than in the first year. In fact, the opposite was found: The differences between these students significantly declined after two years. On the average, "late bloomers" had a 3.80 IQ point advantage over controls at the end of the first year, but only a 2.67 IQ point advantage at the end of the second year.

B. RIST (1970)

Rist (1970, described previously) followed a class of kindergarten students through second grade. Unfortunately, he provided no quantitative information regarding students' learning, IQ scores, or achievement in first or second grade. Thus, it is impossible to determine whether expectancy effects accumulated. Although Rist (1970) concluded that he had observed a rigid cast-like system based on social class, which suggests large and powerful accumulation effects, his own observations actually suggest dissipation instead. As did the kindergarten teacher, the first-grade teacher assigned students to three tables (apparently according to her beliefs about the smart, average, and dumb students). All of the Table 1 ("smart") students in kindergarten were assigned to Table 1 in first grade. However, students at Tables 2 and 3 in kindergarten were all assigned to Table 2. Thus, if table assignment is the criterion, kindergarten differences between Tables 2 and 3 disappeared by first grade, although differences between those children and Table 1 students were maintained.

Rist (1970) reported further reduction of apparent differences in second grade. In the second-grade class, the students who had been assigned to Table 1 in first grade were all assigned to their own table (they were referred to as "tigers"). Students who had been assigned to Tables 2 and 3 in first grade, in the second-grade class were assigned to a second table (referred to as "cardinals"). None of the students from the first-grade glass Rist observed were assigned to the "slow" table (called "clowns"). In addition, Rist (1970) observed that in January, two of the tigers were moved to the cardinals' table, and two of the cardinals were moved to the tigers' table. Thus, although some of the differences among students in kindergarten were maintained through second grade, overall differences between the groups seem to have declined.

C. WEST AND ANDERSON (1976)

West and Anderson (1976) examined relationships between teacher expectations and student achievement in a period running from the freshman through the senior year of high school. The accumulation hypothesis predicts that the coefficients relating freshman-year teacher expectations to senior-year achievement will be larger than those relating freshman-year teacher expectations to sophomore-year achievement. However, their results showed dissipation: The coefficient relating freshman-year teacher expectations to senior-year achievement (.06) was smaller than the coefficient relating to sophomore-year achievement (.12).

D. FRIEZE ET AL. (1991)

Frieze et al. (1991) addressed the accumulation issue by comparing the extent to which the attractiveness of MBAs predicted starting salary versus salary in 1983 (several years later). The unstandardized coefficients relating attractiveness to 1983 salary (2.60 for men and 2.13 for women) were higher than those relating to starting salary (1.13 and 0.28, respectively). Whether these results indicate accumulation of self-fulfilling prophecy effects or accumulation of greater rewards to more socially skilled managers (as discussed previously, the more attractive tend to be more socially skilled), however, is unclear.

These are the only four studies (Frieze et al., 1991; Rist, 1970; Rosenthal & Jacobson, 1968; West & Anderson, 1976) to our knowledge that have directly assessed whether expectancy effects accumulate. These paint a decidedly mixed picture, and all have major conceptual or methodological limitations (see also Elashoff & Snow, 1971; Jussim & Eccles, 1995). Although expectancy effects may accumulate over time, there is currently no evidence clearly demonstrating that they actually do. Strong, empirical evidence on this issue is sorely needed.

E. CONCURRENT ACCUMULATION EFFECTS

The sparce empirical research on accumulation effects has all focused on accumulation over time. However, it is also possible that, within a single time frame (e.g., 1 school year), the effects on targets of multiple perceivers' expectations may accumulate. To distinguish such effects from the accumulation of expectancy effects over time, we refer to these as "concurrent accumulation effects."

The notion of concurrent accumulation effects is implicit in most perspectives that emphasize the potentially self-fulfilling nature of social stereotypes (e.g., Deaux & Major, 1987; Hamilton et al., 1990; Jones, 1990; Snyder, 1984). Because stereotypes are often shared, multiple perceivers will often develop similar expectations for individual members of the stereotyped group. Perceiver after perceiver will presumably heap self-fulfilling prophecy after self-fulfilling prophecy upon stereotyped targets.

Such a perspective appears to imply that the self-fulfilling prophecy effects observed in most individual studies probably underestimate the true extent to which individual targets' are influenced by others' expectancies, because all previous research has focused on the potentially self-fulfilling effects of only one perceiver on each target. If multiple perceivers influence targets, then one might expect that, in the course of daily life, people would be more influenced by self-fulfilling prophecies than is implied by existing research.

Figure 10 presents a simplified general model of concurrent accumulation effects. The model includes two self-fulfilling prophecy paths: Path A (linking one perceiver's expectations to targets) and Path B (linking other perceivers' expectations to targets). r_1 is the correlation between perceivers' expectations. The displayed models are simplified in three ways. First, if there are many "other perceivers," there really could be many more paths and correlations. Second, none of the control variables necessary to actually assess expectancy effects are displayed. Third, we assume all paths are standardized.

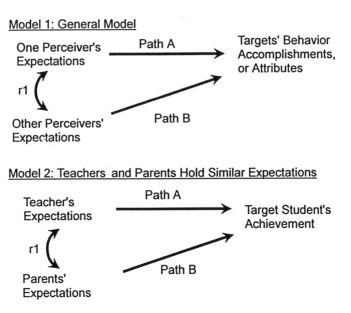

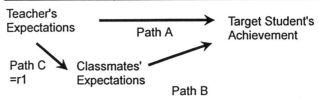

Fig. 10.   Models of concurrent accumulation of expectancy effects. For simplicity of presentation, none of the models displayed here include the control variables that would be necessary to actually assess expectancy effects.

Nonetheless, simply making this model explicit leads to some surprising insights. Model 2 presents a concrete hypothetical example. The model assumes that both teachers' expectations and parents' expectations have self-fulfilling effects on students (Paths A and B, respectively). The similarity between parents' and teachers' expectations is represented by r_1. One might be tempted to conclude that studies focusing only on effects of teacher expectations, for example, would underestimate total expectancy effects because they do not assess effects of parents' expectations.

Figure 10 shows that such a conclusion is not warranted. This analysis is a variant on the omitted variable problem (see our earlier discussion of limitations to naturalistic research on expectancies). In the hypothetical teacher expectation study shown in Model 2, parental expectations correlate with teacher expectations and also cause student outcomes. If effects of parental expectations are not explicitly included in the model, the effects of teacher expectations will be overestimated. In fact, the estimated path coefficient linking teacher expectations to student achievement will equal

$$\text{Path A} + (r_1 * \text{Path B}).$$

Conceptually, the teacher expectation–student achievement coefficient will be biased upward precisely to the extent that parent expectations overlap with teacher expectations and parent expectations themselves cause student outcomes. In other words, the coefficient linking teacher expectations to student achievement will also include the self-fulfilling effect of parental expectations, to the extent that parent and teacher expectations overlap. If they do not overlap, there is no potential for concurrent accumulation, even if parent and teacher expectations are both self-fulfilling.

Model 3 presents another variation on this idea. In this example, teacher expectations cause both classmates' expectations and target students' achievement. However, if classmates' expectations are not assessed, the estimated path coefficient linking teacher expectations to student achievement will equal

$$\text{Path A} + (\text{Path C} * \text{Path B}).$$

In this case, failure to assess the classmates' mediating paths does not "overestimate" teacher expectation effects at all. Model 3 is a classic example of a direct and indirect effects model (e.g., Alwin & Hauser, 1975; see Jussim, 1991, for several examples applied to social perception and expectancies). The total effect of teacher expectations on student achievement equals the sum of its direct effect (Path A) and its indirect effect (Path C * Path B). In other words, if there are important mediators, even if they are not assessed, the total effect of teacher expectations on student achievement simply equals the path coefficient linking them. In this situation, there is no underestimation of concurrent accumulation.

This analysis leads to several surprising conclusions. Studies that assess effects of only a single perceiver's expectations on each target are not likely to be underestimating concurrent expectancy effects. If there is any bias, it is likely to be in overestimating the effects of the expectations of the perceivers who are included in the study. However, as indicated in the models displayed in Figure 10, the estimated effects on targets of individual perceivers who are included in the study should approximate the total self-fulfilling effect of all perceivers (even those excluded from the study) whose expectations overlap with those of the included perceivers. Thus, studies of individual perceiver–target relationships probably do not underestimate the accumulation of concurrent self-fulfilling prophecies.

One caveat is in order. Concurrent accumulation requires different perceivers to hold similar expectations for the target. This is captured by r_1 in the models in Figure 10. Concurrent accumulation generally will underestimate the total extent to which targets are influenced by self-fulfilling prophecies, because perceivers will rarely hold identical expectations for those targets. To the extent that perceivers hold different expectations for the target, even if their expectations are self-fulfilling, there will be little net accumulation. For example, consider Fred, who is neither introverted nor extraverted. Let us assume, furthermore, that two of Fred's friends believe him to be extraverted and two other friends believe him to be introverted. If all of their expectations are approximately equally self-fulfilling, overall, there will be no accumulation—he will remain neither particularly introverted nor very extraverted.

XI. Conclusion

A. ARE SELF-FULFILLING PROPHECIES OFTEN POWERFUL AND PERVASIVE?

This article has described our own and others' research documenting three main phenomena. First, claims about the power of expectancy effects notwithstanding, current evidence from both naturalistic and experimental studies indicates that, in general, self-fulfilling prophecies are not very powerful (see reviews by Brophy, 1983; Eccles & Wigfield, 1985; Jussim, 1991; Jussim & Eccles, 1995; Wineburg, 1987; see also meta-analyses by Raudenbush, 1984; Rosenthal & Rubin, 1978). To date, only naturalistic studies have attempted to compare the extent to which perceivers' expectations predict targets' behavior because those expectations are accurate versus self-fulfilling. These studies consistently show that teacher perceptions predict student achievement more because those perceptions are accurate than because they lead to self-fulfilling prophecies. The little research that has addressed naturally occurring expectancy effects outside of the classroom generally yields similar findings (see Jussim & Eccles, 1995, for a review).

Despite this repeatedly documented pattern of high accuracy and low self-fulfilling prophecy (see reviews by Brophy, 1983; Brophy & Good, 1974; Jussim, 1990, 1991, 1993; Jussim & Eccles, 1995; Jussim et al., 1994), many social psychological perspectives focusing primarily on experimental research often assume or conclude that self-fulfilling prophecies are common and even powerful (e.g., Fiske & Taylor, 1991; Hamilton et al., 1990; Jones, 1986, 1990; von Hippel et al., 1995). To the extent that the criterion for arriving at such conclusions is the evidence regarding what happens under naturalistic conditions, we would argue that it is time for social psychology to discard its belief that expectancy effects are generally powerful and pervasive.

B. WHEN ARE TEACHER EXPECTATION EFFECTS MORE POWERFUL?

This, of course, does not mean that expectancy effects are never powerful. Since we first discovered this pattern of high-accuracy and low-expectancy effects in our own initial studies (Jussim, 1989; Jussim & Eccles, 1992), we have been on a quest to identify conditions under which expectancy effects are more powerful. We have actually uncovered quite a few (these are the second major phenomena we have documented in this article). Expectancy effects are considerably stronger among students from stigmatized groups (African-Americans, lower SES, and, to a smaller extent, girls), and among students with low self-concepts and records of poor previous achievement. It is likely that different processes partially account for each of these groups' greater susceptibility to expectancy effects. However, we have speculated that reduced social and psychological resources for combating erroneous teacher expectations may at least partially underlie the greater susceptibility to expectancy effects that characterizes each of these groups.

C. THE ROLE OF STEREOTYPES IN TEACHERS' PERCEPTIONS OF STUDENTS

The third major contribution of this chapter has been to provide some of the first evidence regarding the role of stereotypes in naturally occurring person perception. Although the role of stereotypes in person perception has been a hot topic (e.g., Beckett & Park, 1995; Bodenhausen, 1988; Darley & Gross, 1983; Krueger & Rothbart, 1988; Locksley et al., 1980, 1982; Nelson, Biernat, & Manis, 1990), there has been little naturalistic research addressing the question (see Jacobs & Eccles, 1992, for an exception). Thus, another contribution of the research described in this article is to provide some of the first empirical evidence regarding the extent to which stereotypes bias person perception among real people making real decisions in real situations. We think the time is ripe for a flood of naturalistic social psychological studies addressing this issue.

Our results show that, in general, teacher perceptions of sex, social class, and ethnic differences and similarities were highly accurate. Such results would seem to contrast with much emphasis on stereotypes biasing social perception (e.g., Fiske & Neuberg, 1990; Fiske & Taylor, 1991; Hamilton et al., 1990; Jones, 1986, 1990; Stangor, 1995). Although we did find some evidence of bias, for the most part, teachers' perceptions of the groups closely corresponded to the group members' grades, achievement, and motivation. Such findings are actually consistent with a number of perspectives all arguing that stereotypes may be either accurate or inaccurate, and that, in general, issues of stereotype accuracy and inaccuracy are considerably more complex than once thought (see, e.g., Ashmore & Longo, 1995; Brigham, 1971; Eagly, 1995; Fox, 1991; Judd & Park, 1993; Jussim, 1990; Jussim et al., 1995; Mackie, 1973; McCauley et al., 1980; Oakes, Haslam, & Turner, 1994; Ottati & Lee, 1995; Ryan, 1995).

We also presented a simple theoretical model for addressing issues of both content and process in stereotyping. The model shown in Figures 8 and 9 may be used to identify whether perceivers' judgments of the differences between individual members of different groups actually corresponds to the existing group differences, if there are any (see also Beckett & Park, 1995; Jussim, 1991). This model is also useful for determining the extent to which judgments were based on individuating information versus social category membership, and shows that people's use of categorical information does not necessarily lead people to unfairly favor one group over another. When individuating information is less than perfectly diagnostic, and when there are real differences between groups, perceivers who base their judgments of individual targets on those targets' social category will arrive at more valid perceptions of group differences than perceivers who do not base their judgments on those targets' social category (see also Funder, in press; Jussim, 1991; Kahneman & Tversky, 1973).

Of course, we are not claiming that either our model or our empirical results show that bias, prejudice, and discrimination do not exist or are unimportant. Obviously, they do exist, and they are terribly important. However, it is also possible that person perception biases produced by stereotypes exist to a smaller extent than one might assume on the basis of the experimental laboratory research. To challenge the tentative hypothesis that biases produced by stereotypes outside of the laboratory may not be that powerful, social psychologists will have to move their research programs out of their laboratories and investigate stereotype-induced biases in naturally occurring situations.

D. BIAS AND DISCRIMINATION WITHOUT EXPECTANCY EFFECTS

It is also possible that bias and discrimination may be manifest in ways very different from those assessed in the current studies, or that they must be assessed in a manner different from that of the typical social psychology laboratory experiment. Barriers may exist to equal employment opportunities, even in the complete absence of employer bias. For example, different social networks may constitute one such barrier (e.g., Braddock & McPartland, 1987). We live in a (still) highly segregated society—Whites are more likely to associate with Whites; African-Americans are more likely to associate with African-Americans. Whites hold more managerial jobs, and job openings are often filled through informal networks. Because Whites are more likely to be "plugged in" to such networks, they will have greater job opportunities. This may occur even if White employers judge the applicants who come to their attention solely on their merits.

E. SELF-FULFILLING PROPHECIES WITHOUT BIASED OR INACCURATE PERCEIVERS

Similarly, stereotypes may create self-fulfilling prophecies that are in no way the fault of the individual perceiver. A series of studies by Zanna (von Baeyer, Sherk, & Zanna, 1981; Zanna & Pack, 1975) showed that when women believed they were to be interviewed by a traditional or sexist man, they often acted in such a way as to confirm sex stereotypes. One reason these studies are interesting is that many of the dependent variables (how much make-up and accessories the women wore, their performance on a test, etc.) were all assessed prior to the interview (which, in the case of Zanna & Pack, 1975, never took place). Similarly, when targets believed that perceivers viewed them as mentally ill, even if perceivers were blind to targets' mental health status, targets actually evoked more rejection from those perceivers (e.g., Farina, Allen, & Saul, 1968; Farina, Gliha, Boudreau, Allen, & Sherman, 1971). These are still self-fulfilling prophecies in the sense that stereotypes create their own reality. However, the self-fulfilling prophecy trigger in these studies is not the beliefs held by bigoted or error-prone perceivers—it is targets' beliefs about how perceivers view them.

Steele's (1992) analysis of disidentification as a source of African-American underachievement is also consistent with this perspective. Steele argued that, because the cultural milieu devalues African-Americans, they are wounded more deeply by scholastic difficulties than are other students. Note, however, that Steele's analysis predicts African-American underachievement, even if African-American students never take a class with a biased teacher (see also Fordham & Ogbu, 1986). Cultural stereotypes may have a life of their own, and may create self-fulfilling prophecies even when individual perceivers do not.

F. BEYOND THE DYAD: SELF-FULFILLING PROPHECIES AT ORGANIZATIONAL, INSTITUTIONAL, AND SOCIETAL LEVELS OF ANALYSIS

In addition to culturally based self-fulfilling prophecies, institutional policies may also create self-fulfilling prophecies. For example, Merton (1948) documented how, in the early part of this century, most labor unions barred African-Americans from membership. Union members often claimed that African-Americans were strikebreakers and could not be trusted. This severely limited the job opportunities of African-Americans. When faced with a strike, companies often offered jobs to all takers, and African-Americans often jumped at the chance for work. Thus, the union's beliefs about African-Americans were confirmed. It is important to note, however, that if an individual union member, acting alone, held this stereotype of African-Americans, it would have had no effect at all on reducing the job opportunities of African-Americans.

In fact, Merton's (1948) original analysis of self-fulfilling prophecies focused primarily on broad-based sociological patterns and institutional practices. However, self-fulfilling prophecies are probably considerably more easily studied as a dyadic interaction level phenomenon (and, of course, it is important at the dyadic level, too). Elsewhere, however, we (Jussim & Fleming, in press) have attempted to update Merton's (1948) analysis by identifying ways in which modern institutional practices create self-fulfilling prophecies. We have suggested that school tracking may contribute to ethnic self-fulfilling prophecies, that funding schools through local property taxes may contribute to social-class self-fulfilling prophecies, and that the allocation of academic rewards (jobs, article acceptances, etc.) are characterized by self-fulfilling prophecies based on institutional prestige.

In the spirit of Merton's (1948) original essay, we (Jussim & Fleming, in press) have speculated that a sociological level analysis of self-fulfilling prophecies might contribute to understanding the 1992 Los Angeles riots. These riots, among the most destructive civil disturbances of this century, are often considered to be a response to the perceived injustice of the "not guilty" verdicts returned in the case against the police officers who beat Rodney King, an African-American motorist. The riot surely resulted from the interplay of many social forces, and a three-step self-fulfilling prophecy analysis may contribute to understanding some sources of the riots.

The first step is expectations: Many Whites have historically held, and continue to hold, negative stereotypes about many minority groups (see reviews by Allport, 1954; Marger, 1991). These beliefs probably contributed to the second step: discrimination. In the last 20 years, Whites have seemingly become less sympathetic to social programs, such as school desegregation and affirmative action, that are designed to provide greater educational and occupational opportunities for minorities (Marger, 1991). Through blatant and subtle forms of discrimination, many Whites continue to limit and undermine the quality of life for many minority groups.

Discrimination may lead to the final step in this self-fulfilling prophecy— riots—in several ways. First, discrimination may create a deep resentment among many minority group members, a resentment that may be triggered by certain conditions into riotous behavior. Second, discrimination probably reduces support for the general social structure. For example, many African-American teenagers may not vigorously pursue high educational achievement because 1) high achievement may be seen as "acting White" and as rejecting one's own ethnic group (e.g., Fordham & Ogbu, 1986; Steele, 1992); or 2) as a result of later job discrimination, education is seen as producing little or no economic payoff. People who have not greatly invested in the social system are probably more likely to take whatever they can get away with when a golden opportunity, such as a riot, appears. Thus, even when the rioters were inspired more by self-interest than by abstract political agendas, discrimination probably played an important role. This type of violent, antisocial behavior, of course, confirms for many Whites the validity of their negative beliefs about minorities.

Of course, we are not claiming that this type of self-fulfilling prophecy analysis completely accounts for such a large-scale and complex social phenomenon as the Los Angeles riots. Furthermore, empirical research that actually documents such sociological self-fulfilling prophecies is considerably more difficult to perform than research on dyadic self-fulfilling prophecies. However, we suspect that at least sometimes, such effects may be quite powerful.

G. WHENCE RESEARCH ON SELF-FULFILLING PROPHECIES?

Social scientists have learned much about self-fulfilling prophecies in the 50 years since Merton (1948) coined the term and in the 30 years since

Rosenthal & Jacobson (1968) triggered an explosion of interest in the area. We know that the phenomenon is indeed real (an issue that was hotly contested through the 1970s (see, e.g., Elashoff & Snow, 1971, or the commentaries on Rosenthal & Rubin's 1978 meta-analysis). We also know much about how they happen (see reviews by Brophy, 1983; Darley & Fazio, 1980; Eccles & Wigfield, 1985; Jussim, 1986; Rosenthal, 1974; see Harris & Rosenthal, 1985, for a meta-analysis) and something of the conditions under which they are more or less likely. Next, therefore, we offer some suggestions regarding potentially fruitful directions for future research on self-fulfilling prophecies.

1. Moderators

In the last 15 years, much research on self-fulfilling prophecies has focused on moderators (e.g., Brattesani, Weinstein, & Marshall, 1984; Neuberg, 1989; see reviews by Neuberg, 1994; Snyder, 1992; see meta-analyses by Cooper & Hazelrigg, 1988; Raudenbush, 1984). Social scientists are only beginning to understanding how the power of self-fulfilling prophecies depends on characteristics of perceivers, targets, and situations. Research on moderators, therefore, is likely to continue to contribute important insights into the role of expectancies in creating social reality and social problems.

2. Mediators

Research on mediators has consistently supported Rosenthal's (1974) four-factor theory (see Jussim, 1986, for a review; see Harris & Rosenthal, 1985, for a meta-analysis). The four-factor theory claims that perceivers act on their expectations in four broad classes of ways that can be described in these terms: climate, feedback, input, and output. Perceivers provide more socioemotional warmth (climate), clearer and more positive feedback (feedback), spend more time with and lavish more attention on (input), and provide more opportunities for high achievement to (output) high-expectancy targets. Perhaps because this pattern has been so well documented, there has been little research on mediators in the last 10 years.

However, other types of mediators have been underexplored. In performance situations, abundant research attests to the power of setting high goals for students, employees, and athletes, to name a few groups (Locke & Latham, 1990). However, whether high expectations often lead perceivers to explicitly set higher goals for targets is not known. However, even if perceivers do not set explicit goals for targets, perceivers may sometimes explicitly convey high expectations, which may have an effect much the same as setting high goals. However, both the extent to which perceivers do this and its effect on targets, is currently unknown.

Two recent studies suggest that the role of affect in driving "expectancy" effects has been underexplored. The first found that children were less warm, friendly, and involved when playing with other children who were stigmatized (Harris, Milich, Corbitt, Hoover, & Brady, 1992). The second found that perceivers' liking or disliking of (prejudice toward) a target's group was a more potent source of biases in judgments of that target's sanity than were perceivers' beliefs (stereotypes) about that group (Jussim et al., 1995).

In addition, the results of several classic self-fulfilling prophecy studies may be readily interpreted as the result of perceivers' affect. For example, in the classic Snyder et al. (1977) study, college men were more pleasant to the supposedly attractive college women. The interpretation of Snyder et al. (1977) was that the men's behavior was triggered by the physical attractiveness stereotype. Perhaps, however, many of the college-age men liked the supposedly attractive women because of their beauty per se and gave little thought to their personal characteristics. Similarly, in Word et al.'s (1974) classic study of race-based self-fulfilling prophecies, many of the behavioral mediators (more speech errors, greater distance, shorter interview to African-American applicants) seemed to reflect anxiety or dislike more than beliefs. Also, much of what drives teacher-expectancy effects may be that teachers like high-expectancy students more than they like low-expectancy students (Rosenthal, 1989; see also Olson, Roese, & Zanna, in press, for a review of how expectancies influence affect).

Another underexplored mediator is targets' beliefs about perceivers' beliefs. A few experiments have shown that targets sometimes confirm the beliefs that they (erroneously) think perceivers hold (Farina et al., 1968, 1971; von Bayer et al., 1981; Zanna & Pack, 1975). The general question here is: How important is targets' awareness (accurate or not) of perceivers' expectations? We speculate that although awareness is not a necessary mediator of self-fulfilling prophecies (i.e., self-fulfilling prophecies may occur without target awareness of the perceivers' expectancies), awareness will often tend to enhance the power of self-fulfilling prophecies, especially among children and people in new situations. Of course, targets may sometimes intentionally resist confirming expectations when they believe that a perceiver holds inappropriate expectations (Hilton & Darley, 1985; Swann & Ely, 1984). Understanding the role of target awareness in self-fulfilling prophecies, then, poses an important question for both mediation and moderation studies.

3. Naturalistic Research Beyond Teachers and Students

To date, naturalistic studies of expectancies have focused almost exclusively on teachers and students (see Jussim & Eccles, 1995, for a review). There have only been a very few naturalistic studies of self-fulfilling prophecies in other areas (Berman, 1979; Frieze et al., 1991; Jacobs & Eccles, 1992). Although research on teacher expectations will remain important, naturalistic research on expectancy effects among parents and children, employers and employees, clinicians and patients, and so on is greatly needed in order to understand the extent and power of self-fulfilling prophecies in daily life.

4. Accumulation and Sociological Level Self-Fulfilling Prophecies

We believe that the accumulation issue is inherently linked to sociological level self-fulfilling prophecies and to self-fulfilling prophecies resulting from targets' beliefs about the beliefs of others. At the sociological level, many negative stereotypes are widely shared, so that targets will frequently confront others' unfavorable views of them. They may also sometimes face social policies designed to exclude them from full equality with other citizens (e.g., in the United States, neither the federal government nor most states have civil rights laws providing equal protection for gays and lesbians). When group membership is physically salient (gender, race/ethnicity, attractiveness, disability, etc.) the potential for dyadic-level bias, blatant or subtle (e.g., glass ceilings), is increased. Moreover, for many such groups, the societal-cultural discourse focuses on some alleged inferiority (e.g., the ongoing festering and inflammatory "debate" over whether Blacks are intellectually inferior to Whites genetically; the presumption of many people that women and minorities in positions of power and prestige got there through unfair and preferential selection procedures). It does not seem particularly far-fetched to suggest that members of such groups may eventually either internalize some of these beliefs (e.g., Heilman, Simon, & Repper, 1987), become more deeply wounded by the failures that accrue to almost everyone (Steele, 1992), or themselves develop an (at least sometimes) inaccurate but ultimately self-fulfilling expectation that others hold negative views of them. Empirical research on the accumulation of the effects of socially, institutionally, and organizationally shared beliefs and discourses could begin to fulfill the promise of Merton's (1948) original sociological level analysis of self-fulfilling prophecies.

Acknowledgments

This research was supported by NICHD Grant 1 R29 HD28401-01A1 to the first author. Data collection was funded by grants to the second author from NIMH, NICHD, and NSF. We gratefully acknowledge the participants of the 1994 Bryn Mawr Conference on Stereotype Accuracy for their suggestions regarding the stereotype studies. We thank Dan Hart and Victor Ottati whose comments and ideas inspired several additional analyses. We also thank the following people for aid in collecting and processing the data: Bonnie L. Barber, Christy Miller Buchanan, Harriet Feldlaufer, Connie Flanagan, Janis Jacobs, Dave Klingel, Doug MacIver, Carol Midgley, David Reuman, and Allan Wigfield. Finally, we thank the personnel in all of the participating schools for their help in data collection.

References

Adorno, T., Frenkel-Brunswick, E., Levinson, D., & Sanford, R. N. (1950). *The authoritarian personality.* New York: Harper.

Allington, R. (1980). Teacher interruption behavior during primary grade oral reading. *Journal of Educational Psychology, 72,* 371–377.

Allport, F. H. (1955). *Theories of perception and the concept of structure.* New York, Wiley.

Allport, G. (1954). *The nature of prejudice.* Cambridge, MA: Addison-Wesley.

Alwin, D., & Hauser, R. M. (1975). The decomposition of effects in path analysis. *American Sociological Review, 40,* 37–47.

Ambady, N., & Rosenthal, R. (1992). Thin slices of expressive behavior as predictors of interpersonal consequences: A meta-analysis. *Psychological Bulletin, 111,* 256–274.

American Association of University Women (AAUW). (1992). *How schools shortchange girls.* American Association of University Women Education Foundation.

American Psychological Association. (1991). In the Supreme Court of the United States: Price Waterhouse v. Ann B. Hopkins (Amicus curiae brief). *American Psychologist, 46,* 1061–1070.

Andersen, S. M., & Bem, S. L. (1981). Sex typing and androgeny in dyadic interaction: Individual differences in responsiveness to physical attractiveness. *Journal of Personality and Social Psychology, 41,* 74–86.

Archer, D., & Akert, R. M. (1977). Words and everything else: Verbal and nonverbal cues in social interpretation. *Journal of Personality and Social Psychology, 35,* 443–449.

Ashmore, R. D., & Del Boca, F. K. (1981). Conceptual appraoches to stereotypes and stereotyping. In D. L. Hamilton (Ed.), *Cognitive processes in stereotyping and intergroup behavior* (pp. 1–35). Hillsdale, NJ: Erlbaum.

Ashmore, R. D., & Longo, L. C. (1995). The accuracy of stereotypes: Considerations suggested by research on physical attractiveness. In Y. T. Lee, L. Jussim, & C. R. McCauley (Eds.), *Stereotype accuracy: Toward appreciating group differences* (pp. 63–86). Washington, DC: American Psychological Association.

Babad, E., Inbar, J., & Rosenthal, R. (1982). Pygmalion, Galatea, and the Golem: Investigations of biased and unbiased teachers. *Journal of Educational Psychology, 74,* 459–474.

Bandura, A. (1977). Self-efficacy: Toward a unifying theory of behavioral change. *Psychological Bulletin, 84,* 191–215.

Baron, R. M., Albright, L., & Malloy, T. E. (1995). The effects of behavioral and social class information on social judgment. *Personality and Social Psychology Bulletin, 21*, 308–315.

Beckett, N. E., & Park, B. (1995). Use of category versus individuating information: Making base rates salient. *Personality and Social Psychology Bulletin, 21*, 21–31.

Berman, J. S. (1979). Social bases of psychotherapy: Expectancy, attraction, and the outcome of treatment. (Doctoral disertation, Harvard University). *Dissertation Abstracts International, 40,* 5800B.

Bodenhausen, G. V. (1988). Stereotypic biases in social decision making and memory: Testing process models of stereotype use. *Journal of Personality and Social Psychology, 55,* 726–737.

Borkenau, P., & Liebler, A. (1992). Trait inferences: Sources of validity at zero acquaintance. *Journal of Personality and Social Psychology, 62,* 645–657.

Braddock, J. H., & McPartland, J. M. (1987). How minorities continue to be excluded from equal employment opportunities: Research on labor market and institutional barriers. *Journal of Social Issues, 43,* 5–40.

Brattesani, K. A., Weinstein, R. S., & Marshall, H. H. (1984). Student perceptions of differential teacher treatment as moderators of teacher expectation effects. *Journal of Educational Psychology, 76,* 236–247.

Brewer, M. B. (1979). In-group bias in the minimal group situation: A cognitive motivational analysis. *Psychological Bulletin, 86,* 307–324.

Brewer, M. B. (1988). A dual-process model of impression formation. In R. S. Wyer, Jr., & T. K. Srull (Eds.), *Advances in social cognition* (pp. 1–36). Hillsdale, NJ: Erlbaum.

Brigham, J. C. (1971). Ethnic stereotypes. *Psychological Bulletin, 76,* 15–38.

Brophy, J. (1983). Research on the self-fulfilling prophecy and teacher expectations. *Journal of Educational Psychology, 75,* 631–661.

Brophy, J., & Good, T. (1974). *Teacher-student relationships: Causes and consequences.* New York: Holt, Rinehart and Winston.

Bruner, J. S. (1957). Going beyond the information given. In H. Gruber, K. R. Hammond, & R. Jessor (Eds.), *Contemporary approaches to cognition.* Cambridge, MA: Harvard University Press.

Bye, L. (1994). Referral of elementary age students for social skill training: Student and teacher characteristics. Doctoral dissertation, Rutgers University, New Brunswick, NJ.

Carlson, R. (1984). What's social about social psychology? Where's the person in personality research? *Journal of Personality and Social Psychology, 47,* 1304–1309.

Cooper, H. (1979). Pygmalion grows up: A model for teacher expectation, communication, and performance influence. *Review of Educational Research, 49,* 389–410.

Cooper, H., & Hazelrigg, P. (1988). Personality moderators of interpersonal expectancy effects: An integrative research review. *Journal of Personality and Social Psychology, 55,* 937–949.

Covington, M. V., & Omelich, C. L. (1979). Effort: The double-edged sword in school achievement. *Journal of Educational Psychology, 71,* 169–182.

Crocker, J., & Major, B. (1989). Social stigma and self-esteem: The self-protective properties of stigma. *Psychological Review, 96,* 608–630.

Cronbach, L. J. (1955). Processes affecting scores on "understanding of others" and "assumed similarity." *Psychological Bulletin, 52,* 177–193.

Darley, J., & Fazio, R. H. (1980). Expectancy-confirmation processes arising in the social interaction sequence. *American Psychologist, 35,* 867–881.

Darley, J., & Gross, P. H. (1983). A hypothesis-confirming bias in labeling effects. *Journal of Personality and Social Psychology, 44,* 20–33.

Deaux, K., & Major, B. (1987). Putting gender into context: An interactive model of gender-related behavior. *Psychological Review, 94,* 369–389.

DeParle, J. (1994, June 19). Welfare as we've known it. *The New York Times* (The Week in Review), p. 4.

Devine, P. (1989). Stereotypes and prejudice: Their automatic and controlled components. *Journal of Personality and Social Psychology, 56,* 5–18.

Dornbusch, S. (1994, February). *Off the track.* Presidential address at the biennial meeting of the Society for Research on Adolescence, San Diego, CA.

Doyle, W. J., Hancock, G., & Kifer, E. (1972). Teachers' perceptions: Do they make a difference? *Journal of the Association for the Study of Perception, 7,* 21–30.

Duncan, B. L. (1976). Differential social perception and attribution of intergroup violence: Testing the lower limits of stereotyping of blacks. *Journal of Personality and Social Psychology, 34,* 590–598.

Dusek, J., & Joseph, G. (1983). The bases of teacher expectancies: A meta-analysis. *Journal of Educational Psychology, 75,* 327–346.

Eagly, A. H. (1995). The science and politics of comparing women and men. *American Psychologist, 50,* 145–158.

Eagly, A. H., Makhijani, M. G., Ashmore, R. D., & Longo, L. C. (1991). What is beautiful is good, but . . .: A meta-analytic review of research on the physical attractiveness stereotype. *Psychological Bulletin, 110,* 109–128.

Eagly, A. H., & Mladinic, A. (1989). Gender stereotypes and attitudes toward men and women. *Personality and Social Psychology Bulletin, 15,* 543–558.

Eccles Parsons, J., et al. (1983). Expectancies, values and academic behaviors. In J. Spence (Ed.), *Achievement and achievement motivation* (pp. 75–146). San Francisco: W. H. Freeman.

Eccles, J. (1988). *Achievement beliefs and environment.* Final report to National Institute of Child Health and Development.

Eccles (Parsons), J. (1984). Sex differences in mathematics participation. In M. L. Maehr & M. W. Steinkamp (Eds.), *Women in science, Vol. 2, Advances in motivation and achievement* (pp. 93–137). Greenwich, CT: JAI Press.

Eccles (Parsons), J., Adler, T., & Meece, J. L. (1984). Sex differences in achievement: A test of alternate theories. *Journal of Personality and Social Psychology, 46,* 26–43.

Eccles, J., & Blumenfeld, P. (1985). Classroom experiences and student gender: Are there differences and do they matter? In L. C. Wilkinson & C. Marett (Ed.), *Gender influences in classroom interaction* (pp. 79–114). Hillsdale, NJ: Erlbaum.

Eccles, J. S., et al. (1993). School and family effects on the ontogeny of children's interests, self-perceptions, and activity choices. In R. Dienstbier & J. E. Jacobs (Eds.), *Developmental perspectives on motivation* (Vol. 40 of the Nebraska Symposium on Motivation) (pp. 145–208). Lincoln : University of Nebraska Press.

Eccles, J., & Harold, R. D. (1991). Gender differences in sports involvement: Applying the Eccles' expectancy-value model. *Journal of Applied Sports Psychology, 3,* 7–35.

Eccles, J., & Harold, R. D. (1992). Gender differences in educational and occupational patterns among the gifted. In N. Colangelo, S. G. Assouline, & D. L. Ambroson (Eds.), *Talent development: Proceedings from the 1991 Henry B. and Jocelyn Wallace National Research Symposium on Talent Development.* (pp. 3–29) Unionville, NY: Trillium Press.

Eccles, J., & Hoffman, L. W. (1984). Socialization and the maintenance of a sex-segregated labor market. In H. W. Stevenson & A. E. Siegel (Eds.), *Research in child development and social policy* (Vol. 1, pp. 367–420). Chicago: University of Chicago Press.

Eccles, J., & Jacobs, J. E. (1986). Social forces shape math attitudes and performance. *Signs, 11,* 367–380.

Eccles-Parsons, J., Kaczala, C. M., & Meece, J. L. (1982). Socialization of achievement attitudes and beliefs: Classroom influences. *Child Development, 53,* 322–339.

Eccles, J., & Wigfield, A. (1985). Teacher expectations and student motivation. In J. Dusek (Ed.), *Teacher expectancies* (pp. 185–226). Hillsdale, NJ: Erlbaum.

Eccles, J. S., Wigfield, A., Flanagan, C. A., Miller, C., Reuman, D., & Yee, D. (1989). Self-concepts, domain values, and self-esteem: Relations and changes at early adolescence. *Journal of Personality, 57,* 283–310.

Eden, D. (1984). Self-fulfilling prophecy as a management tool: Harnessing Pygmalion. *Academy of Management Review, 9,* 64–73.

Eden, D. (1986). OD and self-fulfilling prophecy: Boosting productivity by raising expectations. *Journal of Applied Behavioral Science, 22,* 1–13.

Eden, D., & Shani, A. B. (1982). Pygmalion goes to boot camp: Expectancy, leadership, and trainee performance. *Journal of Applied Psychology, 67,* 194–199.

Elashoff, J. D., & Snow, R. E. (1971). *Pygmalion reconsidered.* Worthington, OH: Charles A. Jones.

Esses, V. M., Haddock, G., & Zanna, M. P. (1993). Values, stereotypes, and emotions as determinants of intergroup attitudes. In D. Mackie & D. L. Hamilton (Eds.), *Affect, cognition, and stereotyping: Interactive processes in group perception* (pp. 137–166). San Diego: Academic Press.

Evertson, C. (1982). Differences in instructional activities in higher and lower achieving junior high English and math classes. *Elementary School Journal, 82,* 329–350.

Farina, A., Allen, J. G., & Saul, B. B. B. (1968). The role of the stigmatized person in affecting social relationships. *Journal of Personality, 36,* 169–182.

Farina, A., Gliha, D., Boudreau, L. A., Allen, J. G., & Sherman, M. (1971). Mental illness and the impact of believing others know about it. *Journal of Abnormal Psychology, 77,* 1–5.

Feingold, A. (1992). Good-looking people are not what we think. *Psychological Bulletin, 111,* 304–341.

Fine, M., & Gordon, S. M. (1989). Feminist transformations of/despite psychology. In M. Crawford (Ed.), *Gender and thought* (pp. 146–174). New York: Springer-Verlag.

Finn, J. (1972). Expectations and the educational environment. *Review of Educational Research, 42,* 387–410.

Fiske, S. T., & Neuberg, S. L. (1990). A continuum of impression formation, from category-based to individuating processes: Influences of information and motivation on attention and interpretation. In M. P. Zanna (Ed.), *Advances in experimental social psychology* (Vol. 23, pp. 1–74). New York: Academic Press.

Fiske, S. T., & Taylor, S. E. (1984). *Social cognition.* Reading, MA: Addison-Wesley.

Fiske, S. T., & Taylor, S. E. (1991). *Social cognition* (2nd ed.). New York: McGraw-Hill.

Fordham, S., & Ogbu, J. U. (1986). Black students' school success: Coping with the burden of "acting White." *The Urban Review, 18,* 176–206.

Fox, R. (1991). Prejudice and the unfinished mind: A new look at an old failing. *Psychological Inquiry, 3,* 137–152.

Frieze, I. H., Olson, J. E., & Russell, J. (1991). Attractiveness and income for men and women in management. *Journal of Applied Social Psychology, 21,* 1039–1057.

Funder, D. C. (1987). Errors and mistakes: Evaluatinig the accuracy of social judgment. *Psychological Bulletin, 101,* 75–90.

Funder, D. C. (1995). Stereotypes, base rates, and the fundamental evaluation mistake: A content-based approach to judgmental accuracy. In Y. T. Lee, L. Jussim, & C. R. McCauley (Eds.), *Stereotype accuracy: Toward appreciating group differences* (pp. 141–156). Washington, DC: American Psychological Association.

Funder, D. C., & Colvin, C. R. (1988). Friends and strangers: Acquaintanceship, agreement, and the accuracy of personality judgments. *Journal of Personality and Social Psychology, 55,* 149–158.

Gage, N. L., & Cronbach, L. J. (1955). Conceptual and methodological problems in interpersonal perception. *Psychological Review, 62,* 411–422.

Gibson, J. J. (1979). *The ecological approach to visual perception.* Boston: Houghton Mifflin.

Gilbert, D. T., & Malone, P. S. (1995). The correspondence bias. *Psychological Bulletin, 117,* 21–38.

Gilbert, D. T., & Osborne, R. E. (1989). Thinking backward: Some curable and incurable consequences of cognitive busyness. *Journal of Personality and Social Psychology, 57,* 940–949.

Goldman, W., & Lewis, P. (1977). Beautiful is good: Evidence that the physically attractive are more socially skillful. *Journal of Experimental Social Psychology, 13,* 125–130.

Gordon, R. A. (1968). Issues in multiple regression. *American Journal of Sociology, 73,* 592–616.

Graham, S. (1992). "Most of the subjects were White and middle class": Trends in published research on African Americans in selected APA journals, 1970–1989. *American Psychologist, 47,* 629–639.

Greenwald, A. G., & Banaji, M. R. (1995). Implicit social cognition: Attitudes, self-esteem, and stereotypes. *Psychological Review, 102,* 4–27.

Haddock, G., Zanna, M. P., & Esses, V. M. (1993). Assessing the structure of prejudicial attitudes: The case of attitudes toward homosexuals. *Journal of Personality and Social Psychology, 65,* 1105–1118.

Hamilton, D. L., Sherman, S. J., & Ruvolo, C. M. (1990). Stereotype-based expectancies: Effects on information processing and social behavior. *Journal of Social Issues, 46,* 35–60.

Harris, M. J. (1989). Personality moderators of expectancy effects: Replication of Harris and Rosenthal (1986). *Journal of Research in Personality, 23,* 381–387.

Harris, M. J., Milich, R., Corbitt, E. M., Hoover, D. W., & Brady, M. (1992). Self-fulfilling effects of stigmatizing information on children's social interactions. *Journal of Personality and Social Psychology, 63,* 41–50.

Harris, M. J., & Rosenthal, R. (1985). Mediation of interpersonal expectancy effects: 31 meta-analyses. *Psychological Bulletin, 97,* 363–386.

Harter, S., & Connell, J. P. (1984). A model of the relationship among children's academic achievement and their self-perceptions of competence, control, and motivational orientation. In J. G. Nicholls (Ed.), *Advances in motivation and achievement* (pp. 219–250). Greenwich, CT: JAI Press.

Heilman, M. E., Simon, M. C., & Repper, D. P. (1987). Intentionally favored, unintentionally harmed? The impact of gender-based preferential selection on self-perceptions and self-evaluations. *Journal of Applied Psychology, 72,* 62–68.

Herrnstein, R. J., & Murray, C. (1994). *The bell curve.* New York: The Free Press.

Higgins, E. T., & Bargh, J. A. (1987). Social cognition and social perception. In M. R. Rosenzweig & L. W. Porter (Eds.), *Annual Review of Psychology, 38,* 369–425.

Hilton, J., & Darley, J. (1985). Constructing other persons: A limit on the effect. *Journal of Experimental Social Psychology, 21,* 1–18.

Hilton, J. L., & Darley, J. M. (1991). The effects of interaction goals on person perception. In M. P. Zanna (Ed.), *Advances in experimental social psychology* (Vol. 24, pp. 235–267). New York: Academic Press.

Jacobs, J. E., & Eccles, J. S. (1985). Gender differences in math ability: The impact of media reports on parents. *Educational Researcher, 14,* 20–25.

Jacobs, J. E., & Eccles, J. S. (1992). The impact of mothers' gender-role stereotypic beliefs on mothers' and children's ability perceptions. *Journal of Personality and Social Psychology, 63,* 932–944.

Jones, E. E. (1986). Interpreting interpersonal behavior: The effects of expectancies. *Science, 234,* 41–46.

Jones, E. E. (1990). *Interpersonal perception.* New York: W. H. Freeman.

Jones, R. A. (1977). *Self-fulfilling prophecies: Social, psychological, and physiological effects of expectancies.* Hillsdale, NJ: Erlbaum.

Judd, C. M., & McClelland, G. H. (1989). *Data analysis: A model-comparison approach.* Orlando, FL: Harcourt Brace Jovanovich.

Judd, C. M., & Park, B. (1993). Definition and assessment of accuracy in social stereotypes. *Psychological Review, 100,* 109–128.

Jussim, L. (1986). Self-fulfilling prophecies: A theoretical and integrative review. *Psychological Review, 93,* 429–445.

Jussim, L. (1987). Interpersonal expectations in social interaction: Self-fulfilling prophecies, confirmatory biases, and accuracy. (Doctoral dissertation, University of Michigan). *Dissertation Abstracts International, 48,* 1845B.

Jussim, L. (1989). Teacher expectations: Self-fulfilling prophecies, perceptual biases, and accuracy. *Journal of Personality and Social Psychology, 57,* 469–480.

Jussim, L. (1990). Social reality and social problems: The role of expectancies. *Journal of Social Issues, 46,* 9–34.

Jussim, L. (1991). Social perception and social reality: A reflection-construction model. *Psychological Review, 98,* 54–73.

Jussim, L. (1993). Accuracy in interpersonal expectations: A reflection-construction analysis of current and classic research. *Journal of Personality, 61,* 637–668.

Jussim, L., Coleman, L., & Lerch, L. (1987). The nature of stereotypes: A comparison and integration of three theories. *Journal of Personality and Social Psychology, 52,* 536–546.

Jussim, L., & Eccles, J. (1992). Teacher expectations II: Construction and reflection of student achievement. *Journal of Personality and Social Psychology, 63,* 947–961.

Jussim, L., & Eccles, J. (1995). Naturalistic studies of interpersonal expectancies. *Review of Personality and Social Psychology, 15,* 74–108.

Jussim, L., & Eccles, J. (1995). Are teacher expectations biased by students' gender, social class, or ethnicity? In Y. T. Lee, L. Jussim, & C. R. McCauley (Eds.), *Stereotype accuracy: Toward appreciating group differences* (pp. 245–271). Washington, DC: American Psychological Association.

Jussim, L., & Fleming, C. (in press). Self-fulfilling prophecies and the maintenance of social stereotypes: The role of dyadic interactions and social forces. In N. Macrae, M. Hewstone, & C. Stangor (Eds.), *The foundations of stereotypes and stereotyping.* New York: Guilford.

Jussim, L., Madon, S., & Chatman, C. (1994). Teacher expectations and student achievement: Self-fulfilling prophecies, biases, and accuracy. In L. Heath, R. S. Tindale, J. Edwards, E. J. Posavac, F. B. Bryant, E. Henderson-King, Y. Suarez-Balcazar, J. Myers (Eds.), *Applications of heuristics and biases to social issues* (pp. 303–334). New York: Plenum.

Jussim, L., Nelson, T., Manis, M., & Soffin, S. (1995). Prejudice, stereotypes, and labeling effects: Sources of bias in person perception. *Journal of Personality and Social Psychology, 68,* 228–246.

Jussim, L., McCauley, C. R., & Lee, Y. T. (1995). Why study stereotype accuracy and inaccuracy? In Y. T. Lee, L. Jussim, & C. R. McCauley (Eds.), *Stereotype accuracy: Toward appreciating group differences* (pp. 3–27). Washington, DC: American Psychological Association.

Kahneman, D., & Tversky, A. (1973). On the psychology of prediction. *Psychological Review, 80,* 237–251.

Katz, D., & Braly, K. (1933). Racial stereotypes of one hundred college students. *Journal of Abnormal and Social Psychology, 28,* 280–290.

Kenny, D. A. (1994). *Interpersonal perception: A social relations analysis.* New York: Guilford.

Kenny, D. A., & Albright, L. (1987). Accuracy in interpersonal perception: A social relations analysis. *Psychological Bulletin, 102,* 390–402.

Kimball, M. M. (1989). A new perspective on women's math achievement. *Psychological Bulletin, 105,* 198–214.

Krueger, J., & Rothbart, M. (1988). Use of categorical and individuating information in making inferences about personality. *Journal of Personality and Social Psychology, 55,* 187–195.

Kunda, Z. (1990). The case for motivated reasoning. *Psychological Bulletin, 108,* 480–498.

LaPiere, R. T. (1936). Type-rationalizations of group antipathy. *Social Forces, 15,* 232–237.

Lareau, A. (1987). Social-class differences in family-school relationships: The importance of cultural capital. *Sociology of Education, 60,* 73–85.

Lee, Y. T., & Ottati, V. (1993). Determinants of in-group and out-group perceptions of heterogeneity. *Journal of Cross-Cultural Psychology, 24,* 298–318.

Lerner, M. (1980). *The belief in a just world.* New York: Plenum.

Levesque, M. J., & Kenny, D. A. (1993). Accuracy of behavioral predictions at zero acquaintance: A social relations analysis. *Journal of Personality and Social Psychology, 65,* 1178–1187.

Linville, P. (1982). The complexity-extremity effect and age-based stereotyping. *Journal of Personality and Social Psychology, 42,* 193–211.

Linville, P., & Jones, E. E. (1980). Polarized appraisal of out-group members. *Journal of Personality and Social Psychology, 38,* 689–703.

Locke, E. A., & Latham, G. P. (1990). *A theory of goal setting and task performance.* Englewood Cliffs, NJ: Prentice-Hall.

Locksley, A., Borgida, E., Brekke, N., & Hepburn, C. (1980). Sex stereotypes and social judgment. *Journal of Personality and Social Psychology, 39,* 821–831.

Locksley, A., Hepburn, C., & Ortiz, V. (1982). Social stereotypes and judgments of individuals: An instance of the base-rate fallacy. *Journal of Experimental Social Psychology, 18,* 23–42.

McArthur, L. Z., & Baron, R. M. (1983). Toward an ecological theory of social perception. *Psychological Review, 90,* 215–238.

Mackie, M. (1973). Arriving at "truth" by definition: The case of stereotype inaccuracy. *Social Problems, 20,* 431–447.

Madon, S., Jussim, L., & Eccles, J. (1995). *In search of the powerful self-fulfilling prophecy.* Manuscript in preparation.

Marger, M. N. (1991). *Race and ethnic relations* (2nd ed.). Belmont, CA: Wadsworth.

Marger, M. N. (1994). *Race and ethnic relations* (3rd ed.). Belmont, CA: Wadsworth.

McCauley, C. (1995). Are stereotypes exaggerated? Looking for perceptual contrast and cognitive miser in beliefs about group differences. In Y. T. Lee, L. Jussim, & C. R. McCauley (Eds.), *Stereotype accuracy: Toward appreciating group differences* (pp. 215–243). Washington, DC: American Psychological Association.

McCauley, C., Jussim, L., & Lee, Y. T. (1995). The time is now: Stereotype accuracy and intergroup relations. In Y. T. Lee, L. Jussim, & C. R. McCauley (Eds.), *Stereotype accuracy: Toward appreciating group differences* (pp. 293–312). Washington, DC: American Psychological Association.

McCauley, C., & Stitt, C. L. (1978). An individual and quantitative measure of stereotypes. *Journal of Personality and Social Psychology, 36,* 929–940.

McCauley, C., Stitt, C. L., & Segal, M. (1980). Stereotyping: From prejudice to prediction. *Psychological Bulletin, 87,* 195–208.

McCauley, C. R., & Thangavelu, K. (1991). Individual differences in sex stereotyping of occupations and personality traits. *Social Psychology Quarterly, 54,* 267–279.

Meece, J. L., Eccles-Parsons, J., Kaczala, C. M., Goff, S. E., & Futterman, R. (1982). Sex differences in math achievement: Towards a model of academic choice. *Psychological Bulletin, 91,* 324–348.

Merton, R. K. (1948). The self-fulfilling prophecy. *Antioch Review, 8,* 193–210.

Midgley, C., Feldlaufer, H., & Eccles, J. S. (1989). Change in teacher efficacy and student self- and task-related beliefs in mathematics during the transition to junior high school. *Journal of Educational Psychology, 81,* 247–258.

Miller, D. T., & Turnbull, W. (1986). Expectancies and interpersonal processes. In M. R. Rosenzweig & L. W. Porter (Eds.), *Annual Review of Psychology* (Vol. 37, pp. 233–256). Stanford, CA: Annual Reviews.

Mook, D. G. (1983). In defense of external invalidity. *American Psychologist, 38,* 379–387.

Nelson, T. E., Biernat, M. R., & Manis, M. (1990). Everybody base rates (sex stereotypes): Potent and resilient. *Journal of Personality and Social Psychology, 59,* 664–675.

Neuberg, S. L. (1989). The goal of forming accurate impressions during social interactions: Attenuating the impact of negative expectancies. *Journal of Personality and Social Psychology, 56,* 374–386.

Neuberg, S. L. (1994). Expectancy-confirmation processes in stereotype-tinged social encounters: The moderating role of social goals. In M. P. Zanna & J. M. Olson (Eds.), *The psychology of prejudice: The Ontario symposium* (Vol. 7). Hillsdale, NJ: Erlbaum.

Nisbett, R., & Ross, L. (1980). *Human inference: Strategies and shortcomings of social judgment.* Englewood Cliffs, NJ: Prentice-Hall.

Oakes, P. J., Haslam, S. A., & Turner, J. C. (1994). *Stereotyping and social reality.* Cambridge, MA: Blackwell.

Olson, J. M., Roese, N. J., & Zanna, M. P. (in press). Expectancies. In E. T. Higgins & A. W. Kruglanski, (Eds.), *Social psychology: Handbook of basic principles.* New York: Guilford.

Ottati, V., & Lee, Y. T. (1995). Accuracy: A neglected component of stereotype research. In Y. T. Lee, L.Jussim, & C. R. McCauley (Eds.), *Stereotype accuracy: Toward appreciating group differences* (pp. 29–59). Washington, DC: American Psychological Association.

Palardy, J. M. (1969). What teachers believe—what children achieve. *Elementary School Journal, 69,* 370–374.

Parsons, J. E. (1980). *Final Report to the National Institute of Education,* Washington, DC (ERIC Document Reproduction Service No. ED 186 477).

Pedhazur, E. J. (1982). *Multiple regression in behavioral research* (2nd ed.). New York: Holt, Rinehart and Winston.

Pettigrew, T. F. (1979). The ultimate attribution error: Extending Allport's cognitive analysis of prejudice. *Personality and Social Psychology Bulletin, 5,* 461–476.

Pyszczynski, T., & Greenberg, J. (1987). Toward an integration of cognitive and motivational perspectives on social inference: A biased hypothesis-testing model. In L. Berkowitz (Ed.), *Advances in experimental social psychology* (Vol. 20, pp. 297–340). New York: Academic Press.

Raudenbush, S. W. (1984). Magnitude of teacher expectancy effects on pupil IQ as a function of the credibility of expectancy inductions: A synthesis of findings from 18 experiments. *Journal of Educational Psychology, 76,* 85–97.

Rist, R. (1970). Student social class and teacher expectations: The self-fulfilling prophecy in ghetto education. *Harvard Educational Review, 40,* 411–451.

Rosenthal, R. (1974). *On the social psychology of the self-fulfilling prophecy: Further evidence for Pygmalion effects and their mediating mechanisms.* New York: MSS Modular Publications.

Rosenthal, R. (1989, August). *Experimenter expectancy, covert comunication, & meta-analytic methods.* Invited address at the 97th annual convention of the American Psychological Association, New Orleans, LA.

Rosenthal, R., & Jacobson, L. (1968). *Pygmalion in the classroom: Teacher expectations and student intellectual development.* New York: Holt, Rinehart and Winston.

Rosenthal, R., & Rubin, D. B. (1978). Interpersonal expectancy effects: The first 345 studies. *The Behavioral and Brain Sciences, 3,* 377–386.

Ryan, C. (1995). Motivation and group membership: Consequences for stereotype accuracy. In L. Jussim, Y. T. Lee, & C. R. McCauley (Eds.), *Stereotype accuracy: Toward appreciating group differences* (pp. 189–214). Washington, DC: American Psychological Association.

Schuman, H., Walsh, E., Olson, C., & Etheridge, B. (1985). Effort and reward: The assumption that college grades are affected by quantity of study. *Social Forces, 63,* 945–966.

Sedikedes, C., & Skowronski, J. J. (1991). The law of cognitive structure activation. *Psychological Inquiry, 2,* 169–184.

Skrypnek, B. J., & Snyder, M. (1982). On the self-perpetuating nature of stereotypes about women and men. *Journal of Experimental Social Psychology, 18,* 277–291.

Snyder, M. (1984). When belief creates reality. In M. P. Zanna (Ed.), *Advances in experimental psychology,* (Vol. *18,* pp. 247–305). Orlando, FL: Academic Press.

Snyder, M. (1992). Motivational foundations of behavioral confirmation. In M. P. Zanna (Ed.), *Advances in experimental social psychology* (Vol. *25,* pp. 67–114). San Diego: Academic Press.

Snyder, M., Tanke, E. D., & Berscheid, E. (1977). Social perception and interpersonal behavior: On the self-fulfilling nature of social stereotypes. *Journal of Personality and Social Psychology, 35,* 656–666.

Stangor, C. (1995). Content and application inaccuracy in social stereotyping. In Y. T. Lee, L. Jussim, & C. R. McCauley (Eds.), *Stereotype accuracy: Toward appreciating group differences* (pp. 275–292). Washington, DC: American Psychological Association.

Steele, C. M. (1992). Race and the schooling of black Americans. *Atlantic Monthly,* April, 68–78.

Stephan, W. G., & Stephan, C. W. (1985). Intergroup anxiety. *Journal of Social Issues, 41,* 157–175.

Swann, W. B. (1984). Quest for accuracy in person perception: A matter of pragmatics. *Psychological Review, 91,* 457–477.

Swann, W. B., Jr., & Ely, R. J. (1984). A battle of wills: Self-verification versus behavioral confirmation. *Journal of Personality and Social Psychology, 46,* 1287–1302.

Swim, J. K. (1994). Perceived versus meta-analytic effect sizes: An assessment of the accuracy of gender stereotypes. *Journal of Personality and Social Psychology, 66,* 21–36.

Taft, R. (1955). The ability to judge people. *Psychological Bulletin, 52,* 1–23.

Tuckman, B. W., & Bierman, M. L. (1971). *Beyond Pygmalion: Galatea in the schools.* Paper presented at the meeting of the American Educational Research Association, New York City.

Vernon, P. E. (1933). Some characteristics of the good judge of personality. *Journal of Social Psychology, 4,* 42–58.

von Baeyer, C. L., Sherk, D. L., & Zanna, M. P. (1981). Impression management in the job interview: When the female applicant meets the male (chauvinist) interviewer. *Personality and Social Psychology Bulletin, 7,* 45–51.

von Hippel, W., Sekaquaptewa, D., & Vargas, P. (1995). On the role of encoding processes in stereotype maintenance. In M. P. Zanna (Ed.), *Advances in experimental social psychology* (Vol. *27,* pp. 177–254). San Diego: Academic Press.

Weber, M. (1930). *The Protestant ethic and the spirit of capitalism.* New York: Scribner.

Weiner, B. (1979). A theory of motivation for some classroom experiences. *Journal of Educational Psychology, 71,* 3–25.

Wentzel, K. R. (1989). Adolescent classroom goals, standard for performance, and academic achievement: An interactionist perspective. *Journal of Educational Psychology, 81,* 131–142.

West, C., & Anderson, T. (1976). The question of preponderant causation in teacher expectancy research. *Review of Educational Research, 46,* 613–630.

Wigfield, A., Eccles, J. S., MacIver, D., Reuman, D., & Midgley, C. (1991). Transitions at early adolescence: Changes in children's domain-specific self-perceptions and general self-esteem across the transition to junior high school. *Developmental Psychology, 27,* 552–565.

Williams, T. (1976). Teacher prophecies and the inheritance of inequality. *Sociology of Education, 49,* 223–236.

Wineburg, S. S. (1987). The self-fulfillment of the self-fulfilling prophecy. *Educational Researcher, 16,* 28–37.

Word, C. O., Zanna, M. P., & Cooper, J. (1974). The nonverbal mediation of self-fulfilling prophecies in interracial interaction. *Journal of Experimental Social Psychology, 10,* 109–120.

Yee, D., & Eccles, J. (1988). Parent perceptions and attributions for children's math achievement. *Sex Roles, 19,* 317–333.

Zanna, M. P., & Pack, S. J. (1975). On the self-fulfilling nature of apparent sex differences in behavior. *Journal of Experimental Social Psychology, 11,* 583–591.

Yee, Fairchild, Weizmann, & Wyatt, (1993). Addressing psychology's problems with race. *American Psychologist, 48,* 1132–1140.

NONVERBAL BEHAVIOR AND NONVERBAL COMMUNICATION: WHAT DO CONVERSATIONAL HAND GESTURES TELL US?

Robert M. Krauss
Yihsiu Chen
Purnima Chawla

I. The Social Psychological Study of Nonverbal Behavior

A. NONVERBAL BEHAVIOR AS NONVERBAL COMMUNICATION

Much of what social psychologists think about nonverbal behavior derives from a proposal made more than a century ago by Charles Darwin. In *The Expression of the Emotions in Man and Animals* (Darwin, 1872), he posed the question: Why do our facial expressions of emotions take the particular forms they do? Why do we wrinkle our nose when we are disgusted, bare our teeth and narrow our eyes when enraged, and stare wide-eyed when we are transfixed by fear? Darwin's answer was that we do these things primarily because they are vestiges of *serviceable associated habits*—behaviors that earlier in our evolutionary history had specific and direct functions. For a species that attacked by biting, baring the teeth was a necessary prelude to an assault; wrinkling the nose reduced the inhalation of foul odors; and so forth.

However, if facial expressions reflect formerly functional behaviors, why have they persisted when they no longer serve their original purposes? Why do people bare their teeth when they are angry, despite the fact that biting is not part of their aggressive repertoire? Why do they wrinkle their noses when their disgust is engendered by an odorless picture? According to Darwin's intellectual heirs, the behavioral ethologists (e.g., Hinde, 1972;

389

ADVANCES IN EXPERIMENTAL
SOCIAL PSYCHOLOGY, VOL. 28

Tinbergen, 1952), humans do these things because over the course of their evolutionary history such behaviors have acquired communicative value: They provide others with external evidence of an individual's internal state. The utility of such information generated evolutionary pressure to select sign behaviors, thereby schematizing them and, in Tinbergen's phrase, "emancipating them" from their original biological function.[1]

B. NONCOMMUNICATIVE FUNCTIONS OF NONVERBAL BEHAVIORS

So pervasive has been social psychologists' preoccupation with the communicative or expressive aspects of nonverbal behaviors that the terms nonverbal behavior and nonverbal communication have tended to be used interchangeably.[2] Recently, however, it has been suggested that this communicative focus has led social psychologists to overlook other functions that such behaviors serve. For example, Zajonc contends that psychologists have been too quick to accept the idea that facial expressions are primarily expressive behaviors. According to his "vascular theory of emotional efference" (Zajonc, 1985; Zajonc, Murphy, & Inglehart, 1989), the actions of the facial musculature that produce facial expressions of emotions serve to restrict venous flow, thereby impeding or facilitating the cooling of cerebral blood as it enters the brain. The resulting variations in cerebral temperature, Zajonc hypothesizes, promote or inhibit the release of emotion-linked neurotransmitters, which, in turn, affect subjective emotional experience. From this perspective, facial expressions do convey information about the individual's emotional state, but they do so as an indirect consequence of their primary, noncommunicative function.

An analogous argument has been made for the role of gaze direction in social interaction. As people speak, their gaze periodically fluctuates toward and away from their conversational partner. Some investigators have interpreted gaze directed at a conversational partner as an expression of intimacy or closeness (cf. Argyle & Cook, 1976; Exline, 1972; Exline, Gray, & Schuette, 1985; Russo, 1975). However, Butterworth (1978) argues that gaze direction is affected by two complex tasks that speakers must manage concurrently: planning speech, and monitoring the listener for visible indications of comprehension, confusion, agreement, interest, and so forth (Brun-

---

[1] See Fridlund (1991) for a discussion of the ethological position.

[2] For example, the recent book edited by Feldman and Rimé (1991) reviewing research in this area is titled *Fundamentals of Nonverbal Behavior,* despite the fact that all of the nonverbal behaviors are discussed in terms of the role that they play in communication (see Krauss, 1993).

ner, 1979; Duncan, Brunner, & Fiske, 1979). When the cognitive demands of speech planning are great, Butterworth argues, speakers avert their gaze to reduce visual information input, and when those demands moderate, they redirect their gaze toward the listener, especially at places where feedback would be useful. Studies of the points in the speech stream where changes in gaze direction occur and of the effects of restricting changes in gaze direction (Beattie, 1978, 1981; Cegala, Alexander, & Sokuvitz, 1979), tend to support Butterworth's conjecture.

C. INTERPERSONAL AND INTRAPERSONAL FUNCTIONS OF NONVERBAL BEHAVIORS

Of course, nonverbal behaviors can serve multiple functions. Facial expression may play a role in affective experience—by modulating vascular blood flow as Zajonc has proposed or through facial feedback as has been suggested by Tomkins and others (Tomkins & McCarter, 1964)—while also conveying information about the expressor's emotional state. Such communicative effects could involve two rather different mechanisms.

First, many nonverbal behaviors are to some extent under the individual's control and can be produced voluntarily. For example, although a smile may be a normal accompaniment of an affectively positive internal state, it can at least to some degree be produced at will. Social norms, called "display rules," dictate that one exhibit at least a moderately pleasant expression on certain social occasions. Kraut (1979) found that the attention of others greatly potentiates smiling in situations that can be expected to induce a positive internal state.

Second, nonverbal behaviors that serve noncommunicative functions can provide information about the noncommunicative functions they serve. For example, if Butterworth is correct about the reason speakers avert gaze, then an excessive amount of gaze aversion may lead a listener to infer that the speaker is having difficulty formulating the message. Conversely, the failure to avert gaze at certain junctures, combined with speech that is overly fluent, may lead an observer to infer that the utterance is not spontaneous.

Viewed in this fashion, we can distinguish between *inter*personal and *intra*personal functions that nonverbal behaviors serve. The interpersonal functions involve information that such behaviors convey to others, regardless of whether they are employed intentionally (i.e., the facial emblem) or serve as the basis of an inference the listener makes about the speaker (i.e., dysfluency). The intrapersonal functions involve noncommunicative purposes that the behaviors serve. The premise of this chapter is that the primary function of conversational hand gestures (unplanned, articulate hand movements that accompany spontaneous speech) is not communicative, but rather to aid in the formulation of speech. It is our contention that the information they convey to an addressee is largely derivative from this primary function.

II. Gestures as Nonverbal Behaviors

A. A TYPOLOGY OF GESTURES

All hand gestures are hand movements, but not all hand movements are gestures, and it is useful to draw some distinctions among the types of hand movements people make. Although gestural typologies abound in the literature, there is little agreement among researchers about the sorts of distinctions that are necessary or useful. Following a suggestion by Kendon (1983), we have found it helpful to think of the different types of hand movements that accompany speech as arranged on a continuum of lexicalization—the extent to which they are "word-like." The continuum is illustrated in Figure 1.

1. Adapters

At the low lexicalization end of the continuum are hand movements that tend not to be considered gestures. They consist of manipulations either of the person or of some object (e.g., clothing, pencils, eyeglasses)—the kinds of scratching, fidgeting, rubbing, tapping, and touching that speakers often do with their hands. Such behaviors are most frequently referred to as *adapters* (Efron, 1941/1972; Ekman & Friesen, 1969b, 1972). Other terms that have been used are *expressive movements* (Reuschert, 1909), *body-*

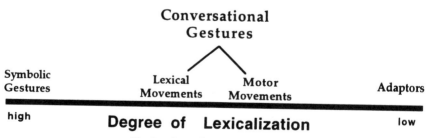

Fig. 1. A continuum of gesture types.

focused movements (Freedman & Hoffman, 1967), *self-touching gestures* (Kimura, 1976), *manipulative gestures* (Edelman & Hampson, 1979), *self-manipulators* (Rosenfeld, 1966), and *contact acts* (Bull & Connelly, 1985). Adapters are not gestures as that term is usually understood. They are not perceived as communicatively intended, nor are they perceived to be meaningfully related to the speech they accompany, although they may serve as the basis for dispositional inferences (e.g., that the speaker is nervous, uncomfortable, bored, etc.). It has been suggested that adapters may reveal unconscious thoughts or feelings (Mahl, 1956, 1968), or thoughts and feelings that the speaker is trying consciously to conceal (Ekman & Friesen, 1969a, 1974), but little systematic research has been directed to this issue.

2. Symbolic Gestures

At the opposite end of the lexicalization continuum are gestural signs—hand configurations and movements with specific, conventionalized meanings—that we call *symbolic gestures* (Ricci Bitti & Poggi, 1991). Other terms that have been used are *emblems* (Efron, 1941/1972), *autonomous gestures* (Kendon, 1983), *conventionalized signs* (Reuschert, 1909), *formal pantomimic gestures* (Wiener, Devoe, Rubinow, & Geller, 1972), *expressive gestures* (Zinober & Martlew, 1985), and *semiotic gestures* (Barakat, 1973). Familiar symbolic gestures include the "raised fist," "bye-bye," "thumbs-up," and the extended middle finger sometimes called "flipping the bird." In contrast to adapters, symbolic gestures are used intentionally and serve a clear communicative function. Every culture has a set of symbolic gestures familiar to most of its adult members, and very similar gestures may have different meanings in different cultures (Ekman, 1976). Subcultural and occupational groups also may have special symbolic gestures not widely known outside the group. Although symbolic gestures often are used in the absence of speech, they occasionally accompany speech, either echoing a spoken word or phrase or substituting for something that was not said.

3. Conversational Gestures

The properties of the hand movements that fall at the two extremes of the continuum are relatively uncontroversial. However, there is considerable disagreement about movements that occupy the middle part of the lexicalization continuum, movements that are neither as word-like as symbolic gestures, nor as devoid of meaning as adapters. We refer to this heterogeneous set of hand movements as *conversational gestures*. They also have been called *illustrators* (Ekman & Friesen, 1969b, 1972), *gesticulations* (Kendon, 1980, 1983), and *signifying signs* (Reuschert, 1909). Conversational gestures are hand movements that accompany speech and seem related to the speech they accompany. This apparent relatedness is manifest in three ways. First, unlike symbolic gestures, conversational gestures do not occur in the absence of speech, and in conversation they are made only by the person who is speaking. Second, conversational gestures are temporally coordinated with speech. Third, unlike adapters, at least some conversational gestures seem related in form to the semantic content of the speech they accompany.

Different types of conversational gestures can be distinguished, and a variety of classification schemes have been proposed (Ekman & Friesen, 1972; Feyereisen & deLannoy, 1991; Hadar, 1989a; McNeill, 1985). We find it useful to distinguish between two major types that differ importantly in form and, we believe, in function.

a. Motor Movements. One type of conversational gesture consists of a simple, repetitive, rhythmic movement, that bears no obvious relationship to the semantic content of the accompanying speech (Feyereisen, Van de Wiele, & Dubois, 1988). Typically the hand shape remains fixed during the gesture, which may be repeated several times. We will follow Hadar (1989a; Hadar & Yadlin-Gedassy, 1994) in referring to such gestures as *motor movements;* they also have been called "batons" (Efron, 1941/1972; Ekman & Friesen, 1972) and "beats" (Kendon, 1983; McNeill, 1987). Motor movements are reported to be coordinated with the speech prosody and to fall on stressed syllables (Bull & Connelly, 1985; but see McClave, 1994), although the synchrony is far from perfect.

b. Lexical Movements. The other main category of conversational gesture consists of hand movements that vary considerably in length; are nonrepetitive, complex and changing in form; and, to a naive observer at least, appear related to the semantic content of the speech they accompany. We call them *lexical movements,* and they are the focus of our research.[3]

---

[3] A number of additional distinctions can be drawn. Butterworth and Hadar (1989) and Hadar and Yadlin-Gedassy (1994) distinguish between two types of lexical movements: conceptual gestures and lexical gestures. The former originate at an earlier stage of the speech production process than the latter. Other investigators distinguish a category of *deictic* gestures that point to individuals or indicate features of the environment; we find it useful to regard them as a kind of lexical movement. Further distinctions can be made between types of lexical movements (e.g., *iconic* vs. *metaphoric* (McNeill, 1985, 1987)), but for the purposes of this chapter the distinctions we have drawn will suffice.

III. Interpersonal Functions of Conversational Gestures

A. COMMUNICATION OF SEMANTIC INFORMATION

Traditionally, conversational hand gestures have been assumed to convey semantic information.[4] "As the tongue speaketh to the ear, so the gesture speaketh to the eye" is the way the eighteenth century naturalist Sir Francis Bacon (1891) put it. One of the most knowledgeable contemporary observers of gestural behavior, the anthropologist Adam Kendon, explicitly rejects the view that conversational gestures serve no interpersonal function—that gestures "are an automatic byproduct of speaking and not in any way functional for the listener"—contending that

> gesticulation arises as an integral part of an individual's *communicative* effort and that, furthermore, it has a direct role to play in this process. Gesticulation . . . is important principally because it is employed, along with speech, in fashioning an effective utterance unit. (Kendon, 1983, p. 27, italics in original)

1. Evidence for the "Gestures As Communication" Hypothesis

Given the pervasiveness and longevity of the belief that communication is a primary function of hand gestures, it is surprising that so little empirical evidence is available to support it. Most writers on the topic seem to accept the proposition as self-evident and proceed to interpret the meanings of gestures on an ad hoc basis (cf. Birdwhistell, 1970).

The experimental evidence supporting the notion that gestures communicate semantic information comes from two lines of research: studies of the effects of visual accessibility on gesturing, and studies of the effectiveness of communication with and without gesturing (Bull, 1983, 1987; Kendon, 1983). The former studies consistently find a somewhat higher rate of gesturing for speakers who interact face-to-face with their listeners, compared to speakers separated by a barrier or who communicate over an intercom (Cohen, 1977; Cohen & Harrison, 1972; Rimé, 1982). Although differences in gesture rates between face-to-face and intercom conditions may be consistent with the view that they are communicatively intended,

---

[4] By semantic information we mean information that contributes to the utterance's "intended meaning" (Grice, 1969; Searle, 1969). Speech, of course, conveys semantic information in abundance, but also may convey additional information (e.g., about the speaker's emotional state, spontaneity, familiarity with the topic, etc.) through variations in voice quality, fluency, and other vocal properties. Although such information is not, strictly speaking, part of the speaker's intended meaning, it nonetheless may be quite informative. See Krauss and Fussell (in press) for a more detailed discussion of this distinction.

this is hardly conclusive evidence. The two communication conditions differ on a number of dimensions, and differences in gesturing may be attributable to factors that have nothing to do with communication. Moreover, all studies that have found such differences also have found a considerable amount of gesturing when speaker and listener could not see each other, something that is difficult to square with the "gesture as communication" hypothesis.

Studies claiming to demonstrate the gestural enhancement of communicative effectiveness report small, but statistically reliable, performance increments on tests of information (e.g., reproduction of a figure from a description, answering questions about an object on the basis of a description) for listeners who could see a speaker gesture, compared to those who could not (Graham & Argyle, 1975; Riseborough, 1981; Rogers, 1978). Unfortunately, all the studies of this type that we have found suffer from serious methodological shortcomings, and we believe that a careful assessment of them yields little support for the hypothesis that gestures convey semantic information. For example, in what is probably the soundest of these studies, Graham and Argyle had speakers describe abstract line drawings to a small audience of listeners who then tried to reproduce the drawings. For half of the descriptions, speakers were allowed to gesture; for the remainder, they were required to keep their arms folded. Graham and Argyle found that audiences of the nongesturing speakers reproduced the figures somewhat less accurately. However, the experiment does not control for the possibility that speakers who were allowed to gesture produced better *verbal* descriptions of the stimuli, which, in turn, enabled their audiences to reproduce the figures more accurately. For more detailed critical reviews of this literature, see Krauss, Dushay, Chen, and Rauscher (in press) and Krauss, Morrel-Samuels, and Colasante (1991).

2. Evidence Inconsistent with the "Gestures as Communication" Hypothesis

Other research has reported results inconsistent with the hypothesis that gestures enhance the communicative value of speech by conveying semantic information. Feyereisen, Van de Wiele, and Dubois (1988) presented subjects with videotaped gestures excerpted from classroom lectures, along with three possible interpretations of each gesture: the word(s) in the accompanying speech that had been associated with the gesture (the *correct response*), the meaning most frequently attributed to the gesture by an independent group of judges (the *plausible response*), and a meaning that had been attributed to the gesture by only one judge (the *implausible response*). Subjects tried to select the response that most closely corresponded to the gesture's meaning. Not surprising, the plausible response (the meaning most often spontaneously attributed to the gesture) was the one most often chosen; more surprising is the fact that the implausible response was chosen about as often as the correct response.

Although not specifically concerned with gestures, an extensive series of studies by the British Communication Studies Group concluded that people convey information just about as effectively over the telephone as they do when they are face-to-face with their coparticipants (Short, Williams, & Christie, 1976; Williams, 1977).[5] Although it is possible that people speaking to listeners they cannot see compensate verbally for information that ordinarily would be conveyed by gestures (and other visible displays), it may also be the case that the contribution that gestural information makes to communication typically is of little consequence.

Certainly reasonable investigators can disagree about the contribution that gestures make to communication in normal conventional settings, but insofar as the research literature is concerned, we believe we are justified in concluding that the communicative value of these visible displays has yet to be demonstrated convincingly.

B. COMMUNICATION OF NONSEMANTIC INFORMATION

Semantic information (as we are using the term) involves information relevant to the intended meaning of the utterance, and it is our contention that gestures have not been shown to make an important contribution to this aspect of communication. However, semantic information is not the only kind of information that people convey. Quite apart from its semantic content, speech may convey information about the speaker's internal state, such as attitude toward the addressee, and in the appropriate circumstances such information can make an important contribution to the interaction. The two messages may be identical semantically, but it can make a great deal of difference to passengers in a storm-buffeted airplane whether the pilot's announcement, "Just a little turbulence, folks—nothing to worry about," is delivered fluently in a resonant, well-modulated voice or hesitantly in a high-pitched, tremulous one (Kimble & Seidel, 1991).

It is surprising that relatively little consideration has been given to the possibility that gestures, like other nonverbal behaviors, are useful commu-

---

[5] More recent research has found some effects attributable to the lack of visual access (Rutter, 1987; Rutter, Stephenson, & Dewey, 1981), but these effects tend to involve the perceived social distance between communicators, not their ability to convey information. There is no reason to believe that the presence or absence of gesture per se is an important mediator of these differences.

nicatively because of the nonsemantic information they convey. Bavelas, Chovil, Lawrie, and Wade (1992) have identified a category of conversational gestures they have called *interactive gestures,* whose function is to support the ongoing interaction by maintaining participants' involvement. In our judgment, the claim has not yet been well substantiated by empirical evidence, but it would be interesting if a category of gestures serving such a function could be shown to exist.

In the next section, we describe a series of studies that examines the information conveyed by conversational gestures and the contribution such gestures make to the effectiveness of communication.

IV. Gestures and Communication: Empirical Studies

Establishing empirically that a particular behavior serves a communicative function turns out to be less straightforward than it might seem.[6] Some investigators have adopted what might be termed an *interpretive* or *hermeneutic* approach, by carefully observing the gestures and the accompanying speech, then attempting to infer the meaning of the gesture and assign a communicative significance to it (Bavelas et al., 1992; Birdwhistell, 1970; Kendon, 1980, 1983; McNeill, 1985, 1987; Schegloff, 1984).

We acknowledge that this approach has yielded useful insights, and we share many goals of the investigators who employ it; at the same time, we believe a method that relies so heavily on an investigator's intuitions can yield misleading results because there are no independent means of corroborating the observer's inferences. For a gesture to convey semantic information, there must be a relationship between its form and the meaning it conveys. In interpreting the gesture's meaning, the interpreter relates some feature of the gesture to the meaning of the speech it accompanies. For example, in a discussion that we videotaped, a speaker described one object's position relative to that of another as "a couple of feet behind it, maybe oh [pause], ten or so degrees to the right." During the pause, he performed a gesture with a vertical palm and extended fingers that moved away from his body at an acute angle from the perpendicular. The relationship of the gesture to the conceptual content of the speech seems transparent; the direction of the gesture's movement illustrates the relative positions of the two objects in the description. However, direction was only one property of the gesture. In focusing on the gesture's direction, we ignored its velocity, extent, duration, and the particular hand configuration—all

---

[6] Indeed, the term *communication* itself has proved difficult to define satisfactorily (see Krauss & Fussell, in press for a discussion of this and related issues).

potentially meaningful features—and selected the one that seemed to make sense in that verbal context. In the absence of independent corroboration, it is difficult to reject the possibility that the interpretation is a construction based on the accompanying speech and owes little to the gesture's form. Without the accompanying speech, the gesture may convey little or nothing; with the accompanying speech, it may add little or nothing to what is conveyed verbally. For this reason, we are inclined to regard such interpretations as a source of hypotheses to be tested rather than useable data.

Moreover, because of differences in the situations of observer and participant, even if such interpretations could be corroborated empirically, it is not clear what bearing they would have on the communicative functions the gestures serve. An observer's interpretation of a gesture's meaning typically is based on careful viewing and re-viewing of a filmed or videotaped record. The naive participant in the interaction must process the gesture online, while simultaneously attending to the spoken message, planning a response, and so forth. The fact that a gesture contained relevant information would not guarantee that it would be accessible to an addressee.

What is needed is an independent means of demonstrating that gestures convey information, and that such information contributes to the effectiveness of communication. We later describe several studies that attempt to assess the kinds of information conversational gestures convey to naive observers and the extent to which gestures enhance the communicativeness of spoken messages.

A. THE SEMANTIC CONTENT OF CONVERSATIONAL GESTURES

For a conversational gesture to convey semantic information, it must satisfy two conditions. First, the gesture must be associated with some semantic content. Second, that relationship must be comprehensible to listeners. "Gestionaries" that catalog the meanings of gestures do not exist. Indeed, there is no reliable notational system for describing gestures. Therefore, it is not obvious how one establishes a gesture's semantic content. We next report three experiments using different methods to examine the semantic content of gestures.

1. The Semantic Content of Gestures and Speech

We can examine the semantic content of gestures by looking at the meanings that naive observers attribute to them. If a gesture conveys semantic content related to the semantic content of the speech that it accompanies, then the meanings observers attribute to the gesture should have semantic content similar to that of the speech. Krauss et al. (1991, Experiment 2) showed videotaped gestures to subjects and asked them to write an impression of each gesture's meaning. We refer to these impressions as *interpretations*. We then directed another sample of subjects to read each interpretation and rate its similarity to each of two phrases. One of the phrases had originally accompanied the gesture, and the other had accompanied a randomly selected gesture.

The stimuli used in this and the next two experiments were 60 brief ($M = 2.49$ s) segments excerpted from videotapes of speakers describing pictures of landscapes, abstractions, buildings, machines, and people. The process by which this corpus of gestures and phrases were selected is described in detail elsewhere (Krauss et al., 1991; Morrel-Samuels, 1989; Morrel-Samuels & Krauss, 1992) and is only summarized here. Naive subjects, provided with transcripts of the descriptions, viewed the videotapes sentence by sentence. After each sentence, they indicated 1) whether the movement they had seen was a gesture, and 2) if it was, the word or phrase in the accompanying speech that they perceived to be related to it. We refer to the words or phrases judged to be related to a gesture as the gesture's *lexical affiliate*. The 60 segments whose lexical affiliates were agreed on by 8 or more of the 10 viewers (and that met certain other technical criteria) were randomly partitioned into two sets of 30 and edited in random order onto separate videotapes.

Six subjects (3 males and 3 females) viewed each of the 60 gestures, without hearing the accompanying speech, and wrote down what they believed to be its intended meaning. The tape was stopped between gestures to give the subjects sufficient time to write down their interpretations. Each of the 60 interpretations produced by one interpreter was given to another subject (judge), along with two lexical affiliates labeled "A" and "B." One of the two lexical affilitates had originally accompanied the gesture that had served as the stimulus for the interpretation; the other was a lexical affiliate that had accompanied a randomly chosen gesture. Judges were asked to indicate on a six-point scale with poles labeled "very similar to A" and "very similar to B" which of the two lexical affiliates was closer in meaning to the interpretation.

On 62% of the trials ($SD = 17\%$), judges rated the gesture's interpretation to be closer in meaning to its original lexical affiliate than to the lexical affiliate of another gesture. This value is reliably greater than the chance value of .50 ($t_{(59)} = 12.34, p < .0001$). We also coded each of the 60 lexical affiliates into one of four semantic categories: *Locations* (e.g., "There's another young girl to the woman's *right*," "passing it *horizontally* to the picture"[7]); *Actions* (e.g., "rockets or bullets *flying out,*" "seems like it's going to *swallow them up*"); *Objects* (e.g., "scarf or *kerchief* around her head," "actual *frame* of the window and the Venetian blind"); and *Descriptions* (e.g., "one of those *Pointillist* paintings," "which is *covered* with paper and books").[8] Accuracy varied reliably as a function of the lexical affiliate's semantic category ($F_{(3,56)}$ = 4.72, $p < .005$). Accuracy was greatest when the lexical affiliates were Actions (73%), somewhat lower for Locations (66%) and considerably lower for Objects and Descriptions (57% and 52%, respectively). The first two means differed reliably from 50% ($t_{(56)}$ = 5.29 and 4.51, respectively, both $ps < .0001$); the latter two did not ($ts < 1$).

Gestures viewed in isolation convey some semantic information, as evidenced by the fact that they elicit interpretations more similar in meaning to their own lexical affiliates than to the lexical affiliates of other gestures. The range of meanings they convey seems to be rather limited when compared to speech. Note that our gestures had been selected because naive subjects perceived them to be meaningful *and* agreed on the words in the accompanying speech to which they were related. Yet interpretations of these gestures, made in the absence of speech, were judged more similar to their original lexical affiliates at a rate that was only 12% better than chance. The best of our six interpreters (i.e., the one whose interpretations most frequently yielded the correct lexical affiliate) had a success rate of 66%; the best judge–interpreter combination achieved an accuracy score of 72%. Thus, although gestures may serve as a guide to what is being conveyed verbally, it would be difficult to argue on the basis of these data that they are a particularly effective guide. It needs to be stressed that our test of communicativeness is a relatively undemanding one (i.e., whether the interpretation enabled a judge to discriminate the correct lexical affiliate from a randomly selected affiliate that, on the average, was relatively dissimilar in meaning). The fact that, with so lenient a criterion, performance was barely better than chance undermines the plausibility of the claim that gestures play an important role in communication when speech is fully accessible.

2. Memory for Gestures

An alternative way of exploring the kinds of meanings that gestures and speech convey is to examine how they are represented in memory (Krauss

---

[7] The italicized words are those judged by subjects to be related in meaning to the meaning of the gesture.

[8] The 60 lexical affiliates were distributed fairly equally among the four coding categories (approximately 33%, 22%, 22%, and 23%, respectively), and two coders working independently agreed on 85% of the categorizations ($k = .798$).

et al., 1991, Experiments 3 and 4). We know that words are remembered in terms of their meanings, rather than as strings of letters or phonemes. If gestures convey meanings, we might likewise expect those meanings to be represented in memory. Using a recognition memory paradigm, we can compare recognition accuracy for lexical affiliates, for the gestures that accompanied the lexical affiliates, and for the speech and gestures combined. If gestures convey information that is different from the information conveyed by the lexical affiliate, then we would expect that speech and gestures combined would be better recognized than either speech or gestures separately. However, if gestures simply convey a less rich version of the information conveyed by speech, we might expect that adding gestural information to speech would have little effect on recognition memory, compared to memory for the speech alone.

The experiment was run in two phases: a presentation phase, in which subjects saw and/or heard the material that they would later try to recognize and a recognition phase, in which they heard and/or saw a pair of segments and tried to select the one they had seen before. We examined recognition in three modality conditions: an *audio-video* condition, in which subjects attempted to recognize the previously exposed segment from the combined audio and video; a *video-only* condition, in which recognition was based on the video portion with the sound turned off; and an *audio-only* condition, in which subjects heard the sound without seeing the picture. We also varied the presentation phase. In the *single-channel* condition, the 30 segments were presented in the same way that they would later be recognized (i.e., sound only if recognition was to be in the audio-only condition, etc.). In the *full channel* condition, all subjects saw the audiovisual version in the presentation phase, irrespective of their recognition condition. They were informed of the recognition condition to which they had been assigned, and told that they would later be asked to distinguish segments to which they had been exposed from new segments on the basis of the video portion only, the audio portion only, or the combined audio-video segment. The instructions stressed the importance of attending to the aspect of the display that they would later try to recognize. About 5 min after completing the presentation phase, all subjects performed a forced-choice recognition test with 30 pairs of segments seen and/or heard in the appropriate recognition mode.

A total of 144 undergraduates, 24 in each of the 3 × 2 conditions, served as subjects. They were about equally distributed between males and females.

The means for the six conditions are plotted in Figure 2. Large effects were found for the recognition mode ($F_{(2,33)} = 40.23, p < .0001$), the presentation mode ($F_{(1,33)} = 5.69, p < .02$), and their interaction ($F_{(2,33)} = 4.75, p < .02$). Speech accompanied by gesture was no better recognized than

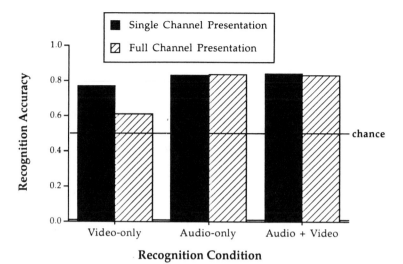

Fig. 2. Recognition accuracy (proportion correct) for videotaped segments from video-only, audio-only, and audio-video presentations.

speech alone ($F < 1$). For the audio-only and audio-video conditions, recognition rates were virtually identical in the two presentation mode conditions, and hearing speech in its gestural context did not improve subsequent recognition. However, in the video-only condition there were substantial differences in performance across the two initial presentations. Compared to subjects who initially saw only the gestures, subjects who had viewed gestures and had simultaneously heard the accompanying speech were subsequently *less* likely to recognize them. Indeed, their mean recognition rate was only about 10% better than the chance level of 50%, and the difference in video-only recognition accuracy between the two conditions (.733 vs. .610) was reliable ($F_{(1,33)} = 14.97$, $p < .0001$).

Conversational gestures seen in isolation do not appear to be especially memorable, and, paradoxically, combining them with the accompanying speech makes them significantly less so. We believe that subjects found it difficult to recognize gestures they had seen in isolation a few minutes earlier because the gestures had to be remembered in terms of their physical properties rather than their meanings. Why then did putting them in a communicative context make them more difficult to recognize? Our hypothesis is that subjects used the verbal context to impute meanings to the gestures, then used these meanings to encode the gestures in memory. If the meanings imputed to the gesture were largely a product of the lexical affiliate, they would be of little help in the subsequent recognition task.

The transparent meaning a gesture has when seen in the context of its lexical affiliate may be illusory—a construction deriving primarily from the lexical affiliate's meaning.

3. Sources of Variance in the Attribution of Gestural Meaning

Our hypothesized explanation for the low-recognition accuracy of gestures initially seen in the context of the accompanying speech is speculative because we have no direct way of ascertaining the strategies our subjects employed when they tried to remember and recognize the gestures. However, the explanation rests on an assumption that is testable, namely, that the meanings people attribute to gestures derive mainly from the meanings of the lexical affiliates. We can estimate the relative contributions gestural and speech information make to judgments of one component of a gesture's meaning: its semantic category. If the gesture's form makes only a minor contribution to its perceived meaning, then remembering the meaning will be of limited value in an effort to recognize the gesture.

To assess this, we asked subjects to assign the gestures in our 60 segments to one of 4 semantic categories (actions, locations, objects, and descriptions) in one of two conditions: a video-only condition, in which they saw the gesture in isolation, or an audio-video condition, in which they both saw the gesture and heard the accompanying speech. Instructions for the audio-video condition stressed that it was the meaning of the gestures that was to be categorized. Two additional groups of subjects categorized the gestures' lexical affiliates—one group from the audio track and the other from verbatim transcripts. From these four sets of judgments, we were able to estimate the relative contribution of speech and gestural information to this component of a gesture's perceived meaning. Forty undergraduates, rather evenly divided between males and females, served as subjects, 10 in each condition (Krauss et al., 1991, Experiment 5).[9]

Our experiment yielded a set of four 4 × 4 contingency tables displaying the distribution of semantic categories attributed to gestures or lexical affiliates as a function of the semantic category of the lexical affiliate (Table I). The primary question of interest here is the relative influence of speech and gestural form on judgments of a gesture's semantic category. Unfortunately, with categorical data of this kind there is no clear "best" way to pose such a question statistically.[10] One approach is to calculate a multiple regression model using the 16 frequencies in the corresponding cells of

---

[9] The subjects in the transcript condition were paid for participating. The remainder were volunteers.

[10] Because many cells have very small expected values, a log-linear analysis would be inappropriate.

TABLE I

SUBJECTS' ASSIGNMENTS OF GESTURES OR SPEECH TO SEMANTIC CATEGORY AS A FUNCTION OF THE SEMANTIC CATEGORY OF THE LEXICAL AFFILIATE, SHOWN FOR JUDGMENTS MADE FROM (A) AUDIO-VIDEO, (B) VIDEO-ONLY, (C) AUDIO-ONLY AND (D) TRANSCRIPT. (A = ACTIONS; L = LOCATIONS; O = OBJECT NAMES; AND D = DESCRIPTIONS.) N = 600 (10 SUBJECTS × 60 JUDGMENTS) PER MATRIX

		Semantic Category Judged from								
		a. Audio-video				b. Video-only				
		A	L	O	D	A	L	O	D	%
Semantic category	A	91	7	5	27	54	13	20	43	21.7
of lexical affiliate	L	32	110	6	52	55	44	28	73	33.3
	O	4	28	52	46	28	22	32	48	21.7
	D	12	31	12	85	26	21	20	73	23.3
	Σ	139	166	85	210	163	100	100	237	
	%	23.2	27.7	14.2	35.0	27.2	16.7	16.7	39.5	
		c. Audio-only				d. Transcript				
		A	L	O	D	A	L	O	D	%
Semantic category	A	69	9	6	46	91	1	2	36	21.7
of lexical affiliate	L	18	100	16	66	28	107	11	54	33.3
	O	3	5	47	75	0	0	109	21	21.7
	D	9	21	30	80	5	20	6	109	23.3
	Σ	99	135	99	267	124	128	128	220	
	%	16.5	22.5	16.5	44.0	20.7	21.3	21.3	36.7	

video-only, audio-only, and transcript condition tables as the independent variables, and the values in the cells of the audio-video table as the dependent variable. Overall, the model accounted for 92% of the variance in the cell frequencies of the audio-video matrix ($F_{(3,12)}$ = 46.10; $p < .0001$); however, the contribution of the video-only matrix was negligible. The β-coefficient for the video-only matrix is $-.026$ ($t = .124$, $p < .90$); for the audio-only condition, $\beta = .511$ ($t = 3.062$, $p < .01$); and for the transcript condition, $\beta = .42$ ($t = 3.764$, $p < .003$). Such an analysis does not take between-subject variance into account. An alternative analytic approach employs multivariate analysis of variance (MANOVA). Each of the four matrices in Table I represents the mean of 10 matrices—one for each of the 10 subjects in that condition. By treating the values in the cells of each subject's 4 × 4 matrix as 16 dependent variables, we can compute a MANOVA using the four presentation conditions as a between-subjects variable. Given a significant overall test, we could then determine which contrasts of the six between-subjects conditions (i.e., audio-video vs. audio-only, audio-video vs. transcript, audio-video vs. video-only, audio-only vs. transcript, audio-only vs. video-only, transcript vs. video-only) differ reliably. Wilk's test indicates the presence of reliable differences among the four conditions ($F_{(36,74.59)} = 6.72$, $p < .0001$). F ratios for the six between-condition contrasts are shown in Table II. As that table indicates, the video-only condition differs reliably from the audio-video condition, and from the audio-only and transcript conditions as well. The latter two conditions differ reliably from each other, but not from the audio-video condition.

Both analytic approaches lead to the conclusion that judgments of a gesture's semantic category based on visual information alone are quite different from the same judgments made when the accompanying speech is accessible. What is striking is that judgments of a gesture's semantic category made in the presence of its lexical affiliate are not reliably different from judgments of the lexical affiliate's category made from the lexical affiliate alone. Unlike the regression analysis, the MANOVA takes the within-cell variances into account, but it does not readily yield an index of the proportion of variance accounted for by each of the independent variables.

Taken together, the multiple regression and MANOVA analyses lead to a relatively straightforward conclusion: At least for the 60 gestures in our corpus, when people can hear the lexical affiliate, their interpretation of the gesture's meaning (as that is reflected in its semantic category) is largely a product of what they hear rather than what they see. Both analyses also indicate that the audio-only and transcript conditions contribute unique

TABLE II
VALUE OF MULTIVARIATE F-RATIOS (WILK'S λ) FOR BETWEEN-CONDITION CONTRASTS. ALL CONTRASTS WITH 12,7 DF

	A + V	Aud	Tran	Vid
Audio-video	—	1.61	3.14	6.52**
Audio-only	—	—	5.33*	17.6***
Transcript	—	—	—	12.85***
Video-only	—	—	—	—

$*p < .05.$
$**p < .01.$
$***p < .0001.$

variance to judgments made in the audio-video condition. Although judgments made in the audio-only and transcript conditions are highly correlated ($r_{(15)}$ = .815, p < .0001), the MANOVA indicates that they also differ reliably. In the regression analysis, the two account for independent shares of the audio-video variance. Because the speech and transcript contain the same semantic information, these results suggest that such rudimentary interpretations of the gesture's meaning take paralinguistic information into account.

B. GESTURAL CONTRIBUTIONS TO COMMUNICATION

The experiments described in the previous section attempted, using a variety of methods, to assess the semantic content of spontaneous conversational hand gestures. Our general conclusion was that these gestures convey relatively little semantic information. However, any conclusion must be tempered by the fact that there is no standard method of assessing the semantic content of gestures, and it might be argued that our results simply reflect the imprecision of our methods. Another approach to assessing the communicativeness of conversational gestures is to examine the utility of the information they convey. It is conceivable that, although the semantic information that gestures convey is meager quantitatively, they nevertheless play a critical role in communication, and that the availability of gestures improve a speaker's ability to communicate. In this section we describe a set of studies that attempt to determine whether the presence of conversational gestures enhances the effectiveness of communication.

If meaningfulness is a nebulous concept, communicative effectiveness is hardly more straightforward. We will take a functional approach: Communication is effective to the extent that it accomplishes its intended goal. For example, other things being equal, directions to a destination are effective to the extent that a person who follows them gets to the destination. Such an approach makes no assumptions about the form of the message: how much detail it contains, from whose spatial perspective it is formulated, the speech genre it employs, and so on. The sole criterion is how well it accomplishes its intended purpose. Of course, with this approach the addressee's performance contributes to the measure of communicative effectiveness. In the previous example, the person might fail to reach the destination because the directions were insufficiently informative or because the addressee did a poor job of following them. We can control for the variance attributable to the listener by having several listeners respond to the same message.

The procedure we used was a modified referential communication task (Fussell & Krauss, 1989a; Krauss & Glucksberg, 1977; Krauss & Weinheimer, 1966). Reference entails using language to designate some state of affairs in the world. In a referential communication task, one person (the speaker or encoder) describes or designates one item in an array of items in such a way that another person (the listener or decoder) can identify the target item. By recording the message the encoder produces, we can present it to several decoders and assess the extent to which it elicits identification of the correct stimulus.

1. Gestural Enhancement of Referential Communication

In three experiments, we examined the extent to which conversational gestures enhanced the communicative effectiveness of messages in a referential communication task (Krauss, et al., in press). The experiments were essentially identical in design. By varying the nature of the stimuli that encoders described, we varied the content of communication from experiment to experiment. To examine whether the communicative value of gestures depended upon the spatial or pictographic quality of the referent, we used stimuli that were explicitly spatial (novel abstract designs), spatial by analogy (novel synthesized sounds), and not at all spatial (tastes).

Speakers were videotaped as they described the stimuli either to listeners seated across a small table (*face-to-face* condition), or over an intercom to listeners in an adjoining room (*intercom* condition). The videotaped descriptions were presented to new subjects (decoders), who tried to select the stimulus described. Half of these decoders both saw and heard the videotape; the remainder only heard the soundtrack. The design permitted us to compare the communicative effectiveness of messages accompanied by gestures with the effectiveness of the same messages without the accompanying gestures. It also permitted us to examine the communicative effectiveness of gestures originally performed in the presence of another person (hence potentially communicatively intended) with gestures originally performed when the listener could not see the speaker.

a. Novel abstract designs. For stimuli we used a set of 10 novel abstract designs taken from a set of designs previously used in other studies (Fussell & Krauss, 1989a, 1989b). A sample is shown in Figure 3. The designs were described by 36 undergraduates (18 males and 18 females) over an intercom to a listener in another room or to a same-sex listener seated in face-to-face situation across a small table. Speakers were videotaped via a wall-mounted camera that captured a frontal view from approximately the waist up.

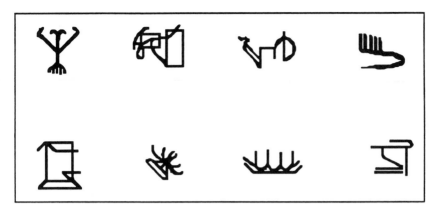

Fig. 3. A sample of the novel graphic designs used as stimuli.

To construct stimulus tapes for the decoder phase of the experiment, we drew 8 random samples of 45 descriptions (sampled without replacement) from the 360 generated in the encoder phase, and edited each onto a videotape in random order. Then 86 undergraduates (32 males and 54 females) either heard-and-saw one of the videotapes (audio-video condition), or only heard its soundtrack (audio-only condition) in groups of 1 to 5.

The mean proportions of correct identifications in the four conditions are shown in the left panels of Table III. As inspection of that table suggests, accuracy does not vary reliably as a function of the decoder condition ($F_{(1,168)} = 1.21$, $p = .27$). Decoders were no more accurate in identifying graphic designs when they could both see and hear the person doing the describing than they were when they could only hear the describer's voice. A

TABLE III
ACCURACY OF IDENTIFICATION (proportion correct) OF NOVEL FIGURES AND SOUNDS AS A
FUNCTION OF ENCODING AND DECODING CONDITION

Encoding condition	Decoding condition					
	Designs			Sounds		
	Audio-only	Audio-video		Audio-only	Audio-video	
Intercom	.696	.692	.694	.669	.685	.677
Face-to-face	.614	.667	.642	.635	.644	.639
	.655	.679		.652	.664	

reliable effect was found for the encoder condition ($F_{(1,168)}$ = 5.72, p = .02). Surprisingly, decoders were somewhat more accurate in identifying the designs from descriptions that originally had been given in the intercom decoding condition. However, regardless of the encoding condition, being able to see the encoder did not affect the decoder's accuracy either positively or negatively. The encoder × decoder interaction was not significant ($F_{(111,168)}$ = 1.61, p = .21).

b. Novel Sounds. The same 36 undergraduates who described the novel designs also listened to 10 pairs of novel sounds using headphones and described one sound from each pair to their partners. Half of the encoders each described the sounds to a partner seated in the same room; the partner for each of the remainder was located in a nearby room. The sounds had been produced by a sound synthesizer and resembled the sorts of sound effects found in a science fiction movie. Except for the stimulus, conditions for the encoding phase of the two experiments were identical. From these descriptions, 6 stimulus tapes, each containing 60 descriptions selected randomly without replacement were constructed. For the next step, 98 paid undergraduates (43 males and 55 females) served as decoders in groups of 1 to 4. They either heard (in the audio-only condition) or viewed and heard (in the audio-video condition) a description of one synthesized sound from the pair, then heard the two sounds and indicated on a response sheet which of the two sounds matched the description.

As was the case with the graphic designs, descriptions of the synthesized sounds made in the intercom coding condition elicited a somewhat higher level of correct identifications than those made face-to-face ($F_{(1,168)}$ = 10.91, p < .001). However, no advantage accrued to decoders who could see the speaker in the video, compared to those who could only hear the soundtrack. The means for the audio-video and audio-only conditions did not differ significantly ($F_{(1,168)}$ = 1.21, p = .27); neither did the encoder × decoder interaction (F < 1). The means for the four conditions are shown in the right panel of Table III.

c. Tea Samples. As stimuli, we used eight varieties of commercially available tea bags that would produce brews with distinctively different tastes. The encoders were 36 undergraduates, approximately evenly divided between males and females. They were given cups containing two tea samples, one of which was designated as the target stimulus. They tasted each and were videotaped as they described the target to a same-sex partner so that it could be distinguished from its pairmate. Half of the encoders described the sample in a face-to-face condition, the remainder in an intercom condition. From these videotaped descriptions, two videotapes were constructed, each containing 72 descriptions, half from the face-to-face condition, the remainder from the intercom condition. Then 43 undergraduates (20 males and 23 females) either heard or heard-and-saw one of the two videotapes. For each description, they tasted two tea samples and tried to decide which one matched it.

Overall identification accuracy was relatively low ($M = .555$; $SD = .089$), but better than the chance level of .50 ($t_{(85)} = 5.765$, $p < .0001$). The means are shown in Table IV. As was the case for the designs and sounds, the analysis of variance (ANOVA) of the proportion of correct identifications revealed a significant effect attributable to the encoding condition, but for the tea samples, the descriptions of face-to-face encoders produced a slightly, but significantly, *higher* rate of correct identifications than those of intercom encoders ($F_{(1,41)} = 5.71$, $p < .02$). Nevertheless, as in the previous two experiments, no effect was found for the decoding condition, or for the encoding–decoding interaction (both Fs < 1).

Thus, in none of the three experiments did we find the slightest indication that being able to see a speaker's gestures enhanced the effectiveness of communication, as compared to simply hearing the speech. Although the logic of statistical hypothesis testing does not permit positive affirmation of the null hypothesis, our failure to find differences cannot be attributed simply to a lack of power of our experiments. Our three experiments employed considerably more subjects, both as encoders and decoders, than is the norm in such research. By calculating the statistical power of our test, we can estimate the least significant number (LSN) (i.e., the number of subjects that would have been required to reject the null hypothesis with $a = .05$ for the audio-only vs. audio-video contrast, given the size of the observed differences). For the novel designs it is 548; for the sounds it is 614. The LSNs for the encoder condition–decoder condition interactions are similarly large: 412 and 7677 for designs and sounds, respectively.

It was not that speakers simply failed to gesture, at least not in the first two experiments. On the average, speakers gestured about 14 times per minute when describing the graphic designs, and about 12 times per minute

TABLE IV

ACCURACY OF IDENTIFICATION OF TEA SAMPLES (proportion correct) AS A FUNCTION OF ENCODING AND DECODING CONDITION

Encoding condition	Decoding condition		
	Audio-only	Audio-video	
Intercom	.528	.541	.535
Face-to-face	.586	.566	.575
	.557	.554	

when describing the sounds; for some speakers, the rate exceeded 25 gestures per minute. Yet no relationship was found between the effectiveness with which a message was communicated and the amount of gesturing that accompanied it. Given these data, along with the absence of a credible body of contradictory results in the literature, it seems to us that only two conclusions are supportable: Either gestural accompaniments of speech do not enhance the communicativeness of speech in settings such as the ones we studied, or the extent to which they do so is negligible.

2. Gestural Enhancement of Communication in a Nonfluent Language

Gestures may not ordinarily facilitate communication in settings such as the ones we have studied, but perhaps they do in special circumstances (e.g., when the speaker has difficulty conveying an idea linguistically). Certainly many travelers have discovered that energetic pantomiming can make up for a deficient vocabulary and make it possible to "get by" with little mastery of a langauge. Dushay (1991) examined the extent to which speakers used gestures to compensate for a lack of fluency, and whether the gestures enhanced the communicativeness of messages in a referential communication task.

Dushay's procedure was similar to that used in the studies described in the preceding section. As stimuli he used the novel figures and synthesized sounds employed in those experiments, and the experimental setup was essentially identical. His subjects (20 native English-speaking undergraduates taking their fourth semester of Spanish) were videotaped describing stimuli either face-to-face with their partner (a Spanish–English bilingual) or communicating over an intercom. On half of the trials the subjects described the stimuli in English, and on the remainder in Spanish. The videotapes of their descriptions were edited and presented to eight Spanish–English bilinguals, who tried to identify the stimulus described. On half of the trials, they heard the soundtrack but did not see the video portion (audio-only condition), and on the remainder they both heard and saw the description (audio-visual condition).

Speakers did not use more conversational gestures when describing the stimuli in Spanish than when doing so in English.[11] When they described

---

[11] Although this was true of conversational gestures, the overall rate for all types of gestures was slightly higher when subjects spoke Spanish. The difference is accounted for largely by what Dushay called "groping movements" (repetitive, typically circular bilateral movements of the hands at about waist level), which were about seven times more frequent when subjects spoke Spanish. Groping movements seemed to occur when speakers were having difficulty recalling the Spanish equivalent of an English word. Different instances of groping movements varied little within the conversation of each speaker, although there was considerable variability from speaker to speaker. Therefore, it is unlikely that such movements were used to convey information, but most likely that the speaker was searching for a word.

the novel figures, their gesture rates in the two languages were identical, and when they described the synthesized sound their gesture rate in Spanish was slightly, but significantly, lower. Moreover, being able to see the gestures did not enhance listeners' ability to identify the stimulus being described. Not surprising, descriptions in English produced more accurate identifications than descriptions in Spanish, but for neither language (and neither stimulus type) did the speaker benefit from seeing the speaker.

C. GESTURES AND THE COMMUNICATION OF NONSEMANTIC INFORMATION

The experiments described previously concerned the communication of semantic information, implicitly accepting the traditionally assumed parallelism of gesture and speech. However, semantic information is only one kind of information that speech conveys. Even when the verbal content of speech is unintelligible, paralinguistic information is present that permits listeners to make reliable judgments of the speaker's internal affective state (Krauss, Apple, Morency, Wenzel, & Winton, 1981; Scherer, Koivumaki, & Rosenthal, 1972; Scherer, London, & Wolf, 1973). Variations in dialect and usage can provide information about a speaker's social category membership (Scherer & Giles, 1979). Variations in the fluency of speech production can provide an insight into the speaker's confidence, spontaneity, involvement, and so on. There is considerable evidence that our impressions of others are, to a great extent, mediated by their nonverbal behavior (DePaulo, 1992). It may be the case that gestures convey similar sorts of information, and thereby contribute to participants' abilities to play their respective roles in interaction.

1. Lexical Movements and Impressions of Spontaneity

Evaluations of spontaneity can affect the way we understand and respond to others' behaviors. Our research on spontaneity judgments was guided by the theoretical position that gestures, like other nonverbal behaviors, often serve both intrapersonal and interpersonal functions. An interesting characteristics of such behaviors is that they are only partially under voluntary control. Although many self-presentational goals can be achieved nonverbally (DePaulo, 1992), the demands of cognitive processing constrains a speaker's ability to use these behaviors strategically (Fleming & Darley, 1991). Because of this, certain nonverbal behaviors can reveal information about the cognitive processes that underlie a speaker's utterances. Listeners may be sensitive to these indicators and may use them to draw inferences about the conditions under which speech was generated.

Chawla and Krauss (1994) studied subjects' sensitivity to nonverbal cues that reflect processing by examining their ability to distinguish between spontaneous and rehearsed speech. Subjects either heard (audio condition), viewed without sound (video condition), or heard and saw (audio-video condition) eight pairs of videotaped narratives, each consisting of a spontaneous narrative and its rehearsed counterpart. The rehearsed version was obtained by giving the transcript of the original narrative to a professional actor of the same sex who was instructed to prepare an authentic and realistic portrayal.[12] Subjects were shown the spontaneous and the rehearsed versions of each scene and tried to identify the spontaneous one. They also were asked to rate how real or spontaneous each portrayal seemed to be. Comparing the performances of subjects in the three presentation conditions allowed us to assess the role of visual and vocal cues while keeping verbal content constant.

In the audio-video presentation condition, subjects correctly distinguished the spontaneous from the rehearsed scenes 80% of the time. In the audio and video conditions, accuracy was somewhat lower (means = 66% and 60%, respectively) although in both cases it was reliably above the chance level of 50%. The audio-video condition differed reliably from the audio and video conditions, but the latter two conditions did not.

Subjects evidenced some sensitivity to subtle nonverbal cues that derive from differences in the way spontaneous and rehearsed speech are processed. A scene's spontaneity rating in the audio-video condition was significantly correlated with the proportion of time the speaker spent making lexical movements, and with the conditional probability of nonjuncture pauses. Given that nonjuncture pauses and lexical movements both reflect problems in lexical access, and that the problems of lexical access are much greater in spontaneous speech than in posed or rehearsed speech, we would expect these two behaviors to be reliable cues in differentiating between spontaneous and rehearsed speech. Interestingly, the subjects' judgments of spontaneity were not related to the total amount of time they spent gesturing or to the total number of pauses in their speech.

Unfortunately, we were not able to get any direct corroboration of our hypothesis from subjects' descriptions of the cues they used to make their judgments. It appears that subjects used nonverbal information in complex ways they were unable to describe. Our subjects appeared to have no insight into the cues they had used and the processes by which they had reached their judgments.

---

[12] Additional details on this aspect of the study are given in Section VI,A,1.

The results of this experiment are consistent with our view that gestures convey nonsemantic information that could, in particular circumstances, be quite useful. Although our judges' ability to discriminate spontaneous from rehearsed scenes was far from perfect, especially when they had only visual information to use, our actors' portrayals may have been unusually artful; we doubt that portrayals by less skilled performers would have been as convincing. Of course, our subjects viewed the scenes on videotape, aware that one of them was duplicitous. In everyday interactions, people often are too involved in the situation to question others' authenticity.

V. Intrapersonal Functions: Gestures and Speech Production

An alternative to the view of gestures as devices for the communication of semantic information focuses on the role of gestures in the speech production process.[13] One possibility, suggested several times over the last 50 years by a remarkably heterogeneous group of writers, contends that gestures help speakers formulate coherent speech, particularly when they are experiencing difficulty retrieving elusive words from lexical memory (DeLaguna, 1927; Ekman & Friesen, 1972; Freedman, 1972; Mead, 1934; Moscovici, 1967; Werner & Kaplan, 1963), although none of the writers who have made the proposal provide details on the mechanisms by which gestures accomplish this. In an early empirical study, Dobrogaev (1929) reported that preventing speakers from gesturing resulted in decreased fluency, impaired articulation, and reduced vocabulary size.[14]

More recently, three studies have examind the effects that preventing gesturing has on speech. Lickiss and Wellens (1978) found no effects on verbal fluency from restraining speakers' hand movements, but it is unclear exactly which dysfluencies they examined. Graham and Heywood (1975) compared the speech of the six speakers in the Graham and Argyle (1975) study who described abstract line drawings and were prevented from ges-

---

[13] Another alternative, proposed by Dittmann (1977), suggests that gestures serve to dissipate excess tension generated by the exigencies of speech production. Hewes (1973) has proposed a theory of the gestural origins of speech in which gestures are seen as vestigial behaviors with no current function—a remnant of human evolutionary history. Although the two theories correctly (in our judgment) emphasize the connection of gesturing and speech, neither is supported by credible evidence, and we regard both as implausible.

[14] Unfortunately, like many papers written in that era, Dobrogaev's includes virtually no details of procedure, and describes results in qualitative terms (e.g., "Both the articulatory and semantic quality of speech was degraded"), making it impossible to assess the plausibility of the claim. In Section VI we describe an attempt to replicate the finding.

turing on half of the descriptions. Although statistically significant effects of preventing gesturing were found on some indices, Graham and Heywood concluded that "elimination of gesture has no particularly marked effects on speech performance" (p. 194). Given their small sample of speakers and the fact that significant or near-significant effects were found for several contrasts, the conclusion seems unwarranted. In a rather different sort of study, Rimé, Schiaratura, Hupet, and Ghysselinckx (1984) had speakers converse while their head, arms, hands, legs, and feet were restrained. Content analysis found less vivid imagery in the speech of these speakers who could not move.

Despite these bits of evidence, support in the research literature for the idea that gestures are implicated in speech production, and specifically in lexical access, is less than compelling. Nevertheless, this is the position we take. To understand how gestures might accomplish this, it is necessary to consider the process by which speech is produced.[15]

A. SPEECH PRODUCTION

Although several different models of speech production have been proposed, virtually all distinguish three stages of the process. We will follow Levelt (1989) in referring to these stages as *conceptualizing, formulating,* and *articulating.* Conceptualizing involves, among other things, drawing upon declarative and procedural knowledge to construct a communicative intention. The output of the conceptualizing stage—what Levelt refers to as a *preverbal message*—is a conceptual structure containing a set of semantic specifications. At the formulating stage, the preverbal message is transformed in two ways. First, a grammatical encoder maps the to-be-lexicalized concept onto a lemma (i.e., an abstract symbol representing the selected word as a semantic-syntactic entity) in the mental lexicon whose meaning matches the content of the preverbal message. By using syntactic information contained in the lemma, the encoder transforms the conceptual structure into a *surface structure.* Then, a phonological encoder transforms the surface structure into a *phonetic plan* (essentially a set of instructions to the articulatory system) by accessing word forms stored in lexical memory and constructing an appropriate plan for the utterance's prosody. Finally, the output of the articulatory stage is overt speech. The process is illustrated schematically by the structure in the shaded portion of Figure 4.

---

[15] In discussions of speech production, "gesture" often is used to refer to what are more properly called *articulatory gestures* (i.e., linguistically significant acts of the articulatory system). We will restrict our use of the term to hand gestures.

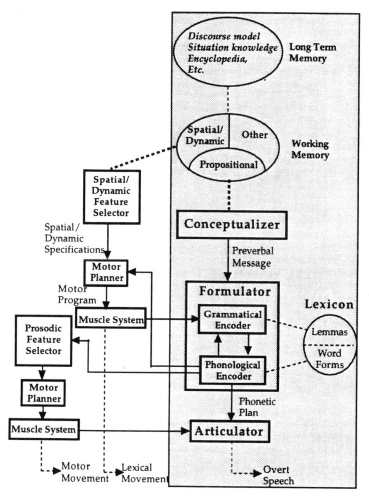

Fig. 4. A model of speech and gesture production processes. Boxes represent processing components; circle and ellipses represent knowledge stores. The speech-production (shaded) section is adapted directly from Levelt (1989); components of the gesture-production section were suggested by a rather different global architecture proposed informally by Jan Peter de Ruiter.

B. GESTURE PRODUCTION

The foregoing description of speech production leaves out many details of what is an extremely complex process, and many of these details are matters of considerable contention. Nevertheless, there is reason to believe that the account is essentially correct in its overall outline (see Levelt, 1989, for a review of the evidence). Unfortunately, we lack even so rudimentary a characterization of the process by which conversational gestures are generated, and because there is so little data to constrain theory, any account that we offer must be regarded as highly speculative.

In explaining the origins of gesture, we begin with the representation in short-term memory that finally is expressed in speech. For convenience, we will call this representation the *source concept*. The conceptual representation output by the conceptualizer that the grammatical encoder transforms into a linguistic representation will incorporate only some of the source concept's features. To put it somewhat differently, in any given utterance, only certain aspects of the source concept will be relevant to the speaker's communicative intention. For example, one might recall the dessert served with the previous evening's meal, and refer to it as the "cake." The particular cake represented in memory had a number of properties (e.g., size, shape, flavor, etc.) not included in the semantics of the word "cake." Presumably if these properties were relevant to the communicative intention, the speaker would have used some lexical device to express them (e.g., a "heart-shaped" cake).[16]

Our central assumption is that lexical movements are made up of representations of the source concept expressed motorically. Just as the linguistic representation often does not incorporate every feature of the source concept, so lexical movements reflect these features even more narrowly. The incorporated features are primarily spatiodynamic.

1. A Gesture Production Model

By adapting Levelt's speech production model, we have tried to formalize some of our ideas in a model that is capable of generating both speech and conversational gestures. Although the diagram in Figure 4 is little more than a sketch depicting one possible architecture for such a system, we find it useful because it suggests some of the mechanisms that might be necessary to account for the ways that gesturing and speaking interact.

The model requires that we make several assumptions about memory and mental representation:

1. Human memory employs a number of different formats to represent knowledge, and much of the contents of memory is multiply encoded in more than one representational format.

[16] The difference between the source concept and the linguistic representation is most clearly seen in reference, in which the linguistic representation is formulated specifically to direct a listener's attention to some thing, and typically incorporates only as much information as is necessary to accomplish this. Hence one may refer to a person as "the tall guy with red hair," employing only a few features of the far more complex and differentiated conceptual representation.

2. Activation of a concept in one representational format tends to activate related concepts in other formats.

3. Concepts differ in how adequately (i.e., efficiently, completely, accessibly, etc.) they can be represented in one or another format.

4. Some representations in one format can be translated into the representational form of another format (e.g., a verbal description can give rise to a visual image, and vice versa).

None of these assumptions is particularly controversial, at least at this level of generality.

2. Lexical Movements

We follow Levelt in assuming that inputs from working memory to the conceptualizing stage of the speech processor must be in propositional form. However, much of the knowledge that represents the source concept is multiply encoded in both propositional and nonpropositional representational formats, or is encoded exclusively in a nonpropositional format. In order to be reflected in speech, nonpropositionally encoded information must be "translated" into propositional form.

Our model posits a spatial/dynamic feature selector that transforms information stored in spatial or dynamic formats into a set of *spatial-dynamic specifications*. How this might work can be illustrated in a hypothetical example? Consider the word "vortex." Conceptually, a state of affairs called "a vortex" would include such spatial elements as size and form, and such dynamic elements as rate and path of motion. The conceptual structure would also include other elements—that the vortex is composed of a liquid, that it is capable of drawing things into it, and so forth. Let us say that the linguistic representation "vortex" includes the elements 1) movement, 2) circular, 3) liquid, 4) mass, and 5) in-drawing. A speaker having thus conceptualized a state of affairs, and wanting to convey this characterization, would search the lexicon for an entry that incorporates the relevant features, and ultimately arrive at the word "vortex." At the same time the spatial-dynamic feature selector might select the elements of motion and circularity, and transform them into a set of spatiodynamic specifications—essentially abstract properties of movements.[17] These abstract specifications would, in turn, be translated by a motor planner into

---

[17] We can only speculate as to what such abstract specifications might be like. One might expect concepts incorporating the feature FAST to be represented by rapid movements, and concepts incorporating the feature LARGE to be represented by movements with large linear displacements. However, we are unaware of any successful attempts to establish systematic relations between abstract dimensions of movement and dimensions of meaning. For a valiant but less-than-successful attempt, see Morrel-Samuels (1989).

a *motor program* that provides the motor system with a set of instructions for executing the lexical movement.

3. Motor Movements

Relatively little is known about the origins of motor movements or the functions they serve. Unlike lexical movements, which we believe have a conceptual origin, motor movments appear to be a product of speech production. Their coordination with the speech prosody suggests they could not be planned before a phonetic plan for the utterance had been established. As is illustrated in the speech production portion of the diagram in Figure 4, the phonetic plan is a product of the phonological encoder. Hence, by this account, motor movements originate at a relatively late stage of the speech production process. We hypothesize that a prosodic feature detector reduces the output of the phonological encoder to a relatively simple set of *prosodic specifications* marking the timing, and, perhaps the amplitude, of primary stresses in the speech. A motor planner translates the specification into a motor program expressing the cadence of stressed syllables in terms of the periodicity of strokes of the gesture, and the loudness of the stressed syllables in terms of the gesture's amplitude.

C. INTEGRATION OF SPEECH AND GESTURE PRODUCTION

Up to this point in our discussion, the processes of lexical movement production and speech production have proceeded independently, and at least one view of gestures holds that the two processes are essentially autonomous (Levelt, Richardson, & La Heij, 1985). However, our contention is that both lexical and motor movements play a role in speech production, and indeed, that this is their primary function.

1. Lexical Movements and Lexical Access

We believe that the primary effect of lexical movements is at the stage of grammatical encoding, where they facilitate access to the lemmas contained in the mental lexicon. A lexical movement represents some of the same conceptual features contained in the preverbal message. In large part, lexical search consists of an attempt to retrieve entries from the lexicon that satisfy the preverbal message's specifications. In the example of "vortex" previously described, the conceptual features of motion and circularity are represented both in the lexical movement and in the meaning of the word "vortex," which is the movement's lexical affiliate. We hypothesize that when the speaker is unable to locate the lemma for a lexical entry whose meaning matches the specifications of the preverbal message, motorically represented features in the lexical movement aid in the process of retrieval by serving as a cross-modal prime. Hadar and Butterworth (1993) have suggested that the gestural representation serves to "hold" the conceptual properties of the sought-for lexical entry in memory during lexical search, and this seems plausible to us.

In our model of the process (Figure 4) we have represented the role that lexical movements play in lexical access by showing the output of the muscle system (an implementation of the motor program produced by the motor planner) affecting the grammatical encoder. Our assumption is that the motorically represented features of the lexical movement are apprehended proprioceptively (i.e., that it is the lexical movements rather than the program that prime the grammatical encoder). The diagram also shows the output of the phonological encoder affecting the motor planner. Such a path is necessary so that the gesture production system knows when to terminate the gesture. If the purpose of gestures is to facilitate lexical access, there is no reason to produce them once the sought-for lexical item has been retrieved, and the gesture system needs some way of knowing this.

2. Lexical Movements and Conceptualizing

Some theorists have proposed that the conversational gestures we are calling lexical movements also can influence speech production at the conceptualizing stage. Hadar and Yadlin-Gedassy (1994) draw a distinction between lexical gestures and conceptual gestures. Conceptual gestures could be used by speakers to frame the conceptual content that will become part of the intended meaning of the utterance. It is not unreasonable to think that some gestures serve this function. Speakers trying to describe the details of a highly practiced motor act (e.g., tying shoelaces, hitting a backhand in tennis) often will perform the act in a schematic way as they construct their description. Doing so presumably helps them work out the steps by which the act is accomplished, and this may be necessary because the motoric representation better represents the content (e.g., is more complete, more detailed, etc.) than an abstract or propositional representation.

Although the idea that gestures aid in conceptualizing is not implausible, we are unaware of any relevant empirical evidence pro or con. As a practical matter, it is not clear how one would go about distinguishing conceptual gestures from lexical movements. Hadar and Yadlin-Gedassy (1994) suggest that the gestures used during hesitations are likely to be lexical gestures, and we agree (see Section VI,A,1), but lexical access can take place during juncture pauses, too, so there is no reason to believe that gestures at junctures are exclusively, or even predominantly, conceptual. Hadar, Burstein, Krauss and Soroker (1995) speculate that conceptual gestures will tend to be less iconic than lexical gestures.[18] However, because the iconicity of many lexical movements is difficult to establish (see Section VII,B,1), the distinction at best will be one of degree. Hence, for reasons of parsimony and because we do not have a principled way of distinguishing between the two kinds of gestures, we have not included conceptual gestures (or movements) in our model, and have simply assumed that the conversational gestures in our corpora are either lexical or motor movements.

3. Motor Movements and Speech Prosody

The function of motor movements is obscure, even though they, along with other coverbal behaviors (e.g., head movements, eye blinks, etc.), are ubiquitous accompaniments of speech. It has been claimed that motor movements along with other coverbal behaviors aid the speaker in coordinating the operation of the articulators (cf. Hadar, 1989b). We know of no data relevant to this claim, but it strikes us as plausible. In our schematic diagram we have represented this by showing the output of the motor system feeding the articulators, as well as producing motor movements.[19] Our account of the origins and functions of motor movements, of course, is highly speculative, and we include it only for completeness. None of the data we present is relevant.

In the next section we describe the results of several studies of the role that gestures play in speech production.

VI. Gestures and Lexical Access: Empirical Studies

In this section we examine evidence relevant to our conjecture that gesturing serves to facilitate speech production—specifically that the conversational gestures we call lexical movements help the speaker access

[18] This will be so, according to Hadar et al., because "iconicity is usually determined by reference to a particular word: the lexical affiliate. Because there are mediating processes between conceptual analysis and lexical retrieval, there is a higher probability that the eventually selected word will fail to relate transparently to the conceptual idea that shaped the gesture. This will result in judging the gesture as 'indefinite.'"

[19] In contrast, Heller, Miller, Reiner, Rupp, and Tweh (1995) reported that motor movements are more frequent when speakers are discussing content that is novel rather than familiar. If such a relationship could be established, it might follow that motor movements are affected by events occurring at the conceptual stage of processing.

entries in the mental lexicon. The data is drawn from several studies, and focuses on four aspects of the speech-gesture relationship: gesture production in rehearsed versus spontaneous speech, the temporal relationship of speech and gesture, the influence of speech content on gesturing, and the effect on speech production of preventing a speaker from gesturing.

A. GESTURING IN SPONTANEOUS AND REHEARSED SPEECH

1. Lexical Movements in Spontaneous and Rehearsed Speech

The microstructures of spontaneously generated speech and speech that has been rehearsed reveal that lexical access presents different problems under the two conditions. For example, while 60 to 70% of the pauses in spontaneous speech are found at grammatical clause junctures (*juncture pauses*), speech read from a prepared text (where neither planning nor lexical access is problematic) contains many fewer pauses, with nearly all of them falling at grammatical junctures (Henderson, Goldman-Eisler, & Skarbek, 1965). Repeatedly expressing the same content produces similar results. Butterworth and Thomas (described in Butterworth, 1980) found that when subjects first described a cartoon, 59% of their pausing time fell at clause boundaries, but by the seventh (not necessarily verbatim) repetition, they spent considerably less time pausing, and 85% of their pauses fell at clause boundaries. Nonjuncture pauses (i.e., pauses that fall within the body of the clause) are generally believed to reflect problems in lexical access, and their infrequent occurrence in read or rehearsed speech is consistent with the conclusion that lexical access in such speech is relatively unproblematic.

As part of the experiment described in Section IV,C,1, Chawla and Krauss (1994) videotaped professional actors spontaneously answering a series of questions about their personal experiences, feelings, and beliefs. Their responses were transcribed and turned into "scripts" that were then given to another actor of the same sex along with instructions to portray the original actor in a convincing manner. Videotapes of both the spontaneous original responses and the rehearsed portrayals were coded for the frequency of lexical movements. Although the overall amount of time spent gesturing did not differ between the spontaneous and rehearsed portrayals, the proportion of time spent making lexical movements was significantly greater in the spontaneous than in the rehearsed scenes ($F_{(1,12)} = 14.14$, $p = .0027$). Consistent with other studies, the conditional probability of a pause being a nonjuncture pause (i.e., probability (nonjuncture pause | pause)) was significantly greater for spontaneous speech ($F_{(1,12)} = 7.59, p =$

.017). The conditional probability of nonjuncture silent pauses and the proportion of time a speaker spent making lexical movements were reliably correlated ($r_{(14)} = .47$, $p < .05$). If speakers use lexical movements as part of the lexical retrieval process, it would follow that the more hesitant a speaker is, the more lexical movements he or she will make.

B. TEMPORAL RELATIONS OF GESTURE AND SPEECH

If lexical movements facilitate lexical access, then their location in the speech stream relative to their lexical affiliates should be constrained. We can specify a number of constraints on the temporal relations of gesture and speech that should be observed if our hypothesis is correct.

1. Relative Onsets of Lexical Movements and Their Lexical Affiliates

It makes little sense to argue that a gesture helped a speaker produce a particular lexical affiliate if the gesture was initiated after the lexical affiliate had been articulated, and it has been known for some time that gestures tend to precede or occur simultaneously with their lexical affiliates (Butterworth & Beattie, 1978). Morrel-Samuels and Krauss (1992) carefully examined the time course of the 60 lexical movements described in Section IV,A,1 relative to the onsets of their lexical affiliates. All 60 were initiated either simultaneously with or prior to the articulation of their lexical affiliates. The median gesture-lexical affiliate asynchrony (the interval by which the movement preceded the lexical affiliate) was 0.75 s, and the mean was .99 s ($SD = 0.83$ s). The smallest asynchrony was 0 s (i.e., movement and speech were initiated simultaneously) and the largest was 3.75 s. The cumulative distribution of asynchronies is shown in Figure 5.

2. Speech–Gesture Asynchrony and Lexical Affiliate Accessibility

Although all of the lexical movements in our 60-gesture corpus were initiated simultaneously with or before the initiation of their lexical affiliates, there was considerable variability in the magnitude of the gesture–speech asynchrony. Our hypothesis that these gestures aid in lexical access leads us to expect at least some of this variability to be attributable to the lexical affiliate's accessibility. Other things being equal, we would expect lexical movements to precede inaccessible lexical affiliates by a longer interval than lexical affiliates that are highly accessible.

Unfortunately, there is no direct way to measure a lexical entry's accessibility, but there is some evidence that accessibility is related to familiarity

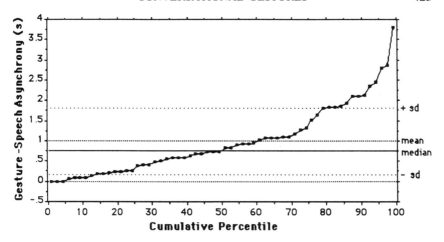

Fig. 5. Cumulative distribution of lexical movement–lexical affiliate asynchronies.

(Gernsbacher, 1984). We had 17 undergraduates rate the familiarity of the 60 lexical affiliates on a seven-point scale;[20] 32 of the 60 were single words and the remainder were two- or three-word phrases. We hypothesized that the asynchrony for a given lexical affiliate would be negatively correlated with its rated familiarity. The correlation, although in the predicted direction, was low $r_{(60)} = -.16, F_{(1,58)} = 1.54, p < .20$. However, a multiple regression model that included the gesture's spatial extent (i.e., the total distance it traversed) and the lexical affiliate's syllabic length and rated familiarity accounted for 30% of the variance in asynchrony ($F_{(3,56)} = 7.89, p < .0002$). The right panel of Figure 6 is a partial residual plot (sometimes called a leverage plot) showing the relationship of familiarity to gesture–speech asynchrony after the effects of spatial extent and syllabic length have been removed; the correlation between the two variables after partialling is $-.27$ ($F_{(1,58)} = 4.44, p < .04$). The left panel shows the relationship before partialling. Consistent with our hypothesis, familiarity accounts for some of the variability in asynchrony, although, perhaps not surprising, the relationship is affected by a number of other factors.

It is possible to manipulate lexical access by restricting the types of words the speaker can use. Rauscher, Krauss, and Chen (in press) videotaped subjects describing the plots of animated action cartoons to a partner. The difficulty of lexical access was independently varied either by requiring subjects to use obscure words (obscure speech condition) or to avoid using

[20] In cases where the lexical affiliate contained more than one word, the familiarity rating of the least familiar word was assigned to the lexical affiliate as a whole.

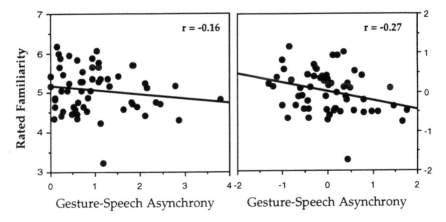

Fig. 6. Mean familiarity ratings for the 60 lexical affiliates plotted against its lexical movement-lexical affiliate asynchrony (in s). The left panel shows the relationship before spatial extent and number of syllables have been partialled, and the right panel shows the relationship after partialling.

words containing the letter "c" (constrained speech condition); these were contrasted with a natural speech condition. The narratives were transcribed and all of the phrases containing spatial prepositions were identified. We called these spatial content phrases (SCPs), and they comprised about 30% of the phrases in the corpus. Gesture rates were calculated by dividing the amount of time the speaker spent in gesturing during SCPs by the number of words in SCPs; the same was done for time spent in gesturing during nonspatial phrases. As lexical access was made more difficult, the rate of gesturing increased in SCPs, but not elsewhere; the interaction of spatial content × speech condition produced a statistically reliable effect ($F_{(2,80)}$ = 6.57, $p < .002$). The means are shown in Figure 7.

3. Gestural Duration and Lexical Access

The durations of lexical movements vary considerably. In the 60-gesture corpus examined by Morrel-Samuels and Krauss, the average lexical movement lasted for 2.49 s (SD = 1.35 s); the duration of the briefest was 0.54 s, and the longest 7.71 s. What accounts for this variability? If, as we have hypothesized, a lexical movement serves to maintain conceptual features in memory during lexical search, then it should not be terminated until the speaker has articulated the sought-for lexical item. Of course, there is no way that we can ascertain the precise moment lexical access occurs, but it would have to occur before the lexical affiliate is articulated.

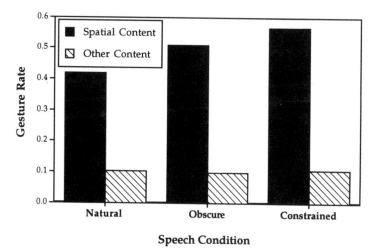

Speech Condition

Fig. 7. Gesture rate (time spent in gesturing/number of words in phrase) in spatial content phrases and elsewhere in the natural, obscure, and constrained speech conditions.

We would therefore expect a lexical movement's duration to be positively correlated with the magnitude of the lexical movement-lexical affiliate asynchrony.

In their 60-gesture corpus, Morrel-Samuels and Krauss found this correlation to be +0.71 ($F_{(1,58)}$ = 57.20, $p \leq .0001$). The data points are plotted in Figure 8. The heavy line in that figure is the unit line (i.e., the line on which all data points would fall if the lexical movement terminated at the precise moment that articulation of the lexical affiliate began); the lighter line above it is the least-squares regression line. Data points below the unit line represent cases in which the lexical movement was terminated before articulation of the lexical affiliate began, and points above the line represent cases in which the articulation of the lexical affiliate began before the lexical movement terminated. Note that all but 3 of the 60 data points fall on or above the unit line, and that the 3 points below the unit line are not very far below it. It seems quite clear that a lexical movement's duration is closely related to the time it takes the speaker to access its lexical affiliate, as our model predicts. This finding poses a serious problem for the "modular" view of the relation of the gesture and speech production system proposed by Levelt et al. (1985) which claims that "the two systems are independent during the phase of motor execution, the temporal parameters having been preestablished in the planning phase" (p. 133). If gesture and speech are independent during the execution phase, the lexical movement's

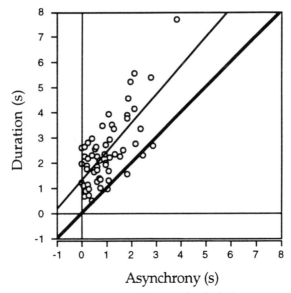

Fig. 8. Duration of lexical movement plotted against lexical movement-lexical affiliate asynchrony (both in s). The heavy line is the unit line; the lighter line above it is the least-squares regression line (see text for explanation).

duration would have to be specified prior to execution, and planning a gesture of sufficient duration would require the speaker to know in advance how long lexical access will take. It is not clear to us how a speaker could know this.

C. GESTURING AND SPEECH CONTENT

If our assumption is correct, that lexical movements reflect spatiodynamic representations in nonpropositional memory, then we should be able to observe an association between gesturing and the conceptual content of speech. We are aware of very few systematic attempts to relate gesturing and speech content, and the data we have are less than conclusive.

1. Gesturing and Description Type

a. Abstract Graphic Designs. The messages describing novel graphic designs and synthesized sounds obtained in the experiments by Krauss et al. (in press) were coded into categories of description types, and the rate of gesturing associated with these description types was examined. For the novel designs, we used a category system developed by Fussell and Krauss (1989a) for descriptions of these figures that partitions the descriptions into three categories: *literal descriptions,* in which a design is characterized in terms of its geometric elements—as a collection of lines, arcs, angles, and the like; *figurative descriptions,* in which a design is described in terms of objects or images it suggests; and *symbol descriptions,* in which a design is likened to a familiar symbol, typically one or more numbers or letters.[21] When a message contained more than one type of description (as many did), we coded it for the type that predominated. Overall, about 60% of the descriptions were coded as figurative, about 24% as literal, and the remaining 16% as symbolic.

For the descriptions of the graphic designs, a one-way ANOVA was performed with description type (literal, figurative, or symbolic) as the independent variable and gesture rate as the dependent variable to determine whether gesturing varied as a function of the kind of content. A significant effect was found ($F_{(2,350)} = 4.26$, $p = .015$). Figurative descriptions were accompanied by slightly more gestures than were literal descriptions; both were accompanied by more gestures than were the symbol descriptions (14.6 vs. 13.7 vs. 10.6 gestures per m, respectively). Both figurative and literal descriptions tended to be formulated in spatial terms. Symbol descriptions tended to be brief and static—essentially a statement of the resemblance.

b. Sound Descriptions. We tried to adapt the coding scheme used in the content analysis of the graphic design descriptions for the analysis of the sound descriptions, but the sound analogs of those categories did not adequately capture the differences in the descriptions of the synthesized sounds, and it was necessary to develop a five-category system that was considerably more complicated than the one used for the pictures. The first three categories referred to straightforward acoustic dimensions: *pitch, intensity,* and *rate of periodicity.* The fourth category, *object–sound,* described the stimulus sound in terms of some known sound source, most often a musical instrument. Finally, the fifth category

[21] Some abridged examples of the three types of descriptions are: *literal* ("On the right-hand side there's an angle, about a 45-degree angle, that seems to form an arrow pointing toward the top. Then at the top of that, at the point of that angle, there's a 180-degree horizontal line that goes into a part of a rectangle. . . ."); *figurative* ("It's sort of like a bird. Reminds me of pictures I've seen of like the phoenix, rising up to regenerate or whatever. . . ."); *symbol* ("This looks like a Greek letter psi, and looks like somebody wrote this letter with their eyes closed, so it's like double-lined all over the place. . . .").

contrasted elements of the sound in terms of *background–foreground*.[22] For graphic design descriptions, it was relatively easy to determine the predominant category type, but the overwhelming majority of the sound descriptions employed more than one category or dimension, and often no single type clearly prevailed. For this reason we have to resort to a less satisfactory multiple-coding scheme in which each description received a score of 0 to 10 on all five categories. Scores were constrained to sum to 10 for any description, with the value for each category representing its relative contribution to the total description.

Because the coding scheme used for the sound descriptions did not assign each description to one, and only one, category, it was not possible to perform the same analysis on all of them. Instead, we computed correlations between a description's score on each of the five coding categories and the rate of gesturing that accompanied it. This was done separately for each category. Only the object–sound category was significantly associated with gesture rate ($r_{(329)} = -0.14$, $p = .012$); the more that one of the sounds was likened to a sound made by some object, the lower the rate of gesturing that accompanied it. The correlations for the four other description types were small (all r's ≤ 0.07) and nonsignificant.

2. Lexical Movement and Spatial Content

In the Rauscher et al. (in press) experiment described in Section VI,B,2, gesture rates were calculated separately for phrases with spatial content (SCPs) and phrases with other content. Overall, gesture rates were nearly five times higher in SCPs than elsewhere (.498 vs. .101), and the difference was highly reliable ($F_{(1,40)} = 204.5$, $p < .0001$). The means are plotted in Figure 7 shown earlier.

---

[22] Some abridged examples of descriptions incorporating these three dimensions could be these: *pitch* ("The one you want here is the higher pitched one. It's a vibrating thing that increases. It ascends the scale. . . ."); *intensity* ("What I perceive are two largely similar tones, the difference between the two being one is louder than the other. The one I would like you to select is the loudest of the two tones."); *rate of periodicity* ("Listen for the frequency of certain intervals and the one you're looking for is slower. You're going to have . . . a certain number of notes played and then they'll repeat. So the one you are looking for, the intervals will be much slower."); *object-sound* ("Sound two sounds more like someone is playing an electric organ or something fairly musically."); *background–foreground* ("This one . . . almost sounds like one tone, and then in the background you can just barely hear, sort of . . . like a ticktock or something like that, whereas the other one, is more of two separate things, going on at the same time. . . .").

D. EFFECTS ON SPEECH OF RESTRICTING GESTURING

If lexical movements help in the process of lexical access, it is not unreasonable to suppose that preventing a speaker from gesturing would make lexical access more difficult, and that this would be directly reflected in less fluent speech. The experiment by Rauscher et al. (in press) referred to in Section VI,C,2 crossed three levels of lexical access difficulty (obscure, constrained, and natural speech conditions) with a gesture/no gesture factor. Subjects were prevented from gesturing under the guise that we were recording skin conductance from their palms. This permitted assessment of the effects of not gesturing on several speech indices.

1. Speech Rate and Speech Content

We know that lexical movements are more likely to occur when the conceptual content of speech is spatial (see Section VI,C,2). If our hypothesis is correct that they enhance lexical access, then the detrimental effects of preventing a speaker from gesturing should be particularly marked for speech with spatial content. Rauscher et al. (in press) calculated their subjects' speech rates in words per minute (wpm) during spatial content phrases and elsewhere in the natural, obscure, and constrained speech conditions. The speech conditions were designed to represent increasing levels of difficulty of lexical access, and it can be shown that they accomplished that goal.[23] Speakers spoke significantly more slowly in the obscure and constrained speech conditions than they did in the normal condition ($F_{(2,80)} = 75.90$, $p < .0001$). They also spoke more slowly when they were not permitted to gesture, but only during SCPs ($F_{(1,40)} = 13.91$, $p < .001$); during nonspatial content, speakers spoke somewhat more rapidly when they could not gesture. Means for the $3 \times 2 \times 2$ conditions are shown in Figure 9. It seems clear that the detrimental effects on fluency of preventing speakers from gesturing are limited specifically to speech whose conceptual content is spatial.

The fact that the effects of gesturing are restricted to speech with spatial content also reduces the plausibility of an alternative explanation for the results of this experiment. It might be argued that keeping one's hands still while talking is unnatural and requires cognitive effort, and that our results simply reflect diminished processing capacity because of having to remem-

---

[23] For example, both the mean syllabic length of words and the type–token ratio (TTR) were greater in the latter two conditions than in the normal condition; syllabic length is related to frequency of usage (Zipf, 1935), and the TTR [the ratio of the number of different words in a sample (types) to the total number of words (tokens)] is a commonly used measure of lexical diversity. Both are related to accessibility.

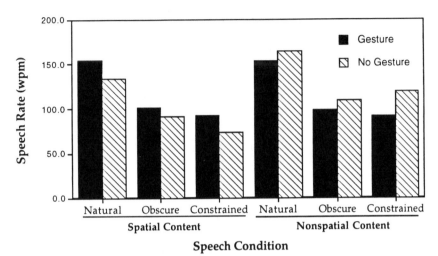

Fig. 9.   Speech rate (words per minute) in the natural, obscure, and constrained speech conditions for spatial and nonspatial content when subjects could and could not gesture.

ber not to gesture. However, such a "cognitive overload" explanation fails to account for the fact that the deleterious effects of preventing gesturing is specific to speech with spatial content. When the content of speech is nonspatial, speech rate actually *increases* slightly when gesturing is not allowed.

2. Dysfluency and Speech Content

Problems in lexical access are a common cause of speech errors. Because speech production is an online process in which conceptualizing, formulating, and articulating must occur in parallel, it is not unusual for a speaker to experience momentary difficulty in locating a lexical item that will fulfill the semantic specifications set out at an earlier stage of the process. When this happens, the speaker may pause silently, utter a filled pause ("uh," "er," "um," etc.), incompletely articulate or repeat a word, or restart the sentence.

Rauscher et al. counted the total number of dysfluencies (long and short pauses, filled pauses, incompleted and repeated words, and restarted sentences) that occurred in SCPs, and divided that number by the number of words in SCPs in that narrative; they did the same for dysfluencies that occurred in phrases without spatial content. These values were then subjected to a 2 (gesture condition) × 3 (speech condition) × 2 (content: spatial vs. nonspatial) ANOVA. Results paralleled those found for speech rate. Significant main effects were found for speech condition and content. Subjects were more dysfluent overall in the obscure and constrained speech conditions than in the natural condition ($F_{(2,78)}$ = 38.32, $p < .0001$), and they were considerably more dysfluent during SCPs than elsewhere ($F_{(1,39)}$ = 18.18, $p < .0001$). The two variables also interact significantly ($F_{(2,78)}$ = 11.96, $p < .0001$). Finally, a significant gesture × speech condition × content interaction ($F_{(2,78)}$ = 4.42, $p < .015$) reflects the fact that preventing gesturing has different effects on speech depending on whether its content is spatial or nonspatial. With spatial content, preventing gesturing increases the dysfluency rate, and with nonspatial content preventing gesturing has no effect. The means are shown in Figure 10.

3. Filled Pauses

Preventing speakers from gesturing has a negative effect on their ability to produce fluent speech when the content of that speech is spatial. However, a variety of factors can affect speech and dysfluency rates. Is it possible to ascertain whether this adverse effect is due specifically to the increased difficulty speakers experience in accessing their lexicons when they cannot gesture, or to some other factor? The measure that seems to reflect difficulty in lexical access most directly is the filled pause. Schachter, Christenfeld, Ravina, and Bilous (1991) argued that filled-pause rate is a consequence of the size of the lexicon from which words are selected; the filled-pause rate in college lectures is predicted by the lecture's type–token ratio

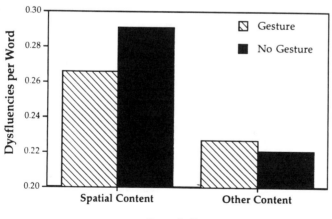

Speech Content

Fig. 10. Dysfluency rates (number of long and short pauses, filled pauses, incompleted and repeated words, and restarted sentences per word) in gesture and no-gesture conditions for spatial and nonspatial content.

(TTR).[24] A high TTR indicates that more alternatives are being considered in lexical selection, which, by Hick's Law (Hick, 1952; Lounsbury, 1954), should make lexical choice more difficult. A pause (filled or otherwise) can fall either at the boundary between grammatical clauses or within a clause. The former are often called juncture pauses, and the later are referred to as hesitations or nonjuncture pauses. Although juncture pauses have a variety of causes, nonjuncture pauses are believed to be attributable primarily to problems in lexical access (Butterworth, 1980).

Rauscher et al. (in press) computed a 2 (gesture condition) × 3 (speech condition) ANOVA using as their dependent variable the conditional probability of a nonjuncture filled pause (i.e., the probability of a nonjuncture filled pause, given a filled pause) in spatial content phrases. The means are plotted in Figure 11. Significant main effects were obtained for both the speech condition ($F_{(2,80)} = 49.39$, $p < .0001$) and the gesture condition ($F_{(1,40)} = 8.50$, $p < .006$). Making lexical access more difficult by requiring speakers to use obscure words or forcing them to avoid words containing a particular letter increased the proportion of nonjuncture filled pauses in their speeches. Preventing speakers from gesturing had the same effect. With no constraints on speaking (the natural-gesture condition), about 25% of the filled pauses were nonjuncture (intraclausal). When subjects could not gesture, that number was increased to about 36%. Because nonjuncture filled pauses are most likely due to problems in word finding, these results

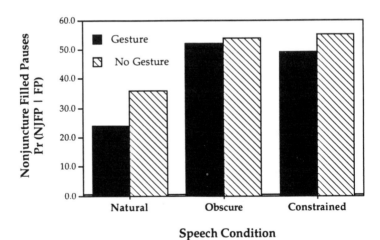

Fig. 11. Conditional probability of nonjuncture filled pause [Pr (NonJ) FP/FP] in three speech conditions when subjects could and could not gesture.

[24] See footnote 23.

indicate that preventing speakers from gesturing makes lexical access more difficult, and support the hypothesis that lexical movements aid in lexical access.

VII. General Discussion

It probably is fair to say that our work raises as many questions as it has answered. In the next section we consider some of the important issues that remain unresolved.

A. HOW DO GESTURES FACILITATE SPEECH?

Taken as a whole, our data support the contention that lexical gestures facilitate lexical access. However, many of the details about the process by which gesturing affects speaking remain obscure and under-specified at the theoretical level. Among them are the details discussed next.

1. Gesturing and Speech Content

Although our data suggest that the generation of words and phrases with spatial content is affected by lexical gesture production, the limited nature of the corpora we have examined needs to be kept in mind. Without systematically sampling content areas, we can only speculate about the relationship of content and gesturing. If our theory about the origins of lexical movements is correct, we would expect that, along with spatial content, words expressing motion and action also would be activated by gestural cross-modal priming. However, it is only fair to admit that our present understanding of word properties likely to be accompanied by gestures is quite rudimentary.

Complicating matters is the fact that many concepts represented in speech have spatiodynamic features that may not be relevant to the discourse at a given time. For example, the same lexical item can be used both to designate a category of objects and a particular member of that category; "The *cake* was served by the bride" versus "Coffee and *cake* are usually served at the end the meeting." When the reference is to a particular cake ("the" cake), the object in question will have a definite shape, but the generic "cake" leaves this feature unspecified. Cakes can be round, square, oblong, heart-shaped, and so on, and this may or may not be part of the concept "cake" as it functions in the speaker's communicative intention.

Now imagine a speaker saying, "He was completely surprised when a waiter put the birthday cake in front of him," while accompanying the utterance with an encircling gesture. The presence of the definite article ("the") implies that the speaker had a specific cake in mind, and we would infer from the shape of the accompanying gestural movement that that cake was round. If English had different words for round and not-round cakes, or if, like Navaho, it obligatorily inflected concrete nouns for shape, the cake's shape would have been conveyed by the utterance regardless of its relevance to the speaker's communicative intention. Because English does not have such grammatical devices available, the speaker would have to employ a more complex expression to convey that information ("a round cake," "a heart-shaped cake," etc.). Consistent with a Gricean perspective (Grice, 1969, 1975), we would not expect speakers to do this unless shape was relevant to their communicative intention.

This brings us to the theoretical question. If shape is not a relevant feature of the word–concept "cake," how could a gesture reflecting shape enhance lexical access? Three possibilities occur to us: 1) It is possible that not all of what we are calling lexical gestures actually play a role in lexical access—that only gestures representing features incorporated in the lexical item's lemma serve this function; 2) alternatively, the gesture may be thought of as communicatively intended—a way for the speaker to convey information that is not part of the verbal message. This, we take it, is what Kendon (1983) meant when he contended that gesturing ". . . is employed, along with speech, in fashioning an effective utterance unit" (p. 27); 3) finally, it is possible that gestures of the sort we have described have an effect at the conceptualizing stage of speech production, acting as a kind of "motoric" imagery to help the speaker retrieve from declarative memory the specific object or situation that will become part of the communicative intention. We pursue this issue further in our discussion of "conceptual gestures" later.

2. Activation and Termination of Lexical Movements

The model represented in Figure 4 presents a general view of the way gesture and speech production systems interact. Within the broad outlines of this architecture, there are a number of ways that the process could be implemented, and they each have somewhat different theoretical implications. For example, the model is not specific about the mechanism that generates lexical movements (i.e., whether they are triggered by problems in lexical retrieval, or simply occur as an automatic product of the process that produces speech). One possibility (that might be called a *failure-activation mechanism*) is that lexical movements are elicited by the inability to retrieve a sought-for lexical entry: Difficulties encountered in lexical access generate signals to the motor planner to initiate the motor program that results in a lexical movement; when lexical access is achieved, the absence of the signal terminates the lexical movement. Alternatively, the motor programs might be initiated independent of the speech processor's state, and their execution could be truncated or aborted by retrieval of a lemma that satisfies the specifications of the preverbal message. This might be termed a *retrieval-deactivation mechanism*. In this latter case, the gesture system must receive feedback from the speech processor when lexical retrieval has been accomplished in order to terminate the gesture.

3. "Conceptual" versus "Lexical" Gestures

Although our model stresses the importance of gesturing for lexical access, it is likely the case, as others have argued (Butterworth & Hadar, 1989; Hadar & Yadlin-Gedassy, 1994), that gestures also play a role at the conceptualizing stage of speech production. Speakers sometimes seem to use gestures to frame the contents of their communicative intentions, especially when the conceptual content relates to some overlearned motor act. Unfortunately, as we have noted above, distinguishing between lexical and conceptual gestures on formal grounds is unlikely to be satisfactory, and systematic study of conceptual gesture functions probably will require experiments that manipulate the conceptual content of speech.

4. Gestural Representation of Abstract Concepts

It is not difficult to imagine how gesturing might play a role in the production of speech that is rich in spatial or dynamic information. Many features of spatial or dynamic concepts can be depicted gesturally, and there are a number of potential ways that information contained in such lexical movements could aid the speaker. But people also gesture when their speech deals with such abstract matters as justice, love, finances, and politics, and it is not always obvious how conceptual content of this sort can be represented gesturally. McNeill (1985) dealt with this problem by distinguishing between "iconic" and "metaphoric" gestures. An *iconic* gesture represents its meaning pictographically; the gesture bears a physical resemblance to what it means. For *metaphoric* gestures, the connection between form and meaning is less direct, or at least less obvious. As McNeill (1985) puts it:

Metaphoric gestures exhibit images of abstract concepts. In form and manner of execution, metaphoric gestures depict the vehicles of metaphors. . . . The metaphors are independently motivated on the basis of cultural and linguistic knowledge. (p. 356)

Essentially, McNeill's contention is that metaphoric gestures are produced in the same way that linguistic metaphors are generated. However, we lack a satisfactory understanding of the processes by which linguistic metaphors are produced and comprehended (cf. Glucksberg, 1991; in press). To say, therefore, that such gestures are visual metaphors may be little more than a way of saying that their iconicity is not apparent.

An alternative view is that many abstract concepts that are not spatial or dynamic per se incorporate spatial or dynamic features. Such spatial and dynamic terms, often used to refer to states of affairs in the world, are spatial or dynamic only in a figurative or nonliteral sense. For example, we use terms like "above" or "below" to refer to individuals' positions in social organizations, implicitly formulating social hierarchies in spatial terms. Such phrases as "he grasped the idea" and "time moved slowly" would be anomalous if taken literally (Clark, 1973; Jackendorf, 1985). The process by which terms from one domain of experience are extended to other domains is called *semiotic extension* (McNeill, 1979).

5. Functions of Motor Movements

Although there is evidence that lexical movements play a role in lexical access, it is not clear what function is served by the other ubiquitous type of conversational gesture: motor movements. Theorists have proposed a number of quite different functions: They exert a structuring influence in the control of discourse production (Rimé, 1982); they disambiguate syntax (McClave, 1991); they serve as "extranarrative comments" (McNeil & Levy, 1982); they reflect the organization of the discourse (Kendon, 1980, 1983). The evidence offered thus far in support of these proposals is, in our judgment, inconclusive.

Neurolinguistic evidence underscores the differences between lexical and motor movements. For example, motor movements show a compensatory increase in Broca's, but not in Werneicke's, aphasia; the opposite is the case for lexical movements (Hadar, 1991). We have speculated that the two kinds of gestural movements are generated at different stages of the speech production process (Section V,B,3). Motor movements appear more closely related to the motor aspects of speech production than to its conceptual content, and like Hadar, we see similarities between them and other coverbal behaviors, such as head movments. Hadar's (1989a, 1989b) proposal that coverbal behaviors serve to coordinate the activities of the articulators seems plausible, although we know of no relevant evidence to prove it.

6. The Significance of Individual Differences in Gesturing

Although we have not presented the data here, in all of our studies we have observed substantial individual differences in the rate at which speakers gesture. For example, in the referential communication experiment involving novel abstract designs (described in Section IV,B,1), gesture rates across speakers ranged from 1.0 to 28.1 gestures per minute. These differences are reasonably consistent across content; the correlation between mean rates describing graphic designs and synthesized sounds was $r = 0.775$ ($p < .001$). In the Rauscher et al. (in press) study, gesture rates ranged from 0.5 to 30 gestures per minute. Gestural frequency and form also are said to vary markedly from culture to culture, although the evidence for the claim is largely anecdotal. In an early study, Efron (1941/1972) reported his impressions of differences in the form and amplitude of conversational gestures of Italian and Jewish immigrants in New York. Certainly the belief that ethnic groups differ greatly in how frequently and energetically they gesture is common.

What accounts for interindividual and intercultural differences in gesturing? One possibility is that they are stylistic, with no particular significance for the individual's cognitive functioning. To draw an analogy with linguistic variation, spoken languages differ in a variety of ways (i.e., they employ different speech sounds, different prosodic patterns, place the voice differently in the vocal range, etc.). Similar sorts of variation can be observed among speakers of the same language. Generally speaking, these variations are not thought to have great cognitive significance, and the same may be true of intercultural or interindividual differences in gesturing.

However, it is intriguing to speculate on the possibility that differences in the quantity and quality of gestures do reflect differences in underlying cognitive processes. Unfortunately, the evidence available at this point is far too sketchy to permit more than conjecture. In the dataset from the Rauscher et al. (in press) experiment, the single variable that best predicted individual differences in gesturing was speech rate; the more rapidly a person spoke, the more he or she gestured ($r_{(127)} = .055$, $p < .0001$). The density of the information conveyed by each of the narratives from that experiment was assessed by counting the number of "idea units" per word (Butterworth & Beattie, 1978). Speech rate and idea rate were orthogonal ($r = 0.05$). The density of idea units in a narrative was modestly (but significantly) correlated with the amount of gesturing that accompanied it ($r_{(127)} = .18$, $p < .04$). Using a median split, we divided the narratives between those that were informationally dense (high idea unit rate) and those that were informationally sparse (low idea unit rate), and then recomputed the within-group correlations of speech rate and gesturing. For the informationally sparse narratives, speech rate accounted for more than 50% of the variability in gesturing ($r_{(62)} = 0.72, p < .0001$), whereas for the informationally dense narratives it accounted for considerably less ($r_{(58)} = 0.42, p < .001$). Similarly although dysfluency rate is uncorrelated with idea unit rate overall, the relationships within the two groups differ markedly (low idea rate group: $r_{(123)} = -0.54, p < .0001$; high idea rate group: $r_{(122)} = -0.04$), These data (and others like them) point to the possibility that gestures may serve different strategic purposes for different speakers. A high rate of gesturing may mean something quite different in an information-rich narrative than in one that is information-sparse and, perhaps, for speakers who habitually speak succinctly as compared with those whose speech is more discursive.

The varied strategies might derive from different ways that speakers habitually conceptualize the world. For example, a person can be described as "grasping" the point or "understanding" the point. In both cases, it is clear that the reference is to an act of comprehension, and "grasping" might be thought of as a metaphoric description of comprehending. Are "grasping" and "understanding" simply synonyms in this context conveying the same intended meaning, or does the fact that the speaker metaphorically likens comprehension to a physical act reveal something about the way comprehension is conceived in his or her mind? We know that gesturing is associated with spatial content, and believe that it is likely to accompany motoric content as well. What we do not know is whether "grasping the point" and "grasping the rope" are equally likely to be accompanied by gestures.

It may seem farfetched, and we certainly know of no relevant data, but is it possible that some people gesture more than others because they habitually think about the world in spatial or motoric terms? In the Rauscher et al. experiment, subjects differed systematically in the extent to which they used spatial language. In each narrative, we calculated the percentage of phrases that were spatial. It ranged from 10% to 53%, with a median of 31%. Each subject contributed six narratives, and we would expect the numbers greater than and less than 31% to be roughly equal if subjects are not consistent in their use of spatial language. In fact the value of χ^2 for the 2 (above/below the median) $\times$ 41 (subjects) contingency table was 127.21 ($p = .001$). These differences are not attributable to content, since subjects were describing the same six "Roadrunner" cartoons. Apparently subjects differed in the extent to which they conceptualized the events of those cartoons in spatial terms, and this was reflected in their speech. It also was reflected in their gesturing. A multiple regression with percentages of spatial phrases and speech rate as independent variables accounted for one-third of the variance in the proportion of speaking time during which the speaker gestured ($r_{(127)}$ = .578, p < .0001).

7. The Role of Gesturally Conveyed Nonsemantic Information

Most studies of the communicative value of conversational gestures have focused on the way they help to convey a message's intended meaning—what we are calling semantic information—with little consideration of the possibility that they may be a rich source of other kinds of information. Our data have led us to conclude that the amounts of semantic information that conversational gestures typically convey is small and, except under special circumstances, probably insufficient to make an important contribution to listener comprehension. At the same time, we recognize that communicative interchanges do not end with the addressee's identification of the speaker's communicative intention. The response to a communicative act often takes into account the addressee's perception of the speaker's *perlocutionary intention* (i.e., the result that the communicative act is designed to accomplish) (Krauss & Fussell, in press). When a used car salesman represents a battered jalopy as having been owned by a retired teacher who drove it only on Sundays to and from church, certainly the addressee will comprehend the salesman's intended meaning, but any response to the assertion is likely to be tempered by the addressee's perception of what it was intended to achieve.

It has been suggested that nonverbal behaviors can play a role in such judgments, and in this way make an important contribution to communication. Nonverbal behaviors, or certain aspects of nonverbal behavior, can provide information about the individual's internal state independent of the message's intended meaning. Discrepancies between this information and the information in the message are a likely source of attributions about the communicator's perlocutionary intentions (cf. DePaulo, 1992). The term often used to describe this process is "nonverbal leakage" (Ekman & Friesen, 1969a, 1974), but that may represent too narrow a view of the process. The nonverbal behaviors that form the basis for perceptions of state are intrinsic parts of the communicative act. We expect some pitch elevation in the voices of people responding to a stress-inducing question, but when they respond the same way to a neutral question, we are likely to seek an explanation (Apple, Streeter, & Krauss, 1979).

As the research described in Section IV,C,1 indicates, subjects can discriminate spontaneous from rehearsed versions of the same narrative by viewing the video track without hearing the accompanying sound (Chawla & Krauss, 1994), suggesting that the visual information contains cues relevant to the speaker's spontaneity. Although spontaneous and rehearsed speakers gestured equally often, a greater proportion of the spontaneous speakers' gestures were lexical movements. Judgments of spontaneity were reliably correlated with the proportion of time the speakers spent making lexical movements, but not with the total time spent gesturing, which suggests that lexical movements served as a cue to spontaneity. However, despite this correlation, raters seldom mentioned gesturing as one of the cues that they used to judge spontaneity. We appear to have an intuitive appreciation of the way lexical movements relate to spontaneous speech production, just as we intuitively understand the significance of dysfluency for speech production. It remains to be seen what other sorts of inferences listeners/ viewers can draw from their partners' gestural behavior.

B. A SUMMING UP: WHAT *DO* CONVERSATIONAL HAND GESTURES TELL US?

On closer examination, this chapter's subtitle (What Do Conversational Hand Gestures Tell Us?) reveals itself to be pragmatically ambiguous. It can be interpreted in at least three different ways, depending upon who is taken to be the referent of us, and what is understood as the implicit indirect object ("What do they tell us *about what?*").

1. How Do Gestures Contribute to Comprehension?

According to one interpretation, *us* refers to the addressee, and *about what* denotes the information the gesture conveys to that addressee. This is the question traditionally asked about gestures that focuses on their *inter*personal function—how do they contribute to our understanding of the speaker's message? Our brief answer is that in the situations we have studied, they contribute relatively little. Contrary to Edward Sapir's familiar aphorism, gestures do not seem to contribute ". . . an elaborate and secret code that is written nowhere, known to none, and understood by all" (Sapir, 1949, p. 556). Certainly it is true that our methods for measuring the amount of semantic information gestures convey are indirect and crude. Nevertheless, such evidence as we have indicates that the amount of information conversational gestures convey is very small—probably too small, relative to the information conveyed by speech, to be of much communicative value. Could there be special circumstances in which conversational gestures are especially useful? Certainly one can imagine the possibility of that being the case, but at this point we have little understanding of what the circumstances might be or precisely how the gestures might contribute to comprehension.

There is, however, some evidence that gestures can convey nonsemantic information, and it is not too difficult to think of circumstances in which such information could be useful. From this perspective, the study of speech and gestures overlaps with the study of person perception and attribution processes, because gestures, in their cultural and social context, may enter into the process by which we draw conclusions about people (e.g., their backgrounds, their personalities, their motives and intentions, their moods and emotions, etc). Further, since the significance of gestures can be ambiguous, it is likely that our beliefs and expectations about the speaker–gesturer will affect the meanings and consequences we attribute to the gestures we observe.

Another way of pursuing this question is to ask how gesturing affects the way listeners process verbal information. Do gestures help engage a listener's attention? Do they activate imagistic or motoric representations in the listener's mind? Do they become incorporated into representations that are invoked by the listener when the conversation is recalled? One hypothesis, currently being tested in our laboratory, is that gestures facilitate the processes by which listeners construct mental models of the events and situations described in a narrative. Communication has been defined as the process by which representations that exist in one person's mind come to exist in another's (Sperber & Wilson, 1986). If our hypothesis is correct, gestures may affect the nature of such representations, and thus contribute importantly to at least some kinds of communication.

2. How Does Gesturing Affect Speech?

On a second construal, the question about what conversational hand gestures tell us concerns the *intra*personal functions of gesture—the role they play in speech production. The question might be paraphrased to ask, "How does gesturing affect us when we speak?" The *us* in this interpretation is the speaker, and the *about what* has to do with the ideas the speaker is trying to articulate in speech. Our response to this question is that gestures are an intrinsic part of the process that produces speech, and that they aid in the process of lexical access, especially when the words refer to concepts represented in spatial or motoric terms. They "tell us" about the concepts underlying our communicative intentions that we seek to express verbally. In this way, conversational gestures may indirectly serve the function conventionally attributed to them. That is, they may indeed enhance the communicativeness of speech, not by conveying information that is apprehended visually by the addressee, but by helping the speaker to formulate speech that more adequately conveys the communicative intention.

3. What Can We Learn from Studying Conversational Gestures?

In a third interpretation the *us* refers to those of us who study behaviors such as gestures, and the *about what* refers to the process by which speech and gesture are generated. Our response to this question is the most speculative, but in some ways it is to us the most interesting. It involves the ways in which we represent and think about the experienced world, and the ways in which such representations come to be manifested in speech when we communicate.

Considering the functions of conversational gestures reminds us that although linguistic representations derive from propositional representations of experience, not all mental representation is propositional. Spatial knowledge and motoric knowledge may have their own representational formats, and some components of emotional experience seem to be represented somatically. These representations (perhaps along with others) will be accessed when we recall and think about these experiences. However, when we try to convey such experiences linguistically, we must create new representations of them, and there is some evidence that so doing can change how we think about them. For example, describing a face makes it more difficult to recognize that face subsequently (Schooler & Engsteller-Schooler, 1990), and this "verbal overshadowing" effect, as it has been termed, is not limited to representations of visual stimuli (Schooler, Ohlsson, & Brooks, 1993; Wilson et al. 1993; Wilson & Schooler, 1991). Linguistic representations may contain information that was not part of the original representations, or omit information that was. It is possible that gestures affect the internal representation and experience of the conceptual content of the speech they accompany, much as facial expressions are believed to affect the experience of emotion.

Acknowledgments

We gratefully acknowledge the advice, comments, and suggestions of Susan Fussell, Uri Hadar, Julian Hochberg, Lois Putnam, and Mark Zanna. Christine Colasante, Robert Dushay, Palmer Morrel-Samuels, and Frances Rauscher were part of the research program described here, and their contributions are indicated in conjunction with the specific studies in which they participated. They also contributed to the development of the theoretical view of the functions of gesturing described in this chapter. The research and preparation of this report were supported by National Science Foundation Grants BNS 86-16131 and SBR 93-10586 to the first author. Correspondence should be addressed to the first author at the Department of Psychology, 1190 Amsterdam Avenue, 402B Schermerhorn Hall, Columbia University, New York, NY 10027. E-mail: rmk@paradox.psych.columbia.edu

References

Apple, W., Streeter, L. A., & Krauss, R. M. (1979). Effects of pitch and speech rate on personal attributions. *Journal of Personality and Social Psychology, 37*, 715–727.

Argyle, M., & Cook, M. (1976). *Gaze and mutual gaze.* Cambridge, England: Cambridge University Press.

Bacon, F. (1891). *The advancement of learning, Book 2.* (4th ed.). London: Oxford University Press.

Barakat, R. (1973). Arabic gestures. *Journal of Popular Culture, 6*, 749–792.

Bavelas, J. B., Chovil, N., Lawrie, D. A., & Wade, A. (1992). Interactive gestures. *Discourse Processes, 15*, 469–489.

Beattie, G. W. (1978). Sequential patterns of speech and gaze in dialogue. *Semiotica, 23*, 29–52.

Beattie, G. W. (1981). A further investigation of the cognitive interference hypothesis of gaze patterns during conversation. *British Journal of Social Psychology, 20*, 243–248.

Birdwhistell, R. L. (1970). *Kinesics and context.* Philadelphia: University of Pennsylvania Press.

Brunner, L. J. (1979). Smiles can be backchannels. *Journal of Personality and Social Psychology, 37*, 728–734.

Bull, P. (1983). *Body movement and interpersonal communication.* London: Wiley.

Bull, P., & Connelly, G. (1985). Body movement and emphasis in speech. *Journal of Nonverbal Behavior, 9*, 169–187.

Bull, P. E. (1987). *Gesture and posture.* Oxford, England: Pergamon.

Butterworth, B. (1978). Maxims for studying conversations. *Semiotica, 24*, 317–339.

Butterworth, B. (1980). Evidence from pauses in speech. In B. Butterworth (Ed.), *Speech and talk.* London: Academic Press.

Butterworth, B., & Beattie, G. (1978). Gesture and silence as indicators of planning in speech. In R. N. Campbell & P. T. Smith (Eds.), *Recent advances in the psychology of language: Formal and experimental approaches.* New York: Plenum.

Butterworth, B., & Hadar, U. (1989). Gesture, speech and computational stage. *Psychological Review, 96*, 168–174.

Cegala, D. J., Alexander, A. F., & Sokuvitz, S. (1979). An investigation of eye gaze and its relation to selected verbal behavior. *Human Communications Research, 5*, 99–108.

Chawla, P., & Krauss, R. M. (1994). Gesture and speech in spontaneous and rehearsed narratives. *Journal of Experimental Social Psychology, 30*, 580–601.

Clark, H. H. (1973). Space, time, semantics and the child. In T. E. Moore (Ed.), *Cognitive development and the acquisition of language.* New York: Academic Press.

Cohen, A. A. (1977). The communicative functions of hand illustrators. *Journal of Communication, 27*, 54–63.

Cohen, A. A., & Harrison, R. P. (1972). Intentionality in the use of hand illustrators in face-to-face communication situations. *Journal of Personality and Social Psychology, 28*, 276–279.

Darwin, C. R. (1872). *The expression of the emotions in man and animals.* London: Albemarle.

DeLaguna, G. (1927). *Speech: Its function and development.* New Haven, CT: Yale University Press.

DePaulo, B. M. (1992). Nonverbal behavior and self-presentation. *Psychological Review*, *111*, 203–243.

Dittmann, A. T. (1977). The role of body movement in communication. In A. W. Siegman & S. Feldstein (Eds.), *Nonverbal behavior and nonverbal communication*. Hillsdale, NJ: Erlbaum.

Dobrogaev, S. M. (1929). Ucnenie o reflekse v problemakh iazykovedeniia [Observations on reflexes and issues in language study]. *Iazykovedenie i Materializm*, 105–173.

Duncan, S. J., Brunner, L. J., & Fiske, D. W. (1979). Strategy signals in face-to-face interaction. *Journal of Personality and Social Psychology*, *37*, 301–313.

Dushay, R. D. (1991). *The association of gestures with speech: A reassessment*. Unpublished doctoral dissertation. Columbia University, New York.

Edelman, R., & Hampson, S. (1979). Changes in non-verbal behavior during embarrassment. *British Journal of Social and Clinical Psychology*, *18*, 385–390.

Efron, D. (1941/1972). *Gesture, race and culture*. (First edition, 1941.) The Hague: Mouton.

Ekman, P. (1976). Movements with precise meanings. *Journal of Communication*, *26*, 14–26.

Ekman, P., & Friesen, W. V. (1969a). Nonverbal leakage and clues to deception. *Psychiatry*, *32*, 88–106.

Ekman, P., & Friesen, W. V. (1969b). The repertoire of nonverbal communication: Categories, origins, usage, and coding. *Semiotica*, *1*, 49–98.

Ekman, P., & Friesen, W. V. (1972). Hand movements. *Journal of Communication*, *22*, 353–374.

Ekman, P., & Friesen, W. V. (1974). Detecting deception from body or face. *Journal of Personality and Social Psychology*, *29*, 288–298.

Exline, R. V. (1972). Visual interaction: The glances of power and preference. In J. K. Cole (Ed.), *Nebraska symposium on motivation* (Vol. 19, pp. 163–206). Lincoln: University of Nebraska Press.

Exline, R. V., Gray, D., & Schuette, D. (1985). Visual behavior in a dyad as affected by interview content and sex of respondent. *Journal of Personality and Social Psychology*, *1*, 201–209.

Feldman, R. S., & Rimé, B. (1991). *Fundamentals of nonverbal behavior*. New York: Cambridge University Press.

Feyereisen, P., & deLannoy, J.-D. (1991). *Gesture and speech: Psychological investigations*. Cambridge, England: Cambridge University Press.

Feyereisen, P., Van de Wiele, M., & Dubois, F. (1988). The meaning of gestures: What can be understood without speech? *Cahiers de Psychologie Cognitive*, *8*, 3–25.

Fleming, J. H., & Darley, J. M. (1991). Mixed messages: The multiple audience problem and strategic social communication. *Journal of Personality and Social Psychology*, *9*, 25–46.

Freedman, N. (1972). The analysis of movement behavior during the clinical interview. In A. W. Siegman & B. Pope (Eds.), *Studies in dyadic communication*. New York: Pergamon.

Freedman, N., & Hoffman, S. (1967). Kinetic behavior in altered clinical states: Approach to objective analysis of motor behavior during clinical interviews. *Perceptual and Motor Skills*, *24*, 527–539.

Fridlund, A. J. (1991). *Darwin's anti-Darwinism in the expression of the emotions in man and animals*. Unpublished paper, University of California, Santa Barbara.

Fussell, S., & Krauss, R. M. (1989a). The effects of intended audience on message production and comprehension: Reference in a common ground framework. *Journal of Experimental Social Psychology*, *25*, 203–219.

Fussell, S. R., & Krauss, R. M. (1989b). Understanding friends and strangers: The effects of audience design on message comprehension. *European Journal of Social Psychology*, *19*, 509–526.

Gernsbacher, M. (1984). Resolving 20 years of inconsistent interactions between lexical familiarity, orthography, concreteness, and polysemy. *Journal of Experimental Psychology: General, 113*, 256–281.

Glucksberg, S. (1991). Beyond literal meanings: The psychology of allusion. *Psychological Science, 2*, 146–152.

Glucksberg, S. (in press). How metaphors work. In A. Ortony (Ed.), *Metaphor and thought* (2nd edition). Cambridge, England: Cambridge University Press.

Graham, J. A., & Argyle, M. (1975). A cross-cultural study of the communication of extra-verbal meaning by gestures. *International Journal of Psychology, 10*, 57–67.

Graham, J. A., & Heywood, S. (1975). The effects of elimination of hand gestures and of verbal codability on speech performance. *European Journal of Social Psychology, 5*, 185–189.

Grice, H. P. (1969). Utterer's meaning and intentions. *Philosophical Review, 78*, 147–177.

Grice, H. P. (1975). Logic and conversation. In P. Cole & J. L. Morgan (Eds.), *Syntax and semantics: Speech acts*. New York: Academic Press.

Hadar, U. (1989a). Two types of gesture and their role in speech production. *Journal of Language and Social Psychology, 8*, 221–228.

Hadar, U. (1989b). Gestural modulation of speech production: The role of head movement. *Language and Communication, 9*, 245–257.

Hadar, U. (1991). Speech-related body movement in aphasia: Period analysis of upper arm and head movement. *Brain and Language, 41*, 339–366.

Hadar, U., Burstein, A., Krauss, R. M., & Soroker, N. (1995). *Visual imagery and word retrieval as factors in the generation of ideational gestures in brain-damaged and normal speakers.* Unpublished paper, Tel Aviv University, Israel.

Hadar, U., & Butterworth, B. (1993). *Iconic gestures, imagery and word retrieval in speech.* Unpublished manuscript, Tel Aviv University, Israel.

Hadar, U., & Yadlin-Gedassy, S. (1994). Conceptual and lexical aspects of gesture: Evidence from aphasia. *Journal of Neurolinguistics, 8*, 57–65.

Heller, J. F., Miller, A. N., Reiner, C. D., Rupp, C., & Tweh, M. (1995). Beat gesturing during conversation: Markers for novel information. Poster presented at meetings of the Eastern Psychological Association.

Henderson, A., Goldman-Eisler, F., & Skarbek, A. (1965). Temporal patterns of cognitive activity and breath control in speech. *Language and Speech, 8*, 236–242.

Hewes, G. (1973). Primate communication and the gestural origins of language. *Current Anthropology, 14*, 5–24.

Hick, W. E. (1952). On the rate of gain of information. *Quarterly Journal of Experimental Psychology, 4*, 11–26.

Hinde, R. (1972). *Nonverbal communication.* Cambridge, Eng.: Cambridge University Press.

Jackendorf, R. (1985). *Semantics and cognition.* Cambridge, MA: MIT Press.

Kendon, A. (1980). Gesticulation and speech: Two aspects of the process of utterance. In M. R. Key (Ed.), *Relationship of verbal and nonverbal communication*. The Hague: Mouton.

Kendon, A. (1983). Gesture and speech: How they interact. In J. M. Weimann & R. P. Harrison (Ed.), *Nonverbal interaction*. Beverly Hills, CA: Sage.

Kimble, & Seidel (1991). Vocal signs of confidence. *Journal of Nonverbal Behavior, 15*, 99–105.

Kimura, D. (1976). The neural basis of language qua gesture. In H. Whitaker & H. A. Whitaker (Ed.), *Studies in neurolinguistics*. New York: Academic Press.

Krauss, R. M. (1993). Nonverbal behaviors à la carte (Review of Robert S. Feldman & Bernard Rimé (Eds.), Fundamentals of nonverbal behavior). *Contemporary Psychology, 38*, 507–508.

Krauss, R. M., Apple, W., Morency, N., Wenzel, C., & Winton, W. (1981). Verbal, vocal and visible factors in judgments of another's affect. *Journal of Personality and Social Psychology, 40,* 312–320.

Krauss, R. M., Dushay, R. A., Chen, Y., & Bilous, F. (in press). The communicative value of conversational hand gestures. *Journal of Experimental Social Psychology.*

Krauss, Dushay, Chen, Rauscher (in press). *Psychological Science.*

Krauss, R. M., & Fussell, S. R. (in press). Social psychological models of interpersonal communication. In E. T. Higgins & A. Kruglanski (Eds.), *Social psychology: A handbook of basic principles.* New York: Guilford.

Krauss, R. M., & Glucksberg, S. (1977). Social and nonsocial speech. *Scientific American, 236,* 100–105.

Krauss, R. M., Morrel-Samuels, P., & Colasante, C. (1991). Do conversational hand gestures communicate? *Journal of Personality and Social Psychology, 61,* 743–754.

Krauss, R. M., & Weinheimer, S. (1966). Concurrent feedback, confirmation and the encoding of referents in verbal communication. *Journal of Personality and Social Psychology, 4,* 343–346.

Kraut, R. E. (1979). Social and emotional messages of smiling: An ethological approach. *Journal of Personality and Social Psychology, 37,* 1539–1553.

Levelt, W. J. M. (1989). *Speaking: From intention to articulation.* Cambridge, MA: The MIT Press.

Levelt, W., Richardson, G., & La Heij, W. (1985). Pointing and voicing in deictic expressons. *Journal of Memory and Language, 24,* 133–164.

Lickiss, K. P., & Wellens, A. R. (1978). Effects of visual accessibility and hand restraint on fluency of gesticulator and effectiveness of message. *Perceptual and Motor Skills, 46,* 925–926.

Lounsbury, F. G. (1954). Traditional probability, linguistic structure, and systems of habit-family heirarchies. In C. E. Osgood & T. Sebeok (Eds.), *Psycholinguistics: A survey of theory and research problems.* Bloomington: University of Indiana Press.

Mahl, G. (1956). Disturbances and silences in the patient's speech in psychotherapy. *Journal of Abnormal and Social Psychology, 53,* 1–15.

Mahl, G. F. (1968). Gestures and body movement in interviews. In J. Schlien (Ed.), *Research in psychotherapy.* Washington, DC: American Psychological Association.

McClave, E. Z. (1991). *Intonation and gesture.* Unpublished doctoral dissertation, Georgetown University.

McClave, E. (1994). Gestural beats: The rhythm hypothesis. *Journal of Psycholinguistic Research, 23,* 45–66.

McNeill, D. (1979). *The conceptual basis of language.* Hillsdale, NJ: Erlbaum.

McNeill, D. (1985). So you think gestures are nonverbal? *Psychological Review, 92,* 350–371.

McNeill, D. (1987). *Psycholinguistics: A new approach.* New York: Harper & Row.

McNeil, D., & Levy, E. (1982). Conceptual representations in language activity and speech. In R. Jarvella & W. Klein (Eds.), *Speech, place and action.* Chichester, Eng.: Wiley.

Mead, G. H. (1934). *Mind, self and society.* Chicago University of Chicago Press.

Morrel-Samuels, P. (1989). *Gesture, word and meaning: The role of gesture in speech production and comprehension.* Unpublished doctoral dissertation, Columbia University, New York.

Morrel-Samuels, P., & Krauss, R. M. (1992). Word familiarity predicts the temporal asynchrony of hand gestures and speech. *Journal of Experimental Psychology: Learning, Memory and Cognition, 18,* 615–623.

Moscovici, S. (1967). Communication processes and the properties of language. In L. Berkowitz (Ed.), *Advances in experimental social psychology.* New York: Academic Press.

Rauscher, F. B., Krauss, R. M., & Chen, Y. (in press). Conversational hand gestures, speech and lexical access: The role of lexical movements in speech production. *Psychological Science*.

Reuschert, E. (1909). *Die gebardensprache die taubstummen*. Leipzig: von University Press.

Ricci Bitti, P. E., & Poggi, I. A. (1991). Symbolic nonverbal behavior: Talking through gestures. In R. S. Feldman & B. Rimé (Eds.), *Fundamentals of nonverbal behavior* (pp. 433–457). New York: Cambridge University Press.

Rimé, B. (1982). The elimination of visible behaviour from social interactions: Effects on verbal, nonverbal and interpersonal behaviour. *European Journal of Social Psychology, 12*, 113–129.

Rimé, B., Schiaratura, L., Hupet, M., & Ghysselinckx, A. (1984). Effects of relative immobilization on the speaker's nonverbal behavior and on the dialogue imagery level. *Motivation and Emotion, 8*, 311–325.

Riseborough, M. G. (1981). Physiographic gestures as decoding facilitators: Three experiments exploring a neglected facet of communication. *Journal of Nonverbal Behavior, 5*, 172–183.

Rogers, W. T. (1978). The contribution of kinesic illustrators toward the comprehension of verbal behaviors within utterances. *Human Communication Research, 5*, 54–62.

Rosenfeld, H. (1966). Instrumental affiliative functions of facial and gestural expressions. *Journal of Personality and Social Psychology, 4*, 65–72.

Russo, N. F. (1975). Eye contact, interpersonal distance, and the equilibrium theory. *Journal of Personality and Social Psychology, 31*, 497–502.

Rutter, D. (1987). *Communicating by telephone*. Oxford, England: Pergamon.

Rutter, D. R., Stephenson, G. M., & Dewey, M. E. (1981). Visual communication and the content and style of communication. *British Journal of Social Psychology, 20*, 41–52.

Sapir, E. (1949). The unconscious patterning of behavior in society. In D. Mandelbaum (Ed.), *Selected writing of Edward Sapir in language, culture and personality* (pp. 544–559). Berkeley: University of California Press.

Schachter, S., Christenfeld, N., Ravina, B., & Bilous, F. (1991). Speech disfluency and the structure of knowledge. *Journal of Personality and Social Psychology, 60*, 362–367.

Schegloff, E. (1984). On some gestures' relation to speech. In J. M. Atkinson & J. Heritage (Eds.), *Structures of social action*. Cambridge, England: Cambridge University Press.

Scherer, K. R., & Giles, H. (1979). *Social markers in speech*. Cambridge, England: Cambridge University Press.

Scherer, K. R., Koivumaki, J., & Rosenthal, R. (1972). Minimal cues in the vocal communication of affect: Judging emotion from content-masked speech. *Journal of Psycholinguistic Research, 1*, 269–285.

Scherer, K. R., London, H., & Wolf, J. J. (1973). The voice of confidence: Paralinguistic cues and audience evaluation. *Journal of Research in Personality, 7*, 31–44.

Schooler, J. W., & Engstler-Schooler, T. Y. (1990). Verbal overshadowing of visual memories: Some things are better left unsaid. *Cognitive Psychology, 22*, 36–71.

Schooler, J. W., Ohlsson, S., & Brooks, K. (1993). Thoughts beyond words: When language overshadows insight. *Journal of Experimental Psychology: General, 122*, 166–183.

Searle, J. R. (1969). *Speech acts: An essay in the philosophy of language*. Cambridge, England: Cambridge University Press.

Short, J., Williams, E., & Christie, B. (1976). *The social psychology of telecommunications*. Chichester, England: Wiley.

Sperber, D., & Wilson, D. (1986). *Relevance: Communication and cognition*. Cambridge, MA: Harvard University Press.

Tinbergen, N. (1952). Derived activities: Their causation, biological significance, origin, and emancipation during evolution. *Quarterly Review of Biology, 27*, 1–32.

Tomkins, S. S., & McCarter, R. (1964). What and where are the primary affects? Some evidence for a theory. *Perceptual and Motor Skills, Monograph Supplement 1, 18,* 119–158.

Werner, H., & Kaplan, B. (1963). *Symbol formation.* New York: Wiley.

Wiener, M., Devoe, S, Rubinow, S., & Geller, J. (1972). Nonverbal behavior and nonverbal communication. *Psychological Review, 79,* 185–214.

Williams, E. (1977). Experimental comparisons of face-to-face and mediated communication: A review. *Psychological Bulletin, 84,* 963–976.

Wilson, T. D., Lisle, D. J., Schooler, J. W., Hidges, S. D., Klaaren, K. J., & LaFleur, S. J. (1993). Introspecting about reasons can reduce post-choice satisfaction. *Journal of Personality and Social Psychology, 19,* 331–339.

Wilson, T. D., & Schooler, J. W. (1991). Thinking too much: Introspection can reduce the quality of preferences and decisions. *Journal of Personality and Social Psychology, 60,* 181–192.

Zajonc, R. B. (1985). Emotion and facial efference: A theory reclaimed. *Science, 228,* 15–21.

Zajonc, R. B., Murphy, S. T., & Inglehart, M. (1989). Feeling and facial efference: Implications of the vascular theory of emotion. *Psychological Review, 96,* 395–418.

Zinober, B., & Martlew, M. (1985). Developmental change in four types of gesture in relation to acts and vocalizations from 10 to 21 months. *British Journal of Developmental Psychology, 3,* 293–306.

Zipf, G. K. (1935). *The psychobiology of language.* New York: Houghton-Mifflin.

INDEX

A

Absence emotions, 147–148
Abstract concepts, gestural representation, 437–438
Abstract designs, communication studies, 408–410, 428–429
Academic abilities, spontaneous trait inferences, 259
Acceleration, valence, 135
Accumulation, teacher expectancy, 364–370, 378
Accuracy
  research, 281–286, 288–293
  stereotypes, 322–328, 337–345
Achievement, student, teacher expectancy, 289–292
Action identification, 99–100
Actor–observer bias, 201–202
Adaptation-level theory, 127–128, 130
Adapters, 392–393
Aggressiveness, spontaneous trait inferences, 263
Alcohol use, pluralistic ignorance, 165–188, 197, 203, 204
Alienation, pluralistic influence, 176–180
Allocentrism, 263
Animals, human autonomic arousal, 23–24, 40
Appraisal
  challenge, 26
  cognitive, 11–12, 24–44
Approach strategies, 99, 112–114, 134–135, 139
Arousal, 1–8
  cardiovascular, challenge appraisal, 3–5, 19–21, 24–44

Arousal regulation, 8–9, 44–46
  biopsychosocial model, 9–20
  empirical model, 18–20
  primary process, 10–16, 17
  secondary process, 17
  situation-arousal studies, 20–44
Articulatory gestures, 416
Articulatory stage, speech production, 416, 417
Aspiration, levels of
  shifts, 114
  valence of event, 98, 103
Attitudes
  autonomic arousal, 33–35
  formation, 144–145
  outcome-biased inferences, 67–72
  valence, 142–145
Attribution, causal, spontaneous trait inferences, 250–252
Attribution error
  fundamental, 57, 256–257
  group, 57
Attribution theory, 54–55
  spontaneous trait inferences, 235, 237
Authoritarianism, spontaneous trait inferences, 262–263
Automatic processes, 240–241
Autonomic arousal, *see* Arousal
Autonomous gestures, 393
Avoidance, 134–135
Avoidance motivation, costs and benefits, 141–142
Avoidance strategies, 112–114, 141
  valence, 139–142
Awareness, spontaneous trait inferences, 253–254

451

CONTENTS OF OTHER VOLUMES

ISBN 0-12-015228-2

90051